S0-DUT-146

The Passenger Pigeon

ITS NATURAL HISTORY AND EXTINCTION

The Passenger Pigeon

ITS NATURAL HISTORY AND EXTINCTION

A.W. Schorger

UNIVERSITY OF OKLAHOMA PRESS   NORMAN

BY A. W. SCHORGER

The Chemistry of Cellulose and Wood (New York, 1926)
The Wild Turkey: Its History and Domestication (Norman, 1966)
The Passenger Pigeon: Its Natural History and Extinction (Madison, 1955; Norman, 1973)

Library of Congress Cataloging in Publication Data

Schorger, Arlie William, 1884–1972.
    The passenger pigeon.

    1. Passenger pigeons. I. Title.
QL696.C6S3 1973   598.6′5   72–3990
ISBN 0–8061–1035–X

Copyright 1955 by the Regents of the University of Wisconsin. Copyright assigned to the University of Oklahoma Press, 1973. Manufactured in the U.S.A.

DEDICATED TO MY WIFE

WHOSE PATIENCE SURMOUNTED EXTINCTION

PREFACE

Deep, youthful impressions are not easily effaced. One day while I was riding along the old Kilbourn Road in northern Ohio with my uncle, we came to a segment of the highway then bordered by fields. He told me that the area was once covered with a large beech forest. In spring when there were beechnuts on the ground, huge flocks of wild pigeons would appear. Their numbers were so great that the earth was shadowed and dung struck the dry leaves like hail. Men stood in the rift in the forest and fired at the passing birds until the road was dotted with their blue bodies, and more were killed than could be carried. He ended by saying, "We will never see the like again."

The extinction of a species once so numerous seemed incredible. Recourse in later years to the formal literature failed to answer many questions that occurred to me. The life history of the passenger pigeon, including its extermination, contained many lacunae and contradictions. It was my good fortune eventually to reside in Wisconsin, one of the last states in which the species strove to maintain its existence. Conversations with men who had shot and trapped pigeons furnished the final stimulus for this history. The unrivaled collection of newspapers in the library of the State Historical Society of Wisconsin provided information on movements, roosts, and nestings manyfold greater than could be found in the scientific and sporting journals. The spare time of a score of years was spent on interviews, correspondence, and a search of the literature.

It is unfortunate and most regrettable that no competent ornithologist attempted to make a comprehensive study of the nesting and other phases of the life history of the passenger pigeon while it existed in large numbers. Writers from Wilson to Brewster recorded largely what they were told by local residents and trappers. Many of the statements are inaccurate, but they appear repeatedly. It is understandable that a unique bird like the passenger pigeon would produce a vast literature. In the preparation of this book I compiled a bibliography of approximately 2,200 titles, which has now been deposited in the Library of the University of Wisconsin. Where possible, each title carries the name of the commonwealth to which the information in the title pertains. If there were included all the references in the newspapers of the various states, the list would readily extend to 10,000. It is not an easy task to reconstruct the life history of an extinct species in the face of a large and contradictory literature since much is beyond absolute proof. The reader may not agree with some of the conclusions, but these have been reached after much sifting and reasoning.

Viewed from all angles, the passenger pigeon was the most impressive species of bird that man has known. Elegant in form and color, graceful and swift of flight, it moved about and nested in such enormous numbers as to confound the senses. Equally dramatic was its disappearance from the earth due to the thoughtlessness and insatiable greed of man. In 1909, at least a decade too late, a concerted effort was made to determine if the passenger pigeon was among the living and to save it from extinction. The pigeon was gone but its passing was a sober lesson to mankind. It brought to sharp attention the fact that a species can become a nonrenewable resource. The wanton slaughter and extinction of this bird did more than all the laws put together to focus the attention of the American people on the necessity of protecting what we have before it is too late. One of the aims of this book is to give the record of a great transgression in the hope that future generations will avoid a similar one.

For access to the rare literature, examination of specimens, or other favors, I wish to express my indebtedness to Dean Amadon, E. R. Blake, W. J. Breckenridge, Herbert Friedmann, James C. Greenway, Jr., the late James L. Peters, L. L. Snyder, Mrs. L. M. Terrill, Josselyn Van Tyne, Alexander Wetmore, John T. Zimmer, Monica de la Salle, and

A. L. Rand. I am under special obligation to J. J. Hickey and R. A. Mc-Cabe for the reading of the manuscript.

A. W. S.

Madison, Wisconsin

CONTENTS

Preface, vii
List of Tables, xiii
List of Figures, xiii

xii *Contents*

TABLES

FIGURES

The following illustrations appear between pages 194 and 195

The
Passenger
Pigeon

ITS NATURAL HISTORY AND EXTINCTION

CHAPTER I: EARLY ACCOUNTS

The recorded history of the passenger pigeon began on July 1, 1534. On this day Cartier saw an infinite number of "wood pigeons" (*ramiers*) and other birds at Cape Orleans (Kildare), Prince Edward Island.[1] Infinite they seemed for three centuries, and it was their very numbers that repeatedly amazed the colonists. In 1536, during his second voyage, Cartier saw them again at Hochelaga, modern Montreal, on the lower St. Lawrence.[2] Cartier was primarily a navigator and spent little time on land. Alphonse of Xanctoigne in 1542 followed nearly the same route as Cartier and reported: "Fowle there are in abundance, as bustards, wild geese, cranes, turtle doves ... and many other birds."[3]

Sailing down the New England coast, Champlain arrived, on July 12, 1605, at Kennebunkport, Maine, where: "Upon these islands grow so many red currants that one can hardly see anything else; and there are countless numbers of pigeons, whereof we took a goodly quantity."[4]

Two years later a French expedition under de Monts occupied Isle Saint Croix, Maine. Lescarbot says: "Wee made there also good Pasties of Turtle Doves, which are very plentifull in the Woods, but the grasse is there so high that one could not find them when they were killed and fallen in the ground."[5]

During 1624–26, the Franciscan, Gabriel Sagard-Theodat, was in the country of the Hurons where there was a great number of pigeons.[6] He published a more complete statement in 1636: "There are here ... an infinite multitude of turtle doves, which they call *Orittey,* that feed in part on acorns which they easily swallow whole. In the beginning they were so stupid that they allowed themselves to be knocked down by blows of stones and poles from beneath the trees, but at present they are a little more wary." [7]

The great flight of pigeons at Quebec in 1663 was a mixed blessing. A Jesuit said of it:

Among the birds of every variety to be found here, it is to be noted that Pigeons abound in such numbers that this year one man killed a hundred and thirty-two at a single shot. They passed continually in flocks so dense, and so near the ground, that sometimes they were struck down with oars. This season they attacked the grain fields, where they made great havoc, after stripping the woods and fields of strawberries and raspberries, which grow here everywhere underfoot. But when these Pigeons were taken in requital, they were made to pay the cost very heavily; for the Farmers, besides having plenty of them for home use and giving them to their servants, and even to their dogs and pigs, salted caskfuls for the winter. [8]

A good description of this pigeon is given by Boucher:

There are birds of another kind called *Tourtes* or *Tourterelles,* (as you choose). They are almost as large as pigeons, and of an ash-colored plumage. The males have a red breast, and are of an excellent taste. There are such prodigious quantities of them that forty or forty-five can be killed at a single discharge of a gun. This is not done ordinarily, but it is common to kill eight, ten, or twelve. They come usually in the month of May, and return in the month of September. They are found everywhere in this country. The Iroquois take them with nets as they fly by, sometimes catching from three to four hundred at a draw. [9]

Pigeons were taken easily. Baron Lahontan came to Canada in 1683 and remained a decade. Through wide travel and a passion for hunting, he was well qualified to write:

In a word, we eat nothing but Water-fowl for fifteen Days; after which we resolv'd to declare War against the Turtle-Doves, which are so numerous in Canada, that the Bishop has been forc'd to excommunicate 'em oftener than once, upon the account of the Damage they do to the Product of the Earth. With that view, we imbarqued and made towards a Meadow, in the Neighborhood of which, the Trees were cover'd with that sort of Fowl, more than with Leaves: For just then 'twas the season in which they retire from the North Countries, and repair to the Southern Climates; and one would have thought, that all the Turtle-Doves upon Earth had chose to pass thro' this place. For the eighteen or twenty days that we stay'd there, I firmly believe that a thousand men might have fed upon 'em heartily, without putting themselves to any trouble. [10]

The passenger pigeons, according to Mather, came at their "appointed season" and did not winter in New England. A summary of his view on their departure runs: "As to the Itinerants; he [Mather] takes notice of vast Flights of Pigeons, coming and departing at certain Seasons: And as to this, he has a particular Fancy of their repairing to some undiscovered Satellite, accompanying the Earth at a near distance." [11] Clearly he was less well informed than Lahontan.

The ill-fated colony of Sir Walter Raleigh at Roanoke Island, now part of North Carolina, seems to have provided the first English account of the passenger pigeon. Thomas Hariot was resident from June, 1585, to June, 1586. On returning to England he wrote that the country provides "Turkie cocks and Turkie hennes, Stockdoues." [12] Captain John Smith gave a modest appraisal of the ornithological resources of Virginia in 1607: "In winter there are great plenty of Swans,...Parrats, and Pigeons." [13]

William Strachey, writing of the period 1610–12 in Virginia, placed himself on the defensive against incredulity:

A kind of wood-pidgeon we see in the winter time, and of them such numbers, as I should drawe (from our homelings here, such who have seen, peradventure, scarce one more than in the markett) the creditt of my relation concerning all the other in question, yf I should expresse what extended flocks, and how manie thousands in one flock, I have seen in one daie, wondering (I must confesse) at their flight, when, like so many thickned clowdes, they (having fed to the northward in the day tyme) retourne againe more sowardly towards night to their roust; but there be manie hundred witnesses, who maie convince this my report, yf herein yt testifieth an untruth.[14]

The abundance of pigeons in Virginia is confirmed by Hamor as follows: "There are...wilde Pidgeons (in Winter beyond number or imagination, my selfe have seene three or four houres together flockes in the Aire, so thicke that even they have shadowed the Skie from us)...." [15]

The prevalence of pigeons in Pennsylvania is mentioned briefly by several early writers.[16] Paskel wrote in 1683: "There are very great quantities of birds and one hardly thinks it worth while to shoot at ring pigeons and pheasants." [17] Some of the residents of the state became lyrical. In 1729, there appeared a poem in Latin and English, by Thomas Makin. It has the lines:

> Here in the fall, large flocks of pigeons fly,
> So num'rous, that they darken all the sky.[18]

A poem, "The Wild Fowl," was written by John Holme on an unknown date. Though late in appearing in print, it is believed to be the first metrical composition by a Pennsylvanian. The merit of quaintness cannot be denied.

> Here is much wild fowl near to us resorts,
> I know not how to name you half the sorts.
> The pidgeons in such numbers we see fly
> That like a cloud they do make dark the sky;
> And in such multitudes are sometimes found,
> As that they cover both the trees and ground:
> He that advances near with one good shot,
> May kill enough to fill both spit and pot.[19]

Shortly after the founding in 1620 of the first settlement in Massachusetts, an anonymous writer said: "The country aboundeth with diversity of wild fowl, as turkeys, ... many doves, especially when strawberries are ripe." [20]

The reticence of the English in recording seemingly unbelievable phenomena is again illustrated by the letter of Thomas Dudley sealed at Salem, Massachusetts, March 28, 1631 (O. S.; April 8, N. S.), and sent to the Countess of Lincoln. He wrote:

Upon the eighth of March from after it was faire day light, until about eight of the clock in the forenoon, there flew over all the towns in our plantations, so many flocks of doves each flock containing many thousands, and some so many, that they obscured the light, that it passeth credit, if but the truth should be written; and the thing was the more strange, because I scarce remember to have seen ten doves since I came into the country: they were all turtles, as appeared by divers of them we killed flying, somewhat bigger than those of Europe, and they flew from the northeast to the south-west; but what it portends I know not.[21]

Higginson, writing of Massachusetts about 1630, described the pigeon as follows: "In the winter time I have seene flockes of pidgeons, and have eaten of them: They doe fly from tree to tree as other birds doe, which our pidgeons will not doe in England: They are of all colours as ours are, but their wings and tayles are far longer, and therefore it is likely they fly swifter to escape the terrible hawkes in this country." [22]

In 1634 William Wood wrote graphically of this pigeon in New England:

The Pigeon of that Countrey, is something different from our Dove-house Pigeons in England, being more like Turtles, of the same colour; but they have long tayles like a Magpie: And they seeme not so bigge, because they carry not so many feathers on their backes as our English Doves, yet are they as bigge in body. These Birds come into the Countrey, to goe to the North parts in the beginning of our Spring, at which time (if I may be counted worthy, to be believed in a thing that is not so strange as true) I have seene them fly as if the Ayerie regiment had beene Pigeons; seeing neyther beginning nor ending, length, or breadth of these Millions of Millions. The shouting of people, the ratling of Gunnes, and pelting of small shotte could not drive them out of their course, but so they continued for foure or five houres together: yet it must not be concluded, that it is thus often; for it is but at the beginning of the Spring, and at Michaelmas, when they returne backe to the Southward; yet are there some all the yeare long, which are easily attained by such as looke after them. Many of them build amongst the Pine-trees, thirty miles to the North-east of our plantations; joyning nest to nest, and tree to tree by their nests, so that the Sunne never sees the ground in that place, from whence the Indians fetch whole loades of them. [23]

Two voyages to New England were made by Josselyn in 1638 and 1663. He seems to have paraphrased Wood's account of the passenger pigeon. [24]

A quaint description of pigeons feeding on grapes in New England is given by Morton. In 1637 he wrote: "[I] discovered, besides, Millions of Turtledoves on the greene boughes, which sate pecking of the full ripe pleasant grapes that were supported by the lusty trees, whose fruitfull loade did cause the armes to bend." [25]

The specter of famine hovered over the New England colonists for years and the coming of the pigeons was dreaded. Governor Winthrop wrote of the year 1642:

The immediate causes of this scarcity were the cold and wet summer, especially in the time of the first harvest; also, the pigeons came in such flocks, (above 10,000 in one flock,) that beat down, and eat up a very great quantity of all sorts of English grain.

Again:

This month [August, 1648], when our first harvest was near had in, the pigeons came again all over the country, but did no harm, (harvest being just in,) but proved a great blessing, it being incredible what multitudes of them were killed daily. It was ordinary for one man to kill eight or ten dozen in half a day, yea five or six dozen at one shoot, and some seven or eight. Thus the Lord showed us, that he could make the same creature, which formerly had been a great chastisement, now to become a great blessing.[26]

The summer visitants to New England impressed Reverend William Hubbard in 1680 in this way: "Turkies also, and pigeons, (that come in multitudes every summer, almost like the quails that fell round the camp of Israel in the wilderness)."[27]

Hand in hand with quaint credulity, we find in Mather's writings the highly important statement that the young pigeon was fed "milk" by the parent:

Among other Curiosities of *Nidification,* I will mention one that is observed in Pidgeons of my own Country. They build their nests with little Sticks laid athwart one another, at such distances, that while they are so near together as to prevent the falling through of their *Eggs,* they are yet so far asunder that the *cool Air* can come at their *Eggs.* And the REASON for this *Architecture* of their *Nests!* 'Tis this; their *Bodies* are much hotter than those of other *Birds;* and their *Eggs* would be perfectly addled by the *Heat* of their Bodies in the Incubation, if the *Nests* were not so built, that the *cool Air* might come at them to temper it.

I will add a Curiosity relating to the Pidgeons, which annually visit my own Country in their *Seasons,* in such incredible numbers, that they have commonly been sold for *Two-pence* a dozen; yea, one Man has at one time surprised no less than *two hundred dozen* in his Barn, into which they have come for Food, and by shutting the door, he has had them all. Among these *Pidgeons,* the *Cocks* take care of the *young* ones for one part of the day, and the *Hens* for the other. When they are taken, we generally take but *one Sex* at a time. In the Crops of the *Cocks,* we find about the quantity of half a Gill of a Substance like a tender *Cheese-Curd:* the *Hens* have it not. This *Curd* flows naturally into their *Crops,* as *Milk* does into the

Dugs of other Creatures. The *Hens* could not keep their *young* ones alive when first hatched; but the *Cocks* do fetch up this *thickned Milk,* and throw it into the Bills of their *young* ones, which are so nourished with it, that they grow faster and fly sooner than any other Bird among us. None but the *Cocks* which have young ones to care for, have this *Curd* found in their *Crops.* Kill one of those *Cocks,* and all the young ones pine away to death in the *Nest,* notwithstanding all that their Dams can do for them.[28]

About 1625, shortly after the Dutch settled on Manhattan Island, Wassenaer wrote: "The Birds most common are wild Pigeons; these are so numerous that they shut out the sunshine." [29] The Dutch colony at Lewes, Delaware, was visited by De Vries in 1633, where: "Whilst we were lying here, there came in during this month of April, hundreds of thousands of wild pigeons, flying from the land over the bay [Chesapeake]. Indeed, the light could hardly be discerned where they were. Sometimes they flew upon the ship, pressed down by numbers as they flew over the bay." [30]

An account of the pigeons at Albany, New York, in 1639, was also given by De Vries: "There are many partridges, heath-hens, and pigeons which fly together in thousands, and our people sometimes shoot thirty, forty, and fifty of them at a shot." He further states: "Pigeons, at the time of year when they migrate, are so numerous, that the light can hardly be discerned where they fly ... they are not larger than turtle-doves, and their bodies are exactly like those of the turtle-doves in Fatherland, except they have longer tails." [31]

The best early account of the passenger pigeon in New York was written by Van der Donck. In 1649 he stated that our pigeon resembled the "coal" pigeon but was smaller. The more complete statement made by him in 1656 follows:

The pigeons, which resemble coal pigeons [*Streptopelia turtur*], are astonishingly plenty. Those are most numerous in the spring and fall of the year, when they are seen in such numbers in flocks, that they resemble the clouds in the heavens, and obstruct the rays of the sun. Many of these birds are shot in the spring and fall, on the wing, and from the dry trees whereon they prefer to alight and will sit in great numbers to see around them, from which they are easily shot. Many are also shot on the ground, and it is not uncommon to kill twenty-five or more at a time. The Indians, when they find the breeding places of the pigeons, (at which they assemble in numberless thousands,) frequently remove to those places with their wives and children, to the number of two or three hundred in a company, where they live a month or more on the young pigeons, which they take, after pushing them from their nests with poles and sticks.[32]

The expedition of de Soto landed on the west coast of Florida in 1539 and extended its explorations northward to Georgia and westward to Arkansas. The entire region was long known as Florida. The account mentions, "There are in Florida . . . ducks, pigeons, thrushes, and sparrows." [33]

The Huguenot fort on the St. Johns River, Florida, was amply supplied with passenger pigeons in 1564. Laudonnière wrote: "In the meane while there came unto our fort a flocke of stock-doves in so great number, and that for the space of seven weeks together, that every day wee killed with harquebush shot two hundred in the woods about our fort." [34]

The ubiquitous French were the first in the Upper Mississippi Valley. Hennepin noted in 1680 that the country afforded wood pigeons. While at the mouth of the Wisconsin River, the small remaining supply of ammunition was reserved to shoot at pigeons.[35] Father Menard was at Chequamegon Bay on the southern shore of Lake Superior in 1661 where pigeons provided part of the means of subsistence.[36]

Marquette wrote in 1669 that there was fine hunting of pigeons in Illinois.[37] He spent the winter of 1674/75 on the present site of Chicago, and provided one of the earliest dates of migration: "On the very next day [March 26, 1675] game began to make its appearance. We killed 30 pigeons, which I found better than those down the great river; but they are smaller both old and young." [38]

The first vessels to enter the Mississippi were fitted out by the elder Coxe. In 1698 they were sailed up the river for one hundred miles. The son, Daniel Coxe, based his description on the journals and reports of those who had been on the river. He was so impressed by the reported amount of dung produced by the great flocks of pigeons that he thought saltpeter could be made profitably from it:

. . . Salt-Peter, which may probably be here procur'd, cheap and plentifully, there being at certain Seasons of the Year most prodigious Flights of Pidgeons, I have been assur'd by some who have seen them, above a League long, and half as broad. These come, many Flocks successively, much the same course, roost upon the Trees in such Numbers, that they often break the Boughs, and leave prodigious Heaps of Dung behind them; from which with good Management, and very little Expence, great Quantities of the best Salt-Peter may be extracted.[39]

Du Pratz, although believing erroneously that this pigeon beat the acorns from the trees with its wings, gives an interesting account of the bird in Louisiana:

There are such prodigious numbers of pigeons that I do not fear exaggerating when I assert that they sometimes darken the sun. One day I was on the bank of the Mississippi which they were following in a flock the length of the woods. This flock was so long that having fired my first shot, I had time to reload three times; but the rapidity of their flight was so great that although I am not a bad shot, my four discharges knocked down only two.

These birds come to Louisiana only in winter, and remain in Canada during the summer, where they eat the grain like they do acorns in Louisiana.... Although what I have said of these birds up to the present is sufficient to show that their number exceeds what can be said, I wish to give an instance which proves their prodigious abundance and at the same time shows their ingenuity in securing food.

.   .   .   .

On this voyage I crossed the river several times, and after setting out from one of these crossings, I heard a dull noise which came from the edge of the river below us, and which was carried faintly by the wind which blew from this side. Noticing that the noise continued to be uniform, I quickly prepared the canoe. I embarked with four men and descended, taking the middle of the stream in order that when necessary I could be carried to whichever side of the river I desired. The more we descended, the more the noise increased. But what was my surprise at what met my view, when I was almost at the place where the noise arose? I observed that the noise came from a thick and short column of pigeons on the bank of the river. I then approached sufficiently close to recognize that this was a legion of wood pigeons which rose and fell continually from the top to the bottom of a live-oak, in which every pigeon rose in succession in order to give two or three blows of the wings to knock down the acorns; then descended to eat his own or those which the others had knocked down. The activity with which they rose and fell made a perpetual motion which formed the column of which I have spoken. The noise was caused by the hum of this multitude, and it was this noise which justly piqued my curiosity since we were then forty leagues from any habitation. This general performance caused me to admire the industrious life of these animals, there being no evidence of any sign of avarice or of indolence in the instinct which gave them this industry; each trying to do an equal share of the work and to gather only about the quantity of acorns which it could have knocked down.[40]

While voyaging up the Mississippi, Bossu noted: "When one approaches the country of the Illinois, one sees during the day, clouds of doves, a kind of wood or wild pigeon. A thing that may perhaps appear incredible is that the sun is obscured by them; these birds living only on the beechnuts and acorns in the forests, and are excellent in autumn; sometimes as many as 80 of them are killed with one shot." [41]

The Greeks and Romans believed that ominous coming events could be foretold by flights of birds. It is incredible that superstitions of this nature should have existed for so many centuries. The vast flights of passenger pigeons afforded the colonists an unusual opportunity to give full sway to fear.

Concerning Bacon's Rebellion in Virginia, Mathew wrote:

About the year 1675, appear'd three prodigies in that country, which from th' attending disasters, were look'd upon as ominous presages . . . .

Another was, fflights of pigeons in breadth nigh a quarter of the mid-hemisphere, and of their length was no visible end; whose weights brake down the limbs of large trees whereon these rested at nights, of which the ffowlers shot abundance and eat 'em; this sight put the old planters under the more portentous apprehensions, because the like was seen (as they said) in the year 1640 when th' Indians committed the last massacre, but not after, untill the present year 1675.[42]

The most common belief was that large flights of pigeons would be followed by sickness. Barton wrote:

It is a common observation in some parts of this state [Pennsylvania], that when the Pigeons continue with us all the winter, we shall have a sickly summer and autumn. There is, perhaps, some foundation for this notion. Large bodies of these birds seldom do winter among us unless the winter be very mild; and the experience of some years has taught us, that such winters are often followed by malignant epidemics. The mild winter of 1792–1793, was succeeded by a dreadful malignant fever, which destroyed between four and five thousand people in Philadelphia; and I am assured, that the same fever in 1762 was preceded by an extremely open winter, during which the pigeons remained about Philadelphia, and in other parts of the state.[43]

Watson said of this epidemic:

In 1793, just before the time of the yellow fever, like flocks flew daily over Philadelphia, and were shot from numerous high houses. The markets were crammed with them. They generally had nothing in their craws besides a single acorn. The superstitious soon found out they presaged some evil; and sure enough sickness and death came! [44]

The incident was used by Longfellow in *Evangeline* (Part II, Book V).

> Then it came to pass that a pestilence fell on the city,
> Presaged by wondrous signs, and mostly by flocks of wild pigeons,
> Darkening the sun in their flight, with naught in their craws but an acorn.

The superstition nearly outlived the pigeon in Wisconsin, as testified by the following statement in the Lancaster *Herald* of March 28, 1846: "Some are prophesying sickness, predicting their fears upon the flight of pigeons."

CHAPTER 2: BEHAVIORAL
CHARACTERISTICS

The passenger pigeon, with its small head and neck, long tail, and beautiful plumage, had an air of uncommon elegance. The male in life had a length of about 16.5 inches. Its color ranged from slaty blue on the head to grayish blue on the back. The throat, foreneck, and breast were vinaceous. A metallic iridescence of bronze, green, and purple tinged the hindneck. The female was about an inch smaller and duller in color. The massive breast muscles and long, pointed wings were commensurate with its speed, grace, and maneuverability in the air, for which it justly earned the title of "blue meteor." In addition, it had a red and sparkling eye. As Schaff has expressed it, "No bird ever had a bolder, more unflinching eye." [1] A more complete, technical description is given in Chapter 10.

VOICE

The pigeon had a repertoire of notes, each peculiar to the activity in hand. It is difficult to make the sounds understandable. Craig has distinguished this pigeon from the mourning dove as a bird that shrieked, chattered, and clucked, but did not coo. [2] Its voice was more distinctive than that of any other pigeon with which he was acquainted. The notes were classified as follows: (1) the copulation note; (2) the keck (peculiar to the species); (3) scolding, chattering, clucking (also peculiar to it); (4) the vestigial coo or keeho; (5) the nest call. [3]

The notes uttered during the breeding season are described by Audubon as a soft *coo-coo-coo-coo* much shorter than that of the domestic pigeon. [4] These cooing notes were delivered with fewer gesticulations than by the domestic bird.[5] This sound corresponds with the vestigial coo or *keeho* of Craig.[6] It was uttered after the more unmusical sounds both in wooing the female and in dealing with an enemy. The sound was weak and apparently the vestige of a louder coo that had gradually become diminished since in the loud noise of community life it could scarcely be heard.[7] When every pigeon gave the loud note, it is difficult to understand why the individual could be heard any more clearly than if all had made soft sounds. The copulation note has been described as similar to that of the mourning dove, a faint growling note, and also as a soft toneless note.[8]

The sounds issuing from a nesting have left various impressions. Mactaggart wrote: "They breed together in the woods by millions, and the singular noise they make in their crowded nursery, or matrimonial haunt, surpasses any sound I have ever heard—it is a loud and confused buzz of love." [9] Most observers were impressed by the tremendous noise, a combination of "twittering and cooing" that could be heard for miles both by day and night.[10] The noise has also been expressed as a blending of the "fluttering of the wings and the cooing." [11] Brewster wrote: "Pigeons are very noisy when building. They make a sound resembling the croaking of wood-frogs. Their combined clamor can be heard four or five miles away when the atmospheric conditions are favorable." [12] To J. B. Oviatt, the sound made by the thousands of birds while building their nests was a "friendly call." [13]

The sound was very musical at the time of mating. Pokagon speaks of the "strange, bell-like wooing notes," and Edwin Haskell of the "peculiarity of the gentle cooing sounds that filled the woods." [14]

The ordinary note of the pigeon was a monosyllabic *kee-kee-kee-kee,* diminishing in power from first to last.[15] It appears to correspond with the loud, shrill, piercing *keck* of Craig, the first *k* being aspirated like the German *ch.*[16] It was intended to command attention and overpower the female before whom the male was displaying, or to intimidate an enemy. In making the sound, the head was drawn back and as the beak opened all the breath was expelled in a single effort. At the same time the wings were flirted upward and forward.[17] This was followed in a few seconds by a single guttural *coo.* The latter was produced by the bird raising its head and lengthening its neck, the upper part of which became swollen as if the air that was forced into it was prevented from escaping.

The call used by sedentary pigeons to those passing has been described by Behr:

Its friendly nature was particularly noticeable when one flock passed another. Birds on the ground, despite their interest in feeding operations, would always take time to hail newcomers with a call peculiar to the occasion. It was a long-drawn and moderately loud repetition of one note, which sounded like "tweet" and this would cause the flying birds to alight in nearby trees, giving in their turn a low call, "tret, tret, tret." To me these seemed to be notes of greeting, while other sounds were indicative of sex. For instance, the female call-note is similar to the "tweet" above but the male response is a low "oorn," which cannot be heard farther than two or three hundred feet. My knowledge of these notes is due to the fact that I learned to imitate them perfectly, in order to call the birds up within good shooting distance.[18]

The call to passing flocks by birds gorged with food and sitting in trees is given as follows: "The call does not at all resemble the cooing or call of our tame pigeon, but on the contrary, is more like the quack of some of our small ducks in tone, not prolonged like the duck, rather more harsh and very quickly repeated; once heard by the sportsman, never forgotten." [19]

The common flight call, sometimes given from trees and from the ground, was a shrill, somewhat screechy *tweet, tweet, tweet-tweet-tweet,* or with several more *tweets* on the end.[20] To Thoreau the sharp *prating* or *quivet* was like the grating of one bough on another, or the creaking of a tree. On April 27, 1855, he wrote: "Heard a singular sort of screech, somewhat like a hawk, under the cliff, and soon some pigeons flew out of a pine near me." [21]

Pigeons, particularly in small flocks, could be brought down by imitating their call with a special instrument that has been described by H. T. Blodgett as follows:

The call was one in imitation of the pigeon's own call, given either as a peculiar throat sound (liable to make the throat sore if too often repeated) or with a silk band between two blocks of wood ... held between the lips and teeth and blown like a blade of grass between the thumbs. By biting or pressing with the teeth ...

the tension upon the silk band would be increased, raising the tone of the call or relaxing for a lower note.[22]

An entirely different interpretation of the sounds made by the pigeons while sitting in trees before dropping to the ground to feed has been given by A. B. Welford. The calls were sweet and plaintive, similar to those of the domestic pigeon, but with a much prettier trill and accentuation, and had a peculiar ventriloquial effect.[23] Other interpretations are: a "peevish scream"; "screaming noise"; *freez; keek, keek, keek; tete-tete-tete; see-see-see;* and "crowing."[24]

A pigeon kept by Howitt had a few notes, each of presumably definite import: *tweet, twee, tweet,* meaning "come here," "good," and "safety"; and *twee* in a low tone, "danger."[25]

Pigeons struggling beneath a net gave grunt-like chirps. The only sounds heard from stall-fed birds by J. B. Oviatt were very similar.[26]

The female was very quiet in comparison with the male. She had a toneless *krk, krk, krk, krk* uttered in self-defense; also while in the nest with the male a *kŭ-ss, kŭ-ss, kŭ-ss, kŭ-ss,* the first note of each pair being a low cluck, the second a high squeak.[27]

Pigeons were most vociferous during the breeding season, which I believe was quite short for the wild bird, when nesting in colonies. The captive bird had a prolonged season and the mating notes could be heard from January or February through August.[28] Strangely, Brewster never heard a note from this pigeon in the wild at any season.[29]

FEAR

It was believed that the pigeon at times had sentinels posted to sound an alarm by note or by clapping of the wings. Pokagon wrote:

> While feeding, they always have guards on duty, to give alarm of danger. It is made by the watch-bird as it takes its flight, beating its wings together in quick succession, sounding like the rolling beat of a snare drum. Quick as thought each bird repeats the alarm with a thundering sound, as the flock struggles to rise, leading a stranger to think a young cyclone is being born.[30]

Bethune states that sentinels were stationed at the edges of the grain fields in which the flock was feeding.[31]

The posting of sentinels seems to have depended upon the degree of exposure of the feeding birds. When they were feeding in the open, according to Moore, at least one sentinel was posted in a tree and when its scream was uttered the flock arose immediately; however, when they were feeding in the woods, a sentinel was rarely posted.[32] Dury found that birds feeding in the woods could be approached within shotgun range by approaching behind the trunk of a tree; however, if one pigeon flew up in alarm, the entire flock was certain to follow.[33] Others had no difficulty in approaching them in grain fields in autumn.[34] Possibly in these cases most of the birds were young.

Shyness while feeding was not considered a usual trait by Gentry: "When they alight for the purposes of feeding, they cluster close together, and do not diffuse themselves over a considerable scope of country. They are not ordinarily shy, and can be approached with the least difficulty, so intent are they upon feeding." [35] A flock alighted and fed in a wild cherry tree beneath which a speech was being made to a large gathering of people.[36]

Wariness in animals usually decreases with hunger and fatigue. It was often impossible for the farmers to keep the pigeons off a newly sowed field by shooting or other devices. Kalm remarked on their timidity after they had had sufficient food.[37] When fatigued by a long flight, they could be killed with a stick.[38] Weary birds paid scarcely any attention to the volleys poured into their resting ranks.[39]

The favorite perch of the pigeons was a dead tree that gave a clear field of vision. Under this condition they were difficult to approach by a pedestrian, but little attention was paid to a horse or wagon.[40] The snapping of a twig or the mere sight of a person approaching would put them to flight.[41]

Often they were fearless. Brewster found that pigeons feeding on berries in a pasture would rise out of range, but once settled in a tree they could be approached with ease. After being fired at repeatedly, they would return again and again. Occasionally it was necessary to pound the tree with a stick or throw stones to put the birds to flight.[42] Thoreau found some pigeons resting in white pines and unwilling to move.[43]

Fear was completely lacking during the nesting period, and the old birds could almost be touched.[44] This confidence was lost during the last nestings, the brooding birds flying from the nests on the approach of a man. The parents then stole into the nesting to feed the young and departed quickly.[45] Squabs in the nests were fearless.

A characteristic behavior is given by Maynard:

They sit near the top of the tree and generally close together, their bills resting on their breasts and their feathers puffed out, apparently without a motion; at such times, these birds may, with caution, be approached very closely but should the Pigeons have the slightest suspicion of one's approach, they will give a note of alarm, sounding something like a laugh made with a child's trumpet; this same note is occasionally used when not in danger.[46]

The behavior on capture has been described by Whitman: "The passenger pigeon, when captured, emits a cry of distress or terror, and struggles hard to escape. If it finds its struggles of no avail, it will soon stop and often *lie motionless* in the hand, *feigning dead,* for some moments after the hand is open. It will lie for nearly a minute on a shelf if left undisturbed." [47] This reaction is common to most species of pigeons, but was most marked with the passenger pigeon and its hybrids.

Pigeons reared in captivity never lost their fear of man even after reaching an age of three or four years. At times they appeared terror-stricken and would dash against the wire of the cage with considerable injury to the wings and tail feathers.[48] J. B. Oviatt found that pigeons taken as squabs became quite tame, some so much so that on escaping they could be retaken.[49] Thoreau mentions that a trapper released some of his pigeons which stayed about the stands and attracted others.[50] When a flock of its kind passed over, the domesticated bird of Howitt evidenced recognition with its wings and other movements, watched until the flock was out of sight, but never tried to join it.[51]

The behavior of a flock when attacked in the air by a hawk has been described by Wilson: "Sometimes a Hawk would make a sweep on a particular part of the column, from a great height, when almost as quick as lightning, that part shot downwards out of the common track, but soon rising again, continued advancing at the same height as before." [52]

A tame pigeon kept by Howitt flew to him, or to a member of his family, when a hawk was sighted.[53] A wild pigeon when pursued by a duck hawk sought refuge among the men and horses of an expedition in the Dakotas.[54] I have seen domestic pigeons, at which a trained duck hawk was flown, take refuge at the feet of the observers.

The pigeon behaved towards other aerial danger in the same manner as to hawks to which it was alone accustomed. There is an interesting case of its reaction to rockets reported in the Cleveland *Plain Dealer* (Ohio) of March 12, 1860:

A few days since, while the wild pigeons were flying in innumerable quantities over the city, Mr. Geo. N. Baker, proprietor of the pyrotechnic establishment . . . , thought that he would see what effect his fire-works would have upon the feathered tribe . . . . Just as a large flock approached he sent hissing through their midst a half dozen heavy rockets, producing a wild and irrepressible consternation; at once the vast flock would change its course, dividing in all directions, and in many instances great numbers would come to the ground and alight, others would reverse their course, while the greater number would come down within a few yards of the ground, wandering about in wild confusion. One heavy rocket bursting just beneath a large flock and shooting out its hundred firey serpents, had the effect of sending the whole brood flying upward until it was lost to the sight. In many instances large numbers, diving in wild confusion to the earth, were captured by boys in the neighborhood.

The passenger pigeon and other members of the family have been long considered peculiar for the ease with which the feathers are shed.[55] Audubon wrote that, when the passenger pigeon and mourning dove were taken alive in the hand, the feathers became loosened at the slightest touch, a trait peculiar to the genus *Columba* and certain gallinaceous birds.[56] With this assertion Dixon is in full agreement.[57]

The statement of Audubon that the passenger pigeons roosted in masses on the backs of one another, coupled with the remark that they lost their feathers at the least touch, laid him open to criticism by Waterton.[58] This gentleman suffered from real or fancied wrongs dating back to Queen Mary, and life for him was a continual joust. He went so far as to call Audubon an arrogant fool. As to the pigeons:

From this we may infer, to a certainty, that every pigeon which was unlucky enough to be undermost in the solid masses would lose every feather from its uppermost parts, through the pressure of the feet of those above it. Now I would fain believe that instinct taught these pigeons to resort to a certain part of the forest solely for the purpose of repose, and not to undergo a process of inevitable suffocation, and, at the same time, to have their backs deprived of every feather, while they were voluntarily submitting to this self-inflicting method of ending their days.[59]

The explanation lies in the fact that the feathers of some pigeons and gallinaceous birds are easily loosened by a certain degree of fright. The reaction is well known to poulterers, who take advantage of it for plucking, and is produced by a procedure known as the "stick." [60] The mouth of the fowl is opened and the rear lobe of the brain is pierced by the thrust of a sharp, narrow-bladed knife. Prior to *rigor mortis,* a period of two or three minutes, the feathers are very loose in the follicles and can be knocked off easily by downward strokes of the hand held vertically. The physiology of the "stick" was investigated by King. He found that the cerebellum was the essential part of the brain to be pierced. Electrical stimulation, chloroform, and several other chemicals also caused loosening of the feathers.[61]

The sympathetic system by which the erector, depressor, and re-tractor muscles of birds control the feathers was studied by Langley; [62] however, the exact nature of the loosening process is not known. A captured eastern nighthawk (*Chordeiles minor minor*) shed wing and tail feathers due to a "violent nervous shock." [63] The ringdove (*Turtur risorius*) and blue peafowl (*Pavo cristatus*) shed profusely when handled.[64] Among the Columbidae there is a specific as well as intra-specific variation in the degree of attachment of the feathers, or a failure of the appropriate stage of nervous shock to coincide with the death of the bird. I have prepared skins of the mourning dove (*Zenaidura macroura*) and the rock dove (*Columba livia*) of Morocco without ab-normal loss of feathers.

There is little doubt that the passenger pigeon associated danger with loose feathers that might be seen on the ground and became frightened. The trapper on resetting his net removed every feather from the bed for, as long as any remained, the pigeons would not alight.

INTELLIGENCE

The two characteristics of the passenger pigeon to impress Dillin were timidity and stupidity.[65] Whitman had a low opinion of its in-telligence: "The passenger-pigeon's instinct is wound up to a high point of uniformity and promptness, and her conduct is almost too blindly regular to be credited even with that stupidity which implies a grain of intelligence." [66]

There is no assurance that the intelligence tests applied to birds warrant the conclusions drawn by the experimenters. Whitman removed the egg of a passenger pigeon to a distance of two inches outside the edge of the nest: "The passenger pigeon ... leaves the nest when approached, but returns soon after you leave. On returning she looks at the nest, steps into it, and sits down as if nothing had happened. She soon finds out, not by sight, but by feeling, that something is missing. Her instinct is keenly attuned and she acts promptly, leaving the nest after a few minutes without heeding the egg. The conduct varies relatively little in different individuals." [67] The ringdove was satisfied with the recovery of one egg, while the domestic pigeon tried to recover both.

Generations of experience have taught most of the tree-nesting birds that if the eggs, or nest, are not in place they have been destroyed. The condition is different with the domestic pigeon or rock dove nesting on ledges. An egg that rolls from the nest may lodge near it and be readily recoverable. The pied-billed grebe (*Podilymbus podiceps*) when frightened from the nest will frequently dislodge one or more eggs. On returning she recovers the eggs with facility. The Atlantic murre (*Uria aalge aalge*) will roll its egg back to the original site over a distance of at least eighteen inches.[68] Several species of gulls will also retrieve their eggs.[69] The reaction in these cases should be considered as the result of conditioning to the ecological environment rather than to intelligence.

PHYSICAL HABITS

The bearing of the passenger pigeon was regal (Fig. 7). A friend of Dixon wrote to him: "They sit up as if they had a wire drawn through them." [70] In an attitude of alarm the long tail was held on a level with the back, the wings were compressed against the body, and the raised head gave an air of complete attention. Thoreau spoke most aptly of their "inquisitive necks." [71]

Their attitude when concerned has been described by Brewster: "They usually chose conspicuous perches on dead prongs, or among leafless branches, and sat there erect, with necks elongated and almost perfectly in line with the body and tail, looking very long and slender, and remaining motionless save for occasional nodding, or oscillating movements of the head as they gazed fixedly at the advancing sportsman with what seemed an expression of blended timidity and curiosity." [72]

A pigeon in repose rested its body on a limb and its head on its chest especially after eating.[73] Dillin wrote: "On the approach of danger he generally stood up and stretched out his neck; if his head moved slowly about, you were safe in the belief that he was not alarmed; but if on the contrary a rapid motion was observed, it was a case of shoot quickly, for he had decided to fly, and when he did fly he was off like a whirl-wind." [74] A friend of Dixon to whom a pair of pigeons was given commented on their predilection for a sloping perch and curious grebe-like fashion of resting upon it.[75]

The raising of the head and nodding when the bird was approached impressed Green as highly characteristic and indicative of curiosity.[76] The nodding has been described by Craig as follows:

The nod of the Passenger Pigeon was utterly different from that of the Mourning Dove. The specific manner of nodding seemed an integral part of the bird's general bearing. The nod consisted of a movement of the head in a circle, back, up, forward and down, as if the bird were trying to hook its bill over something. Often two or three such nods were given with no pauses between, following one another much more rapidly than in the Mourning Dove, because body and tail remained all the while stationary. Thus the nod, being performed by the head alone, fell in with the general mannerism of the species—the body generally executing strong and ample movements, the short and quick glances and nods being executed by the head alone.[77]

Unfortunately we are left in the dark as to the conditions under which nodding was indulged in, except under alarm, and whether it had various stimuli.

The passenger pigeon when sleeping held its bill in the middle of the breast where it became well covered by the feathers. The tail was held at an angle of about 45°.[78]

The pigeon with its quite short legs was rather awkward on the ground, advancing with a "jerky, alert step." [79] The ordinary walking pace of the male was twelve to thirteen steps in five seconds.[80]

Like all other members of the family, this pigeon immersed its head up to the eyes while drinking and did not remove it until satiated.[81] Bryant remarks that they were "great drinkers, going to water as regularly as to feed." [82] The small ponds were the favored drinking places in southern Michigan. The pigeon drank at least once daily, usually at dawn. A salt spring in Michigan was visited by countless thousands of pigeons at daybreak during the nesting season.[83] Pigeons in autumn repaired uniformly to the banks of the Ohio for water between dawn and sunrise.[84] In the Indian territory they drank on the return to the nesting after feeding.[85]

The alighting of a flock of pigeons to drink must have made a charming picture. Green wrote:

One of the most beautiful sights I ever had of wild pigeons was seen while fishing along Honeoye Creek . . . near Rochester, N. Y., above the ripples of the creek where the stones were plainly visible, the water dashing down between the stones and rocks. Suddenly a marvelously large flock of pigeons circled over the spot and alighted in the stream upon these stones and rocks. Their object was to alleviate their thirst in the pure waters of the stream.[86]

When the state of the shoreline did not permit the customary approach, the passenger pigeon would alight on the water with wings half-spread and, after drinking, clear the water with a single sweep of its wings.[87] This behavior was not peculiar to the species. Darwin mentions that the domestic pigeon alighted on the water of the Nile to drink and the same habit in this country has been observed.[88] The flock pigeon (*Histriophaps histrionica*) of Australia alighted on the water to drink in large numbers.[89]

Pigeons seeking water, particularly salt water, have been known to pile upon one another two and three deep.[90] An instance is recorded of pigeons stopping to drink at a pond in New Jersey. The birds in the rear alighted upon the backs of the first arrivals, pressing them into the water, and tens of thousands were drowned.[91] A destruction of this magnitude while drinking must have been very unusual.

The only description of bathing is that furnished by Whitman:

I watched a young ectopistes a little more than 2 months old, take its bath in a shallow glass basin. After trying the water by immersing its beak and shaking it, it plunged in and gave itself a vigorous shaking several times. After each shaking it would lie over on one side and lift up the wing of the other side, stretching it vertically or a little inclined and as far as it could reach. I have often noticed this habit of lifting the wing during a bath in other pigeons. They frequently perform these same motions when it rains, especially if they are disposed to a bath. The wing is raised so as to expose its under surface to the falling rain. The same movements are also often employed in "sunning" themselves.[92]

Feathers were sometimes abundant in shallow water where the wild birds had evidently bathed.[93]

SOCIABILITY

The truculence attributed to the passenger pigeon must have been due in part to the circumstance that most of the observations were made on captives. Dixon had a pair that quarreled incessantly. The male, smaller and weaker than the female, was constantly abused by her.[94] Craig had this opinion:

The male Ectopistes was a particularly quarrelsome bird, ever ready to threaten or strike with his wings (though perhaps not quite so ready with his beak), and to shout defiance in his loud strident voice. With such a quick temper, such a grand air, and such an unusual voice and method of attack, he generally put to flight a pigeon of any other species at the first onslaught. Nevertheless he was a coward at heart. In short, he was a splendid bluffer.[95]

The literature has a wealth of contradictory statements. The birds kept in Cincinnati became very tame, were quiet and never fought with each other.[96] Pugnaciousness was no more peculiar to the passenger pigeon during the mating season than to any other species of pigeon. Fighting for food by the young began early.[97] The only cases of fighting ever observed by J. B. Oviatt were mild encounters over food. He never chanced to observe fighting in a nesting over either mates or nesting sites.[98]

Two young passenger pigeons kept by Whitman never slept side by side but insisted on an open space of six or more inches.[99] This behavior is entirely out of keeping with that of birds in the wild, where gregariousness was highly developed in flight, resting, roosting, and nesting. Roberts mentions that on alighting in trees they formed "crowded rows," and Maynard that they generally sat "close together" (Fig. 14).[100] The crowding at the roosts was proverbial.

A passenger pigeon, hatched and reared by a different species, was very apt when fully grown to attempt to mate with the species by which it had been fostered. This type of conditioning is not unusual among birds. In confinement, males were known to mate with each other when there were several unmated females desirous of mating in the same pen.[101]

The passenger pigeon associated with only the mourning dove and domestic pigeon, and cases of this are few. Occasionally a mourning dove was netted with the pigeons.[102] W. B. Barrows never knew the dove and pigeon to mingle.[103] Most of the accounts of a pigeon being in the company of mourning doves came at the time when the species was nearly extinct. In Maryland single pigeons were seen frequently in flocks of mourning doves.[104] A wild pigeon was seen in the company of two mourning doves over a period of two weeks in Charles City, Iowa, in 1898, while the last bird taken in Wisconsin was shot from a flock of mourning doves.[105] Trippe saw "wild pigeons and doves" feeding in the streets of a town in Iowa but does not state that they were actually associated.[106]

The tame pigeon kept by Howitt would not associate with domestic pigeons; however, C. S. Osborn saw a wild pigeon flying about with domestic pigeons at Sault Ste. Marie, Michigan, in 1897.[107]

DOMESTICATION

Passenger pigeons were held in captivity for use as decoys at an early date. Attempts to domesticate them met with little success. Kalm wrote that in 1748 he had seen wild pigeons so tame that they would fly out and return again.[108] Elsewhere he said:

The French in Canada, who annually catch a number of young Pigeons alive which they thereafter rear at their homes, have taken much pains to tame these birds, although with but little success. It is very easy, when they are kept in suitable quarters to make them so tame as to feed from one's hands ... ; but as soon as they are let out into the open hardly a few days pass before they fly away to the woods, nevermore to return. It was, however, emphatically asserted, that some had succeeded in taming them to the same extent as the domesticated Pigeons.[109]

In April, 1827, Bullock spent a day at a home in Kentucky where the farmyard abounded with wild pigeons as tame as domestic ones.[110] We are left in the dark as to the origin of these pigeons.

Recorded attempts to breed them are few. Janson, who resided near Edenton, North Carolina, claims to have enticed wild pigeons into his barn by cutting holes in the roof and placing food upon it. The birds became very tame, fed with the fowls, and bred in his dovecote.[111] It is difficult to believe that this pigeon would enter the compartments of a dovecote of the usual construction. He had the passenger pigeon in mind, for he speaks of its occurrence in enormous numbers at intervals of seven to ten years.

The experiments of Paul Clark of Albany, New York, have been described by Clinton. Old birds that had been taken in nets would not breed. Success was finally attained by mating a male captured in a net and held in a cage for three years, so that it was quite tame, with a female taken as a squab from a nest in the woods and held in a cage to maturity. In the year 1822, two pairs nested seven and eight times, respectively, from May to September. Thirteen of the young survived. The young were said to have been completely feathered within eight days after hatching and to have flown from the nest.[112] At this rate, the development was considerably greater than in the wild. It is also unbelievable that a pair would nest seven or eight times within a period of five months. Whittaker's pigeons had a breeding period of seven months. During this time some females laid seven to eight eggs, but the average was three to four.[113]

Pigeons taken to England by Audubon bred in the London Zoological Gardens in 1832.[114] Squabs captured at the nesting on Bell's Run in Pennsylvania in 1870 were kept in a large cage in Potter County by Herman Lehman. They bred indifferently, never laying more than one egg to a clutch. Frequently nests were built without ovulation, or the egg was not incubated.[115] In 1879 Owen was successful in raising young from pigeons brought from Pennsylvania. Mates were changed after each nesting.[116] Limited breeding was obtained with stool pigeons.[117]

The history of the pigeons kept at the Cincinnati Zoological Gardens is hopelessly confused. Thompson states that three pairs of trapped birds were purchased in the spring of 1877.[118] According to Dury, when the

Gardens opened in 1875, they had a flock of about 22 birds.[119] S. A. Stephan, General Manager of the Gardens, wrote Deane on November 9, 1907, that in 1875 there were purchased 26 birds that came from Michigan.[120] Years later, in letters, Stephan varied this figure to 17 captured in 1876 and to six pairs purchased in 1878.[121] Thompson states that these pigeons began to breed in March, 1878, but an earlier note by him indicates March, 1879.[122] By 1881 they had increased to 20.

Our best knowledge of the life of this pigeon began with the breeding experiments conducted by David Whittaker in Milwaukee, Wisconsin. One writer states that Whittaker had 50 birds, the descendants of a pair given him by an Indian in 1887.[123] Deane was in Milwaukee on March 1, 1896 and learned from Whittaker that he obtained from an Indian in the fall of 1888 a pair of adult and a pair of young pigeons that had been trapped in Shawano County, Wisconsin. Shortly after confinement one of the adults died and the other escaped. It was several years before the remaining pair was successful in rearing young. At the time of Deane's visit there were 15 birds in the flock.[124] The University of Chicago in 1896 became the center of interest. Prof. C. O. Whitman in a letter to Ames dated May 20, 1901, states that he purchased about one-half of Whittaker's flock of 15 birds. These pigeons increased slowly. In 1899 and 1900 not a single egg hatched. Whitman at this time was trying to get a new bird to counteract the effects of inbreeding.[125] On finding that his pigeons ate earthworms avidly and improved in vigor, he thought that if he had known of this diet earlier his flock could have been kept from dying out.[126] Had he read Bendire,[127] he would have learned that they were very fond of earthworms.

A history of the condition of the pigeons held in Milwaukee, Chicago, and Cincinnati up to 1908 is given by Deane.[128] In February, 1908, four males remained in the Whittaker flock in Milwaukee, while in November, 1907, there were two males and a female in Cincinnati, making a total of seven birds. Whitman's flock by 1906 was reduced to two females and these had died by 1907. Fleming states that Whitman had five birds left in 1906.[129] The four males in Milwaukee died between November, 1908, and February, 1909. A male died in Cincinnati in April, 1909.[130] Finally on July 10, 1910, the remaining male died in

Cincinnati.[131] This left as sole survivor of the species a female, the celebrated Martha, named after Martha Washington.

It would be difficult to find a more garbled history than that of Martha. The more that was written about her, the worse the confusion. The following dates and times of death in 1914 occur in the literature: 2:00 P.M., August 29, 1914; 2:00 P.M., September 1; 1:00 A.M., September 1; 1:00 P.M., September 1.[132] Bridges unfortunately made further inquiry and was informed by Director Joseph A. Stephan that she died at 5:00 P.M., September 1.[133] That she died at 5:00 P.M. "surrounded by a hushed group of distinguished ornithologists" is sheer romance.[134] The latest direct information derived from S. A. Stephan is that her lifeless body was found on the ground on September 1 at 1:00 P.M.[135]

This pigeon was promised to the Smithsonian Institution when she died. The body was suspended in water and the whole frozen. Encased in a 300-pound cake of ice, she arrived in Washington, D. C. September 4, 1914, where a detailed anatomical examination of the body was made by Shufeldt.[136]

The last passenger pigeon was mounted and now reposes in a glass case in the U. S. National Museum. The two labels read as follows:

Ectopistes migratorius (Linnaeus)
Passenger Pigeon
Exterminated. Formerly very abundant
throughout a large part of North America.
This is the last known individual. It died
in captivity in September, 1914.

Ectopistes migratorius (Linnaeus)
Passenger Pigeon
Last of its race. Died at Cincinnati
Zoological Garden, September 1st, 1914.
Age 29 years.
Presented by the Cincinnati Zoological
Garden to the National Museum.
Adult female, 236,650

Martha in consonance with her sex was of indefinite age at the time of her death. A letter dated November 9, 1910, from S. A. Stephan to Pearson gave her age as "about eighteen years." [137] According to information given by S. A. Stephan to Deane she was about 12 years old in 1907 and about 13 years old in 1909.[138] In 1911 Deane reported her in good health and plumage and about 14 years of age.[139] Her age at death was accordingly 19, 18, or 17 years. Stephan wrote to Shufeldt at the time of her death that she was 29 years of age.[140] Other ages given are: 20 years, 27 years, 28 years, and 29 years.[141] A letter received from N. S. Hastings, Zoological Society of Cincinnati, dated February 13, 1950, states that she was hatched in the Zoo in 1888, giving an age of 26 years. It could not be determined that any records of her age were kept at Cincinnati, or at Chicago by Professor Whitman. It is not known if any one of the ages ranging from 17 to 29 years is correct.

One fact is known about Martha. Her ancestors were captured in Wisconsin. A post card distributed by the Cincinnati Zoological Society states erroneously that she was hatched in Cincinnati. All the birds in possession of Professor Whitman originated from the Wisconsin birds obtained by Whitman. Deane gives the reliable statement of Professor Whitman that in 1902 he sent a female to the Gardens of the Cincinnati Zoological Company. He also quotes in the same paper a letter from S. A. Stephan, General Manager of the Gardens, in which the latter mentions three pigeons remaining, two old males and "one female that we obtained from Prof. Whitman's flock in 1902." [142]

CHAPTER 3 : FOOD

The passenger pigeon had a varied diet. The staple foods during fall, winter, and spring were acorns, chestnuts, and beechnuts, and during the summer soft fruits of many kinds. Included in the diet were weed seeds, insects, and worms. Succulent plants appear to have been eaten very sparingly. Aside from gravel and a few feathers, the stomach contents of eleven birds showed 9.36 per cent animal food, the remainder being vegetable.[1]

This pigeon was a prodigious eater due to the energy expended in swift and long flights. At times birds had their crops so distended with beechnuts that they burst open on striking the ground after being shot.[2] Dury mentions having shot pigeons with crops so distended with mast that they were as large as an orange, while Roberts states that a well-filled pigeon had a neck and crop almost the size of the body.[3] Seventeen acorns were removed from one bird. The crop of a pigeon has contained: half a pint of beechnuts;[4] a teacupful of acorns;[5] 28 beechnuts, 11 grains of corn, 100 maple "leaves" (seeds or samaras), and other material;[6] "a good handful of the kernels of beech nuts, intermixed with acorns and chestnuts";[7] 104 kernels of corn, 14 beechnuts, and 22 maple seeds, in volume over a gill;[8] and 30 acorns.[9]

The daily food requirement for the multitude of pigeons was enormous. Wilson gives half a pint of mast as the daily consumption,[10] so that the flock of 2,230,272,000 pigeons seen by him would require 17,424,000 bushels per day. Audubon estimated that 1,115,136,000 birds would consume daily 8,712,000 bushels of mast.[11] It is to be noted that his estimates are Wilson's figures divided by two. Some fantastic calculations are given by Révoil based on a single pigeon's daily consumption of a quarter of a bushel of seeds or fruits: "Quel formidable appétit!" [12]

It is doubtful if the average daily consumption of food by the passenger pigeon was equal to one-half a pint, or two gills per day. Some figures are available on the quantity of corn consumed by captive birds. According to the La Crosse *Democrat* (Wis.) of June 1, 1871, a shipment of 10,200 birds from Milwaukee to Buffalo consumed in three days 34 bushels of corn. This is 0.28 gill per pigeon per day. In another case, 3,000 pigeons being fattened for the market consumed 15 bushels of corn in a week, or only 0.18 gill per pigeon daily.[13] Knapp states that 8,400 captive pigeons ate "over eight bushels of grain per day," or 0.24 gill per bird.[14] Martin mentions that in a pen 1,000 birds were given one-half a bushel of corn in the morning.[15] Since two feedings were customary, they received a bushel per day or 0.256 gill per bird. The four cases show approximately a daily consumption of 0.25 gill. While a bird in the wild would consume considerably more food than when in captivity, it is questionable if it would be eight times this amount. The average volume of food eaten by seven wild band-tailed pigeons was 45.2 cubic centimeters.[16] Allowing 90 cubic centimeters for two feedings a day, there is obtained only 0.65 gill. The passenger pigeon was of similar size, so it is doubtful if its daily consumption of food averaged more than 0.5 gill.

The thoroughness with which the pigeons gleaned the mast had a decided effect on other forms of wildlife. In 1728 Byrd wrote: "In their Travels they make vast Havock among the Acorns and Berries of all Sorts, that they waste whole Forrests in a short time, and leave a Famine behind them for most other Creatures." [17] Wilson also calls attention to the serious loss to other creatures of the forest due to the consumption of mast by the pigeons.[18] Bears, squirrels, and wild turkeys would have been especially affected, and the depletion might well have caused their emigration from the denuded region.

The pigs of the settlers lived largely on mast during the winter. A visitation by pigeons caused great harm. The difficulty in finding any mast where the pigeons had fed is commented upon by Kalm.[19] Catesby wrote: "Where they light, they so effectively clear the Woods of Acorns and other Mast, that the Hogs that come after them, to the detriment of the Planters, fare very poorly." [20] After removal of the mast, some hogs actually starved to death in the north.[21]

The gathering of the mast was not always as thorough as indicated. Scherer writes: "Mr. Oviatt ... told me that they would feed over a place many times and still not get everything. He had observed that beech nuts might sprout quite thickly from an area of forest floor, even though the torn-up leaves gave evidence that pigeons had fed there." [22]

METHODS OF FEEDING

A flock of pigeons feeding on the ground followed a characteristic procedure that has been often described. It has been well pictured by Wheaton:

In the fall of 1859 ... I had an opportunity of observing a large flock while feeding. The flock, after a little circling by the foremost ranks, alighted upon the ground, presenting a front of over a quarter of a mile, with a depth of nearly a hundred yards. In a very few moments those in the rear, finding the ground nearly stripped of mast, arose above the tree tops and alighted in front of the advance column. This movement soon became continuous and uniform, birds from the rear flying to the front so rapidly that the whole presented the appearance of a rolling cylinder having a diameter of about fifty yards, its interior filled with flying leaves and grass. The noise was deafening and the sight confusing to the mind.[23]

The behavior of a small flock was different:

It was in the late autumn, after the leaves had fallen from the trees. There were about 120 birds in the flock. They lighted in the top of a large beech tree; and, finding that the beechnuts had fallen out of the hulls, dropped in rapid succession from branch to branch till all had reached the ground. I never have seen more intense activity or seeming system in feeding than those birds displayed. They worked in a wing-shaped group, moving nervously forward in one direction around the tree, gleaning the entire nut-covered space as they went. Those falling to the rear of the flock, where the nuts were picked up, kept flopping across to the front so as to get the advantage of unpicked ground. A few that wandered apart in search of scattered nuts kept scurrying about and tilting as they picked them up and then hurried back to the flock as if they feared the flock would soon be through feeding and off on the wing. This restless, voracious activity was continued till the flock took fright and burst into the air, to fly away and disappear as a small cloud.[24]

There was a constant "twittering and squeaking" as the pigeons fed.[25] To Burroughs the sound, which could be heard for half a mile, was soft and sweet like the voices of little girls.[26] A babble of tongues is seldom musical except at a distance.

The procedure by which the pigeons fed on the mast *in situ* has been incorrectly described. Du Pratz and Wilson have pictured the pigeons detaching by blows of the wings the acorns and nuts, then dropping to the ground to eat them.[27] This produced a column of pigeons rising and descending. French also tells of the beating of beechnuts from a tree with the wings.[28] The fluttering of the pigeons in the bur oaks in Michigan is mentioned by Ferris but not interpreted.[29]

No bird in the wild would put its safety in jeopardy by injuring its flight feathers. The correct method of securing the mast is given by Bryant. He writes: "One of their methods of feeding on acorns and beechnuts was peculiar. After the frost had fallen a time or two the nuts and acorns became loosened from their holds, but did not fall at once. Then the pigeons would light on the outer ends of the limbs of the oak or beech, and seizing a beechnut or acorn in their bill, winnow backward with their wings and pull the nut from its fastening and swallow it whole."[30] Owing to the precarious footing the winnowing was necessary to maintain a balance. E. Haskell adds that the birds maintained themselves in suspension in the air in an upright position by a peculiar flapping of the wings while the nuts were being extracted.[31] It is doubtful if the pigeons could do this without some footing, however unstable.

The passenger pigeon was usually reluctant to alight immediately to feed. "When a suitable feeding-place is discovered, the birds move in circles over the spot, then descend to a lower level and make a movement as if to alight, when all of a sudden, they take to flight, but speedily return and pass through the same manoeuvers, as if undecided, or apprehensive of hidden dangers."[32]

In view of the small mouth of the passenger pigeon, its ability to swallow an acorn as large as that of the red oak is surprising; however, the mouth could be expanded to one inch. Audubon wrote: "Whilst feeding, their avidity is at times so great that in attempting to swallow a large acorn or nut, they are seen gasping for a long while, as if in the agonies of suffocation."[33]

The pigeon never obtained its food by "scratching" with its feet as has been sometimes stated. Leaves and earth were turned with the bill. Behr never saw the feet used for this purpose.[34] In a letter to me M. A. Schmitz stated that in autumn, when snow came prior to migration, the pigeons sought food with their bills and never scratched like chickens. At times, while nesting, the pigeons were obliged to search for food in from four to six inches of snow. Pokagon on such occasions has seen the snow and leaves intermingled for many miles where the birds had been feeding.[35]

Having filled their crops, the pigeons lined up on branches as closely as they could sit. While so perched they called to any passing flock and usually brought them down.[36] With bills resting on the distended crops, the birds gave themselves over to the pleasures of digestion. This was so rapid that a crop filled with acorns in the evening was empty by morning.

An interesting habit of the passenger pigeon was the disgorging of the contents of the crop when food more to its liking was found.[37] Both old and young pigeons could throw up food.[38] In the process the head was held down with the bill open, while the crop was shaken, an operation involving movement of the entire body, especially the wings. Kalm was told that they would disgorge rye to eat wheat on arriving at a field of the latter.[39] During an interview with John Willsey, Lake Mills, Wisconsin, in 1937, I was assured that he had seen pigeons alight on shocks of wheat and throw up acorns in order to eat the grain. In connection with this habit, it was believed that pigeon grass was widely distributed in Michigan by the pigeons disgorging the seeds upon the wheat fields when the more desirable food was found.[40]

It is doubtful if any of the seeds eaten by the passenger pigeon escaped digestion. Cox fancied that the spread of the forests westward was aided by the acorns and nuts carried by the great flocks of passenger pigeons.[41] The seeds of the apple, grape, strawberry, and cherry fed to domestic pigeons were crushed and digested beyond power of germination.[42] How the pigeons could have aided in the spread of the forests is not clear. Normally they rested after eating and the process of digestion was rapid. Mast was the preferred diet and it is unlikely that it would have been disgorged for any of the other native foods. Forests attained their present distribution long before any cultivated grains, other than corn possibly, were available.

The principal foods of the passenger pigeon are discussed below.

PLANT FOODS

BEECH (*Fagus grandifolia*).—Beechnuts were the favored food of the passenger pigeon and other forms of wildlife. The beech ranged from New Brunswick westward to the northern shore of Lake Huron, northern Michigan, eastern Wisconsin; south through eastern Illinois to eastern Texas; and in the east south to Florida. The most important stands occurred in Kentucky, Indiana, Ohio, Michigan, West Virginia, Pennsylvania, New York and central Ontario. The beechnut is very high in both fat and protein. (See Table 1.)

While Charles Martin was trapping in Michigan, the beechnuts removed from the crops of the pigeons accumulated to such an extent that hogs were brought in to devour them.[43]

The beech for a period in the latter part of the nineteenth century seems to have had a good crop of nuts every two years. A biennial crop of nuts in southeastern New York was long considered a regular event.[44] Merriam wrote of the Adirondack region: "My notes show that the beechnut crop was good in the autumns of 1871, 1873, 1875, 1877, 1879, 1881, 1883,—always on the odd years—while on the alternate seasons it failed." [45] A large crop of beechnuts in the fall of an odd year meant that the pigeons might nest in the spring of the even year. Roney, without comment on mast, stated that nestings occurred in Michigan only in even alternate years, 1868, 1870, 1872, 1874, 1876, and 1878.[46] Gunn mentions that the main colony of pigeons visited Michigan every two years due to the abundance of mast one year and the scarcity the next.[47] From 1937 to 1950, I sent annually about thirty inquiries to people living throughout the range of the beech to determine the yield of nuts. No regularity in bearing was shown, and no region showed a good crop of nuts every second year. A good crop might be followed in two years by a small or medium yield with large crops occurring only once in three to seven years. The principal reason given for a failure was a late frost.

OAK (*Quercus*).—It is probable that the acorns of all species of oaks were eaten. Acorns in quantity are borne at irregular intervals, usually three to five years. In Wisconsin the bur and red oaks show the greatest regularity in bearing. A large crop of acorns may be so heavily infested

TABLE 1

ANALYSES OF BEECHNUT AND ACORNS

SPECIES	PORTION	WATER	ETHER EXTRACT	PROTEIN	FAT	NITROGEN-FREE EXTRACT
Beechnut, Fagus silvatica *	Kernel	...	...	28.52%	42.22%	...
	Shell	...	...	4.35	1.14	...
	Whole Nut	...	...	20.22	28.12	...
Acorn — Quercus alba †	Kernel	24.29%	4.41%	5.92	...	61.51%
Quercus velutina †	"	9.04	20.90	6.29	...	59.23
Quercus borealis maxima †	"	14.88	16.06	5.92	...	58.07
Quercus rubra ‡	Kernel with integument	38.20	12.87	3.81	...	41.45
Quercus prinus ‡	"	50.10	2.52	3.13	...	41.52
Quercus ilicifolia ‡	"	42.00	11.61	5.56	...	37.48
Quercus prinoides ‡	"	44.20	3.52	3.81	...	45.57
Quercus alba ‡	"	47.30	3.33	3.13	...	43.37

* The American beech (*Fagus grandifolia*) is very similar to the European (*Fagus sylvatica*), the nuts of which on a dry basis have the composition given in the above table. Figures after Engels, "Eicheln und Bucheckern," *Land. Vers. Stat.*, LXXXII (1913), 139.
† Figures after Baumgras, "Experimental Feeding of Captive Fox Squirrels," *J. Wildlife Management*, VIII (1944), 296–300.
‡ Figures after Wainio and Forbes, "The Chemical Composition of Forest Fruits and Nuts from Pennsylvania," *J. Agr. Research*, LXII (1941), 627–35.

with the larvae of weevils, particularly of the genus *Balaninus,* that it is almost impossible to find a sound acorn the following spring. In the autumn of 1937, at Madison, Wisconsin, from 83 to 100 per cent of the acorns of *Quercus ellipsoidalis* were parasitized.

In the South the pigeons ate chiefly the acorns of the willow oak (*Quercus phellos*), water oak (*Q. nigra*), and turkey oak (*Q. flammula = laevis* Walter = *catesbaei*).[48] Use of the acorns of the turkey oak and *Q. obtusifolia* (?) is mentioned by others.[49]

The acorns of the white oak (*Q. alba*), post oak (*Q. stellata*), blackjack oak (*Q. marilandica*), and bur oak (*Q. macrocarpa*) were eaten in Missouri.[50] Those of the white oak, red oak (*Q. rubra = borealis*), and pin oak (*Q. palustris*) were consumed in the eastern states.[51]

Large nestings in Wisconsin were dependent on the presence of the acorns of the black oak (*Q. velutina*) and Hill's oak (*Q. ellipsoidalis*). The acorns of the white oak sprout soon after falling so that their value as food is brief.

Pigeons obtained from Chicago were on sale in Cleveland in February, 1878.[52] The impression is left that they had been captured alive and fed acorns instead of grain. In view of the season and the belief that the acorns were from the blackjack oak (*Q. marilandica*), it is improbable that these acorns would have been fed in Chicago. It is logical to assume that these were dead birds shipped originally from the southwest.

Acorns are low in fat and protein, and high in carbohydrates. Decided preferences are shown by game animals. They will avoid the acorns of the red oak almost completely if those of the white and black oak are available. Analyses are given in Table 1.

CHESTNUT (*Castanea dentata*).—Chestnuts must have been an important food, but they are mentioned rarely in comparison with acorns and beechnuts.[53] The utilization of the nuts of the chinquapin (*Castanea* sp.), a species found in the southeastern part of the United States, has been reported from Ontario.[54]

HEMLOCK (*Tsuga canadensis*).—There are several statements that the pigeons ate the seeds of conifers, but none of these seeds has been reported from the stomach contents. Forbush gives hemlock and pine seeds as important in their diet, and Wilson states that the seeds of "some conifers" were eaten in Michigan.[55] Thoreau wrote: "Minott says that pigeons alight in great flocks on the top of hemlocks in March, and he thinks they eat the seed. (But he also thought for the same reason that they ate the white pine seed at the same season, when it is not there!)" [56]

During the nesting near Sheffield, Pennsylvania, in 1863, according to E. Osborn, the pigeons fed on hemlock seed; and he had known them to depend on this food entirely during the nesting season.[57] J. B. Oviatt considered hemlock seeds second in importance to beechnuts in Pennsylvania.[58]

PINE (*Pinus*).—Pigeons, while nesting in Michigan, are said to have fed on pine seeds after the beechnuts were exhausted.[59] Eating the seeds of the white pine (*Pinus strobus*) is mentioned specifically.[60]

Pine seeds are a staple food of mourning doves in the South. Wayne found that they remain in the pine woods for weeks at a time, walking out on the branches and extracting the seeds from the cones.[61]

JUNIPER (*Juniperus virginiana*).—Eating the berries of this tree, as mentioned by Gentry,[62] must have been unusual. The "buds" are stated to have been eaten in the Hudson Bay region when the various berries were covered with snow.[63] Forster interpreted this to mean that the buds were eaten in winter, which is improbable.[64]

ELM (*Ulmus*).—It is probable that the seeds of all three of the native elms were eaten. The rock elm (*Ulmus racemosa*) was never plentiful, but the American elm (*U. americana*) was abundant. The seeds of the latter were eaten in large quantities.[65] In 1940 Ernest Thompson Seton wrote to me: "It was understood that they came *each year* to feed on the seeds of the slippery elm [*Ulmus fulva*], which covered the ground in early spring." This applied to the Toronto region. One writer mentions the eating of young elm buds after the beechnuts had sprouted.[66]

MAPLE (*Acer*).—The seeds were eaten regularly,[67] specifically those of the red maple (*Acer rubrum*) [68] and the sugar maple (*A. saccharum*). Twenty-five seeds of the latter, with the wings removed, were found in the crop of a dried specimen of a female passenger pigeon.[69] The eating of maple buds is also mentioned.[70]

BIRCH (*Betula*).—The nutlets of the river birch (*Betula nigra*) and the nutlets and catkins of the yellow birch (*B. excelsa*) were eaten.[71] Cottam and Knappen mention a samara of the yellow birch (*B. lutea*).[72]

ALDER (*Alnus*).—The catkins of the alder (*Alnus serrulata = rugosa*) were sometimes consumed.[73]

HACKBERRY (*Celtis occidentalis*).—The berries were eaten.[74]

CHERRY (*Prunus*).—In autumn the pigeons fed liberally on the fruits of the black cherry (*Prunus serotina*), choke cherry (*P. virginiana*), and pin cherry (*P. pennsylvanica*).[75] The pin cherry was commonly known as pigeon cherry in New England, New York, Ontario, and North Dakota.[76] Of the sand cherry (*P. pumila*), Traill wrote: "So eagerly is the fruit sought by the Pigeons and Partridges that it is difficult to obtain any quantity in its most favoured localities." [77]

As to hunting in the glades of the Allegheny Mountains, Hallock said: "The wild cherries are, while they last, eagerly sought by the pigeons, and large bags are made by sitting beneath these trees and shooting at the incoming flocks." [78]

The black cherry bears abundantly nearly every year. The soil of a farm in Simcoe County, Ontario, contained so many cherry pits that a pan of it when sifted yielded a small teacupful of the seeds. Their abundance was attributed to a pigeon roost a few miles distant.[79] Normally the seeds were crushed and the kernel digested.

Byrd was surprised to find that the wild pigeons had eaten all the "black-heart" cherries in his orchard at Westover, Virginia.[80] Cultivated cherries were also eaten in the gardens at Waukegan, Illinois,[81] and at Cleveland, Ohio.[82]

JUNEBERRY (*Amelanchier*).—Pigeons were fond of the fruits of the various species of juneberry or service berry.[83] Pigeon berry, applied to *A. spicata*,[84] was probably used for the other species of juneberry as well. In autumn in western Montana they fed chiefly on the fruit of *A. alnifolia*.[85] This tree was known in the west as pigeon berry.[86]

SASSAFRAS (*Sassafras variifolium*).—The blue drupes were consumed.[87]

HOLLY (*Ilex*).—Wilson mentions that pigeons ate the berries of the holly of which there are several species in the eastern states.[88] The fruit of *Ilex verticillata*, commonly known as black alder or pigeon berry,[89] was a favorite food in Ontario.[90]

BLACK GUM (*Nyssa sylvatica*).—The references to the eating of gum berries must refer to this species.[91] The fruit of the tupelo gum (*N. aquatica*), a southern species, may have been utilized also.

DOGWOOD (*Cornus*).—The berries of the flowering dogwood (*C. florida*) were eaten regularly.[92] In New York the blue dogwood (*C. alternifolia*) was known as pigeon berry.[93]

With respect to the shrubs of the genus *Cornus,* the gray-barked dog-wood (*C. paniculata*) was known as pigeon berry.[94] The berries of the common red osier (*C. stolonifera*) were eaten in Manitoba.[95] The pigeon collected by Ridgway in Nevada had eaten the fruit of *C. pubescens.*[96] In Nova Scotia the fruit of the bunchberry (*C. canadensis*), also known as pigeon berry, was eaten.[97]

MOUNTAIN ASH (*Sorbus americana*).—The fruits were eaten, especially when snow covered the ground,[98] and in late summer.[99]

MULBERRY (*Morus rubra*).—"These ripen in Pennsylvania in the beginning of June (new style), and are relished by these Pigeons almost above everything else." [100]

POPLAR (*Populus*).—According to Maximilian, pigeons collected in autumn in the tall poplar forests in Missouri had their crops filled with the fruits of these trees.[101] It is probable that he was mistaken. The fruits of the various species of poplars ripen in spring and are so small that it is doubtful if a pigeon would search for them. The seeds of *P. tremuloides* run 3,600,000 to the pound.[102] Hearne states: "They usually feed on poplar buds, and are good eating, though seldom fat." [103]

SUMAC (*Rhus*).—Pigeons caught in spring in Pennsylvania by a heavy snowfall ate the seeds of sumac.[104] This was a starvation diet as the nutritive value of the seeds is very low.

RAGWEED (*Ambrosia artemisiifolia*).—The seeds were eaten.[105]

SMARTWEED (*Polygonum pennsylvanicum*).—The seeds were a minor item.[106]

PIGWEED (*Amaranthus hybridus*).—Eating the seeds is mentioned by Gentry.[107]

BENT GRASS (*Agrostis* sp.).—Seed in traces.[108]

PIGEON GRASS (*Setaria*).—There are several species and it is probable that the seeds of all of them were eaten. The pigeon weed or "red-rod" mentioned by Purdy [109] was probably *S. glauca,* an importation from Europe. Both *S. viridis* and *S. glauca* are known as pigeon grass.[110] Cottam and Knappen report a few seeds.[111]

CANE (*Arundinaria*).—The seeds were eaten according to Lincecum.[112]

PARTRIDGE BERRY (*Mitchella repens*).—The berries of this plant persist through the winter, hence were available in the spring.[113] It is also known as pigeon berry and pigeon plum.[114]

WINTERGREEN (*Gaultheria procumbens*).—The eating of the berries is mentioned by Wilson.[115]

POKEBERRY (*Phytolacca decandra*).—Pigeons were so exceedingly fond of the fruit of this plant that it was commonly known as pigeon berry.[116] It is one of the foods to receive early mention.[117] Pigeons shot by Dury had all the fluids of the body stained by these berries.[118]

MYRTLE (*Myrica*).—Pigeons are reported to have eaten the berries of the myrtle, from which candles were made, along the Atlantic Coast from North Carolina to Florida.[119]

ROSE (*Rosa*).—Two passenger pigeons shot in September, 1877, and one in July, 1878, at Magnolia, Massachusetts, had eaten rose hips.[120]

STRAWBERRY (*Fragaria*).—Roger Williams wrote in 1643 that pigeons were abundant "especially in Strawberrie time when they pick up whole large Fields of the old grounds of the Natives." [121] An anonymous writer mentions that in New England there are "many doves, especially when the strawberries are ripe." [122] Pigeons near Quebec stripped the fields and woods of strawberries and raspberries.[123] They also fed on straw-berries in the Nipigon country, northern Canada, and in New Bruns-wick.[124] An unknown New England poet wrote in 1648:

> Bespread with Roses Sommer 'gins take place with hasty speed,
> Whose parching heate Strawberries coole doth moderation breed,
> Ayre darkening sholes of pigeons picke their berries sweet and good.[125]

GRAPE (*Vitis*).—Wild grapes were eaten in New England.[126] The summer grape, *V. aestivalis,* is also known as pigeon grape.[127] Seeds of the frost grape (*V. cordifolia*) were found.[128]

CROWBERRY (*Empetrum nigrum*).—Eaten in Labrador; one of the common names is pigeon berry.[129]

BLUEBERRY (*Vaccinium*).—A food eaten abundantly in summer and fall.[130]

HUCKLEBERRY (*Gaylussacia*).—The berries were eaten in large quan-tity.[131] At times their plumage was stained by the berries.[132]

ELDERBERRY (*Sambucus*).—The berries of the black and red species were eaten.[133] The berries of the red elder (*S. pubens = racemosa*) are mentioned specifically.[134] The crop and the flesh around the crop was stained by these fruits.[135]

BLACKBERRY (*Rubus*).—The berries were eaten to some extent.[136]

RASPBERRY (*Rubus*).—The berries of all species were eaten.[137]

GOOSEBERRY (*Ribes*).—There are numerous species, the berries of which were eaten.[138]

CURRANT (*Ribes*).—When Champlain was at Kennebunkport, Maine, July 12, 1605, he found countless pigeons feeding upon the red currants, probably *Ribes tristes,* that grew upon the islands in great profusion.[139] Wild currants attracted the pigeons to the Nipigon region.[140] Brewster found them eating currants in his garden.[141]

CRANBERRY (*Vaccinium*).—The fruit was eaten in Canada.[142] North of the Lake of the Woods and Rainy Lake the cranberry and blueberry "constitute their chief food supply as they remain on the bushes and retain much of their food properties until well on into the summer following their growth." [143]

WILD RICE (*Zizania aquatica*).—Crèvecoeur wrote at Carlisle, Pennsylvania: "I fancy they breed towards the plains of Ohio, and those about Lake Michigan, which abound in wild oats; though I have never killed any that had that grain in their craws. In one of them, last year, I found some undigested rice. Now the nearest rice fields from where I live, must be at least 560 miles; and either their digestion must be suspended while they are flying or else they must fly with the celerity of the wind." [144]

The finding of cultivated rice (*Oryza*) in the crops of pigeons killed hundreds of miles north of the nearest rice plantations became a favorite tale.[145] According to Audubon, pigeons killed in the vicinity of New York with their "crops full of rice" must have flown 300 to 400 miles in this condition.[146] In March, 1850, two pigeons with rice in their crops were killed near Detroit and it was estimated that the nearest place where this food could have been obtained was 700 miles distant.[147] It is very doubtful if any pigeon would start on so long a migration with a full crop. When they were satiated with food, it was their habit to seek repose. Sterling found that captive pigeons with a full crop would by choice remain on a perch until the process of digestion was finished;[148] and Schaff mentions seeing pigeons after filling their crops with acorns fly into trees where, with their heads resting on their breasts, they apparently dozed.[149]

Information on the stomach contents of birds in migratory flight is meager. Thompson states that it is well known that geese with wild rice in their stomachs have been killed at Fort Churchill, the nearest known source of the rice being at Turtle Lake, distant 780 miles.[150] Thirteen hours would be required to make this trip at a speed of 60 miles an hour. Neither the presence of rice in the stomach nor a flight of this duration is believable.

Attention has been called to the fact that when the pigeons have young, the milk in the crops of the parents sometimes granulates and in this state could be readily mistaken for rice.[151]

The evidence for the presence of rice, particularly cultivated, in the crop of the passenger pigeon is unsatisfactory. Bachman, while in the state of New York, examined the crops of several pigeons said by the country people to contain "rice" and found it to be wild rice (*Z. aquatica*).[152] Unfortunately the season when the pigeons were taken is not stated. As a food for land birds, wild rice is available for only a comparatively short time in autumn and must be gleaned from the stock. The grain matures the latter part of August or in September and then falls into the water. The stem of the wild rice sometimes attains an inch in diameter. It is probable, however, that while securing the grain it was necessary to use the wings as in obtaining mast from twigs.

In September, 1857, there was a large pigeon roost in a swamp 30 miles south of Cleveland, Ohio. Sterling states: "The crops in the majority of these birds, on their arrival at night, were full or partially filled, with rice and a good sprinkling of rice hulls. The grains were in every state of maceration, from mere pulp to those just swollen by the heat and secretions of the crop."[153] He was obsessed with the opinion that the grain had been obtained from the rice fields of the South. Wild rice, formerly at least, was locally common in northern Ohio and the shallow portions of Lake Erie.

Wild rice appears to have been eaten extensively in the north central states.[154] Writing of Michigan and the Northwest Territories, Morse reported: "This rice invites, at the proper season, and furnishes food for, and fattens, immense flocks of ducks, geese, pigeons, and other wild fowl."[155] Large numbers of pigeons were reported feeding on the wild rice growing along the Tittabawassee River, Michigan.[156]

There is no direct statement of Canadian source that wild rice was eaten. Hind found pigeons at "an immense marshy area covered with wild rice" on the Pennawa River, a tributary of the Winnipeg.[157]

The fruits of the following plants, judging from the common names,[158] may have been eaten by the pigeon: corn gromwell, or pigeon weed (*Lithospermum arvense*); European vervain, or pigeon grass (*Verbena officinalis*); bristly sarsaparilla, or pigeon berry (*Aralia hispida*); and Hercules' club, or pigeon tree (*Aralia spinosa*).

CULTIVATED GRAIN.—All the cultivated grains were eaten. Buckwheat was the first choice.[159] Wheat came second.[160] References to driving pigeons from the wheat fields are many. Wheat was commonly used for bait when trapping. Alexander Henry shot pigeons in his field of barley at the Terre Blanche, Manitoba, "as they pluck it up by the roots and devour it." [161]

As to rye, Kalm wrote: "They ate Rye, although not with particular avidity, but rather as if in the absence of something else more palatable." [162] Oats was consumed,[163] but Forbush seems alone in stating that it was a favorite food.[164] In 1860, at Manitowoc, Wisconsin, fields recently sown to oats were reported covered with pigeons.[165]

Corn was eaten extensively.[166] Bond mentions the eating of corn that had escaped digestion by cattle.[167] Kalm was erroneously informed that they would not touch corn.[168] This grain was used almost exclusively for feeding the pigeons prior to marketing and frequently for baiting. At Monroe, Wisconsin, in 1862 over 500 bushels were used on one trapping bed.[169]

The eating of the seeds of hemp (*Cannabis sativa*) is mentioned.[170]

PEAS.—Cultivated peas were eaten eagerly. Colonel Gordon wrote on June 16, 1760: "Planting peas the second time, the pigeons had pulled them up." [171] Langton complained of the great flocks of pigeons that devoured his peas.[172] A curious instance is given by Mitchell of pigeons being killed or disabled by filling their crops with dry peas, then drinking water that caused them to swell.[173] It is strange that the power of the passenger pigeon to disgorge food was not utilized in this case of extreme distress.

The squabs taken by Pike's men in Illinois in 1806 had their crops filled with acorns and the "wild pea." [174] The latter was probably a variety of *Lathyrus palustris,* once locally abundant in the Upper Mississippi Valley.

SUCCULENT PLANTS AND ROOTS.—There is no satisfactory information on the consumption of succulent plants. Whitman states that lettuce is eaten quite freely by pigeons generally.[175] Some species liked grass and the leaves of plantain. Based on her experience with wild birds, the following statement was made by Wilson: "We never found any green herbage or trace of garden crops." [176] There are numerous references to the "pulling" of corn and spring wheat, but the pigeons here sought the grain.

Evidence for the eating of small tubers and rootlets is equally unsatisfactory due to the want of any report of foods of this nature in the stomach contents. The digging by pigeons in marshy soil to obtain worms and insects, whereby roots were exposed, led to the conclusion that vegetable food was being sought. Barrows doubted that roots were eaten to an appreciable extent.[177]

While at Martin Creek, Pennsylvania, in 1807, Pursh took a walk with a friend who wished to show him the pigeon pea. He wrote: "In howing up some ground they showed me the roots by which I found them to be probably nothing else, than the tuberculis of a species of Glycine, resembling marrow fat peas very much; the pigeons scrach them up at certain times of the year and feed upon them very greedily." [178] The description fits the tubercles of *Amphicarpa bracteata* (L.), a widely distributed plant known as hog peanut, wild peanut, and wild peavine.

The consumption of the small tubers of squirrel corn (*Dicentra canadensis*) is recorded by Mitchell.[179] She also quotes William Pope on the eating by pigeons of the crisp roots of a plant growing in low ground and having the flavor of horseradish. This corresponds with the pepper-root (*Dentaria diphylla*).

BUDS.—The utilization of the buds of several species of trees has been mentioned above. Mactaggart, writing of Canada, says: "They seem to live in the wilderness, on the buds of various hard-wood trees, as the contents of their crops affirm." [180] Buds were probably eaten only when other foods were not available.

A considerable stir was created in 1878 by the publication of a letter from East Saginaw, Michigan, to the effect that the flesh of the pigeons was poisonous from feeding on the buds of the laurel.[181] There are two species in Michigan, *Kalmia angustifolia* and *Kalmia polifolia,* the latter being the more widely distributed. Confirmation of the eating of the buds is lacking. The game dealers considered the statement to be propaganda.[182]

ANIMAL FOODS

EARTHWORMS.—These worms were sought and eaten with avidity, but a reference to this fact was late in appearing in the literature.[183] Earthworms were acceptable at all times but especially when there were young to be fed.[184] At this time they sought "marsh feed," [185] a procedure known as "worming." [186] The food of the pigeons at the nesting at Shelby, Michigan, in 1876, consisted entirely of beechnuts and worms.[187] Barrows mentions that a trapper, failing to entice the pigeons with grain, resorted to earthworms with great success.[188] Invariably after a rain Wilson found earthworms together with other small worms and insects, in their crops.[189]

It was several years after Professor Whitman acquired his flock of passenger pigeons that he discovered their fondness for earthworms.[190] Gifford mentions several species of exotic pigeons that were fond of mealworms and earthworms.[191]

The adult passenger pigeons, especially the females, kept by Whitman searched the ground thoroughly for worms and insects.[192] A young passenger pigeon, 32 days of age, hatched by ring-doves, ate several earthworms that were given it, after a little testing. Even a hybrid *Ectopistes* ate worms, indicating an inherited instinct: "Here, then, is a case where the instinct, received from the father, acts independently of imitation. The bird's instinct led it to be attracted by the worm at first sight, and the wriggling of the worm stimulated the bird to snatch it quickly from its burrow, just as the adult *Ectopistes* does. The birds had never before tasted of worms, having been bred under ring-doves and having received only seed and bread." [193] This is not a clear case of inheritance from the passenger pigeon, since ring-doves also ate worms when there were young to feed.

INSECTS.—The recognition of insects in the diet was also long in coming. Wheaton wrote: "It will be noticed that insects do not enter into their diet, and this is true of them and their young at all times."[194] In a letter to me M. A. Schmitz stated that insects were fed the young before they received mast.

Grasshoppers were eaten at times. In the spring of 1851 great numbers of pigeons in northern Ohio were observed feeding on the dead grasshoppers remaining from the hordes present the preceding summer and fall.[195] Their nutrient value must have been low. Five of the pigeons examined by Aughey contained in their stomachs from 7 to 15 locusts, while the sixth contained 15 other insects.[196]

The crop of a passenger pigeon examined by Hollister was filled with acorns and grasshoppers.[197] King found in one stomach two large caterpillars, one being *Edema albifrons,* a harvestman (Arachnida), nine black crickets [*Gryllus?*], and four grasshoppers.[198] In 1858, Hind mentioned the abundance of grasshoppers (*Acrydium femur-rubrum*) and pigeons in the same breath at the Lake of the Woods and the Blue Hills, Manitoba, but did not actually state that the pigeons were eating them.[199]

Ants (*Lasius* sp.), a cocoon of an anthomyiid fly (*Helina* sp.), cynipid larvae from oak galls, and a May-beetle (*Phyllophaga tristis*) were reported by Cottam and Knappen.[200]

The insects found by Gentry in the crops were click beetle (*Cratonychus cinereus*), ground beetle (*Harpalus compar* and *H. pennsylvanicus*), band-winged locust (*Oedipoda nebulosa* and *O. sulphurea*).[201]

Caterpillars were consumed in quantity. Peabody says: "One office of the pigeon seems to be to protect the oak forests. It is stated, on excellent authority, that for some years after they have occupied a particular spot as their breeding place, the oaks, for many miles around, are remarkably free from the green caterpillars, by which they are apt to be infested."[202] There was a plague of army worms (*Leucania*) in Coos County, New Hampshire, the summer of 1770.[203] In this case immense numbers of pigeons are stated to have arrived *after* the worms had disappeared. Peters mentions that a similar army of worms invaded the Connecticut Valley in 1768 and so many pigeons arrived subsequently that 30,000 people in Vermont lived on them for three weeks.[204] He did not state that the pigeons ate the worms as inferred by Allen.[205] It is possible that there was but one coincidence and that one of the dates is incorrect.

All of the fourteen pigeons shot by C. W. Nash in Manitoba on June 27, 1885, had their crops crammed with green caterpillars, mainly *Geometra*.[206]

SNAILS.—Snails were sought eagerly by the pigeons. M. W. Smith of Taylor, Wisconsin, wrote in a letter to me: "The crops of the first birds that were killed after their arrival were filled with such food as acorns and strange to say snails, shells and all." Snails are also mentioned by Pokagon and Roberts.[207]

Snails are eaten extensively by mourning doves in Iowa, as many as 125 being found in a single crop.[208] They are fed to the young and it is inferred that the calcium of the shells enters into the metabolism.

MINERAL SUBSTANCES

SALT.—All species of pigeons are fond of salt and seek it eagerly, especially when raising young. The opinion has existed that the passenger pigeon could not raise its young successfully without salt.[209] McClure considers salt highly important in the rearing of the young of the mourning dove and in some manner essential to the viability of the eggs.[210] The comparatively high salt content of snails may be the reason why they are consumed in quantity.

Chief Pokagon wrote to Mershon: "Certain it is, while feeding their young they are frantic for salt. I have seen them pile on top of each other, about salt springs, two or more deep. I wonder if your friend gives his birds, while brooding, salt." [211]

The desire for salt was not limited to the breeding season. Kalm was astonished by the number of pigeons taken by the Indians at the salt springs at Onondaga, New York, in August, 1750.[212] These springs had long been famous for their attractiveness to pigeons.[213] They also repaired to the Montezuma salt marshes, Cayuga County, and to the saline springs at Saratoga.[214]

Shooting stands were commonly erected at places along the seacoast where the pigeons repaired to drink the water or eat the salty earth.[215] The saline Caledonia Springs on the Ottawa River, Canada, are said to have been discovered from the great numbers of pigeons frequenting them.[216]

The salt springs and marshes of Michigan were equally attractive.[217] A hundred acres of the salt meadows near Grand Rapids were at times densely covered with pigeons.[218] Concerning their fondness for salt, Audubon wrote: "I have seen the Negroes at the United States' Salines or Saltworks of Shawanee Town [Gallatin County, Illinois], wearied with killing Pigeons, as they alighted to drink the water issuing from the leading pipes, for weeks at a time." [219]

Beds of bare earth treated with salt were extremely effective in drawing pigeons for netting. When they came to the bed in abundance, a barrel of salt, weighing 280 pounds, lasted about four days.[220] Salted beds were used extensively in Michigan [221] and in Pennsylvania.[222] They were not successful in Wisconsin where the pigeons fed mainly on acorns and grain. Proof is lacking that there is any connection between this condition and the following: "When they fed on beech-nuts they would eat salt like sheep but when feeding on acorns or grain they would take no salt." [223]

Salt was found very necessary for captive pigeons.[224] The staple diet of the passenger pigeons consisted of salt, mixed seed, grit, oyster shells, and green food such as lettuce.[225]

GRIT.—Fine gravel or sand was found in the stomachs of the passenger pigeons dressed for eating.[226] Where possible they alighted on sand bars where both water and grit were available.[227]

Immense numbers of pigeons were observed by Washington Irving in November, 1832, on sandbars in the Verdigris River, eastern Oklahoma, and in the Arkansas River, western Arkansas.[228] In 1879 large numbers occurred on the sandbars of the Arkansas near Little Rock: "The wild pigeons are in greater abundance than for many years. Every second morning they light on the sand bars of the river to get sand, and they are in such numbers, that as many as one hundred have been killed at the discharge of both barrels of a gun.... They sometimes huddle so close together in lighting on the bar that they are three feet deep, and a few get their wings broken, so the little negroes go out and catch them." [229]

The performance of the pigeons seeking gravel and water at Marietta, Ohio, in 1806 was so remarkable that school was dismissed to permit the children to witness the phenomenon:

They were actually so numerous as to obscure the light of the sun like a cloud. This continued for some time. The sand-bar at the foot of the island above Marietta contained about fifty acres of land. Far above the island the birds checked their flight, and began to descend upon the bar in a dense mass. The descent, at a distance, appeared like an inverted cone, or an enormous waterspout, as an old sailor describes it. The birds apparently came down to the bar for water and sand. They crowded the shore, and dipped their beaks into the water, and took to the air again, and continued their flight. The whole town turned out to witness the novel spectacle, and many persons hastened to the sand-bar, and large numbers of the birds were killed with sticks. Their crops were supplied with small gravel and sand.[230]

EFFECT ON AGRICULTURE

Due to the preciousness of grain, pigeons were at times an intolerable nuisance to the early settlers. Winthrop wrote of the summer of 1642 that the pigeons beat down and ate a very great quantity of grain.[231] Lahontan mentions that the pigeons did so much damage to the crops of the farmers that the Bishop of Quebec was more than once forced to excommunicate them. Whether this ever had the desired effect, is not stated.[232]

The general attitude towards the passenger pigeon was that it provided no direct benefit to agriculture and was frequently very destructive: "The *Columbae* (pigeons) are injurious in some districts, eminently so by their ravages in the grain fields. Some species are gregarious and their immense flocks sweep through the rich fields of wheat with a destructiveness hardly credible; they have no redeeming traits, economically speaking, as they destroy but very few insects, and the best use to which they can be put is to furnish food to some of their former victims."[233] Michener considered it granivorous and at times destructive.[234]

Pigeons were particularly destructive to newly sown fields in the prairie states where mast was scarce. Goss mentions that in Wabasha County, Minnesota, in the spring of 1863, they picked up in an incredibly short time about four and one-half bushels of newly sown wheat.[235] At Baldwin, Wisconsin (Baldwin *Bulletin,* May 20, 1875), they were considered as second only to the grasshoppers in destructiveness to a crop of wheat. In the spring of 1867, a pigeon was killed with two tablespoonfuls of wheat in its crop at Vinton, Iowa (Vinton *Eagle*, May 15, 1867), and farmers were said to have planted their wheat two and three times. Some farmers tried to postpone sowing until the migration was at an end.[236]

After quoting Audubon on the amount of food consumed by the passenger pigeon, Wilson wrote: "We wonder, after this, that any farmer should ever dare to migrate to America." [237]

Various devices were employed to frighten the pigeons from the fields. These included scarecrows, shooting, netting, cowbells, and tin pans.[238] In Susquehanna County, Pennsylvania, in 1834, Galusha A. Grow "was assigned a post upon the ridge of a barn, which stood between the cornfield and the oats, that he might with two small sticks rattle upon the roof and scare off the pigeons. So he spent the days, after the corn came up till it was too large for the pigeons to disturb. He was obliged to be up early in the morning, and to carry his dinner with him, as the pigeons were so numerous they would destroy a whole field in a very short time." [239]

Corn was sometimes pulled as soon as the shoot appeared above ground. It was suggested that ears of corn be left on the ground for the pigeons so that they would not pull the growing grain.[240] Before planting, attempts were made to make the corn unpalatable. It was recommended that the grain be soaked in water containing saltpeter or creosote, then rolled in slaked lime or ashes, or smoked over a wood fire.[241]

Suggestions of poisoning pigeons were few. A letter from Reedsburg, Wisconsin (*Free Press*, June 1, 1861) recommended treating the grain with strychnine. This appears to have been tried in Minnesota, for a strong protest appeared against it.[242] It was dangerous to people capturing and eating pigeons, since they were known to fly miles and live several hours after taking the poison. Pigeons are killed by quite small amounts of strychnine, but most of the gallinaceous birds have a high tolerance.

A method employed at Brandon, Wisconsin, consisted in scattering wheat soaked in alcohol around the edges of the field.[243] The inebriated pigeons gathered in clusters and were easily captured.

Pigeons were never known to alight on the ripening grain.[244] Rieber goes so far as to state that they never fed on standing grain or that in the shock.[245]

Opinion that the pigeons were destructive to agricultural products was by no means uniform. Mitchell, in her questionnaire sent to residents of Ontario, requested information on the effect of the birds on crops. Of the 96 replies received, 56 stated that they were destructive and 40 that they were not.[246] The reason for this was that as long as beechnuts and other natural foods were available, the pigeons would seldom touch grain.[247] Rieber wrote: "The pigeon was not destructive to agriculture. Their principal food was acorns. The only time they picked grain was at seeding time. This was before the advent of the seeder, or grain drill, when grain was sown by hand. Then I used a long whip with a cracker at the end and walked up and down the field cracking my whip so the birds would keep off until the grain was covered by a drag." [248]

It is believed that Daniel C. Van Brunt, in 1860, built at Horicon, Wisconsin, the first underground seeder. The effort was made in response to requests from farmers for a means of preventing the passenger pigeons from eating the grain as rapidly as sown.[249]

The passenger pigeon consumed a wide variety of foods, but only a few items were of importance. Animal matter, consisting of insects and earthworms, bulked small in the diet and was eaten principally during the breeding season. The summer months were spent in the Transition and Canadian zones, where there was an abundance of soft fruits. During almost nine months of the year, September into May, mast in some form was eaten very largely. The order of importance was the beechnut, acorn, and chestnut. Mast, when available, was generally preferred to cultivated grains. No food was as acceptable as the beechnut. In view of the abundance of pigeons, the damage to agriculture was relatively small.

CHAPTER 4 : MOVEMENTS

The immense flocks of passenger pigeons twisting and undulating over the landscape were spectacular—even awesome. The earth was darkened by their numbers causing chickens to start to their roost prematurely.[1] Their dung fell like hail, leaving a characteristic odor in the air. The large flights caused fear in man and beast unaccustomed to them. Geikie, whether fictitiously or not, mentions a hunter who threw himself to the ground in terror of the thousands of birds that brushed past him.[2] The English geologist Featherstonhaugh wrote of a flight in northeastern Arkansas in November, 1834:

But when such myriads of timid birds as the wild pigeon are on the wing, often wheeling and performing evolutions almost as complicated as pyrotechnic movements, and creating whirlwinds as they move, they present an image of the most fearful power. Our horse, Missouri, at such times has been so cowed by them that he would stand still and tremble in his harness, whilst we ourselves were glad when their flight was directed from us.[3]

FLIGHT

Their flight has been described by Audubon as follows: "The Passenger Pigeon ... moves with extreme rapidity, propelling itself by quickly repeated flaps of the wings, which it brings more or less near the body, according to the degree of velocity which is required."[4] Unlike the mourning dove it did not make a whistling sound with its wings when in rapid flight or when it rose in flight.[5]

According to Kalm, as soon as the pigeon alighted in a tree it had the habit of making a clapping sound with its wings.[6] This was believed

54

by some to be a signal for others to alight. The sound was undoubtedly made during the process of alighting and not afterwards.

The passenger pigeon had a deep keel to which powerful breast muscles were attached. The long and pointed wings permitted great speed and remarkable aerial evolutions.

Flight from tall trees was begun by a downward plunge:

In starting upon a journey from perches in the tall trees, passenger pigeons, at first dipped slightly toward the earth and tobogganed down the decline with increasing velocity, in the general direction they wished to go, and skimmed along the valley between the hills. Then they began to rise above the hills and when high in the air they trimmed their course by curving toward the exact place they sought, accelerating the pace until a speed of nearly a hundred miles an hour was attained, and maintained to the end of their trip, when they circled in a wide, declining plane and gently alighted upon the ground, with a roaring of wings like a fearful tempest, or sought the branches of trees beyond, in a graceful upward sweep that absorbed much of the momentum they had attained.[7]

The habit of dipping then rising before alighting in a tree is described by Beck.[8] He observed a flock at York, Pennsylvania, flying towards and somewhat higher than the tip of a large white oak. Before reaching the tree the pigeons dropped sharply downward, formed a funnel-shaped mass near the ground, then rose sharply almost against the trunk before spreading out into the branches. Prior to alighting the pigeon broke its momentum by repeated flapping of the wings, which were lifted at the moment of alighting.[9]

The pigeons showed nearly the same command of the air when flying in woods as in the open. Though adept in flying through timber, they usually moved above it.[10] The flight through timber in northern Louisiana has been well described:

Flocks of small size can at times be seen flying through the timber and generally a few feet below the tops of the trees, just where the limbs appear thickest and present the most impediments to fast flight. A mount of only a yard or two would put them above all obstructions; yet they continue their flight upon the lower plane and apparently with as much speed as in the open. They dash and wheel, this way and that, now under, now over obstructions, and now seemingly hang momentarily in the air, before entanglements of limbs that present an almost impervious front, but the next second they have passed on; how, one cannot exactly tell, breaking their line of formation, however, before reforming it in the next open space beyond, and all this breakneck racing continued for miles without ever touching a limb with a feather.[11]

The pigeon, like the ruffed grouse, was expert in threading its way through the woods, but the structures reared by man sometimes resulted in fatalities. On the morning of April 9, 1876, a flock of pigeons passed through the village of Sturgeon Bay, Wisconsin. The Sturgeon Bay *Expositor* for April 14, 1876, reported that four of the flock struck a house and were killed. According to the Green Bay (Wis.) *Gazette* for August 16, 1888, another flock was more fortunate, passing unharmed through a store as both the rear and front doors were open.

The speed and grace of the passenger pigeon in flight was proverbial and had no counterpart. This is most happily expressed by Audubon: "When an individual is seen gliding through the woods and close to the observer, it passes like a thought, and on trying to see it again, the eye searches in vain; the bird is gone." [12]

There is now no way of determining the speed of the passenger pigeon. It is doubtful if the statements in the literature are in most cases more than estimates, since the procedure by which the speed was determined is given rarely. Audubon on October 21, 1826, while in England, gave to Mrs. Rathbone a speed of two miles per minute.[13] Later he reduced the speed to sixty miles an hour. This figure was based on the killing of wild pigeons in New York having in their crops undigested rice which could have been obtained only from Georgia or the Carolinas. He reasoned as follows: "As their power of digestion is so great that they will decompose food entirely in twelve hours, they must in this case have travelled between three hundred and four hundred miles in six hours, which shews their speed to be at an average about one mile in a minute. A velocity such as this would enable one of these birds, were it so inclined, to visit the European continent in less than three days." [14] None of his premises are based on facts. Other speeds given in the literature are in Table 2.

A method used in Michigan for determining the speed is given by Thompson.[15] Two men took their positions on section lines, i. e., a mile from each other. When a flock reached his section line, one man gave notice by waving a handkerchief, and the time was taken by the other

TABLE 2

ᴇꜱᴛɪᴍᴀᴛᴇᴅ Fʟɪɢʜᴛ Sᴘᴇᴇᴅ ᴏꜰ Pᴀꜱꜱᴇɴɢᴇʀ Pɪɢᴇᴏɴ

ᴀɴᴅ Cᴏᴍᴘᴀʀɪꜱᴏɴ ᴡɪᴛʜ Oᴛʜᴇʀ Sᴘᴇᴄɪᴇꜱ

SPECIES	MILES PER HOUR	REMARKS	REF.
Passenger Pigeon	40	....	1
	40–60	....	2
	60	....	3
	60–70	....	4
	60–90	....	5
	75	....	6
	100	....	7
Blue Rock	45	frightened	8
Homing Pigeon	45	average maximum	8
	43	400–mile distance	9
	39	522–mile distance	8
Mourning Dove	26–41	....	10
Pigeon	60	top speed with tail wind	8
Wood Pigeon	45	frightened	8

[1] John Bachman, "On the Migration of the Birds of North America," *Am. J. Sci.*, XXX (1836), 83. [2] Ludlow Griscom, "The Passing of the Passenger Pigeon," *Am. Scholar*, XV (1946), 213. [3] De Witt Clinton in *N. Y. Med. Phys. J.*, II (1823), 210; Henry D. Minot, *The Land-Birds and Game-Birds of New England* (Salem, Mass., 1877), p. 378; Moritz Fischer, "A Vanished Race," *Bird-Lore*, XV (1913), 78; W. W. Thompson, *Passenger Pigeon*, p. 13; William Welsh, "Passenger Pigeons," *Can. Field-Naturalist*, XXXIX (1925), 165–66. [4] Charles Mann in *Jahres-Bericht des naturhistorischen Vereins von Wisconsin*, 1880–81, p. 43. [5] H. B. Roney in *Chicago Field*, X (1879), 345. [6] George N. Lawrence, "An Account of the Former Abundance of Some Species of Birds on New York Island, at the Time of Their Migrations to the South," *Auk*, VI (1889), 201–2. [7] J. C. French, *Passenger Pigeon*, p. 81. [8] Roy C. Andrews, "Wings Win," *Nat. Hist.*, XL (1937), 560. [9] Editor in *Osprey*, I (1897), 149. [10] May T. Cooke, *Flight Speed of Birds* (U. S. Dept. Agr., Circular No. 428; Wash., 1937), p. 8.

person. When the flock reached his section line, the time was again noted. A large number of observations gave a speed of one mile per minute. Bachman says that the speed was determined at forty miles per hour, but he fails to mention how.[16]

Pigeons going to a roost were studied by Greenleaf in March, 1855, at Madison, Indiana.[17] He thought that their speed did not exceed greatly that of a steamer then going up the Ohio. Since the pigeons were flying against the wind and going in a direction opposite to that of the river steamer, the conditions were poor for a comparison of the relative speeds.

It would be reasonable to assume that the contour of the passenger pigeon and the shape of its wings would permit it to outfly most species of pigeons. This was essential for preservation since it traveled great distances for food and was forced frequently to retreat suddenly from snowstorms. The speeds of some species of pigeons are given in Table 2.

An indirect approach to arriving at the speed of the passenger pigeon is given by Grinnell's observations on the capture of a pigeon on the plains of South Dakota by a duck hawk.[18] Portal determined the average level speed of the latter to be 62 miles per hour.[19] Welsh states that he has seen the "blue hawk" catch the passenger pigeon in direct flight. The speed of the pigeon was estimated at 60 miles per hour and that of the hawk when stooping at 80 to 180 miles.[20]

It is probable that the normal speed of the passenger pigeon was about 60 miles per hour when migrating, with a potential speed of 70 miles when pressed.

The passenger pigeon performed inconceivably complicated maneuvers at high speed. Audubon wrote of a flock passing over the Ohio:

I cannot describe to you the extreme beauty of their aerial evolutions, when a Hawk chanced to press upon the rear of a flock. At once, like a torrent, and with a noise like thunder, they pushed into a compact mass, pressing upon each other towards the centre. In these almost solid masses, they darted forward in undulating and angular lines, descended and swept close to the earth with inconceivable velocity, mounted perpendicularly so as to resemble a vast column, and when high, were seen wheeling and twisting within their continued lines which then resembled the coils of a gigantic serpent.[21]

The evolutions of a flock were repeated at exactly the same place by succeeding flocks though the reasons for the deviations had long passed. In a letter to me O. B. Stephens of Deerfield, Wisconsin, stated that he had witnessed a spring flight of pigeons, consisting of an endless string of rather small flocks, when there was a strong, gusty wind from the northwest. The pigeons flew low and when gusts of wind struck them dove nearly to the ground, gradually rising again. Each succeeding flock dove at the same places. The terrain was open, nearly level prairie.

This trait of "following the leader" has been aptly described by Audubon:

It is extremely interesting to see flock after flock performing exactly the same evolutions which had been traced as it were in the air by a preceding flock. Thus, should a Hawk have charged on a group at a certain spot, the angles, curves, and undulations that have been described by the birds, in their efforts to escape from the dreaded talons of the plunderer, are undeviatingly followed by the next group that comes up. Should the bystander happen to witness one of these affrays, and, struck with the rapidity and elegance of the motions exhibited, feel desirous of seeing them repeated, his wishes will be gratified if he only remain in the place until the next group comes up.[22]

The habit of following an indirect, set course in certain localities is difficult to explain. At Racine, Wisconsin, in autumn the pigeons came southward around Wind Point and followed the curve of the shore until they reached the mouth of Root River. Here they followed the general course of the stream and disappeared in the west.[23]

The sudden evolutions of the pigeons at times led to a momentary congestion described by one writer as follows: "They have a habit of suddenly swerving from a direct course, as if each individual at the same identical instant of time was moved by the self-same impulse. Surprising, indeed, is the rushing noise of their wings when performing one of these curious gyrations. Frequently when stationed on their line of flight, I have succeeded in catching them as they bunch up in a dense mass with an impetuous rush." [24]

The complicated massed evolutions seldom caused injuries to the pigeons. Heriot, however, states that when two columns moving in opposite directions at the same level came into contact, many birds fell stunned to the ground.[25]

SHAPE OF FLOCKS

The passenger pigeon had what French has called "ingenuity for massing great flocks in flight in narrow columns, in numerous strata." When the congestion became too great, numbers of the birds would descend in great spirals and resume the flight at a lower level.[26]

There has been controversy over the form of the flying flocks. Almost every conceivable shape has been mentioned. The latter varied seemingly according to whether the pigeons were flying on a long migration, searching for food, or leaving or returning to a roost or a nesting. Numbers also had an effect on the form of the flocks.

The small flocks had no particular shape. Blakiston writing from

Fort Carlton, Saskatchewan, described the numerous flocks as passing in no particular order. They could be distinguished from the waterfowl and shorebirds at a great distance since they flew on the principle of "every one for himself, and the devil take the hindermost." [27]

The flocks were likened to clouds, an indication of irregularity of shape. Hebert witnessed a flight at Harmony, Indiana, in September, 1823, when the pigeons passed over in a succession of clouds as far as the eye could reach.[28] At times they caused a rush of air sufficient to induce motion in the trees over which they flew. Mactaggart wrote, "They move with great rapidity, not in strings as waterfowl do, but in irregular clouds; those before are often flung behind, while they warp and veer round one another." [29]

Pigeons when traveling leisurely, flew in open order.[30] When frightened or moving at full speed they flew in close rank. The large and small flocks of pigeons during the spring migration in Pennsylvania were irregular in shape.[31] In 1870, they flew northwest over Rock Island Arsenal, Illinois, in "broken droves." [32]

The various shapes of the flocks in Pennsylvania have been described by J. B. Oviatt:

The migrating flocks were huge. Sometimes a moving flock would be split by a hill in its path; sometimes two flocks would merge. The flocks were of no definite shape; they might be oval; they might be strung out in one or more long arms. The haphazard, irregular mass might be of nearly any conceivable shape. In some flocks the birds all flew substantially in a single plane, and in others the flock was many birds deep. Some flocks were so dense that they obscured the sky above them; others were very loose.[33]

A contemporary sketch (Fig. 18) by Bennett shows a flock in the shape of a large V, while another by an anonymous hand (Fig. 19) shows a long, narrow column.[34] Almost every shape imaginable has been assigned to the flocks, showing that there was little uniformity. The most that can be said is that the migrating flocks were usually in long columns that twisted and undulated like aerial serpents.

The flight of the passenger pigeon was mercurial. The appearance of a hawk, a gust of wind, a change in terrain, or a mere whim could cause an instantaneous change in the direction of the flight and the shape of the flock. Wilson wrote:

In descending the Ohio, by myself, in the month of February, I often rested on my oars to contemplate their aerial manoeuvers. A column, eight or ten miles in length, would appear from Kentucky, high in air, steering across to Indiana. The leaders of this great body would sometimes gradually vary their course, until it formed a large bend of more than a mile in diameter, those behind tracing the exact route of their predecessors. This would continue sometimes long after both extremities were beyond the reach of sight, so that the whole, with its glittery undulations, marked a space on the face of the heavens resembling the windings of a vast and majestic river. When this bend became very great, the birds, as if sensible of the unnecessary circuitous course they were taking, suddenly changed their direction, so that what was in column before became an immense front, straightening all its indentures, until it swept the heavens in one vast and infinitely extended line.[35]

The change from a columnar to a regimental front is described by Pender as taking place at Benton Harbor, Michigan.[36] His description reads like a paraphrase of Wilson.

The extended or regimental front was used in the search for food;[37] however, it appears to have been a common form of the migrating flocks. Some descriptions are so loosely worded that it is impossible to determine the direction of movement relative to the long axis of the flock. Brown described the flights at Cleveland, Ohio, proceeding westward along the shore of Lake Erie. Evidently this was a post-breeding movement for it began about the middle of May and continued about a month. He adds: "They arrive in flocks of from three hundred yards to three miles broad, flying in nearly a straight line, and about twenty deep; and flock succeeds flock so fast, that a person having a single-barrelled gun cannot load his gun after he has fired before another flock passes over his head."[38] Here the birds were flying with a broad front.

The migration at Toronto, Ontario, in April 1876, was witnessed by Seton.[39] The birds were moving due north in flocks of hundreds of thousands about twenty deep and extending east and west until lost in hazy lines. Bethune likewise describes the flights northward over Toronto as being of great width east to west and one hundred yards or less in depth from north to south.[40]

One morning in May, 1878, C. K. Sober, while riding westward on a train from Kane, Pennsylvania, saw a constant stream of adult pigeons twenty miles wide.[41] This resembles the "break-up" of a nesting.

The vernal migration in west-central Dubuque County, Iowa, has been described by McGee. His home was on the edge of the belt of timber bordering the Mississippi, while four miles to the westward was another belt of timber along the Maquoketa River. The flocks appeared from the south as dark bands. When overhead they were about one hundred yards in depth and extended eastward over the woodland and westward nearly, if not to the Maquoketa. He adds:

The flocks were always irregular in width and height, occasionally thinning out or even separating into a phalanx of fairly distinct flocks maintaining about the same height and rate of movement in the same latitudinal line; but the large flocks were always more extended at right angles to the line of flight, though those of only a few thousand birds preceding or following the main flights were longer front to rear, sometimes tailing out in irregular lines of stragglers evidently unable to keep up with those of greater strength.[42]

The flocks passing through Johnson County, Iowa, between 1872–76, likewise flew with a broad front extending from horizon to horizon.[43] The distance between the flocks varied from a few hundred yards to a mile or more. Nauman describes the flights in southeastern Iowa as great "windrows" at a right angle to the direction of flight.[44]

The predominating shape of the flocks in migration was serpentine. In contrast with the wide front of the flocks over the prairie regions of Iowa, Leffingwell describes the columnar shape along the Mississippi at Lyons, Iowa, as follows:

In going to their roosting- [nesting-]places, they annually flew up the Valley of the Mississippi, following the river in its windings. In this vicinity, they flew about a mile west of the city, sweeping up and down over the hills and valleys, resembling the long tail of a kite, that would be changed into serpentine form by the fitful wind. East of us, drifting rapidly and gracefully over the tops of the willows, oaks and elms in the bottom-land, they darkened the shores of the western boundary of the State of Illinois. The tall bluffs of Fulton, sloping gently from the south, terminate abruptly at the north, and sink into miles and miles of bottom-lands, islands, and verdant fields; when they reached these bluffs, instead of dropping down and flying over the islands, they crossed the Mississippi River, meandered over the bluffs in Iowa, swelling the numbers that had passed over us, and disappeared in their tireless flight.[45]

The flight in Michigan, as pictured by Mershon, was in columns. When the birds were numerous there might be two or three strata, each separated from the other by a distance of thirty or forty feet. There was nearly a steady stream of flocks, each being large at the head and trailing out to a few birds in the rear. The rear of each flock overlapped the head of the succeeding one.[46]

The columnar formation occurred in New Hampshire during the spring migration.[47] A continuous stream of birds, about two hundred yards in width and in two layers, is mentioned by Hall.[48] During the spring migration of 1875, near Pittsburgh, Pennsylvania, the pigeons flew in "streams," not compact flocks. The lines were usually columns, broad and dense in some parts, and narrow in others, the ends being too distant to see clearly.[49] The long narrow column is mentioned also by Hough.[50]

The pigeons flew southward in northern Louisiana in 1873 in columns, some of which were miles in length.[51] The path followed had a maximum width of approximately one half of a mile; but most of the flocks, of which there were several hundred, passed over a space considerably narrower. There were numerous tiers in the large flocks and one tier in the small flocks. With the latter, they seemed to prefer to advance with a regimental front, each bird as far forward as the other. The wings of the birds in the dense flocks appeared to almost touch.

During the fall migration at Cincinnati, Ohio, the pigeons flew in columns.[52] A flock returning to a roost in Missouri was like a "mighty river winding its way through the air."[53]

A continuous column of pigeons, averaging nearly a mile in width, required the whole of one day in May to pass over Fort Mississisaugua, Ontario.[54]

A good description of the shape of the flocks arriving at Guelph, Ontario, is given by Howitt.[55] The pigeons arrived from the east in parallel columns extending in straight lines westward as far as the eye could reach. The number of tiers in a flock varied with size. The small ones had two to three tiers, the larger thirty or more, but always less than forty. The lowest tier was always the greater in length and width, decreasing in dimensions to the uppermost tier. In every flock the front slope was shortest and the rear the longest of all. The slope at the sides was considerably longer than that of the front. The distance between the tiers was about a foot. The birds in each tier had just enough side-room to move their wings, which seemed to synchronize in movement with those of the leader.

The height at which the pigeons flew varied greatly. In a strong wind the flight was only a few feet above the earth. In rising over a prominence, the birds barely cleared it. Flocks at Cleveland, Ohio, flew about nine feet above the trees and buildings.[56] During the spring migration over the prairies of Iowa the height was 100 to 150 feet.[57] A height of a quarter of a mile is given by Howitt.[58] Schaff states that in the spring migration of 1870, they flew almost on a level with the sandhill cranes, which are noted for the elevation of their flight.[59] Audubon mentions a flight that was beyond the range of a good rifle.[60]

The duration and extent of the flights differed greatly. During migration the main flight usually took place in a single day. The flight at Fort Mississisaugua, near Niagara, described by King began at 4:00 A.M. and lasted until 6:00 P.M., a period of fourteen hours. He states that the column could not have been less than 300 miles in length.[61] If the speed were 60 miles per hour, as assumed, the actual length of the column would have been the improbable figure of 840 miles. The flights continued for several days in diminishing numbers.

The flight at Bloomington, Indiana, observed by Hall lasted five hours, there being no greater than 30-second intervals between the flocks.[62] That observed by Seton at Toronto lasted all day.[63] At Cleveland the flights continued without slackening from 8:00 A.M. to 12:00, were resumed at 4:00 P.M., and continued until dark.[64] A flight in Louisiana lasted from 10:00 A.M. to 2:00 P.M.[65]

The migrations in Iowa lasted two to three days, the bulk of the birds passing through in a single day.[66] In Michigan, according to Bryant, the large flights were over in two or three days but small flocks continued to arrive for two to four weeks. The flocks appeared soon after daylight and continued until noon; however on cloudy or rainy days the birds often flew all day.[67] McClintock states that the flights were stopped by rain.[68]

A flight in Ontario is described by Weld as follows:

During particular years, these birds come down from the northern regions in flights that it is marvellous to tell of. A gentleman of the town of Niagara assured me, that once as he was embarking there on board ship for Toronto, a flight of them was observed coming from that quarter; that as he sailed over Lake Ontario to Toronto, forty miles distant from Niagara, pigeons were seen flying over head the whole way in a contrary direction to that in which the ship proceeded; and that on arriving at the place of his destination, the birds were still observed coming down from the north in as large bodies as had been noticed at any one time during the whole voyage; supposing, therefore, that the pigeons moved no faster than the vessel, the flight according to this gentleman's account, must at least have extended eighty miles.[69]

In the fall of 1813, Audubon journeyed from Henderson to Louisville, Kentucky, and encountered an immense flight of pigeons that lasted three days in undiminished numbers.[70] In Pennsylvania, Robinson observed flights lasting from morning until night and continuing for several successive days.[71]

The flocks did not have definite leaders as with wildfowl.[72] O. B. Stephens in a letter to me stated that he could detect no more leadership than occurred in a flock of blackbirds. No note was uttered by the pigeons while flying.[73]

There was limited flying by night. Many birds returned to the roost or nesting long after dark. However, it was not often that they migrated in darkness. According to Smith, they sometimes flew both night and day in New Jersey in order to avoid the northeastern storms.[74] Concerning the migration, Bachman wrote: "Wild pigeons are frequently seen, at early dawn, in the high atmosphere. They fly higher by night than by day, and thus experience less inconvenience from darkness." [75] He seems to have concluded from seeing pigeons in the early morning that they had been flying by night. It was usual during migration for the pigeons to set out at break of day and fly a few hours before stopping to feed. McGee mentions that the spring flights sometimes extended into the night and were detectable by the whistling of the wings.[76] Collins believed that near his home in Pennsylvania the pigeons flew over at night and rested by day during the fall migration, since no one saw them by day.[77] This is doubtful. J. B. Oviatt heard flocks passing over by moonlight, but attributed their passage to shooting at the nestings.[78]

The pigeons arrived in the evening at the autumn roosts in Ohio in tiers of immense extent.[79] The main flight lasted about twenty minutes. The arrival and departure from a roost near Wadsworth, Ohio, has been described by Brown:

They would come in vast flocks from the west, in the evening. For a long time before they appeared in sight, we could hear the roar of their wings, like a distant cataract. Then they would come, spreading like a cloud over the whole horizon, for several minutes. In the morning they would fly westward, breaking up into smaller flocks as they proceeded; so their morning flight was not, like the evening, in clouds, but in chains. In the fall of 1823, I watched such a chain flying over these grounds that continued without a break from 6 to 9 o'clock.[80]

EFFECTS OF WEATHER

The passenger pigeon was so hardy a bird that it sometimes met disaster by attempting to winter in the north or by migrating too early in the spring. Some of the earlier writers believed that the migration to the southern states was made largely for the purpose of escaping the rigors of the northern winter. The combination of a mild winter and abundance of mast might hold some of the birds in the northern states, but there was no consistency in their behavior under these conditions. When snow covered the supply of food, migration southward was a necessity.

The movement of pigeons through the southeastern states bordering the Atlantic was erratic and not necessarily due to weather. Catesby wrote that few or no pigeons were present in the Carolinas during a mild winter, but that they appeared during a hard winter in the north in order to obtain a plentiful supply of mast.[81] A similar opinion was expressed by Bartram.[82] Bachman did not share the belief that the southward movement was induced by cold and wrote:

The wild pigeon is another of those birds, that are supposed to be driven among us by the extreme cold of the north. This is a mistake. These birds appear in Carolina, only at very long and uncertain intervals. Sometimes they visit us in cold, but frequently in mild winters. I have seen wild pigeons in immense flocks, in Canada, in the coldest winters, when the thermometer was below zero. It is to be remarked, that the previous autumn had produced an abundance of beech nuts and buckwheat, their favorite food, and that the ground was not covered with snow. It is only when the forests of the west have failed in their usual supply of mast and berries that the pigeons come among us, to claim a share of the acorns and berries of our woods, and the refuse grains scattered over our rice fields.[83]

It is stated by Turner that on one occasion the mild weather and abundance of beechnuts attracted the pigeons to Wayne County, New York. The weather changed suddenly to severe cold and the woods were covered with pigeons that had frozen to death.[84] In Iowa, pigeons migrating early in the spring once encountered a storm that caused the death of many.[85] The winter of 1876/77 was mild in Pennsylvania. Many of the migratory birds, presumably including pigeons, remained all winter. A heavy snowstorm in March caused death by starvation.[86]

Cold alone generally had little effect on the pigeons. The migration northward frequently took place early in March when the temperature was twenty degrees below freezing.[87] Professor Whitman kept his birds in an open cage protected from the wind.[88] Clinton remarks on their ability to withstand severe cold and mentions that in January and February, 1819, large flocks were observed at Albany, New York, and in the northwestern part of this state.[89] Once the pigeons arrived in the north in spring, they were seldom routed by inclement weather, according to Bryant; but in the fall, the first cold days usually sent them southward.[90] In common with some other species of birds, there was a tendency on the part of the passenger pigeon, having stayed into the winter in the north, to attempt to hold on. They were found frozen to death in Indiana during a severe winter.[91]

Late spring snows were a frequent source of trouble. The pigeons that had arrived at Albany, New York, in the spring of 1830 were overwhelmed by a snowstorm.[92] A snowstorm with high winds that began on the evening of March 25 continued throughout the following day, and the snow attained a depth of 18 inches. The birds took refuge in Wendall's Hollow, in the southern part of the city, where they were shot and netted in large numbers. I have determined that this storm originated in the northeast along the New England coast and extended southward beyond Philadelphia. A tremendous snowstorm that occurred at Titusville, Pennsylvania, on March 25, 1852, drove the bewildered birds to the ground where they were killed by hundreds.[93]

A wet snow could be disastrous. Pigeons were caught in a snowstorm in Chautauqua County, New York, in May, 1833. Large numbers of dead birds were found widely spread in the fields and woods, and floating on Lake Erie and on the lakes and streams in the county.[94]

A condition that the pigeons sometimes met was recorded by Alexander Henry on April 11, 1800: "The Terre Blanche [Manitoba] having been clear of ice for some time, I embarked in my canoe for Portage la Prairie. Weather excessively hot. Wild pigeons passing N. in great abundance. In a few days we experienced a dreadful snowstorm, which continued with great violence for three days, when there were three feet of snow upon the ground; but it did not remain long." [95]

There is no claim that the pigeons could sense a storm hours in advance. Deane wrote of captive birds:

On the approach of a storm the old birds will arrange themselves side by side on the perch, draw the head and neck down into the feathers and sit motionless for a time, then gradually resume an upright position, spread the tail, stretch each wing in turn, and then, as at a given signal, they spring from the perch and bring up against the wire netting with their feet as though anxious to fly before the disturbing elements. Mr. Whittaker has noticed the same trait while observing Pigeons in the woods. [96]

The pigeons became desperate for food after a snowstorm. A heavy fall of snow caught them one spring at Muncy, Pennsylvania: "On the edges of the streams and around ponds, where the snow melted first, there was a blue border of pigeons trying to find a little food. They went into the farmyards and into the barns where doors were left open. It was a hard time for them." [97] A similar condition is mentioned by Collins. [98] When snow prevailed, the pigeons would sometimes tear down entirely the heaps of manure with which the houses were banked, "probably for worms." They also fed where manure had been scattered on the snow-covered fields. [99]

The persistence of pigeons when they had decided to remain after a snowstorm is described by Marsden from his diary. On April 7, 1868, the day the pigeons arrived, a foot of snow fell at Forksville, Pennsylvania. On the tenth he found them feeding on sumac berries and those shot were in fair condition, but by the twelfth they were too lean to eat. On the fourteenth many birds were found dead, others being too weak to fly; and by the sixteenth only dead birds were to be found. The snow remained until the twentieth. In the interim the ground in the forest for many miles was covered with dead pigeons. [100]

Nesting sometimes took place before all of the snow had disappeared. This gave rise to the opinion that the pigeon always nested on "the borders of the snow." [101] Mershon mentions a large nesting near Georgian Bay, Ontario, Canada, in 1865, the snow being two feet deep under the nesting.[102] It is doubtful if this condition obtained at the time of nesting, as the difficulties in finding food and nesting materials would have been too great.

It was quite common for a nesting to be abandoned, due to snow, after the eggs were laid. Dr. I. Voorheis informed Barrows that in 1880 a nesting in Benzie County, Michigan, was broken up by a snowfall of 8 inches. Though most of the nests had an egg, the pigeons left and never returned.[103] J. B. Oviatt informed Scherer that the eggs in early nestings would often freeze.[104] The brooding bird covered the egg so well that it is difficult to believe that a low temperature unaccompanied by snow was sufficient to cause destruction of the egg. The dropping of eggs at random when a snowstorm drove the pigeons from the nesting when they were ready to lay, will be discussed in the chapter on nesting.

The Winnebago Indians of Wisconsin informed Radin that pigeons (squabs) were obtained by poking them from the nest with a long pole. Then follows the ambiguous statement: "Often it is unnecessary to hunt for them after a storm because large quantities die from exposure to inclement weather." [105]

The pigeons usually scudded southward in the face of a heavy snowstorm. Their behavior at Chicago on March 13, 1855, was described in the Chicago *Daily Journal* for the next day as follows: "During the storm yesterday, clouds of pigeons were circling in the snow-laden air, now over the city, and now above the lake, evidently bewildered and at loss what to make of the wild winter that met them on their way northward. This morning, however, having recovered their self-possession, large flocks of them bore away to the south."

Little has been recorded on the effect of rain. Greenleaf mentions that the pigeons migrating at Madison, Indiana, on March 10, 1855, were driven by a heavy rain to drop into the trees. The rain of the following day prevented continuation of the flight.[106] On the other hand, Bryant states that in cloudy or rainy weather the pigeons frequently flew all day.[107]

A sleetstorm brought the pigeons to earth quickly. Pigeons returning to a roost in Medina County, Ohio, settled in a sugar grove on encountering a storm of sleet and snow accompanied by a high wind.[108] Ingells was in Emmet County, Michigan, six miles south of the Straits of Mackinac in the fall of 1881. Pigeons crossing the Straits from the north encountered a heavy sleetstorm that caused them to drop into the water and drown. The following day there was a windrow of dead pigeons about five miles in length on the shore of the cove at Cross Village. The Indians lived on the dead pigeons during the following winter.[109] A similar account was given to Mershon in 1905 by B. O. Bush; however, he has the disaster occurring in the spring of 1881 while the pigeons were nesting near Petoskey.[110] Ingells claims to have been an eyewitness, while Bush's information was hearsay.

CROSSING LAKES

The pigeons at times crossed large bodies of water, generally with reluctance. In most cases in the region of the Great Lakes the shore line was followed until a comparatively narrow crossing was available. Migrants usually entered Ontario between Lakes Erie and Huron, over the Niagara Peninsula, and the eastern end of Lake Ontario.[111] The finding of drowned pigeons along the shore of a lake was not a proof of a deliberate attempt at crossing, as they may have become bewildered in a fog while flying along the shore.

Descriptions of the behavior of the pigeons on arriving at a large body of water are meager, particularly as to the procedure in crossing. Immense numbers arrived from the south at Cleveland, Ohio, in January, 1851, according to the Cleveland *Plain Dealer* of January 24. On reaching Lake Erie, they performed a "somersault" and returned in the direction from which they came. Migrants arriving in spring at Rochester, New York, on reaching the shore of Lake Ontario, followed it eastward, refusing to cross the lake.[112]

The Straits of Mackinac, Michigan, are narrow, being approximately five miles in width. B. F. Beaudreau, Ludington, Michigan, was informed by an old resident that the pigeons commonly crossed at this place, as he related in a letter to me. Even here reluctance to cross was sometimes shown. Etta Wilson lived at Northport on the western shore of Grand Traverse Bay. During the spring migration the upper tiers of pigeons were flying southward, the lower northward. Evidently on reaching the tip of the Leelanau Peninsula, they returned, refusing even to cross the mouth of the bay.[113]

A peculiarity of the pigeon, according to Sellar, was skimming the surface when crossing water, then rising on reaching land.[114] It is doubtful if they usually flew this low unless tired, or the day windy. Those arriving at Toronto over Lake Ontario, in 1876, were flying at a height of about 500 feet.[115]

The best accounts of crossing large lakes relate to Lake Michigan. Schoolcraft was on the Door Peninsula, Wisconsin, on August 25, 1820, when he wrote:

In walking along some parts of the shore, I observed a great number of the skeletons and half consumed bodies of the pigeon, which, in crossing the lake, is often overtaken by severe tempests, and compelled to alight upon the water and thus drowned, in entire flocks, which are thrown up along the shores. This causes the shores of Lake Michigan to be visited by vast numbers of buzzards, eagles, and other birds of prey. The Indians also make use of these pigeons, as food, when they are first driven ashore, preserving such in smoke, as they have not immediate occasion for.[116]

The drowning of pigeons on the western shore of Lake Michigan by violent thunderstorms is also mentioned by Lanman.[117] Windrows of pigeons that had met death in a tornado were formed on the beach north of Milwaukee.[118]

Pigeons were hunted by Kellogg at the lighthouse north of Milwaukee in the early days. He states that every spring they came over the lake and then rose to clear the high bluff.[119] In this case, the pigeons may merely have crossed Milwaukee Bay. There could be no incentive to cross the lower end of Lake Michigan. In the spring migration, the birds usually followed the eastern or western shore.

A writer who was hunting pigeons at Milwaukee in the autumn of 1841 observed that the flocks flew very low, just skimming the tops of the bushes as they arrived from their long flight over Lake Michigan.[120] Here again, it is doubtful that they crossed the lake. Their arrival in Milwaukee Bay from North Point could give this impression. An anonymous writer in the Milwaukee *Free Press* of July 29, 1905, also stated that in the fall they crossed Lake Michigan to Milwaukee in great flocks. The young dropped exhausted into the brush and were killed easily with clubs. The shortest crossing from the state of Michigan to Milwaukee is

110 miles. Crossing Lake Michigan and arriving exhausted at Pentwater, Michigan, is mentioned by Dawson. Thousands were killed with sticks and whips.[121] The distance mentioned, in itself, was no inconvenience to the pigeon, so that the exhaustion may well have resulted from a much longer flight.

Crossing the lake to Sheboygan, Wisconsin, was considered a regular procedure.[122] An account of the arrival of pigeons at Manitowoc in the Manitowoc *Tribune* of June 10, 1858, leaves a doubt that a crossing was made:

On Monday last [June 7, 1858], millions of pigeons were seen breasting the land breeze far out on the Lake, and alighting in large numbers as soon as they reached the shore. Some of them rested for a short time on the pier at Two Rivers, indicating considerable fatigue, as men were working there at the time . . . whether they were blown out to sea in a fog, is difficult to conjecture. Such a circumstance has no precedent in the memory of the oldest inhabitant.

Pigeons in the spring migration sometimes flew northeasterly through Wisconsin and entered Michigan by following the western shore of Green Bay, or crossing Lake Michigan. The nesting at Petoskey, Michigan, in 1876, consisted of two distinct groups of birds. S. S. Stevens informed Brewster that one group followed the Wisconsin shore and that it crossed to Michigan over the Manitou Islands. The pigeons appeared about three o'clock in the afternoon as a compact mass at least a mile wide and five miles long.[123] Roney mentions that during the nesting of 1878 many of the pigeons came from the Wisconsin shore with the speed of a dart.[124] The distance from the Door Peninsula, Wisconsin, to the nearest of the Manitou Islands is not over fifty miles; and the route from Rawley Point, Two Rivers, Wisconsin, to Big Sable Point, Michigan, is even less.

E. C. Burke, in a letter to me, stated that pigeons on reaching Peshtigo Harbor in the fall of 1880 flew across Green Bay towards Sturgeon Bay. A similar crossing may have been made in spring.

A catastrophe to pigeons crossing the Great Lakes was due most frequently to fog. In 1937 I sent inquiries to people living in ports on Lakes Michigan and Superior for information on crossing during migration, and on drowning. Frank Kaufman of Two Rivers, Wisconsin, wrote:

The great destruction to which your letter refers occurred in the late fifties or early sixties. It was caused not by a storm but by a dense fog that overhung Lake Michigan for days at a time, and because of this fog the birds were drowned. It so happens that the narrowest point [Rawley Point] for their flight across Lake Michigan is just six miles north of Two Rivers and I can remember one morning seeing the dead pigeons piled three and four feet high along the beach.

Large numbers of dead pigeons were seen by E. Osborn off Sleeping Bear Point, Michigan, which is south of the Manitou Islands. He attributed their death to drowning as a result of fog and wind while crossing Lake Michigan.[125] McConnell obtained information, third hand, on the finding of large numbers of pigeons on the shore of Lake Michigan after a great storm.[126]

There is no clear case of the drowning of adult birds. The victims appear to have been the young birds, weak of wing and inexperienced. Anburey was at Lake Champlain on June 23, 1777, when the pigeons were crossing. They reached the opposite shore with difficulty, some dropping into the water.[127] This lake is so narrow that only young birds would have had difficulty in crossing. S. S. Stevens saw the shores of Crooked Lake, a small lake four miles in length in Emmet County, Michigan, covered for miles with a foot or more of dead, young pigeons that had become bewildered in a fog. No old birds were killed, so they were supposed to have risen above the fog.[128] This is not an entirely satisfactory explanation, since the old and young did not generally associate until the fall migration.

The passenger pigeon was so powerful a flyer that a fog was one of the few meteorological conditions with which it could not cope. Like all land birds, it became bewildered. Susan Fenimore Cooper wrote on June 8, 1848:

Rainy morning. It appears that yesterday we missed a fine sight; about dawn it was foggy; a large flock of wild pigeons passing over the valley, became bewildered in the mist, and actually alighted in the heart of the village, which we have never known them to do before. The trees in the churchyard, those in our own grounds, and several other gardens, were loaded with them.... When the fog rose, they took flight again. What a pity to have missed so unusual a sight! [129]

Harriet Martineau was on a ship off Cape Sable, Michigan, on July

3, 1836, a foggy day. A flock of pigeons flew around and over the ship. Shooting at the birds prevented determining if they would have alighted on the vessel.[130]

The lethal effect of a fog is mentioned by Moore, who lived in Kewaunee County, Wisconsin. In early spring a fog arising on Lake Michigan would sweep inland several miles. Pigeons caught in flight would become lost, and wander over the lake where they would fly about until exhausted. Millions of dead pigeons were subsequently washed ashore.[131]

It was customary for the pigeons to alight on trees during a fog when this was possible. Head was camping on Kempenfeldt Bay, Ontario, early in April. He awoke to the sound of pigeons that thickly covered a dead tree. When these arose, large numbers invisible in the fog followed them. Though some were shot, a few birds continued to fly about in circles.[132] Early on the morning of July 21, 1881, while Glazier was camped near Lake Itasca, Minnesota, a fog limited the visibility to a distance of twenty yards. Before the fog lifted, a small flock of pigeons alighted in the tops of some adjacent pines.[133]

There is no clear evidence of pigeons crossing large bodies of water and perishing in numbers in the absence of fog or snow. Etta Wilson wrote of the crossing of Lake Michigan:

Surely many perished in this manner, for one day in early summer we got up in the morning to find Grand Traverse Bay covered with dead Pigeons and the shore strewn with their bodies where the undulating back wash of the night had brought them in from the big lake. The night had been quiet. There had been no storm and no fog. Strong of wing, summer storms never overcame them and the season of sleet storms had passed. True it had sometimes happened that small numbers of the birds had been lost in lake fogs, had flown around until their strength was spent, and had fallen and died; but there seemed to have been no possible cause for the death of so many.

Later in the day the merciful wind came up from the southwest and carried back to the bosom of the great lake the vast and silent caravan of gentle birds whose very attractiveness and usefulness had led to their extinction.[134]

Had the pigeons perished during a fog far out in the lake, days might have passed before they were washed ashore.

There are statements on the crossing of each of the Great Lakes.

While McKenney was off Keweenaw Point in Lake Superior, an exhausted, immature wild pigeon alighted on his canoe. He adds: "Thousands of them perish in crossing every season and I am told they are often seen on the lake shore fastened together by their feet, looking like ropes of onions. The lake, in the direction in which this one came, must be at least sixty miles across."[135]

There is a more specific account by Moulton. While he was on a steamer on Lake Superior, the captain informed him that, while running down the lake one fall, he encountered a terrible snowstorm with the wind blowing a gale. The snow was wet and froze to the vessel. In the midst of the storm he ran into countless pigeons that had been beaten down to the water by the wet snow. Later he was told by the Chippewa dwelling on the north shore that a windrow of pigeons extending for miles formed on the beach.[136] That portion of the shore extending from Duluth to the international boundary is customarily known as the North Shore.

Fog again seems to have been the chief source of difficulty on Lake Superior. Alexander McDougall wrote to Mershon: "The pigeon was numerous on Lake Superior in 1872, for I have recollections of catching some that year while captain of the Steamer *Japan*. During foggy weather and at night, they would alight on the boat in great numbers, tired out. On foggy mornings, the blowing of our whistle would start them up. Often, when they would light on the eave of our overhanging deck, we could sneak along under the deck and quickly snatch one."[137] I was informed in a letter by B. F. Beaudreau that an old timber cruiser and surveyor of his acquaintance who worked in the western part of the Upper Peninsula of Michigan had often seen flocks of pigeons start across Lake Superior.

Large numbers of pigeons were known by H. T. Phillips to have drowned in crossing Lake Huron from southern Ontario. Captains on the lake told him of passing for three hours through birds that had died during a fog.[138] Stone was also informed by J. G. Dille[i]n in 1895 that about twelve years previously large numbers were washed up on the northern shore of this lake.[139]

Pigeons in 1876 flew from the Township of Ashfield, Huron County, Ontario, to Michigan, across the narrow southern end of Lake Huron.

In June they flew northward over Manitoulin Island, presumably from Bruce County, Ontario.[140]

The crossing of Lake Erie to Canada from Chautauqua County, New York, was considered a normal procedure.[141] Jones mentions large flights at Cedar Point, Ohio, both northward and southward, indicating that they crossed the lake.[142] In spring and fall, large numbers collected on Long Point on the northern shore of Lake Erie. This point projects far into the lake, but there is no mention of crossing.[143] No specific statement of crossing Lake Erie through Point Pelee was found. Mann makes the bold statement that during a nesting on the north shore about 1878 the pigeons crossed the lake to the vicinity of Cleveland, fed, and returned.[144]

The large flights at the western end of Lake Ontario took place over the Niagara River.[145] The immense flight described by Weld followed the north shore from Toronto to Niagara.[146] Bethune mentions large flocks crossing the lake from the south and arriving at both Toronto and Coburg.[147] The distance in either case is not over forty miles. The flock observed by John Townson to arrive at Toronto from the southeast could hardly have covered a greater distance.[148] According to Vieillot, this lake was crossed where it was eight to ten miles wide.[149]

Information on flights over water along the Atlantic coast is meager. De Vries observed pigeons crossing the mouth of Delaware Bay from Cape Henlopen to Cape May, in April, 1633.[150] There is a tradition that Pigeon Cove, Massachusetts, received its name from a large number of pigeons washed up on the beach. These birds in flying over the sea from New Hampshire and Maine toward Cape Ann were overwhelmed by a storm.[151] Five pigeons are known to have been shot on the island of Nantucket.[152]

There are two early accounts of destruction by drowning of large numbers of pigeons along the Atlantic seaboard. Mather wrote in 1712: "When ye time of their Departure has been at hand about *Michaelmas* [September 29], they have in horrible storms miss'd their way; & thousands of Millions have perished in the sea, where o^r Ships have afterward sailed thro' them lying on ye Surface of ye Water, for some Leagues together." [153]

Kalm wrote in a similar vein regarding a large flight of pigeons in 1740:

About a week or a little later subsequent to the disappearance of this enormous multitude of Pigeons from Pennsylvania and New Jersey, a sea-captain by the name of Amies, who had just arrived at Philadelphia, and after him several other seafaring men, stated that they had found localities out at sea where the water, to an extent of over 3 French miles, was entirely covered by dead Pigeons of this species. It was conjectured that the Pigeons, whether owing to a storm, mist or snowfall, had been carried away to the sea, and then on account of the darkness of the following night or from fatigue, had alighted on the water and in that place and manner met their fate. It is said that from that date no such tremendous numbers of this species of Pigeon have been seen in Pennsylvania.[154]

Factual, or traditional, accounts of large numbers of pigeons being found dead at sea were still current in the days of Giraud.[155]

The "roost" was perhaps the most impressive feature in the life of the passenger pigeon. Immense numbers remained together in fall and winter, roosting nightly in a selected woodland or swamp. Scouring the surrounding country for food during the day, the pigeons returned at night to break frequently even the large limbs of the trees on which they roosted, by sheer weight of numbers, and cover the ground with excrement inches deep. The food exhausted, they moved on to repeat the performance elsewhere. The roost is well described by Wilson:

It sometimes happens that having consumed the whole produce of the beech trees in an extensive district they discover another at the distance perhaps of sixty or eighty miles, to which they regularly repair every morning, and return as regularly in the course of the day, or in the evening, to their place of general rendezvous, or as it is usually called the *roosting place*. These roosting places are always in the woods, and sometimes occupy a large extent of forest. When they have frequented one of these places for some time, the appearance it exhibits is surprising. The ground is covered to the depth of several inches with their dung; all the tender grass and underwood destroyed; the surface strewed with large limbs of trees broken down by the weight of the birds clustering one above another; and the trees themselves, for thousands of acres, killed as completely as if girdled with an axe. The marks of this desolation remain for many years on the spot; and numerous places could be pointed out where for several years after, scarce a single vegetable made its appearance.[1]

Audubon's description of a roost in Kentucky is more colorful:

My first view of it was about a fortnight subsequent to the period when they had made choice of it, and I arrived there nearly two hours before sunset. Few Pigeons were then to be seen.... The dung lay several inches deep, covering the whole extent of the roosting-place, like a bed of snow. Many trees two feet in diameter, I observed, were broken off at no great distance from the ground; and the branches of many of the largest and tallest had given way, as if the forest had been swept by a tornado. Every thing proved to me that the number of birds resorting to this part of the forest must be immense beyond conception.... The sun was lost to our view, yet not a Pigeon had arrived.... Suddenly there burst forth a general cry of "Here they come!" The noise which they made, though yet distant, reminded me of a hard gale at sea, passing through the rigging of a close-reefed vessel. As the birds arrived and passed over me, I felt a current of air that surprised me.... The Pigeons, arriving by thousands, alighted everywhere, one above another, until solid masses as large as hogsheads were formed on the branches all around. Here and there the perches gave way under the weight with a crash, and, falling to the ground, destroyed hundreds of the birds beneath, forcing down the dense groups with which every stick was loaded. It was a scene of uproar and confusion. I found it quite useless to speak, or even to shout to those persons who were nearest to me. Even the reports of guns were seldom heard, and I was made aware of the firing only by seeing the shooters reloading.[2]

It is desirable at this point to consider the density in which the pigeons roosted in order to produce such havoc to the trees. Audubon's statement that the roosting birds formed masses as large as hogsheads was attacked by Waterton with great sarcasm: "Solid Masses! Our European pigeons, in a similar situation, would have been all smothered in less than three minutes." [3] Rev. Cotton Mather was even less modest in his statement: "Yea, they satt upon one another like Bees, till a Limb of a Tree would seem almost as big as an House." [4]

There are many references to the habit of these pigeons piling on one another in roosting, feeding, and drinking. Catesby says that the limbs of oaks were broken since they roosted on the backs of others.[5] The thicker branches, according to Kalm, had piles of pigeons a yard high.[6] Burnaby mentions that the large branches were broken by the pigeons sitting upon each other.[7] Faux likened the roosting birds to swarms of bees covering a bush.[8]

A roost near Salem, North Carolina, in November, 1760, is described by a Moravian as follows: "... an incredible Number of wild Pidgeons assembled there every night for a Month together, in a small District, perching manyfold upon one another, so as by their Weight to break down the largest Limbs of Oaks, bending the Tops of others to the Ground, which was covered more than one foot high with their Dung. The ruins of the Wood as well as the remains of the Dung could be seen several Years after." [9]

A roost in Knapp's Creek Valley, Richland County, Wisconsin, was visited by Johnson in April, 1841. Nearly every limb was piled with pigeons "three ... to twelve" high, and he was able to kill five to thirteen birds at a shot with a rifle.[10]

The pigeons arriving late at the roost did not hesitate to alight on the backs of others.[11] Displaced by the breaking of a limb, the pigeons sought a high perch elsewhere or descended to the bushes from which they could be taken by the hand.[12]

An observer could be deceived readily as to the number of pigeons in masses as large as hogsheads. It is probable that these consisted of small branches so weighted with the birds as to form a canopy. This was certainly true where the pigeons roosted in bushes and small trees. A roost in an alder thicket near Oakland, Maryland, was said to contain pigeons piled upon each other one to two feet high, according to the Cumberland *Daily News* (Md.) of October 2, 1872. Cook went to a pigeon roost in the Lodi Swamp, Medina County, Ohio, and what seemed haystacks proved to be alders, small elms, and willows loaded with pigeons.[13] In these cases the birds formed a mere shell.

Alighting on the backs of one another was not confined to the roost. The pigeons alighted two and three deep on the shooting poles, at times in such numbers that the poles were broken.[14]

It is not to be expected that a pigeon long endured one or more companions on its back.[15] In fact it is stated by one writer that settling on the back was momentary.[16] A roost was a bedlam throughout the night due to the struggles of the late arrivals and displaced birds to find a perch.

The largest summer roosts consisted of young birds that remained in close association as if for mutual protection. They roosted by hundreds of thousands in the alder swamps until the mast was exhausted. On being attacked by men with torches, "they move to and fro, they flutter, but do not attempt to quit the bushes, seemingly determined to retain possession of their roosting-place regardless of consequences. ... It is exceedingly strange that among the thousands of pigeons taken in the manner here described, there never happens, by any chance, to be any old birds!" [17]

Descriptions of the effect on the timber of the large numbers of roosting birds are numerous. James Hall was in Mississippi from December, 1800, to April, 1801. Some months previously, there was a roost in the Hurricane Swamp on which most of the large trees had been razed by the wind. The roost was on a branch of the Big Black River, sixty miles from the Chickasaw nation. Since the towns of these Indians were in Union and Pontococ Counties, the roost was probably in Clay County. He describes the condition of a hickory tree a foot in diameter:

The tree had gone down by an easy descent, which was evident from its roots having raised a bank on the opposite side, and the bracers not torn out of the earth. That the tree had been considerably straight is evident from this circumstance, that a heap of dung lay round the root. The pigeons appear to have kept their station when the tree went down, for when the top rested on the ground, the body bent into a bow, the middle being about three feet high in which position it still stands. Many similar instances may be there seen, and many of a more brittle texture were broken off in the middle.[18]

Flocks alighting temporarily during the day were also destructive to trees. Mather mentions that orchards were ruined by them.[19] During a large flight at Lititz, Pennsylvania, in the spring of 1846, the pigeons settled so thickly in an apple orchard that thick limbs were broken off.[20] Cook records that one November the pigeons were caught in a sleet and snow storm while returning to their roost in the Lodi Swamp in Ohio. They stopped in a sugar maple grove covering twenty acres and within half an hour the grove was ruined by the breaking of the branches through the combined weight of the birds and the sleet.[21] In this connection it may be mentioned that in the 1870's pigeons were very numerous between Kane and Sargeant, Pennsylvania.[22] They alighted in such numbers on the telegraph wires that the line was broken down for a distance of eleven poles.

The type of vegetation selected for a roost varied greatly. Wilson states that the pigeons always roosted in the woods, and Audubon that they selected the largest trees, with undergrowth.[23] The roost on Pine Creek, Iowa, was also in heavy timber.[24] A roost twenty-five miles southwest of Marietta, Ohio, the winter of 1832/33 was in large trees.[25]

Pines, low and high, were favored and their use is mentioned frequently.[26] The pigeons that spent the summer in Sullivan and Wyoming Counties, Pennsylvania, roosted in thick clumps of hemlock or spruce about twenty-five feet tall.[27] Junipers were also used.[28]

Pigeons were seen to go to roost in fall at Smethport, Pennsylvania, in beech brush to which the leaves still clung. Frequently they could be reached from the ground.[29] During the fall flight of pigeons at Cincinnati, Ohio, in 1865, Langdon found at dusk several hundred pigeons in a tall, untrimmed hedge of osage orange, where they had evidently gone to roost for the night.[30] The osage orange hedge remains a favorite roost for mourning doves.

The autumn of 1866 there was a roost in a dense growth of oak saplings in Newaygo County, Michigan.[31] The small oaks were bent to the ground by the weight of the birds. The same area had been occupied as a roost six years previously. The roost at Marietta, Ohio, in the fall of 1840, was in second growth, i.e., small trees and saplings.[32]

Rarely, the pigeons roosted on a man-made structure. In December, 1865, vast numbers of pigeons roosted along the railroad between Louisville and Nashville.[33] It is said that one night so many pigeons settled on a bridge over the Green River as to endanger it.

Swamps, particularly alder, had preference as a roost over every other type of terrain.[34] No satisfactory reason can be advanced for the use of these swamps.

Throughout the whole of the beechwoods [in New York and Pennsylvania] there are low and swampy pieces of ground designated "Beaver Meadows." Those swamps, for the most part, are overgrown with tall coarse grass; and around many of their margins grows a profusion of alder bushes, seldom attaining more than fifteen or twenty feet. Why or wherefore the pigeons select those bushes for their roosting places might be somewhat difficult to conceive, since the forest trees in the immediate vicinity would afford them much greater security; but such is the case at present, and such it is known to have been.[35]

If the alder bushes were selected to avoid the destruction resulting from the falling of large limbs, low growth on high land was even more plentiful. That this type of vegetation was sometimes used, is shown by the description of a roost at Deer Park, Maryland: "Our forests here are composed almost entirely of oaks of various kinds, the white, red, black, yellow, chestnut, pin and jack oaks being the principal varieties; the latter (jack oaks) form the underbrush in most places, and are the favorites with the pigeons, who crowd so thickly upon them that many of the smaller branches were broken off." [36]

The large swamps in Ohio were famous for their roosts, particularly: Lodi Swamp, Medina County; Copley and Mud Brook Swamps, Summit County; Bloody Run Swamp, Licking County; Bloomfield Swamp, Trumbull County; Aurora Swamp, Portage County; and Newman's Swamp, Wayne County. [37]

The Bloody Run Swamp, two and one-half miles long by one-half mile wide, "was a thickly matted growth of willows, young elms, water beeches and alders. In the middle were several islands covered with big timber.... The pigeons set toward the roost an hour before sundown, often lighting on the intermediate timber for a while, and passed on in a broad stream as far as the eye could reach. After arriving at the swamp they circled round and round till dark, when they settled down, covering every limb and twig." [38] In the early days, 1815, they flew directly into the swamp.

The Lodi Swamp covered several thousand acres. The center was a cranberry bog bounded by a ring of alders one-half mile in width and growing ten feet high. The whole was surrounded by tall timber consisting of ash, maple, and bur oak. On arriving at the roost in the evening, the pigeons alighted in the timber before retiring to the alders. This was done also in the morning before leaving for feeding. [39]

The arrival of the pigeons at a roost in Iowa is described as follows:

The pigeons checked their flight and settled down on the largest limbs of the tallest trees, beginning about 5 o'clock in the evening and continuing until dark to fill tree after tree until every available inch of space on the limbs was occupied, those arriving toward the last often flying against those already in possession and knocking them from their perch.... As far as the eye could see the air was filled with the flying birds, not in flocks but a steady downpour of feathered life. There did not seem to be any diminution in the velocity of their flight, or any lessening to the height in the air at which they were traveling until they were within a few rods of the earlier arrivals and then a downward swoop with distended wings. The nearness of bird to bird, and their continuous arrival resembled the pouring of a sheet of water over the incline of an apron in a dam across a stream.[40]

The pigeons began to arrive at the roost at dusk. The cessation of the flight depended on the size of the colony and the distance from the feeding grounds. Audubon states that they appeared at sundown and that there was no apparent diminution in the number of arrivals until after midnight.[41] Révoil visited a roost on the Green River, Kentucky, in the fall of 1847. The inward flight lasted from sundown to 11:00 P.M.[42] At other roosts the influx lasted from: dusk to one hour after dark; 4:00 P.M. to dark; and 5:00 P.M. to dark.[43] The pigeons using the famous roost in Scott County, Indiana, the fall of 1879 went so far for food that many did not return until midnight.[44] Departure in the morning took place uniformly at dawn.

The size of the roosts was usually much smaller than that of the nestings. The smallest mentioned is six acres.[45] Audubon visited a roost on Green River, Kentucky, that was forty miles long and over three wide.[46] This is very exceptional. Lincecum mentions a roost covering forty or fifty square miles.[47] Other roosts are stated to have covered an area: a mile in diameter, one mile by three, four square miles, "several hundred acres," and 2,000 to 2,500 acres.[48] The Milwaukee weekly *Wisconsin* for March 1, 1854, reported that the roost in Franklin County, Indiana, occupied in the first months of 1854, was five by ten miles. In February, 1879, a roost in Oklahoma was reported to be forty miles long and eighteen wide.[49] These dimensions are very doubtful.

The period of time that a roost was occupied depended upon its size, the amount of food in the region, the weather, and the degree of freedom from molestation. Hildreth wrote on February 1, 1833, from Marietta, Ohio, that a roost on the Little Hockhocking had been occupied for three months.[50] In contrast a roost near Marietta in the fall of 1840 was abandoned after two weeks, due possibly to nightly disturbance by hunters.[51] A large roost at Brookville, Indiana, was occupied throughout January and February, 1854.[52] Lincecum has described a roost in Mississippi that was occupied for six weeks. The acorns having been exhausted, all the pigeons left in a single day.[53] A heavy snowstorm in

January, 1761, drove away all the pigeons from the Petersback River, North Carolina, where they had had a roost for two months.[54] In the same locality, pigeons remained throughout January and into February, 1799.[55]

Many of the roosts were occupied with such regularity as to give names to the localities. Perhaps the most famous was that in Finley Township, Scott County, Indiana.[56] The settlement at this place, known as the "Pigeon Roost," was attacked by the Potawatomi in 1812 and twenty-four of the thirty inhabitants slain.[57] B. S. Miner, who was familiar with this roost since 1840, informed Butler that it would be occupied for two or three years, then after an absence of a few years the pigeons would return.[58] It was occupied at intervals at least until 1880.[59] Britton states that the roosts in southwestern Missouri were occupied nearly every year and that the pigeons did not winter.[60]

The amount of dung that collected in a roost used for a long time was immense. The possibility of making saltpeter from the heaps of this dung in Louisiana impressed Coxe.[61] The roost in Mississippi inspected by Hall contained thousands of wagonloads, though eighteen months had passed since deposition.[62] The dung under a roost at Waterford, Ohio, was a foot thick.[63] At a roost, used for many years, in southwestern Missouri, it was two to three feet thick in places.[64] Rev. David Zeisberger wrote that the pigeons appeared on the Muskinghum River in Ohio in 1777 and that over a foot of dung was formed in the roost in one night.[65] It is to be noted that in the history of this pigeon, data involving the highest figures are given by men of the cloth, a trait not inconsistent with belief in the miraculous. Brickell wrote: "Their Dung will lie above half a Foot thick about those Trees, which kills Shrubs, Grass, and everything that grows near where it falls." [66]

A roost that had been used for some time had a desolate appearance. Hulme wrote on July 5, 1819: "Come to Judge Chamber's [now Chambersburg, Orange County, Indiana] a good tavern. . . . Some of the trees near the Judge's exhibit a curious spectacle; a large piece of wood appears totally dead, all the leaves brown and the branches broken, from being roosted upon lately by an enormous multitude of pigeons. A novel sight for us, unaccustomed to the abundance of the backwoods." [67] When the dung became sufficiently thick, the trees and every plant beneath them were killed by what Wailes called the "heating effects of the large accumulations of the ordure about the roots." [68] The excrement of birds is rich in uric acid and ureates. Bacterial action soon converts them into readily soluble ammonia and nitrates which, at a certain concentration, kill the roots of the plants.

A pigeon roost on agricultural land was a blessing to the pioneer who had the problem of clearing the land. The trees were often killed and the soil enriched greatly by the dung. A pigeon roost occupied for many years was the most fertile land in the town of Troy, Geauga County, Ohio.[69] Lincecum thought that the soil was improved 100 per cent.[70] The high fertility of Bloody Run Swamp after draining was attributed to the pigeons that had used it as a roost for centuries.[71]

Natural growth, when resumed, frequently differed greatly from that without the roost. Price found that on an old roosting tract near Marlinton, Pocahontas County, West Virginia, the growth of pokeweed (*Phytolacca*) was luxuriant, and that there were many plants not natural to the type of soil.[72] There was a widespread belief among gatherers of ginseng (*Panax*) that this plant grew most abundantly at the old roosts.

CHAPTER 6: NESTING

The great colonial nestings of the passenger pigeon have obscured the fact that it also nested widely as single pairs and loose groups of a dozen or more pairs.[1] The degree of success attending the latter type of nestings is not known, but it must have been very low.

COLONIAL NESTINGS

It was characteristic of this pigeon to breed in large colonies. The nestings varied in size from many thousands of acres to a score or less. The large nestings were narrow in comparison with the length. Presumably a long, narrow line facilitated the arrival and departure of the parents and led to a minimum of confusion.[2] Disregarding the few large nestings forty or more miles in length, I have computed the average area of forty-seven nestings, the dimensions of which are given in the literature. This area is thirty-one square miles, so that a nesting three miles in width and ten in length can be considered typical.

There is little to support the contention of some writers that the nestings were constructed with the precision of cities with their streets and wards. French says: "Their colonies were generally regular in the border lines, being parallelograms, squares and circles, even to leaving the branches of an occupied tree that was outside the boundary line, bare of nests; while inside the boundary lines the branches were all covered with them, except a few near the tops of the trees. ..."[3] John C. French never heard of or saw a round nesting.[4]

The nesting might be two, three, or even twenty miles wide, between the "wards" of which there were avenues in the forest where no nests were constructed.[5] The avenues might be one to five miles wide, so that only 3 per cent, or less, of the entire area would be occupied. Apparently the description applies to a group of nestings.

The sharp limitation of nest-construction on the boundaries of a colony was not by design. Before expanding, every available nesting site within the colony was occupied. The passenger pigeon was never comfortable unless it was crowded. The nucleus of a nesting having been established, a density of nesting consistent with sites available was maintained to the borders of the colony. John H. Chatham wrote: "The nesting was built in compact form, with a certain length and width. So closely did they comply with this method, that trees on the sides of the nesting often would have from twenty-five to fifty nests on the inside and not a single nest on the opposite side of the tree." [6]

A nesting in the bottoms of the Tombecbee (Tombigbee) River, Mississippi, was studied by Lincecum. He wrote: "It is a subject worthy of notice, that no nest was found on any tree that stood on ground higher than the level of the bottom, not even on those trees whose branches interlocked with the limbs of the lowland timber, but having their roots on higher ground at the foot of the up-land slope." [7] The nesting at Montrose, Pennsylvania, was nine miles in length and four in breadth, the boundary lines being "regular and straight," according to the Montrose *Register* of May 8, 1829.

The size of the nestings reached its maximum in the North Central States, and was only average in New England and west of the Mississippi. Josselyn simply states that in New England the pigeons join nest to nest and tree to tree for many miles.[8] The nesting that occurred in New Hampshire in 1741 was only three miles in length.[9]

Some of the nestings were of extraordinary size. The two descriptions of the nestings seen by Alexander Wilson in Kentucky in the spring of 1810 are difficult to reconcile. Preference should be given to the letters by him written to Alexander Lawson and published by Ord.[10] On April 4 he wrote that between Shelbyville and Frankfort he went out of his way to visit a "pigeon-roost," no details of which are given. He states in his *Ornithology* that this was an old nesting used about five years previously, speaking evidently from the time of writing the chapter, so that it was probably occupied about 1808.[11] He goes on to say that this nesting was several miles in width and reported to have extended *forty* miles north and south. Remains of *ninety* nests were found in a single tree. The pigeons had abandoned this place and were then (1810) nesting on Green River.

On April 28 he wrote that he had passed through a nesting forty-nine miles from Danville that was three miles wide and said to be *forty* miles in length. The route followed and distance traveled would place this nesting near the Green River, Green County. Here he counted more than *ninety* nests in a single tree. In his text he states that he crossed this nesting for a distance of more than three miles. Wilson's journal for this period is lost, so that a further check is impossible. It may be inferred that in his publication he confused the dimensions of the old nesting with those of the new, or that they were identical, which is improbable. Ninety is given as the number of nests in a single tree at both nestings.

The large nestings were rarely continuous, due to topography, and it is a matter of opinion if they should be considered a single nesting or a chain of nestings. C. W. Dickinson states: "The writer's home was near these nestings. From one-half mile to four miles we could find eight or ten colonies of nesting birds, and we have been in six or eight that were farther away." [12] The nesting in McKean and Potter counties, Pennsylvania, in 1870 was from one-half to two miles in width. It zig-zagged for about forty miles through an unbroken forest, keeping near the range of mountains separating the waters of the Allegheny and Susquehanna rivers.[13]

The Petoskey, Michigan, nesting of 1878 was first described by Martin, a game dealer, as consisting of seven or eight distinct nestings; and he said that the areas actually occupied by the nestings would be a tract about fifteen miles long with an average width of three miles.[14] Later he mentioned the nesting as a unit that was thirty miles in length with an average width of one mile.[15] Mann has two nestings at Petoskey in 1878, his date of 1879 being incorrect. One was five by thirty miles, the other five by twelve miles.[16]

The dimensions of the large nestings were estimates. The difficulties of the terrain and lack of interest precluded a survey in the manner of a timber cruiser. The same nesting at Petoskey was visited by Professor

Roney. He states that in the opinion of qualified judges, the nesting was forty miles long and three to ten miles wide.[17] In close agreement are the dimensions given by Bond and Ellsworth, forty miles in length and six in width.[18] Disregarding Martin's data, the three remaining estimates vary from 210 to 260 square miles. This is a reasonable variation.

The nesting of 1876 at Crooked Lake, Emmet County, Michigan, began at Round Lake and extended past Crooked Lake towards Cheboygan for a total distance of thirty miles. U. P. Hedrick in a letter to me stated that the width was three to four miles. S. S. Stevens informed Brewster that this was the largest nesting that he ever visited.[19] It was twenty-eight miles in length, and three to four in width. This nesting is sometimes referred to as the Petoskey nesting, since it began near this town.

There is fair agreement on the area of the nesting at Shelby, Allegan County, Michigan, in 1876. The following sizes have been given: twelve by three miles, thirty miles in length and varying in width from one to five miles, and thirty square miles.[20]

Several nestings of exceptional size occurred in New York. About the year 1847 there was a nesting that extended from the vicinity of Annsville, Oneida County, nearly to Watertown, Jefferson County.[21] It was thirty miles in length and averaged three in width. A considerably larger nesting occurred in 1823. It began near the Allegheny River, Cattaraugus County, and extended north to the town of Collins, Erie County. It covered part or all of the townships of South Valley, Cold Spring, Napoli, New Albion, Dayton, and Tonawanda. The length was thirty miles and the average width was said to be six miles.[22]

A nesting in Pennsylvania in 1863 was reported by the Smethport *Democrat* to have extended from the Second Fork in McKean County through Elk County to Tionesta, Forest County.[23] This would be a length of sixty miles in a straight line.

The nestings in Pennsylvania in 1870 do not appear to have been of abnormal size despite the statement of Knapp that one was said to be one hundred miles long and one to seventy-five miles wide.[24] The width is preposterous. J. B. Oviatt informed Scherer that the largest nesting that he ever saw occurred in this year in McKean County. It extended from the east branch of Potato Creek to the head of Colgrave Brook, which streams are in the Township of Norwich.[25] If the nesting began at the source of the east branch, ran down Potato Creek to the junction with Colgrave Brook, then up this stream to its source, the length of the nesting would not have been over fifteen miles. Disturbed by shooting, the pigeons abandoned the nesting and moved to Potter County.

The information given by Thompson on the Pennsylvania nestings is not sufficiently specific. He states: "In 1870 there were nestings in Potter, McKean and Elk Counties about forty miles in length. They commenced nestings in McKean County." [26]

The nesting in the bottoms of the Mississippi River at La Crosse, Wisconsin, mentioned by Bunnell was about forty-five miles in length.[27] Due to its location, it must have been less than a mile in average width. Bunnell came to Wisconsin in June, 1842, so that the nesting must have occurred in 1843 or shortly thereafter.

The nesting in Wisconsin in 1871 was the largest of record. Muir quotes Chief Pokagon as follows: "I saw one nesting-place in Wisconsin one hundred miles long and from three to ten miles wide." [28] A letter from Pokagon to Deane shows that he was at the nesting of 1871.[29] Mershon has the following statement from H. T. Phillips, a game dealer, of Detroit: "In Wisconsin I have seen a continual nesting for 100 miles, with from one to possibly fifty nests on every oak scrub." [30] The nesting of 1871 is the only one that ever approached this size. Where it has been possible to check from independent sources, I have found the statements of Phillips to be very reliable, particularly as to dates and localities.

It was determined from contemporary sources that the nesting of 1871 was in the shape of a huge ell (Fig. 1).[31] The long arm, having an average width of six miles, extended from Black River Falls to Kilbourn, a distance of seventy-five miles. The short arm extended from Kilbourn towards Wisconsin Rapids for a distance of fifty miles and had an average width of eight miles. The entire area within the lines of the nesting was not occupied. Unfortunately it was not possible to determine the number and size of the gaps. Insofar as can be determined, nearly all the pigeons in North America nested in Wisconsin this year, acorns being abundant. The statement of Bishop that the main body of pigeons nested in Forest County, Pennsylvania, in 1871 cannot be confirmed.[32]

The largest credible nesting reported in the extreme South was lo-

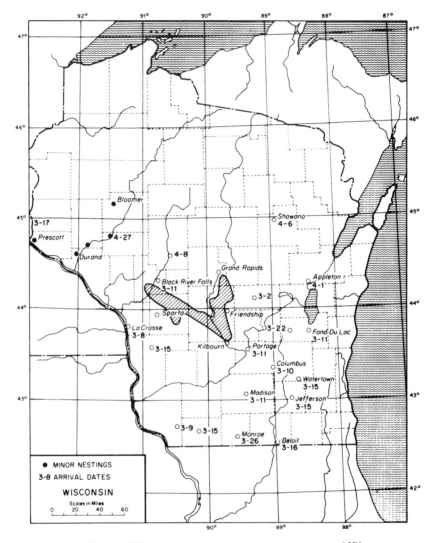

Fig. 1.—Wisconsin passenger pigeon nesting of 1871.

cated on the Tombigbee River, Mississippi, in 1832. Lincecum states that it was fifteen miles in length and one and one-half to two miles in width.[33]

The nesting in Oklahoma in 1881, as described by Thomas, was located in the Potawatomi Reservation. The region was thickly covered with post oak (*Quercus stellata*). He went into this nesting for ten miles without finding indications of an end and estimated its dimensions as twenty miles long and fifteen broad.[34] The shape is very unusual. Bryant states that in 1882 there was a nesting in the Panhandle of Texas that was forty miles in length and twenty in width. The nesting was so far from a shipping point that the pigeons were not trapped.[35] The location is unlikely and no further information on this nesting was found. The pigeons nested in Wisconsin in this year.

The finding of food, according to Audubon, depended entirely on distant vision. He wrote:

This great power of flight is seconded by as great a power of vision, which enables them, as they travel at that swift rate, to inspect the country below, discover their food with facility, and thus attain the object for which their journey has been undertaken. This I have also proved to be the case, by having observed them, when passing over a sterile part of the country, or one scantily furnished with food suited to them, keep high in the air, flying with an extended front, so as to enable them to survey hundreds of acres at once. On the contrary, when the land is richly covered with food, or the trees abundantly hung with mast, they fly low, in order to discover the part most plentifully supplied.[36]

Pigeons flying at a great height have been seen to descend suddenly to feed. Gentry also attributed this maneuver to their powerful vision.[37]

It is doubtful if pigeons could see mast or other food, either in summer or winter, from a great height. It is more probable that they could recognize the vegetation producing their accustomed foods; but the actual finding must have been largely by trial and error. This would certainly be the case in late fall and winter when the mast on the ground was largely concealed by leaves. Burs of the beech, when subjected to an early frost, frequently remain on the trees until spring and are plainly visible.

The most interesting phase of the problem is the procedure by which the pigeons discovered an area with sufficient food to support a nesting.

It was believed by some that the small flocks first seen in spring were "scouts" whose duty it was to return to the main flock and report on the condition of the mast.[38] There is nothing to support this opinion. Frequently the first arrivals were in very large flocks. To return and report is to assume a high degree of intelligence.

A region without mast would be passed over without hesitation during the spring flights, or the pigeons would not appear at all. Bryant mentions that a crop of pigeons, like any other crop, could be counted upon in Michigan every second year due to the mast.[39] In the off year the pigeons flew over without stopping to nest. J. B. Oviatt states that in Pennsylvania, "the spring flocks usually stayed for at least a short time to rest and feed—though in years when there was no crop of beech nuts the birds usually passed quite rapidly, stopping only a little to look about for food." [40]

There is no information showing the relative numbers of pigeons migrating through a given region in the spring of good and poor mast years. Generally the inhabitants of a region where there was no mast did not expect pigeons in large numbers. It is difficult to believe that the birds on arrival in the north always indulged in random wanderings until food sufficient for nesting was located. Pigeons entering Michigan, e.g., during a mastless year would be compelled to leave the state by following the northern shores of Lakes Michigan or Huron, by crossing these lakes at some point, or returning southward. The well established crossing of Lake Michigan from the Wisconsin shore would seem even more senseless unless it were known that there was mast in Michigan. In fact, the known crossings were in mast years.

In autumn the pigeons were widely distributed and assembled gradually into large flocks during the southward migration. There was abundant opportunity to learn where mast was plentiful. The autumn of 1881 there was a large crop of acorns in Wisconsin. Large numbers of pigeons passed through the state in the fall migration, many remaining into October. They returned in February of the following year and remained until breeding was completed at Sparta and Kilbourn. There is no reason to suppose that the return was not due to memory. Whitman defines memory as the capacity to form habits. He was so impressed by the memory of his pigeons as to say: "I am inclined to think that these birds have as good a memory as we have."[41] Based on food box tests, Porter concluded that the passenger and other pigeons have a fairly good memory.[42] The song sparrows of Margaret Nice were frightened by a mounted barred owl resting on a piano. After an interval of several months, the same alarm was shown at the sight of the piano though the owl had been removed. The association was remembered.[43] It does not seem to me any more difficult to attribute memory to conditioning by food than by a place or object.

The only suggestion found in the literature that the pigeons remembered the fall supply of mast is in the description of the nesting in Forest and Warren counties, Pennsylvania, in 1886:

The vast beech forests that cover much of the area afford the food that attracts the pigeons to the locality, every fruitful beechnut year being sure to be followed by the appearance of the birds in greater or less numbers. The beech tree is uncertain in its yield of nuts, and never bears two years in succession. When the trees bear well thousands and thousands of bushels of the nuts fall to the ground after the frosts of Autumn.... The condition of the nut crop is learned in the Fall by the birds, flocks of scouting pigeons visiting the woods in the flight south, and it is supposed, informing the great body of birds as to the result of their investigations.[44]

It is to be assumed that the old pigeons remembered the localities supplied with mast and, in the spring migration, led the flocks to them.

The nestings generally started along a stream. Valleys afforded protection from high winds. William French states that in Pennsylvania the pigeons selected a clump of evergreens by a small stream with the ground rising on the eastern side. If the colony was large, the nesting spread to high ground.[45] Otis Lyman has the nestings following the bends of creeks and spreading to the hilltops.[46] Occasionally the nestings were placed on ridges.[47] According to J. B. Oviatt, highlands at the heads of streams were usually selected in Pennsylvania.[48] If the nesting was large, it extended across hollows and little valleys.

It was not uncommon for a nesting to be located on an island. In 1806, Pike found one on an island in the Mississippi off Pike County, Illinois.[49] There was a nesting on Nine Mile Island in the Chippewa River, three miles north of Durand, Wisconsin, in 1871, reported in the Durand *Times* for May 2 of that year. In the same year the Prescott *Jour-*

nal of June 21 reported a nesting on an island in the Mississippi below Prescott, Wisconsin. Pigeons were reported nesting on an island in the Mississippi four miles below Hastings, Minnesota, in the Hastings *Independent* for June 13, 1861, and June 19, 1862.

The pigeons never nested twice in the same place,[50] or at least until several years had elapsed.[51] Pigeons were said to breed regularly in Leelanau County, Michigan, in a tract of timber 22.5 miles long and 1.5 to 3 miles wide lying between Lake Leelanau and Grand Traverse Bay.[52] This does not mean necessarily that the same area within the tract was occupied in successive nestings. Furthermore, they rarely nested oftener than once in two years in Michigan, as there was not a crop of beechnuts more frequently than this.

Pigeons nested near Chatfield, Minnesota, three years in succession.[53] This was due to feeding in part at least on wheat. These nestings did not occupy the same areas. In 1863 the nesting was two miles west of Chatfield, in 1864 three miles west, and in 1865 "much the same territory as the past two years."

A nesting having started, every tree, regardless of species, contained nests. In Pennsylvania a preference for evergreens, especially hemlocks, was shown.[54] John C. French states that they chose hollows where hemlocks grew thickly over an area of about twenty acres. The area contained from 800 to 1,000 trees.[55] In contrast, Scherer reported: "The birds chose chiefly hardwood timber for their cities. They preferred to build their nests in hardwood trees and in hemlocks of open growth—never in thick hemlocks. Mr. Oviatt never saw a nest in a white pine." [56]

The use of beech trees was common. In Kentucky the nestings were mainly in beech forests.[57] Edwin Haskell visited a nesting on Dingman Run, Potter County, Pennsylvania, where hundreds of acres of beech trees were being felled to obtain the squabs.[58] All the nests seen by C. K. Sober were in beechwoods and mostly in beech trees.[59]

A variety of trees was used in New York. The large nesting along Bell's Run, Allegany County, New York, in 1868 was in hemlock, pine, and deciduous trees.[60] This forest was thick.[61] A group of less than a dozen birds was found nesting in small spruce trees along the Moose River, Herkimer County, New York, in 1878.[62]

The nesting at Tupper's Lake, Franklin County, New York, in 1853, is described by Hammond: "The trees were not of large growth, being mostly of spruce and stunted birch, hemlock, and elm, but every one was loaded with nests."[63] In the vicinity of Guelph, Ontario, the nestings were located along streams where fir trees were numerous.[64]

A preference for nesting in "cedar," probably *Thuja occidentalis,* was shown in the northern part of the lower peninsula of Michigan.[65] Gunn visited the nesting of 1878 at Crooked Lake, Emmet County. The woods occupied consisted mainly of pine with a few beech and maple.[66] Maynard was informed by E. H. Bowers that in Benzie County a preference was shown for deciduous trees.[67]

The statements on the nesting at Shelby, Michigan, in 1876, are in conflict. According to "Tom Tramp" the belt of timber occupied consisted of hemlock and pine with a few beech and other species.[68] Ingells, writing many years later of the same nesting, said that they built only in the best timber, maple and beech, and not in pine, cedar, or hemlock.[69] This is incorrect.

Two small nestings of a few hundred birds in southern Michigan were known to Bryant.[70] One was on a beech ridge flanked on one side by a tamarack swamp and on the other by a lake surrounded by an impassable marsh; the other was in a tamarack swamp. The big nesting at Grand Haven, Michigan, in 1866, was in a large tamarack swamp three miles from the town.[71]

The statement of Knapp that in Pennsylvania and Michigan the pigeons nested in beech, birch, and cherry and that in Wisconsin scrub oak and dwarf pine were sometimes used adds little to our knowledge.[72] In fact most of the nestings in Wisconsin occurred in forests of Hill's oak (*Quercus ellipsoidalis*) and jack pine (*Pinus banksiana*). Thickets of young pines were used in Sheboygan County, Wisconsin.[73]

Pigeons nested in the alder swamps along the west branch of Pine River, Richland County, Wisconsin, in 1855, according to a notice in the Richland Center *Observer* for January 17, 1878. It is improbable that the nests were placed in the alders. The last attempt at colonial nesting in this state was in a swamp north of Wautoma, Waushara County, in 1887, as reported in the Wautoma *Argus* for May 20 and 27 and June 3 of this year. A few scattered pairs nested in oak trees along the Wolf River, in a swampy area in southwestern Waupaca County, Wisconsin, in 1885.[74] The area was timbered with swamp oak, ash, and elm, and contained many marshes and sloughs.

Species of poplar were used rarely. P. H. Woodworth by interview informed me that he was at a nesting in poplars in the township of Caseville, Huron County, Michigan. In a letter O. B. Stephens informed me that an attempt was made to nest in a poplar grove near Deerfield, Wisconsin, but the branches proved to be too brittle. Poplars were also used in Manitoba.[75]

High trees were used, but less frequently than low ones. Kalm has the pigeons nesting in high pine and deciduous trees.[76] The nesting along Wood Creek, near Lake Oneida, New York, in 1793, was in lofty sugar maples, elms, and hickories.[77] Rintoul visited a nesting south of Altona, Clinton County, New York, in 1867 or 1868, that was built in heavy hardwood timber.[78] The trees in the nesting in Mississippi described by Lincecum were very tall and consisted of hickory, oak, beech, sweet gum, and cypress.[79]

NESTING PROCEDURES

The selection of a nesting site was not made until some time after the pigeons appeared in a region. The pigeons arrived in Wisconsin in 1882 on February 9 and did not begin nesting until the middle of April. In the interim the entire southern portion of the state as far north as Green Bay was covered in their wanderings. Firstly, a region was surveyed for its food resources. By some instinct only enough pigeons arrived, or remained, to form a nesting that was certain to be supported by the amount of food available. We are entirely in the dark as to the reason for selecting a given area for the building of the nests. A location central with respect to the food supply was often disregarded. In Michigan the nestings were frequently placed so close to Lake Michigan that food could not be obtained westward, or northward, or both.

The nesting area seems to have been selected in advance of occupation. The pigeons might be few or altogether absent from the area prior to courtship. A flock would suddenly arrive and mill about over the area showing definitely that nesting would soon begin. The main body might arrive the following day or over a period of two or three days. C. W. Dickinson states that prior to nesting the pigeons would be scattered over three or four counties; but they roosted in one large body a night or two before building of the nests began.[80]

An experienced person could tell at once by the actions of the birds where a nesting would start. E. Haskell mentions having his attention called to the pigeons circling in and out of an upland woods one April day at Coudersport, Pennsylvania.[81] The informant stated that the main flock would appear the next day and nesting would begin soon. This proved to be true.

The beginning of a nesting is described by J. B. Oviatt:

It was a dense, oval bunch coming in to drop to its new nesting ground just before dark.... The birds were milling about among themselves, so that the flock moved slowly. They were going in the direction of the Denton Hill country, twelve miles away, where a day or two later it was reported that they had begun nesting. For a number of days afterward, smaller flocks came in from all around, to nest with them. Hundreds probably of such additional flocks came in, and it is likely that they more than doubled the size of the nesting.[82]

Increase in the size of a nesting after it had reached the point of nest construction was not normal. All the stages in breeding were remarkably synchronized. There are statements of a nesting being increased by the arrival of "new bodies" of pigeons. This sometimes occurred when a nesting was abandoned on account of a snowstorm or shooting. J. B. Oviatt states that after the first nests were built pigeons continued to arrive over a period of two weeks and built on the edges of the colony;[83] however, the growth of the nesting of 1870 continued for about a month. His statements appear to have been based on finding eggs ready to be laid in birds trapped two weeks after nesting had started. This is not proof that these birds were new arrivals. There was continuous destruction of nests during the nesting period, and some at least of the females would make a second attempt to rear young.

Various stages in breeding have been noted occasionally in the same colony. At the Tupper Lake, New York, nesting in 1853, Hammond found squabs with down, while others were about ready to fly.[84] Hedrick has old birds mating and squabs just flying at the Petoskey, Michigan, nesting of 1876.[85] This would be most unusual. Hedrick was but six years of age at the time.

A nesting with sections in every degree of advancement was considered normal by Roney. He entered only a section where squabs were being collected but states that in others the pigeons were building nests or hatching.[86] It is evident that he relied on hearsay for some of his information or he would never have made the wholly erroneous statement that the old birds abandon the young when one week old and move a mile or two to begin nesting anew.

The courtship of the passenger pigeon is described by Audubon as follows:

The male assumes a pompous demeanour, and follows the female whether on the ground or on the branches, with spread tail and drooping wings, which it rubs against the part over which it is moving. The body is elevated, the throat swells, the eyes sparkle. He continues his notes, and now and then rises on the wing, and flies a few yards to approach the fugitive and timorous female. Like the domestic Pigeon and other species, they caress each other by billing, in which action, the bill of the one is introduced transversely into that of the other, and both parties alternately disgorge the contents of their crop by repeated efforts. These preliminary affairs are soon settled, and the Pigeons commence their nests in general peace and harmony.[87]

Audubon (Plate LXII) shows a female passenger pigeon standing on a branch over a male on a lower limb. She has inserted her bill directly into that of the male, that can be barely reached, as if he were begging for food. Craig finds Audubon incorrect in several particulars.[88] When the birds billed, they were always side by side and the tail was not spread. The bill was inserted directly and not transversely as described in the above paragraph. If food is passed among pigeons, the female is the sole recipient. In the case of the passenger pigeon, it is not certain that she was ever so favored.

The male was described by Audubon as flying in circles with wings elevated at an angle, as with the domestic pigeon, the tips of the primaries occasionally meeting over the back to produce a sound that could be heard at a distance of thirty or forty rods. There is doubt that the clapping is produced by contact between the wings. It may be due to a downstroke like the crack of a whip.[89]

Flapping of the wings occurred also when the bird was perched. It was considered as mainly a mating display by Craig, since it took place most frequently during the breeding season.[90] The male raised its wings until the carpi were about one and one-half inches apart over the back. The entire body, head, and tail rose with each stroke. Propulsion was prevented by the slowness of the flapping and by a firm grasp on the perch with the feet. Although the bird usually stood obliquely so that the wings came down on each side, the perch was frequently struck with a very audible sound.

Our knowledge of mating depends largely on the behavior of birds in captivity. This behavior should not be fundamentally different from that of the bird in the wild. Craig writes:

The courting behaviour of this species, as is evident from what has been said about voice and gestures, was very different from the courting behaviour of other Pigeons and Doves. Instead of pirouetting before the female, or bowing to her, or running and jumping after her on the ground, the passenger pigeon sidled up to her on the perch and pressed her very close; and if she moved a little away from him he sidled up to her again and tried to put his neck over her.

The male was very jealous of his mate. And when they had a nest he was a most truculent fellow, attacking any other bird that came into the vicinity.... He was not really a good fighter: he made a bold attack, but if the attacked one showed fight, *Ectopistes* generally retreated.[91]

Quarrelsomeness within a nesting colony with its crowded conditions would have been disastrous after the birds were mated. J. B. Oviatt never saw fighting over either mates or nesting sites.[92] There was, however, belligerence over the females. Bishop wrote:

As soon as a colony of wild pigeons is settled in its roosting place the mating of the birds begins. The cooing of the thousands upon thousands of pigeons in the roost during the courting period is kept up constantly for three days. This is the love note of the male. A tom pigeon, as the male is called, selects the hen he fancies and woos her alone. If another tom wants her, there must be a fight among the rivals, which is always a fierce one. The hen perches on a limb near by while the fight for her possession is going on, and when it is over she is claimed by the winner and she becomes his at once.[93]

The choosing of mates and nesting sites was indicated when the flocks scattered and the gently cooing birds sidled up to each other to form pairs.[94]

A good description of the courtship period is given by Pokagon as witnessed on the headwaters of the Manistee River, about the middle of May, 1850. Millions of pigeons passed through the forest, filling the space between the ground and the tops of the trees, with a sound resembling a mixture of sleigh bells and the rumble of an approaching storm. So fearless were the pigeons that they fluttered all about him, even alighting on his head and shoulders. He adds:

I now began to realize that they were mating, preparatory to nesting. It was an event which I had long hoped to witness; so I sat down and carefully watched their movements, amid the greatest tumult. I tried to understand their strange language, and why they all chatted in concert. In the course of the day the great onmoving mass passed by me, but the trees were still filled with them sitting in pairs in convenient crotches of the limbs, now and then gently fluttering their halfspread wings and uttering to their mates those strange bell-like wooing notes which I had mistaken for the ringing of bells in the distance.

On the third day after, this chattering ceased and all were busy carrying sticks with which they were building nests in the same crotches of the limbs they had occupied in pairs the day before.[95]

Copulation with pigeons in general persists until the first egg is laid, ceasing then, or soon thereafter. There is normally no courting or copulation during incubation.[96]

The best description of the act of copulation is that in Whitman:

The female, if disposed, often takes the initiative, giving the call and then hugging the male while she pressed with body against him. He returns the call and the hugging and the billing. He reaches over, so that the front of his neck bears on the back of her neck or the top of her head, and often jerks or pulls her head towards him by means of his beak, which is held like a hook over her head. He may often mount several times before the female is ready. When she is ready she stoops and raises both wings to support him. Sometimes she begins to stoop only after he has mounted, gradually and slowly lowering her body to a horizontal position. The male expects her to raise her tail to contact with his; if she does not at once do this he touches her with his beak, with a single stroke first on one side then on the other, or touches her beak near the base, as if to make her lower her head and raise her tail. It is more probable, however, that he does this to excite her to the point of responding to his movements. The pressure of the body and neck against the female is to induce her to active participation in the act. The pull with the beak hooked over the head and the side stroke of the beak, as well as the fondling of the head feathers, all tend to excitement, and they are the expression of the sexual impulse.[97]

An unusual amount of scrambling on the back of the female was believed to serve the same purpose as the prolonged billing in other species. "Each time they copulate, female stands up very straight when male mounts; this compels him to flap his wings for long time, scrambling up near her neck, till she becomes tired [?] and sinks down, then he copulates." [98] Following copulation both birds uttered soft, toneless clucks, the female striking the male two or three times, an act peculiar to the species. In one instance, following copulation, each bird tickled the head of the other "with nervous rapidity for several seconds."

The female was never seen to place her beak within that of the male; [99] however, there was a brief, perfunctory billing.[100]

The male would often utter a loud squawk and rush towards a female a foot or two distant and hug her strenuously. The female in a proper state of amorousness pursued the male in similar fashion. When either a male or female passenger pigeon showed this behavior with other species of pigeons, the latter were frightened and usually retreated.[101] This trait made crossbreeding difficult.

The three days of courtship having passed, construction of the nest was started. The selection of the nesting site was done with considerable ceremony involving caressing and cooing. The male brought all of the nesting material, one piece at a time in his bill, to the female who performed all the labor of construction. The male mounted on the back of the female and placed the stick or straw in front of her, this being apparently the most convenient way to receive it.[102] When the male found a suitable straw, he uttered a few "kecks" on starting and guttural clucks on delivering it to the female.[103] Deane mentions that the female uttered a specific signal for the delivery of nesting material.[104]

According to Gibbs, a twig dropped was never reclaimed by the bearer but was taken by another bird.[105] His statement that the birds were flying in every direction, seemingly bent on securing twigs at a distance, would indicate that nesting material was not plentiful. In building, according to J. B. Oviatt, they merely flew up and down from the ground.[106]

The great majority of the nests were constructed of small twigs only (Fig. 8). Usually the nest was so loosely built that the egg could be seen from the ground. The saucer-shaped edifices were six to seven inches in diameter and not more than two and one-half inches in height.[107] Gibbs gives the diameter as six to twelve inches.[108] A nest found by Thoreau in Minnesota was six inches in diameter and the cavity only three-fourths of an inch deep.[109]

The time required for the building of the nest depended upon the availability of twigs of the proper dimensions, and probably on the urgency for laying. Simpson was informed by a man who had often visited the nestings that a pair required only about forty minutes to build a nest.[110] This is beyond belief. A pair in captivity began a nest on the morning of April 25, 1832, and finished it by evening.[111] The egg was laid the morning of April 26. Pokagon has the nest built and the egg laid within twenty-four hours.[112] Gibbs states that it required four to six days for the building.[113] The birds in the Cincinnati Zoological Gardens constructed a nest in three to four days, but at times six were taken.[114] Other data are: three days, a day or two at most, two days to build the nest and lay the egg, and two or three days for construction and laying.[115] It appears accordingly that three days may be considered the average time required to build the nest and deposit the egg.

The foundation of the nest consisted of coarse twigs, described as half the size of the little finger,[116] and scarcely as large as the stem of a clay pipe.[117] The lining was usually of fine twigs. Pokagon frequently counted the number of twigs in a nest and found from 70 to 110.[118] Occasionally there was found in the lining: leaves, dry stubble (straw), feathers, and moss.[119] It is questionable if moss was deliberately selected. The twigs of the black spruce and tamarack in the northern coniferous swamps generally have "moss" (*Usnea*) attached to them.

The solidarity of the nest depended largely on the availability of suitable twigs. Barrows' statement that the nests were so loosely interwoven as to be easily dislodged or shaken apart is typical.[120] It is not, however, in accord with the fact. Concerning the nests found in New York, Merriam wrote: "They were all much more substantial than the published accounts had led me to believe. In fact they were not frail structures at all, but were so compactly built of twigs, that one could by no means see daylight through them." [121]

The loose structure was deceptive. "Antler" states that the twigs were so cleverly interwoven with the branches on which the nest was built that winds and storms did not dislodge them.[122] Several nestings, wherein the nests were very compact, were seen by Gunn.[123]

The persistence of the nests in old nestings is indicative of an adequate permanence. An uprooted yellow birch in an old nesting in the Adirondacks had several nests still in place.[124] Any number of nests could be counted in nestings that were two to three years old.[125] Schaff could detect the remains of nests eleven or twelve years after they were made.[126]

Want of proper structural materials was sometimes a handicap; hence the nests in some colonies were barely serviceable. It was a source of wonder to "Antler" where all the twigs could be found to build the millions of nests.[127] At a nesting on the Genesee River, New York, in 1782, the pigeons so exhausted the supply of twigs that the floor of the forest was entirely bare.[128] The exhaustion of the nesting materials is described concisely by Lincecum: "They made their nests of small dry twigs, bits of sticks, dry leaves, all kinds of trash found on the ground, and by the time they had completed their work, the entire bottom looked black and clear of litter as if it had been swept with a broom. Not a leaf nor a stick was left, and to judge from the appearance of the scanty nests, the birds didn't have half enough." [129]

The captive passenger pigeons of Whitman when ready to select a place for a nest, stretched their heads forward, raised their wings, and moved them slightly. The search for a location is thus described:

They flew several times against the wire of their cage, and seemed to wish to get out in order to find a new place for a nest.... Two days later these passengers were very active, but not yet decided where to place the nest. The male was especially active, taking the lead in the search. He kept alighting on a small tree inclosed in their large pen, and here he would put down his head and call the female. I repeatedly saw this pair flying about in search for a nesting place. I note, too, that when the male flew back and forth he called to his mate *while on the wing.*[130]

A pair in the Zoological Society's Gardens, London, spent three or four days in selecting a building site in a fir tree.[131]

The nests were placed, while a choice remained, on a limb near the trunk of the tree. The tops of the trees and the ends of limbs were rarely used since the wind would dislodge the nest or its contents. Gibbs states that the position of the nests varied greatly, being even located well out on slender branches.[132] The use of strong limbs, or a position close to the trunk, was general.[133] Often the nests were placed close together in rows on suitable limbs. The limbs of the hemlock furnished flat, substantial bases for nests in large numbers. During an interview with W. Dunwoody of Monroe, Wisconsin, in 1934, I was informed that oak trees not over twenty feet high were selected for the nestings in the southern part of Green County. The nests were placed in crotches.

The height of the nest varied with the type and height of trees in the nesting. Pokagon found in Wisconsin nests only five to six feet from the ground.[134] Some of the heights given are: generally twelve feet and from this distance up to twenty-five feet; twelve feet, usually higher, to top of trees; six to sixty-five feet; seven to thirty feet; twelve to fifty feet; and thirty to sixty feet.[135]

It has been stated in the literature that as many as 500 nests were built in one tree. Any number of this magnitude is a product of the imagination. Bryant and a companion counted 317 nests in a large hemlock at one of the nestings at Shelby, Michigan.[136] A friend reported to Dümling that he counted 140 nests in a broadly branched tree in Ozaukee County, Wisconsin.[137]

Gibbs was told by a man that he counted 110 nests in one tree.[138] One hundred nests in a tree was considered common by Proctor, and Loskiel stated that the Indians sometimes obtained 200 squabs (200 nests) from one tree.[139] Other numbers given are: about one hundred, sixty to seventy, twenty to fifty, fifty, thirty-six, and twenty-four.[140] In Wisconsin as many as forty nests were counted in scrub oaks not over twenty-five feet in height.[141] C. W. Dickinson counted 57 nests in a large birch and believed that there were three times as many in hemlocks.[142]

The laying of the egg by captives is described by Whitman: "An *Ectopistes* was observed in laying an egg at 5:25 P.M. She moved forward in the nest and held herself in a more or less erect position. When she dropped the egg she lifted her wings a little, just as I saw her do in laying a previous egg. Another *Ectopistes* female stood up for 5 minutes after laying and then sat on the egg. She gave a few low calls shortly before laying."[143] The eggs were laid in the afternoon between 4:00 and 6:25 P.M.[144]

Dates of the deposition of eggs are few and are wanting almost entirely for the large colonies. Regarding the large nestings in Pennsylvania in 1870, Thompson states that eggs were laid the middle and 26 of

April, and that additions were made to the colonies on May 3 and 9 by pigeons from the West.[145] The latter would not have laid much before the middle of May. The nesting of single pairs, frequent in late spring and extending throughout the summer, bore little relationship in time to that of the colonies.

The dates of nests with eggs for single pairs or for groups are as follows:

CONNECTICUT. May 29 and June 6 (Sage, Bishop, and Bliss, as in Chap. 8, n. 138); late in May (Merriam, as in Chap. 14, n. 16).

IOWA. First week in April (Bendire, as in Chap. 3, n. 183); June 14 (Keyes and Williams, as in Chap. 6, n. 169).

MANITOBA. May 21 and 31 (Thompson, as in Chap. 2, n. 118); June 1 (Reed, as in Table 3, n. 10); June 23 (Macoun, as in Chap. 6, n. 75).

MASSACHUSETTS. April to July (Forbush, as in Chap. 10, n. 26); May 22 (Brewster, as in Chap. 3, n. 141); a trapper at Concord informed Thoreau on September 28, 1859, that a day or two previously he had found a fully developed egg in a pigeon (Thoreau, as in Chap. 8, n. 36).

MICHIGAN. Nesting began frequently the middle of April, and extended normally into late June, or even into July (Barrows, as in Chap. 4, n. 103); May 20 (Covert, as in Chap. 14, n. 133); June 1 (Gibbs, as in Chap. 6, n. 163); June 18 (Coale, as in Chap. 15, n. 15).

MINNESOTA. Early April (Cantwell, as in Chap. 9, n. 135); April 29 to May 17 (Vernon Bailey quoted in Roberts, as in Chap. 14, n. 149); May 1 (E. S. Stebbins and W. O. Emerson quoted in Roberts, *ibid.*); about the first of May (Hatch, as in Chap. 14, n. 149); W. Otto Emerson is incorrect in stating June (in *Warbler,* 2nd ser., I [1905], 74–76); June 6 (Thoreau, as in Chap. 6, n. 109); June 21 (Jones, as in Chap. 15, n. 44); Roberts gives six records for May 9 to June 2, an egg ready to hatch on August 20, and a fresh egg on September 6 (as in Chap. 14, n. 109).

NEW YORK. Began nesting early in April and height of nesting was reached the middle of May (Eaton, as in Chap. 3, n. 184); May 18 (Pennock, as in Chap. 6, n. 62); June (Bagg, as in Chap. 6, n. 21); early in June (Merriam quoted in Eaton, as in Chap. 3, n. 184).

North Dakota.   June 13 (Coues, as in Chap. 10, n. 5).

Pennsylvania.   First eggs about the first of April, which checks with earliest record of squabs almost ready to fly on April 27 (J. B. Oviatt quoted in Scherer, as in Chap. 14, n. 308); as early as the middle of April (Gentry, as in Chap. 10, n. 30).

Wisconsin.   First week in April (Bendire, as in Chap. 3, n. 183); April 27 to September 10 (Kumlien, as in Chap. 9, n. 127); May 2 (A. L. Kumlien and N. Hollister, *The Birds of Wisconsin* [Milwaukee, Wis., 1903], p. 59); June 3 (date of egg in the Milwaukee Public Museum); June 11 and 21 (Gruntvig, as in Chap. 6, n. 1).

There are no specific dates for nesting for March in the wild. Pigeons taken at Albany, New York, March 10, 1872, were found to have in the oviduct fully formed eggs ready for laying.[146] Birds received in Chicago on April 15, 1882, from New Lisbon, Wisconsin, contained eggs the size of the "end of a lead pencil," some slightly larger.[147]

Pigeons in confinement in Milwaukee "usually laid from the middle of February to the middle of September," [148] and those in Chicago from February 24 to August 29.[149] Single pairs in the wild have laid eggs from early in April to September 10, so that the breeding season for non-colonial nestings was as prolonged as that of the mourning dove in the northern latitudes.

The dates of the various stages in the nesting of colonies have not been recorded. In many cases the dates when the squabs were collected are given. Allowing thirty days for the nesting cycle, it is possible to determine within two or three days the dates of the beginning of nesting. An analysis of these nestings showed that the great majority began in April, and this was true throughout the breeding range. Nesting began the first of April in New York and Michigan if the weather permitted.[150] Most of the nestings in Wisconsin did not start until the middle of April.

The eggs are pure white, elongate, elliptical, or elliptical ovate, and considered by Barrows as scarcely distinguishable from those of the domestic pigeon.[151] There is a slight gloss, but without the "polish" of the egg of the domestic pigeon.[152]

It would appear simple to have determined the number of eggs laid

TABLE 3

Size of Passenger Pigeon Eggs

NUMBER OF EGGS MEASURED	AVERAGE		EXTREME		REF.
	LENGTH	WIDTH	LENGTH	WIDTH	
32	38.2 mm.	27.0 mm.	45.2 mm.	29.7 mm.	1
"	....	....	36.2	24.9	1
"	....	....	33.5	26.0	2
20	37.5	26.5	39.5	28.5	3
"	....	....	33.5	26.0	3
unknown	36.8	26.7	....	....	4
"	37.3	25.9	....	....	5
"	38.1	25.4	(with little variation)		6
"	38.1–39.4	25.4–28.5	....	....	7
"	38.1	25.9	....	....	8
"	38.1	26.2	....	....	9
"	38.1	27.9	....	....	10
"	39.0	27.25	....	....	11

[1] A. C. Bent, *Life Histories of N. Am. Gallinaceous Birds*, p. 386. [2] *Ibid.* Bent obviously took these last figures from Bendire. [3] C. Bendire, *Life Histories of N. Am. Birds*, Part I, p. 138. [4] J. M. Wheaton, "Report on the Birds of Ohio," *Rept. Geol. Survey Ohio*, IV (1882), 442. [5] W. B. Barrows, *Mich. Bird Life*, p. 241. [6] "Pericles" (R. M. Gibbs) in *Oologist*, XI (1894), 237–40. [7] Charles J. Maynard, *Eggs of North American Birds* (Boston, 1890), p. 53. [8] Chester A. Reed, *North American Birds Eggs* (N.Y., 1904), p. 148. [9] Oliver Davie, *Nests and Eggs of North American Birds* (5th ed.; Columbus, Ohio, 1898), p. 187. [10] Henry D. Minot, *The Land-Birds and Game-Birds of New England* (Salem, Mass., 1877), p. 378. [11] F. L. Grundtvig, "On the Birds of Shoicton in Bovina, Outagamie County, Wisconsin, 1881–83," *Trans. Wis. Acad. Sci.*, X (1895), 106.

by the passenger pigeon, yet the number has been the subject of endless dispute. Even the most recent reference books state cautiously, one and sometimes two. Wilson was told correctly that only one egg was deposited.[153] The first to challenge this statement was Governor Clinton.[154] To him it would be an anomaly for the passenger pigeon to lay but one egg when all the other members of the pigeon family laid two. He marshaled the observations of friends who asserted that when only one egg was found in a nest it was due to the second having fallen out. He was informed by Paul Clark of Albany that his captive pigeons sometimes laid one egg but more often two. This is the only statement to be found of this pigeon laying more than one egg in confinement, and it may have resulted from executive courtesy.

Audubon stated that the passenger pigeon lays two eggs, but there is nothing in his writings indicating that this statement resulted from personal observations.[155] The opportunity to prove Wilson incorrect would not have been overlooked. In 1830 Audubon took most of a lot of 350 pigeons to England for the London Zoological Society and several noblemen. Hunt reported that one pair held by the Society bred in 1832 and that only one egg was laid.[156] Audubon was not satisfied with the performance of the pigeons given to Lord Derby since they too refused to lay more than one egg.[157] On his visit to England in 1834, he took some pigeons to John Heppenstall to determine if they also would lay but one egg. The outcome is not known; but it is to be assumed that, if there was any change in the number of eggs, the fact would have been announced in the last volume of *Ornithological Biography* that was not published until 1839.

In support of his position Audubon quoted the statement of his friend John Bachman that two eggs were laid invariably.[158] Frequently only one young was to be found in a nest, but this was due to the loss of an egg or young. Giraud was assured that there were two eggs which hatched a few days apart, the first-born ejecting the second egg or young.[159] Nuttall claimed that two eggs were laid, but only one young was produced, since, according to Wilson, one egg was "abortive." [160] No such statement by Alexander Wilson can be found. As late as 1875 it was stated, on the authority of Audubon, that the eggs are never more than two in number and that the young usually represent both sexes.[161]

It is not unusual for even noncolonial birds to lay in nests not their own. Some species of ducks are very careless in this respect. Three to five eggs have been found in the nest of the mourning dove and there is general agreement that they were deposited by two or more females.[162]

There is little doubt that two females were involved when two eggs were found in the nest of the passenger pigeon.[163] The males were the more easily trapped and this resulted in numerous "widows" that had to leave the nest exposed in order to feed. Females that had lost their nests by accidents would lay in the exposed nests or appropriate abandoned nests containing one egg. The belief in two eggs was adhered to by French, one being lost by accident: "Under the trees, during the first days after nest building started, there were thousands of eggs testifying plainly to these casualties." [164] It is to be expected that a female that had lost her nest would try to lay in that of another rather than drop the egg on the ground.

There is the possibility that unmated females, motivated by the breeding activities of the colony, would lay unfertilized eggs; also, that they would not attempt to construct a nest in the absence of a male to bring the twigs. Pigeons are stimulated to ovulation by the mere presence of the male without copulation.[165] Bryant mentions the solitary squab or egg and quotes a letter from a pigeon-netter: "I have seen two eggs in a nest, but I never saw two young birds or squabs in one nest. I have seen one squab and one bad egg in a nest when the squabs were small, but as they grew, soon got rid of the egg."[166] Gunn records a nest with one egg and a young about two days old, and Gibbs a nest with one egg and a half-grown young.[167] In each instance the egg must have been infertile, or the two eggs originally in the nest were not laid by the same female.

It was asserted by Mann and W. J. Hoxie that one egg was laid in large nestings, but that the nests of single pairs or small colonies frequently had two eggs.[168] Under these conditions, capable ornithologists never found more than one egg.[169] Pigeons held in captivity never laid more than one egg.[170] Many writers report only one egg to a nest in the large nestings.[171] More observers state that two are rare.[172]

It is certain, biologically, that only one egg was laid during a nesting. Whitman found that a minimum of five days was required before a second egg could be laid.[173] The times required for the deposition of an egg under various conditions were:

5 days after removal of egg (2 cases)
6 days after removal of egg
7 days after removal of egg (4 cases)
8 days after removal of egg
6 days after breaking egg
5 days after first courting
6 days after first billing
7 days after pairing
12 days after hatching of young

Mr. Willard, of Ashburnham, Massachusetts, who had had wide

experience with the pigeons at their nestings, informed Hodge that "in dressing many thousands of the birds for market, he has found but a single developed egg." [174] Birds laying more than one egg have eggs sufficiently well developed that ovulation takes place daily, or at most at intervals of two days.

There are several cases mentioned of the eggs being dropped prematurely. Mann states that in 1878 the pigeons were so persecuted in Wisconsin that they flew to the islands in the Mississippi River at the lower end of Lake Pepin and deposited their eggs on the ground. [175]

Adverse weather sometimes caused the egg to be dropped before the nest was ready. [176] The effect of a snowstorm on a nesting at Petoskey, Michigan, is described by Martin:

A fact in connection with the nesting of 1878 which the writer has never seen in print is that when the first body of birds reached the Crooked River country, before their nests were completed, a heavy snowstorm came which caused the birds to drop millions of eggs on the frozen ground. After the storm abated and the snow melted, part of the swamp still was white, the eggs being so thick for several miles as to give the appearance of a snow-covered ground. These birds moved around for a week or two, roosting at night near those nesting, then built for themselves close by the others and raised their young as if nothing had happened. [177]

A snowstorm during the nesting along the Platte River, Benzie County, Michigan, in 1880, also caused the eggs to be dropped prematurely. [178] The morning of April 21, 1865, in Wisconsin, a cold rain was followed by a snowstorm from the northwest and a freezing temperature. Before noon the pigeons began to appear in Dane County and by the afternoon there was a continuous stream going southward. [179] The following day eggs were found scattered about in the woods and brush where the pigeons had stopped to rest.

It has been stated by Knapp that the eggs on a few occasions would be dropped if the food were insufficient to raise the young. [180] This is doubtful since the incentive to breed would not be expected to proceed to the egg stage unless the food supply was ample.

Incubation was shared by both parents. The male sat on the nest from about 10:00 A.M. to about 3:00 P.M., the female the remaining hours. The passenger pigeon in confinement began to "incubate" a day or two in advance of deposition of the egg.[181] In one instance the female began sitting on the nest on Monday and continued to do so much of the time prior to laying of the egg at 4:00 P.M. on Wednesday. The male took his turn incubating just as though there were an egg in the nest.

The time required to hatch the egg is reported as follows: twelve days (eleven days after the egg was laid), twelve days, twelve to fourteen days, thirteen days, about fourteen days, fourteen days.[182] The period of eighteen to twenty days given by Bendire is much too long.[183]

The experimental data accumulated by Whitman show that twelve to thirteen days were required to hatch the egg, twelve and one-half days being considered the average normal time. In one case of intermittent incubation the time was fourteen to fifteen days.[184] It appears therefore from the information available that thirteen days would be the average length of incubation for the bird in the wild. This is the shortest known period for any species of pigeon.

A low temperature suspended breeding.[185] Incubation having begun, the passenger pigeon often stuck to its nest in spite of adverse weather. A snowstorm on March 16, 1878, piled the snow so high about three pigeons incubating in the Zoological Garden, Cincinnati, Ohio, that they were nearly invisible. During the next four to five nights the temperature registered 14° to 19°. One nest was deserted, but the remaining two eggs hatched.[186] It is not clear that a nest was ever deserted due to cold alone. J. B. Oviatt states that in a period of cold weather the eggs in the entire colony would freeze. The pigeons might remain and lay again when warm weather arrived or, as usually happened, abandon the locality.[187]

Long experience with the fickle weather of early spring had taught the parents how to keep the egg warm. "When the birds are sitting during cold weather, the egg is tucked up under the feathers, and the primaries of one wing are drawn under the body as though to support the egg in its position. At such times the Pigeon rests on the side of the folded wing instead of squatting on the nest." [188]

An egg that did not hatch within a few hours after the incubation period had passed was deserted.[189] Whitman states in one place that this pigeon never waited more than ten or twelve hours after the normal time, even though the shell was cracked and the young in process of appearing;[190] but in another, the time is extended to twelve to twenty hours. The eggs hatched from about 6:00 A.M. to 3:00 P.M.[191]

The male occupied the nest during the middle of the day, the female the remainder of the time, while the egg was being incubated and the young attaining an age of about eight days. The male departed at daybreak, or earlier, to feed and returned in the late forenoon to relieve the female. The latter then fed and returned in the middle of the afternoon. The male then went to feed again, returning at dusk. When the young was old enough to be left uncovered, both parents were absent from the nest. The bird on the nest did not leave "until the bill of its incoming mate nearly touches its tail."[192] This constant coverage supposedly prevented an appreciable loss of eggs even in a powerful wind.

The literature contains misinformation on the feeding times of the sexes. Ben O. Bush states that the male and female sat on alternate days; again that the male sat in the morning and was relieved by the female.[193] Rintoul has the females feeding at dawn.[194] Cook says that the male sat one-half of the time, and Bishop that he sat for one to two hours in the afternoon.[195]

There are several excellent accounts of the manner by which the mates exchanged places. Three are given in order to cover all phases of the procedure.

At early dawn the male birds set out flying to the east and north to seek a breakfast of seeds and berries, ten, twenty, or fifty miles away, and by six or half-past six the sky is black with the departing birds. They tower up in great armies to a considerable height, each sheet of birds—sheet is the word that best describes them —wavering a moment like the needle of the compass when disturbed, then taking flight in the appointed direction with a unanimity and evenness of speed that would make one believe that every bird was animated by the same impulse at the same instant. An hour later not a bird is to be seen, but towards eight o'clock the rush of the returning armies is heard. Squadron after squadron arrives, cleaving the air with unwearied wing and unfailing sense, fluttering, wheeling, and descending, each division over its own district, each bird over the nest of its faithful mate. As "tom" after "tom" returns to take his trick at the domestic helm, "hen" after "hen" rises upward, and the armies of the Amazons go out to the east and the north. Towards nine o'clock the scene is indescribable. It is a very atmosphere of wings, earth and forest have been converted into feathers....[196]

The relief at the nesting in Benzie County, Michigan, in 1874, is described by Starr:

Previous to the nest building the air was continually alive with the flyers in the wild frolic of the mating season. As the building began order was established to a degree, but it was not until the eggs were laid that a regular system prevailed. Then the males would take wing together at sunrise, rising from their roosts in a column, then spreading like a cloud through the air. Then an instant's delay and all were flying easily and steadily in the direction of the chosen feeding-ground. Thousands of hens and eggs were ensconced in the branches, but not a bird rose above them, and all was still. A few hours later and the advance returned; then another flight and another, until finally the main body appeared, hovered over the forest for an instant, then each bird dropped to the perch beside the nest and mate. In the dense thicket of nests and birds each seemed to know its own. In a moment the whir and rush of wings told that the hens had left the nest. There was the same column and cloud with which the males departed, and the same course was taken—no confusion, no delay, no apparent hesitation. At 3 o'clock in the afternoon these returned and the males again took wing, to be absent until near sundown.[197]

A picturesque description of the return of the females is given by Cooper, who wrote from experience. The males dropped from the nests into the space between the ground and the lower branches until the females had settled on the nests.

The air was suddenly darkened, and the place where we stood was as sombre as a dusky twilight. At the same instant, all the pigeons near us, that had been on their nests, appeared to fall out of them, and the space immediately above our heads was at once filled with birds.... This part of the scene may have lasted a minute, when the space around us was suddenly cleared, the birds glancing upward among the branches of the trees, disappearing among the foliage. All this was the effect produced by the return of the female birds which had been off at a distance, some twenty miles at least to feed on beech-nuts, and which now assumed the places of the males on the nests; the latter taking a flight to get their meal in their turn.[198]

The captive male passenger pigeons of Whitman occupied the nest from about 10 A.M. to 4 P.M.[199] The males of several other species of pigeons resigned the nest at 4 P.M. Stephens informed Brewster that all males were regularly on the nest by 10 A.M.[200] The periods when the male occupied the nest, as given by various writers, are:

8–9 A.M. to afternoon.—Thomas (as in Chap. 6, n. 34).

8–9 A.M. to middle of afternoon.—New York *World,* July 4, 1874.

9 A.M. to 1 P.M.—Dickinson (as in Chap. 6, n. 202).

About 9 A.M. to 4 P.M.—Bowers (as in Chap. 6, n. 67).

9 or 10 A.M. to 2 P.M.—McKnight (as in Chap. 9, n. 46) and Stevens (as in Chap. 4, n. 123).

9–10 A.M. to 3–4 P.M.—Ingells (as in Chap. 6, n. 69).

10 A.M. to 2 P.M.—Gunn (as in Chap. 9, n. 169).

10 A.M. to 3 P.M.—F. E. S. (as in Chap. 3, n. 66) and Pokagon (as in Chap. 6, n. 95).

11 A.M. to 2 P.M.—Gunn (as in Chap. 6, n. 66).

11 A.M. to 3 P.M.—Eaton (as in Chap. 3, n. 184) and Knapp (as in Chap. 6, n. 24).

Females returned at 3 P.M.—Starr (as in Chap. 6, n. 197).

The average time for the male to occupy the nest in the wild was from 10 A.M. to 3 P.M. If he remained on the nest until 4 P.M., there would be insufficient time to feed again at any considerable distance.

Evening flights of females are mentioned.[201] C. W. Dickinson states that, if the weather was not too rough, the females made a short flight before occupying the nest for the night.[202] The evening flight of the females presupposes that the young were sufficiently advanced to be left alone.

The males seldom, if ever, roosted in the trees within the nesting. The trees surrounding a nesting bore witness by the broken limbs to mass roosting that would have been highly destructive to the nests within the breeding area. However, C. W. Dickinson has stated that the males roosted within the nesting or on surrounding trees.[203] A similar statement was made by William French.[204] The comment of J. B. Oviatt on the morning flight of the males indicates that the latter came directly from the nesting.[205] E. Haskell and Hammond have them in a roosting place outside the nesting.[206] Fountain states specifically that the males did not roost in the same tree with the females: "Strange to relate, the cocks go nightly to the juniper-swamps, and roost on the bushes, within a dozen or fifteen feet of the ground, breaking down the bushes by hundreds, as I have myself witnessed." [207] They also roosted on the alders in old beaver meadows.

An egg having been laid, it is a general instinct for the captive males of the various species of pigeons to roost as far as possible from the females.[208] This was a protective measure and cannot be interpreted as mere reluctance on the part of the males to roost in contiguity with the females.

The brooding of the young is described by Deane: "During the first few days, after the young is hatched, to guard against the cold, it is, like the egg, concealed under the feathers of the abdomen, the head always pointing forward. In this attitude, the parents, without changing the sitting position or reclining on the side, feed the squab by arching the head and neck down, and administering the food." [209] On the other hand, Whitman states that almost invariably the young passenger pigeon, after feeding, turned so that its head pointed backward beneath the parent. The young after eight days of age was left uncovered during the day, but covered during the ninth and tenth nights.[210]

In feeding the young, the head and neck of the parent were drawn down, and the mouth opened wide.[211] The young thrust its bill into that of the parent and ate the regurgitated food. Audubon was incorrect in stating that the parent introduced its bill into that of the young.[212]

No accurate data are available on the length of time that the young was fed milk exclusively. C. W. Dickinson says that they were so fed for twelve days; and Pokagon, until nearly ready to fly.[213] On the other hand, Knapp states that they would take beechnuts and even acorns when four or five days old.[214] It is doubtful if milk was fed exclusively for more than about six days. It was then gradually replaced by the food, softened in the crop, normally eaten by the parent. Abandoned squabs were found with their crops filled with beechnuts with the shells intact. It has been said by Whitman that the young of pigeons will pick up food a day or two after leaving the nest.[215] That the "parental example is the guiding instinct" could not apply to the passenger pigeon since the young were abandoned while still in the nest.

There was a belief that any squab bereft of parents, or one begging loudly for food, would be fed by foster parents.[216] Pokagon states that he saw as many as a dozen young assemble about a male and with drooping wings beg plaintively for food. They were never abused by either sex under these circumstances.[217] In another case a male was observed to feed seven young in succession.[218]

It is doubtful that a parent would feed any crying young. Martin wrote: "It is a well proved fact that the old bird coming in will stop and feed any squab heard crying for food, that in this way they look out for one another's young, and the orphans or half orphans are cared for. . . . As proof of the pigeons feeding squabs indiscriminately, I may mention that one of the men in my employ this year, at the Shelby nesting in 1876, in one afternoon shot and killed *six* hen pigeons that came to *find* the *one squab* in the *same nest*." [219] Caring for orphans in this way is very questionable, for it would seem to be a unique trait for any species of pigeon.[220]

It is probable that this pigeon did not show deliberate attention to a young, other than its own, begging for food. The parent had no control over the formation of the milk, this being ready when the egg hatched. If the young died, or would not take all the food, the parent was in great distress.[221] Within six to ten hours it was willing to feed any bird that would place its bill in its mouth. Even weaned young and adults would be fed. According to C. W. Dickinson, the parents died if there were no young to take the milk.[222]

The "white strings" on the breast, considered proof that the bird was brooding,[223] must refer to the "curds" or milk. Sometimes the curds were wasted, dropping from the corners of the mouth to the breast.

The young passenger pigeon grew with astonishing rapidity. The length of time that the young remained in the nest has been reported as: 13 days, 13 to 14 days, 14 days, about 15 days.[224] Whitman mentions a case in which the young was abandoned at the end of 12 days and a new cycle begun.[225]

The young on the fourteenth day was filled with food by the parents and abandoned. The statements that the young was pushed from the nest by the parents are overshadowed by the more logical ones of the old birds leaving suddenly, en masse. The young was then a mass of fat and frequently equaled if not exceeded the weight of the adult. It sat crying in the nest for a day or so, then fluttered to the ground. Within three or four days it could fly sufficiently well to escape capture. Within a week it was barely edible, nearly all the fat having disappeared.

The cycle of the average nesting was 30 days:

Building nest and laying egg	3 days
Incubation	13 days
Feeding young	14 days

Knapp gives 28 to 31 days.[226] Ingells states that in 30 days after the nesting started, nearly all the young had left the nests.[227]

The abandonment of the young was a spectacular affair.

When the old birds deserted the nesting city, they left in a great mass. Mr. Oviatt has seen them fill the skies for half an hour, passing over Smethport in a stream as wide as the valley. In places the flock was so dense that one could not see the sky beyond. It was the bulk of the parent birds, but not the entire population of the city, that so left at one time, for the birds that had been late in beginning to nest were not yet finished. The birds that were leaving for good and all went out with the daybreak flight, and those that were still nesting soon dropped out, to feed and return to their young.[228]

The breaking up of a nesting was shown, according to the White-water *Register* (Wis.) for June 3, 1880, "when the toms and hens arise from the tops of the trees like a great cloud and are quickly lost to sight."

The distances that the parents traveled from the nesting for food must have been short, compared with those during the fall and winter roosts, since they were absent but a few hours at a time. All the distances given appear to be estimates as there is no indication how they were arrived at. Examples are: 25 miles, 10 to 50 miles, 40 miles, 20 to 60 miles, 50 to 100 miles, 100 miles, 75 to 100 miles, and 150 miles.[229]

One evening, while at Columbus, Mississippi, Lincecum shot one of the numerous pigeons returning to a nesting 50 miles northward. The crop contained acorns of the live oak, *Quercus virens* (*virginiana*), and he concluded that they must have been obtained from Florida or Alabama at a distance of 500 miles.[230] This oak grows abundantly in southern Mississippi.

There was a nesting in the township of Fenelon, Colborne County, Ontario, which Strickland states was 40 or 50 miles from his residence in the township of Douro. The pigeons passed over his place in going for food, but never returned by the same route.[231] Smith's map of Canada West, dated 1847, shows that the distance from Strickland's place to the nesting could not have been over 35 miles. It appears that most of the feeding was done within a radius of 50 miles of the nesting.

ABERRANT NESTING

A peculiar nesting is described by Pokagon.

Thirty-two years ago [1864] there was a big nesting between South Haven and St. Joseph on Lake Michigan. About one week after the main body commenced nesting, a new body of great size, covering hundreds of acres, came and joined them.... I found they were all young birds less than a year old, which could be easily explained from their mottled coloring. To my surprise, soon as nests were built, they commenced tearing them down—a few eggs scattered about told some had laid; within three days they all left, moving in a body up the lake shore north. I have had like facts told me by others who have witnessed the same thing.[232]

This nesting is beyond explanation, since by March or earlier all the young should have been in adult plumage. Audubon states that the young are capable of breeding when six months of age.[233] If so, breeding in the wild did not occur until they were approximately a year old.

NUMBER OF NESTINGS

There was a very general belief that the passenger pigeon nested several times a year. This is difficult to prove or disprove. Kalm stated that some people thought that they raised two broods each summer.[234]

Wilson was told that they bred three, and sometimes four times in the same season.[235] Macauley goes the limit and has a hatching every month of the year.[236]

The statements on the number of nestings annually emanated largely from trappers who were anxious to implant the conviction that a species that bred so frequently was in no danger of extinction. Roney was led to believe that there was a nesting every month over a period as long as five months.[237] Mershon and French mention three or four nestings, and Heddon four to eight.[238] When food was plentiful, according to C. W. Dickinson, there were three nestings in a season: the latter part of March, early May, and about June 10.[239] The shooting in September at Cincinnati, Ohio, of young one-half grown led Dury to the conclusion that they came from a second brood.[240] Some pairs nested as late as September, but there is no proof that these were second nestings.

There was no doubt in the mind of Gibbs that two or three young might be raised in a season. An old trapper gave him the fanciful tale that, when an egg was ready to hatch, a second egg was deposited. The squab assisted in incubating this egg and the process continued until three young were hatched.[241] Sutton had the same story from Nelson Gehr.[242]

An incredible second nesting is described by Owen. He arrived at a breeding place near Marionville, Forest County, Pennsylvania, on March 20, 1878, when the pigeons had not finished building. On April 6, the squabs were large enough to take from the nest, as they had been filled with beechnuts by the parents preparatory to abandonment. It would have been utterly impossible for an egg to hatch and the young to develop to this stage in sixteen days. He states that on April 9 the old birds began building nests again within one-half mile of the old nesting. The same pigeons never re-nested in the same locality, so that a new flock must have arrived. He admitted that the oldest trappers from Sheffield had never heard of the like before.[243]

It was the opinion of S. S. Stevens that breeding continued throughout the summer.[244] He and other netters believed that the pigeons bred in the South in winter, since young birds in considerable number often accompanied the earliest spring flights. If these were juveniles, their presence would have been extraordinary. It would have been necessary for them to be capable of long flights by the end of February, and no young are known to have reached this stage of advancement in the South at so early a date. Colonial breeding south of the Ohio had practically ceased by the middle of the nineteenth century. Furthermore, it was unusual for young and old to mix until after the breeding season. C. W. Dickinson mentions that there were always quite a number of non-nesting birds, "strays," and birds "too young" to breed attached to a nesting colony.[245] If he refers to juveniles, they must have come from an early hatch in the region and attached themselves to a colony making a second attempt at nesting. J. B. Oviatt, who has furnished the soundest information that I have encountered on the habits of the pigeon, said that there were no young birds in the spring migration in Pennsylvania.[246] This would be the logical expectation.

Doubts regarding a second nesting did exist. The majority of the contributors to Bendire asserted that there was one nesting, a few that there were two.[247] The pigeons in the Cincinnati Zoological Gardens are said to have laid but one egg and to have had only one brood a year.[248] Captive birds usually laid more than one egg in a season. J. B. Oviatt did not believe that the pigeons ever nested a second time in the same year in Pennsylvania.[249] The nearest approach was when a nesting colony, broken up by shooting, would move a few miles distant for a second attempt. If again disturbed, they might leave the region entirely before young were raised. Thompson states that there is evidence that in some years the same birds nested two or three times, but this was not often.[250] It is also stated: "In case the temptation is exceedingly strong, the old birds will sometimes nest and breed again." [251]

There was no possible way, without marking, to determine if the same group of birds nested twice or more. Most of the first nestings occurred in April. If nestings were found in May and June, many trappers inferred that these were second and third nestings. The late nestings may well have been due to interference by man or the weather. A wind storm would precipitate thousands of eggs.[252] In this case other nests would be built. Snowstorms could destroy a nesting completely.

The diary of Leroy Lyman, Coudersport, Pennsylvania, furnished the following information: "About the middle of April, 1854, the pigeons commenced nesting west of Coudersport, snow all gone. Soon after came high winds and for several days around zero weather, with snow several inches deep, breaking up the nesting and thousands of birds freezing to death. By May 20, the surviving birds were nesting again." [253] This nesting lasted until June 20, yet it was the only successful attempt of that season.

The Wisconsin literature has been covered thoroughly. There is no clear record of a large nesting after the middle of May. The small nestings that occurred after this date appear to have been due to a failure of the first nesting. The huge nesting that took place in the state in 1871 "broke" about May 15, most of the birds leaving the state. The only possible case where the pigeons could have nested twice that year occurred at Durand. This nesting dissolved about June 15. It was so small as to have formed but a few per cent of the birds that nested earlier.[254] There was a nesting in the bottoms of the Mississippi River, near Wabasha, Minnesota, that must have been started about May 1, since the Wabasha *Herald* for June 1, 1871, reported that the squabs were sufficiently large to be eaten by that time. Aside from the above, no other cases of nesting for the Great Lakes region were found for the year 1871.

The problem of the number of nestings can be approached from two angles. Firstly, did the passenger pigeon nest sufficiently early in the South to permit nesting subsequently in the North? Secondly, did mast last sufficiently long to permit two or more nestings?

Nestings south of Kentucky were so rare that it may be concluded that the passenger pigeon nested in the North by choice, or that the mast was consumed by the wintering hordes. The most southern nesting of definite record is the one that took place on the Tombigbee River, Mississippi, in 1832. The young left this nesting by May 1, so that breeding was no earlier than if the pigeons had nested in the North.[255] The nesting in Oklahoma in 1881, mentioned by Thomas, began about April 20.[256]

The nesting visited by Wilson on April 17, 1810, on the Green River, Kentucky, according to report, was vacated by the young the middle of

March.[257] If this report was correct, the nesting must have started the middle of February, making it the earliest nesting known. It was extraordinary also that a "few bodies" of pigeons remained in the nesting a month after it had been abandoned. The nesting at Shelbyville, Kentucky, about 1808, was abandoned the end of May, showing nothing abnormal in time.

The men of Pike's Expedition landed on Pike Island, Illinois, on April 28, 1806, and in a few minutes captured 298 squabs barely able to fly.[258] It was stated on May 1, 1858, that the squabs in the nesting in Decatur County, Indiana, were barely able to fly.[259] Again there is nothing abnormal about the season for both nestings.

Very few nestings are specifically recorded for March. Martin states that about the middle of March, 1878, a nesting began at Pickerel Lake, Emmet County, Michigan, which is about 13 miles east of Petoskey.[260] This date is supported by Roney, who found squabs ready to fly at this nesting on April 16.[261] The nesting on the Platte River, Benzie County, Michigan, in 1880, began on March 29.[262]

The nestings in Michigan in 1878 are said to have covered so great a space of time, the middle of March to early July, that they should be examined in as great detail as possible to determine if there was more than one nesting by the same colony. The pigeons arrived at Petoskey, according to a letter quoted by Bryant, on February 23, 1877,[263] the correct year being 1878. Another reference states that the first birds appeared in Oceana and adjoining counties early in March.[264] Ingells, who was living at Petoskey at the time, also gives March.[265] As shown above, some of these pigeons began a successful nesting the middle of March.

According to Martin, a very large number of birds began nesting about April 8 near Cross Village (Emmet County), along Maple and Indian rivers, and Burt Lake (Cheboygan County); there were altogether seven or eight distinct nestings. The nestings along Maple and Indian rivers "broke" about May 25.[266] If the latter date is correct, then these nestings must have started about April 25 instead of April 8.

Another nesting is said to have started at Boyne Falls (Charlevoix County) about May 25 and to have broken early in July.[267] No further information on this nesting is available and the dates are doubtful.

Martin mentions another nesting on the Manistee River (Manistee County) covering 130 square miles. Here the birds hatched *three times,* but not a pigeon was caught, since the nesting was in an impenetrable swamp. Martin is not to be believed on details. The length of the season in 1878 is fixed definitely by a letter of H. T. Phillips to Mershon: "In regard to dates, would say that the last nesting of birds set in about 5 P.M. May 5, 1878, on the southeast side of Crooked Lake."[268] The young should have left this nesting the first week in June. Martin was told that, when the Crooked River nesting dissolved the last of May or the first of June, millions of old birds crossed the straits into the Upper Peninsula of Michigan where many of them nested again.[269] There is not one record of a colonial nesting in the Upper Peninsula of Michigan.

The so-called Petoskey nestings did extend over a period of two and one-half months, from the middle of March to the first week in June, but this was not from choice on the part of the pigeons. The main reason for the erratic nestings was the occurrence of periods of inhospitable weather. A snowstorm in March caused most of the birds to drop their eggs on the ground, as the nests were not ready.[270] Some of the birds had laid. A sitting pigeon caught in a snowstorm would not desert the nest for several days, and then only if the weather continued unfavorable. This accounts for the squabs flying at Pickerel Lake the middle of April. In view of the time covered by the various nestings, it would have been impossible for any colony to nest more than twice.

The length of the breeding period and the number of nestings in a season must also be considered in the light of the *availability of mast.* If there was any one factor in the life of the passenger pigeon on which there was unanimity of opinion, it was the necessity for an abundance of mast as a requisite for nesting. Knapp states that there were two seasons in which there was so little mast that very few young were raised.[271] One of these years was 1873. This receives confirmation from E. Osborn, who failed to find a nesting in that year.[272]

The nestings in Pennsylvania, Michigan, and other states where beech was plentiful were almost invariably based on beechnuts. Acorns were a second choice. In Wisconsin and Minnesota, acorns were the principal food. The beechnut sprouted comparatively early in the spring. J. B. Oviatt mentions that in late spring the crops of the pigeons were filled with sprouted beechnuts.[273] The sprouted nuts were considered of little use to the pigeons.[274] Thompson believed that, when the beechnuts began to sprout, the old birds scratched up the leaves to prevent further growth and so maintain food for the young.[275] No such foresight is to be believed, but the statement shows that the nutritive value of the sprouted nuts was of short duration. In June, 1868, the young pigeons were feeding on sprouted beechnuts at Roxbury, New York.[276] By this time all of the nuts had sprouted. C. H. Merriam collected old birds and squabs in the Adirondacks in June, 1878, and found the crops of all crammed with beechnuts.[277] The condition of the nuts is not stated. It is probable that at high altitudes during late seasons some unsprouted beechnuts could be found in June.

The state of the mast in Michigan in the spring of 1878 does not support the assumption of a long breeding season. The weather was mild in most of the northern states the beginning of spring. The mean temperatures at Madison, Wisconsin, were: January, 25°; February, 32°; and March, 44°. In February, due to the mildness of the season, there was a large pigeon roost in Trumbull County, Ohio.[278] As evidence of the advancement of the season in Michigan, sprouted beechnuts were taken from the crops of pigeons at Petoskey the first of April.[279] In view of this, it is inconceivable that the pigeons nested three times and that the nestings extended into July. The use of pine mast has been mentioned after the beechnuts were exhausted.[280] Apparently pine mast was used to finish a nesting rather than to start one. Nestings on conifer seeds were exceptional.

There are but four species of oaks in the northern states that could be relied upon to furnish sufficient acorns for colonial nestings. These are the black (*Quercus velutina*), scarlet (*Q. coccinea*), Hill's (*Q. ellipsoidalis*), and red oak (*Q. borealis*). In Wisconsin and Minnesota, Hill's oak was the most abundant source of acorns. The acorns of the white oak sprout in autumn and have little food value the following spring. The bur oak bears abundantly, but the keeping quality of the acorns is very poor. Few sound ones are to be found in spring.

There is little information in the literature on the seasonal availability of plant foods. In Tennessee beechnuts are available from September 30 to March 10 and acorns from October 7 to May 1, but a few are to be found throughout the year.[281] The acorns of the black oaks sometimes remain edible in small quantities until June in the northern states. Near Minneapolis, on May 22, 1849, Seymour passed a grove of oaks filled with pigeons, the ground of which was covered with acorns.[282] The quality of these acorns is not mentioned. At Madison, Wisconsin, the acorns of the black oaks begin to sprout about May 10, and a few unsprouted ones persist into the following month. The sprouting of these oaks in the vicinity of Minneapolis varies from year to year but usually takes place between April 15 and May 15, according to a letter I received from the Lake States Forest Experiment Station.

There was a huge crop of acorns, principally of *Quercus ellipsoidalis,* in central Wisconsin the autumn of 1951. Counts made by Frances Hamerstrom on four plots of one square foot each in the Town of Bear Bluff, Jackson County, on May 18, 1952, showed 10 to 45 sound acorns, two-thirds of which were sprouted. A plot near Crex Meadows, Burnett County, on May 23 showed 16 good acorns, none sprouted; and four plots examined near Keystone Rock, Adams County, on May 26, gave 11 to 25 sound acorns, none sprouted.

Large colonial nestings were typical of the passenger pigeon. However, individual to a few pairs nested widely. The size of the colony was adjusted to the food resources of the region. There is reason to believe that in some cases due to memory the pigeons returned in spring to an area where mast was plentiful in the preceding fall, and that the discovery of food sufficient for a nesting was not always the result of random search. The distance traveled from the nesting for food was generally within a radius of fifty miles.

Only one egg was laid to a set. This is shown by the fact that only one egg was laid in captivity and that only one was ever found in isolated nests in the wild by capable ornithologists. Also, this pigeon was biologically incapable of laying more than one egg to a set.

It is doubtful that more than one brood was raised in a season. If there were two nestings, only a small part of the total population was involved. There was very little difference in time between the extreme southern and northern nestings. In the North, where by far the largest number of nestings occurred, breeding began on the average the middle of April and the nesting was completed by the middle of May. After this time, insufficient nutritive mast remained to permit more than a small number of birds to nest a second time.

CHAPTER 7: UTILIZATION

Pigeons were an important source of food, but opinions differed greatly as to the tastiness of the flesh. Byrd had this to say: "In these long Flights they are very lean, and their Flesh is far from being white or tender, tho' good enough upon a March, when Hunger is the sauce, and makes it go down better than Truffles and Morels wou'd do." [1]

The old birds were not a delicacy and when nesting were as "palatable as a setting hen." [2] The adults were dry and tough, though well flavored.[3] Cockrum had a low opinion of the flesh, it being dark, stringy and with a peculiar odor.[4] The appetite was soon cloyed when the birds were served frequently.[5] When they were served three times daily, even the name became sickening.[6] The meat of the mourning dove was thought superior.[7]

Its flesh was considered by Kalm more palatable than that of any bird that he had tasted.[8] Loskiel remarked on the excellent taste of pigeons, the Indians eating them fresh, dried, and smoked; however, some Indians preferred the flesh of the skunk to that of the pigeon.[9] Much depended on the method of cooking.[10] Wilson never ate a pigeon of any age that was not delicate and delicious.[11]

There was general agreement that a fat pigeon afforded superior eating.[12] In order of desirability were squabs, birds fed in captivity, and those taken in September and October. Occasionally adults were exceedingly fat in spring.[13] The fattening of trapped pigeons was common practice and persisted as long as they were obtainable. At Montreal they were fed until the first frosts, then killed and placed in the storeroom for winter use.[14] Kalm mentions also that squabs, with their wings clipped to prevent escape, were fed for future use in Canada.[15] Feeding was also in vogue in New England.[16] Hoy states: "Mr. Cox ... used to catch them in a net by the five hundred at a time. He sold them for from six to ten cents a dozen. He used to take a great number, put them in a cage and feed them with salted wheat, boiled. After a month the breasts became light-colored and much improved, commanding double price." [17]

The pigeon was a boon to the poor.[18] Its importance as food during the periods of migration may be gleaned from the fact that Burnaby found it the only food available at the inns where he stopped, and the common people were living almost entirely on its flesh.[19] More wrote from Pennsylvania in 1686: "We have had so great abundance of *Pigeons* this Summer, that we have fed all our Servants with them." [20]

These pigeons were of great value as a source of food on the frontiers. Ashton Blackburne wrote to Pennant

I think this as remarkable a bird as any in *America*. They are in vast numbers in all parts, and have been of great service at particular times to our garrisons, in supplying them with fresh meat, especially at the out-posts ... I have heard many say they think them as good as our common Blue Pigeon, but I cannot agree with them by any means. They taste more like our Queest, or Wild Pigeon; but are better meat. .... I have been at *Niagara* when the centinel has given the word that the Pigeons were *flying;* and the whole garrison were ready to run over one another, so eager were they to get fresh meat.[21]

"Pigeon" shot was carried very generally in the storerooms of the fur-trading posts on the Great Lakes. Adair remarks that the traders in the South had plenty of pigeons in winter.[22] The trader Robert Dickson wrote from Lake Winnebago, Wisconsin on March 10, 1814: "As we shall be early in the Lake [Michigan] we shall find Sturgeon & Trout &c. in abundance and perhaps Pidgeons, we cannot starve." [23]

The wide distribution of the pigeon in summer made it one of the most certain sources of food in cases of distress. In the summer of 1847, government surveyors while working in the swamps of the St. Croix River in Wisconsin ran short of provisions. The consequences might have been fatal to some had they not succeeded in killing a few pigeons.[24] Pigeons were counted upon to help support the colony of Niagara.[25] Their extinction was deplored in the province of Quebec for it meant a loss to the people of an important resource.[26]

On long voyages roasted pigeons and other game were packed in casks and covered with molten fat. In this way the air was excluded and the pigeons could be kept for several months.[27] The commonest method of preserving pigeons was by the use of salt. This method was in vogue along the St. Lawrence as early as 1662.[28] Anne Cary Randolph wrote to Jefferson on March 18, 1808: "there has been the greatest number of wild pigeons this spring that I ever saw. Mr. Craven they say, by means of his net has caught nearly three thousand. he kills some days 700 & seldom less than three or four hundred. he salts & barrels them like fish for his people."[29] They were also salted by the barrel in Sullivan County, New York.[30] Wilson considered a salted pigeon, freshened over night in sweet water, about as palatable as a freshly killed bird.[31]

The pigeons were also pickled. Birds preserved in spiced apple cider in sealed jars were served to guests as an especially choice dish.[32]

Often only the breasts were preserved, frequently by smoking. The pigeons nested at Wauwatosa, Wisconsin, in 1838. In four days Mrs. Earles preserved, by the use of brine and by drying, the breasts of about 1700 squabs obtained from the Indians in exchange for brass rings.[33] The squabs were dried, or "jerked," over hardwood fires by both whites and Indians.[34] The drying at the nesting at Kilbourn, Wisconsin, in 1871, was described in the Fond du Lac *Commonwealth* (Wis.) for May 20, 1871, as follows: "The old men and squaws were engaged in picking and drying pigeons. A full grown pigeon, when fully dried and smoked is about the size, shape and hardness of an old, last year's butternut."

The fat of the pigeons was used for culinary and other purposes. Both whites and Indians in Virginia knocked the pigeons, which were usually very fat, from their roosts at night.[35] Tubs full of the fat were made for kitchen use, it being sweet as butter and not deteriorating for a year. It is stated that at a nesting in northeastern Pennsylvania, in about 1805, millions of squabs were collected for their fat, barrels of which were shipped down the Susquehanna River.[36] The oil was sometimes used as soap-stock.[37]

The extensive feeding of pigeons to hogs is unworthy of comment.

The feathers from the body of the pigeon were used in large quantities for bedding.[38] They were soft but did not last as long as those from the goose or duck.[39] According to Chauncey E. Kent, about fifty pigeons were required to obtain a pound of feathers.[40] Pigeons were so plentiful in Grafton County, New Hampshire, the summer of 1770 that picking bees were organized and operated two or three times a week. "Those who went had the meat of all they picked and the Tylers had the feathers; and they made says Jonathan Tyler, 'four very decent beds of those feathers.' " [41]

There was more than one source of comfort in the possession of a bedtick filled with pigeon feathers. A letter, dated January 13, 1936, was received by me from Alvin McKnight of Augusta, Wisconsin, reading in part:

In the year 1877, Chas. Martin, who was my uncle, was trapping near here and told my wife that if she would pick the pigeons he would buy her the ticking to make a feather bed. This was shortly after we were married so she gladly accepted the offer and picked just 144 dozen pigeons. We are still using that bed. We were told years ago that a person would never die on a bed of pigeon feathers, and we are beginning to have some faith in the saying as I am nearing my 84th birthday and my wife is 77 and both enjoying very good health, so we have decided to test it out and see if the saying is true.

It must be reported with regret that the experiment eventually failed.

Formerly no girl in the vicinity of St. Jerome, Quebec, ever married without having a bed and pillows of pigeon feathers in her dowry.[42]

Pigeons were sometimes taken for the feathers alone. In the spring of 1822, a family living on the shore of Lake Erie in Chautauqua County, New York, killed with poles in one day 4,000 pigeons. Only the feathers were saved.[43] At Granby, Massachusetts, where the feathers were used extensively for bedding, the bodies of the pigeons were given to the hogs.[44]

Curative properties were assigned to the passenger pigeon in an age when nothing was too noisome to be used in medicine. Dr. John Brickell wrote: "The Blood helps disorders in the Eyes, the Coats of the Stomach in Powder, cures bloody Fluxes. The Dung is the hottest of all Fowls, and is wonderful attractive, yet accompanied with an *Anodyne* force, and helps the Head-ach, Megrim, pain in the Side and Stomach, Pleurisy, Cholick, Apoplexy, Lethargy, and many other Disorders." [45]

The principle underlying the administration of the dung is not clearly disclosed, but we are not left in doubt when it comes to the use of the gizzard in the treatment of gallstones.

An old woman, part Indian, used to save the gizzard ... when the pigeons were prepared for market and would string them on a thread and hang them up to dry. The gizzards when dry became shiny and transparent and were used by this old woman, who was a sort of medicine-woman, in the treatment of gallstones. The reasoning was as follows: the *tourte* would sometimes take up small stones ... instead of grain but that did not matter as its gizzard was strong enough to dissolve the stones. Therefore when the gizzard came in contact with the gall stones it would dissolve them too and cure the patient. My informant did not make it quite clear how the remedy was taken but it is certain that it was taken internally as the gizzard had to come in contact with the stone.[46]

When Morse was on St. Helena Island, Straits of Mackinac, in 1820, he became ill. His Indian cook went into the woods, shot and dressed a pigeon, and roasted it with pork on the ends of sticks. This was considered "savoury meat." [47]

A superstition regarding the eating of pigeons existed in New York. Cooper wrote: "They are not thought very healthy food, however, when eaten repeatedly in succession. There is a tradition that the Indians, at the time of the year when they lived chiefly on these birds, were not in a healthy condition." [48] A somewhat similar belief arose in Ontario. McIlwraith mentions that large numbers of pigeons occurred at Hamilton in 1854, the year of the cholera. Taking the birds ceased when a rumor arose that the eating of too many caused the disease.[49]

THE INDIAN AND THE PIGEON

The passenger pigeon was of importance in the economy of the Indian. Netting was practiced in a few localities where conditions favored visitation by pigeons with some regularity. By far the greater number were taken at the nestings, and at the temporary roosts where the birds could be killed easily at night with long poles. A nesting place having been discovered, frequently an entire tribe would move to the site and feast on the squabs.[50] Wood, writing of New England in 1634, mentions that the Indians brought loads of them from a nesting.[51] Among the game birds, the passenger pigeon was second in importance to the wild turkey to the Indians of the southeastern states.[52] Lawson wrote that in the Carolinas, "You may find several Indian towns of not above seventeen houses, that have more than one hundred gallons of pigeon's oil or fat; they using it with pulse or bread as we do butter." [53]

The bones of the passenger pigeon found in archeological investigations give some indication of the widespread utilization of this bird by the Indians. The bones, being small, would under ordinary conditions disintegrate rapidly. Of the bird bones found at a village site in Grenville County, Ontario, those of the pigeon ranked sixth in order of abundance; and at a site in Middlesex County, Ontario, third.[54] In Quebec, its bones were found at Tadousac by Father Thomas-Louis Doré, who informed me of his discovery by letter, in the summer of 1949. Some were found in July, 1948, in the Sleeping Bear sand dune, Leelanau County, Michigan, according to a letter I received from W. O. Pruitt, Jr. In Wisconsin they were found at Ancient Aztalan and at the village sites near Oshkosh.[55]

The following terms used by the Mohawk in hunting pigeons are extant: *ata,* a small piece of bark or dry wood serving as a torch for hunting pigeons at night; *ataseront,* hunting by the above method; *kannhi,* a long pole for dislodging the nests of the pigeons; and *te hokxaton onte,* "he has brought down a pigeon." [56]

The gathering of the squabs at a nesting along the Genesee River, New York, in 1782, is described by Horatio Jones, who at the time was living with the Indians.

As the annual nesting of the pigeons was a matter of great importance to the Indians, who depended largely upon the supply of food thus obtained, runners carried the news to every part of the Seneca territory, and the inhabitants, singly and in bands, came from as far west as Seneca Lake and as far north as Lake Ontario. Within a few days several hundred, men, women and children gathered in the locality of the pigeon woods....

The Indians cut down the roosting trees to secure the birds, and each day thousands of squabs were killed. Fires were made in front of the cabins and bunches of the dressed birds were suspended on poles sustained by crotched sticks, to dry in the heat and smoke. When properly cured they were packed in bags or baskets for transportation to the home towns. It was a festival season for the red men and even the meanest dog in camp had his fill of pigeon meat.[57]

Apparently this was the same nesting described by Gilbert.[58]

The cuisine of the Indians was not for the squeamish. Colonel Proctor attended a feast given by the Onondaga near Buffalo on May 3, 1791. He records that the feast consisted principally of squabs, "some boiled, some stewed, and the mode of dishing them up was, that a hank of six were tied with a deer's sinew around their necks, their bills pointing outwards; they were plucked but of pen feathers, there plenty remained; the inside was taken out, but it appeared from the soup made of them, that water had not touched them before. The repast being the best I had seen for a long time, I ate of it very heartily." [59]

A settler in Waushara County, Wisconsin, in 1849, gave several pigeons that he had shot to "Menominee John." [60] The squaws put the heads of the pigeons, stomach upwards, in their mouths and blew them up as a boy would a bladder. The crop, intestines, and feathers were then removed before cooking.

The Chippewa had three methods of cooking pigeons: boiling with rice or potatoes and meat; cooking in hot ashes without removing the feathers or intestines; and impaling the plucked birds on sticks and roasting before a fire.[61]

The pigeon played a part in the religion of the northern Indians. Le Jeune wrote in 1636: "At the feast of the Dead, which takes place about every twelve years, the souls quit the cemetaries, and in the opinion of some are changed into Turtle-doves (*Tourterelles*), which they [the Hurons] pursue later in the woods, with bow and arrow, to boil and eat." [62]

The Seneca did not take the squabs without making to the old birds what was considered an adequate payment in prayers and gifts. After they had put tobacco on a fire to create a smoke, a brass kettle or other small receptacle filled with wampum, brooches, and various other articles was deposited on the ground and left for the pigeons.[63]

The gatherings for the collection of squabs had all the aspects of a feast and a council.[64] Among the Winnebago, passenger pigeons were known as "chief" birds since they were used when the chief decided to give the "chief feast" to which the entire tribe was invited.[65]

The Indians' appreciation of the pigeon is shown in the statement of Proctor: "Red Jacket and Captain O'Beel came to see me, when the former acquainted me with the reason why no council would be held this day, to wit: that it was their pigeon time, in which the Great Spirit had blessed them with an abundance; and that such was his goodness to the Indians that He never failed sending them season after season, and although it might seem a small matter to me, the Indians will never lose sight of those blessings." [66]

The pigeon was the source of several myths and legends among the Seneca. A white pigeon was "chief" of the colony. This is in accordance with the respect held for a white animal of any kind. The White Pigeon informed the Indians that at a council of the birds it was decided that the pigeons must pay tribute with their bodies since, unlike other birds, they were colonial. The pigeon dance and offerings at the nesting were forms of thanksgiving.[67]

The serious attitude of the Seneca toward the pigeon is illustrated by the following quotation from French:

Standing upon the flattened top of a high hill, overlooking the Allegheny valley, in 1870, Dan Gleason, the Indian Wolf hunter, told me about the pigeons, which were flying past us then in many strata, some overhead and many below us, in the valley between our hill and others, south of the river; with waving arms, swaying body and nimble feet he illustrated the sacred pigeon dance of the Redmen in America, based upon the flight of their sacred bird; in soft cadences he sang the song of "Wah-ho-pah," and in solemn words explained the wonderful birds and their beneficence to his race, and to their ancestors when they began life upon the earth; how a warrior's hair must not be lost, for it represents the feathers of the sacred bird and preserves his soul for the immortal bliss of the Happy Hunting Ground. When the hair is lost there can be no blessed immortality, for on the journey after death they would become confused and take the wrong trail, followed by all who offend the Great Spirit—the trail that had no end and led to no place, an eternity of wandering.[68]

This bird appeared in the imagery of the Indian. On the eve of Braddock's defeat a Delaware told Smith that the soldiers were marching in close formation and that the Indians would get behind trees and "shoot um down all one pigeon." [69]

The Indians were careful not to kill or disturb in any way the old birds when a nesting was in progress. This precaution was observed as long as nestings existed.[70] Kalm states:

While these birds are hatching their young, or while the latter are not yet able to fly, the savages or Indians in North America are in the habit of never shooting or killing them, nor of allowing others to do so, pretending that it would be a great pity on their young, which would in that case have to starve to death. Some of the Frenchmen told me that they had set out with the intention of shooting some of them at that season of the year, but that the savages had at first with kindness endeavoured to dissuade them from such a purpose, and later added threats to their entreaties when the latter were of no avail.[71]

The real purpose in protecting the nestings was the fear that the pigeons might abandon their nests and thus prevent the tribe from securing squabs with ease and in abundance. Regarding a nesting in Wisconsin in the Mississippi bottoms, Bunnell says: "Some of the young Sioux were watching the 'roost,' to see if any had commenced laying, for some were already building nests, and when I told Mr. Reed of the Indians being there and not a shot fired at the pigeons, he told me that the Indians never disturbed pigeons or ducks by shooting at them when nesting, and that the life of a man so doing would not be safe among the Sioux, as the whole tribe would feast upon the squabs as soon as big enough." [72]

It has been said that the Indian was the most dangerous of any of the wild enemies of the pigeon.[73] While possibly true in a literal sense, there is no reason to believe that their raids had an appreciable effect until a large commerce was established by the whites. A fair statement is that of Chief Pokagon, a Michigan Potawatomi: "A pigeon nesting was always a great source of revenue to our people. Whole tribes would wigwam in the brooding places. They seldom killed the old birds, but made great preparation to secure their young, out of which the squaws made squab butter and smoked and dried them by thousands for future use. Yet, under our manner of securing them, they continued to increase." [74]

The Indians behaved no better or worse at a nesting than the whites.

Regarding the nesting in northeastern Forest County, Pennsylvania, in 1880, we have the following: "Three weeks ago, just before the 'squabs' ... could fly, about two hundred Cornplanter Indians left their reservation above Warren, and moved bag and baggage, upon the pigeon roost. They remained a week, and during that time cut down thousands of trees in order to get squabs. When the marauders departed they left the ground blue with dead birds, having killed twice as many as they knew how to dispose of." [75]

An equally severe indictment is given by Roney, who gives 900 as the number of Indians that had moved to the nesting at Petoskey, Michigan in 1878. They were provided with camping equipment and containers for the squabs, intending to remain as long as the birds were available. In his opinion the loss of pigeons would have been incalculable if the Indians had not been driven away. [76]

The destruction of pigeons at a nesting was so great that the Indians were not always singled out for blame. The Fond du Lac *Commonwealth* (Wis.) for May 20, 1871, gave the following description of their customary procedure at the nesting at Kilbourn, Wisconsin, in 1871:

Likewise attracted there were several tribes of Indians. We met numerous squads, the men and boys armed with bows and arrows, the squaws carrying long poles. When the nest was within reach the squaws punched the young pigeon from its home, and caught it as it fell. When too high to reach, the skillful archer generally at the first shot drove the large headed arrow plump to the center of the nest, and the young bird, shot first upward, then fell dead. We saw one young Indian shoot three pigeons on the wing, with his arrow, killing his bird on each occasion.... The old men and squaws were engaged in picking and drying pigeons.

Pigeons nested in the same locality in 1882. Then the censure fell on the white buyers for hiring the Indians to collect the squabs.

A complete description of the pigeon hunts of the Cornplanter Seneca is given by Fenton and Deardorff. [77] Though scouts were sent out to locate the nestings, watch their development, and inform the people, the hunt itself was not organized. Each person or family acted independently in collecting the pigeons. The squabs were dislodged from the nests by the use of long poles, shooting into the nests with blunt arrows, and cutting down the trees. The climbing of trees at night to secure the squabs, attributed to the Cayuga,[78] could not have been practiced extensively since it was much simpler to secure them by daylight.

The Indians took pigeons in nets, but doubt has been expressed that netting was a native art. Nevertheless, it is clear that they netted fish, wildfowl, and other birds before the arrival of the Europeans. When the English landed in Virginia in 1607, they found that the Indians "make nets for fishing...as formally braded as ours." [79] Williams wrote in 1643 that the Indians catch geese, turkeys, and cranes with nets.[80] Nets of native manufacture by the Hurons were known by 1636.[81] In 1669 the Indians had nets set in Green Bay, Wisconsin, and sometimes captured 50 waterfowl in a night, while they were feeding on the wild rice.[82] Dablon is more explicit regarding the netting at Green Bay. He states that the nets were set in like manner as for fish, frequently both fish and waterfowl being caught in the same net, and that the Indians were the *inventors*.[83] The Sauteurs at Sault Ste. Marie, Michigan, had dip-nets about three feet in depth for taking whitefish.[84] According to Kalm, the Delaware made fish nets from the dogbane (*Apocynum cannabinum*) centuries before the arrival of Europeans.[85]

There is ample information to show that some methods of netting pigeons were original with the Indians. If there were nothing novel in their procedure, the Europeans would not have gone to the trouble of describing them. In July, 1656, Le Jeune wrote from Lake Gannentaa (Onondaga), New York, that "in the Spring, so great numbers of Pigeons collect around these salt-springs, that sometimes as many as seven hundred are caught in the course of one morning." [86] Radisson was at this lake in 1657 when he thought that 1,500 or 1,600 might be taken in a net at one time.[87]

The snaring of 700 to 800 pigeons at a time by the Iroquois on Lake Cayuga is also mentioned by Raffeix.[88] Boucher is more specific in that he states that the pigeons are taken in *nets*, three and four hundred at a draw.[89] The design of the nets used is not disclosed; but Kalm, who visited the Iroquois in August, 1750, gives an inkling. He wrote: "The savages in Onondago had built their huts on the sides of this salt field, and here they had erected sloping nets with a cord attachment leading to the huts where they were sitting: when the Pigeons arrived in swarms to eat of this salty soil, the Savages pulled the cords, enclosing them in the net, and thus at once secured the entire flock." [90]

A clear description of the construction and operation of a net by the Indians at Green Bay, Wisconsin, in the period 1640–60, is given by La Potherie. In view of the time and remoteness from the Atlantic coast, it is improbable that netting was a borrowed culture. He wrote: "To take pigeons in nets in summer, they make large aisles in the woods, where they attach to two trees on both sides a net made like a completely open bag. They build a small hut of boughs in which they sit, and when the pigeons in their flight get within this opening, they pull a small cord which runs through the edge of the opening to the net and so sometimes take five or six hundred in one morning, especially when it is windy." [91]

The Cayuga are said to have set up nets on high places and when the pigeons were blown into them by a high wind, the net was pulled.[92] A modern Cayuga told Dodge that the netting of pigeons as practiced by the whites was never followed.[93] It is not clear if this means that no net was used or that the more complicated clap-net of the whites was not employed. The Chippewa informed Densmore that they formerly took pigeons by erecting long fish nets on poles in the same manner that fish were caught in the water.[94]

SQUABS

Squab is derived from the Swedish *sqvabb* meaning a soft, fat body. Peter Yarnall wrote from Jersey, Pennsylvania on March 17, 1850: "When the young pigeons become fledged, they are so fat, that they are much heavier than the old ones, and can not do much at flying, the surrounding inhabitants ... come to the encampment to supply themselves with squabs, they strike the trees with their axes, and frighten them out of their nests ... they had much more fat on than was required to cook them and I thought it the most delicious meat I ever tasted of the wild kind." [95]

Squabs that had been fed on beechnuts were especially fine eating. Beechnuts are rich in fat. When an animal feeds on a particular fat for some time, it will resynthesize the same fat. Eventually over one-half of the fat in its body will have the same chemical composition as that of the fat ingested. All of the various kinds of mast produce soft fats.

The young in the nest were unceremoniously abandoned by the parents.[96] S. S. Stevens told Brewster that he had twice seen the squabs driven from the nest.[97] Possibly these actually were instances where the begging for food, by a squab not belonging to the parent, was resented.

The young on abandonment by the parents were quite helpless. The following description is given in the Whitewater *Register* (Wis.) of June 3, 1880:

The squabs lie blinking in their nests for hours. On finding themselves deserted, they toddle to the rims of their baskets [nests] and balance themselves. After a preliminary flutter of the wings they strike out for a limb, reach it, lose their equilibrium and tumble to the ground. They then wander about like drunken men for three or four days ere they know enough to seek food or water. Fully a week elapses before they are in good flying condition. When they become lean they readily take wing and skirmish for themselves. The wing feathers grow much faster than the feathers in their tails, and when flying gives them a ludicrous appearance. They resemble boys in monkey jackets. A lack of tail feathers sends them rudderless through the air. They are forced to fly in a straight line swerving gently between the trees. On alighting they frequently pitch head over heels, and appear dumfounded. At first they form small flocks, but as they grow stronger of wing these flocks come together, and the downy brigade pitches for a good feeding ground.

It was impossible to drive along a road when the squabs were learning to fly, especially after a rain, without killing a considerable number of them.[98]

The time during which the squabs could be collected lasted but two or three days after abandonment. When the squabs began leaving the nests on their own volition, squabbing was nearly over.[99] In some nestings the squabs could be punched from the nests with long poles. When the trees were of moderate size, many squabs could be jarred from the nests by striking the tree with the head of an axe or by using a small log as a battering ram. Squabbing reminded Ingells of picking apples since when the trees were shaken the squabs struck the ground with a thud like that of large apples.[100] The greater number were taken both by whites and Indians by felling trees with axes, care being taken that the falling tree struck another in order to dislodge the squabs from it as well.[101] At the nesting on the Genesee River, New York, in 1782, the

Indians secured thousands of squabs daily in this manner.[102] During the last nestings in Pennsylvania, the owners of the land prohibited the cutting of trees for this purpose.[103]

The shooting of blunt-headed arrows against the bottom of the nest to dislodge the squab was practiced by the Indians.[104] Even the children were efficient with the bow.

The depth of depravity was reached when squabs were obtained by firing the loose, highly combustible bark of the birch trees.

These outlaws to all moral sense would touch a lighted match to the bark of the trees at the base, when with a flash, more like an explosion, the blast would reach every limb of the tree and while the affrightened young birds would leap simultaneously to the ground, the parent birds with plumage scorched, would rise high in air amid flame and smoke. I noticed that many of these squabs were so fat and clumsy they would burst open on striking the ground. Several thousand were obtained during the day by that cruel process.[105]

Between the vile odor and coating of excrement, there was nothing aesthetic within a nesting, especially when squabs were being gathered.

Day and night the horrible business continued. Bird lime covered everything and lay deep on the ground. Pots burning sulphur vomited their lethal fumes here and there suffocating the birds. Gnomes in the forms of men wearing old, tattered clothing, heads covered with burlap and feet encased in old shoes or rubber boots went about with sticks and clubs knocking off the birds' nests while others were chopping down trees and breaking off the over-laden limbs to gather the squabs. Pigs turned into the roost to fatten on the fallen birds added their squeals to the general clamor when stepped on or kicked out of the way, while the high, cackling notes of the terrified Pigeons, a bit husky and hesitant as though short of breath, combined into a peculiar roar unlike any other known sound, and which could be heard at least a mile away.

Of the countless thousands of birds bruised, broken and fallen, a comparatively few could be salvaged yet wagon loads were being driven out in an almost unbroken procession, leaving the ground still covered with living, dying, dead and rotting birds. An inferno where the Pigeons had builded their Eden.[106]

A squab spoiled quickly unless the crop was removed. Accordingly when the squab was caught, the crop was grasped between the first and second fingers and with a snap the crop and head were removed in one operation.[107] The last stuffing with food so distended the crop that it was as large or larger than the body, giving the appearance of two birds with one head.[108]

The behavior of the young pigeons is described by William French: "When the young birds fluttered from the nests in large numbers they started at once and kept going ahead, in spite of the wild animals and hawks that killed many of them. If they came to a road they crossed it; a stream, they flew over; or they fell exhausted into the water and, flapping their wings, swam to the other shore and ran on until night." [109]

The young at first gathered into numerous small flocks, eventually forming large ones.

For about a week after they could fly they were too weak to rise high and keep the pace of the old ones. They seldom flew higher than twelve feet above the ground except to pass over obstructions in their way. These flights were in the course of least obstruction from the rookery to a place where food was plentiful and back; they were never straight and often followed the course of a creek. In formation these flocks were longish, small, numerous and followed one another closely. The morning flight took place at dawn, and the evening about 4 P.M.[110]

The habit of following openings in the forest rendered the young an easy prey. C. K. Sober relates that on May 11–13, 1880, he saw hundreds killed with clubs at Kane, Pennsylvania, as they followed an opening cut for a pipe line. Their flight was from six to twelve feet above the ground.[111] Great numbers were killed by flying against telegraph wires when these lay in the line of flight.[112]

The young are said to have remained together until they reached maturity. In fall, however, the young were mixed with the old birds in the migration southward.[113]

There is no foundation for the claim that the young within a week followed the line of flight taken by the old birds.[114] The statement that the young joined the old birds at Sydenham, Ontario, within three days after leaving Pennsylvania is preposterous.[115] It was not uncommon for the young to remain within 100 miles of the nesting throughout the summer. For example, E. Osborn in July, 1866, had a busy time with young pigeons near Port Huron, Michigan.[116] These birds came from the nesting at Forestville, Sanilac County, less than 50 miles distant. When the young left the Crooked River nesting in Emmet County, Michigan, in 1878, millions of young were seen flying *southward* over a period of three days.[117]

It has been stated repeatedly that the old birds never fed near the nesting, but left the food for the young birds. E. Haskell states that when the pigeons arrived in a forest in Potter County, Pennsylvania, that they had selected for nesting, they soon stripped the ground of beechnuts.[118] Accordingly, the attributed foresight did not exist. It is true that, once incubation started, the pigeons usually flew several miles from the nesting before beginning to feed. It was for this reason that the trappers set their nets five to ten miles from the nesting as the birds would not decoy well near it. This trait may have been developed to prevent congestion when the millions of birds were arriving or departing from the nesting. In some cases mast was absent in the immediate vicinity of the nesting. According to J. B. Oviatt, the departure from the vicinity of the nesting took place as soon as the young could fly well. "For quite a while many young birds remained in the woods in the neighborhood of the city [nesting], while others in small flocks spread out in every direction. As they learned to fly better, they spread faster." [119]

COMMERCE

The trade in pigeons did not become important until the railroads offered rapid transportation to the city markets. Rail transportation from the Atlantic coast to Chicago was not available until 1852, and the Mississippi was not reached until 1854. In the spring of 1842, 3,000 live pigeons taken in Michigan arrived in Boston by rail.[120] Transportation of pigeons eastward through the Great Lakes continued for many years. On June 3, 1868, the Milwaukee *News* reported that the ship *Messenger* stopped that day at Milwaukee with 49 crates numbering 5,000 pigeons that had been taken aboard at Manistee, Michigan. Their destination was Buffalo, New York, where they were to be used in shooting matches.

The effect of a railroad is illustrated by the Erie which was extended from New York City to the southwestern corner of New York in 1851. Up to April 25, 1851, according to the New York *Evening Post* of April 26, 75 tons of pigeons were shipped over this road to New York City from Steuben and Allegany counties, New York. This was a new industry for the region, since prior to this time it was impossible to get the pigeons to New York in salable condition. The game market of New York, in 1855, was estimated to dispose of 300,000 pigeons annually. The Milwaukee *Wisconsin* for November 28, 1855, reported that a dealer in the Fulton Market received in one day 60 barrels, or 18,000 pigeons, caught in New York and Pennsylvania and shipped over the Erie Railroad.

A nesting was reported in April, 1882, as located in the mountains in northern Potter County, Pennsylvania, 37 miles from a railroad.[121] The distance and terrain would make the cost of transportation high. In the same year it was announced that a railroad had just been completed from Sheffield, Pennsylvania, to the vicinity of the old nesting places in Forest County and that transportation would accordingly be greatly facilitated if a nesting again occurred.[122]

The Plattsburg *Republican* of August 2, 1851, estimated that not less than 150,000 dozen or 1,800,000 pigeons were sent to market from the nesting near Plattsburg, New York, in 1851. The dealers paid from 31 to 56 cents a dozen. From 15 to 25 people were employed in dressing the birds for which labor they received about eight cents per dozen.

In the spring of 1861, up to April 5, 750 barrels or 212,500 pigeons, weighing 67.5 tons, were shipped east from Circleville, Ohio, by express. In addition to the large numbers consumed locally, wagonloads were taken to Columbus, and many sent to Cincinnati.[123]

The pigeon trade became thoroughly organized in the latter half of the nineteenth century. The large commission houses had buyers and trappers in the field and followed the movements of the pigeons the year around. Some of the large dealers were: Henry Knapp, Utica, New York; H. T. Phillips and Company, Detroit; Bond and Ellsworth, Chicago; Holmes and Sears, Chicago; Edward T. Martin, Chicago; W. P. Thomas, Peoria, Illinois; and N. W. Judy and Company, St. Louis.

Advertisements were run in the trade journals, of which the following are typical:

Wild Pigeons.—I leave for the Petoskey nesting, April 10th, and by the 15th, can fill all orders for birds.—E. T. Martin, 79 Clark St., Chicago.

Wild pigeons for sale, a limited number; price $2.50 per doz. on cars here. No shipments made to strangers without cash accompanies the order. Two and a half per cent discount in price on all orders accompanied by the money.—E. T. Martin.[124]

The express companies obtained so great a revenue from the shipments that their agents kept the trappers informed on the location of the
pigeons. The business was conducted in this fashion:

From 100 to 200 men have been engaged in the business of netting these birds all
the time, and this number is increased by a great many local netters wherever the
birds happen to nest. . . .

In this very large country there would seem to be every chance of losing a body
of birds and not finding out where they are. But a very good system has been established for keeping track of them, which is specially looked after by the different
express companies and the shippers and handlers of live and dead birds, who form
another section of those interested in the history of the wild pigeon, before the
epicure meets him at the table. When the body of birds leaves the South the local
superintendents of the express companies are instructed to keep their eyes out for
indications of a nesting, and the messengers generally are to report on their route.
A correspondence of an inquisitive nature is carried on by every regular netter in
order that he or his chums may strike the birds first. One may judge of the importance of the receipts to the express companies from the fact that a total of four to
five thousand barrels of birds are shipped from each nesting, averaging thirty dozen
to the barrel [1,440,000 to 1,800,000 birds], on which the charges are from $6 to
$12 per barrel, which sometimes includes re-icing on the trip. This does not include
the stall-fed birds for later market, nor the live birds for trap-shooting, and on
which charges are 75 cents per crate of seventy-two birds to $300 per carload, nor
the squabs, so that it is of considerable importance that no nesting be overlooked.[125]

The estimated number of birds shipped from every nesting is too high.

There are no accurate figures on the number of professional trappers
who followed the pigeons throughout the year. According to H. T.
Phillips, "In 1874 there were over six hundred professional netters, and
when the pigeons nested north, every man or woman was either a
catcher or a picker." [126] Roney gives 5,000 as the number of habitués and
says that at the nesting at Petoskey in 1878 at least 2,000 people were con-
nected with the pigeon trade in one way or another.[127] The number of
netters operating at this nesting is also given as 700.[128] In 1881 the number of professional trappers was placed at 1,200.[129] Aside from the pro-
fessionals, the northern states had hundreds of people who trapped in
their communities during the migrations, and every nesting attracted
swarms of Indians.

A brief description of the pigeon trade and its rewards was furnished by Alvin McKnight of Augusta, Wisconsin in a letter to me:

The nesting season lasted about three weeks, and I have known as many as 1500 barrels of birds, with from 30 to 35 dozen to the barrel, being shipped to New York City every day during that period. . . . In packing for shipment, the ends of the wings were chopped off, but very few were ever plucked or drawn. . . . My uncle Chas. Martin used to make around $500 a season trapping pigeons at from one to two dollars per dozen and I presume that this is a fair average of what the other trappers did. Sometimes when his catches were light, he would put them into crates alive, take them home and put them in a feeding pen and feed them about ten days. Then he would kill and ship them as plucked, stall-fed birds. For these he used to realize a fancy price, sometimes as much as $3.50 per dozen.

Pigeons appeared in the market in various conditions. The term "flight" was generally applied to a pigeon taken in passage to and from a nesting, but sometimes to one taken in migration. In either case it was generally lean. A dressed bird had the entrails and sometimes the head removed, and a "feathered" bird had the feathers removed. If both operations were performed, it was dressed and plucked. The choicest bird was one fed grain for several days and known as stall-fed. Squabs always had the crop removed, as otherwise they deteriorated rapidly. Live birds were seldom sold except for shooting tournaments.

Sometimes the pigeons were as neatly dressed for the market as domestic fowls. Usually this was not the case, as the trappers could not go to this trouble when large catches were being made. In order to conserve space the ends of the wings were cut off, or the wing and tail feathers pulled out. The pigeons were then packed in barrels with ice. The number placed in a barrel depended upon whether the birds were completely dressed or not and the necessity of using ice. The numbers given most frequently are 25, 30, and 35 dozen.

The enormous numbers of pigeons sold in the city markets are a source of wonder. In spite of individual opinions to the contrary, the population in general must have considered them a delicacy. There was a nesting near Grand Rapids, Michigan, in 1860. The records of the express office, given in the Grand Rapids *Eagle* of July 23, 1860, provided the following figures on shipments:

Shipper	Barrels	Pounds	Express Charges
A. Paxson	66	1,300	$ 404.50
B. G. Parke	37	7,400	203.50
B. Goodhart	75	15,600	475.50
M. H. Latten	238	47,600	1,355.27
Osborn and Co.	129	29,955	801.50
L. Sexton	27	5,400	148.50
Gilder and Knight	14	2,800	90.00
G. T. Fowler	2	400	10.20
	588	110,455	$3,488.97

Since the shipments of M. H. Latten averaged 400 pigeons to the barrel, the total number shipped was approximately 235,200.

It is stated by Cook that in 1869 the pigeons nested in Deerfield Township, Van Buren County, Michigan, and that during a period of 40 days there were shipped daily from Hartford three carloads of pigeons.[130] Since each car contained 150 barrels of 35 dozen each, the total daily shipment amounted to 24,750 dozen, equivalent to 11,880,000 birds. These figures were quoted by Hornaday and by Mershon without checking.[131] Martin, the game dealer, hopped upon Hornaday with pleasure. Aside from denying that this nesting occurred in 1869, he pointed out that the facilities available at the time would have rendered it utterly impossible to market anything like this number of pigeons.[132] There is an error in the calculations of Cook, as the daily shipment was only 15,750 dozen, or 7,560,000 birds for the season. Even this number passes credulity.

The large nesting in Wisconsin in 1871 occurred in an area where transportation was a simple problem. S. S. Duffie of the American Merchants' Union Express furnished the following data on shipments by express, which were given in the Portage *Register* (Wis.) for May 6, 1871:

Station	Time	Barrels
Kilbourn	April 21 to May 3	255
Greenfield	April 12 to April 28	108

Station	Time	Barrels (*cont.*)
New Lisborn	April 17 to April 29	71
Sparta	April 19 to April 29	75
Tomah	April 18 to April 28	103
		612

He thought that if all the figures were available the total shipments would amount to 1,000 barrels, or 300,000 birds, allowing 25 dozen to the barrel. The above does not include the pigeons shipped by fast freight, the live birds in crates, and the great number of birds shot by hunters.

There was an important nesting near Shelby, Oceana County, Michigan, in 1874, concerning which H. T. Phillips gives this information: "they made the heaviest catches I have ever known of: 100 barrels of dead birds daily on an average of thirty days, besides the live ones, of which I shipped 175,000." [133] At 300 birds to the barrel, at least 1,075,000 pigeons were accounted for. The nesting was a bonanza to the local people, who had an income of $50,000. [134]

Estimates of the number of squabs destroyed at the nestings in Michigan in 1874 are given by Roney, the information being second-hand. He gives 1875 for the year, which is incorrect. The last nestings in Oceana County were in 1874 and 1876, and 1874 is the year in which there were several large nestings in the state. The shipments of squabs from the nesting in Newaygo County was estimated at 40 to 50 tons. He adds: "At another large nesting in Oceana County, of which I could not obtain statistical information, residents and those qualified to speak said there were shipped *ten barrels of squabs for every one barrel* at the Newaygo County nesting." [135] The two nestings and another in Grand Traverse County furnished for the market 1,000 tons of squabs and 2,400,000 adult birds.

The credibility of the estimates of the number of pigeons killed at a particular nesting is clouded by the motives of the contributor. The conservationist overestimated the numbers, while the game buyers pursued the opposite course. Professor Roney in his very sincere efforts to have the law enforced, overstated the number killed at the nesting at Petoskey, Michigan, in 1878:

The first shipment of birds from Petoskey was upon March 22, and the last upon August 12, making over twenty weeks or five months that the bird war was carried on. For many weeks the railroad shipments averaged fifty barrels of dead birds per day—thirty to forty dozen old birds and about fifty dozen squabs being packed in a barrel. Allowing 500 birds to a barrel, and averaging the entire shipments for the season at twenty-five barrels per day, we find the rail shipments to have been 12,500 dead birds daily, or 1,500,000 for the summer [based on a week of six days]. Of live birds there were shipped 1,116 crates, six dozen per crate, or 80,352 birds. These were the rail shipments only, and not including the cargoes by steamers from Petoskey, Cheboygan, Cross Village, and other lake ports, which were as many more. Added to this were the daily express shipments in bags and boxes, the wagon loads hauled away by the shot-gun brigade, the thousands of dead and wounded ones not secured, and the myriads of squabs dead in the nest by the trapping off of the parent birds soon after hatching, (for a young pigeon will surely die if deprived of its parents during the first week of its life) and we have at the lowest possible estimate a grand total of 1,000,000,000 pigeons sacrificed to Mammon during the nesting of 1878.[136]

The statements of Roney were challenged by Martin.[137] He gave the shipments, purporting to be official, from Petoskey and Boyne Falls as follows:

Point of Origin	Number of Birds
Petoskey, dead by express	490,000
Petoskey, alive by express	86,400
Boyne Falls, dead	47,100
Boyne Falls, alive	42,696
Petoskey, dead by boat estimated	110,000
Petoskey, alive by boat estimated	33,640
Cheboygan, dead by boat estimated	108,300
Cheboygan, alive by boat estimated	89,730
Other points, dead and alive estimated	100,000
	1,107,866

Martin assumed that 1,500,000 would include all of the birds killed.

There are many accounts of the number of pigeons taken at the nesting at Shelby, Oceana County, Michigan, in 1876. The number taken was large owing to the accessibility of the nesting. One writer states that the season lasted from April 20 to May 20 and that over 400 netters were at work. The day that he was in Shelby 124 barrels, 25 dozen to the barrel, or 37,200 birds, were shipped by express.[138] Spoiled and trapped birds would increase this sum by 5,000. Over 40,000 pigeons were being held in coops. It was estimated that there was a daily shipment of 25,000 pigeons over a period of four weeks. This would amount to 600,000 pigeons with a week of six days. The best prices paid the catchers were thirty cents per dozen for dead, and fifty cents for live birds, delivered at the depot. Another visitor saw 100 barrels of dead pigeons shipped in one day from Shelby, and he gives 300 as the number of men engaged in the pigeon trade.[139]

The firm of H. T. Phillips and Company secured during the month of April, at the Shelby nesting, 15,000 live birds and expected to have 100,000 before the season closed. In addition five to ten barrels of dressed pigeons, each barrel holding about 350 birds, were shipped daily.[140]

The estimates made by Owen of the number of pigeons taken at this nesting were influenced by his indignation. He gives a weekly shipment of 352,800 dead birds.[141] The firms of H. T. Phillips and Company and E. T. Martin were each obtaining 15,000 live birds each week, with a total of 45,000 being taken by all the purchasers. This gives a total of 397,800 birds per week or 1,591,200 for a season of four weeks.

The express agent at Shelby, A. Z. Moore, received 10 per cent of the receipts for shipping pigeons. In 1876, this amounted to $1,553.30.[142] There were expressed 1,781 barrels and 1,982 crates, and 2,000 dozen birds were held for feeding. It was estimated that over 700,000 birds were shipped. This is correct, for at 300 birds to the barrel, 72 to the crate, and with the birds withheld, a total of 701,104 birds is obtained. This is less than one-half of Owen's estimate.

A game dealer was not inclined to overestimate the size of the pigeon trade, hence the data given by Bond on the nestings in Benzie and Emmet counties, Michigan, in 1880, are of special interest.[143] The following estimates are based on reports from dealers:

Shipper	*Live Pigeons*
Bond and Ellsworth	65,000
E. T. Martin	50,000
Thomas Stagg	30,000
P. C. Sears	25,000
H. T. Phillips	20,000
Other parties	20,000
	210,000

Shipping Facts	*Dead Pigeons*
490 barrels from Traverse City by express	147,000
300 barrels from Petoskey by express	90,000
150 barrels from Petoskey by boat	45,000
150 barrels from Cheboygan by boat	45,000
1090	327,000

Unit Price	*Value*
Live birds, 210,000 at 15 cents each	$31,500.00
Dead birds, 327,000 at 6 cents each	19,620.00
537,000	$51,120.00

These figures are of particular interest, since the pigeons were on the verge of a precipitous decline. Including the birds taken at the nestings in Pennsylvania the same year, the total value of the pigeons marketed was placed at $100,000.

The year 1882 marks the end of the taking of pigeons in any number approaching those of former years. There was a nesting about four miles in length in Potter County, Pennsylvania. Two larger ones in Wisconsin, in the counties of Monroe and Adams, were known as the Sparta and Kilbourn nestings. The former was about nine miles in length by two in width, and the latter six by one and one-half miles. The following figures, given in the La Crosse *Chronicle* (Wis.) of June 13, 1882, are recorded for the shipments by express from Sparta, Wisconsin:

460 crates of 100 birds each	46,000
205 barrels of 540 birds each	110,700
	156,700

Total weight, pounds	62,070
Express charges	$1,700

No data are available on shipments from other points along the railroad. The Milwaukee *Evening Wisconsin,* May 23, 1882, states: "About 75 crates of live wild squabs and several hundred barrels of dead salted [?] wild pigeons pass through the city by way of the American Express Co., daily."

A man from Milwaukee, on May 30, made the following estimate of the number of pigeons destroyed:

The nestings were formed some six weeks ago, and the shipments of dead birds have averaged 75 bbls. per day.... One barrel of pigeons equals 44 dozen, or 528 birds; 75 barrels, one day's shipment, equals 39,600, and six weeks' shipment 1,425,600. Now add to this number 475,200 live birds shipped in the same time, which is a fair estimate according to the best information I can get; again add one-half as many (237,600) as the least number of birds killed by gunners and others ...and we have a total of 2,138,400.[144]

Very similar data are used by another writer, who arrives at the sum of 2,494,800 pigeons destroyed.[145] It is very doubtful if the total number of pigeons destroyed at the Wisconsin nestings attained this number in view of the shipment by express of only 156,700 birds from Sparta. The worst aspect was the almost total destruction of the squabs, a large part of which were taken at so underdeveloped a stage that they were scarcely fit for food.

The pigeon trade was considered highly profitable by Roney.

The prices of dead birds range from thirty-five cents to forty cents per dozen at the nesting. In Chicago markets fifty to sixty cents. Squabs twelve cents per dozen in the woods, in metropolitan markets sixty cents to seventy cents.... Live birds are worth at the trapper's net forty cents to sixty cents per dozen; in cities $1 to $2. It can thus be easily seen that the business, when at all successful, is a very profitable one, for from the above quotations a pencil will quickly figure out an income of $10 to

$40 a day for the "poor and hard working pigeon trapper." One "pigeoner" at the Petoskey nesting was reported to be worth $60,000, all made in that business.[146]

It is claimed by Martin that pigeons were so abundant during the nestings in Michigan in 1876 and 1878 that at the height of the catches the shipment of dead birds would not pay the cost of the barrels and ice. Had it not been for the good demand for live birds for trap shooting, the netters would have been forced to cease operations.[147]

The traffic in pigeons was accompanied by tremendous waste even after the birds were taken. H. T. Phillips wrote: "I have lost 3,000 birds in one day because the railroad did not have a car ready on the date promised. I threw away what cost me $250 in eight hours, fat birds, because the weather was too hot. I have bought carloads in Wisconsin at 15 and 25 cents per dozen, but in Michigan we usually paid from 50 cents to $1 a dozen. I have fed thirty bushels of shelled corn daily at $1.20 per bushel, and paid out from $300 to $600 per day for pigeons." He adds: "Express charges on barrels to New York from Michigan were $6.50, from Wisconsin $8; on live birds $3 per cwt." [148]

Special care was necessary in the shipment of live birds in order to prevent high losses. Knapp purchased 8,400 pigeons at a nesting in Van Buren County, Michigan, in 1872. It was necessary to build a large shed to accustom the pigeons to confinement for a few days. If placed immediately in close quarters in the shipping crates, all would die in a very short time. At every station during shipment the attendants removed the coops from the cars to give the pigeons fresh, cool air. "Still, immense numbers die in the coops." [149]

Some figures on the losses of captives are: of 60,000 secured from Missouri, 40,000 died before they could be marketed; of 20,000 secured from Missouri, 16,700 died; and from another lot of 13,000, the loss was 6,000. The birds were shipped in crates four feet long, three feet wide, and three inches high. (The standard crate held 72 birds.) Death was attributed to the birds being held several days without water.[150]

Pigeons intended for trapshooting were kept in cages preparatory to marketing. There is little information on the losses suffered while in captivity. Birds were held in Chicago in rooms twelve feet square, 500 to the room. During the first day in the cage 30 to 50 died, the second day five or six, and few thereafter.[151] The probable loss was about 15 per cent. Martin mentions pigeons held in rooms sixteen feet square, 1,000 to a room.[152] The density in both cases is about four birds to the square foot. It is to be expected that the congestion was relieved by perches.

The price at which pigeons sold depended strictly on the law of supply and demand. They were so plentiful at times that they were given away or fed to hogs. Josselyn wrote in 1674: "I have bought at Boston a dozen of Pidgeons ready pull'd and garbidged for three pence."[153] They were considered excellent food, though at times a penny would purchase as many as could be carried away.[154]

The range of prices in Massachusetts for over one hundred years is given by Judd: "In August, 1736, pigeons fell in Boston to two pence per dozen (not a penny, lawful) and many could not be sold at that. In Northampton, from 1725 to 1785, pigeons when sold brought usually three pence to six pence per dozen. In 1790, they were nine pence, and a few years after 1800, 1s. 6d. Since 1850 they have been sold from 75 cents to $1.50 per dozen."[155] The price of six shillings charged for 18 pigeons at Needham, Massachusetts, in 1755 indicates a temporary scarcity.[156]

Schooners, in 1805, arrived in New York with so many pigeons in bulk, caught up the Hudson, that they sold for a cent apiece.[157] On another occasion the arrival of 75,000 pigeons in New York caused the price to drop to one shilling (12.5 cents) for 50 birds.[158]

They sold in Quebec, about 1807, at 1s. 6d. to 4s. sterling per dozen, sometimes less.[159] So many pigeons were netted at Circleville, Ohio, in 1850 that they sold in Columbus at 5 to 6 cents per dozen.[160] When in danger of spoiling, pigeons sold in Cincinnati, Ohio, as low as 25 cents a dozen, but the usual price was 50 cents to $1.00.[161]

The prices received by trappers and shooters varied widely. The father of Etta A. Wilson received 5 to 10 cents a dozen for pigeons sold to the cooks of ships in northern Michigan.[162] At Traverse City, Michigan, on May 3, 1880, live pigeons sold at the net at 75 to 85 cents a dozen, or at $1.25 to $1.50 in crates on board the cars.[163] J. B. Oviatt, in Pennsylvania, received as low as 10 cents a dozen, the maximum, $2.65, being reached in 1882.[164] Some prices are given in Table 4.

TABLE 4

Market Prices of Passenger Pigeons by Year

PRICE PER DOZEN	DATE	DESCRIPTION	PLACE	REF.
$0.50	9 Sept. 1834	....	Boston, Mass.	1
0.75	7 Nov. 1853	....	Chicago, Ill.	2
0.50–1.50	1855	....	New York City	3
1.50	July 1858	....	Hartford, Conn.	4
0.25	1870's	....	Little Rock, Ark.	5
0.40–0.85	Spring, 1871	....	Milwaukee, Wis.	*
0.50–0.75	Sept. 1871	....	"	*
0.75–0.85	Spring, 1872	....	"	*
1.00	3 Sept. 1872	....	"	*
0.70–1.50	Spring, 1873	....	"	*
1.25	4 May 1874	....	"	*
0.60–0.75	Fall, 1874	....	"	*
0.65–1.25	Spring, 1875	....	"	*
1.25–1.50	March, 1875	Flight	Chicago, Ill.	6
1.25–1.50	March, 1875	Dressed	"	6
1.75–2.00	March, 1875	Feathered	"	6
1.75	March, 1875	Live	"	6
0.50–0.75	Fall, 1875	....	Milwaukee, Wis.	*
2.00–2.25	Oct., 1875	Live	Chicago, Ill.	6
1.00–1.25	Oct., 1875	Dressed & Feathered	"	6
0.35–1.25	Spring, 1876	....	Milwaukee, Wis.	*
2.50	30 Mar. 1876	....	New York City	7
1.50	6 Apr. 1876	....	"	7
0.60–0.75	Fall, 1876	....	Milwaukee, Wis.	*
0.60–0.75	Fall, 1877	....	"	*
0.40–0.90	Spring, 1878	....	"	*
1.75	10 Apr. 1880	Live	Chicago, Ill.	8
1.50	10 Apr. 1880	Dead	"	8
1.50	17 Apr. 1880	Live	"	8
1.25	17 Apr. 1880	Dead	"	8
0.60–1.00	Fall, 1881	....	Milwaukee, Wis.	*
0.75–1.00	1 Mar. 1882	....	"	*
1.25	6 Apr. 1882	....	"	*
0.60–1.00	1 May 1882	....	"	*
1.00	23 May 1882	....	"	*
1.00–1.25	24 May 1882	....	"	*
.80–1.00	24 May 1882	Squabs	"	*
0.50–0.65	27 May 1882	Squabs	"	*
1.00–1.25	2 June 1882	....	"	*
0.75–1.00	2 June 1882	Squabs	"	*
0.75–0.90	13 June 1882	....	"	*
0.50	22 June 1882	Squabs	"	*
0.40	26 June 1882	Squabs	"	*
0.90–1.00	Dec. 1882	....	"	*
2.50	11 Sept. 1884	....	New York City	9
3.50	11 Sept. 1884	Stall-fed	"	9

* All Milwaukee figures are taken from the Milwaukee *Sentinel*.

[1] Boston *Evening Transcript*, Sept. 9, 1834. [2] Chicago *Daily Journal*, Sept. 7, 1853. [3] Milwaukee *Wisconsin*, Nov. 28, 1855. [4] *Porter's Spirit of the Times*, IV (July 17, 1858), 318. [5] Paul R. Litzke, "Wild Pigeons," *Forest and Stream*, LIV (1900), 24. [6] Holmes and Sears in *Field and Stream*, III (Mar. 13, 1875), 61. [7] Editor in *Forest and Stream*, VI (1876), 122. [8] Editor, "Wild Pigeons," *Chicago Field*, XIII (1880), 152. [9] Editor, "Game in New York Markets," *Forest and Stream*, XXIII (1884), 125.

TRAPSHOOTING

There is uncertainty when the shooting of pigeons from traps began in the United States. It has been stated that it started in 1825 and that Cincinnati, Ohio, is recognized as the home of the organized sport, a club having been established in this city in 1831.[165] One writer has 1830 as the beginning of the shooting of wild pigeons in Cincinnati.[166] An account of a match held by the Cincinnati Independent Shooting Club in 1842 mentions that the club had been in existence about three years.[167] By the middle of the century, the avocation had attained wide popularity. Regarding a trapshoot in Chicago on June 9, 1849, the Chicago *Daily Journal* for June 12 of that year stated: "The birds were wild pigeons, caught the day before, and most of them flew very well."

A long poem on trapshooting appeared in 1831, a few lines of which will be ample.

> Of all the themes that writers ever chose
> To try their wits upon in verse or prose,
> A Pigeon-shooting match would surely be
> The last selected for sweet poesy.[168]

There was some difference of opinion on whether the passenger pigeon or domestic pigeon made the most difficult mark. Krider wrote: "The passenger pigeon ... has been frequently shot from traps in this country, and when not disabled by confinement, affords excellent sport. It flies very swiftly, and, in general, straight from the trap, and cannot be brought down unless covered immediately. They should, however, be used for this purpose as soon as possible after being netted, as they soon beat themselves to pieces in captivity."[169] Leffingwell thought that the passenger pigeon was easier to kill than the domestic one, in spite of its greater speed, since it flew in a straight line.[170] Since this bird was a strong flyer, it was necessary to shoot the passenger pigeon as soon as it was "up"; otherwise, though wounded fatally, it might fall out of bounds.[171]

Mutilation was sometimes practiced to induce sluggish birds to fly well. Levinge states: "They have a long wedge-shaped tail; and, if the

ends are cut off previously to putting them in a trap, they are so astonished at the moment they attempt to fly, that they go off quite as game
as the best blue rocks of 'Red House' celebrity." [172] When sluggish
birds had their toes clipped before being placed in the trap, they flew
like a rocket when released. [173]

The first trap used was of simple construction. It consisted of a
hickory pole, or other piece of flexible wood, about fourteen feet in
length. One end was fastened into the ground at an acute angle. A support about three feet high was provided for the pole and so placed that
about two-thirds of the length of the pole was available for furnishing
the power. To the free end of the pole was nailed a small box, with a
hinged lid, in which the pigeon was placed. When the pole was pulled
down and released, the lid of the box flew open and the pigeon was
catapulted into the air. [174] Regarding the pigeon's behavior when
released from a trap of this type, Dury wrote: "In this connection, I
have noticed that the wild pigeon, when thrown into the air, quickly
righted itself and made a bee line for the woods; but the domestic bird
... made for the nearest building." [175]

The pigeon was thrown into the air with such force by the spring-
trap that, before it could gain control of its wings, it offered a no more
difficult mark than an inanimate object. About 1850, when trapshooting
was in vogue, other types of traps were devised to give the bird free
use of its wings at the moment of release. Krider states specifically
that the spring-trap was discarded as it gave the bird too little chance
to escape. [176] However, this trap continued in use for many years at
small, local matches.

The "H" and "T" designations for traps had no bearing on their
design. The referee flipped a coin; and if the head or tail came up, the
shooter took the H or T trap, accordingly. [177] The apparatus in use for
releasing the pigeon were generally known as ground- or plunge-traps.
The simplest type of ground-trap consisted of a small metal box, placed
on the ground, the lid of which was raised by a rope to permit the
pigeon to escape. [178] In another type, the box was pyramidal in shape,
the four triangular sides dropping flat on the ground when the trap was
sprung. [179] The Hawes' trap (Fig. 2) consisted of a semicylindrical box

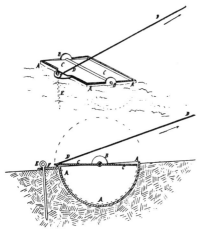

Fig. 2.—Hawes' pigeon trap or releaser.

Fig. 3.—Rosenthal's pigeon starter.

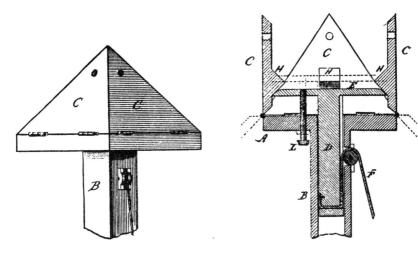

Fig. 4.—The Parker pigeon trap.

159

sunk into the ground and provided with a pivoted lid.[180] When the latter was turned by a rope, the enclosed pigeon was literally scooped into the air. This trap did not meet with much favor. The pigeon could not avoid an excellent start and was liable to fly in any direction; hence too much skill was required from the marksman.

The plunge-traps were the most popular. As the name implies, the mechanism consisted essentially of a "plunger," or follower, surmounted by a plate on which the pigeon rested. The housing was a pyramid with the sides hinged at the bottom (as shown in Fig. 4). When a rope was pulled, the pigeon was forced upwards and released by the collapsing of the sides of the housing. There were several modifications of the plunge-trap.[181] The Parker trap made by Parker Brothers, Meriden, Connecticut, was in great favor. A pair cost $25.00. [182]

A pigeon, due to weakness or bewilderment, would frequently refuse to fly when the trap was sprung. Often it would run along the ground a considerable distance before flying. The refusal of a bird to fly created an intolerable situation, as it "tends to make the sportsman nervous, and frequently causes him to lose his shot," according to the description of the Rosenthal patent.[183] To correct this grievous lack of co-operation, "pigeon-starters" were invented.[184] The most ingenious was the mechanical cat of Rosenthal. The crouched animal was placed with its head towards the pigeon. If the latter refused to fly when the trap was sprung, a pull on a rope caused the cat to spring erect (Fig. 3).

The rules governing trapshooting underwent constant change and varied with the different clubs.[185] During the last years of shooting live birds, five traps were used. The distance from the marksman on the dead line, to the traps varied from 25 to 30 yards, depending on the gauge of the gun. Any bird falling outside of a circle having a radius of 50 yards, the shooter being the center, could not be counted. Some of the rules were:

Birds Refusing to Fly.—When a bird refuses to fly, such artificial means as have been provided by the management may be used to start it, by direction of the referee. A bird hit with a missile shall be declared "No Bird."

Birds Killed on the Ground.—A bird killed on the ground with the first barrel is "No Bird." But it may be killed on the ground with the second barrel if the first is fired while the bird is on the wing. If a bird is shot at on the ground with the first barrel, and the shooter uses the second barrel, but fails to kill, it is "Lost bird." But if the bird is killed, it shall be "No Bird."

Mutilating Birds.—No mutilation of birds will be allowed, and if it is proved to the referee that any contestant has wilfully mutilated a bird, or is a party thereto, the referee shall declare all his rights in the match forfeited.[186]

The inhuman manner in which many of the matches were held is described by Arthur W. Du Bray:

The greatest backset trap shooting has ever had was when "find, trap, and handle" matches came into vogue. The brutality of many of these contests was simply horrible; the most barbarous methods were used to accomplish certain damnable results, and no wonder that when fiends calling themselves men, sportsmen forsooth, disgraced humanity by torturing harmless birds in order to win a few paltry dollars or acquire a degree of fame (?), no wonder, I say, that the rest of mankind tabooed pigeon shooting as a whole, making all suffer alike as a penalty for the trickery of cruel blacklegs bent on winning a stake or reputation regardless of the commonest laws of decency. These "find, trap, and handle" matches were in a great measure merely gambling schemes. . . .

Birds killed at the traps are invariably used as food, hence it is that they are well cared for, first to insure their being good, rapid flyers, and secondly, so that when dead they can readily be sold for the table. . . . It was, or has been, a cruel sport, but when properly carried on there is absolutely nothing of that character about it. On some grounds, I admit, birds are allowed to suffer; wing-broken birds or birds shot so they can fly off are permitted to limp around the traps or lie stretched on the ground, bleeding and crippled, writhing in their agony, but this is entirely due to want of management and can not in fairness be charged against the sport itself, such birds being actually detrimental to it, as they serve as decoys and materially interfere with the flight of all birds subsequently released. . . .

It is to be regretted that men still continue to import pigeons long distances, generally by rail, when they come packed too solidly in crates, and where their feathers must perforce become soiled and stuck together to such an extent they can not fly. Such shooting is entirely devoid of sport. . . .[187]

The condition of the pigeons used in many of the matches prevented a semblance of sportsmanship. The La Crosse *Democrat* for June 15 and 17, 1864, stated that of the 2,000 pigeons provided for a match at La Crosse, Wisconsin, all were young and some could not even fly. Concerning the young being held by H. D. Gardiner in Milwaukee, the Milwaukee *Wisconsin* for July 1, 1882, reported: "The loft contains about 3,000 wild birds, and the din and confusion made by them flying about, is terrific. Two boys are kept busy feeding them and they are sold to supply birds for matches. They are obtained by visiting the breeding places of the birds, where they are shaken out of the nest by jarring the trees." Squabs fed in pens could not possibly attain sufficient strength of wing to make strong flyers.

The methods of handling the captured pigeons often resulted in high losses and left many in a weakened condition. Thomas Stagg, of Chicago, converted a barn into a loft in which he kept as many as 5,000 birds. Concerning the supplying of birds for matches, Coale states: "When the pigeons were put into this huge cage they were so thirsty, that many drank themselves to death, or were killed in the mad scramble for water." He also states that in 1876 R. A. Tuttle "took 3500 Passenger Pigeons in crates to the annual live pigeon shoot in New York, which was run by Seth Greene. . . . When this shipment reached its destination, most of the birds had worn the skin and feathers off the top of their heads from contact with the crates."[188] Confinement in the foul shipping crates left many birds unable to fly after reaching New York.[189] Of 10,800 pigeons shipped from Milwaukee to Buffalo by boat, the La Crosse *Democrat* (Wis.) of June 1, 1871, reported that about 8,000 arrived in "good condition" at Utica, where a match was to be held.

Trapshooting was a popular, though expensive pastime. The cost of each pigeon to the contestant ran from 20 to 30 cents.[190] The cost of the birds in quantity varied with the time, locality, and type of match. Mershon wrote: "We used to buy them for trap shooting at about $70 per thousand, but after 1886, they were positively unknown."[191] Normally, the supplier received one to two dollars per dozen, depending on the supply and demand. Losses and shipping costs raised the cost considerably by the time the birds reached the shooting grounds.

The total number of pigeons used during the hundreds of matches held annually throughout the country was enormous in the aggregate. As early as 1862, according to the Milwaukee *Wisconsin* for June 17 of that year, a shipment of 1,500 pigeons was sent from Monroe, Wisconsin, to the Monroe County (N.Y.) Sportsmen's Club. After 1870, most of the pigeons used came from states west of the Alleghenies. There were many large dealers. Bond and Ellsworth, of Chicago, had facilities for keeping 12,000 birds, and Stagg advertised that he was holding 23,000 birds, in fine condition, in coops in Chicago.[192]

The New York State Sportsmen's Association was reported in the New York *World* of July 4, 1874, to have taken 40,000 to 45,000 pigeons, captured at Frankfort, Michigan, for the shoot of 1874. Henry Knapp supplied the state match at Geneseo, New York, with 10,000 birds brought from Michigan.[193] It is of interest that at this match only about half a dozen muzzle loaders were in use among the 150 contestants. According to one writer, 12,000 birds were supplied for the state match and 7,000 for another held at Syracuse; and it was estimated that 1,000,000 were netted annually.[194] A contract was let for 20,000 pigeons for the shoot at Syracuse, New York in 1877.[195] In 1881, Thomas contracted to supply the state match at Coney Island, New York, with 20,000 birds, and he expected to get a total of 40,000 from the Indian Territory.[196] The number of the pigeons to be used at Coney Island was also given as 25,000.[197]

As examples of the toll in the West, it may be mentioned that the St. Paul (Minnesota) Club shot 8,400 pigeons in the month of June, 1875, and that 10,000 were received for the state shoot at St. Paul in 1878.[198] Following mention of the 14,000 wild pigeons to be used at a match at Peoria, Illinois, and the potential extermination of the species, the suggestion was made that redwinged blackbirds be used in the traps.[199]

There are no reliable data on the number of pigeons used annually in trapshooting. Thomas states that about 500,000 wild birds were used and two or three times that number of domestic ones.[200] Martin claims that in no year did the demand exceed 500,000 and that he was in a position to know that the peak year was 1878, when 250,000 were used.[201]

Very few of the pigeons that were released from the traps escaped with their lives. Those that were missed by the contestants had to run the gauntlet of a crowd of men and boys with firearms stationed beyond the boundary.[202] It was estimated that of 62,868 birds shot at by contestants, 44,668 (72 per cent) were killed.[203] At a match in 1872 at Seneca Falls, New York, 4,310 birds were shot at and 2,780 (65 per cent) killed. Experts made some remarkable scores. Leffingwell mentions four men who shot at 5,161 birds and killed 4,763, an average of 92.3 per cent.[204] At a match held in Dexter Park, Chicago, May 15, 1869, Bogardus was to kill 500 pigeons in 645 minutes and load his own gun. The wager was $1,000. The feat was accomplished in 528 minutes.[205] In killing this number, he shot at 605 birds, therefore hitting 82.6 per cent of them.

Many matches were promoted by the large dealers in wild pigeons. The tournament held in St. Louis in 1876 was sponsored by E. T. Martin of Chicago, who also supplied the birds.[206] Martin personally killed 27,378 pigeons at trapshooting over a period of years.[207] A match held in Milwaukee in July, 1882, netted the promoters, W. P. Thomas and W. H. Cash, only $600. Of the 6,200 pigeons shipped, only 3,000 were used, according to the Milwaukee *Wisconsin* for June 24 and July 7, 1882.

The practice of shooting pigeons from traps aroused so great protest that by 1880 few would defend it. Knowles claimed that 90 per cent of the birds were domestic and that the sport was no more cruel than field shooting.[208] Nevertheless, most of the birds shot at tournaments up to this time were wild pigeons.[209] By 1887, very few live birds of any kind were used. The custom did not disappear completely until passenger pigeons were no longer obtainable. Hough mentions that in 1890 the Lake George Club obtained a crate of wild pigeons but did not shoot them at the traps.[210] As late as 1891 there was an inquiry from Dayton, Ohio, for 2,000 wild pigeons for a tournament.[211]

Public sentiment against the shooting of pigeons at traps was growing rapidly, but the history of all humane or social legislation shows that it is usually very slow in reaching fruition. The following protest, signed "Observer," in the Madison *State Journal* (Wis.) of June 24, 1875, is typical:

Large numbers of pigeons are closely confined for a length of time, until their powers of flight are almost gone, then the helpless birds are tossed, one by one, from a spring-trap, and as, dazed and startled, they flutter in their new liberty, a scientific butcher, standing near, brings them down with his fowling-piece. This is continued through the day and until night falls, and thousands of birds quiver and die on the bloody sod.

On June 30, 1875, the editor of the Madison *Democrat* published an equally typical reply to such a protest: "Although the [Madison] Common Council, at its last meeting, passed a resolution instructing the Mayor and Police officers to stop all further shooting within the city limits, we noticed on the ground yesterday four Aldermen, one acting as referee, one as scorer, the other two being around as spectators."

The most persistent and effective protagonist of the pigeon was Henry Bergh of New York City, founder and president of the American Society for the Prevention of Cruelty to Animals. After seven years of effort, he succeeded in having a bill passed by the Senate of the State of New York prohibiting the trapshooting of pigeons.[212] Section 1 of the bill read:

Any person who shall keep or use any live pigeon, fowl or other bird or animal for the purpose of a target, or to be shot at, either for amusement or as a test of skill in marksmanship, and any person who shall shoot at any pigeon, fowl, or other bird or animal, as aforesaid, or be a party to any such shooting of any pigeon, fowl, or other bird or animal; and any person who shall rent any building, shed, room, yard, field, or other premises, or shall suffer or permit the use of any building, shed, room, yard, field, or other premises for the purpose of shooting any pigeon, fowl, or other bird or animal as aforesaid, shall be guilty of a misdemeanor.[213]

Efforts to stop the trapshooting of pigeons became widespread. At a shoot in St. Louis in 1879, an ineffectual attempt was made to convict the famous shot, Captain Adam H. Bogardus, under a statute prohibiting the needless killing of any living creature, as reported in the New York *Tribune* of July 19, 1879. The act that fully aroused the public occurred on June 21, 1881, while the New York State Association for the Protection of Fish and Game was holding its tournament at Brighton Beach. Henry Bergh appeared with several small boys who distributed to the spectators a pamphlet, *So-called Sport and its Victims*. One of the paragraphs, quoted in the New York *Tribune* of June 22, 1881, read:

A practical marksman requiring only recreation, sallies forth in search of amusement. Suddenly he experiences a strange desire to kill—to destroy a hapless being and disfigure the scene which lies like a dream of Paradise before him. He is not alone; friends and admirers of his aim are with him; and among them—horribly out of place—fair women are also seen. An unresisting creature is in the trap, and the life which God gave for the support and profit of our race awaits its unrequited sacrifice. American citizens, abolish this cruel and unsportsmanlike pastime.

Bergh was supported by a vigorous editorial in the New York *Tribune* of June 24, 1881, and sketches of the scenes at a tournament were printed by Leslie.[214]

The acts of past generations must not be judged too harshly in the light of the present. Many estimable men considered the trapshooting of pigeons a clean sport. Carter relates that, in 1872, he and Ruthven Deane purchased 200 wild pigeons for a shoot that was held near Concord, Massachusetts. Among the fourteen contestants was William Brewster.[215] In 1888, Brewster was to travel to Michigan to determine if the passenger pigeon was in actual danger of extinction; and Deane was to become assiduous in collecting the last records for the species.

I t cannot be said that any particularly important method of taking pigeons originated in America. Centuries of poaching in Europe had virtually exhausted man's ingenuity. The burning of sulphur under the trees in which the pigeons roosted to suffocate them was first practiced in Louisiana; [1] however, it was an old custom in Europe to burn sulphur under the trees in which pheasants roosted, so that the idea was probably imported. Sulphur was used also in Kentucky.[2] It was employed in Tennessee as late as 1881.[3] William G. Hayes informed Sutton that pigeons roosting in the Pymatuning Swamp in Pennsylvania were killed with "gas fumes." [4]

The use of sulphur is described by Du Pratz:

In walking among the high forest trees, it is necessary to look at the base of the trees with the most limbs and observe if a large quantity of dung is to be seen; then having found such a place as I have described, note the manner by which it can be recognized and go there a little before dark. Before setting out provide yourself with fragments of coffee pots, or in default of them, take earthen vessels to the number of five or six; add about two ounces of powdered sulphur and do not forget to provide three or four sacks and a torch. Having arrived there, distribute the sulphur in the vessels and set them equally spaced around the base of the tree. Set fire to the sulphur in the order placed and withdraw to the side from which the wind comes for fear of being annoyed by the odor of sulphur. All being arranged, it will not be long until there is heard to fall a shower of wood pigeons. These are collected when they cease to fall, this being when the sulphur is exhausted. In order to gather them easily, and with greater success, it is necessary to have ready torches of dry canes or of straw, (according to the country), to produce sufficient light to be able to carry away all the game that has fallen under the tree. This hunting is easy. Women can take part with pleasure since there is neither fatigue nor danger of being wounded.[5]

The practice of burning sulphur was not extensive, since the method was not as effective as it might appear. The pigeons suffered little if they were roosting high or if there was any movement of the air.

An original villainy was the burning of the grass and leaves beneath the roost. Faux was told of the birds being knocked from their roost with long poles: "But the grand mode of taking them is by setting fire to the high dead grass, leaves, and shrubs underneath, in a wide blazing circle, fired at different parts, at the same time, so as soon to meet. Then down rush the pigeons in immense numbers, and indescribable confusion, to be roasted alive, and gathered up dead next day from heaps two feet deep." [6]

Grain soaked in alcohol was used as bait by one trapper. After eating it the pigeons fluttered, fell on their backs and sides, kicking and quivering. Pokagon helped catch about one hundred of them.[7]

The pigeons when roosting sufficiently low could at times be taken at night with the bare hands. Thomas Tanner was one of a number of persons to visit a roost in West Virginia in 1854. Each carried a meal bag for the game. He states:

So we got there about nine o'clock at night. On nearing the place it sounded like a windy rainstorm in the woods. They were so crowded on every branch of some two or three acres of trees, that here and there, every once in a while, a branch would break, bringing to the ground most of its load of birds. These joined those yet searching for an alighting place and filled the air about our heads.... All one had to do was to reach out and grab them on the fly and stick them in the bag.[8]

Pigeons when in flight were taken by various methods. If the large flocks flew low, considerable execution was done by throwing stones or sticks. The pigeons leaving a roost in the morning in Oklahoma flew low over the ridges where the Cherokee Indian boys assailed them with clubs. The nearest pigeons, attempting to turn aside, caused a blockade as a result of the swiftness of those following. Clubs thrown into the struggling mass brought down hundreds.[9] Where the birds rose to skim the brow of a hill, a pole could be swung with deadly effect. Edwin Haskell wrote: "All the young pigeons seemed to leave their nests about the same time. At first their flight was quite near the ground. People would take advantage of this, and station themselves on the brow of the hill, with long flexible poles, and whip into the low-flying flocks, killing in this manner many birds." [10] The adult birds were killed with almost equal ease when conditions were favorable. The direction in which the pole was swung was of importance. [11] When the pole was swung haphazardly, the flocks parted and suffered little damage. Swinging in the direction from which the flight was coming reduced the visibility of the pole so that many more could be killed.

An improved "pigeon-killer," used at Racine, Wisconsin, is described by Stone: "They planted a long hickory pole in the ground and attached cords to it extending in opposite directions. At this point the birds generally flew low, and as they passed over the bluff the boys would vibrate the pole rapidly by pulling the cords alternately, the top of the pole knocking hundreds of them to the earth." [12] A pole of this type was sometimes operated by a single person who, standing at one side could, with his hands, make it to swing rapidly back and forth.

They were readily knocked from their roosts at night with poles. A family at Lynn, Massachusetts, was known to have killed in this manner more than 1,200 in one night. [13]

Young pigeons, when just able to fly, could be caught in large numbers near a nesting in pens made of slats. Brewster wrote: "A few dozen old Pigeons are confined in the pens as decoys, and a net is thrown over the mouth of the pen when a sufficient number of young birds have entered it. Mr. Stevens has known over four hundred dozen young Pigeons to be taken at once by this method." [14]

Fall-traps were used to capture pigeons on farms. The simplest type was a box made of slats, one edge of which was propped with a stick to which a string was attached. When the pigeons went beneath the box to get the bait, the prop was jerked away. May used a sap-trough. [15] At Fort Garry, Manitoba, Hind saw a trap made of a net 15 feet wide and 20 feet long stretched on a frame and held up in front by a pole eight feet in length. When the prop was released twenty or more pigeons might be caught. [16] A trap of this type could not close with sufficient speed to make a large catch. The figure-four trap, held in high esteem by boys, was much used. It was also in operation in Canada.[17] The pigeons in struggling to get the bait, struck the trigger, allowing the cover to fall. Large numbers were taken in quail traps.[18]

The trapping of pigeons in Pennsylvania in 1850 is described by Peter Yarnall as follows: "our traps are made of sticks, like partridge traps, and we take them alive.... James made a trap just 4 feet square and set it, in about two hours he went to it and found twenty-one pigeons in it, yesterday we caught one hundred and three altogether." [19]

An unusual capture was related to Cotton Mather by a friend: "I have catched no less than Two Hundred Dozens of Pigeons, in Less than two minutes of Time & all in one Trap.... Such a Number broke into my Barn, & bin—by shutting ye Door, I had y^m all at my Mercy." [20]

NETTING

The colonials were prompt in netting pigeons. Josselyn, following his voyages to New England in 1638 and 1663, wrote that the English took them in nets.[21] Nets are stated to have been used around Boston by 1700, and in Hampshire County, Massachusetts, prior to 1740.[22] Mather wrote on November 19, 1712, that it was incredible how many pigeons were taken in a net at one time; and Douglass mentions that they were taken alive in "nets or snares" (Fig. 15).[23]

Writing from New York, June 21, 1770, Ashton Blackburne informed Pennant that: "They catch vast quantities of them in clap-nets, with stale [stool] pigeons. I have seen them brought to this market by sacksfull." [24] The netting of pigeons became such common practice that every farmer was equipped to net them.[25] Among the items in the estate of John Mills of Needham, Massachusetts, appraised in 1763, were two pigeon nets.[26]

Pigeons were taken in New Brunswick in 1791 in nets like those used in Germany for taking fieldfares (*Turdus pilaris*). Campbell thought it probable that the net was introduced from the latter country.[27] A clap-net with two tension poles for taking fieldfares in Germany is described by Macpherson.[28]

It is uncertain when the French Canadians began to net pigeons. Charlevoix wrote from Montreal, April 22, 1721, that they had means for taking them alive.[29] The net (Fig. 5) used by the French at Quebec in the early part of the nineteenth century does not appear to have been in operation in the United States. Cockburn describes it as follows:

Fig. 5.—Pigeon net used in Quebec. From R. A. Cockburn, *Quebec and Its Environments* (1831).

The nets, which are very large, are placed at the end of an avenue of trees, (for it appears the pigeons choose an avenue to fly down). Opposite a large tree, upon erect poles two nets are suspended, one facing the avenue, the other the tree; another is placed over them, which is fixed at one end, and supported by two pullies and two perpendicular poles at the opposite; a man is hid in a small covered house under the tree, with a rope leading from the pullies in his hand—directly the pigeons fly against the perpendicular nets, he pulls the rope, when the top net immediately falls and encloses the whole flock; by this process vast numbers are taken.[30]

Upright nets were fairly effective where the terrain caused the pigeons to follow a certain route as in many places along the shores of the Great Lakes.[31] At Racine, Wisconsin, a seine 100 feet in length was suspended between two trees. The pigeons struck the seine with great force.

Some fell to the ground while others remained entangled in the meshes.[32]

Upright and tunnel nets attached to long poles were frequently used to catch the pigeons on their roosts at night. Their use in Iowa is described as follows:

I remember at one time seeing three large farm wagons, with side boards above the usual boxes, filled to their top with wild pigeons that had been netted the night before. These nets were of two kinds, and were made especially for this work; one funnel-shaped, with wings stretched out from either side, and the other a long and wide affair fastened at each end to a long pole. Two or three men at each of these poles held them aloft as far as possible, stretching the net to its full length. Torches were lit on the opposite side of the trees from that on which the net was held and sticks and clods thrown among the birds, and thus startled they flew into the darkness away from the lights. When the pressure against the net indicated that it was well filled the men in charge hurriedly carried the poles together, and they and the nets were thrown to the ground. Lights were then brought, the birds removed from their entanglement and killed.[33]

The use of upright nets at roosts was practiced at Madison, Wisconsin, and elsewhere. It was particularly effective in swamps where the pigeons were roosting in low trees and alders. According to the Warren *Trumbull County Democrat* of December 22, 1855, on the night of December 8, 1855, three men in a tamarack swamp in the township of Bloomfield, Trumbull County, Ohio, took 1,800 pigeons at one haul. In addition, 816 birds were killed by shooting.

The most pretentious trap encountered was that built by E. Osborn near a nesting in Wisconsin. A pen 100 feet long, 20 feet wide, and 4 to 5 feet high was baited for several days, as much as 40 bushels of corn being used at a time. Means were provided for springing three nets over the top whereby as many as 3,500 pigeons were caught at one time.[34]

A net thrown over a bed by spring-poles was in general use in the United States. There are many descriptions, but only a few of them are specific as to the construction and operation. The first step in netting was the preparation of the baited "bed," which was somewhat larger than the area of the net. The bed was of smooth bare earth. Generally it was spaded to bury the grass and leaves, then raked. Food was scattered over the bed for a few days prior to netting to get the pigeons accustomed to coming to it. Acorns, buckwheat, rye, corn, and wheat, which was particularly effective, were the chief baits used.[35] A trapper informed Thoreau that crushed acorns of the white oak formed the best bait.[36] The use of the seed of pigeon grass (*Setaria*) is mentioned by Inman.[37] In New England, for baiting in early fall before the corn was ripe, corn shaved from the ear with a knife was used.[38] According to J. B. Oviatt, corn could be used successfully in Pennsylvania while there was snow on the ground, but not when the ground was clear, since the pigeons preferred beechnuts and other natural foods.[39]

The pigeon beds used in Michigan were described to Brewster by S. S. Stevens as follows: "Two kinds of beds are used, the 'mud' bed and the 'dry' bed. The former is the most killing in Michigan, but, for some unknown reason, it will not attract birds in Wisconsin. It is made of mud, kept in a moist condition and saturated with a mixture of saltpetre and anise seed. . . . When they are feeding on beech mast, they often will not touch grain of any kind, and the mast must then be used for bait." [40]

Seeds having an aromatic odor have long been considered especially attractive to pigeons. The pigeon trappers had as many superstitions regarding lures as the beaver trappers had for "scent." Some trappers refused to divulge the composition of the lure.[41] Moore wrote: "The Cummin Seed, which has a strong Smell in which Pigeons delight, will keep your own Pigeons at home, and allure others that are straying about, and at a Loss where to fix upon a Habitation." [42] Seeds of coriander, anise, and caraway were used by netters of wood pigeons in Germany.[43] Cumin seed, or its oil, was considered best in New England; [44] however, anise, or its oil, was preferred by some. Most netters were content with a mixture of salt and grain. One netter used two teaspoonfuls each of salt and molasses to half a bucket of grain.

Pigeons were extremely fond of common salt and it was a more effective bait than grain. Trappers took advantage of this trait by placing their nets at salt springs, which were to be found in Michigan and New York especially. Lacking a natural salt "bed," they cleared a section of marshy ground of vegetation and scattered salt over it. Ingells added to the salty "muck" sugar, oil of "rodium," and oil of roses; and Roney mentions sulphur.[45] Alum on rare occasions was used in place of salt. Decoys were not necessary on salt beds.[46]

The value of salt in trapping may be gained from the information furnished by H. T. Phillips: "I knew of a man paying $300 for the privilege of netting on one salt spring near White River Michigan. It was a spring dug for oil, boarded up sixteen feet square. He cut it down a little and built a platform, and caught once or twice each week. He got 300 dozen at one haul in this house. He said they piled there three feet deep." [47]

Netting on a salted muck bed had a serious disadvantage aside from the impediment of the movement of the trapper by the deep mire. The captured birds became so soiled that they could not be marketed without plucking. If they were to be sold alive, it was necessary to keep them in a cage over running water until their plumage had been cleaned. The netting operation possessed nothing pleasing to the eye. Roney gives a vivid description:

On one side of the bed of a little creek was spread the net, a double one, covering an area when thrown, of about ten by twenty feet. Through its meshes were stretched the heads of the fluttering captives, vainly struggling to escape. In the midst of them stood a stalwart pigeoner up to his knees in the mire and bespattered with mud and blood from head to foot. Passing from bird to bird, with a blacksmith's pincers he gave the neck of each a cruel grip with his remorseless weapon, causing the blood to burst from the eyes and trickle down the beak of the helpless captive, which slowly fluttered its life away, its beautiful plumage besmeared with filth and its bed dyed with its crimson blood. When all were dead, the net was raised, many still clinging to its meshes with beak and claws in their death grip and were shaken off. They were then gathered, counted, deposited behind a log with many others and covered with bushes, and the death trap set for another harvest. [48]

An improvement over the muck bed was made by F. E. S. Around it was constructed a bait pen of notched logs 24 to 28 feet long and 4 feet high. The earth was then spaded, covered with a network of saplings, and sprinkled with salt mixed with sulphur and oil of anise. A holding pen of similar size was built adjoining it with a sliding door between. When the net was sprung over the walls of the bait pen, the trapper entered it through this door and drove the captured birds into the holding pen. By this procedure, the plumage of the pigeons was not soiled. [49]

A water hole, under the proper conditions, made an effective "bed" for netting. This was an excavation filled with water to which salt was sometimes added. Thomas saw 67 dozen caught at one cast of the net at a water bed.[50] On the Canadian River, Oklahoma, the water was too alkaline to draw the birds, but they were netted along the river banks where they alighted to get gravel. Baldwin placed his net at a water hole near Sparta, Wisconsin.[51]

The net, generally of a diamond-shaped mesh 2 inches in width, was frequently made by the trapper during the winter months. The dimensions were not standard. Roney gives a width of 6 feet and a length of 20 to 30 feet.[52] A single net with a width of 6 feet was too narrow to be efficient. A width as low as 3 feet as given by French is preposterously small.[53] Other dimensions given are: 12 by 18 feet, 15 by 30 feet, 28 by 36 feet, 20 by 40 feet.[54]

The complete outfit for netting was simple in construction and operation (Fig. 6). The power for throwing the nets was provided by two saplings, approximately 10 feet in height, of hickory or other strong, flexible wood. These were planted firmly in the ground about 100 feet

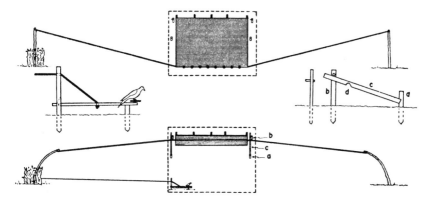

Fig. 6.—Net and stool used in capturing passenger pigeons.

from the front corners of the net. The net was spread over the bed and the back edge secured to the ground with small stakes. At each end, approximately 4 feet from the back, a foot-stake (a) was driven into the ground. Two trigger-stakes (b) were then placed at the rear corners of the net. These stakes had a notch in the side, or preferably a round peg with its lesser bearing surface, to hold the latch. The "latch," or "throw-stick," (c) having a groove (d) to hold the net-rope, was 4 to 5 feet in length. A long rope was tied near the middle to the front of the net. The free ends of the rope were approximately 100 feet in length and were tied to the tops of the spring-poles. The tension on the rope was insufficient to raise the front edge of the net from the ground. This edge was provided with small lead weights to retard escape of the pigeons when the net was sprung.

Two men were required to set the net. Each man, carrying a latch, took his station at a front corner of the net, pushing back the rope to the rear of the bed. The end of the latch was butted against the foot-stake (a), the rope slipped into the groove (d) in the latch, then the free end of the latch was pressed down and under the peg of the trigger-stake (b). Knots in the rope, or tightly wound cord to form a button, rested against the side of the groove in the latch, to insure release of both latches simultaneously when the net was sprung. The net was folded compactly at the rear of the bed to render it as inconspicuous as possible and concealed with cut grass, weeds, or powdered earth.[55]

The net described was that in general use, but there were many variations in the mechanism for springing it. John H. Chatham used for latches sections of broom handle two and one-half feet in length, notched in the ends to receive the rope. In setting the net, the end of the latch was placed against the foot-stake, the rope placed in the groove and pressed down at an angle that would hold it stationary. If this proved impossible, sufficient stones were placed on the latch to hold it down. The trigger-stake was not used.[56]

Small nets usually had but one spring-pole. The opposite end of the rope was fastened to a stake driven into the ground. In some cases only one latch was used. There was a stake at the corner opposite the latch over which, in setting the net, the rope was pushed just far enough to hold it in place. The rope rose over this stake when the latch was released.

The use of double nets was particularly effective in capturing large numbers of pigeons. When a net was sprung, the birds attempted to fly away from it. Escape was rendered difficult by using two nets which were sprung simultaneously towards each other. There was slight overlapping.[57]

The apparatus described by Mitchell consists of two saplings bent down to engage at their ends two notches in stakes inserted at the rear corners of the net. Two heavy iron rings attached to the front corners of the net were slipped over the free ends of the spring-poles. When the latter were released and attained an upright position, the rings slipped rapidly to the ground.[58] It is doubtful if this net could close with the speed of the typical clap-net.

A hut, or "bough house," about 10 feet in diameter was constructed around one of the spring-poles. It was made by placing upright in the ground small conifers or their branches, or branches of the white oak, the leaves of which are retained until spring. In some cases the house was constructed between one of the spring-poles and the net, with the rope running through it within easy reach. Within the house were stored the grain for bait, and barrels and crates for the captured birds.

Important to netting was the stool pigeon. This was a passenger pigeon "blinded" to prevent it from trying to leave the stool. The operation was performed by thrusting a needle through the edge of the lower eyelid from the inside, bringing a thread over the top of the head and through the lower lid on the opposite side. Sufficient tension was applied to draw the lids over the eyes. The ends of the thread were tied on top of the head.

The blinding of stool pigeons is an ancient custom. Tristram states that for taking wood pigeons the Arabs of Mount Gilead used as decoys wild birds, the eyelids of which were sewn together, and tied them to a perch.[59] Flow of blood or soreness did not follow when the operation was properly performed.[60] The hole became permanent after the needle had been used a few times. The thread used to "blind" the decoys was usually not removed from the eyes during the trapping season to prevent irritation by blinding anew each day.[61]

Captured birds used for decoys were kept through the winter in pens sufficiently large that they could fly a little, but not so large that they remained wild. Some birds became so tame that it was not necessary to blind them.[62] Others remained wild and flapped so much that they could not be used. Males were preferable to females, being larger and more brightly colored. About one-fourth of the birds used were females. Only one bird in a dozen made a good stool pigeon.[63]

The birds were fed by hand. The great care given the stool pigeons is described by Thompson:

I spent a few evenings watching the care of the birds used in netting. At night all the birds were fed, watered and exercised. A Pigeoner would take a bird from the box or basket, the birds eyes sewed up, place it upon his knee and with one hand over the bird's shoulders press the beak with thumb and forefinger until its mouth opened, with fingers of the other hand put kernels of corn in its mouth until the crop was filled; then the beak is pushed into a small cup of water and in less time than it takes to write this the feeding and watering is over. About the second feeding the bird is ready to do its part fully. Next the boots are put on, buckskin strings made into slip knots over the feet, and the bird transferred to the forefinger, the strings drawn taut through the hand and the exercise begins. The hand is raised slowly and dropped quickly. As the bird drops the wings are outstretched, quickly recovering as the hand stops, and this is repeated a number of times. Every motion is carefully watched and the action of the bird soon determines whether or not it will do for netting purposes. The least wrong motion or misplacing of a wing or feather on recovery condemns the bird as a Stooler. A coming flock of birds seem to be eagle-eyed as to the stool-bird, paying little or no attention to Bedders and Flyers.[64]

The training of a young pigeon for the stool is described by John H. Chatham. The bird, after being fed, was placed on the trapper's hand, his thumb holding the toes, then moved up and down to cause it to flutter. It had to learn to fold its wings without allowing them to droop.[65]

The stool pigeon generally cost $5 to $10. According to Roney, a good stool pigeon, one that would stay upon the stool, was worth $5 to $25.[66] Lincoln states that some birds would fall off the stool.[67] The stool pigeon was always so securely tied to the stool that it could not fall off, but might lose its balance.

There were two types of "stools" in use. In one a broom handle was inserted in a hole in a stake about two and one-half feet in length and pinned in the middle so that the handle could work up and down. Fastened to one end of the handle was an upright piece of wood to which was attached a cord that ran back to the bough house. On the opposite end of the handle was a circular, padded platform, four inches in diameter, supported by a small stick driven into the ground. The stool customarily used (Fig. 17) had the cord attached to the handle near the platform and run through a hole in the top of the stake. The stool was held in position by driving the stake into the ground. The pigeon was attached firmly to the stool with "boots," which were made of material that would not abrade the feet. The boots were made by cutting slits in the ends of buckskin thongs through which the opposite ends were inserted to form loops. The feet of the bird were placed through the loops, which were drawn tight. The ends of the boots were then tied to staples at the side of the stool. Boots were also made with woolen yarn. The operator, by pulling the cord, raised the stool three to four feet, then allowed it to drop quickly. The pigeon, sensing falling, began to flutter. The illusion that the stool pigeon was alighting to feed drew the attention of a passing flock.

Additional decoys were generally used. One to six "flyers," or "flutterers," were employed frequently. These were generally made "blind" also.[68] A long cord attached to the pigeon's leg ran to the bough house. This cord was usually 50 to 60 feet in length; however, Purdy states 200 feet.[69] When released, the flyer ascended the length of the string, then dropped to the ground. One writer claims that they flew about until exhausted, then struck the ground with a thud.[70] In many cases the flyers were pulled down and not allowed to drop. Sometimes the flyer was placed on the ground near the bed and held there by laying a stone on the cord. At the right moment the cord was pulled from beneath the stone and the flyer released.

The use of a "hoverer" in Maine is mentioned by Sibley. A pigeon was tied to a stake in the middle of the bed by a string sufficiently long to give freedom of movement. Desiring to join a passing flock, it would flutter and call. He adds: "Although there was no bait, they would thus be decoyed. As they would not alight unless there was bait, the catcher was ready to spring the net upon the flock the moment it struck down where the hoverer was." [71] The only decoy used by Conyngham in Jefferson County, Wisconsin, was a wild captured pigeon used as a "hoverer." A crotched stick was driven into the middle of the baited bed. A fishline, tied to the pigeon, ran to the bough house through the opening formed by the crotch. When a flock was sighted, a few jerks and slackening of the line sent the pigeon into the air. The bird when drawn gradually downward resembled exactly a pigeon alighting on the bed.[72]

Dead pigeons were customarily propped up on the bed to simulate feeding; however, dead birds placed on the bed with their backs upward were just as effective.[73] Stuffed birds were also used.[74]

The passenger pigeon, before dropping to the ground to feed, preferred to survey the area from trees. The nets, accordingly, were usually placed near trees, preferably dead ones (Fig. 16). In default of these, small trees were placed in the ground, or use was made of poles resting on crotched posts, called "stands." On September 12, 1851, Thoreau wrote: "Saw a pigeon-place on George Heywood's cleared lot,—the six dead trees set up for the pigeons to alight on, and the brush house close by to conceal the man. I was rather startled to find such a thing going on now in Concord. The pigeons on the trees looked like fabulous birds with their long tails and pointed breasts. I could hardly believe they were alive and not some wooden birds used for decoys, they sat so still; and even when they moved their necks, I thought it was the effect of art." [75] When the flocks were small or not hungry they were slow in dropping to the ground. Sibley mentions that they might sit an hour.[76] One pigeon would descend, then two or three more, and soon the entire flock. When the net was sprung, the pigeons instinctively flew towards the trees or stands, so the net was placed to spring in the opposite direction for better interception.

Netting was never very successful close to a nesting, as it was a habit of the pigeons to fly several miles from the colony before stopping to feed. J. B. Oviatt considered ten miles the optimum distance from the nesting for netting.[77] One writer states: "In the immediate vicinity of a nesting the nets may be set at any time of the day, but the catch at each cast is apt to be small, rarely exceeding six or eight dozen. Some of the most successful catches this year have not been within five miles of the nesting." [78]

The time of day had a big influence on the size of the catches. The largest numbers were taken at daybreak when the males ("toms") came out to feed, the middle of the forenoon when the females ("hens") left the nesting, and the middle of the afternoon when the males fed a second time. The result was that, depending on the time of day, the netter would get all males or all females.

The maximum distance at which a flock could be attracted by the decoys was one-half of a mile.[79] A flock might pass this distance beyond the bed before turning back.[80] Usually the flock was within 25 to 30 rods before the flyers were released.[81]

The pigeons on a bed became frightened with extreme ease. The snapping of a twig in the bough house, the arrival of other pigeons or a hawk would cause them to leave the bed with explosive violence.[82] The beds were cleaned after each catch. Every feather had to be removed or the pigeons would not alight.[83] S. S. Stevens warned against shedding blood, as its presence alarmed the birds greatly.[84] If necessary, the bed was raked and rebaited.

All being in readiness, the trappers watch for the pigeons. When a flock is seen approaching, the flyers are tossed into air. They rise to the length of the string, sail about in circles, then drop to the ground. The stool is raised and dropped quickly. The stool pigeon, sensing falling, begins to flutter. The repeated raising and lowering soon draws the attention of the passing flock. As soon as the birds are about to touch the bed, the net is sprung, and the slaughter commences.

Pigeons, arrested in flight and alighting directly on the bed, would whirl about and descend in the shape of a funnel. The netting operation is described as follows:

Presently, a scattered flock of some two or three hundred appears. We both sally out, and when we think [it] near enough, toss our flyers into the air. They go up the length of their lines, fifty or sixty feet, and find they are anchored, and return to the ground, wherever their blinded lot may light them. Then we rush in and "play the stool"—pulling on the cord and lifting it from the ground where it rests on a small pod of grass.

We lift it about three feet and let it drop instantly. In this operation, the stool flutters on its way downward, imitating pigeons feeding on the ground, when other flocks are passing. Soon we see the flock beginning to sail, they whirl, sail over the bed, turn and sail for alighting. We never wait a second. As soon as we think we have a fair amount of them alighting and about to alight, we surge on the spring pole and spring the net, rush out and hold down the sides, to keep them in, for with their united effort, they carry the net off the ground, and the ones near the sides escape....

The trappers now went in on top of the nets, walked over them, and stooping down, placed their thumb on top of the pigeon's head, their finger under the bill, and pressed the skull down till it crushed, and the bird's life went out. After all the birds had been treated, the nets were reset, the dead pigeons carried into the bough house, in bags, and another "lookout" kept.[85]

When trees were available near the bed, the pigeons first alighted in them, then dropped to the ground. The behavior of the birds in this case was as follows:

On the occasion I speak of we arrived at the bower just before daybreak. The birds were well baited, and I expected to see a fine catch, as no net had as yet been sprung over that bed. With the first streaks of light we could hear the flutter of wings as they lit in the trees about the bed. As the light increased they came faster and thicker, until soon the trees were alive with them, and the woods were filled with their calls. Soon a single pigeon dropped upon the bed, and had hardly folded its wings before others began to pour from the trees in a stream. When they seemed to be standing on each other's backs and you could see nothing but pointed tails sticking up, and while they were still flying thickly down on the bed, we both jerked the line with all our might. There was a loud swish as the net sprang over, and the lead line knocking feathers from those still in the air and in the way of the net. We rushed from our cover, and while I stood in astonishment at the boiling mass under the meshes, the netter proceeded to fasten down the corners of the net and remove the birds to coops.[86]

There follows a graphic description of netting:

Just then the first flock of about a dozen stragglers went through the valley to our right. I am told to keep down in the left corner under cover of the side and look out behind and see if the birds notice the flyers. The netter now buttons his coat, and taking a flyer on his hand, strokes it so as to calm it, while his eye travels every foot of the valley behind us. Suddenly I hear "Hist!" and the sound of wings as the first flyer leaves his hand, and the second follows a moment later. I at once forget the birds and look at the two flyers. Right up to the end of their lines they go, strongly and well, then round in graceful circles until they light suddenly on the ground. Then I notice that he has taken hold of the stool line, and I can hear the hover of his bird, while the flock, having seen the flyers light, evidently desire company, for after circling once they set their wings and come broadside to the bed. He holds the stool up until they are about fifty feet from the bed, when he gives the lighting hover with the stool bird and releases the stool line. His eyes tell him when the bulk of the flock strike the bed, and as their wings close, a quick pull on the spring line and a tumble out through the back speedily follow.

I note a small bunch of birds making their way to the woods, but he is at the net, pincers in hand, and wherever a head shows through it they are applied and the neck is broken. Out of breath from nervousness he says, "Eight out of fourteen; pretty good!" A pat to the stool bird, a hurried setting of the net, and with flyers gathered in we are ready once more. A flock passes out of range, but no effort is made to halt them, as he says the flocks will follow their leaders and more will come to our point. I am interested now, and only anxious to throw a flyer or do something to help. He says, "Take it easy now and we won't be disappointed to-day. The birds you see dead and those you see flying are all toms, and the nesting is ready to commence a regular flight. We will need help before evening and won't tire a flyer for nothing." As he spoke he made a quick jump into the house and I lie flat on my face. I don't know that a large flock is directly upon us. No time to throw a flyer, so under his coat it goes, and the stool birds and the bedders which were increased by the ones just killed, were used for all they were worth. I could hear him breathing hard, when suddenly he sprung the net and yelled, "Now hustle, we have something worth going out for." [87]

The net was sprung as soon as some of the pigeons were touching the ground and others about to do so. The correct time to spring the net was a matter of fine judgment. When the birds were wary, a fraction of a second meant the difference between success and failure. Scherer wrote: "The net was sprung just as some of the incoming pigeons were touching the ground and others almost touching, for then the birds could not turn quickly enough to escape the net. If the pigeons were allowed to settle before the net was sprung, they might see it and fly quickly from under it. Mr. Oviatt said that it was quite a trick to spring the net at the right instant to get the most birds." [88]

The net having been sprung, the men rushed quickly from the bough house and held down the front side of the net, or placed stones upon it, to retain as many of the pigeons as possible. The density of the birds on a bed was sometimes so great as to be an embarrassment to the netter. Under normal conditions about one-third of them were too quick for the net and escaped.[89] When too many pigeons were covered, they raised the net and a large number recovered their liberty. Expressions such as "so thick they will stand on one another," "a foot deep," and "three feet deep" are encountered.[90] Regarding the nesting at Petoskey, Michigan, in 1876, Pokagon states: "I think I am correct in saying the birds piled one upon another at least two feet deep when the net was sprung, and it seemed to me that most of them escaped the trap, but on killing and counting, there were found to be over one hundred dozen, all nesting birds." [91] Often as many as 2,400 would alight on a bed. [92]

An extreme case of congestion is recorded in the New York *World* of July 4, 1874, for the nesting near Frankfort, Michigan: "The biggest catch of the year has been 800 birds, though it is of record that one trapper secured nearly 1,300 at one strike. This probably would have been exceeded by Mr. Fisher a few days ago when he struck into a flight so thick that the birds raised nets, stakes, and all, breaking the meshes and flying off by hundreds."

The heads of the birds projected through the net and they were killed in three principal ways. The commonest procedure was to crush the skull between the thumb and forefinger. It was difficult to continue this method without fatigue when many birds were handled. Some trappers broke the necks with a special pair of pliers, the tips of which did not meet when closed. Others crushed the skull between their teeth. Weld mentions that old women killed wood pigeons netted in the Pyrenees by biting their necks. [93] Not all of the pigeons were killed. Many were placed in crates to be fattened for the market or to be sold for trap-shooting.

The number of pigeons taken at a throw depended on the size of the net and the behavior of the birds. At times the net was not sprung unless there was a certain number of pigeons on the bed. The requirement varied from 120 to 600. [94]

There are many records of the number of pigeons taken at a single spring of the net. Usually there is no information on the size of the net, or whether it was single or double. Crèvecoeur never caught more than 168 at once. [95] The evening of September 8, 1834, a catch of 960 was made at Chelmsford, Massachusetts, according to the Boston *Evening Transcript* of the following day. De Voe mentions 648 as the largest number of which he had heard. [96] An average catch in Ohio was 240 birds, but sometimes 360 to 480 were taken with a net 15 feet by 30 feet. [97] Two men trapping at a nesting in Potter County, Pennsylvania, in 1861, averaged 100 birds for each spring of the net during the first day. Thereafter the catch decreased rapidly. [98] Single nets at the nesting in Benzie County, Michigan, in 1880, are stated to have taken in one haul as high as 360 to 600 birds, indicating that the average was considerably below these figures.[99] Often only 120 to 144 were taken, and a good "strike" was 480 to 600.[100]

Some very large single catches were made. Dr. Isaac Vorheis, Frankfort, Michigan, took 1,316 birds.[101] H. T. Phillips, using a net 28 feet by 36 feet, once saved 1,584 pigeons, but many escaped as they were too numerous on the bed. The taking of 1,200 was rather common.[102] The following catches were made with double nets: 1,320, 1,332, 1,528, 1,560, and 1,680.[103]

The daily catches varied greatly. On some days not a single pigeon would go to the beds. Roney gives 720 to 1,080 pigeons as a fair average, though at natural salt licks 3,600 to 4,800 were sometimes taken. One trapper averaged 2,400 daily over a period of ten days. The large catches at the salt licks were made with double nets.[104] Audubon knew a man in Pennsylvania who caught 6,000 in one day; and a day's catch of 5,076 is recorded for Perry County in the same state.[105] A catch of 360 to 480 per day was considered large, and one of 735 as exceptional.[106] The largest daily catch by Baldwin was 1,320.[107]

There are few data available on the number caught by a netter in one season. Luther Adams, Townsend, Massachusetts, in the fall of 1847, caught 5,028 pigeons, nearly all being taken in September; and 1,962 from May 1 to September 11, 1848.[108] Ingells and two companions caught between 50,000 and 60,000 at Petoskey, Michigan, in 1878.[109]

The majority of the netters operated only in the spring and then near a nesting. Fall trapping was done on a considerable scale in New England, but not elsewhere. One netter has stated: "In the fall, after they have got their winter plumage and are bound for the South, they are scarce [?] and shy, for they are well fed and the young are fully grown. . . . A few may be caught on bait, but it is only by the greatest care and skill aided by fortune." [110] S. S. Stevens informed Brewster that the young birds could be netted in autumn in the wheat stubble, but it was seldom attempted.[111]

It is evident that nearly every conceivable method of capturing pigeons was employed. The numbers taken by the use of clubs, the burning of sulphur, and traps were inconsiderable in comparison with netting. The worst feature of netting was that it was most successful near the nestings and resulted not only in the death of the breeding birds but the young as well. The annual toll by the hundreds of netters was fearful. A constant stimulus to the decimation during the latter half of the nineteenth century was the demand for live birds for shooting tournaments. Only the netters could provide them.

SHOOTING

The passenger pigeon was shot so easily that up to the middle of the nineteenth century it was not even considered a game bird.[112] Charlevoix wrote that it seemed to court death.[113] Wherever there was a naked branch on a tree, these birds chose to sit upon it in such a manner that an amateur could not fail to bring down at least half a dozen at one shot. The people of Philadelphia and New York shot them from balconies and housetops during the flights.[114]

The shooting of pigeons at Chambly, Quebec, in 1777, is described by Madam Riedesel:

As we were passing through a wood, I saw, all at once, something like a cloud rise up before our wagon. We were at first frightened, until we discovered that it was a flock of wild pigeons, which they call here *tourtes* (turtle doves), and which are found in such numbers that the Canadian lives on them for more than six weeks at a time. He goes to one of these pigeon hunts with a gun loaded with the smallest shot; and when he comes in sight of them he makes a noise. They fly up, and he fires into the midst of them, generally with considerable luck; for sometimes he wounds two or three hundred, which are afterwards beaten to death with sticks.[115]

This pigeon preferred to rest after eating, or when tired, on the dead branches of trees. Several hunters have told me that in their boyhood it was simple to shoot them. The hunter, having found a dead tree that the pigeons frequented, concealed himself nearby, and it was only a question of time until the birds appeared and alighted in rows on the branches. In Pennsylvania they showed a preference for pine trees, and Dillin always hunted for them among these trees.[116]

The hunter could get within range of a flock feeding in the woods by approaching behind a tree.[117] If one bird took alarm and arose, the entire flock was certain to follow. Little caution was necessary with the young birds feeding in grain stubble in autumn. The hunter crept up on the rear of the feeding flock and fired just as the rear rank rose to take its place in front.[118] The second barrel was fired as the flock arose. In Maine they could be secured in a similar manner while feeding in a buckwheat field. They settled on the rails of the enclosing fence so as to appear "like a chain of living birds." [119] By firing from the proper angle, a hunter could kill eight or ten at a shot. Decoys were sometimes placed on the rails.[120]

Much of the shooting for the market was done near the nestings. The procedure at the nesting near Shelby, Michigan, is described by "Tom Tramp":

Often these flights out [from the nesting] would continue without a break in the string of birds across a favored point, for an hour or two, and all one . . . had to do was to sit down in some small clearing and shoot until it became monotonous, as there would be no lack of birds. Shooters who put in the day, would secure twenty-five to thirty dozen to a gun. The shooting had to be done on the wing, though fine shots were presented in the woods where large lots of birds were feeding. By screening one's-self in the direction of the birds and waiting until they worked up to you with their never ceasing roar, as they fluttered one over the other in search of nuts, stepping out you would have a solid mass of birds to fire into as far as your shot would carry. As they thundered up from the ground, two or three dozen were several times killed at a double discharge; but this was mere slaughter of the innocents.[121]

Accounts of shooting pigeons at the nesting at Grand Haven, Michigan, in 1866, are contained in the diary of Franc B. Daniels, an enthusiastic sportsman who attended school in Grand Rapids and was seventeen years of age at the time. The diary is in the possession of Professor Farrington B. Daniels of the University of Wisconsin and through his courtesy the following extracts are quoted:

Grand Haven, May 12. Arose at 4.30 after a very poor night's sleep as we had a poor bed and were in a room with two other men who started off at 3.00. We did not get started until after five and then went off without our breakfast which as I expected made me sick. Reached the nest[ing] about seven, going to the old one first but found but very few there; so we went over to the new one which we reached at 9.00. Here we found pigeons to our heart's content, *thousands*, yes *millions* of them. Doc and I were *completely sick* of it by eleven. Always before supposed I could load & fire as long as anything showed itself but for once was beat. We went over to the wagon for a drink & some lunch which we had brought and did not begin again until one and then both our heads ached so that they seemed to crack when we fired.

They were much thicker than in the morning and we shot sixty or seventy in an hour when we had all our birds, about one hundred and sixty to carry half a mile, with all our traps.

. . . .

Grand Haven, May 18. Awoke and rose about five and immediately took our rods and fished out to the end of the pier.... Never before did I see so many pigeons, flock after flock swept over the village, fairly clouds of them, and continued all the time we were out. Came to breakfast at 7 and afterwards immediately went out back of the village and remained until noon. Had some good shooting at single birds mostly however, or twos or threes. Kill about fifty by noon. Fished again after dinner and Doc caught two beauties, the largest bass I think that I ever saw. As the pigeons again began to fly, came in about 3 and taking all our traps crossed the river and climbed the largest bank this way. It was the hardest tug I ever took and not a thing did we get to pay us. Followed the bank around to another about half a mile, descended from it & climbed another where we remained for some time without any shooting, when they began to come in earnest. Such a sight I never saw before nor expect to again. Thousands, yes millions swept through the valley before us, two or three feet from the ground & up the bank into our faces. As we could not shoot over us, (for they fell in the woods,) we did not get but about forty having to shoot them in the face. My gun got dirty awfully & myself as badly excited. If I had had a fish pole could have killed a hundred for they came within two feet of me.

His last shoot was on May 19. He and a companion went to the nesting three miles from the village and "back of the school house." The colony now had young but one egg was found in a nest and three eggs on the ground. Fifty birds were shot. They returned to Grand Rapids with 160 birds, obtained during the hunt of two days' duration.

In the Fond du Lac *Commonwealth* (Wis.) for May 20, 1871, there is a vivid description of shooting at the nesting at Kilbourn (Wisconsin Dells) in 1871:

The idea was to get an opportunity to rake the immense flocks of pigeons as they left the roost for the fields and feeding places throughout the State. The indescribable cooing roar produced by uncounted millions of pigeons, as arousing from their slumbers, they saluted each other and made up their foraging parties for the day, arose from every side, creating an almost bewildering effect on the senses, as it was echoed and re-echoed back by the mighty rocks and ledges of the Wisconsin [River] bank. As the first streakings of daylight began to break over the eastern horizon, small scouting parties of the monstrous army of birds to follow, every now and then darted like night spirits past our heads. Soon the skirmish line ... swept past in small and irregular bodies. Our guide now told us to get into position as quick as possible as the large flocks would follow in rapid succession. We quickly ranged ourselves along the crest of a hill overlooking a cleared valley through which the birds would fly on their outward passage. It was yet a long way from being light. ...

And now arose a roar, compared with which all previous noises ever heard, are but lullabys, and which caused more than one of the expectant and excited party to drop their guns, and seek shelter behind and beneath the nearest trees. The sound was condensed terror. Imagine a thousand threshing machines running under full headway, accompanied by as many steamboats groaning off steam, with an equal quota of R. R. trains passing through covered bridges—imagine these massed into a single flock, and you possibly have a faint conception of the terrific roar following the monstrous black cloud of pigeons as they passed in rapid flight in the grey light of morning, a few feet before our faces. So sudden and unexpected was the shock, that nearly the entire flock passed before a shot was fired. The unearthly roar continued, and as flock after flock, in almost endless line succeeded each other, nearly on a level with the muzzle of our guns, the contents of a score of double barrels was poured into their dense midst. Hundreds, yes thousands, dropped into the open fields below. Not infrequently a hunter would discharge his piece and load and fire the third and fourth time into the same flock. The slaughter was terrible beyond any description. Our guns became so hot by the rapid discharges, we were afraid to load them.* Then while waiting for them to cool, lying on the damp leaves, we used ... pistols, while others threw clubs, seldom if ever, failing to bring down some of the passing flock. Ere the sun was up, the flying host had ceased. It continued scarcely an hour in all. Below the scene was truly pitiable. Not less than 2,500 birds covered the ground. Many were only wounded, a wing broken or something of the kind. These were quickly caught and their necks broken.

A favorite spot for shooting pigeons in autumn was in the "glades" in the Allegheny Mountains. These are described by Hallock as open spaces in the vast forest covered with tall grass and alder bushes. They were to be found in an area fifteen to twenty miles wide and about fifty miles long. Immense numbers of pigeons visited the glades in autumn to feed on acorns and wild cherries.[122]

The best pigeon shooting in northern Minnesota in autumn was also in the "openings," particularly if swampy and surrounded by scrub oaks. The birds were shot from the tops of dead oaks.[123]

* A considerable number of breech-loaders were in use by 1871.

The trait of associating in large numbers permitted the killing of many pigeons at one shot. Mather mentions the killing at one discharge of 384 birds, a number so high that it is doubtful if a shoulder weapon was used.[124] They were so plentiful in 1662 on the St. Lawrence that 132 were killed at one discharge.[125] Sir William Johnson reported that he killed with one discharge of a blunderbuss 120 or 130 from stands on the salt marshes.[126] Other high kills are 144 and 124.[127]

The pigeons were commonly shot from "stands," "poles," "ladders," or "spars." Anburey wrote that the Canadians "go into the woods, and make ladders by the side of the tall pines, which the pigeons roost on, and when it is dark they creep softly under and fire up this ladder, killing them in great abundance." [128] An identical description is given by Lamb.[129]

The stands appear to have been used first along the salt marshes.[130] The craving of the pigeons for salt and their desire to perch before dropping to the ground to drink made the stands very effective.[131] They were equally useful inland. Their construction is given by De Voe:

A few days previous to their usual flight, a "bough-house" is made by placing cedar bushes in the ground, in a circle, large enough for one or two persons to go behind or out of sight. A "floor" is then prepared by levelling the ground about twenty feet square—say fifteen or twenty yards from the "bough-house"; then, on the left side of this "floor," four crotched sticks are driven into the ground. The two nearest the "bough-house" are placed quite close together, or about one foot apart, and the other two some fifteen feet further off, and some three or four feet apart, ranging a little higher than the first two, on a line from the "bough-house," when two poles, of about twenty feet length, are placed on those crotched sticks. The further end of the poles should set high enough, that when the pigeons alight they can be all seen from the "bough-house." [132]

The stands were placed one to two hundred yards from trees, since if any of the latter were near, the pigeons would alight on them. The floor or bed was baited and live decoys used as in netting. Leffingwell states: "The flocks after making two or three wide circles, would settle on the poles, and then the hunter quickly fired at them; experience had demonstrated that it would not do to wait too long before firing, but the shots must be made just after the first birds had settled on the poles, and while their companions were hovering over them." [133] The enfilading fire was very destructive with a ten-gauge gun with an ounce and three-quarters of shot. Sometimes thirty-six were killed with one barrel, and as high as seventy-one were killed with both barrels.

A single pole six inches in diameter and twenty feet long, from which the pigeons were swept by the discharge of an old musket, was in use in Massachusetts in 1832. A pigeon shooter, who had been following the profession for about forty-five years, attracted the pigeons by the use of "flutterers" and by "prating."[134] Flutterers were pigeons "blinded" with thread, placed on the tops of poles twelve feet high, and attached by strings about five feet long. Strings running from the bough house to the pigeons permitted setting them in motion at the proper time.

Prating, or imitating with the lips the call of the pigeon, was practiced more extensively in New England than elsewhere. It is clear from the above that it was in use prior to 1800. Thoreau recorded on March 29, 1853, that Dugan "saw two pigeons to-day. *Prated* for them; they came near and then flew away." On September 12, 1854, he called *prating* the sound made by the pigeons.[135] Fletcher Osgood described the art to F. H. Allen as follows: "Wild pigeon prating consisted of voice delivered through *tightly* approximated lips, with a buzz or vibration of those lips, in two somewhat prolonged, high-pitched monotones (a very brief interval of silence between the monotones, of course) followed by a somewhat more prolonged monotone on a decidedly higher pitch, this immediately followed by two scale-descending monotones, the descent approximately an octave or more, each descending monotone *briefly* uttered, no prolongation."[136]

Frequently poles were placed in the tops of trees. Cockburn states that at St. Ann, near Quebec, innumerable poles with crosspieces were fastened at a slant in the highest trees. When enfiladed, few of the pigeons escaped.[137] At New Haven, Connecticut, the poles were placed at an angle of about thirty degrees. The pigeons alighted on these poles in the early morning on their way to the salt marshes of Quinnipiac.[138]

The water of Crystal Lake, Benzie County, Michigan, was lowered in 1873. During the large nesting near Frankfort in 1874, a level ring of sand about one-half mile in width and twenty-five miles in circumference surrounded the lake. This was dotted thickly with the stands of hunters with their bough houses. Dozens of pigeons were secured at one discharge of a gun, according to the New York *World* of July 4, 1874.

Another method of killing the birds in quantity was to dig a long trench in which wheat or other grain was placed. The gunner fired along this trench from his bough house.[139]

The pigeons after alighting in a leafy tree were very difficult to see.[140] Thompson killed a dozen pigeons in one shot by firing at random into a maple tree where they had alighted, and where not a single bird was visible.[141] Vigne hunted pigeons on Mackinac Island, Michigan, the summer of 1831 and wrote: "I amused myself with shooting pigeons, which are to be found on the island in great numbers. I was quite surprised at the extraordinary facility and quickness of eye, with which my guide, half Indian and half Canadian, discovered them sitting in the thickest foliage; his sight seemed to me to be far keener than that of an English sportsman when looking for a hare." [142]

Shooting pigeons in flight was not so simple. The individual pigeon in timber made a very difficult mark due to its twisting and turning. A writer in the La Crosse *Democrat* (Wis.) of June 1, 1871, stated regarding the shooting at the nesting near Sparta, Wisconsin, in 1871: "In the woods the birds do not fly in flocks as generally supposed, but are scattered, and fly in and out more like mosquitoes, so that it is very hard, although there seems to be millions of pigeons around, to kill large numbers at one shot." Evidently the shooting was within the nesting.

The high speed and dense coat of feathers on the passenger pigeons rendered them very hard to kill when approaching head on.[143] The only certain method of killing them was to wait until the flock had passed. The flight shooting is described in French as follows:

The lowest stratum of birds was just above the orchard trees, and many young men, with shot-guns, fired into the passing flocks, as they came into range; but they obtained few birds in that manner. The speed of the flocks made of their feathers coats of mail, impervious to small shot. Their heads alone were vulnerable, in a flock coming towards the shooters. Those who shot into the rear of the birds that had passed them, killed many birds which were usually precipitated into the fields of the farms beyond, or into brush and briars, far away; so, many dead birds were never found, for they hid away in their death-struggles.[144]

The pigeons in Arkansas, in 1808, flew so close to Schultz in numberless flocks, that he could distinguish their eyes. The smallness of his bag was attributed to the failure of the shot to scatter at the close range.[145]

Expert shots under favorable circumstances could make enormous bags. C. W. Stark, shooting for the market in Wisconsin, averaged the almost incredible number of 1,200 pigeons daily over a period of one week in May, as reported in the Milwaukee *News* of June 9, 1867. His highest kill for one day was 1,458 birds. In May, 1851, according to the Rochester *Daily American* of May 24, two men at Rochester, New York, shot and brought home in one day 991 pigeons. About 200 other birds were picked up by boys. It is probable that these were young birds recently on the wing. Two good marksmen, in April, 1878, killed about 1,200 birds in ten days near Erie, Pennsylvania.[146] This gives an average of 60 birds per gun per day. Near Ottawa, Ontario, a gunner killed 3,500 pigeons between April 10 and July 15, about the year 1859, in their flight northward.[147]

The terrain in many localities along the large rivers and lakes caused the pigeons to take a fixed line of flight during the migrations. Taber states that at Red Wing, Minnesota, a Sioux chief took his father to a point on the Mississippi that was considered the best pigeon-pass in the West.[148] The father of Etta S. Wilson shot for the market in an exceptionally favorable locality in northern Michigan. Frequently 70 pigeons were killed at one discharge, and he seldom came to breakfast before he had knocked down 1,000 to 1,200 birds. The largest bags were made in early spring when the flocks moved in close formation.[149]

Shooting at the roosts was sheer murder. As many as 61 birds were killed by using both barrels; when a shot was fired, the birds arose en masse, then soon settled again.[150] Shooting at the roost in the Bloody Run Swamp, Licking County, Ohio, is described by Schaff:

We all went in together, but not more than a few rods, when the men began to shoot. The birds would rise in throngs with thundering noise, but would soon come back, for there were hunters apparently, all along the margins of the swamp, and firing was like that of a closely engaged skirmish line. When the pigeons returned they would light all over and around us, and no aim was necessary or possible, for that matter. We carried away two large three-bushel bags full by nine o'clock, and doubtless did not get one half of what we killed.[151]

Occasionally pigeons were shot by the whites with bow and arrow. Byrd recorded in his diary on May 22, 1711: "Mr. Mumford cut my young horse and then he and I went and shot wild pigeons with bows and arrows." [152]

Even a cannon was used sometimes. Taylor mentions that a garrison on Lake Ontario fired a charge of grapeshot into a flock and killed hundreds.[153] Cooper voiced his indignation when a small swivel loaded with duck shot was brought into play.[154]

Gunfire had various effects on the pigeons. Faux, while in Ohio in 1819, thought that they courted death since the discharge of a gun seemed to call them together rather than to frighten them away.[155] The birds, especially the young, would often return to the spot from which they had been driven by shooting or alight nearby.[156] Taylor was at Crown Point, New York, in September, 1768, when word was brought that a flock of pigeons, numbering 1,500 to 1,600, had settled nearby. Five guns brought down seventy-two birds. The pigeons alighted at a short distance and a second discharge brought down eighty-five.[157]

The young pigeons flew densely massed. A shot fired into the flock caused them to huddle more closely together than ever, as if safety lay in companionship. Wilson added: "I have seen a flock of hundreds of inexperienced birds fly up the hill top and meeting the barrage of guns, falter, hesitate, turn and pass the entire gamut of the line thus exposing themselves twice to the attack, and return whence they came. If twenty-five individuals survived the double onslaught they were lucky." [158]

Pigeons at Cleveland, Ohio, flew east and west at a low altitude over Doan Street. Shots fired into the flocks at times so confused the birds that they alighted in the low trees, on wagons, and even on the backs of hitched horses! [159]

Shooting into the migrating flocks usually caused but temporary scattering, the ranks closing immediately. Leffingwell has described their reaction to shooting during the spring migration along the Mississippi in Iowa:

At this time, the advancing flock seemed to rise out of the hilltops far ahead of us, and everyone, man and boy, quickly secreted himself behind the first bush or tree

Fig. 7.—Adult male passenger pigeon.

The passenger pigeon, with its small head and neck, long tail, and beautiful plumage, had an air of uncommon elegance. The length of the male was about 16½ inches, and color ranged from slaty blue on the head to grayish blue on the back. The throat, foreneck, and breast were vinaceous; a metallic iridescence of bronze, green, and purple tinged the hindneck. The massive breast muscles and long, pointed wings were commensurate with its speed, grace, and maneuverability in the air, for which it justly earned the title of "blue meteor." (Courtesy American Museum of Natural History, New York.)

Fig. 8.—NEST AND EGG OF PASSENGER PIGEON COLLECTED BY
DR. THOMAS S. ROBERTS IN 1874.

The nest, usually placed on a limb near the trunk of a tree, was 6 to 7 inches in diameter and not more than 2½ inches in height. The single white egg could usually be seen from the ground through the loose construction of twigs. When squabbing, the Indians punched the young from their nests with long poles, although frequently the nests were so near to the ground that a man could reach them with his hand. (Courtesy Museum of Natural History, University of Minnesota.)

Fig. 9.—YOUNG PASSENGER PIGEON.
(Courtesy American Museum of Natural History, New York.)

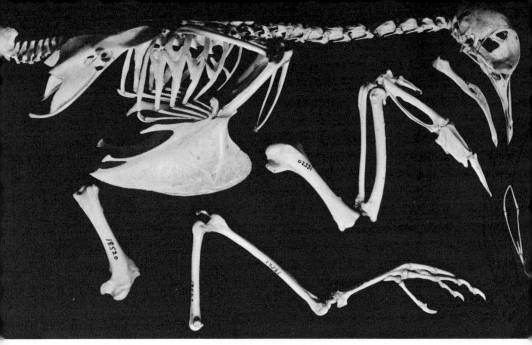

Fig. 10.—SKELETON OF THE PASSENGER PIGEON.

Only fourteen complete skeletons and one partial skeleton of the passenger pigeon are known to have been preserved. Photographs, the mounted specimens, and the fund of information on the habits of the passenger pigeon provide ample material for an evaluation of the many illustrations discussed in Chapter 16.

Fig. 11.—Granville's drawing of the passenger pigeon made about 1701.
Fig. 11 from Marc de Villiers, *Les Raretés des Indes. "Codex Canadensis"* (1930),
Plate 45, Fig. 1.

The primitive sketch of Charles Bécard de Granville, for example, is marred
by a distorted, forked tail. This drawing is accompanied by a French legend which
reads in translation: "*Oumimi* or *ourite*, or pigeon, we find in such huge quantities at the first migration in spring and autumn that the thing is scarcely
believable."

Fig. 12.—UNPUBLISHED DRAWING OF THE MALE PASSENGER PIGEON BY JOHN ABBOT.

Abbot's watercolor is preserved in the library of Harvard University. Abbot lived in Jacksonborough, Screven County, Georgia, from 1790 to 1810, when this drawing was made. (Courtesy Harvard University.)

Fig. 13.—PASSENGER PIGEON OF FRISCH. From Johann L. Frisch, *Vorstellung der Vögel in Teutschland*, Vol. I (*ca.* 1743), Tab. 142.

The Frisch drawing is of a juvenile.

Fig. 14.—Passenger pigeons of Studer. From Jacob H. Studer, *The Birds of North America* (1903).

The gregariousness of the passenger pigeon in the wild, its preference for crowded roosts and nesting conditions, is illustrated by the Studer drawing. From both pictures one may gain some idea of what Morris Schaff meant when he said "no bird ever had a bolder, more unflinching eye."

Fig. 15.—CATCHING PIGEONS. From Samuel G. Goodrich, *Recollections of a Lifetime* (1857), Vol. I.

No particularly important method of taking pigeons originated in America. Centuries of poaching in Europe had virtually exhausted man's ingenuity. Trappers concentrated on special formulas for baiting muck or dry beds, on nets used with the greatest possible dexterity, and on the training of stool pigeons. One trapper, at least, intoxicated his quarry by baiting beds with grain soaked in alcohol. Others devised larger or double nets by which a greater number of birds could be taken at a throw, the required number varying from 120 to 600 birds. Many trappers depended upon trained stool pigeons or decoys. Only one bird in a dozen made a good stool pigeon, and the price was $5 or $10, or might even be as high as $25 for a particularly effective bird.

Fig. 16.—Netting wild pigeons in New England. From *Leslie's Illustrated Newspaper*, Sept. 21, 1867.

The bough house of the hunters is located near dead trees, a favorite resting place. Before dropping to the ground to feed, the passenger pigeon preferred to survey the area from trees. When flocks were small or not hungry, they were slow in dropping to the ground and might sit an hour before the entire flock would finally descend.

Fig. 17.—STOOL, NET, AND BASKET FOR DECOYS.
(Courtesy Alexander Wetmore, Smithsonian Institution, Washington, D.C.)

Fig. 18.—SHOOTING WILD PIGEONS IN NORTHERN LOUISIANA. From Smith Bennett. "Winter Sports in Northern Louisiana: Shooting Wild Pigeons," *Illustrated Sporting and Dramatic News*, July 3, 1875.

Fig. 19.—Shooting wild pigeons in Iowa.
From *Leslie's Illustrated Newspaper*, Sept. 21, 1867.

Figures 18 and 19 give some idea of the density of flight and the variety of flight formations. Almost every shape imaginable has been assigned to the flocks, indicating that there was little uniformity. Although the density of the flocks varied, one observer estimated ten pigeons per square yard. It is understandable, then, how a professional hunter in Michigan frequently killed 70 pigeons at one shot, when the pigeons were in close formation in the spring, and seldom came to breakfast before he had knocked down 1,000 to 1,200 birds.

Fig. 19a.—Male passenger pigeon. (Courtesy National Cowboy Hall of Fame, Rockwell Foundation Collection, Oklahoma City.)

and awaited the congregated flock's approach; then, when near enough, the shooter would arise and pour from his destructive gun the leaden hail, while the frightened flock would break its solid ranks and sheer from the dangerous place; but of no avail, for there were hunters secreted all through the woods, and "bang!", "bang!" the guns roared out, until, within a few acres space, perhaps twenty different hunters fired into the flock, while the birds separated at each report, and quickly came together again, veering from the spot where the ascending smoke was, or at times turning completely around, and then advancing by another route.[160]

The passenger pigeon did not surrender its life easily. Regarding this trait "Snap Shot" wrote:

They are a peculiarly tenaceous bird, and notwithstanding their size, they cannot be shot successfully with a bullet finer than No. 6; even with that they will fly a hundred yards and alight in a tree apparently unharmed, from which they will afterwards fall dead, from the wounds, to the ground. Always after gathering my birds after a shot on the field, I would follow the course of the retreating flock, and under the nearest tree find from one to six additional birds; and it is quite surprising to observe what a diversity of wounds and hurts one will discover in dressing a quantity of them—the scars of previous assaults. Broken and disjointed legs; bills that have been shot half away, and grown curiously out again; missing toes, or even a whole leg, and even healed-up breast wounds I have seen.[161]

A good example of the hardiness of the pigeon is given by Kumlien: "I have seen pigeons with a considerable branch dangling beneath them. I have one specimen with a beech twig about nine inches long, that had entered the bird from beneath and pierced the femoral muscles, projecting about four inches on the back. It had undoubtedly fallen from the nest when a "squab" and been impaled on a twig. It was an old bird and as the stick was much worn, it must have been unpleasant in walking." [162] It is more probable that the bird, while in rapid flight, was pierced by striking the twig, as happens occasionally with the ruffed grouse.

The expenditure of ammunition in the aggregate was enormous. The usual size of shot used was No. 5 or 6.[163] No. 8 is also mentioned.[164] According to the Sparta *Herald* of May 23, 1882, J. H. Baldwin handled three tons of powder and sixteen tons of shot during the nesting at Sparta, Wisconsin, in 1871 and 75 kegs of powder and 360 sacks (9,000 pounds) of shot during that of 1882.

It has been stated by Manlove that the companions of a wounded pigeon would attempt to aid it. The speed of the bird and this aid would sometimes carry it several hundred yards after receiving a mortal wound. He adds: "It was pathetic to see the efforts of the comrades of a wounded pigeon to support him in his flight. One after another would dart under the stricken one as he began to sink, as if to buoy him with their wings. They would continue these efforts long after he had sunk below the general line of flight, and not until all hope was lost would they reluctantly leave him and rejoin the flock."[165] It was the habit of the passenger pigeon to follow closely every motion of the bird ahead of it. A wounded bird might be followed for a considerable distance before the follower realized that there was anything abnormal. Though the same solicitude is mentioned by Brandt,[166] there is probably an error in the interpretation.

The sportsman had two methods for "stringing" pigeons. A slender limb, at the bottom of which a shortened twig was left to preserve a crotch, was sharpened at the tip. The tip was thrust through the soft area in the lower mandible of the pigeon.[167] Stringing on the tail feathers was a custom of wide distribution.[168] The four longest tail feathers were pulled from the tail and knotted together at the tips. The quill ends were thrust through the lower mandibles of the dead birds, then tied together to form compact bunches.

A flight of pigeons was the occasion for a general holiday. Mrs. Grant wrote that at Albany, New York, "This migration, as it passed by, occasioned . . . a total relaxation from all employments, and a kind of drunken gaiety, though it was rather slaughter than sport."[169]

So little discrimination was shown by gunners that the first legal acts were for the protection of the inhabitants rather than the pigeons. In 1720, an ordinance was passed in Philadelphia imposing a fine of five shillings for the shooting of pigeons and other fowls from the streets, gardens, or orchards within the city.[170]

The problem in Quebec induced Dupuy, Intendant of Canada, to promulgate an ordinance against shooting. It is written in the customary legal style, without punctuation, under date of August 8, 1727.

On account of the complaints which we receive daily from many people who spend their days here in various parts of the city of Quebec and as much as they trust in the security which accords with being in a city closed and policed they have nevertheless received blows from shot which have reached them and others have gone into their yards and have wounded fowls and ducks which happens only because whenever there is a flight of pigeons and because of the eagerness to have them without taking the trouble of going out [of town] and going to those places where hunting is permitted every one takes the liberty of shooting thoughtlessly from his windows the threshold of his door the middle of the streets from their yards and gardens without thinking not only of the danger in which they place the passer-by the old people and the children who cannot take shelter sufficiently quickly from the danger to which they are exposed by indiscrete and clumsy people of whom the greater part know nothing about the handling of guns but more to the danger which they run for themselves in setting fire to their own homes and to other houses of the city as has happened several times from the wads of the firearms which have fallen all lighted upon the roofs of the houses the greater part of which are only shingled and upon the enclosures so dried out that they are susceptible to the least touch of fire as well as the accumulations and stores of fire-wood stacked the length of these enclosures considerations for which our predecessors and on the last occasion M. Begon drew his general ordinance of 21 May 1721 carrying prohibitions for all people from shooting in the city under a penalty of a fine of 50 livres and of confiscation of the guns in conformity with which we would cite our special ordinance of the 10th of May last on the subject of the discharge of a gun which was fired before the house of Jacques Parent Desbutes and of which a portion of the lead went through a window of the said house having reason to believe that in having that particular order posted and making it public in the same way as we have done it would be sufficient with the ordinance of M. Begon produced and published 21 May 1721 to stop and forestall any such disorder but we remark to the contrary that in scorn of the most wise precautions taken upon this subject by our predecessors this trouble has only increased to the point where the day laborers and apprentices manage to shoot every work-day dropping for it their wages and abandoning their work to the detriment of their masters and of the citizens who hire them *we now make* express prohibitions to the day laborers and apprentices against leaving their work on work-days to go shooting at all either within or without the city under penalty of a fine of fifty livres for those who are in a condition to pay and a fine of ten livres and fifteen days in prison for the others ...[171]

The hunters were rampant at Montreal also. Raudot by decree of June 22, 1710, forbade the hunting of pigeons on any field sown to peas or grain, the penalty for violation being ten livres.[172] An ordinance by the Intendant Hocquart of May 29, 1748, prohibited the hunting of pigeons on the lands of J. B. Hervieux at Point au Trembles, Isle of Montreal. The list of complaints includes damage to the grain, setting the woods on fire, and burning and breaking down the fences so that the domestic animals could enter the sown fields.[173]

The enforcing of ordinances against shooting within many incorporated communities was almost impossible up to the end of the nineteenth century. However, a spirit of intolerance was arising, for in 1853 the citizens of Madison, Wisconsin, objected to being shot in the back by quail hunters. A typical example of the holiday spirit during a flight of pigeons is given by Dunlop for York (Toronto), Canada:

Some two summers ago, a stream of them took it into their heads to fly over York; and for three or four days the town resounded with one continuous roll of firing, as if a skirmish were going on in the streets—every gun, pistol, musket, blunderbuss, and fire-arm of whatever description, was put in requisition. The constable and police magistrate were on the alert, and offenders without number were *pulled up*—among them were honourable members of the executive and legislative councils, crown lawyers, respectable, staid citizens, and last of all, the sheriff of the county; till at last it was found that pigeons, flying within easy shot, were a temptation too strong for human virtue to withstand;—and so the contest was given up, and a sporting jubilee proclaimed to all and sundry.[174]

In the final analysis, shooting was most destructive to the pigeons. The number of hunters exceeded greatly that of the trappers. Pigeons were the favorite game of the small boy; and any indifferent marksman could look forward to some success if stationed on a flight-way. When the birds were plentiful, no pains were taken to search for all of the dead and fatally wounded, so that it is improbable that more than one-half of them were recovered. During the last nestings, men traveled two hundred miles or more to get the shooting. In one case a special train for gunners was run from Chicago to a nesting in Michigan. Securing the birds was at times secondary to the sport of shooting. Two men killed about 150 pigeons at a roost at Deer Park, Maryland, and left them as there were no means of transportation.[175] The most deplorable feature was the shooting near or within a nesting. Time and again the birds were driven away before young were raised.

CHAPTER 9

DECREASE AND
EXTINCTION

N̲o other species of bird, to the best of our knowledge, ever approached the passenger pigeon in numbers. Champlain, in 1605, encountered them in "countless numbers," while Sagard-Theodat wrote
of an "infinite number." [1] Lahontan thought that all the doves on earth
had congregated in his locality.[2] To Strachey, they flew in "thickened
clowdes." [3] Wood wrote: "I have seene them fly as if the Ayerie regiment had beene Pigeons; seeing neyther beginning nor ending, length,
or breadth of these Millions of Millions." [4] Mather adds: "I affirm to
you then; That sometimes we have mighty Flocks of those *Pigeons*
flying over us; thousands in a Flock; ye best part of a mile square occupied by a Flock; These passing along, ye Welkin in a manner obscured & covered with y^m; & several Hours have run out, before y^e
appearance of these Birds thus making ye best of their way have been
over." [5]

Their numbers were beyond belief even after the decline was well
under way. Strickland wrote: "Persons unacquainted with the country
and the gregarious habits of this lovely bird, are apt to doubt the accounts they have heard or read respecting their numbers: since my
return to England I have repeatedly been questioned upon the subject.
In answer to these queries, I can only say that in some parts of the
province, early in the spring and directly after wheat-harvest, their
numbers are incredible." [6]

POPULATION FIGURES

It is an insuperable problem to determine the total population of
the passenger pigeon at any one time. This could only be done with

a fair degree of accuracy if we had a record of all the nestings in a given year, their size, and the number of nests per acre. No data of this kind are available. Estimates based on the number in a single flock, or in a flight lasting a day, are of little value since they could represent but a portion of the population. The vast food requirements of this species prohibited an assemblage of the entire population. The data available on shipments of pigeons are of little assistance since we do not know what percentage of the adults at a nesting were trapped or shot, or what percentage of the squabs were taken.

The first attempt to estimate the number of pigeons seen was made by Wilson. He wrote:

I had left the public road, to visit the remains of the breeding place near Shelby-ville, and was traversing the woods with my gun, in my way to Frankfort, when about one o'clock the Pigeons, which I had observed flying the greater part of the morning northerly, began to return in such immense numbers as I never before had witnessed. Coming to an opening by the side of a creek called the Benson, where I had a more uninterrupted view, I was astonished at their appearance. They were flying with great steadiness and rapidity, at a height beyond gunshot, in several strata deep, and so close together, that could shot have reached them, one discharge could not have failed of bringing down several individuals. From right to left as far as the eye could reach, the breadth of this vast procession extended; seeming everywhere equally crowded. Curious to determine how long this appearance would continue, I took out my watch to note the time, and sat down to observe them. It was then half past one. I sat for more than an hour, but instead of a diminu-tion of this prodigious procession, it seemed rather to increase both in numbers and rapidity; and, anxious to reach Frankfort before night, I rose and went on. About four o'clock in the afternoon I crossed the Kentucky river, at the town of Frankfort, at which time the living torrent above my head seemed as numerous and as exten-sive as ever. Long after this I observed them, in large bodies that continued to pass for six or eight minutes, and these again were followed by other detached bodies, all moving in the same south-east direction, till after six in the evening. . . .

To form a rough estimate of the daily consumption of one of these immense flocks, let us first attempt to calculate the numbers of that above mentioned, as seen passing between Frankfort and the Indiana territory. If we suppose this column to have been one mile in breadth (and I believe it to have been much more), and that it moved at the rate of one mile in a minute; four hours, the time it continued pass-ing, would make its whole length two hundred and forty miles. Again supposing that each square yard of this moving body comprehended three Pigeons, the square yards in the whole space, multiplied by three, would give two thousand two hundred and thirty millions, two hundred and seventy-two thousand pigeons! An almost inconceivable multitude, and yet probably far below the actual amount.[7]

Audubon made the following calculation:

It may not, perhaps, be out of place to attempt an estimate of the number of Pigeons contained in one of those mighty flocks.... The inquiry will tend to shew the astonishing bounty of the great Author of Nature in providing for the wants of his creatures. Let us take a column of one mile in breadth, which is far below the average size, and suppose it passing over us without interruption for three hours, at the rate mentioned above of one mile in the minute. This will give us a parallelgram of 180 miles by 1, covering 180 square miles. Allowing two pigeons to the square yard, we have One billion, one hundred and fifteen millions, one hundred and thirty-six thousand pigeons in one flock.[8]

An example of an unusual flight in the month of May at Fort Mississisaugua, Ontario, is given by Major King:

Early in the morning I was apprised by my servant that an extraordinary flock of birds was passing over, such as he had never seen before. Hurrying out and ascending the grassy ramparts, I was perfectly amazed to behold the air filled and the sun obscured by millions of pigeons, not hovering about, but darting onwards in a straight line with arrowy flight, in a vast mass a mile or more in breadth, and stretching before and behind as far as the eye could reach.

Swiftly and steadily the column passed over with a rushing sound, and for hours continued in undiminished myriads advancing over the American forests in the eastern horizon, as the myriads that had passed were lost in the western sky.

It was late in the afternoon before any decrease in the mass was perceptible, but they became gradually less dense as the day drew to a close. At sunset the detached flocks bringing up the rear began to settle in the forest on the Lake-road, and in such numbers as to break down branches from the trees.

The duration of this flight being about fourteen hours, viz., from four A.M. to six P.M., the column (allowing a probable velocity of sixty miles an hour, as assumed by Wilson), could not have been less than three hundred miles in length, with an average breadth, as before stated, of one mile.

During the following day and for several days afterwards, they still continued flying over in immense though greatly diminished numbers, broken up into flocks and keeping much lower, possibly being weaker or younger birds.[9]

It is of interest to calculate the number of pigeons seen by King.

Since the flight lasted for 14 hours during the first day and continued in diminished intensity for several days thereafter, it will be conservative to assume that the total flights at the original density would have continued for ten consecutive hours. At a speed of 60 miles per hour we would have a column of pigeons 600 miles in length by one mile in width, or 600 square miles. Since there were usually several strata of pigeons in the large flocks, it is equally conservative to allow two birds to the square yard. This gives a total of 3,717,120,000 pigeons. In order to obtain a figure that is comprehensible, it will be advantageous to calculate the number of pigeons per acre. All of these pigeons were coming from the United States. The land area roamed over by this species in the eastern United States was approximately 1,493,176 square miles. This includes, in the western part of its range, all of Texas, Oklahoma, Arkansas, Missouri, Iowa, and Minnesota. The inclusion of all of Texas and Oklahoma will compensate amply for the small areas in Kansas, Nebraska, North Dakota, South Dakota, and Montana where pigeons were occasionally found. This gives 955,632,640 acres, and a population density of approximately four pigeons per acre. It is inconceivable that at this period all of the pigeons in the United States were in the flights witnessed by King. With sufficient optimism the population could accordingly be estimated at five or six birds per acre.

Another example of the number of pigeons is furnished by Révoil:

One autumn morning of 1847, before day I was wandering along the heights which overhang the town of Hartford, in Kentucky, ... when all at once, on emerging from the wood, I observed that the horizon was darkling; and after having attentively examined what could have caused so sudden a change in the atmosphere, I discovered that the clouds—as I had supposed them to be—were neither more nor less than numerous flocks of pigeons. These birds flew out of range, ... so I conceived the idea of counting how many troops flew over my head in the course of an hour. Accordingly, I seated myself tranquilly; and drawing from my pocket pencil and paper, I began to take my notes. In a short time the flocks succeeded each other with so much rapidity that the only way I could count them was by tracing manifold strokes. In the space of thirty-five minutes, two hundred and twenty bands of pigeons had passed before my eyes. Soon the flocks touched each other, and were arrayed in so compact a manner that they hid from my sight the sun. The ordure of these birds covered the ground, falling thick and fast like winter's snow....

An arithmetician of the district made a sufficiently curious approximative calculation of the number of individuals composing these extraordinary legions, and of the enormous quantity of food necessary to their sustenance. Taking for example, a column about five hundred yards in breadth—which is much below the ordinary measurement—and allowing three hours for the birds composing it to accomplish their flight, as its swiftness was five hundred yards a minute, its length would be two hundred thousand yards. Supposing now, that each square yard was occupied by ten pigeons, we may conclude that their total number amounted to a billion, one hundred and twenty millions, one hundred and forty thousand.[10]

Either the arithmetician or the author became hopelessly entangled. If the birds flew at a speed of 500 yards per minute, then the speed per hour was only approximately 17 miles. At a speed of 500 yards per minute the flock would have covered a distance of only 30,000 yards in one hour, or 90,000 yards in three hours, in place of the 200,000 mentioned. Even if the flock had had a length of 200,000 yards and a width of 500 yards, the number of square yards would have been only 100,000,000. At 10 pigeons per square yard, the number of birds would have been 1,000,000,000 in place of the 1,120,140,000 given.

The Allen brothers lived in Wayne County, New York, until 1854. An opinion on the abundance of pigeons at this time follows:

It would be hard to make any estimate of their numbers that people would believe at this late day. I was going to say that a thousand million could have been seen in the air all at once. There would be days and days when the air was alive with them, hardly a break occurring in a flock for half a day at a time. Flocks stretched as far as a person could see, one tier above another. I think it would be safe to say that millions could have been seen at the same time.[11]

It was the opinion of Nuttall that the entire continental population of the passenger pigeon was always found together at one particular place.[12] This we know was not the case, particularly from the wide distribution of the nestings. A numerical estimate of a single flight is accordingly of little avail in determining the total population. Mershon mentions that on April 8, 1873, a continuous stream of pigeons passed over Saginaw, Michigan, from 7:30 A.M. to nearly 4:00 P.M.[13] Further data on this flight are wanting. The number of pigeons in migration in eastern Iowa, flying in regimental front, has been estimated by McGee as follows:

A rough estimate of the number of birds passing a given point in a spring may be useful. The cross-section of an average flock was, say, a hundred yards from front to rear, and fifty yards in height, and when the birds were so close as to cast a continuous shadow there must have been fully one pigeon per cubic yard of space, or 5000 to each linear yard of east-west extension—i.e. 8,800,000 to the mile, or (with reasonable allowance for the occasional thinning of the flock) say 30,000,000 for a flock extending from one woodland to the other. Since such flocks passed repeatedly during the greater part of the day of chief flight at intervals of a few minutes, the aggregate number of birds must have approached 120,000,000 an hour for, say five hours, or six hundred million pigeons virtually visible from a single point in the culminating part of a single typical migration.[14]

The examples given above of the data available show the impossibility of arriving at a satisfactory estimate of the original population of the passenger pigeon. As a guess, I would place this population at 3,000,000,000 at the time of the discovery of America, with a possibility of 5,000,000,000. Of all the pigeons, apparently only the flock pigeon (*Histriophaps histrionica*) of Australia ever even approached it in numbers. According to Carter, the flock pigeon once occurred in "countless myriads." [15]

The question immediately arises how the passenger pigeon attained such enormous numbers when it laid but one egg. Quite a few members of the pigeon family lay, or laid, but one egg. This is true of *Raphus cucullatus, Pezophaps solitaria, Didunculus strigirostris, Columba maculosa, C. gymnothalma, Goüra coronata* (*cristata*), *G. victoria, Ptilinopus ewingii, Histriophaps* and *Lophophaps leucogaster* (probably only one), *Ptilinopus regina regina, P. r. livingii, P. superbus* (usually one), *Megaloprepia magnifica magnifica, M. m. assimilis, Ducula* (*Myristicivora*) *spilorrhoa spilorrhoa, Lopholiamus antarcticus, Columba norfolciensis* (usually one), *Macropygia phasianella phasianella*.[16] Among the North American pigeons laying almost invariably a single egg are the band-tailed pigeon (*Columba fasciata*) and the red-billed pigeon (*Columba flavirostris*).[17]

It is commonly assumed that the passenger pigeon, and other pigeons laying one egg, nested more than once a season. Regarding so well known a bird as the band-tailed pigeon, Neff writes: "Observers have recorded successive broods from the same nest, without proof, however, that the same adults were concerned. The long nesting period alone has led some observers to believe that at least in the South some bandtails may rear two or possibly three broods. In the northern part of the bird's range it seems that normally only one brood is produced." [18] There is also a marked similarity in the wide range of foods consumed by the passenger pigeon and the band-tailed pigeon, and it is significant that the presence or absence of both species in a region was dependent on the state of the mast.

It is not necessary to conclude that the passenger pigeon must have laid more than one egg a year in order to attain a large population. There are several examples to the contrary among the Alcidae. The great auk (*Plautus impennis*) apparently laid but one egg a year, yet it occurred in "immense numbers" in the North American waters.[19] Other examples are the puffins (*Lunda* and *Fratercula*), auklets (*Cerorhinca, Ptychoramphus, Phaleris,* and *Aethia*), murres (*Uria*), razor-billed auk (*Alca torda*), and dovekie (*Alle alle*). It seems to be a general rule among birds that the lower the mortality of the adults and young, the fewer are the eggs laid.

We are totally in the dark as to the approximate number of birds that bred in the United States under primitive conditions. In view of drainage and the great acreage devoted to corn and other grains that support a low breeding population, it is probable that the original population was considerably higher than at present. Peterson believes that the present population of all breeding birds in the United States is around 6,000,000,000, or a density of about three birds per acre.[20] Wing arrived at comparable figures. He estimated from census data that the winter population is 3,776,000,000 and the summer population 5,660,-000,000 birds.[21]

The passenger pigeon appears to have had a longer life than the average land bird due to the protection afforded by high speed and mass association. There is a probability that the population attained 3,000,000,000 birds. This figure is not beyond reason for a species laying but one egg a year and having an apparently low rate of mortality under normal conditions. It is possible that at one time this pigeon formed 25 to 40 per cent of the total bird population in the United States.

DECREASE

The irregularity of the movements of the passenger pigeons in the states along the Atlantic seaboard was not at first recognized. This gave rise to assertions that they were not as abundant as formerly long before the colonists could have had a noticeable effect on their numbers. As early as 1674 Josselyn wrote: "But of late they are much diminished, the English taking them with Nets." [22] Cotton Mather expressed the same opinion in 1712.[23] In the year 1721 Charlevoix wrote from Montreal that, while they no longer darkened the air, "a very great number still come to rest themselves upon the trees, even in the neighborhood of the towns." [24]

At least one European, in contrast, was impressed by a huge flight of pigeons after residing in the country for a year and seeing but few. Dudley came to Massachusetts in 1630. In 1631 he wrote of a flight that spring that obscured the light. To him, "the thing was the more strange, because I scarce remember to have seen ten doves since I came into the country." [25] After his arrival in Virginia, Clayton heard of the vast number of pigeons that had appeared a few years before. He wrote in 1688 that the story was all the more wonderful since he himself had never seen a flock larger than ten in number.[26]

The irregularity of the flights in New Jersey and eastern Pennsylvania is mentioned by Kalm. From information obtained from the oldest inhabitants, he concluded that pigeons appeared in multitude at intervals of eleven to twelve years. A decrease in numbers was attributed to clearing the land, the competition for mast given by hogs, and a feeling of insecurity in placing their nests in inhabited regions.[27] A decrease in New Jersey was mentioned by Smith in 1765. The reason for the former abundance was the plentiful supply of acorns, there being no hogs, and the Indians firing the woods so that the acorns were easily obtainable.[28]

There was a decrease in the number of pigeons appearing in the East during the latter part of the eighteenth century, but there is no way to show that there was a material decline in the total population. Blackburne wrote from New York in 1770: "Some years past they have not been in such plenty as they used to be. This spring I saw them fly one morning, as I thought in great abundance; but every body was amazed how few there were; and wondered at the reason." [29]

Pigeons ceased to nest in Ohio by 1838, if we are to believe Atwater, as the country was too well settled.[30] Three years later Hildreth wrote:

"Although this beautiful bird has been subject to the depredation of man for more than fifty years in Ohio, in addition to the multitudes that annually fall a prey to their feathered enemies, they still exist in vast numbers. What then must have been the amount of their winged hosts...before civilization had made any inroads on the vast forests which had for ages supplied them with food." [31]

Writing in 1848, Susan F. Cooper found the number of pigeons visiting Cooperstown, New York, as nothing compared with the flocks that formerly darkened the valley.[32]

The immense numbers that formerly visited Quebec were greatly reduced at the turn of the nineteenth century. Lambert gave as a possible reason retirement from the cleared lands.[33] By 1841 pigeons were few at Toronto in comparison with former years.[34] They were numerous in Ontario only about once in four to five years.[35]

A decline in New Hampshire was noted in 1792 and attributed to clearing of the forests.[36] The paucity of the population, compared with earlier years, in Massachusetts was mentioned by Thoreau in 1852.[37] Allen stressed the decrease during the century, particularly during his generation.[38] There are no data on which the rate of the decline in the state can be based. Baldwin states that 2,800 dozen were taken at Templeton and Winchendon in 1831 and that about the same number had been taken annually for several years past.[39]

The decline in the number of pigeons became precipitous from 1871 to 1880. The number killed during this decade was so great that the species was doomed. A visitor to the nesting at Shelby, Michigan, in 1874, after estimating that 25,000 pigeons were shipped daily over a period of four weeks, realized fully that the end of the pigeon was in sight:

I was speaking with an old pigeoner who had followed the business for twenty-one years, and his opinion was that the birds were rapidly decreasing, but that there was enough for all practical purposes yet; and one would think so to see a good day's flight at this roost.... With the number of pigeons left, the steadily increasing demand for them dead and alive, and the fearful increase in the rank and file of professional netters who follow them by telegraph hundreds of miles, it is high time to do something for their protection, or ere long our skillful trap-shooters and all pigeon consumers will have to fall back on something more tame in the pigeon line. There were probably as many, or more, pigeons caught this year than ever, but it was not on account of the increased number of birds; it was done by the more numerous army than ever of pigeoners.[40]

The eventual extinction of the species was foreseen by Révoil, who wrote: "and if the world will endure a century longer, I will wager that the amateur of ornithology will find no pigeons except in select Museums of Natural History." [41]

ENEMIES

The pigeon had numerous enemies, aside from man, but there is no reason to believe that they had a material effect on the population. There is Audubon's description of a roost at dawn: "The howlings of the wolves now reached our ears, and the foxes, lynxes, cougars, bears, raccoons, opossums and pole-cats were seen sneaking off, whilst eagles and hawks of different species, accompanied by a crowd of vultures, came to supplant them, and enjoy their share of the spoil." [42] Some, if not most, of these mammals must be considered scavengers. That the Indians protected the nestings by shooting the wolves, as stated by French, seems farfetched.[43] Hildreth mentions that the wolves and foxes visited a roost to feast on the crippled birds.[44]

Members of the Mustelidae are excellent climbers and probably were the most destructive of the mammals. The number that could invade a roost or nesting must have been so small as to have a negligible effect. Welsh mentions the mink, weasel, and marten as aiding in the destruction of the pigeons.[45] According to McKnight, the weasel climbed the trees to secure eggs, young, and the old birds while at rest, while the fox, lynx, and mink depended on the young that fell from the nests.[46] It is impossible to determine if the statements on mammals are based on observation or inference.

Raptors were numerous at the roosts and nestings. Wrote Wilson: "Great numbers of Hawks, and sometimes the Bald Eagle himself, hover about those breeding places, and seize the old or young from the nest amidst the rising multitudes, and with the most daring effrontery." [47] S. S. Stevens informed Brewster that at a nesting, owls could be heard hooting throughout the night.[48]

In the fall of 1841 hawks attacked the pigeons as they came to the shore in the bay at Milwaukee. An eyewitness states: "I observed some vagrant hawks hovering over some of the flocks just as they approached the shore, and struck down sundry lagging birds as if in mere wantonness; indeed I once nearly captured both hawk and pigeon, for both whirled down into the lake; the hawk got wet, and was only able to fly a short distance from the dead pigeon, when he alighted upon a rock with drooping wings." [49]

Occasionally a hawk was captured by the netters as it attempted to take a stool pigeon. Enraged trappers are said to have released the hawks after plucking all the feathers from the body. [50] In the fall of 1859, a trapper at Concord, Massachusetts, within a short time shot fourteen hawks that were chasing the pigeons. [51]

The Cooper's hawk (*Accipiter cooperi*) was a persistent enemy of the pigeon, exceeding it in swiftness. Known in the southern states as the great pigeon hawk, it "also follows the Wild Pigeons in their migrations, and always causes fear and confusion in their ranks." [52] The "Blue Hawk" had been seen to catch a passenger pigeon in a direct chase. [53] It had also been seen to take young pigeons from the nest. [54] Trautman thinks that this hawk must have been a numerous nesting species in the early days due to the abundance of pigeons. [55] It often took the stool pigeon. S. S. Stevens had twelve of his decoys taken in one season. [56]

The sharp-shinned hawk (*Accipiter velox*), according to Audubon, also captured these pigeons. [57] It must have been difficult for it to kill a bird of the size and speed of the passenger pigeon, yet Hatch saw a hawk strike one with such skill that it was killed instantly. [58]

The goshawk (*Accipiter gentilis*) was a deadly enemy. About 1870, this hawk was a common permanent resident of the counties in northern Pennsylvania where the pigeon bred. [59] It left with the disappearance of the pigeons. The goshawk captured the pigeons under every conceivable condition. [60]

Audubon wrote of this hawk:

Should a flock of Wild Pigeons pass him when on these predatory excursions, he immediately gives chase, soon overtakes them, and forcing his way into the very center of the flock, scatters them in confusion, then you may see him emerging with a bird in his talons, and diving towards the depth of the forest to feed upon his victim....

When the Passenger pigeons are abundant in the western country, the Goshawk follows their close masses, and subsists upon them. A single hawk suffices to spread the greatest terror among their ranks, and the moment he sweeps towards a flock, the whole immediately dive into the deepest woods, where, notwithstanding their great speed, the marauder succeeds in clutching the fattest. While travelling along the Ohio, I observed several Hawks of this species in the train of millions of these Pigeons.[61]

The pigeon hawk (*Falco columbarius*) also preyed upon the passenger pigeon.[62] In Indiana this hawk was seen rarely except when following the migrating pigeons.[63]

The duck hawk (*Falco peregrinus*), when seen, was usually following a flock of pigeons.[64] George B. Grinnell gives an interesting description of the capture of a pigeon by this hawk.

They flew with astonishing velocity, and it was but a short time before they were quite near us. From the manner of their flight, I at first thought they were two falcons engaged in play, but a nearer view showed me that the foremost bird was much the smallest, and that it was making most strenuous efforts to escape from its pursuer by darting and twisting from one side to the other, up or down, or by straight forward flight. In one of its turnings it came quite close to the column, and, forgetting in its intense fear its natural shyness, it darted in among the men and horses. The larger bird, a peregrine falcon, as I could now see, hesitated not an instant, but dashed after, following the object of its pursuit in every cut and twist that it made, now passing under the horses, now low over their backs or close to the men's heads. After, perhaps a minute of rapid pursuit, the smaller bird by a quick double put a group of men and horses between itself and the falcon, and then darted swiftly along the ground to where I was standing, an interested observer. Here, almost exhausted, it alighted on the saddle of a horse standing within arm's length of me, and I was able to distinguish that it was a passenger pigeon, (*Ectopistes migratoria*). Meanwhile, the falcon, baffled for a moment, had risen 30 feet in the air, and was hovering over the group looking for his prey. Hardly ten seconds had elapsed since the pigeon alighted, when he saw his pursuer above him, and, terror-stricken by the sight, the luckless bird darted away again over the open prairie. The falcon followed, and the doubling and twisting recommenced before they had gone a quarter of a mile. The pigeon once tried to regain the shelter of the command, but his relentless pursuer cut him off and drove him toward the plain, and, in a few seconds, by a tremendous burst of speed, caught up to his victim, and, throwing out his powerful feet, seized him, and, without checking his flight, bore him off to a neighboring butte, there to devour him....[65]

The red-tailed hawk (*Buteo jamaicensis*) was known to swoop at pigcons sitting in a dead tree. The pigeons did not leave until the hawk was almost upon them.[66] The pursuit was not serious, the hawk generally returning to the vacated tree.

Apparently the tables were sometimes turned, according to the Janesville *Gazette* (Wis.) of April 16, 1879. A "gray eagle" is stated to have been pursued by a large flock of pigeons. The latter flew at the eagle in squads to its great annoyance. It is common for flocks of starlings and some other species to pursue certain raptors, but for pigeons to do so is improbable.

Crows were never seen to eat the eggs of the pigeon, the only predators being hawks and owls.[67] The sitting bird did not leave the nest until its mate arrived; hence there was seldom an opportunity for a crow to take an exposed egg. The capture of one of the parents would alter the situation.

Predators under normal conditions have little effect on animal populations. Species of hawks long accustomed to preying on the pigeon may have hastened its extinction during the last decade, but there is no information on which to base a conclusion.

EXTINCTION

Almost every conceivable cause has been given for the extinction of the pigeon. One of the most popular explanations was drowning en masse in the Gulf of Mexico or the Atlantic Ocean.[68] Pigeons were reported as having been washed ashore even on the coast of Russia.[69] Another theory was that, under persecution, the pigeons migrated to Chile and Peru.[70] As late as 1939, they were thought to have been seen in Bolivia.[71]

Fire has been assigned as a cause leading to extinction. Bartsch was informed that about 1879 a large roost that existed near Beebe, Arkansas, was accidentally set on fire. The pigeons flew into the flames by the hundreds and died from the singeing of their feathers. This continued during the week that the roost was burning, after which there were no more pigeons in the state.[72] Unfortunately for the tale, this was not the last time that pigeons appeared in Arkansas. Furthermore, the pigeon would not stupidly commit suicide. Mershon quotes from a letter from Philip B. Woodworth who thought that the forest fire at Saginaw Bay, Michigan, in 1871 was the beginning of the end of the pigeon. Mershon points out that the fire would have been ineffective since it occurred in autumn when the pigeons were scattered widely.[73]

The extinction of the pigeon has been attributed often to the cutting of the mast-bearing trees. Audubon was confident that only the decrease in the forests would accomplish its decline.[74] A decade later Hildreth considered the cutting of the forests a definite factor in its decline.[75] Paxson states that the nesting in Pennsylvania in 1880 contained 200,-000,000 birds, this number being increased to 400,000,000 or 500,-000,000 by the end of the breeding season. Since 1,000 persons each taking 1,000 birds per day for 50 days would account for only 50,000,000 pigeons, he was forced to conclude that the destruction of the forests was an important factor in their eventual extinction.[76] The excessively high estimates nullify the conclusion. As early as 1878 the destruction of the beech forests was considered a factor in the decrease of the pigeon.[77] Recently Peattie expressed the opinion that the disappearance of the beech mast was a more important influence than mass slaughter.[78] The fact remains that the supply of beechnuts and acorns was far in excess of the needs of the pigeons throughout the last half-century of their existence.[79]

The most probable cause of extinction, in the opinion of Barrows, was the forcing of the pigeons to nest farther and farther northward by the cutting of the forests and by the persecution by man. Unfavorable weather conditions prevented the raising of sufficient young to prevent the flocks from consisting of essentially old birds, which would naturally become weaker each year and which may have been overwhelmed by ice and snow.[80] This theory is not tenable since the pigeons never nested in large colonies unless there was a supply of mast. Only very small colonies were reported nesting north of Minnesota, Wisconsin, and Michigan, a region where there was very little mast. Latitude 46° N. may be taken as the limit of the typical nestings. Even south of this line it was not unusual for nestings to be destroyed by inclement weather, followed by a second attempt at breeding.

A fanciful cause of extinction was the use by a Michigan trapper of bait containing a "spice." The adults ate it greedily, fed their young, and the latter died.[81] An equally weighty reason for disappearance was the pigeon's lack of foresight as shown by laying white eggs.[82] This is as credible as the belief of the French Canadians that the birds were conjured.[83] A French-Canadian woman gave Larocque the following information: "The depredations were so serious in a parish up the Gatineau that the *curé* decided to invoke the aid of God. He therefore laid a curse (*conjuration*) on the pigeons and from then on their number decreased until now they are no more." [84]

Extinction has been attributed to disease more than to any other cause. Disease acquired from exotic, imported pigeons has been suggested.[85] There is no reliable information at all on pigeons dying of disease in the wild. Howitt states that no epidemic ever occurred in the neighborhood of Guelph, Ontario.[86] C. O. Whitman informed Ames that "they are apparently proof against diseases that carry off many of the other wild species." [87]

The death of the four males in Milwaukee was believed by A. E. Wiedring to have been due to tuberculosis.[88] I have been informed by Reuben M. Strong that these pigeons were kept in a room under wretched sanitary conditions. The birds held in Cincinnati died simply from old age and never had a disease.[89]

Pigeons in captivity, according to Martin, were very susceptible to disease. He mentions that 20,000 were confined in rooms sixteen feet square, 1,000 birds to each room. One morning, an hour after they had eaten their corn with avidity, all the pigeons in one room were dead of "canker." Prompt administration of sulphur and alum checked the disease.[90] If the ailment was canker, it would not have been cured so simply. He wisely asks what became of the dead pigeons if an epidemic of this kind had ever occurred during a nesting.

The most ardent proponent of the disease theory is Thompson. He mentions cases of pigeons sick and dead from canker in Michigan and Pennsylvania, one extending back to 1854. He concludes that during the eighties most of the pigeons died of disease in the wilds of Canada without attracting attention.[91] It would be difficult to rout him from this haven.

It has been supposed that trichomoniasis (canker), due to *Trichomonas gallinae,* spread from domestic pigeons to the passenger pigeons. Some support is lent to this belief by the recent outbreak of this disease among the mourning doves in the South.[92] Canker is an old disease among domestic pigeons. The French in Canada had domestic pigeons in 1606 and from then on the introductions were numerous, extending to Louisiana by 1722 and to Illinois prior to 1768.[93] Since the passenger pigeon was subjected to the possibility of infection for a period of three centuries, it does not seem probable that this disease was important in its extermination.

Pigeons were very numerous at Hamilton, Ontario, the spring of 1854. McIlwraith writes: "The summer was unusually warm, and as the heat increased, the birds seemed weak and languid, with scarcely enough energy left to rise above the houses." [94] No deaths were reported and there is no proof of disease. The behavior was not abnormal for young pigeons.

The disappearance of the pigeon caused Lowe to speculate at some length. He suggested as a possible cause "an abnormal stimulation or feverish exhaustion of the germ plasm," but how, or if ever, it arose could not be shown.[95] Reliance was then placed on microbic infection or destruction by man.

There is now very general agreement that man was responsible for the extinction of the pigeon. Since it was once supposedly "abundant" in Montana and disappeared while the state was very thinly populated, Saunders reasoned that man could not have been responsible solely.[96] He overlooked the fact that, as the numbers of the pigeon decreased, the eastern and western borders of its range contracted to such an extent that they contained merely stragglers. The species was never abundant in Montana.

The key to the problem of extinction lies in mass association. Stone wrote: "The pigeon like the buffalo was a species whose existence seems to have depended upon association in large numbers and once separated and scattered into small flocks and pairs its doom was sealed." [97]

The same view was taken by Todd, coupled with the inability of the pigeon to adapt itself to new conditions.[98] The shortcomings of the species are given in greater detail by Griscom.

The primary cause for the passing of the passenger pigeon was its own specialized habits and a long list of biological "defects." Its low egg-laying capacity, flimsy nest, and herd instinct in migration are three minor ones. Its spectacular gregariousness was disastrous in two respects. The huge flocks could not be overlooked by the birds' enemies, and no effort was made to avoid them. In a primeval wilderness their ravages were overcome by sheer weight of numbers. Every nesting automatically involved an appalling mortality of adults and young and a waste of eggs, caused by the habits of the bird itself. The final "defect" of this pigeon was its inability to learn anything new; it could not change its habits to meet the pressure of new and unfavorable conditions or dangers.[99]

Judged from the standpoint of numbers, the pigeon was enormously successful in its way of life. Failure to change its habits cannot be laid to stupidity without assuming that most of the surviving species have a higher order of intelligence. The greater number of the passerines chanced to develop a mode of life that rendered survival fairly simple after the advent of Europeans. Very many of our game birds, shore birds, and waterfowl would today be extinct, or near extinction, were it not for coddling through refuges and protective laws.

Inbreeding of the small number of survivors has been suggested as having had fatal consequences.[100] On the other hand, Allen thinks that a lack of synchronization of the mating cycle, when only a few males and females were left, might have led to extinction.[101] A quite similar opinion is held by Breckenridge.[102] Colonial nesting afforded a maximum opportunity for the pairing of males and females in a mating condition. This advantage is lost when a colony is reduced below a certain minimum number.

The greater success of large colonies of gulls was due apparently to the better synchronization of the breeding cycle throughout the colony. With herring gulls, a colony of ninety birds lost about one-half of its young, one of thirty-four about two-thirds, and that of twenty about three-fourths.[103]

There was marked synchronization in the mating of the pigeon. Insofar as known, all the eggs in relatively small as well as in large colonies were deposited on almost the same day; and it is certain that the parents abandoned the young in a body. Apparently an assemblage of only a few hundred birds was necessary to bring nearly all of the pigeons to the same state of sexual excitement. While it was characteristic of the pigeon to nest in large colonies, single to a few colonial pairs nested commonly. It is probable that these nestings were by birds entering their second year and late in reaching sexual maturity. They occurred mainly in late May and June, hence considerably later than the large colonial nestings. Craig wrote: "If two inexperienced birds be allowed to mate, they are very slow in coming to the point of mating; and, though they go through all the processes of mating, nest-building, and brooding, yet their efforts lack something of the precision and promptness which signally characterize the work of experienced birds." [104] When an experienced bird took the lead, the young bird was brought to the complete exercise of its functions much more quickly.

It was recognized that the basic difficulty was the inability to raise sufficient young. When a nesting was invaded, thousands of eggs and young were accidentally thrown from the nest by the frightened adults, thereby impairing the perpetuation of the species. [105] Mershon analyzed the problem as follows: "The old birds were netted continually, and had no chance to rear their young. The cutting off of the forests and natural feeding-grounds, and disseminating of the large flights, made it impossible for the scattered bands to adopt a new habit of living and adapt themselves to the changed conditions, and thus the birds that were left after the general extinction of the mighty host failed to reproduce their species and soon became extinct." [106]

Unfortunately the pigeons did not scatter appreciably and continued to nest in colonies even in the decade beginning in 1880. What was left of the former hosts nested in Wisconsin in 1885, in Pennsylvania in 1886, and again in Wisconsin in 1887.

Every species of animal is doomed to extinction when it fails to produce sufficient young to equal the inherent annual losses. This the pigeon was not permitted to do. Fischer estimated that nearly 12,000,000 brooding pigeons met their death during the decade 1866–76. [107] This represented a high loss of nestlings. It is certain, assuming the correctness of his figures, that the loss would exceed 6,000,000 young. If both parents were taken, the young was doomed to die; and if only one adult of a pair was captured, the lone parent could not keep its young alive during the first few days after hatching. His assumption that the number of squabs taken was negligible missed the most potent cause of extinction.

Failure to rear an adequate number of young (Fig. 9) resulted from shooting and trapping the adults, breaking up the nestings by shooting within the limits forbidden by law, and capture of the squabs. As the nestings became smaller, the competition for the squabs became all the keener. The destruction of the young at the nestings near Sparta and Kilbourn, Wisconsin, in 1882 was fearful; and it began before they were ready for the table. Squabs were a glut on the market in Milwaukee, where the retail price ranged during the season from 35 cents to $1.00 per dozen. For the first time known, they were sold "according to size." Protests were raised against the taking of the young before they had attained sufficient growth.[108] On May 21 nearly every team available at Sparta went to the nesting for squabs. Conditions reached the stage where a fruitless petition, received from New Lisbon, was sent to Governor Jeremiah M. Rusk to call out the militia to protect the nesting.[109] As one writer from New Lisbon expressed it in the Mauston *Star* (Wis.) of May 25, 1882: "Some of our prominent business men (?) are busily engaged, and have been the past week in destroying thousands of poor little helpless young pigeons yet without feathers and encouraging others in the wholesale murder, and from a greedy desire to catch a few squabs to ship and sell for 30 cts. per dozen."

The young at the Kilbourn nesting suffered as severely. On May 17, 15,600 were buried due to spoilage, the dealers having purchased more than could be preserved; and on another occasion several tons were thrown into the Wisconsin River for the same reason.[110] According to the Milwaukee *Sentinel* of June 22, 1882, many, too young for consumption, were left under the trees from which they had been dislodged. Thousands of squabs were placed in crates and shipped alive to Milwaukee in an attempt to prevent spoilage during the hot June weather.

A visitor to the nesting at Kilbourn remarked on the "immense number of young birds" that were tumbled from the nests before the squabs were of any use whatsoever.[111] Another statement in the Milwaukee *Sentinel* of March 15, 1883, reads:

The wholesale slaughter of these birds at their nesting place in Monroe County last spring when not half grown, and even before they were feathered, was disgracefully notorious at the time. One man shipped over 2,000,000 [?] of these birds out of the county and the ground was so strewn with the carcasses of young pigeons, too small for shipment, that for three weeks there was an area of several miles where such a stench arose as to sicken travelers.

It will be shown that persecution was unremitting until the last wild bird disappeared. In following the species to extinction, it is to be noted that the end came quite gradually and not with catastrophic suddenness as is popularly believed.

A nesting was reported to have occurred in Missouri the spring of 1883 at which all of the young were taken. One man had 60,000 and several others 10,000 young each. E. S. Bond predicted that "three years will finish them." [112] The following winter there was a roost near Augusta, St. Charles County, Missouri, three by five miles in dimension. A party is stated to have killed 5,415 of the birds. [113]

There was a large flight of pigeons lasting one day over Coudersport, Pennsylvania, in the spring of 1884. Subsequently a flock of about 300 birds nested undisturbed at Cherry Springs. [114]

A nesting, said to cover forty acres, formed in eastern Langlade County, Wisconsin, in 1885. [115] According to information received in a letter from A. C. Weber, of Shawano, this nesting was considerably larger. He states: "This nesting was in Township 31, Range 15, being a part of Oconto County particularly in the following sections: 22–23–26–27–34 and 35 along both sides of the two South Branches of Oconto River which flow through these sections." No young were raised, as the birds were driven away by shooting. The fewer the pigeons the more persistently they were hunted. In the Racine *Times* for September 11 of this year a flock was reported at the "Springs" at Racine, Wisconsin, and within an hour 500 men with shotguns were headed for the locality.

"Millions" are said to have assembled in the mountains twenty-five miles northwest of Bedford, Pennsylvania, in the summer of 1885. [116] Strangely, there is no record of even an attempt at colonial nesting in the East during this year. J. B. Oviatt found a few nests, his last, in McKean County, Pennsylvania, in 1885. [117]

By 1886 only two large flocks were believed to exist, one in Pennsylvania and one in the Indian Territory (Oklahoma). [118] Bishop has the bulk of the pigeons in Missouri. [119] A nesting much smaller than that of 1880 was established in the Spring Creek region on the border of Forest and Warren counties, Pennsylvania. [120] This nesting did not proceed to completion, due apparently to "thousands and tens of thousands" of the nesting birds being killed. [121]

Several flocks of pigeons passed over Coudersport, Pennsylvania, on

March 20, 1886, according to the Coudersport *Potter County Journal* for March 25 of that year. For two or three weeks southeastern Potter County was alive with them. For a time they were in McKean County, where it appeared that they would nest. Later they returned to Potter County and began to nest on Potato and Marvin creeks. Before the nests were completed, the birds were driven away by shooting. After these pigeons left, there was a new flight to the northeast lasting two days. This was the last time that they appeared in numbers in Potter County.[122] J. B. Oviatt visited all the localities in Potter County in 1886 where the pigeons were reported to have nests, but could find none.[123] According to French, the pigeons attempted to nest on Pine Creek, Potter County, but left on account of the shooting. A late nesting took place near Blossburg, Tioga County, Pennsylvania, from which thousands of squabs were taken.[124]

In the spring migration of 1886 pigeons were reported numerous at Darlington, Manitowoc, and Green Bay, Wisconsin, but no nesting was reported. About 600 pairs were found nesting near Lake City, Michigan, by S. S. Stevens.[125] In Missouri, 4,929 pigeons were killed during the year ending March 1, 1886.[126]

Pigeons were reported quite numerous in several localities in Wisconsin in the spring of 1887. They started to nest in the swamp north of Wautoma, and a number of professional trappers arrived upon the scene. Again the pigeons left due to shooting within the nesting. The birds were reported in the Wautoma *Argus* (Wis.) of May 20 and 27 and June 3, 1887, to have failed to nest at Sparta, Wisconsin, for the same reason. Pigeons were found to be abundant in the Ozark Mountains, Arkansas, in 1887 by Kumlien from "December to April." [127]

Pigeons had now become so scarce that Brewster went to Michigan in the spring of 1888 to investigate the reported nesting of large numbers of birds. Accompanied by Jonathan Dwight, Jr., he arrived at Cadillac on May 8. They learned that large flocks had passed this place late in April and they received similar reports from nearly all the counties in the southern part of the state. The flocks reported seen varied from fifty birds to one that "covered at least eight acres." During their stay in the state only single pairs could be found nesting. The netters believed that most of the pigeons had gone through the state to the uninhabited regions north of the Great Lakes. The numbers reported induced Brewster to express the opinion that the species was at present not on the verge of extinction, but unless effectual laws could be passed "our Passenger Pigeons are preparing to follow the Great Auk and the American Bison."[128]

There was a small nesting in Potter County, Pennsylvania, in the spring of 1888; and a flock of 150 to 175 birds was seen at York, Pennsylvania, September 1, 1888.[129] In the spring of this year pigeons appeared in fourteen localities in Wisconsin. There was shooting for a week at Prairie du Chien and a "roost" was reported to exist on the Yellow River, according to accounts in the Prairie du Chien *Courier* for April 17 and 24, 1888. In the same year, Mershon, a resident of Michigan, considered the pigeon virtually extinct, destroyed by netting.[130] Opinion was widespread that it had disappeared from the continent, but hope was expressed that a few flocks had taken refuge in the far West.[131]

The population seems to have dwindled to a few thousands by 1889. White saw a "large flock" on Mackinac Island, Michigan, August 30, 1889, the only definite number given being one hundred seen September 10.[132] Two flocks of about twenty each were seen in Kent County, Michigan, in September of this year, and a flock of sixty was reported.[133] These data are at variance with those given by White to Mershon from memory.[134]

Only stragglers were to be encountered at Lake Mills, Wisconsin, in 1889.[135] On December 25 of this year a flock of three hundred was reported flying northward along the Susquehanna River at Harrisburg, Pennsylvania.[136]

Pigeons were reported from thirteen localities in Wisconsin in the spring of 1890. The Madison *Democrat* of March 27 and 28 reported "thousands" seen in the woods about four miles from Madison, Wisconsin, on March 26. According to Carr, a large flock was seen near Madison in April and a few days afterwards one of twenty.[137] A few flocks passed through Jefferson County in April, and Kumlien secured some specimens.[138]

About one hundred dozen pigeons, said to have come from Pennsylvania and Missouri, were seen in the Boston market in February, 1891.[139] A considerable flight took place at Prairie du Sac, Wisconsin, on April 3, 1891, and some were killed.[140] Hough states that a man living thirty miles west of Fayetteville, Arkansas, netted 2,000 pigeons which were fed and shipped to Boston.[141] Several birds were received at the aviary of Central Park, New York, in June, 1891, and considered rare specimens.[142] (These pigeons may have replaced some that had died, for the American Museum of Natural History has two skeletons prepared from birds received from Central Park in January, 1891.)

According to the report in the Sparta *Herald* (Wis.) for April 5, 1892, the pigeons that appeared in the township of Greenfield, Monroe County, Wisconsin, in the spring of 1892 behaved as though they would nest at Wilsonville, where two large nestings had occurred in former years. In this year three flocks were seen in Potter County, Pennsylvania.[143] Several hundred dozen pigeons, states Brewster, were received in Boston from the Indian Territory in December, 1892, and January, 1893.[144] Fleming was in New York in November, 1892, and was informed by Rowland that he had seen recently several barrels of pigeons, shipped from the Indian Territory, that had been condemned as unfit for the table.[145]

In 1895 Deane had a letter from the game dealers, N. W. Judy & Co., St. Louis, informing him that they had had no pigeons for two seasons and that their netters were idle. The last were received from Siloam Springs, Arkansas.[146] The Wautoma *Argus* (Wis.) of April 14, 1893, reported that a few flocks had been seen that spring but that the species was nearly extinct.

A flock of 150 pigeons was seen at Whitewater, Wisconsin, on May 4, 1894.[147] More pigeons were seen in Indiana in this year than during the preceding two or three years.[148]

The Manitowoc *Pilot* (Wis.) of September 12, 1895, stated that more pigeons had been seen than for several years; and the Prairie du Chien *Courier* (Wis.) of October 8 mentioned that hunters were shooting pigeons. John L. Stockton informed Deane that in June, 1895, he saw a flock of about ten pigeons for several consecutive days on the Menominee Indian Reservation in Wisconsin.[149] A flock of about ten birds was seen at West Branch, Michigan, in this year.[150] Two flocks, numbering twenty-five and sixty pigeons, were seen in Indiana in April, 1895.[151]

The occurrence of a small nesting in 1896 on the headwaters of the Au Sable River, Michigan, was reported to Deane by Chief Pokagon.[152]

Pigeons were considered to be increasing at this time in Michigan.[153] C. H. Holden, Jr., while hunting at "Altie" (Alton), Oregon County, Missouri, saw a flock of about fifty on December 17, 1896. Two birds that he shot were presented to Deane.[154] A similar occurrence is related by Hough. William Knight, while hunting in Missouri and Arkansas in December, 1896, saw a large flock of pigeons, killed two and brought them home for mounting.[155] It is not reported in which state the birds were taken.

Reports by residents of Oshkosh, Wisconsin, of flocks of pigeons ranging in size from ten to fifty in the fall of 1897 were sent to both Deane and Hough.[156] On August 17, 1897, W. F. Rightmire saw a flock of seventy-five to one hundred birds in Johnson County, Nebraska.[157]

No one will ever be satisfied as to the date when the last wild passenger pigeon was shot or seen. Since pigeons were reported seen well into the twentieth century, reliance must be placed on specimens with credible data. The last records are given in Chapter 15.

The year 1900 may be considered as marking the end. As late as 1899 Hollister was so optimistic as to state that the species was in no danger of total extinction, several species of American birds being in a more precarious position.[158] Brewster in 1906 found it difficult to believe that the pigeon was extinct; but as Hegner remarked, another of our "inexhaustible resources" had disappeared.[159]

It was thought by Job that the pigeon could have been saved from disappearance if "applied ornithology" had been in use sufficiently early, since the bird was easily propagated in confinement.[160] The latter was not the case. It will remain a matter of opinion if the pigeon could have been saved had the last few thousands remained free from all persecution. Some of the northern states still contain sufficient mast-bearing forests to have afforded adequate subsistence during the nesting season. The substitution of the seeder for the broadcasting of grain by hand had removed the chief source of loss to agriculture. Whether or not the pigeon would have caused sufficient damage to growing crops to provoke the farmer to seek relief in the customary manner is unanswerable.

The threshold of survival of the pigeon is not determinable. This is at best a vague term and seldom can be defined statistically due to widely varying conditions. The heath hen rose from an estimated population of 120 to 200 birds in 1890 to a maximum estimate of 2,000 in 1916, then dropped to 414 in 1921, and to about 50 in 1926.[161] The last bird disappeared in 1932. This species was in danger of extinction for over a century and it is impossible to fix upon a number that was critical.

No better example of eternal hope, so characteristic of man, can be found than the search for a living wild passenger pigeon long after it had ceased to exist. At the meeting of the American Ornithologists' Union in New York, December 7–9, 1909, Professor A. F. Hodge reported on the problem of determining if the species was actually extinct.[162] Plans were made for an adequate search, and awards totaling $1,220 were offered for the discovery of a nest or a colony. An original offer of $100 for a freshly killed pigeon was withdrawn due to the possibility of exterminating the few birds that might be left. The sum of $400 was contributed by Charles K. Reed and Chester A. Reed for the preparation of a leaflet on the passenger pigeon that included a colored plate.[163] This was distributed widely.

The awards for discovery varied somewhat from time to time. In January, 1910, they were as follows: [164]

Donor and Description	*Value*
Colonel Anthony R. Kuser, for first nest or nesting colony	$300
W. B. Mershon, for first nest or nesting colony in Michigan	100
Professor C. O. Whitman and Ruthven Deane, for Illinois	100
John E. Thayer, five awards of $100 each for the five most likely States, including Canada, for which there were no local offers	500
A. B. Miller, for first discovery in Worcester County, Massachusetts	20
John Lewis Childs, nest or nesting colony anywhere in North America; and an additional award of $500 to be divided among subsequent finds, if more than one is made	700
	500
	$2,220

The search, set to end on October 1, 1911, was finally extended to October 31, 1912. All the reports and specimens investigated confirmed the general opinion that the species was extinct.[165] On the death of the last pigeon in captivity, Stone wrote the following sober admonition: "The reduction of this once abundant bird to absolute extermination by man's greed should be a lesson to us all and stifle all opposition to the efforts now being made by national and state governments in behalf of the conservation of other birds threatened with a like fate. What is a little loss of sport to us compared with the extinction of a wild species—something that the hand of man can never replace?" [166]

CONSERVATION AND LEGISLATION

Attempts to preserve the passenger pigeon were long in coming and were the outgrowth of pity. The sickening slaughter moved Cooper to write this protest:

If the heavens were alive with pigeons, the whole village seemed equally in motion, with men, women, and children. Every species of fire-arms from the French ducking-gun with a barrel near six feet in length, to the common horseman's pistol, was to be seen in the hands of the men and boys; while bows and arrows, some made of the simple stick of a walnut sapling, and others in a rude imitation of the ancient cross-bows, were carried by many of the latter....

So prodigious was the number of the birds, that the scattering fire of the guns, with the hurling of missiles, and the cries of the boys, had no other effect than to break off small flocks from the immense masses that continued to dart along the valley, as if the whole of the feathered tribe were pouring through that one pass. None pretended to collect the game, which lay scattered over the fields in such profusion as to cover the very ground with the fluttering victims....

"This comes of settling a country!" he [Leather-stocking] said; "here have I known the pigeons to fly for forty long years, and, till you made your clearings, there was nobody to skear or to hurt them. I loved to see them come, into the woods, for they were company to a body; hurting nothing; being, as it was, as harmless as a garter-snake. But now it gives me sore thoughts when I hear the frighty things whizzing through the air, for I know it's only a motion to bring out all the brats in the village. Well! The Lord won't see the waste of his creatures for nothing, and right will be done to the pigeons, as well as others, by and by." [167]

An extraordinary example of sentimentality is related by Clarke. While pastor of a church at Louisville, Kentucky, he received a letter, dated January 4, 1834, from the actor J. B. Booth, requesting that he attend the burial of his friends. He adds:

Booth went to another corner of the room, where, spread out upon a large sheet, I beheld to my surprise, *about a bushel of wild pigeons!*

Booth knelt down by the side of the birds, and with evidence of sincere affliction began to mourn over them. He took them up in his hands tenderly, and presented them to his heart. For a few moments he seemed to forget my presence.... So I decided that it was a sincere conviction,—an idea, exaggerated perhaps to the border of monomania, of the sacredness of all life....

I also saw the motive for this particular course of action. During the week immense quantities of the wild pigeon (Passenger Pigeon, *Columba migratoria*) had been flying over the city, in their way to and from a *roost* in the neighborhood. These birds had been slaughtered by myriads, and were for sale at the corners of every street in the city. Although all the birds which could be killed by man made the smallest impression on the vast multitude contained in one of these flocks..., yet to Booth the destruction seemed wasteful, wanton, and, from his point of view, was a wilful and barbarous murder.

I heard, in a day or two, that he actually purchased a lot in the cemetery, two or three miles below the city, had a coffin made, hired a hearse and carriage, and had gone through all the solemnity of a regular funeral. For several days he continued to visit the grave of his little friends, and mourned over them with a grief which did not seem at all theatrical.[168]

Adequate protection for the pigeon never came. The first state law, in fact, was passed for the "biped without feathers." An act passed in Massachusetts in 1848, for the protection of beds for netting pigeons, reads as follows:

If any person shall attempt to kill or frighten pigeons from beds made for the purpose of taking them in nets, by firing guns, or by any other means, within one hundred yards of the same, except on lands owned or occupied by himself, he shall forfeit and pay, to the owner or occupant of such lands, or to the owner or occupant of such beds, the sum of ten dollars, in addition to the actual damages sustained, to be recovered by such owner or occupant in an action of trespass.

The general attitude towards the pigeon was expressed in 1857 by a committee reporting on a game bill to the State Legislature of Ohio: "The passenger pigeon needs no protection. Wonderfully prolific, having the vast forests of the North as its breeding grounds, travelling hundreds of miles in search of food, it is here to-day, and elsewhere to-morrow, and no ordinary destruction can lessen them or be missed from the myriads that are yearly produced."

New York led in 1862 with a law protecting nestings. The pigeons were to be disturbed in no wise at the nesting and the discharge of firearms within a mile of the nesting was prohibited. The distance was changed in 1867 to one-fourth of a mile. Michigan followed in 1869 with a statute prohibiting the disturbance of the pigeons within one-half of a mile of the nesting. This was amended in 1875 to prohibit shooting within five miles and netting within two miles of a nesting.

The statutes of the various states differed little except in the distance from the nesting where protection was afforded. Section 1 of the Wisconsin act of 1877 may be taken as an example.

It shall be unlawful for any person or persons to use any gun or guns or firearms, or in any manner to maim, kill, destroy or disturb any wild pigeon or pigeons at or within three miles of the place or places where they are gathered for the purpose of brooding their young, known as pigeon nestings. Nor shall any person or persons fire at or attempt to kill or destroy any such wild pigeon or pigeons, or disturb their nests within said limits anywhere within this state, at any time from the beginning of such nesting or brooding until the last hatching of such birds, and every person offending against the provisions of this section, shall be punished by a fine of not more than fifty dollars nor less than twenty dollars for each and every offense, together with the costs of suit, and shall be imprisoned in the county jail of the county wherein such offense was committed until such fine and costs are fully paid, or until discharged according to law; and in all convictions under this act one-half of all fines shall be paid over, by the justice of the peace before whom such trial is brought, to the person who shall have made the complaint in such case.

There was a slight modification of the above act in 1883. In 1887 the eggs were protected.

The Pennsylvania act of 1878 specified that the pigeons were not to be disturbed within one-fourth of a mile of the nesting and that nonresident trappers must obtain a license, costing $50.00, from the county in which they operated. The distance from the nesting was subsequently changed to one mile. The act appears in the statutes of 1936 and is still in force. Several states have not repealed their laws protecting pigeons, though their need vanished long ago.

The Ohio law of 1876 not only protected the pigeons within one-half of a mile of a nesting but also within the same distance of a roost. No nestlings or eggs were to be disturbed.

A closed season, similar to those provided for other game birds, was enacted in Massachusetts in 1870. Pigeons were protected except from September through November. In 1888 the law was modified to give a closed season from the first of May to the first of October. This protected the pigeon during most of the months when it was present in Massachusetts.

In spite of the numerous laws of the several states, it cannot be found that sustained efforts were made by the enforcement officials in any state to protect the pigeons. Public opinion, in large part, was apathetic to protection or against it. An editorial in the Elroy *Plain Talker* (Wis.) of March 8, 1878, protests the passage of the Wisconsin law of 1877. It asserts that only hunters and the express companies are interested in protecting pigeons, while: "There are ... but few pests that farmers dread more than they do wild pigeons, and yet the members of the Legislature of the great state of Wisconsin, last winter saw fit to pass this law, notwithstanding that hundreds of families in the state might be left without food, and to the charity of the public, if this law were to be strictly carried out."

It was stated by Gunn that at the nesting at Shelby, Michigan, in 1876, the law prohibiting shooting within five miles and netting within two miles of a nesting was enforced strictly.[169] Another writer found that the law was only partially enforced. Two netters were fined $50 and costs, totaling $60, for netting within the prescribed limits, and several others were fined.[170]

The most earnest attempts to stop the wholesale slaughter of pigeons were made by Professor H. B. Roney of East Saginaw, Michigan. In 1878 he made a plea for legislation sufficiently effective to afford adequate protection.[171] Conditions became so bad in Michigan that in this year Roney and three other men, under the auspices of the Saginaw and Bay City Game Protection Clubs, went to Petoskey to investigate the enforcement of the law at the nearby nesting. The state of affairs was worse than anticipated, for "the shooting done at the nesting was in the most flagrant violation of the protective laws. The five-mile limit was a dead letter. The shot-gun brigade went where they listed, and shot the birds in the nesting as they sat in rows on the trees or passed in clouds overhead. Before we arrived, a party of four men shot 826 birds in one day and then only stopping from sheer fatigue." [172] *One* netter, violating the law, was arrested and fined $50 and costs.

It is unfortunately true that at the time some members of "Audubon

Clubs" and state game protective associations professed protection yet, when in the field, behaved to the contrary. It was stated in 1876 that the State Sportsman's Association of Michigan was the only organization known to have taken steps to reduce the slaughter of pigeons.[173] One of the men arrested at Petoskey was A. B. Turner, ex-officer of the Association, president of the Kent County Game Protection Club, and editor of the Grand Rapids *Eagle*. Prior to going to Petoskey, Turner wrote in his paper (Grand Rapids *Eagle*, April 18, 1878) that it would be almost impossible to get a jury in northern Michigan to convict a violator of the pigeon law.[174] While the evidence against Turner seemed overwhelming, he was acquitted. Subsequently he denied any violation.[175] Roney is supported in his statement concerning violations of the law by Lawrence.[176]

The Michigan law was drawn solely in the interest of netters.[177] Shooters had to remain five miles from the nesting so that the netters could work undisturbed within two miles of it. The law gave protection to the nesting only until *after the last hatching,* so that the squabs could be taken at any stage of growth. There was also no adequate provision for administering punishment in case the conviction of an offender was obtained. In fact, the opinion prevailed that the species would not have been near extinction in 1892 had not netting taken place near the breeding grounds, contrary to law.[178]

Conditions were no better in the other states. Bishop, writing of the last nesting of consequence in Pennsylvania, mentions that "the same ruthless hunting of the birds on and off their nests, by night and by day," continued.[179] During all the years that the Pennsylvania law had been in effect and notoriously violated, not one arrest of an offender had been made.

With the extinction of the pigeon well within sight, we have the following comment:

When the birds appear all the male inhabitants of the neighborhood leave their customary occupations as farmers, bark-peelers, oil-scouts, wild-catters, and tavern loafers, and join in the work of capturing and marketing the game. The Pennsylvania law very plainly forbids the destruction of the pigeons on their nesting grounds, but no one pays any attention to the law, and the nesting birds have been killed by thousands and tens of thousands.[180]

The editors of the journals for sportsmen had an opportunity for effective service in checking the decimation of the pigeon, but the subject was pursued sporadically and halfheartedly. Following the large shipments of pigeons from Petoskey, Michigan, the question is merely raised if it is not advisable to stop the killing of the birds while nesting to avoid extermination.[181]

The wasteful destruction of pigeons at the Wisconsin nestings in 1882 provoked a strong editorial from Rowe, editor of the *American Field*.[182] He pointed out that there was no argument possible against the rapid extermination of the pigeon unless it received complete protection from trapping and shooting during the nesting season. The slaughter of squabs by the Indians hired by W. H. H. Cash is mentioned. According to the latter's interpretation of the Wisconsin law, the old birds were protected while on the nest but not the young. It might be added that, since the Wisconsin law contains the phrase "until the last hatching," it could be argued that any and all protection ceased at this point.

Rowe made the admirable suggestion that every state and territory pass a law prohibiting trapping, shooting, or having in possession any wild pigeons during the months of March, April, and May; and prohibiting a person at any time from approaching a nesting for the purpose of shooting or capturing an old or a young bird. The anticlimax to this solicitude occurs in an item from Sparta in the La Crosse *Republican and Leader* (Wis.) of May 13, 1882: "The editor of the *Field* and other sportsmen from Chicago took the evening train. They expended a large quantity of powder and shot, and in return received all the pigeons they desired."

The only law giving complete protection to the pigeon was enacted in Michigan in 1897. Through the efforts of Chase S. Osborn, State Game and Fish Warden, pigeons were protected until 1905. After that year there was to be an open season from the first of October to the last day in December; and pigeons were to be disturbed in no manner within five miles of their nesting places and roosts. This law came much too late.

The conclusion is inescapable that the passenger pigeon became extinct through such constant persecution that it was unable to raise sufficient young to perpetuate the race. Trapping and shooting were devastating. Drowning, disease if any, and all the other suggested causes of extinction must have been minor in effect. The extremely lax enforcement of the protective laws, engendered by little heed for the morrow, should have a sobering influence when attention is called to any other species that is in danger of vanishing. The sacrifice, however regrettable, was not in vain, for the passing of a bird known to millions has furnished a most poignant example of what will happen when man is heedless of his heritage.

On a bluff in Wyalusing State Park, at the junction of the Mississippi and Wisconsin rivers, stands a monument to the passenger pigeon. It was dedicated on May 11, 1947. The legend on the bronze tablet reads:

Dedicated
To The Last Wisconsin
Passenger Pigeon
Shot At Babcock, Sept. 1899

This Species Became Extinct
Through The Avarice And
Thoughtlessness Of Man

Erected By
The Wisconsin Society For Ornithology

CHAPTER 10: DESCRIPTION

The passenger pigeon was the longest, if not the heaviest, member of the family in America.

GENERIC CHARACTERS.—An arboreal pigeon, the male averaging 410 mm. and the female 350 mm. in length;[1] head small; tail, with twelve rectrices, long, pointed, and graduated for about two-thirds of its length; wing long and pointed, about equal to length of tail; bill small, slender, with a shallow notch and nasal opercula highly swollen.

MALE.—Entire head slaty blue, somewhat paler on chin and upper throat; hindneck with a metallic iridescence of bronze, green, and purple, depending upon the angle of the light; back slate gray tinged with grayish brown or olive brown; lower back and rump clear grayish blue, becoming brownish gray on upper tail coverts; below from throat to abdomen rich russet vinaceous, changing to white on abdomen.

Primaries dark grayish brown and, except for the tenth (counting from the inside), narrowly edged whitish, the inner webs being tinged rufous; near middle of wing, outer webs of first three primaries colored bluish gray to shaft, fading to whitish edging on the ninth primary, and forming a conspicuous band when wing is spread; last three primaries the longest, the ninth of maximum length; relative decreasing lengths in order of numbering of primaries, 9, 10, 8, 7, 6, 5, 4, 3, 2, 1; scapulars and proximal secondaries grayish brown; under wing coverts and axillars pale bluish gray.

Rectrices acuminate; inner pair, 1, 1, brownish black and slightly the longest; 2, 2 light gray on outer web and white on inner web; remaining pairs colored similarly but the inner webs becoming gray at base; the four outer pairs graduated so that 6, 6 are approximately only one-third the length of 1, 1; rectrices, except 1, 1, with concealed spots of black on inner web near base, between which and base are characteristic spots of cinnamon rufous. The number of major coverts equals that of the rectrices.

The relative lengths of the rectrices are given by Clark, and most authorities, as 1, 2, 3, 4, 5, 6.[2] This relationship holds for the majority of, and apparently normal, specimens. In some collections where the rectrices show no evidence of wear, as high as 20 per cent of the specimens will be found to have 2, 2 longer than 1, 1. These cases may represent incomplete development of the middle pair. Unfortunately, most specimens lack the exact date of collection.

Bill black, slender, short, with culmen about one-third the length of the head; iris scarlet; bare orbital ring purplish flesh-colored.

Tibia bluish violet; legs and feet lake red; tarsus short and feathered anteriorly 10 to 12 mm.; acrotarsium with two longitudinal rows of scutella, partially transverse and partially hexagonal; planta tarsi with very small round or hexagonal scales; tarsus nearly equal in length to middle toe.

The following measurements of skins in millimeters are from Ridgway (with extent from Coues): length, 361–459 (412); wing, 196.5–214.5 (204.9); tail, 173–211 (193.5); culmen, 15–18 (16.7); tarsus, 26–29 (27.4); middle toe, 26.5–29.5 (27.7); extent 584–625.[3]

Accurate measurements in the flesh have been scantily recorded. According to Coues, the length is very variable and dependent upon the development of the tail.[4] There are the following rough measurements of males: length, 17 in. (432 mm.); wing, 8.5 (216); extent, 23.5 (597);[5] length, 16.5 (419); wing, 8 (203); tail, 8 (203); extent, 24 (610).[6]

The measurements of five adult males and five adult females given by Mearns appear to have been made on specimens in the flesh.[7] Not only are the average lengths greater than those given by Ridgway for skins,[8] but there is less difference between the sexes. Average measurements for the males were: length, 16.67 in. (423 mm.); extent, 24.30

(617); wing, 7.88 (200); tail, 7.80 (198); culmen, 0.72 (18.3); gape, 1.12 (28.5); tarsus, 1.14 (29); middle toe, 1.16 (29.5); its claw, 0.37 (9.4); middle toe and claw, 1.50 (38.1).

FEMALE.—Similar to adult male but colors decidedly duller; head grayish brown; back brownish; foreneck and underparts light drab becoming pale gray on breast and sides; metallic reflections on hind-neck and sides of neck; scapulars and proximal secondaries brownish; scapulars and wing coverts with more black spots.

Iris orange red; bare orbital ring light grayish blue; legs and feet paler than in male.

Measurements of female skins in millimeters are: length, 290–428 (352); wing, 175–210 (198.1); tail, 141.5–194.5 (176.6); culmen, 15–18.5 (16.9); tarsus 25.5–28.5 (27.1); middle toe, 25–28.5 (26.6).

The following average measurements of five adult females are given by Mearns: length, 15.92 in. (394 mm.); extent, 23.96 (609); wing, 7.76 (197); tail, 7.27 (185); culmen, 0.70 (17.8); gape, 1.06 (26.9); tarsus, 1.07 (27.2); middle toe, 1.09 (27.7); its claw, 0.35 (8.9).[9]

YOUNG.—Sexes alike; similar to adult female but scapulars, wing-coverts, feathers of foreneck and breast tipped with white giving a characteristic scaled appearance; primaries margined with cinnamon; iris brownish with a narrow outer ring of carmen; tarsi and toes pinkish brown to salmon pink; scutella brownish; claws blackish.

Kalm states that all the young birds that he killed in spring had some iridescence.[10] I have examined the plate in Frisch which is clearly that of a juvenile (Fig. 13).[11] It has a small iridescent (pink) spot on the side of the neck. None of the specimens in juvenal plumage that I have examined show this phenomenon and it is not mentioned in any of the descriptions.

The following descriptions of young birds are given by Bent:

A small juvenal female, 8 inches long, is nearly fledged, but the yellowish down filaments still adorn the head, neck and breast; the crown and upper back are "bister" or "warm sepia," shading off to "natal brown" on the breast and to "wood brown" on the lesser wing coverts and scapulars; the feathers of the back, wing coverts, and scapulars are edged with whitish, or pinkish buff; the greater coverts shade from "fawn color" to "French gray," and are more narrowly edged; many of the inner coverts have a large patch of "bister" on the outer web; the inner primaries are tipped and broadly edged on the outer web with "Mikado brown," the edgings gradually disappearing outwardly; the lower back and rump are "Quaker drab" to "mouse gray"; the underparts shade off from "wood brown" on the flanks to whitish on the belly and chin.

Another young bird is fully fledged in juvenal plumage; the feathers of the head, neck and breast, now fully grown have narrow, buffy-white edgings; many of the outer wing coverts, especially the greater, are "French gray"; the tail is shorter than the adult's, the central rectrices are browner and the lateral ones are darker gray, so that there is less contrast in the tail.[12]

NESTLING.—The only nestling known to me is in the Museum of Comparative Zoology, Cambridge, Massachusetts. It was taken in Wisconsin by one of the Kumliens. It measures about 105 mm. in length, of which the bill is about 15 mm.[13] In the opinion of James L. Peters, this bird is less than a week old. It is sparsely covered with antimony yellow, hairlike down. A few pin feathers barely show on the wings, dorsal and crural tracts. The dry skin is light brown. Deane's statement that the downy young is a dark slate color must refer to the skin in life for this would be in accord with Herman.[14]

A layman, writing in the Milwaukee *Republican-Sentinel* (Wis.) of June 14, 1882, has described the nestling as "a little yellow pigeon about as big as one's thumb, and three-fourths mouth." Thoreau found in a nest in Minnesota "one young bird three inches long, of a dirty yellowish and leaden color, with pinfeathers, and with a great bill bare at the base and a blackish tip." [15]

CHEQUERS.—The spots, or chequers, in the wing (Fig. 20), resembling closely those of the chequered rock pigeon, were in process of elimination.[16] The left wing and scapulars of a juvenile had 90 chequers in contrast with 51 for an adult female and only 25 for an adult male. Passing from the juvenile to the adult male, not only the number of the spots but also their size is reduced greatly. The chequers of the female are two or more times larger than those of the male. Among birds in general, evolutionary changes are most advanced in the male,

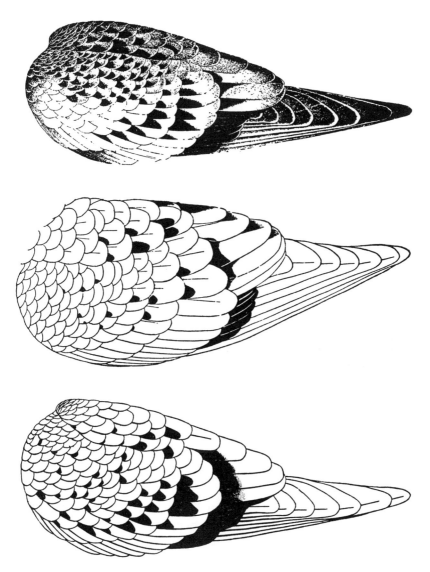

Fig. 20.—Chequers in wings of passenger pigeon. (Upper) Wing of young male. (Middle) Wing of adult male. (Lower) Wing of adult female. From C. O. Whitman, *Posthumous Works,* Vol. I.

the female occupying an intermediate position between the juvenile and male.

The black and cinnamon rufous spots on the tail feathers were considered by Keeler as recognition marks for keeping the small flocks from going astray.[17] This view was severely criticized by J. A. Allen, who contended that the spots were normally concealed by the coverts, hence invisible.[18] Even though the spots were visible when the tail was spread, as in turning or alighting, it is extremely doubtful if they served as recognition marks. Furthermore, it is to be inferred from I. B. Williams that the rufous spots are vestigial.[19]

ALBINISM.—In view of the multitudes of the passenger pigeon, the number of cases of albinism recorded is extremely small. This phenomenon has been reported by Deane and Davis.[20] A white bird killed at Chilton, Wisconsin, September 29, 1875, by David La Count was acquired by the Wisconsin Natural History Society.[21] The Milwaukee Public Museum inherited a partial albino, without data, from the above Society. This is probably the specimen from Chilton. According to C. W. Dickinson, an occasional white pigeon was seen, but a variation from the normal color was rare. The "ten or twelve spotted birds" seen by him were probably partial albinos.[22] A partially albinistic male was reported by Newcomb.[23]

MOLT.—The adults had one complete molt in August and September.[24] The molt of captive birds began in September and required several weeks for completion.[25] According to Forbush, the molt of wild birds took place once a year, usually in September, and was rapid and complete.[26] Thoreau wrote on September 12, 1854, of a flock of passenger pigeons in a white oak, that "their blue-black droppings and feathers spot the road."[27] It seems anomalous that the molt should take place at the time of the main fall migration. The postjuvenal molt took place July to October,[28] or August to October, earlier or later, depending upon the time of hatching.[29] Gentry took birds in eastern Pennsylvania in early August that were in the characteristic juvenal plumage.[30] By early spring the plumage of the young was scarcely distinguishable from that of the adult. Captive birds of all ages were in perfect plumage by March 1.

PTERYLOSIS.—Our knowledge of the distribution and development of the feather tracts in the passenger pigeon is due solely to Clark.[31] The pterylosis differs markedly from that of other species of pigeons, particularly in the development of the pelvic wing in the nestling. This consists of nineteen quills, twelve of which are apparently on the tibia; six and possibly seven are main quills, the remainder coverts. The remaining seven feathers consist of four main quills and three coverts lying along the posterior margin of the femur. All the quills of the pelvic wing are considerably more advanced than those of the wings and tail. The apteria are exceptionally large, the dorsal being 5–6 mm. wide.

The adult shows a striking decrease in the apterial areas from those in the nestling stage. The dorsal surface shows only a few small areas free from contour feathers. The ventral apterium attains a maximum width of 20 mm. at the middle of the sternum, decreasing to a width of 10 mm. on the belly and to 5–6 mm. on the crop.

WEIGHT.—Data on the weight of the adult passenger pigeon are astonishingly meager. Forster gives 9 ounces (255.6 g.) and Eaton 12 ounces (340.8 g.).[32] The squabs when abandoned by their parents weighed 10 (284 g.) to 20 ounces (568 g.).[33] The latter figure appears to be too high. The band-tailed pigeon has an average weight of 340 grams.

But I am pigeon-liver'd, and lack gall
To make oppression bitter.
—Hamlet, *Act II, scene 2*

CHAPTER II: ANATOMY AND

PHYSIOLOGY

The pigeons have been difficult to classify. They have affinities with the gallinaceous birds, *Galliformes,* under which they were once placed. They also show a relationship to the shore birds to the extent that Gadow included them with the *Charadriiformes.* The bill of the pigeon is like that of a plover, and the flight of pigeons is strikingly like that of the larger plovers, the golden and black-bellied.

The pigeons are sufficiently distinct to be placed in a separate order, the *Columbiformes.* They differ from the *Galliformes* and *Charadriiformes* in several important respects. In the pigeons the vomer is absent or rudimentary, the gall bladder is absent, and the caeca, if present, are nonfunctional. The bilobed crop is highly specialized, the lining of which desquamates to form "pigeon milk," the sole food of the young for the first few days after birth. The eggs are unspotted. The young, born blind and naked, at least without real down, must be fed in the nest.

The osteology of the passenger pigeon has been studied thoroughly by Shufeldt.[1] The skeleton may be considered typical of the Columbidae except the genus *Starnoenas.*[2] The skeleton is shown in Figure 10.

There are but few known skeletons. Pitelka and Bryant list the following: one, Museum of Vertebrate Zoology, University of California, Berkeley, California; two, U. S. National Museum, Washington, D. C.; two, Peabody Museum, Yale University, New Haven, Connecticut; one, Charleston Museum, Charleston, South Carolina; one, Science Museum, St. Paul Institute, St. Paul, Minnesota.[3] Elsewhere are: six complete and one partial, American Museum of Natural History, New

York; [4] one, Department of Biology, University of Notre Dame, Notre Dame, Indiana.[5]

Comparative measurements of some of the bones of three native pigeons are given by Pitelka and Bryant: [6]

	Ectopistes migratorius	*Zenaidura macroura*	*Columba fasciata*
(1) Length of coracoid	31.6 mm.	34.1 mm.	37.2 mm.
(2) Length of carpometacarpus	29.8	23.2	33.1
(3) Length of tarsometatarsus (greatest)	28.3	21.1	28.3
(4) Breadth of proximal end of tarsometatarsus	6.4	5.0	7.1
(5) Breadth of distal end	6.6	5.1	7.7
(6) Breadth of shaft	2.3	2.2	3.6
Ratio of Item 4 to Item 3	22.6%	23.7%	25.1%
Ratio of Item 5 to Item 3	23.3	24.2	27.2
Ratio of Item 6 to Item 3	7.8	10.4	12.7

The anatomy of the passenger pigeon was investigated first by William Macgillivray. His description of the digestive and respiratory tracts (Fig. 21) is as follows:

The mouth is very narrow, being only 4½ twelfths [inches] in breadth, but capable of being dilated to the width of 1 inch by means of a joint on each side of the lower mandible. There are two thin longitudinal ridges on the palate, of which the sides slope upwards. The posterior aperture of the nares is ½ inch long, margined with papillae. The tongue is 7½ twelfths long, rather broad and sagittate at the base with numerous small papillae, but at the middle contracted to 1½ twelfth, afterwards horny, very narrow, induplicate, and ending in a rather sharp point. Oesophagus, *a g,* 5½ inches long, immediately dilated to 1 inch, and at the lower part of the neck enlarged into an enormous sac, *b c d,* 3 inches in breadth, and 2½ inches in length, a little contracted in the middle; with its inner surface smooth, and at the lower aperture running into longitudinal prominent plicae; in the rest of its extent, the width of the oesophagus, *e f,* is about 10 twelfths. The stomach, *g h i,* is a very large and strong gizzard, placed obliquely, 2 inches 2 twelfths in breadth, 1 inch 1 fourth in length; its lateral muscles exceedingly thick, the left being 7¼ twelfths, the right 8 twelfths; the lower muscle prominent; the tendons very large; the epithelium of a horny texture, of moderate thickness, with longitudinal broad rugae, and two opposite longitudinal grinding surfaces, of a yellowish colour. In the crop were found three entire acorns, and in the stomach fragments of others, and three pieces of quartz. The intestine, *i j k l m n,* is 4 feet long, 4 twelfths in width, at the narrowest part only 2 twelfths. The duodenum, *i j k,* curves in the usual manner, at the distance of 3 inches. The intestine forms six folds. The coeca, *m,* are extremely diminutive, being only 1½ twelfth in breadth; they are 2 inches distant from the extremity; the cloaca, *n,* oblong.

The trachea passes along the left side, as usual in birds having a large crop: its length is 2¾ inches; its breadth varying from 2¾ twelfths to 1½ twelfth; its rings 105, feeble; the last ring large, formed laterally of two rings, with an intervening membrane. Bronchi of about 15 half rings, and narrow. The lateral muscles strong, as are the sterno-tracheal, which come off at the distance of ½ inch. There is a single pair of inferior laryngeal muscles going to the upper edge of the last tracheal ring.[7]

The specimen examined by Macgillivray was an adult male preserved in alcohol. A more complete anatomical investigation of Martha, the last passenger pigeon, was made by Shufeldt.[8] The much smaller measurements of the crop, 54 x 40 mm. (2.1 x 1.6 inches), and the gizzard, one-half the size given by Macgillivray, may have been characteristic of the female.

A thorough treatment of the anatomy of the domestic pigeon is given by Parker.[9] A colored frontispiece showing the anatomy of the same pigeon is to be found in Coues.[10]

The red blood corpuscles in the blood of the passenger pigeon were found by Gulliver to be remarkably different from those in any other species of Columbidae. The unusually narrow ellipses measured 1/1909 inch in length and 1/4626 inch in width.[11]

The nervous system of the passenger pigeon was investigated by Romano-Prestia.[12]

The digestion of food was rapid. A crop filled in the evening was empty by morning. According to Audubon, the food was digested completely within twelve hours.[13] Dr. E. Sterling states: "I have often experimented with the wild pigeon while in confinement, and have found that it requires about seven hours for corn to pass the crop; wheat, oats,

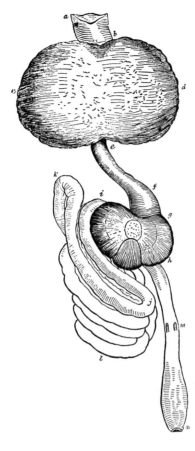

Fig. 21.—Digestive tract of passenger pigeon. From J. J. Audubon, *Ornithological Biography*, Vol. V.

and rice pass in four to five hours. This is when the crop is full." [14] Beechnuts and acorns with their hard shells probably required a longer time than grain.

The ability of a pigeon to produce "milk" is unique and characteristic. It is remarkable that the American Indian had a thorough grasp of the physiological significance of this substance. Cotton Mather in 1712 gave an excellent summation:

The *cocks* were always by far yᵉ fattest, and when we opened them we found in their *craws*, about yᵉ Quantity of half a Gill of a Substance like a Tender *Cheese-Curd*. I asked Some of oʳ Indians, what those *Pigeons* had Eaten; and why the Hens did not feed on the Same. They answered, It was nothing they had eaten, but something that came naturally into their *crops*, as milk does into the Dugs of other

Creatures; and that the Hens could not keep their Young alive, when first hatched; and that this nourished the young Birds, & caused them to grow fatter, & fly in half ye Time, that any other Birds could attain it.[15]

Both sexes produced milk. Mather was of the opinion that only the male passenger pigeon had this ability and that if killed the female could not keep the young alive.[16] The production of milk was smaller in the female due to feeding but once a day and spending many hours on the nest.

The feeding of "milk" to the young, according to Litwer, was observed by Conrad Peyer in 1685.[17] The gifted English physiologist, John Hunter, was the first to throw any scientific light on this phenomenon. After working with the domestic pigeon (*Columba livia*) he wrote:

During incubation the coats of the crop in the pigeon are gradually enlarged and thickened. . . . On comparing the state of the crop when the bird is not sitting, with its appearance during incubation, the difference is very remarkable. In the first case it is thin and membranous; but by the time the young are about to be hatched, the whole, except what lies on the trachea, becomes thicker, and takes on a glandular appearance, having its internal surface very irregular. . . .

Whatever may be the consistence of this substance when just secreted, it most probably very soon coagulates into granulated white curd, for in such form I have always found it in the crop; and if an old pigeon is killed just as the young ones are hatching, the crop will be found as above described, and in its cavity pieces of white curd, mixed with some of the common food of the pigeon, such as barley, beans, &c. If we allow either of the parents to feed the brood, the crop of the young pigeons when examined will be discovered to contain the same kind of curdled substance as that of the old ones, which passes from thence into the stomach, where it is to be digested.

The young pigeon is fed for a little time with this substance only, as about the third day some of the common food is found mingled with it: as the pigeon grows older the proportion of common food is increased; so that by the time it is seven, eight, or nine days old, the secretion of the curd ceases in the old ones, and of course no more will be found in the crop of the young. It is a curious fact that the parent pigeon has at first a power to throw up this curd without any mixture of common food, although afterwards both are thrown up according to the proportion required for the young ones.[18]

The initial feeding of the milk only, with subsequent admixture of softened grain, is also mentioned by Fulton.[19] The assumption that the pigeon can regurgitate the milk and withhold the grain is apparently erroneous. Patel states:

> From the seventeenth day of incubation to the fourth day of feeding, grain is not found in the crops of the parent birds, even just after they are fed. This is apparently due to the enormous hypertrophy of the epithelium, which greatly decreases the cavities of the pouches. The space which remains is occupied by milk, and thus no place is available for the storage of grain. From the fourth day of feeding onward, the processes of cell multiplication and desquamation begin to regress, and consequently more space is available for the collection of grain.[20]

It is apparent, therefore, that the omission of grain for the first two or three days and its subsequent inclusion in the feed of the young is not due to any special regulatory power possessed by the pigeons but is the direct result of the histological changes in the crop during this period.

There is a similarity between pigeon milk and mammalian milk in that both contain salts, fats, and proteins, but in the former there is a total absence of sugar. A recent analysis of pigeon milk was made by Dabrowska. (See Table 5.) As she states, this milk has considerable similarity to that of the rabbit.

TABLE 5

CHEMICAL COMPOSITION OF PIGEON MILK *

	PIGEON MILK	
COMPONENT	FRESH	DRY
Water	76.65%	0.00%
Proteins	13.34	57.41
Fats	7.95	34.19
Ash	1.52	6.51
Carbohydrates	0.00	0.00

* Figures after W. Dabrowska, "Sur la Composition chimique de la sécrétion lactée du jabot du pigeon," *Compt. rend. soc. biol.*, CX (1932), 1093.

Pigeon milk appears to be a combination of secretion and desquamation according to the more recent studies by Litwer, Beams and Meyer, and Patel.[21] The epithelium of the two lobes of the crop consist of an outer layer, the "nutritive" epithelium (Beams and Meyer), and a deeper layer of cells forming the "proliferating" epithelium (Litwer). With the domestic pigeon hypertrophy of the epithelium begins on about the eighth day of incubation. The epithelium gradually becomes thicker and more folded. After eighteen days, the average time for hatching, the hypertrophy reaches its greatest development. The major portion of the lumen is filled with desquamated cells containing fat globules which are apparently secreted from the nutritive epithelium. Regression of the crop of the parent begins one to two weeks after the young have hatched and reaches its normal stage in 14 to 25 days.

The parent has little control of the formation of the milk, which is ready for the young at the time of hatching. With the male the formation seems to be due to the sight of the brooding female; and the changes in the crop can be checked by preventing him from brooding or seeing the female, "psychological brooding." If eggs are replaced by young early in the period of incubation, the formation of milk is not hastened, nor is the formation of milk prolonged by successive substitution of newly hatched young.

A clue to the agent in the formation of the milk was obtained by Riddle and Braucher, and Riddle and Dykshorn.[22] It was found that injection of extracts from the anterior lobe of the pituitary glands would produce the milk in nestling pigeons only a week old, as well as in nonbrooding pigeons. The extracts were effective on the male castrated at the beginning of the incubation period, and even six months after castration. The wall of the crop thickened rapidly. An increased rate of cell division in the epithelium could be detected within 20–30 minutes after treatment.[23] Increase in the thickness of the wall of the crop is limited to the lateral lobes. The crop, liver, pancreas, and intestine are enlarged while the sexual organs are reduced. The active principle is the hormone, prolactin.[24] This hormone likewise stimulates the secretion of milk by the mammary gland.

It was observed by Patel that a mated male castrated 12 to 16 days prior to the laying of eggs by the female had a normal crop development, but never thereafter. He suggests that the action of prolactin is linked with that of a sex hormone.[25] Riddle found that the pituitary releases three hormones which are similar to prolactin and greatly modify its activity.[26]

Many attempts have been made to determine the genetic relationship between the various species of pigeons by crossbreeding. Mitchell mentions two specimens in the collection of the London Zoological Society, the products of *Ectopistes migratorius* male x *Turtur risorius* female. They had neither the long tail of *migratorius* nor the collar of *risorius*. Any person unfamiliar with their origin might think the cross a distinct species.[27] This hybrid appears to be the *Trygon gregaria* of Brehm, according to Salvadori.[28] The ancestry of *Turtur risorius* (*Streptopelia risoria*) is quite obscure.[29] Generally known as the ringdove or blond ringdove, it has been kept in confinement for many centuries. Less commonly it has been called the collared or Barbary dove, though its African origin is denied.[30] Peters considers it a form of *Streptopelia decaocto decaocto*.[31]

Males obtained by crossing the passenger pigeon with the turtledove, *Turtur vulgaris* (*Streptopelia turtur turtur*) were mated with pure females of the passenger pigeon, ringdove (*Turtur risorius*), turtledove, and stock dove (*Columba oenas*). Many eggs were produced but all failed to hatch.[32]

The offspring of crosses of the passenger pigeon and blond ringdove obtained by Guyer were sterile. The testes of the males were small to extremely small.[33] Whitman, in his extensive experiments in crossing the passenger pigeon with *Streptopelia risoria,* obtained males only and these without exception were sterile.[34] The hybrids obtained by crossing a passenger pigeon with a ringdove hybrid were in plumage very uniform intermediates. The pointed, though shortened, tail gave them the general appearance of the passenger pigeon.[35] The general color was lighter, resembling that of the ringdove. The neck had a slight iridescence from the male parent and the characteristic mark of the ringdove. The black spots on the wing of the male parent did not appear in the hybrid except on the posterior edge of the wing.

The great resemblance between the passenger pigeon and the mourning dove would promise successful interbreeding. Starr states that the mating of the passenger pigeon with the "Carolina dove" produced young which proved fertile when again mated with this dove.[36] I have been unable to locate any experimental evidence on which this statement was based. Whitman is silent; however, some original notes kindly loaned by Dr. Wallace Craig show that crossing was attempted in 1903. There is no indication that any fertile eggs were produced.

The line of descent of the passenger pigeon is conjectural. The nest call bore a general resemblance to that of the Japanese turtledove, *Turtur* (*Streptopelia*) *orientalis,* and the European turtledove, *Turtur* (*Streptopelia*) *turtur,* which Whitman believed to be the nearest living representatives of the ancestral type.[37] Subsequently the Japanese turtledove alone was selected.[38] No attempts to cross this dove with the passenger pigeon have been recorded. The phylogeny is based mainly on color patterns and in part on voice. The descent of *Ectopistes* as drawn by Craig is as follows: [39]

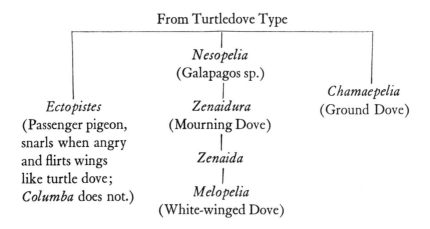

From Turtledove Type

Nesopelia
(Galapagos sp.)

Ectopistes
(Passenger pigeon,
snarls when angry
and flirts wings
like turtle dove;
Columba does not.)

Zenaidura
(Mourning Dove)

Zenaida

Melopelia
(White-winged Dove)

Chamaepelia
(Ground Dove)

The passenger pigeon is considered by Williams an excellent example of the typical family where gray predominates. It is to be assumed that the rufous spots on the tail feathers are vestigial. He points out that the dodo (*Raphus cucullatus*) and solitaire (*Pezophaps solitaria*) were both gray birds.[40]

The behavior of the hybrid between the male passenger pigeon and female collared dove is quoted from Craig:

The "nest-call" is a sort of "caw" resembling that of the male parent, but very much weaker. The tail is held up and slightly spread, and the head bowed, as he looks at the female. In the "note of attack" the bird bristles, drops the head, shortens the neck, and gives a scolding or snarling note. This is given when he flies at another dove, or when he jumps to peck through the wire netting of his pen. He often flies up to the side of his pen against another bird, and while the other bird merely tries to peck, making no noise, this male always emits his snarl.

This snarl is like that of the male parent, but the hybrid gives it with markedly less vigor and shrillness than it is given by the parent.

This hybrid has the up-and-down motion of a ring-dove, to accompany its "coo," but not so pronounced as in the latter. Its "coo" is the same "caw" repeated several times with the up-and-down motion. It solicits the female by offering the open beak, as a ring-dove does (I have never seen *Ectopistes* do this); but it slurs this part and more often omits it entirely. Often before offering the beak the hybrid bills his wing as the rings and common doves nearly always do, and as *Ectopistes* occasionally does.

The hybrids have thus far shown a decided mating preference for female ring-doves over every other species. They give little attention to female passengers. A hybrid brought into the house in January at once became amorous at sight of a female ring-dove. So eager was he that he pursued her in spite of her strokes—not offering to resist, but simply facing the blows, spreading his tail, and jumping like a male ring-dove.

The "call-note" is a "caw" emitted from 5 to 10 or more times in slow succession. The bird sits fairly erect on the perch, with the body, head, and tail inclined a little. The beak is very slightly nodded at each caw. This call-note in *Ectopistes* is usually emitted *once* at a time, and it differs very much from the shriller and louder note of attack or threat. I do not now understand how it comes to pass that the hybrid emits its call so many times in succession. Possibly this is a peculiarity from the ring-dove mother. The ring-dove repeats its coo or call (5 to 15 times) when calling on the perch, and takes the same position. This would be a curious mixture of instincts. . . .

Two of my passenger hybrids have *weak voices;* they are barely able to make the call-note audible. They make the same call in the same way, or attempt to do so, but their vocal organs are too weak or ill-constructed to enable them to vocalize strongly.[41]

The passenger pigeon was very fond of earthworms. The hybrids had the instinct to pull them from their burrows but ate them gingerly. The hybrids also had to a marked degree the passenger pigeon's habit of emitting a cry of distress when caught, struggling to escape, then feigning death.

CHAPTER 12: NOMENCLATURE

The word pigeon is of Norman origin and is derived from the Latin *pipio,* meaning a peeping, nestling bird. There is no real distinction between a pigeon and a dove, but the latter name is applied generally to a small, delicately formed pigeon. The pigeons form a large family, of which about 825 forms have been described.[1] The center of abundance is in the islands of the western Pacific.

The passenger pigeon was kept in suspense for a century and a half as to its proper scientific name. The history of its nomenclature will serve a useful purpose, since this species furnishes an excellent example of the difficulties that sometimes beset the systematic ornithologist. The English saved themselves much trouble in this field by accepting as a starting point the names in the twelfth edition of the *Systema Naturae* of Linnaeus. In America our views are still primordial.

The first adequate description and colored plate of this pigeon was published by Catesby, who called it *Palumbus migratorius.*[2] A few years later a plate, poorly colored but excellent in draughtsmanship, was published by Frisch under the caption *Columba americana.*[3] Klein called it *Columbus, Palumbus caroliniensis* and referred to Catesby's description. He considered the "long-tailed dove" of Edwards an "elegant variety."[4]

A curious trinomen, *Palumbus torquatus migratorius,* based on *P. migratorius* Catesby and *P. torquatus* Aldrovandus, was used by Douglass.[5] *P. torquatus* (the European wood pigeon, *Columba palumbus*), of course, has no relationship to the passenger pigeon.

248

None of the Latin names had true scientific significance until Linnaeus used *Columba macroura* and applied it to both the true passenger pigeon, the *Palumbus migratorius* of Catesby, and the "long-tailed dove" of Edwards.[6] The latter bird is the Cuban mourning dove (*Zenaidura*). This is shown by Edwards' statement that it came from the West Indies and by his plate in which the bird has on the side of the neck the black spot characteristic of the mourning dove.[7]

A very complete description of the passenger pigeon was given by Kalm in 1759, who copied the nomenclature in the tenth edition of Linnaeus.[8] Two years later Kalm used *Columba macroura* only. J. R. Forster in the abridged London edition of Kalm's *Resa* changed this to *Columba migratoria*.[9]

Brisson's *Oenas americana* (*le pigeon sauvage d'Amérique*), based on Frisch and Klein, apparently represents the male passenger pigeon.[10] He then proceeded to describe *Turtur canadensis* (*la tourterelle de Canada*). The description is that of the female passenger pigeon. Mention is made of the red spots (*une grande tache rousse*) at the base of the tail feathers. He considered it to be a male, since the female is mentioned specifically.[11] Temminck viewed Brisson's *tourterelle* as only an accidental variety; and Vieillot as in no wise a variety, but a young passenger pigeon in its first plumage.[12]

The twelfth edition of Linnaeus only added to the confusion. His *Columba canadensis* was based on Brisson's female and his *Columba migratoria* on Catesby's male.[13] Coues, and subsequently Oberholser, showed that *canadensis* had page priority over *migratoria* but suggested that a name (*migratoria*) that had been unchallenged for fifty years or more should stand.[14] Nevertheless *canadensis* was preferred by Hellmayr and Conover.[15]

Buffon indulged in strange reasoning. He recognized that the passenger pigeon differed from the European turtle dove in size and length of tail, but considered it only a variety of the latter produced by climate. He thought it the same as Edwards' long-tailed dove.[16] His plate, No. 175 (*tourterelle de la Caroline*), is possibly a badly colored male passenger pigeon; and plate No. 176 (*tourterelle du Canada*), the female.

Müller in his revised *Systema,* for reasons not apparent, used *Co-*

lumba histrio for *C. migratoria* Linn. and *C. ventrilis* for *C. canadensis* Linn.; however, Gmelin, in the thirteenth edition, retained the Linnaean names.[17] The popular and scientific names "Canada turtle" (*Columba canadensis*) and "passenger pigeon" (*Columba migratoria*) were used by Latham.[18] It remained for Temminck to clarify the synonomy in 1813. He showed that the *Columba canadensis* of Linnaeus was the female passenger pigeon.[19]

In 1827 Swainson placed this pigeon in a new genus, *Ectopistes,* selecting *Columba migratoria* Linn. as the type.[20] Here it stands today. The type locality is South Carolina.[21] *Ectopistes* is masculine. Swainson evidently considered it to be feminine, for in 1831 he used *Columba* (*Ectopistes*) *migratoria.*[22] The correct form of the adjective, *migratorius,* used by Gray was long in receiving general usage.[23] The recent use of *migratoria* by Peters is a *lapsus calami.*[24]

Strictly, *migratorius* is improperly applied and *macrourus* should prevail. Coues used *Ectopistes macroura.* Later he withdrew the name, since he had mistaken Edwards' bird for the passenger pigeon.[25] He was likewise in error in stating that the Linnaean diagnosis and habitat covered both the bird of Edwards and that of Catesby. Bangs approached the problem with greater discernment. He pointed out that Linnaeus had taken his description and habitat directly from Catesby, "pectore purpurascente" and "habitat in Canada; hybernat in Carolina," hence *macrourus* should be used.[26] Bangs was mistaken in stating that the Linnaean references are given chronologically. Edwards appears first, though second in point of time. Bangs's position regarding the use of *macrourus* is perfectly correct;[27] however, "squatter's rights" now prevail and it is unlikely that the position of *migratorius* will be disturbed.[28]

A few attempts have been made to supplant *Ectopistes.* Brehm proposed *Trygon migratoria.*[29] His *Trygon gregaria* is a hybrid between the passenger pigeon and the collared dove.[30] Schlegel used *Turtur migratorius,* then *Peristera migratoria.*[31]

There is but one form of *Ectopistes.* The small race mentioned by Mauduyt as rare in Louisiana is believed to be the female.[32] The *Ectopistes carolinensis* of Bonaparte and Audubon is the eastern mourning dove, while the *Ectopistes carolinensis* of Peale and the *Ectopistes marginellus* of Woodhouse represent the western mourning dove.[33]

There is a strong superficial resemblance between the passenger pigeon and the mourning dove in form and color, but there are also some marked differences. The passenger pigeon has only twelve tail feathers compared with fourteen for the mourning dove. The passenger pigeon has the tarsus partially feathered anteriorly. The nostril is covered with a rounded protuberance and there is a notch in approximately the middle of the upper mandible.

The scientific name of the passenger pigeon is redundant in a sense. Billings thought that *Ectopistes* was derived from the Greek word *ektopisteos,* meaning to change place frequently.[34] Coues, with his usual flair for fitness, translates *ektopistes* as wanderer, which he rightly thinks very appropriate.[35] The adjective *migratorius* is a less happy selection as it is in no wise particular.

A common name of a bird is seldom satisfactory to the layman and he proceeds to coin a large number of synonyms. Were it not for scientific names, the confusion would usually be endless. Scientists eventually agree upon a name, but the public seldom does. Frost expressed himself as follows:

None of the names bestowed upon this species are sufficiently, or at all descriptive of it. Passenger, the English expression, and *migratoria,* the Latin name, fall equally short, inasmuch as every known pigeon is to a greater or less extent migratory as well as this one. The "swarm" pigeon, the "flood" pigeon, or even the "deluge" pigeon would be a more appropriate appellation; for the weight of their numbers breaks down the forest with scarcely less havoc than if the stream of the Mississippi were poured upon it.[36]

The use of the term birds of passage to show that they were migratory was common in the eighteenth century. Catesby's choice of pigeon of passage is subject to the criticism that several other species of pigeons are more or less migratory, however, so far as America is concerned the name expresses one of the most striking habits of the species, passage in multitudes. Pennant used the more direct "passenger pigeon," accepted today as the correct common name in scientific literature.

The name wild pigeon was in common use throughout the last century of the existence of the species. The archaic spelling, pidgeon, persisted long. The editor of the Oconto *Pioneer* (Wis.), twitted by a colleague on his spelling, retorted on September 12, 1861: "The editor of the *Advocate* wants to know what pidgeons are, and queries about our spelling of the article so common in our woods. The pidgeons, as we learned to spell it when we were young, are game of the flybysterous order, dedicated by the gods of Greece to the sons of Mars [Ares] and Oconto. They live on wheat and huckleberries, and they die on pine trees. Are you satisfied?"

Some of the names used in various European languages are given below:

Dutch

BOOM DUIF.—Douglass (as in Chap. 7, n. 18).
RINGLE DUIF.—Douglass (as in Chap. 7, n. 18).
WILDE DUIF.—Douglass (as in Chap. 7, n. 18).

English

BLUE PIGEON.—Billings (as in Chap. 12, n. 34).
DOVE.—Ashe (as in Chap. 3, n. 213).
MERNE ROUCK PIGEON.—Hutchins (as in Chap. 3, n. 63).
PASSENGER PIGEON.—Pennant (as in Chap. 3, n. 215), Audubon (as in Chap. 4, n. 4).
PIDGEON.—Josselyn (as in Chap. 1, n. 24), Mather (as in Chap. 1, n. 28).
PIGEON.—Lawson (as in Chap. 7, n. 53), Du Pratz (as in Chap. 1, n. 40), Anburey (as in Chap. 5, n. 26), Mather (as in Chap. 1, n. 11).
PIGEON OF PASSAGE.—Catesby (as in Chap. 3, n. 20), Douglass (as in Chap. 7, n. 18).
RING DOVE.—Douglass (as in Chap. 7, n. 18).
ROCK PIGEON.—Taylor (as in Chap. 8, n. 153).
STOCK DOVE.—Thomas Heriot (in *Travels and Works of Captain John Smith* [Edinburgh, 1910], I, 320).
TURTLE.—Hennepin (as in Chap. 1, n. 35).
WANDERING LONG-TAILED DOVE.—Audubon (as in Chap. 6, n. 157), Billings (as in Chap. 12, n. 34), Hennepin (as in Chap. 1, n. 35), Lawson (as in Chap. 7, n. 53), John Bartram (*Observations on the Inhabitants, Climate* ... [London, 1751], p. 36).

WILD PIGEON.—Byrd (as in Chap. 14, n. 349), Douglass (as in Chap. 7, n. 18), William Stork (*An Account of East Florida* [London, 1766], p. 51).

WOOD PIGEON.—Hennepin (as in Chap. 1, n. 35), Richard H. Bonnycastle (*The Canadas in 1841* [London, 1841], II, 50).

French

CROISEAU D'AMERIQUE.—Frisch (as in Chap. 12, n. 3).

PIGEON RAMIER.—Gravier (in *The Jesuit Relations and Allied Documents* [ed. R. G. Thwaites; Cleveland, Ohio, 1896–1901], LXV, 109).

PIGEON SAUVAGE.—Vivier (*ibid.,* LXIX, 145).

RAMIER.—Cartier (as in Chap. 1, n. 2), Du Pratz (as in Chap. 1, n. 40), Douglass (as in Chap. 7, n. 18).

TOURTE.—Biard (in *Jesuit Relations,* III, 81), Raffeix (*ibid.,* LVI, 49), Anburey (as in Chap. 5, n. 26).

TOURTERELLE.—Le Jeune (in *Jesuit Relations,* X, 143 and 287), Sagard-Theodat (as in Chap. 1, n. 6).

German

STRICHTAUBE.—Georg H. Borowski (*Gemeinnüzzige Naturgeschichte des Thierreichs* [Berlin, 1782], III, 214).

WANDERTAUBE.—Borowski (*ibid.*), Maximilian (as in Chap. 14, n. 80).

German (of Pennsylvania)

WILTE DOUB.—Herbert H. Beck (in *Auk,* XLI [1924], 292).

Swedish (of New Jersey)

DUFOR.—Pehr Kalm (in *Kong. Svenska Vetenskapsakadimien Handlingar,* XX [1759], 275–95).

VILLA DUFOR.—Kalm (*ibid.*).

It is remarkable that the Massachusetts Indians anticipated Swainson in giving the most suitable name to the passenger pigeon. Cotton Mather wrote about 1712: "Our Indians call these *Pigeons* by a name that signifies Wanderers." [37] Roger Williams' book on the language of the Narragansetts, written in 1643, gives *wuskówhàn* as their name for pigeon.[38] A. Lewis is more explicit as he states that this name means a wanderer.[39] Williams gives in addition: *wuskowhanánnûaog*, pigeons, and *wuskowhannanaûkit*, pigeon country.

O-mi-mi was the common word for pigeon amongst the Algonquian tribes; however, the Narragansetts were of Algonquian linguistic stock. The Micmac, another Algonquian tribe, also did not conform to the usual name. Their word for pigeon was *pŭlés*, or *wĕnjooepŭlĕś*.[40] *O-mi-mi*, or a variant, was used over a wide territory. The name is supposed to express one of the pigeon's notes. The word appears in widely scattered place names as: village of Omémee, Victoria County, Ontario; Memee, or Pigeon River, north of Sheboygan, Wisconsin; village and township of Memee in Manitowoc County, Wisconsin; and the village of Omemee, Bottineau County, North Dakota.

Indian words for, or pertaining to the passenger pigeon are listed below. Spelling of all tribal names follows that of W. B. Hodge in *Handbook of American Indians* (Washington, 1912).

Algonquian Linguistic Stock

AMEMI.—Delaware or Lenape (David Zeisberger, *Zeisberger's Indian Dictionary* [Cambridge, Mass., 1887], p. 143; Daniel G. Brinton and Albert S. Anthony, *A Lenâpé-English Dictionary* [Phila., 1888], p. 19).

ME-ME.—Chippewa of Minnesota (McKenny, as in Chap. 4, n. 135).

O-ME-ME-OO.—Potawatomi (Mershon, as in Chap. 3, n. 35).

OMIHMI, with second *mi* pronounced abruptly.—Chippewa (Maximilian, as in Chap. 14, n. 80).

OMIMI.—Algonquian (J. A. Curoq, *Lexique de la langue algonquine* [Montreal, 1886], p. 298; G. Lemoine, *Dictionnaire français-algonquin* [Quebec, 1911]) and Chippewa of Minnesota (Wells W. Cooke in *Auk*, I [1884], 247).

OMIMIW.—Cree (P. A. Lacombe, *Dictionnaire de la langue des Cris* [Montreal, 1874], p. 264).

Other Indian Linguistic Stocks

Jäh'gowa'son'on, literally "big breads."—Seneca (Fenton and Deardorff, as in Chap. 7, n. 77).

Jă-kó-wä-o-ań-no, pigeon dance.—Seneca (Lewis Henry Morgan, *League of the . . . Iroquois* [Rochester, N. Y., 1851], pp. 290 and 345).

Ka-ko-ee.—Blackfoot (John Palliser, *British North America* [London, 1863], p. 213).

Kun-kai-ğa.—Rocky Mountain Stoney or Assiniboin (*ibid.,* p. 211).

Ma-ra-ka-it-ea.—Gros Ventres (*ibid.,* p. 208).

Ori'te, ourité.—Mohawk (Dodge, as in Chap. 7, n. 78; Villiers, as in Chap. 16, n. 40).

Pachaiasha or pachanusi, pigeon roost.—Choctaw (Cyrus Byington, *A Dictionary of the Choctaw Language* [Bur. Am. Ethnology, Bull. No. 46; Wash., 1915], p. 518).

Pachi.—Choctaw (*ibid.*).

Pachushi, pigeon egg.—Choctaw (*ibid.*).

Poweatha.—Shawnee (Matilda Edgar, *Ten Years of Upper Canada in Peace and War, 1805–1815* [Toronto, 1890], p. 377).

Putchee nashoba, lost dove.—Choctaw (Lincecum, as in Chap. 13, n. 116).

Tcahko'wa.—Cayuga (Dodge, as in Chap. 7, n. 78).

Tshiòchara.—Onondaga (Zeisberger, *op. cit.,* p. 143).

Uti.—Biloxi and Ofo (James O. Dorsey and John R. Swanton, *A Dictionary of the Biloxi and Ofo Languages* [Bur. Am. Ethnology, Bull. No. 47; Wash., 1912], p. 310).

Yu-ak-oo-was.—Seneca (Harris, as in Chap. 7, n. 57).

The range of the passenger pigeon given in the fourth edition of the *Check-List of North American Birds* is: "Bred formerly from middle western Mackenzie, central Keewatin, central Ontario, central Quebec and Nova Scotia south to Kansas, Mississippi, Kentucky, Pennsylvania, and New York. Wintered principally from Arkansas and North Carolina south to central Texas, Louisiana, and Florida. Casual west to Oregon, Nevada, Washington, and eastern Mexico; accidental in Bermuda, Cuba, the British Isles, and Europe." [1]

No reliable records of the occurrence of this species in Oregon, Washington, or Keewatin have been found in the literature. While it was met with at times in Mackenzie, there is no mention of nesting. The limits of its range, illustrated in Figure 22, are given below.

LIMITS OF RANGE

United States

FLORIDA. At Bryan's (Drayton's) Island, lat. 29° 20′ N., in N. end Lake George, John Bartram saw several flocks on Jan. 24 and 25, 1766.[2] Occurred in Alachua Co. at Gainsville and Archer.[3] At times abundant in Wakulla Co.[4]

IDAHO. On Aug. 26, 1805, Lewis and Clark recorded a few at forks of Salmon River, Lemi Co.[5] Area is outside range of band-tailed pigeon and they knew both passenger pigeon and mourning dove. Assumption that Cooper's paper showed presence in Idaho invalid in view of

Fig. 22.—DISTRIBUTION MAP OF THE PASSENGER PIGEON. Solid line encloses area of normal distribution. Dotted line encloses principal nesting area. Solid circles represent casual or accidental occurrences.

Cooper's retraction in 1894.[6] U. S. Nat. Museum has specimen of adult (No. 22,006) taken by C. B. R. Kennerly, June 17, 1860, on Pack River, N. Idaho, lat. 48° 22′ N., long. 116° 28′ W.

KANSAS. Information on W. range extremely slight. Few nested in Neosho Valley, long. 96° 30′ W.[7] If it behaved here as northward, it must have followed timbered valleys of Republican, Salmon, and Arkansas and its tributaries to considerable distance W.

MONTANA. Immature bird, supposedly of this species, seen on branch of Milk River near Bear Paw Mountains, lat. 48° 30′ N., long. 109° 30′ W. Montana ("Nebraska").[8] Lewis and Clark saw pigeons and doves on Medicine (Sun) River, long. 111° 20′ W., on July 12, 1806.[9] Above Great Falls, Cascade Co., Gass saw "wild pigeons and turtle-doves" on July 12, 1805.[10] On following day Lewis shot one and found it to be common wild pigeon of U. S.[11] Male taken on Aug. 8, 1856, above mouth of Yellowstone.[12] Hayden saw small flocks "high up on the Yellowstone" and considered species little more than a straggler in far west, not over a hundred individuals being seen in a season.[13] No record of any taken in W. Montana; but since this region is entirely without range of band-tailed pigeon, reports must refer to passenger pigeon. While in region of Missoula, Lewis and Clark, who distinguished between pigeons and doves, wrote on July 5, 1806: "A great number of pigeons breeding in this part of the mountains." [14] This would be unusual time for many to be nesting. Cooper, referring to same region, saw them almost daily in 1860, and refers to their feeding on service berries at or near Hell Gate River.[15] Young bird taken at Chief Mountain (Waterton) Lake, lat. 49° N., long. 112° 50′ W., on Aug. 23, 1874.[16] Saunders believed it to be an abundant migrant, "evidently throughout the state"; [17] however, it seems to have been rare except along the Missouri. In 1874 none seen along Missouri or Milk river.[18]

NEBRASKA. Coues states it ranged entirely across state, probably following N. Platte into Wyoming.[19] The few reaching Fort Laramie undoubtedly followed this route. U. S. Nat. Museum has immature specimen (No. 8,913) taken July 5 [1857] by F. V. Hayden on Platte River near junction with Loup River, approx. lat. 41° 22′ N., long. 97° 20′ W.

NEVADA. Accidental. Juvenile female collected in W. Humboldt Mountains, lat. 40° 30′ N., long. 118° W., on Sept. 10, 1867.[20]

NORTH DAKOTA. Single bird seen near head of Heart River, Stark Co., long. 102° 45′ W.[21] One taken in July, 1873, in Turtle Mountains, lat. 49° N., long. 100° W., where it was rare.[22]

OKLAHOMA. Found W. at least as far as Potawatomi Reservation, lat. 35° N., long. 97° W.[23]

OREGON and WASHINGTON. No authentic record for either state. Townsend lists passenger pigeon, band-tailed pigeon, and mourning dove in Territory of Oregon. Elsewhere he includes Rocky Mountains.[24] Territory of Oregon at the time had vague boundaries. In 1894 Cooper disclaimed previous statements that he had seen them almost every day in Rocky Mountains until passing Spokane Falls and that they were found as far west as Puget Sound, saying that he had never seen them farther west than Montana.[25] Pigeons reported in Pierce Co., Wash., were unquestionably band-tailed.[26] Lord reported passenger pigeons to arrive at Colville, Stevens Co., Wash., in April in flocks of 20 to 30 and to lay two eggs on the bare ground, generally on a sandy bank.[27] Nidification and locality indicate he confused western mourning dove with passenger pigeon.

SOUTH DAKOTA. Occurred at Grand River Agency, lat. 101° W.[28]

TEXAS. Several shot near Corpus Christi, lat. 27° 48′ in 1889.[29] Occasionally abundant in winter in Nueces Canyon in SE. Edwards and NW. Uvalde counties.[30] In winter of 1881/82 large roost at head of Frio Canyon,[31] which is in S. Real and NW. Uvalde counties, not in Tom Green Co.

WYOMING. Observed on N. Platte River at Fort Laramie, long. 104° 30′ W.[32] One shot by Charles S. McCarty 40 miles W. (long. 105° 15′ W.) of Fort Laramie in 1859.[33]

Canada

ALBERTA. In the middle of June, 1863, Milton and Cheadle found them very plentiful two or three days after crossing Pembina River (roughly lat. 53° 30′ N., long. 117° W.).[34] Southesk saw "a good many pigeons" near Lobstick River, W. of Edmonton, and shot one on Aug. 22, 1859.[35] There is a Pigeon Lake about 40 miles SW. of Edmonton. Passenger pigeon probably entered Alberta along valley of N. Saskatchewan.

BAFFIN BAY. On July 31, 1829, young male came aboard the *Victory* during a storm, lat. 73° 31′ N.[36] This is probably basis for statement of its accidental presence in Greenland.[37]

BRITISH COLUMBIA. The "beautiful long-tailed passenger pigeon" found as far W. as sources of N. Thompson, lat. 52° N., long. 120° W.[38] Pigeons could have arrived from Alberta by crossing Rockies at Yellow-head Pass. Band-tailed pigeon not recorded farther E. than Spuzzum on Fraser River.[39] Lord very indefinite regarding occurrence of species.[40] Much of his collecting done in Wash.[41] One of his specimens in Museum of Royal Artillery Inst., Woolwich, England, catalogued as from British Columbia.[42] Three specimens in British Museum, undated, are recorded as taken "W. side of Rocky Mts." [43] Female in U. S. Nat. Museum (No. 15,993) taken at Chilliwack, June 29, 1859, by C. B. R. Kennerly.[44] This specimen recorded by Ridgway as taken at Puget Sound.[45]

LABRADOR. One casual occurrence at Mealy Mountains, SW. of mouth of Hamilton Inlet, lat. 53° 40′ N., long. 59° 10′ W. Cartwright wrote on Aug. 22, 1775: "Near the mouth of the brook we saw a pair of doves, and I killed one with my rifle; it was much like a turtle dove and fed on the berries of Empetrum Nigrum. I never heard of such a bird in the country before and I believe they are very scarce." [46] It was suggested that these may have been mourning doves.[47] At the time it is much more probable that the passenger pigeon would have wandered to Labrador coast. Mourning dove lives almost exclusively on seeds and a specimen was not taken in Labrador until Sept. 7, 1898.[48]

MACKENZIE. On July 25, 1789, one flew past Mackenzie between Fort Chipewyan and Great Slave Lake, approx. 60° N. lat.[49] While at Fort Simpson (lat. 61° N., long. 120° W.) on June 29, 1837, Simpson wrote: "The fields here looked well, but had a troublesome enemy in the passenger pigeons. Except one at Salt River, we saw none of these grace-ful birds elsewhere throughout our journey." [50] Ross mentions a speci-men taken at Fort Simpson and also states that it occurred N. to Fort Norman (lat. 65° N.) but was not common.[51] Specimen was taken at Fort Good Hope, lat. 66° 30′ N.[52] Occurrence in Mackenzie District must be considered infrequent and breeding is doubtful.

MANITOBA. Common in S. Only northernmost records will be given

here. Alexander Henry found pigeons plentiful at Cedar Lake, lat. 53°
10′ N., long. 100° W., on Aug. 21, 1808, and between Le Pas and Pine
Island, lat. 54° N., long. 101° 30′ W. Some of large numbers seen on
Aug. 23 were shot.[53] Franklin found pigeons at Cross Lake, lat. 54° 40′
N., long. 98° W., on July 28, 1820.[54] Rare at Fort Churchill, Hudson Bay,
lat. 58° 48′ N., long. 94° 14′ W.[55] Bell states unknown at Churchill;
however, adult male and female taken here by Dr. Gillespie, Jr., were
presented to Edinburgh Museum in 1845.[56] About 1756 it appeared at
York Factory.[57] In early Sept., 1878, found on upper part of Nelson
River.[58] In fine summers only it occurred on Hudson Bay as far north as
lat. 58°.[59]

NEWFOUNDLAND. No authentic record.[60] While "stocke dooves"
were mentioned by Peckham in 1583, it is evident that his list of natural
products covers an area larger than that of Newfoundland.[61]

ONTARIO. In 1771 Hutchins received specimen at Fort Severn, lat.
56°.[62] This bird, which may not have been taken in the vicinity, is apparently the specimen mentioned by Forster, who considered it rare this
far north.[63] On Aug. 10, 1840, Barnston found them numerous at Martin
Falls, lat. 51° 40′ N., on the Albany.[64] Considered common at Moose
Factory, lat. 51° 12′ N., near James Bay.[65] One collected here Aug. 16,
1860, by C. Drexler.[66]

PRINCE EDWARD ISLAND. On July 1, 1534, Cartier saw an infinite
number of wood pigeons (*ramiers*) between Cape Orleans (Kildare)
and Cape Savage.[67]

QUEBEC. Low reported species very rare on Labrador Peninsula.[68]
His statement that eggs were obtained at Fort George, on eastern shore
of James Bay, in 1887 is open to doubt. Four seen at Lake St. John, lat.
48° 30′ N., in summer of 1883.[69] Specimen in collection of J. Dwight, Jr.,
taken at Tadousac on July 20, 1889.[70] Bones of species found by Father
Thomas-Louis Doré while excavating at Tadousac the summer of 1949,
as he reported in letter to me. Rare and very irregular visitor at Point de
Monts, 49° 20′ N., 67° 20′ W., on St. Lawrence.[71] Single bird seen at
Heath Point on extreme SE. portion of Anticosti Island in summer of
1861 by Verrill.[72] A few seen on Gaspé Peninsula between June 18 and
Aug. 31, 1858, at Matane, Chat River, Ste. Anne des Monts, Metis, be-

tween Metis and Lake Matapédia, and on Restigouche River.[73] In 17th century abundant on Gaspé.[74]

SASKATCHEWAN.   Small flocks found along entire course of the Saskatchewan.[75] During journey from Manitoba to Rocky Mountain House, Alberta, in 1873 Selwyn found them plentiful.[76] Species observed on the N. Saskatchewan at Fort Carlton in 1858 and at Prince Albert where, according to Coubeaux, it was "common; a straggler during the migration season, and oftenest seen in fall."[77] Hind found them on Qu'Appelle River on July 26, 1858, and some were shot at Fort Qu'Appelle on July 2, 1859, by Southesk.[78] Charles A. Boultbee shot some at Fort Pelley on the Assiniboine in autumn of 1874.[79]

Elsewhere in the Americas

BAHAMAS.   No definite record but more likely to occur here than on Bermudas. Mease states it wintered in southern states and Florida and passed over to Bahamas.[80]

BERMUDAS.   Accidental. Presence considered doubtful by Major J. W. Wedderburn and Willis in absence of specimen.[81] One supposedly seen by Dr. Cole of 20th Regiment in 1846, according to J. L. Hurdis.[82] One shot by a Mr. Bartram on Oct. 24, 1863.[83]

CUBA.   Accidental.[84] Two mounted specimens, taken on island, in Museo Gundlach, Havana.[85] Female killed in mangrove swamp in Bay of Triscornia near Havana and male found in Havana market among Cuban mourning doves.[86]

GUATEMALA.   Nothing more definite than the following: "We have reason to believe that *E. migratorius* wanders as far south as the tablelands near the city of Guatemala."[87]

MEXICO.   Accidental.[88] All records apparently obtained during severe winter of 1872/73 when four sent to Museo Nacional, Mexico City, by Sr. Rincon from Jalapa (lat. 19° 30′ N.), Vera Cruz, and when species seen in other states.[89] Flight lasting several days began Dec. 10, 1872, and several were taken alive in Zacapoaxtela range, state of Puebla.[90] Also occurred in Valley of Mexico and at Ariziba (lat. 19° N.), state of Vera Cruz.[91]

Europe

It is very doubtful if any European record is due to other than escaped or liberated passenger pigeons. Degland states that they had been sighted many times at sea.[92]

AUSTRIA. A curious error, frequently copied, made by Dalgleish in reporting presence in Austria.[93] Bird referred to in Bree is *Turdus migratorius*.[94]

ENGLAND. Thompson remarks many brought to British Isles and kept by bird-fanciers, while Saunders says, "it is notorious that, from 1830 onwards, many have been brought over and turned loose in this country." [95] Female escaped from Dixon while being taken from a basket at Norwich in Feb., 1849.[96] Audubon took large numbers of live birds to England in 1830 and 1834.[97] In 1883 G. F. J. Thompson presented three to Zoological Society, London, but they died in captivity, two in 1884 and third in 1889.[98] Capture of one near Royston, Hertfordshire, early in July, 1844, recorded by Yarrell.[99] Bird appeared exhausted, had nearly empty crop, and showed no signs of confinement. Rev. Williams reported one in woods near Tring in Hertfordshire. On Oct. 12, 1876, one shot at Mulgrave Castle, Yorkshire. Condition of plumage left no doubt it had escaped from cage.[100] Two above cases considered only ones of occurrence in England proper; [101] however, Blanc mentioned pair killed in England in Zoological Museum, Lausanne, Switzerland.[102] J. de Beaumont, Director of the museum, kindly investigated the origin of specimens and reported in a letter to me that he did not find anything to prove they were killed in England.

FRANCE. Marquis de la Galissoniere, Governor-General of Canada, informed Kalm that on two occasions he had taken some to France, a large number in 1749, and liberated them in hope that they would become established.[103] Seebohm's assertion that it never occurred in Europe is incorrect.[104] Museum of Natural History, Nantes, has male from collection of Jules Vian shot in 1840 near Havre by lad named Eyriès.[105] While in Paris in 1910, H. W. Shoemaker saw one, labeled taken in France, in Natural History Museum of Jardin des Plantes.[106] My friend Professor Julian Harris, while in Paris in May, 1950, discussed origin of specimen with Dr. Jacques Berlioz, finding that it came from a private collection and that it was extremely doubtful if it had been taken in France or anywhere in Europe.

IRELAND.   One taken at Tralee, Kerry Co., about 1848 and kept for two years. Because of its exhausted condition when captured, it was assumed to have come directly from America.[107]

RUSSIA and NORWAY.   Mere statements of occurrence in these countries.[108]

SCOTLAND.   One shot at Westhall, parish of Monymeal, Fifeshire, by Rev. A. Esplin on Dec. 31, 1825, and presented to Fleming.[109] Freshness of its plumage as criterion of wildness has been questioned.[110] Incident is probably basis for statement of Keyserling and Blasius that it has flown to England.[111] Another specimen shot at Mellerstain on unknown date by Lord Haddington. Gentleman in Berwickshire had liberated several a short time previously.[112]

BREEDING RANGE

Nesting records on the boundaries of the range of the passenger pigeon are few. It is very probable that the nests of individual pairs occurred more widely within the migratory range than those of the colonies.

United States

GEORGIA.   According to S. W. Wilson, nested on St. Simon Island and presumably in Wayne and MacIntosh counties, but no dates given.[113]

KANSAS.   Few pairs nested in Neosha Valley.[114]

MISSISSIPPI.   Southernmost definite point of breeding in this state and only two instances on record. Wilson in spring of 1810 found remains of large breeding place in country of Choctaws, lat. 32° N.[115] Lincecum described in considerable detail nesting of April, 1832, on Tombigbee River, lat. 33° 16′ N., which would place it in Ala. Latitude evidently should have been 34° 16′ N., for later he mentions Columbus, Miss., as being 50 miles S. of nesting.[116]

MONTANA.   About 1862, some bred at Fort Benton, Chouteau Co.[117]

Questionable if numerous pigeons seen by Lewis and Clark near Missoula in July, 1806, were breeding as stated. Most that reached the Upper Missouri were probably postbreeding wanderers.

NEW JERSEY. Bred occasionally.[118] Smith, writing in 1765, stated they bred chiefly to N.[119]

NORTH and SOUTH CAROLINA. No definite breeding records. Two pairs seen near summit of Caesar's Head, Greenville Co., S. C., in summer of 1882.[120]

NORTH DAKOTA. Many nested along Red River S. of Pembina in 1873.[121] Some nests found along the Missouri S. of Berthold.[122]

OKLAHOMA. Nesting that started about April 20, 1881, reported as located about 70 miles W. of Atoka.[123] Circumstantial description of this nesting given by Thomas, who stated it was located about 110 miles from Atoka in Potawatomi Reservation, which lay on N. bank of Canadian River, about 70 miles NW. of Atoka.[124] On April 18, Judy stated pigeons made first nesting 110 miles from Atoka and on May 17 he reported completion of second hatching.[125] If first nesting began about middle of April, second brood could not possibly have been brought off by middle of May.

SOUTH DAKOTA. Information on breeding in SE. part of state limited to: "Rare in summer; breeds." [126] Nests found by Cooper in small trees along the Missouri from Fort Pierre N.[127]

TENNESSEE. No satisfactory record of nesting. Rhoads was informed by a Mr. Miles that he had heard of isolated nestings at Brownsville, Haywood Co., but he, himself, had never found one.[128]

VIRGINIA. No definite breeding records.

WEST VIRGINIA. Specific information wanting. According to Brooks, it nested extensively in valleys of Ohio and Kanawha rivers.[129]

Canada

MANITOBA. On Waterhan River, lat. about 52° N., "less than a score of nests" were found on June 23, 1881; "breeding in an aspen grove at Northwest Angle, Lake of the Woods, Man., 1873." [130] A few bred at Portage la Prairie.[131]

NEW BRUNSWICK. Apparently bred in very small numbers. It was written of Grand Menan: "Not rare; said to breed in the interior of the island." [132] In 1879 Batchelder found it breeding at Grand Falls, but it was not common. [133]

NOVA SCOTIA.   Once very abundant and bred. [134]

ONTARIO.   About 1860, according to W. J. McLean, great numbers bred in region N. of Lake of the Woods and Rainy Lake. [135] Until 1880 nested at Nipigon, Thunder Bay district, lat. 49° N. [136] One writer states that in May he visited a rookery on the N. shore of Lake Huron where "they were never known by the oldest inhabitant to nest in this locality before." [137] If Hutchins was correctly informed that they bred at Moose Factory, laying *two* eggs, this is northernmost breeding record. [138] Report of taking of eggs at Moose Factory by Miles Spence in June, 1888, is apparently unreliable since it was subsequently omitted. [139] According to information secured by Mitchell, they nested at Smokey Falls, Mattagami River, and from Canyon to Alter Falls, Abitibi River, Cochrane District, at lat. approximately 50° N. [140]

QUEBEC.   Statements of breeding N. of St. Lawrence almost wholly wanting. Kalm wrote that they were to be found about 20 French miles N. of Quebec, but that only a few nested because of scarcity of beech and oak mast. [141] According to Gray, they occurred only during migration. [142]

The passenger pigeon was an early migrant and usually appeared in the northern states as soon as the ground was bare of snow, or even before. At times it persistently clung to the regions where it had arrived in spite of late snowstorms; at others the flocks went scurrying southward. The spring migration was so influenced by the weather that it was a good indication of meteorological conditions; hence, the year is important. The earliest dates of arrival frequently had no bearing on the main migration that followed long afterwards. In 1873, pigeons appeared at Janesville, Wisconsin, on February 18, and at Beloit and Whitewater on February 22. They were not again reported until March 15 and large numbers were still moving on April 15. The entire main migration lasted about a month.

Writing of New York, Grant states that the migrations always began about the time of the spring and fall equinoxes when the weather is generally cloudy.[1] No such regularity existed. Macauley mentions that, depending on the weather, they arrived in New York the latter part of March, or a month later.[2] The spring migration in southern Michigan has been described by Bryant:

In early spring, often while the snow still covered the ground, the northward flight of pigeons commenced. A few warm days in succession and the advance guard of the flight came in small flocks. Often they stopped to feed, seeking the places where hillsides with a southern exposure had been laid bare of snow by the sun. Perching in the trees on these hills the pigeons dropped to the ground to feed on the acorns, beechnuts, etc. which had been left from the previous fall. The advance flight did not remain long, but as soon as they had fed, sped northward in search of nesting places.... Following close on the wake of the pilot flight came the main army of the pigeons. Soon after daylight they began to fly north and continued to pass over until nearly noon, the majority of the flight of the day being over by the time the sun reached the meridian, though on cloudy or rainy days the birds often flew all day. On such days, the pigeons often alighted in large numbers, giving preference at such times to the dry trees, particularly to those which had been "girdled" in the process of clearing the land.... The spring flight never lasted more than about a month altogether. The flight of the flock [height of migration], the thousands and tens of thousands, which came in the spring, often passed over in three or four days. This flight was followed by smaller flocks, and these were often passing a few at a time, for two or three weeks.[3]

According to Gibbs, there was no regularity to either the spring or fall migration in Michigan.[4]

There are few data to show the rate of progress northward. Regarding its migration in the Mississippi Valley, Cooke states:

In the spring of 1884 its northward journey commenced about the middle of March, and by March 16, stations here and there had noticed it up to latitude 42°. It was found [at] about the forty-fourth parallel March 23, and reached Elk River, Minn. (latitude 45° 25'), March 29. The storms of April evidently delayed its progress, as it was not reported from Barton, [N.] Dak., until May 4, and did not reach Oak Point, Manitoba, until May 20. The bulk was reported from Portage la Prairie, Manitoba, May 12, a few having been seen previously.[5]

Reverse migration, due to unfavorable weather, sometimes gave false impressions. A notice signed "Atticus" in the Racine *Advocate* of January 23, 1844, said that at Racine, Wisconsin, the pigeons flew southward, never northward at any season. In some cases the pigeons did migrate in spring along the western shore of Lake Michigan, but most of the migrants entered the state from the southwest. On striking the shore of Lake Michigan and encountering unfavorable weather, they made the return southward along the shore of the lake.

Few migrants appeared in spring in the southeastern states and in Rhode Island and eastern Connecticut. There are many early references to the great number of pigeons in Virginia in fall and winter but few for spring. Byrd, writing in 1728, considered it remarkable that they never returned in spring; and, according to Catesby, this held for South Carolina.[6] The pigeons that went southward in autumn through these states returned in spring mainly through the states west of the Appalachian Mountains. Pigeons that reached the vicinity of New York flew north or northeast so that eastern Connecticut and Rhode Island were by-passed largely.

The fall migration in the northern states began the end of August, usually reached its height during the first two weeks in September, and was completed largely by the end of this month. Contrary to the situation in spring, the first migrants in autumn, if in small numbers, generally did not cause comment; hence the actual dates of migration are earlier than the general statements on movement indicate.

In the early days this pigeon wintered from the Ohio Valley southward. According to Cooke, it spent the winter usually from latitude 37 degrees north, and always from latitude 36 degrees north, southward.[7] "Wintered principally from Arkansas and North Carolina south to central Texas, Louisiana, and Florida."[8]

The technical literature, due to late founding of the publications, contains but few dates of migration. The country newspapers, however, contain a vast amount of information on the movements of the passenger pigeon. An examination of the newspapers of Wisconsin has shown that a large amount of data on migration does exist.[9] A similar review should be made for other states. The following list gives representative migration and wintering data.

City or Region	Spring	Fall	Winter	Ref.
ALABAMA				
Marion	. . . .	17 Nov. 1883	. . . .	10
ARKANSAS				
Arkansas River	. . . .	12 Nov. 1832	. . . .	11
Beebe	. . . .	10 Oct. 1881	. . . .	12
Clinton	9 Apr. 1889	. . . .	. . . .	13
Dardanelle	. . . .	22 Oct. 1879	. . . .	14
Little Rock	. . . .	27 Oct. 1841	. . . .	15
CONNECTICUT				
. . . .	2 Apr. 1875	. . . .	. . . .	16
East Hartford	. . . .	19 Oct.	. . . .	*

* All information marked with an asterisk in the reference column of this list has been taken from Arthur Cleveland Bent, *Life Histories of North American Gallinaceous Birds* (Bull. U. S. Nat. Museum, No. 162; Wash., 1832), pp. 379–402. Bent gives day of the month but not the year.

City or Region	Spring	Fall	Winter	Ref.
CONNECTICUT (*cont.*)				
Gaylordsville	13 Mar.	. . . .	. . . .	*
Hartford	. . . .	. . . .	1882/83	*
New London	. . . .	10–11 Sept. 1876	. . . .	17
Saybrook	21 Mar.	. . . .	. . . .	*
Tolland Co.	. . . .	29 Sept. 1880	. . . .	19
DELAWARE				
Wilmington	. . . .	mid Oct. 1783	. . . .	20
DISTRICT OF COLUMBIA				
Washington	3 Apr.	. . . .	rarely	*21
GEORGIA				
Augusta	. . . .	12 Sept. 1893	. . . .	22
Savannah	. . . .	early Nov. 1776	. . . .	23
ILLINOIS				
NE. region	15 Mar.–mid Apr.	Oct. & Nov.	. . . .	24
S. region	. . . .	. . . .	1881/82	25
Belleville	. . . .	5 Oct. 1854	. . . .	26
Bryn Mawr (Chicago)	. . . .	30 Sept. 1901	. . . .	27
Carthage	12 Mar.	. . . .	. . . .	*
Charleston	3 Feb. 1882	24 Sept. 1878	3 Feb. 1882	28
Chicago	26 Mar. 1675	. . . .	. . . .	29
"	28 Apr. 1833	3 Sept. 1844	. . . .	30
"	10 Mar. 1850	6 Sept. 1853	. . . .	31
"	13 Mar. 1855	3 Sept. 1891	. . . .	32
"	26 Mar. 1856	. . . .	. . . .	33
"	5 Mar. 1860	. . . .	. . . .	34
"	7 Mar. 1865	. . . .	. . . .	35
"	9 Mar. 1882	. . . .	. . . .	36
Ellsworth	6 Feb. 1882	. . . .	. . . .	37
"	15 Mar. 1889	. . . .	. . . .	38
Evanston	11 Feb. 1882	. . . .	. . . .	39
Franklin Grove	. . . .	. . . .	11 Jan. 1882	40
Freeport	4 Apr. 1867	12 Sept. 1866	. . . .	41
"	19 Mar. 1868	. . . .	. . . .	42
Galena	17 Mar. 1846	. . . .	. . . .	43
Glen Ellyn (Chicago)	. . . .	4 Sept. 1892	. . . .	44
Grand Crossing, Cook Co.	. . . .	21 Aug. 1886	. . . .	45
Hanover	14 Feb. 1882	. . . .	. . . .	46

City or Region	Spring	Fall	Winter	Ref.
ILLINOIS (cont.)				
Hennepin	26 Mar. 1885	....	....	47
Highland Park	6 Feb. 1882	....	....	48
Jerseyville	....	6 Sept. 1896	....	49
Lake Forest	4 Mar.	7 Aug. 1895	....	*50
Lebanon	13 Mar. 1876	....	....	51
"	8 Feb. 1878	....	....	52
"	17 Feb. 1878	....	17 Feb. 1878	53
Lena	2 Mar. 1882	....	....	54
Middlegrove	....	5 Sept. 1876	....	55
Morgan Park (Chicago)	....	28 Sept. 1883	....	56
Ohio River mouth	....	16 Oct. 1700	....	57
"	....	24 Oct. 1807	....	58
Palatine, Cook Co.	....	15 Oct. 1874	....	59
Quincy	27 Mar. 1846	....	....	60
Robinson	10 Mar. 1883	....	....	61
Rockford	26 Mar. 1875	....	....	62
St. Clair Co.	11 Feb. 1882	....	....	63
Serena	....	....	11 Jan. 1882	64
Virden	11 Feb.	5 Oct.	....	*
Wabash Valley	15 Jan.–25 Feb.	....	when mild	65
Waukegan	....	....	10 Dec. 1890	66
"	....	....	19 Dec. 1892	67
INDIANA				
....	Feb. & Mar.	....	present	68
Bloomington	....	28 Sept.	....	*
Brookville	28 Feb.	....	Jan. & Feb. 1854	*69
Brown Co.	7 Mar. 1894	....	....	70
"	12 Apr. 1895	....	....	71
Delaware	....	....	Feb. 1880	72
French Lick	....	....	1822/23	73
Indianapolis	12 Apr. 1883	....	....	74
Jonesboro	1 Mar.	....	....	*
Kokomo	13 Mar.	....	....	*
Liverpool	14 Mar. 1894	....	....	75
"	8 Apr. 1894	....	....	76
Madison	9 Mar. 1855	....	....	77
Maxinkuckee Lake	6 Apr. 1885	....	....	78
Miamitown, NE. portion	16 Mar. 1780	....	....	79

City or Region	Spring	Fall	Winter	Ref.
INDIANA (*cont.*)				
Millwood	18 Feb.	. . . .	. . . .	*
New Harmony	. . . .	. . . .	1832/33	80
North Vernon	. . . .	. . . .	13 Mar. 1880	81
Terre Haute	9 Mar. 1855	. . . .	. . . .	82
Vernon	. . . .	. . . .	1831/32	83
IOWA				
Atalissa	13 Mar. 1882	. . . .	. . . .	84
Bear Creek	. . . .	5 Aug. 1820	. . . .	85
Burlington	15 Mar.	. . . .	. . . .	*
Cascade	13 Mar. 1882	. . . .	. . . .	86
Coralville	11 Feb. 1882	. . . .	. . . .	87
Delaware Co.	2 May 1867	. . . .	. . . .	88
Dubuque	22 Mar.	. . . .	. . . .	*
"	18 Feb. 1882	. . . .	. . . .	89
Independence	6 May 1881	. . . .	. . . .	90
Iowa City	13 Mar.	. . . .	. . . .	*
Keokuk	12 Mar. 1855	17 Sept. 1896	. . . .	91
"	5 Feb. 1882	18 Oct. 1896	. . . .	92
"	15 Apr. 1894	. . . .	. . . .	93
La Porte	16 Mar.	. . . .	. . . .	*
Williamstown	. . . .	27 Sept.	. . . .	*
KANSAS				
. . . .	early Mar.	. . . .	. . . .	94
Leavenworth	18 Apr. 1810	. . . .	. . . .	95
KENTUCKY				
. . . .	. . . .	. . . .	Dec. 1865	96
Casky	. . . .	30 Oct.	. . . .	*
Louisville	. . . .	. . . .	8 Dec. 1785	97
"	. . . .	. . . .	1833/34	98
"	. . . .	. . . .	Jan. 1854	99
"	. . . .	. . . .	22 Jan. 1858	100
South Union	. . . .	. . . .	Feb. 1820	101
MAINE				
Lake Umbagog	. . . .	8 Oct. 1882	. . . .	102
North Bridgton	24 Apr. 1877	. . . .	. . . .	103
North Livermore	28 Apr.	. . . .	. . . .	*
Norway	7 Apr.–4 May	. . . .	. . . .	104
Portland	. . . .	8 Oct. 1872	. . . .	105
Warren	30 Apr. 1817	. . . .	. . . .	106

City or Region	Spring	Fall	Winter	Ref.
MARYLAND				
Cumberland	. . . .	. . . .	12 Jan. 1878	107
Deer Park	26 Mar. 1875	18 Sept. 1874	. . . .	108
Hagerstown	. . . .	7 Nov. 1882	. . . .	109
Laurel	. . . .	11 Oct.	. . . .	*
Montgomery Co.	. . . .	12 Oct. 1878	. . . .	110
Oakland	. . . .	30 Sept. 1872	. . . .	111
Prince Georges Co.	. . . .	11 Oct. 1889	. . . .	112
MASSACHUSETTS				
. . . .	present	present	present	113
. . . .	20–31 Mar.	. . . .	rare	114
. . . .	from 10 Mar.	to 21 Oct.	Dec.	115
Amesbury	23 Apr. 1887	24 Aug. 1886	. . . .	116
"	. . . .	29 Nov. 1887	. . . .	117
Amherst	7 Apr.	. . . .	. . . .	*
Ashburnham	30 Mar. 1896	. . . .	. . . .	118
Boston	. . . .	28 Sept. 1834	. . . .	119
Bristol Co.	. . . .	23 Aug. 1889	. . . .	120
Cambridge	. . . .	30 Sept. 1885	. . . .	121
Concord	26 Apr. 1855	. . . .	. . . .	122
East Templeton	. . . .	23 Sept. 1889	. . . .	123
Medford	8 Mar. 1631	. . . .	. . . .	124
Plymouth	. . . .	16 Oct. 1852	. . . .	125
Ponkapog	31 Mar.	. . . .	. . . .	*
Salem	14 Apr. 1879	. . . .	. . . .	126
Siasconset	. . . .	23 Sept. 1878	. . . .	127
Tewkesbury	. . . .	19 Aug. 1793	. . . .	128
Townsend	. . . .	26 Aug.–27 Sept. 1847	. . . .	129
"	. . . .	21 Aug.–11 Sept. 1848	. . . .	130
Waltham	. . . .	5 Oct. 1878	. . . .	131
Woods Hole	20 Mar.	. . . .	. . . .	*
Worcester	. . . .	25 Sept.	. . . .	*
MICHIGAN				
. . . .	Feb.	Oct. & Nov.	occasionally	132
. . . .	late Mar.–mid Apr.	. . . .	. . . .	133
Ann Arbor	. . . .	12 Oct.	. . . .	*
Battle Creek	27 Mar.	. . . .	. . . .	*
Cheboygan	25 Apr. 1881	. . . .	. . . .	134
Delta Co.	. . . .	1 Oct. 1895	. . . .	135

City or Region	Spring	Fall	Winter	Ref.
MICHIGAN (*cont.*)				
Detroit	....	14 Sept. 1898	....	136
Grand Haven	22 Mar. 1865	....	....	137
Grand Marais	....	13–14 Sept. 1835	....	138
Grand Rapids	18 Mar. 1865	....	....	139
Locke	22 Mar.	....	....	*
Mackinac	3 Apr. 1775	....	....	140
Mackinac Island	....	30 Aug.–12 Sept.	....	141
Newberry	....	24 Oct.	....	*
Niles	1 Feb. 1851	....	Nov. & Dec. 1846	142
Petersburg	20 Mar.	....	....	*
Petoskey	23 Feb. 1877	....	....	143
Plymouth	7 Apr.	....	....	*
Pontiac	....	17 Sept. 1875	....	144
Portage Lake	4 May 1857	....	....	145
Sault Ste. Marie	19 Apr. 1762	....	....	146
Tecumseh	3 Mar. 1882	....	....	147
Wayne Co.	21 Mar. 1890	....	....	148
MINNESOTA				
....	7 Apr.	1 Nov.	....	149
Southern region	5 Apr.	13 Sept.–5 Oct.	....	150
Bradford	1 Apr.	....	....	*
Chatfield	8 Apr. 1864	....	....	151
Duluth	....	3 Sept. 1870	....	152
Elk River	29 Mar.–15 Apr.	....	....	153
"	29 Mar. 1884	....	....	154
Grant Co.	9 Mar. 1876	....	....	155
Hokah	9 Mar. 1879	....	....	156
Lake Andrew	9 Apr.	....	....	*
"	....	28 Sept.	....	*
Lake City	8 Apr. 1876	....	....	157
Lanesboro	22 Mar.	5 Oct. 1890	....	*158
Minneapolis	9 Mar. 1878	....	....	159
"	25 Mar. 1880	....	....	160
Rochester	24 Mar. 1859	....	•••••••••••	161
"	24 Apr. 1869	....	....	162
St. Paul	....	6 Sept. 1859	....	163
Winona	12 Apr. 1872	....	....	164
Zumbrota	8 Apr.	15 Nov.	....	*

City or Region	Spring	Fall	Winter	Ref.
MISSOURI				
....	....	21 Nov. 1818	....	165
SW. region	early Feb. 1882	....	....	166
Alton ("Altie")	....	....	17 Dec. 1896	167
Augusta	....	....	Jan. 1884	168
Howell Co.	21 Mar. 1879	....	....	169
Jefferson City	....	29 Sept. 1876	....	170
Johnson Co.	6 Apr. 1874	....	....	171
Mexico	2 Mar. 1878	....	....	172
Oregon Co.	21 Mar. 1879	....	....	173
St. Charles	31 Mar. 1834	....	....	174
St. Louis	5–6 Feb. 1882	30 Sept. 1851	24 Dec. 1851	175
"	....	19 Sept. 1885	....	176
Shannon Co.	21 Mar. 1879	....	....	177
Stoutland	....	18 Oct. 1877	....	178
Thomasville	7 Feb. 1882	....	....	179
NEBRASKA				
Cook	....	17 Aug. 1897	....	180
Omaha	....	28 Nov. 1895	....	181
Papillion	....	9 Nov. 1895	....	182
NEW HAMPSHIRE				
....	1st wk. Apr.	....	....	183
Acworth	....	10 Oct. 1881	....	184
Hollis	6 Apr. 1874	....	....	185
"	8 Apr. 1875	....	....	186
"	2 Apr. 1876	....	....	187
Nashua	....	6 Sept. 1880	....	188
NEW JERSEY				
....	....	Aug. & Sept.	Jan. 1884	189
Barnegat	....	27 Sept. 1874	....	190
Caldwell	31 Mar.	....	....	*
Campgaw ("Camp Gaugh")	9 Mar. 1838	....	....	191
Haddonfield	22 Mar. 1879	....	....	192
Malboro	....	14 Aug. 1875	....	193
Morris Plains	....	16 Sept. 1885	....	194
Morristown	....	16 Sept.	....	*
"	....	7 Oct. 1893	....	195
New Providence	....	12 Nov.	....	*
Plainfield	12 Mar.	....	....	*

City or Region	Spring	Fall	Winter	Ref.
NEW JERSEY (*cont.*)				
Raccoon	3 Mar. 1749	. . . .	. . . .	196
Waretown	. . . .	12 Sept. 1874	. . . .	197
NEW YORK				
. . . .	. . . .	. . . .	Feb. 1842	198
Central region	1st wk. Mar.	. . . .	. . . .	199
Northern region	. . . .	. . . .	1819	200
Albany	25 Mar. 1830	. . . .	. . . .	201
Buffalo	27 Mar.	. . . .	. . . .	*
"	8 Mar. 1878	. . . .	. . . .	202
Canandaigua	. . . .	14 Sept. 1898	. . . .	203
Cherry Valley	31 Mar. 1851	. . . .	. . . .	204
Cooperstown	27 Mar. 1848	8 Sept. 1848	. . . .	205
"	. . . .	29 Sept. 1848	. . . .	206
Cornwall-on-Hudson	4 Mar.	. . . .	. . . .	*
Croton Falls	. . . .	16 Oct.	. . . .	*
Crown Point	. . . .	17 Sept. 1755	. . . .	207
"	. . . .	Sept. 1768	. . . .	208
Deposit	. . . .	30 Sept. 1876	. . . .	209
Eldred	14 Mar. 1879	20 Sept. 1880	. . . .	210
Elmira	12 Mar. 1860	. . . .	. . . .	211
"	7 Mar. 1878	. . . .	. . . .	212
Fredonia	. . . .	. . . .	16–17 Dec. 1846	213
Glasco	20 Mar.	. . . .	. . . .	*
Hopkinton	5 Apr. 1836	. . . .	. . . .	214
"	27 Mar. 1845	. . . .	. . . .	215
Hornellsville	5 Mar. 1878	2 Oct. 1876	. . . .	216
"	1 Apr. 1881	. . . .	. . . .	217
Hudson Highlands	. . . .	. . . .	a few	218
Hudson River valley	. . . .	. . . .	unusual	219
Jamestown	13 Apr. 1872	. . . .	. . . .	220
Lewis Co.	3 Mar. 1882	. . . .	. . . .	221
Liberty	1 Apr. 1856	. . . .	. . . .	222
Locust Grove	3 Mar.	. . . .	. . . .	*
Locust Valley	. . . .	4 Nov.	. . . .	*
Mayville	29 Feb. 1840	. . . .	. . . .	223
Meacham Lake	2 May 1876	. . . .	. . . .	224
Mexico	19 Mar. 1858	. . . .	. . . .	222
Monroe Co.	4 Mar. 1880	. . . .	. . . .	225

City or Region	Spring	Fall	Winter	Ref.
NEW YORK (*cont.*)				
New York City	. . . .	. . . .	31 Jan. 1858	226
Orange Lake	. . . .	17 Nov.	. . . .	*
Ossining	. . . .	1 Oct.	. . . .	*
Painted Post	16 Mar.	. . . .	. . . .	*
Pompey	1 Apr. 1851	. . . .	. . . .	227
Rochester	20 Mar. 1850	. . . .	13 Dec. 1828	228
"	. . . .	. . . .	7 Jan. 1858	229
"	14 Mar. 1860	. . . .	. . . .	230
"	10 Apr. 1876	. . . .	. . . .	231
Wellsville	2 Mar. 1882	. . . .	. . . .	232
NORTH CAROLINA				
. . . .	. . . .	present	present	233
. . . .	. . . .	20 Nov. 1760	1701/2	234
. . . .	. . . .	. . . .	1707	235
Raleigh	18 Apr.	. . . .	19 Feb. 1838	*236
Salem	. . . .	. . . .	1760/61	237
"	. . . .	. . . .	Jan. 1799	238
"	. . . .	. . . .	8 Dec. 1805	239
Surrey Co.	. . . .	. . . .	Feb. 1842	240
NORTH DAKOTA				
Barton	4 May 1884	. . . .	. . . .	241
Dunn Co.	. . . .	23 Aug. 1843	. . . .	242
Larimore	26 Mar. 1892	. . . .	. . . .	243
Pembina River Post	23 Apr. 1802	. . . .	. . . .	244
"	4 May 1804	. . . .	. . . .	245
OHIO				
. . . .	resident	resident	resident	246
Bloomfield	25 Feb. 1878	. . . .	. . . .	247
Bloomfield (Trumbull Co.)	. . . .	. . . .	8 Dec. 1855	248
"	. . . .	. . . .	Jan. & Feb. 1878	249
Canton	. . . .	29 Oct. 1843	. . . .	250
Chillicothe	18 Feb. 1857	. . . .	. . . .	251
Circleville	1 Feb. 1861	. . . .	. . . .	252
Cleveland	. . . .	. . . .	24 Jan. 1851	253
"	. . . .	. . . .	14 Jan. 1880	254
Fayette	15 Mar.	. . . .	. . . .	*
Hudson	8 Mar.	. . . .	. . . .	*
"	30 Apr. 1876	. . . .	. . . .	255

City or Region	Spring	Fall	Winter	Ref.
OHIO (*cont.*)				
Hudson	25–27 Feb. 1880	. . . .	. . . .	256
Jefferson	4 Mar. 1880	. . . .	20 Jan. 1878	257
"	. . . .	. . . .	16 Feb. 1878	258
Marietta	. . . .	4 Sept. 1788	2 Dec. 1792	259
"	. . . .	. . . .	1832/33	260
Mechanicsburg	23 Feb. 1882	. . . .	. . . .	261
"	26 Mar. 1883	. . . .	. . . .	262
Nelsonville	. . . .	5 Oct. 1879	. . . .	263
Oxford	2 Feb. 1880	. . . .	. . . .	264
Ravenna	. . . .	9 Oct. 1850	. . . .	265
Sargents	24 Mar. 1900	. . . .	. . . .	266
Springfield	24 Mar. 1882	. . . .	. . . .	267
Strongsville	18 Feb. 1882	. . . .	. . . .	268
Toledo	6 Mar. 1876	. . . .	. . . .	269
Wayne Co.	. . . .	30 Aug. 1892	. . . .	270
"	. . . .	19 Sept. 1888	. . . .	271
West Liberty	10 Mar.	. . . .	. . . .	*
Woodstock	18 Feb. 1880	. . . .	. . . .	272
Youngstown	. . . .	11 Oct. 1879	. . . .	273
Zanesville	. . . .	14 Oct. 1819	. . . .	274
PENNSYLVANIA				
. . . .	. . . .	. . . .	present	275
Altoona	7 Mar. 1876	. . . .	. . . .	276
Applebacksville	. . . .	2 Nov. 1879	. . . .	277
Bethlehem	. . . .	19 Aug. 1773	. . . .	278
Brockney	18 Mar.	. . . .	. . . .	*
Cambria Co.	. . . .	. . . .	1875 or '76	279
Carlisle	31 Mar. 1841	19 Oct. 1844	rare	280
"	4 Feb. 1842	. . . .	. . . .	281
"	6 Apr. 1843	. . . .	. . . .	282
Chambersburg	13 Feb.	. . . .	. . . .	*
Chester Co.	. . . .	1 Sept. 1886	. . . .	283
"	. . . .	9 Sept. 1887	. . . .	284
Coudersport	20 Mar. 1886	. . . .	. . . .	285
Erie	13 Mar.	. . . .	. . . .	*
"	28 Feb. 1878	. . . .	. . . .	286
Forest Co.	. . . .	. . . .	1881/82	287
Guths Station	20 Mar.	. . . .	. . . .	*
Harrisburg	. . . .	. . . .	25 Dec. 1889	288

City or Region	Spring	Fall	Winter	Ref.
PENNSYLVANIA (*cont.*)				
Lancaster Co.	26 Mar. 1780	. . . .	. . . .	289
"	31 Mar. ("May") 1875	. . . .	. . . .	290
"	1 Apr. 1875	. . . .	. . . .	291
Linden	. . . .	5 Oct. 1890	. . . .	292
McKean Co.	. . . .	. . . .	1879/80	293
Monroe Co.	. . . .	23 Oct. 1895	. . . .	294
"	. . . .	25 Oct. 1895	. . . .	295
Nazareth	. . . .	10 Aug. 1783	. . . .	296
Philadelphia	11–22 Mar. 1740	. . . .	1792/93	297
"	19 Feb. 1804	. . . .	7 Jan. 1804	298
"	. . . .	. . . .	1806/7	299
"	1 Mar.–22 Apr. 1804	. . . .	. . . .	300
"	10 Feb. 1807	. . . .	9 Jan. 1807	301
"	18 Mar. 1882	26 Sept. 1878	. . . .	302
Pike Co.	7 Apr. 1876	. . . .	. . . .	303
"	14 Apr. 1876	. . . .	. . . .	304
Ridgway	22 Mar. 1886	. . . .	. . . .	305
St. Mary's	. . . .	28 Sept. 1877	. . . .	306
Sewickley	present	present	present	307
Smethport	21 Mar. 1870	. . . .	present	308
"	26 Feb. 1880	. . . .	. . . .	309
Somerset Co.	. . . .	. . . .	1875 or '76	310
Springs, Somerset Co.	. . . .	. . . .	1 Jan. 1876	311
Stroudsburg	9 Apr. 1868	. . . .	. . . .	312
Tionesta	Mar. 1878	. . . .	present	313
Titusville	25 Mar. 1852	. . . .	. . . .	314
"	3 Mar. 1878	. . . .	. . . .	315
Warren	Feb. 1882	. . . .	. . . .	316
Wayne Co.	. . . .	2 Nov.	. . . .	*
Wilcox	6 Feb. 1882	. . . .	. . . .	317
York	. . . .	1 Sept. 1888	. . . .	318
RHODE ISLAND				
Cranston	. . . .	2 Nov. 1886	. . . .	319
Kingston	. . . .	18–23 Aug. 1784	. . . .	320
"	. . . .	5 Aug.–20 Sept. 1785	. . . .	321
Newport	. . . .	19 Oct.	. . . .	*
"	. . . .	4 Sept. 1759	. . . .	322

City or Region	Spring	Fall	Winter	Ref.
RHODE ISLAND (*cont.*)				
Providence	. . . .	25 Sept. 1888	. . . .	323
SOUTH DAKOTA				
Missouri River	. . . .	3–6 Sept. 1843	. . . .	324
TENNESSEE				
Eastern region	23–28 Apr. 1797	. . . .	. . . .	325
Clarksville	. . . .	8 Oct. 1877	. . . .	326
Hurricane Springs	. . . .	23 Nov. 1881	. . . .	327
La Grange	. . . .	27 Oct. 1883	. . . .	328
Nashville	. . . .	25 Oct. 1844	. . . .	329
Savannah	. . . .	28 Oct. 1878	. . . .	330
"	. . . .	25 Oct. 1882	. . . .	331
Stewart Co.	. . . .	4 Nov. 1857	. . . .	332
VERMONT				
Tydeville	9 Apr.	. . . .	. . . .	*
VIRGINIA				
. . . .	. . . .	. . . .	present	333
S. boundary region	. . . .	19 Oct. 1728	. . . .	334
Aldie	21 Mar. 1850	. . . .	. . . .	335
Blacksburg	. . . .	18 Sept. 1876	. . . .	336
"	. . . .	8 Oct. 1878	. . . .	337
Culpeper Co.	. . . .	Oct. 1874	. . . .	338
Dunn Loring	. . . .	19 Oct.	. . . .	*
Edgehill, Albemarle Co.	18 Mar. 1808	. . . .	. . . .	339
Fairfax Co.	. . . .	12 Oct. 1878	. . . .	340
Highgate	20 Apr. 1893	. . . .	. . . .	341
Lancaster Co.	. . . .	. . . .	18 Jan. 1763	342
Leesburg	27 Mar. 1876	4 Oct. 1878	. . . .	343
"	. . . .	8 Oct. 1878	. . . .	344
Moore's Fort (St. Paul), Wise Co.	. . . .	29 Sept. 1774	. . . .	345
Norfolk	. . . .	. . . .	16 Jan. 1892	346
Warrenton	. . . .	Nov. 1857	. . . .	347
"	. . . .	18 Sept. 1890	. . . .	348
Westover	21 May 1711	. . . .	. . . .	349
White Sulphur Springs	. . . .	Aug. 1839	. . . .	350
WEST VIRGINIA				
Fairview	19 Mar.	. . . .	. . . .	*
French Creek	27 Feb.	20 Oct.	. . . .	*
"	10 Apr.	. . . .	. . . .	*

City or Region	Spring	Fall	Winter	Ref.
WEST VIRGINIA (*cont.*)				
Oakland	....	Oct. 1874	....	351
Parkersburg	....	7 Nov. 1899	....	352
Stone Coal Creek, Upshur Co.	Apr. 1781	....	....	353
Wood Co.	....	10 Sept. 1788	....	354
WISCONSIN				
Algoma	....	14 Oct. 1875	....	†
Appleton	11 Apr. 1862	23 Sept. 1854	....	†
"	*ca.* 15 Mar. 1870	....	....	†
"	26 Feb. 1874	....	....	†355
Arena	23 Mar. 1884	....	....	†
Babcock	....	9–15 Sept. 1899	....	†356
Baldwin	....	13 Aug. 1877	....	†
Beaver Dam	....	3 Aug. 1853	....	†
Beloit	14 Apr. 1852	16 Sept. 1871	....	†
Black River Falls	9 Mar. 1879	12 Sept. 1868	....	†
"	....	2 Aug. 1873	....	†
Brandon	10 Mar. 1868	....	....	†
Brooklyn	....	late Sept. 1866	....	†
Brown Co.	*ca.* 16 Mar. 1889	....	....	†
Burlington	26 Mar. 1869	....	....	†
Busseyville	26 Mar. 1869	....	....	†
Cassell Prairie, Sauk Co.	....	Oct. 1888	....	†
Cassville	....	2 Sept. 1805	....	357
Clinton	16 Feb. 1876	....	....	†358
Colby	....	8 Aug. 1874	....	†
Darlington	1 Apr. 1881	13 Oct. 1876	....	†
"	19 Mar. 1888	13 Oct. 1882	....	†
"	....	30 Sept. 1887	....	†
Delavan Lake	....	8 Sept. 1896	....	†
Door Co.	....	25 Aug. 1820	....	359
Fairfield, Sauk Co.	7 Feb. 1882	....	....	†
Florence	....	21 Aug. 1886	....	†
Fond du Lac	6 Apr. 1861	....	....	†
"	18 Mar. 1865	....	....	†

† All information marked with a dagger in the reference column has been taken from Wisconsin newspapers. This information was previously published, by yearly listing, in my article, "The Migration of the Passenger Pigeon in Wisconsin," *Passenger Pigeon*, XIII (1951), 101–4 and 144–46. When other sources were also consulted or when pertinent information is necessary for interpretation of the listed data, numbered notes are also given.

City or Region	Spring	Fall	Winter	Ref.
WISCONSIN (*cont.*)				
Green Bay	2 Apr. 1844	6 Sept. 1855	. . . .	†
"	23 Mar. 1854	. . . .	. . . .	†360
Hammond	. . . .	13 Aug. 1875	. . . .	†
Horicon	2 Apr. 1856	21 Aug. 1857	. . . .	†361
"	8 May 1857	. . . .	. . . .	†362
Janesville	9 Feb. 1848	11 Sept. 1858	. . . .	†
"	18 Feb. 1873	23 Oct. 1869	. . . .	†
"	16 Mar. 1875	. . . .	. . . .	†
Juda	. . . .	7 Aug. 1879	. . . .	†
Kenosha	15 Mar. 1855	. . . .	. . . .	†363
Kirby	18 Mar. 1890	. . . .	. . . .	†
"	5 Apr. 1893	. . . .	. . . .	†
"	7 Mar. 1894	. . . .	. . . .	†
"	1 Apr. 1896	. . . .	. . . .	†
"	19 Apr. 1899	. . . .	. . . .	†
La Crosse	. . . .	13 Sept. 1853	. . . .	†
"	. . . .	11 Sept. 1863	. . . .	†
"	. . . .	12 Oct. 1863	. . . .	†
Lake Geneva	25 Feb. 1880	. . . .	. . . .	†
Lancaster	14 Mar. 1855	1 Oct. 1872	. . . .	†364
"	. . . .	25 Sept. 1873	. . . .	†
Madison	12 Mar. 1846	2 Oct. 1857	13 Dec. 1875	†365
"	12 Mar. 1859	7 Sept. 1861	. . . .	†
"	28 Mar. 1864	8 Sept. 1870	. . . .	†366
"	9 Apr. 1867	11 Oct. 1878	. . . .	†
"	20 Mar. 1886	2 Sept. 1891	. . . .	†
Marinette	. . . .	19 Aug. 1884	. . . .	†
Meridian	20 Apr. 1897	. . . .	. . . .	†
"	5 May 1898	. . . .	. . . .	†
Milwaukee	7 May 1845	5–8 Sept. 1843	. . . .	†
"	20 Mar. 1849	5–9 Sept. 1846	. . . .	†
"	25 Mar. 1872	5 Sept. 1848	. . . .	†
"	. . . .	15 Oct. 1856	. . . .	†
"	. . . .	27 Aug. 1864	. . . .	†367
Mineral Point	12 Mar. 1887	6 Oct. 1881	. . . .	†
Monroe	. . . .	16 Oct. 1879	. . . .	†
Muscoda	. . . .	10 Oct. 1880	. . . .	†
New Lisbon	3 Apr. 1883	25 Aug. 1885	. . . .	†368
"	27 Mar. 1885	. . . .	. . . .	†

City or Region	Spring	Fall	Winter	Ref.
WISCONSIN *(cont.)*				
New Richmond	....	30 Aug. 1882	....	†
"	....	12 Sept. 1883	....	†
"	....	28 Sept. 1887	....	†
Oconto	3 Mar. 1860	29 Aug. 1861	....	†
"	....	12 Aug. 1876	....	†
"	....	14 Aug. 1880	....	†
Oregon	....	10 Sept. 1862	....	†
Osceola	....	19 Aug. 1865	....	†
Oshkosh	....	8 Oct. 1867	....	†
"	....	22 Aug. 1868	....	†
"	....	8 Aug. 1872	....	†
"	....	14 Aug. 1897	....	†
Palmyra	....	3 Oct. 1877	....	†
Platteville	....	....	24 Dec. 1881	369
Plover	....	11 Sept. 1856	....	†
Port Washington	....	2 Sept. 1852	....	†
Prairie du Chien	....	6 Oct. 1874	....	†
"	....	4 Sept. 1895	....	†
"	....	8 Oct. 1895	....	†
Prairie du Sac	3 Apr. 1891	....	....	†
Racine	11 Apr. 1866	10 Oct. 1870	....	†
"	....	2 Aug. 1878	....	†
"	....	24 Aug. 1881	....	†
"	....	11 Sept. 1885	....	†
Randolph	late Feb. 1878	....	....	†
Reedsburg	1 Mar. 1878	3 Oct. 1883	....	†
Shawano	....	9 Aug. 1866	....	†
Sheboygan	....	30 Aug. 1854	....	†
"	....	11 Aug. 1855	....	†
"	....	22 Sept. 1864	....	†
Somers	26 Mar. 1870	....	....	†
Sparta	5 Apr. 1892	....	....	†
Sturgeon Bay	19 Mar. 1888	*ca.* 20 Sept. 1865	....	†
"	....	26 Sept. 1867	....	†370
"	....	8 Sept. 1870	....	†
"	....	11 Sept. 1884	....	†371
Superior	....	21 Sept. 1858	....	†
"	....	1 Oct. 1859	....	†
Two Rivers	20 Feb. 1877	....	....	†

City or Region	Spring	Fall	Winter	Ref.
WISCONSIN (*cont.*)				
Watertown	13 Mar. 1858	....	3 Jan. 1876	†372
"	26 Mar. 1863	....	....	†
Waukesha	....	26 Aug. 1871	....	†
Wautoma	2 Mar. 1871	25 Aug. 1869	....	†
West Bend	....	24 Aug. 1881	....	†
Weyauwega	....	3 Aug. 1859	....	†
MANITOBA				
....	early May	Oct.	....	373
Aweme	8 Apr.	21 Sept.	....	*
Carberry	....	30 Aug. 1883	....	374
Dufferin	17 May 1874	....	....	375
Greenridge	17 Apr.	....	....	*
Lake Winnipegosis	10 Apr. 1898	....	....	376
"	14 Apr. 1898	....	....	377
"	13 Apr. 1898	....	....	378
Mount Royal	....	15 Sept.	....	*
Oak Point	20 May 1884	....	....	379
Ossowo	18 Apr. 1885	....	....	380
Park River Post	22 Apr. 1801	....	....	381
Pine Island	....	23 Aug. 1808	....	382
Portage la Prairie	12 May 1884	....	....	383
Riding Mountain	12 May 1892	....	....	384
Swan River	2 May 1802	....	....	385
Terre Blanche	....	31 Aug. 1810	....	386
Terre Blanche River	11 Apr. 1800	....	....	387
ONTARIO				
....	....	Aug.–Nov.	present	388
Ashfield Township, Huron Co.	10 Apr. 1876	....	....	389
Bowmanville	....	12 Sept. 1881	....	390
Dunnville	9 Apr. 1883	....	....	391
Galt	....	....	Jan. 1851	392
Hamilton	10 Apr. 1836	....	....	393
Kempenfeldt Bay, Lake Simco	4 Apr. 1828	....	....	394
"	19 Mar. 1858	....	....	395
Kingston	21 Mar.	....	....	*
Lake Ontario	13 Apr. 1876	....	....	396

City or Region	Spring	Fall	Winter	Ref.
ONTARIO (*cont.*)				
London	21 Mar.	24 Sept. 1885	. . . .	*397
Martin's Falls, Hudson Bay	. . . .	10 Aug. 1840	. . . .	398
Moose Factory	. . . .	16 Aug. 1860	. . . .	399
Niagara	8 Mar. 1779	. . . .	. . . .	400
"	7 Apr. 1847	. . . .	. . . .	401
"	1–4 Apr. 1872	. . . .	. . . .	402
Niagara Falls	20 Mar. 1883	. . . .	. . . .	403
Ottawa	10 Apr. 1859	25 Aug. 1885	. . . .	404
"	15 Apr. 1886	3 Sept. 1887	. . . .	405
Peterborough	6 Apr. 1833	. . . .	. . . .	406
"	1 Apr. 1834	. . . .	. . . .	407
Port Hope	. . . .	. . . .	1826/27	408
Port Rowan	26 Mar.	. . . .	. . . .	*
Toronto	27 Mar. 1815	22 Oct.	. . . .	*409
"	31 Mar. 1851	20 Sept. 1890	. . . .	410
"	25 Apr. 1854	11 Oct. 1890	. . . .	411
"	8 Mar. 1860	. . . .	. . . .	412
"	13 Mar. 1860	. . . .	. . . .	413
"	13 Apr. 1861	. . . .	. . . .	414
"	9 Apr. 1862	. . . .	. . . .	415
"	19 Apr. 1863	. . . .	. . . .	416
"	14 Apr. 1867	. . . .	. . . .	417
"	14 Apr. 1869	. . . .	. . . .	418
"	3 Apr. 1871	. . . .	. . . .	419
"	10 Apr. 1872	. . . .	. . . .	420
"	13 Mar. 1875	. . . .	. . . .	421
"	31 Apr. 1891	. . . .	. . . .	422
QUEBEC				
Gaspé Peninsula	. . . .	31 Aug. 1858	. . . .	423
La Chine	. . . .	Sept. 1796	. . . .	424
Montreal	. . . .	15 Sept.	Dec. 1888	*425
"	. . . .	. . . .	9 Dec. 1888	426
Quebec	. . . .	Sept.	. . . .	427
River Rouge Valley	. . . .	7 Oct. 1858	. . . .	428
SASKATCHEWAN				
Fort Carlton	23 May–mid June 1858	. . . .	. . . .	429

CHAPTER 15: LATE RECORDS

It will be difficult to satisfy everyone on the last date of capture of a passenger pigeon in the wild. Below are given late dates of sight records and captures for the various commonwealths. The last records must be based on specimens taken and accompanied by a satisfactory history. I am willing to accept as the very last record the specimen taken at Sargents, Pike County, Ohio, on March 24, 1900.

Sight records carry interest but little weight. Persons with wide experience with the passenger pigeon have been deceived by a mourning dove under certain circumstances. Brewster wrote: "I have often been unable to satisfy myself respecting the identity of single birds viewed at a distance, or in unfavorable lights. For a Dove seen through mist-laden atmosphere sometimes looked as big as a Pigeon, and when its colour and markings could not be discerned it might easily be mistaken for one, there being really no very obvious points of difference between the two birds in respect to either general appearance or behaviour." [1]

An experienced pigeon trapper who was with Witmer Stone in Sullivan County, Pennsylvania, thought that he had found a pigeon. On collecting the bird, he was astonished to find that it was a mourning dove. [2] Due to similarity in behavior, W. B. Barrows had difficulty on one occasion in persuading a friend that doves in large number were not pigeons. [3] George E. Atkinson, in 1905, shot a mourning dove under the conviction that it was a pigeon. [4]

286

United States

ALABAMA. Edward Pasteur, of Greensboro, shot one in the "winter of 1887." The bird was alone.[5]

ARKANSAS. During Christmas week, 1899, a merchant in Little Rock received with some quail a male passenger pigeon that had been shipped from Cabot, Arkansas. This bird was placed on display for several days with an inscription stating it was the last of its species.[6] Otto Widmann informed Forbush that F. H. Miller, a marketman of St. Louis, received twelve dozen pigeons from Rogers, Arkansas, in 1902, and a single bird shipped from Black River in 1906.[7] Record questionable.

CONNECTICUT. A young male shot at Portland on October 1, 1889, was in the collection of John H. Sage.[8] Wyman has recorded a male in the collection of G. S. Hamlin, the label carrying the data that it was shot at North Bridgeport, August, 1906, by a Swede.[9] James H. Fleming has suggested that the bird was acquired rather than shot on this date.[10] An adult male and three young were seen near Willimantic in October, 1901, by Outram Bangs.[11] Questionable.

GEORGIA. A young male was shot at Augusta, September 12, 1893, by George Jackson. The skin was destroyed by the burning of Science Hall, University of Georgia, Athens.[12]

ILLINOIS. A young female shot at Lake Forest, August 7, 1895, in the collection of John F. Ferry.[13] The latest of the skins in the collection of the Chicago Academy of Sciences was taken in Rogers Park, Chicago, "about 1897." [14] A young male in the collection of the Bryn Mawr High School was collected by William Clingman in the Bryn Mawr district September 30, 1901.[15] In a letter Blair Coursen informed me that this specimen was destroyed by a fire in the school some years ago, so that the date cannot be checked.

INDIANA. A male in the possession of Mr. Kaempher, a taxidermist of Chicago, brought to him March 14, 1894, by a man who shot one of several seen at Liverpool.[16] The wings of a bird killed near Greensburg in the winter of 1895/96, or the spring of 1896, were seen by Professor W. P. Shannon.[17] A flock of sixty was seen in Brown County on April 12, 1895, by V. H. Barnett.[18] There are sight records for 1896 and 1897.[19] Joseph F. Honecker reported to Butler that he saw a wild pigeon with young near Haymond, Franklin County, in the spring of 1905.[20] Questionable.

IOWA. A young male was shot near Keokuk on September 17, 1896, by W. Praeger.[21] A lone pigeon associated with two mourning doves was seen during a period of two weeks in Charles City by C. S. Webster in the summer of 1898.[22] James claims to have seen several flocks, varying in number from 25 to 100, at Edgewood, Clayton County, in the spring of 1902.[23]

KANSAS. There is no specific information. Goss wrote that it was a rare bird, breeding occasionally.[24] Lantz in 1897 considered it a rare summer resident and nearly extinct.[25] Wetmore has written: "I believe that I saw two in flight near Independence, Kansas, in April, 1905, but as the birds were at a little distance this is not entirely certain." [26]

KENTUCKY. On or about November 20, 1898, Seth S. Beckner shot one three miles south of Winchester.[27] It was not preserved. The Smithsonian Institution has an immature male taken at Owensboro on July 27, 1898, by J. G. Taylor.[28]

LOUISIANA. Professor George E. Beyer informed Forbush that two pigeons were taken from a flock of five at Mandeville on January 26, 1895, by J. H. Lamb.[29] An earlier communication gives the date as February, 1895, and states that one specimen is preserved in the Museum of Tulane University.[30] Mrs. Eugene Ellis and a companion killed one near Bains in the autumn of 1895, and McIlhenny shot one from a flock of mourning doves, near Welsh, November 28, 1896.[31]

MAINE. One was taken by Frank Rogers, near Dexter, August 16, 1896.[32] Knight, in May, 1908, was informed by Harry Merrill, of Bangor, that early in the summer of 1904 he saw in a local taxidermist's shop a mounted specimen killed at Bar Harbor. The wrappings were still on it.[33] Palmer considers the date authentic.[34] Since both Knight and Merrill lived in Bangor, it seems strange that four years would elapse before the information was divulged.

MARYLAND. Several flocks of twenty to sixty birds were reported the fall of 1893.[35] Eifrig thought that he saw five July 19, 1901, and two July 17, 1903.[36]

MASSACHUSETTS. Reported seen at Walnut Hill, North Reading, and Plymouth in 1890 and at Woods Hole in the summer of 1891.[37]

The last specimen, an adult female, preserved and mounted, was taken at Melrose by Neil Casey April 12, 1894.[38] The bird was skinned by H. E. Maynard.[39]

MICHIGAN. A lone young female was taken in Delta County on October 1, 1895, by Ernest Copeland.[40] Two mounted specimens in the possession of Otis Watson, Grand Rapids, represent birds killed near that city in July, 1898.[41] His daughter, Mrs. Cora French, informed me by letter that she remembers the specimens but does not now recall what became of them. The last specimen, an immature male, was taken at Chestnut Ridge, near Detroit, September 14, 1898, by Frank Clements (pseudonym of P. E. Moody).[42] This bird, mounted by C. Campion and acquired by J. H. Fleming, is now in the Royal Ontario Museum of Zoology, Toronto.

MINNESOTA. Henry W. Shoemaker has a young male taken on the Root River in August, 1891.[43] A male, nest, and egg taken at Minneapolis June 21, 1895, by O. V. Jones are now in the Museum of Natural History, University of Minnesota.[44]

MISSISSIPPI. No late information was found. A few birds were seen at Corinth in October, 1874.[45] The report of their presence in considerable numbers in February, 1883, at Cedar Grove, Mississippi may be an error in the state.[46] It is probable that at this date the information came from Cedar Grove, Missouri.

MISSOURI. Deane received in the flesh two pigeons, shot from a flock of about fifty, at Altie [Alton?], Oregon County, December 17, 1896, by Charles U. Holden, Jr.[47] Pigeons were reported as last seen at New Haven, Franklin County, September 26, 1902, by A. F. Eimbeck.[48] Questionable.

NEBRASKA. One was shot from a flock of fifteen or twenty birds at Papillion, Sarpy County, November 9, 1895, by Edgar Howard.[49] I was informed by A. M. Brooking in a letter that in 1919 a fine male was found in a collection in an old barn five miles south of Cook, Johnson County. The man from whom it was obtained said that it was mounted by his father twenty or thirty years previously. The specimen is in the Hastings (Nebraska) Museum. A flock of seventy-five to one hundred birds was reported seen in Johnson County in September, 1897.[50]

New Hampshire. A mounted specimen in the Public Library at Acworth was taken near this town on October 10, 1881.[51] Seven were seen feeding in a wild cherry tree at Greenfield in the fall of 1891.[52]

New Jersey. A bird shot at Morris Plains, September 16, 1885, was seen by Thurber.[53] A specimen was taken at Morristown on October 7, 1893, by A. B. Frost.[54] A pigeon was taken at Englewood, June 23, 1896, by C. Irving Wood. When seen by Chapman it was in the possession of the taxidermist, J. Ullrich.[55]

New York. A flock of about 300 pigeons was seen at Constableville, May 22, 1896, by Henry Felshaw who had mounted a male shot near North Western in the spring of 1895.[56] A young male, assuming adult plumage, was taken at Canandaigua, September 14, 1898, by Addison P. Wilbur.[57] One was killed by Michael Healy of the Bolivar (N. Y.) Gun Club on August 10, 1899.[58] The Museum of Cornell University received a mounted adult male from its collector, J. L. Howard of Clyde, New York.[59] According to his memory, he being over eighty years of age, the bird was taken in 1909; however, the mount bore the legend, "Geo. L. Perkins, July 5, 1898." The date of 1909 is considered doubtful.[60]

North Carolina. One was observed by Brimley at Raleigh on April 18, 1891.[61] A female was taken in Buncombe County, October 20, 1894, by J. S. Cairns.[62]

North Dakota. One was killed at Glasston by W. H. Williams in the spring of 1882.[63] A large flock was reported to have been seen at Larimore on April 22, 1891, and another on March 26, 1892.[64]

Ohio. Specimens were taken in Wayne County September 19, 1888, and August 30, 1892.[65] There is a specimen in the Ohio State Museum, killed by a boy March 24, 1900, near Sargents, Pike County, and mounted by Mrs. C. Barnes.[66] Forbush considers the data questionable and Bannon states the bird was killed a mile and one-half east of Wakefield in 1899.[67] Henninger lived in the region where the bird was shot and had ample opportunity to investigate the accuracy of the circumstances surrounding the capture before publishing. The authenticity of the record has never been questioned at Ohio State University. In view of all the information available, it is believed that the record should stand.

OKLAHOMA. Seton had in his collection an adult male and female taken at Fort Holmes in January, 1889, by C. Dewar.[68] Pigeons shipped from Oklahoma (Indian Territory) were in the Boston market in December, 1892, and January, 1893, and in the New York market in November, 1892.[69] A man who spent the winter of 1899/1900 in Oklahoma is reported to have seen a flock of about one hundred pigeons. Five were killed by Cale Ervin.[70]

PENNSYLVANIA. A circumstantial account is given by Norris of the shooting of a pigeon in Monroe County by his brother, Frank Cushing Norris, October 25, 1895.[71] Stone cites a specimen taken on October 23 at Canadensis, in the same county, by George H. Stuart.[72] According to Paxson, the bird taken by Norris on October 23 (?) was presented to Stuart and was still in his possession.[73] There is a mature female in the collection of the Carnegie Institution, Pittsburgh, bearing the label "Pennsylvania," August 15, 1898, no definite locality being given.[74] According to Todd, H. A. Surface exhibited a bird shot in McKean County in 1902.[75] Surface actually stated regarding its supposed extinction: "But last year [1903] I received a specimen of the wild pigeon and I intended to bring it down and show it to this audience at this time. It came from McKean County, where there were about seventy-five or eighty birds in the flock." [76] The date of collection was not stated and efforts to locate the specimen have failed.

RHODE ISLAND. The last bird to be taken was collected at Cranston, November 2, 1886, by Walter A. Angell.[77] One was seen sitting on a telegraph wire by William A. Sprague of Providence on September 25, 1888.[78] A flock of eight was seen by Walter A. Angell in the month of August, 1893.[79]

SOUTH CAROLINA. No specimen from the state is known to exist. Wayne on November 21, 1885, at a station thirteen miles north of Charleston, saw a young female that had been shot by a hunter.[80] The morning of March 18, 1901, a flock of six to eight was seen at Beaufort by Hoxie.[81] According to Davis, one was shot by him in Williamsburg County in the fall of 1895, "as nearly as I can recall the date." [82]

SOUTH DAKOTA. A male was procured by Hoffman while stationed at the Grand River Agency, October 7, 1872 to June 7, 1873.[83] It was listed as rare in summer in the southeastern section of the state in 1885.[84]

TENNESSEE.   In the fall of 1893, a Mr. Riddick of Brownsville, Haywood County, killed one from a flock of eight.[85]

TEXAS.   Large number seen near Lampasas the winter of 1882/83, according to A. S. Eldredge; a few were shot near Corpus Christi in 1889.[86] Three reported killed by market hunters in 1896.[87]

VERMONT.   A few were seen every year at the close of the nineteenth century and some were shot in 1900.[88] Small flocks persisted at Milton where a few bred in 1898.[89] These records are doubtful.

VIRGINIA.   In September, 1890, there were pigeons near Warrenton, Fauquier County, where it was not uncommon to see them yearly.[90] Wild pigeons were on sale in the Norfolk market in January, 1892.[91] A few were stated to be breeding at Highgate, three being seen April 20, 1893, and attempts were being made to protect them.[92]

WEST VIRGINIA.   Some specimens have been preserved.[93] In Roane County, the last were killed in the fall of 1886.[94] Several hundred pigeons nested on Sugar Ridge, on the headwaters of the Greenbrier River, in the spring of 1889 and a few were shot.[95] There is a very questionable report of 700 to 1,000 pigeons being seen near Parkersburg in the fall of 1899.[96]

WISCONSIN.   An immature male shot near Delavan Lake on September 8, 1896, by C. E. Golder came into the possession of Hollister.[97] The specimen is now in the Denver Museum of Natural History. Several small flocks were reported at Oshkosh in the fall of 1897.[98] An immature pigeon, associated with mourning doves, was shot at Babcock between September 9 and 15, 1899, by the guide Varney of E. Hough's party. The bird was recognized as a passenger pigeon by Neal Brown and the skin was preserved.[99] Hough added later: "As to the bird itself, it was identified by scientists, in case it needed any identification other than that of these men perfectly familiar with the passenger pigeon."[100] Coale states that O. L. Wetterhall shot a pigeon at Oconomowoc in the fall of 1905 that was "picked and cooked."[101] This record is too indefinite to be accepted.

Canada

MANITOBA. Fleming had in his collection an adult female taken at Riding Mountain, May 12, 1892, by Walter Brett.[102] A specimen was taken at St. Boniface, near Winnipeg, in the fall of 1893 by Dan Smith.[103] The last specimen was a fine male collected at Winnipegosis, April 10, 1898, and sent to Atkinson to be mounted.[104] Fleming gives the date April 14.[105] What was apparently the same specimen is given by Seton as taken April 13, 1898, by J. J. G. Rosser.[106]

NEW BRUNSWICK. Bred at Grand Falls in 1879.[107] Though formerly abundant, it was seen rarely by the year 1882.[108]

NOVA SCOTIA. The species had apparently disappeared by 1879.[109]

ONTARIO. Two immature females taken at Toronto, September 20, 1890,[110] and October 11, 1890. The latter was in the collection of Fleming.[111] A male pursued for half an hour in University Park Ravine, Toronto, on April 13, 1891, eluded capture.[112] Sight reports through 1902 are given by Fleming.[113]

QUEBEC. Fleming had in his collection an immature bird taken at Montreal in December, 1888, and mentions a specimen in the collection of Jonathan Dwight, Jr., collected at Tadousac July 20, 1889.[114] Five were shot at Pointe des Monts June 27, 1889.[115] That they were still to be seen occasionally as late as 1908 is very doubtful. There is a questionable record of a bird taken by Pacificque Couture of St. Vincent, September 23, 1907. The bird was mounted and identified by A. Learo, a taxidermist of Montreal.[116]

CHAPTER 16: EVALUATION OF
ILLUSTRATIONS

Two brief papers on illustrations of the passenger pigeon have appeared.[1] A more comprehensive list is given below, but it is not to be considered complete. Most of the plates are indifferent in character, coloring, and draughtsmanship. There is a tendency among artists to show for the pigeon too prominent a notch in the bill and too high a forehead. The latter sloped sharply as is shown by reference to photographs of the living bird.

The earliest colored drawing is that of Catesby.[2] Admittedly not trained as an artist, he undertook also the engraving. His classic figure of a male pigeon standing on the leaf of a detached twig of an oak is poorly drawn. The feathers have a hairy appearance and the chequers appear as random, round dots. In the edition of 1754, the entire underparts are colored pink.

The plate in Frisch is highly commendable for the excellence of the drawing.[3] The chief defect is the shortness of the tail. The chequers indicate an adult male, but the body plumage is scaled as in the immature bird. In the copy examined at McGill University there is a minimum of color. There is a pink spot on the side of the neck while the underparts are pale brown.

No illustration was originally included by Buffon. Between 1765 and 1783 (?) Daubenton supervised the preparation of a series of colored plates drawn by Martinet, to accompany Buffon's *Histoire naturelle des oiseaux*. Plate 176, representing a male passenger pigeon (*Tourterelle, du Canada*) about two-thirds natural size, is indifferent.[4] Owing to the limited number of colored plates, a new set in black and white was produced to accompany the special edition in ten volumes (1770–86).

In the Library of Harvard University is a water color of a male pigeon drawn by John Abbot (Fig. 12). Abbot lived at Jacksonborough, Screven County, Georgia, from 1790–1810.[5] The erect posture, in particular, is wholly unlike a pigeon. In life, when the pigeon was perching, the tibia was invisible and the tarsus was held at an angle of about 15°.

The folios on the pigeons, in which Temminck supplied the text and Madame Knip the paintings, contain two plates (Nos. 48 and 49) of a male and female.[6] While pleasing to the eye, the plates are not faithfully drawn or colored. I have not seen the first edition of 1809–11.

The painting by Wilson of a male standing on the sawed surface of a stump is spiritless, but a decided improvement over Catesby.[7] The bird stands too high and its tail is spread to show an exceptional amount of white. The shape of the head is good. In the reproduction by Brown the colors are exaggerated, the breast being crimson.[8]

The famous painting by Audubon (Plate 62) shows a female leaning down to feed a male on a lower branch. That the work is artistic cannot be denied. Audubon was a much better draughtsman than Wilson, but he was too prone to paint his subject in an abnormal pose. Frequently the result was contrary to life, if not grotesque. The feeding of a male by a female was never observed while the species was extant. The painting at Harvard University, though not signed, is considered to be the original. A fine reproduction of the plate occurs in Mershon.[9] In 1937, the History Institute of America, Inc., copyrighted and published a beautiful copy. An exceptionally good drawing of a male made by Audubon at Louisville, Kentucky, December 11, 1809, is to be found in Herrick.[10] The shape of the head and the position of the legs are excellent.

In 1835, Selby published a colored plate in which the drawing of the pigeon is poor.[11] The head is turned to show an incongruously swollen throat. In the same year William Pope painted a male passenger pigeon standing on a curved limb that gives the impression of being the trunk of a tree. The original is in the Toronto Public Library. The eye is not well done and the tarsi are nearly perpendicular, a liberty too frequently taken in mounting specimens. It has been reproduced as a frontispiece by Mitchell and Scott.[12]

The plate by Meÿer, showing a pair of pigeons, has no merit as to drawing and coloring.[13] The tip of the tail of the male is incorrectly shown as curving upward.

In DeKay, we find a good plate of a male standing on a small mound.[14] It was lithographed by Endicott of New York. The drawing is good except that the white tail feathers are too conspicuous. The colors are better than in some modern plates.

The monograph on the pigeons by Reichenbach has, on Plate 154, three small colored drawings (Nos. 1377–79) representing two male and one female passenger pigeons perched on a limb.[15] The colors and draughtsmanship are indifferent in quality. The central tail feathers of the bird on the right are much too short. The middle figure is copied from Selby.

Baird, Brewer, and Ridgway show a colored head only. The orbital ring is exaggerated in size, shape, and color.[16]

A crudely colored plate in Dümling shows a pair of pigeons on the lateral limb of a pine and two birds on a limb in the background.[17] The style is that in Brehm.

The lithograph in Warren is a copy of the male in Audubon's painting except for a modification of the head.[18] The coloring is poor.

In Jasper there is a tinted drawing, 10.5 cm. in size, of a single pigeon perched on a pine branch.[19]

There is a very attractive drawing in Studer of six pigeons sitting on the stubs of branches in pine trees.[20] The stubs may have been intended to show that the limbs had been broken by the weight of roosting birds.

An excellent colored illustration of a male perched on an aspen stub was copyrighted in 1900 by A. W. Mumford of Chicago. The pose and colors are unusually good. The drawing was used by Dawson and several other authors.[21] I have not been able to determine the name of the artist. The plate in Mitchell carries the notation, "From Col. Ruthven Deane." [22]

The pamphlet prepared by Charles K. Reed contains a good plate by his brother, Chester A. Reed, of a pair of adults and a juvenile.[23] On the back of this publication is a small colored plate showing a pair of passenger pigeons and a pair of mourning doves. The painting of the three pigeons appeared on the cover of the *Wisconsin Conservationist,* March, 1920. The original is in the possession of Eva Reed Holden, Worcester, Massachusetts.

Many good colored illustrations have appeared in the present century, the pace having been set by Louis Agassiz Fuertes. He did the frontispiece for Mershon, showing a pair of pigeons with a background of oak and hemlock branches.[24] The illustration in Eaton represents a young bird with an adult male and female.[25] The juvenile is too dark and the breast of the male is crimson. Plate 36 by this artist in Forbush is poorly colored.[26] The subjects are the same as in the preceding. The breast of the male is clay color in place of vinaceous brown. The notch in the bill is exaggerated. A very attractive painting of passenger pigeons done by Fuertes was reproduced in 1911 by the Ithaca Gun Company.

The Japanese artist, K. Hayashi, did three paintings with exceptionally sharp detail for Whitman.[27] Plate 28 shows a male resting on a large limb of a pine tree. The pose is good and the slope of the forehead is more natural than in most drawings. Plate 29 has a female standing on the prostrate trunk of a tree. Barrows reproduced this plate in black and white and attributed it erroneously to a photograph of a mounted specimen.[28] A hybrid between a passenger pigeon and a ring dove is shown in Plate 29. The massive Japanese backgrounds used by the artist are poor settings for the passenger pigeon.

The painting by E. J. Sawyer in the Audubon Society leaflet shows influence by Hayashi, but the bird faces in the opposite direction.[29] In the background a few pigeons rest in trees and there is a large flock in the air. It has been reproduced in Oberholser and in many other publications.[30]

The colored plate by R. Bruce Horsfall in Hornaday is good in most respects.[31] The bird is perched on the dead stub of a tree.

The small colored plates by F. C. Hennessey and Allan Brooks are without distinction due to the limitations of the publications.[32] Brooks had a better opportunity to show his skill in Plate 15 for Wetmore.[33] A male perches on a twig with a particularly pleasing background of three birds in flight and a large flock in the distance.

The colors of a pair painted by Francis Lee Jacques for Roberts were, unfortunately, poorly reproduced.[34]

The author has a fine water color by Owen J. Gromme of a male perched on a limb with the Dells of the Wisconsin in the background.

A lithograph by A. F. Tait, "Playing the Decoy," was published by Currier and Ives in 1862. One of the men in the blind is Frank Forester. The decoys are being "worked" and the pigeons will be shot from the spars.

A Kollner lithograph, "Scenes in the Country," shows a bonneted lady on horseback crossing a stream. Pigeons hang in a row from the saddle. I have been unable to obtain the history of this lithograph.

An engraving in aquatint, made by William Daniel in 1809, shows a pigeon at rest on a branch, another alighting, and an indistinct flock in flight in the river valley in the background.[35]

Walter Thorp, of Baraboo, Wisconsin, made in 1944 a pencil and water-color drawing of large numbers of pigeons, principally in flight. The original is in the Rural Art Collection of the University of Wisconsin. It has been reproduced in *Silent Wings*.[36] The ensemble is pleasing in spite of the stiffness of the style. Four black rectrices are shown in place of two.

A painting by C. H. Shearer, done in 1910–11, shows a flight of wild pigeons in Berks County, Pennsylvania, with the Schuylkill River in the middle distance.[37] It is in the collection of Colonel Henry W. Shoemaker.

A painting by Frank Bond has been published in black and white.[38] The composition is poor, there being merely four distinct flocks of pigeons flying in "company" front.

The Travellers Insurance Company, Hartford, Connecticut, had a colored advertisement in the National Geographic Magazine for September, 1936, showing two pigeons on the branch of an oak. The upper figure is a male and the lower a female preening its extended right wing. The composition is pleasing. I was informed by the company that the original water color in their collection is by an unknown artist.

A large number of woodcuts and black and white drawings have been published. Many, like those in Révoil, are atrocious in execution or without any merit.[39] Some are of historical interest. The drawing by

Charles Bécard de Granville, made about 1701, is the earliest illustration of the passenger pigeon known.[40] As an artist, Granville was a
primitive. The tail of the bird is highly distorted, being forked in place
of wedge-shaped (Fig. 11).

John R. Forster inserted in his edition of Kalm a woodcut of a single
pigeon standing on a branch.[41] The tail is slightly forked and the two
middle rectrices are insufficiently long.

The pigeon in Pennant rests on a rocky ledge.[42] The nasal opercula
are too prominent, the tail is spread, and there are fourteen rectrices in
place of twelve. The small figures in Eyton and Yarrell are a considerable improvement.[43]

The woodcuts in Nuttall were executed by Bowen and Hall.[44]
There is a fair representation of a pigeon standing on the ground, its
tail spread and slightly curved. It is copied from Wilson. Other birds
are shown diagrammatically in flight, some alighting on a baited bed.
The V-formation of one of the flocks, identical with that of waterfowl,
is unnatural. A woodcut of a single bird and a V-shaped flock appears
also in the paper by Frost.[45] The figure in Coues is a poor copy of Wilson or Nuttall.[46]

The drawing of the pigeon in Cooper is characterless.[47] The bird,
with spread tail, rests on a dead branch. The sketch of a head on the
same page is a decided advance in the art. Excellent line drawings of
bill, foot, wing and tail are to be found in Cooper and Ridgway.[48]

Pleasing illustrations occur in Gillmore and Brehm.[49] There can be
mentioned also an artistic sketch of a pigeon roost by moonlight in
Stratton-Porter and a drawing by Sawyer of a bird in flight in the fore-
ground and a flock in the distance.[50] Nash did an attractive headpiece
of three pigeons in flight; also a pair of pigeons, and a bird looking
at a nest containing *two* eggs.[51]

The great advantage of working with a live model is shown by the
exceptionally fine drawing of a male by Charles R. Knight to be found
in Dutcher.[52]

There is a good small drawing by G. M. Sutton in Todd.[53] There
are similar ones in Wright and Sprunt.[54] W. J. Breckenridge made a
fine sketch of a pigeon in juvenal plumage for Roberts.[55]

Many attempts have been made with indifferent success to portray pigeons in numbers. The woodcut by Lossing and Barritt shows a pigeon, drawn in Wilson's style, standing on the trunk of a fallen tree.[56] In a tree are three pigeons, two of which show the influence of Audubon. The background is similar to Nuttall's. A man is concealed in a bough house ready to spring a net on the pigeons descending to the bed. Here again is a V-shaped flock.

There is a woodcut of the same period showing the netting of pigeons in New England. The trees are full of pigeons ready to descend to the bed.[57] Cockburn shows a net used in Quebec.[58] Only four pigeons are visible.

A sketch by Smith Bennett showing the shooting of pigeons in northern Louisiana is highly successful in showing the birds en masse.[59] Nine hunters are collecting dead pigeons or firing into a huge V-shaped flock. A similar shooting scene in Iowa is less well done.[60]

Leslie published five inaccurate sketches of methods of trapping and transporting pigeons for shooting tournaments.[61] The trapping equipment is mainly imaginative. The five sketches of scenes at a shooting tournament give evidence of having been made on the grounds.[62]

Fuertes made for Chapman a drawing of three pigeons on a branch and with indistinct flocks flying in long lines with a narrow front.[63] Townsend, who described the flight formations to the artist, states that they were sketched "rather successfully." [64]

Photographs of mounted birds are numerous. Forbush printed the photograph of a mounted male (American Museum of Natural History, No. 258,154).[65] Barrows has a particularly good photograph to show the comparative sizes of the passenger pigeon and mourning dove.[66] There is an excellent one by Forest R. Poe on the cover of the *Passenger Pigeon,* October, 1949.

A photograph of "Martha" after mounting is shown in Shufeldt.[67] Several good photographs of museum groups, such as that shown by Bishop, are available.[68] Roberts shows a pair of pigeons in a small oak with a genuine nest and egg collected by him in 1874.[69] Other photographs are available from the Chicago Museum of Natural History, American Museum of Natural History (No. 293,027), and the Royal Ontario Museum, Toronto, Canada.

The size and shape of the egg of the passenger pigeon are compared with those of the mourning dove in Forbush.[70]

In the course of the anatomical examination of the last passenger pigeon, several photographs were taken by Shufeldt. There is a good photograph of the head of this bird, with the "eye restored."[71] The anatomical photographs do not even possess clarity to compensate for their gruesomeness.[72] Included is a good drawing of part of the trachea, lower larynx, and bronchial tubes.

There is a photograph of a disarticulated skeleton by Shufeldt.[73]

Invaluable is a series of photographs (Nos. 29,438–29,453) taken by J. G. Hubbard in 1898 of the live passenger pigeons in the aviary of C. O. Whitman at Woods Hole, Massachusetts, in the possession of the American Museum of Natural History, New York. These have been reproduced frequently. The following may be mentioned:

No. 29,440.—Adult female in a characteristically erect pose.[74]

No. 29,441.—Squab.

No. 29,443.—Bird on nest in a vine.

No. 29,444.—Adult male, side view. "A highly characteristic attitude."[75]

No. 29,445.—Adult male. "A characteristic attitude assumed as the bird walked through branches."[76]

No. 29,446.—Adult, facing, head turned to left. "The nearby presence of the bird's offspring induces an alert, defiant pose when confronted by the camera."[77]

No. 29,447.—Back view, very dark, of bird with the white feathers in the tail conspicuous.

No. 29,448.—Male in an alert attitude.

No. 29,449.—Adult male in erect, alert pose.[78] This is the best photograph known to me. The reproduction by Wetmore was incorrectly designated by the supplier of the photograph as the last surviving passenger pigeon, which was a female.[79] The chequers are clearly those of a male.

No. 29,450.—Side view of adult female.

No. 29,451.—Back view of an immature bird.[80]

Other good photographs are: an adult male in Whitman's aviary copyrighted in 1903 by Cole; one of the last survivors of Whitman's flock taken by Hegner; an adult male in repose; and one of an immature bird sent to Mershon by Whitman.[81]

In 1911, Enno Meyer copyrighted a photograph of Martha, the last passenger pigeon. It is a back view of the bird, facing left, and is without character. It was reproduced as a frontispiece by Hornaday and also used by Chapman.[82] It also appears on a post card issued by the Cincinnati Zoological Gardens. Another photograph of this bird, taken by Dr. William C. Herman, is shown in Bent.[83]

A photograph of a nest with an egg occurs in Craig.[84]

REFERENCES AND NOTES

INDEX

REFERENCES AND NOTES

The following references are those of scientific interest most frequently cited in the notes. In the chapter notes, all citations of items in this list occur in abbreviated form. Other sources not listed here are given complete citation at first occurrence in the notes of each chapter; thereafter the reference is also abbreviated.

Audubon, John J. *Ornithological Biography*. Edinburgh, 1831–39. 5 vols.

Baird, Spencer F., Thomas M. Brewer, and Robert Ridgway. *A History of North American Birds. Land Birds*. Boston, 1875. Vol. III.

Barrows, Walter B. *Michigan Bird Life*. Lansing, Mich., 1912.

Bendire, Charles. *Life Histories of North American Birds*. Washington, D. C., 1892. Part I.

Bent, Arthur Cleveland. *Life Histories of North American Gallinaceous Birds*. (Bull. U. S. Nat. Museum, No. 162.) Washington, D. C., 1932.

Bethune, C. J. S. "Recollections of the Passenger Pigeon," *Ottawa Naturalist,* XVI (1902), 40–44.

Brewster, William. "The Birds of the Lake Umbagog Region of Maine," *Bull. Museum Comparative Zool.,* No. 66 (1925), Part II, pp. 306–10.

———. "The Present Status of the Wild Pigeon (*Ectopistes migratorius*) as a Bird of the United States, with Some Notes on Its Habits," *Auk,* VI (1889), 285–91.

Bryant, C. A. "The Passenger Pigeon," *Forest and Stream,* LXXX (1913), 494, 512, 514–15.

Butler, Amos W. "The Birds of Indiana," *22nd Ann. Rept. Indiana Dept. Geol. Nat. Resources,* 1897, pp. 760–64.

Catesby, Mark. *The Natural History of Carolina, Florida and the Bahama Islands.* London, 1731. Vol. I.

Clinton, De Witt. "Remarks on the Columba Migratoria, or Passenger Pigeon, in a

Letter to Dr. J. W. Francis, . . . Albany, April 24, 1823," *N. Y. Med. Phys. J.*, II (1823), 210–15.

Cook, Sullivan. "What Became of the Wild Pigeon," *Forest and Stream*, LX (1903), 205–6.

Craig, Wallace. "The Expressions of Emotion in the Pigeons. III: The Passenger Pigeon (*Ectopistes migratorius* Linn.)," *Auk*, XXVIII (1911), 408–27.

Deane, Ruthven. "Some Notes on the Passenger Pigeon (Ectopistes migratorius) in Confinement," *Auk*, XIII (1896), 234–37.

———. "The Passenger Pigeon (Ectopistes migratorius) in Wisconsin and Nebraska," *Auk*, XV (1898), 184–85.

Dury, Charles. "The Passenger Pigeon," *J. Cincinnati Soc. Nat. Hist.*, XXI (1910), 52–56.

Eaton, Elon H. *Birds of New York*. (N. Y. State Museum, Memoir No. 2.) Albany, N.Y., 1910. Vol. I.

Fenton, W. N., and M. H. Deardorff. "The Last Passenger Hunts of the Cornplanter Senecas," *J. Wash. Acad. Sci.*, XXXIII (1943), 289–315.

Fleming, James H. "The Disappearance of the Passenger Pigeon," *Ottawa Naturalist*, XX (March, 1907), 236–37.

Forbush, Edward H. *Birds of Massachusetts and Other New England States*. Boston, 1927. Vol. II.

———. *Game Birds, Wild-Fowl and Shore Birds*. 2nd ed.; Boston, 1916.

French, John C. *The Passenger Pigeon in Pennsylvania*. Altoona, Penn., 1919.

Gentry, Thomas G. *Life-Histories of the Birds of Eastern Pennsylvania*. Phila., and West Salem, Mass., 1876–77. Vol. II.

Gibbs, Robert Morris ("Pericles"). "Nesting Habits of the Passenger Pigeon," *Oologist*, XI (1894), 237–40.

Gunn, Charles W. "The Ectopistes migratoria," *Oologist*, II (1876), 29–30.

Hatch, Philo L. *Notes on the Birds of Minnesota*. Minneapolis, Minn., 1892.

Herman, William C. "The Last Passenger Pigeon," *Auk*, LXV (1948), 77–80.

Hildreth, S. P. "Columbia migratoria," *Am. J. Sci.*, XL (1841), 348.

———. "Flight and Bivouac of Pigeons," *ibid.*, XXIV (1833), 134–35.

Howitt, Henry. "A Short History of the Passenger, or Wild, Pigeon," *Can. Field-Naturalist*, XLVI (1932), 27–30.

Ingells, James. "The Pigeon Days," Grand Rapids *Press* (Mich.), Oct. 21, 28, Nov. 4, 1933.

Kalm, Pehr. "A Description of the Wild Pigeons Which Visit the Southern English Colonies in North America, during Certain Years, in Incredible Multitudes," *Auk*, XXVIII (1911), 53–66.

———. *Travels into North America*. 2nd ed.; London, 1772. 2 vols.

K[napp], H[enry]. "The Wild Pigeon," *Am. Sportsman*, IV (Sept. 19, 1874), 387.

Lincecum, Gideon. "The Nesting of Wild Pigeons," *Am. Sportsman*, IV (June 27, 1874), 194–95.

McGee, W. J. "Notes on the Passenger Pigeon," *Science,* N. S., XXXII (1910), 958–64.

Mann, Charles L. "Die Wandertaube," *Jahres-Bericht des naturhistorischen Vereins von Wisconsin,* 1880–81, pp. 43–47.

Martin, Edward T. "Among the Pigeons," *Chicago Field,* X (1879), 385–86.

———. "What Became of All the Pigeons?" *Outing,* LXIV (1914), 478–81.

Maynard, Charles J. *The Birds of Eastern North America....* Newtonville, Mass., 1881.

Mershon, William B. *The Passenger Pigeon.* New York, 1907.

Mitchell, Margaret H. *The Passenger Pigeon in Ontario.* Toronto, 1935.

Pennant, Thomas. *Arctic Zoology.* London, 1784–85. Vol. II.

Pokagon, Simon. "The Wild Pigeon of North America," *Chautauquan,* XXII (1895), 202–6.

Purdy, James B. "The Passenger Pigeon in the Early Days of Michigan," *Bull. Mich. Ornithol. Club,* IV (1903), 69–71.

Roberts, Thomas S. *The Birds of Minnesota.* Minneapolis, Minn., 1932. Vol. I.

Roney, H. B. "A Description of the Pigeon Nesting of 1878 and the Work of Protection Undertaken by the East Saginaw and Bay City Game Protection Clubs," *Chicago Field,* X (1879), 345–47, 349.

Schaff, Morris. *Etna and Kirkersville.* Boston and N. Y., 1905.

Scherer, Lloyd E., Jr., "Passenger Pigeon in Northwestern Pennsylvania," *Cardinal,* V (1939), 25–42.

Schorger, A. W. "The Migration of the Passenger Pigeon in Wisconsin," *Passenger Pigeon,* XIII (1951), 101–4, 144–46.

———. "Unpublished Manuscripts by Cotton Mather on the Passenger Pigeon," *Auk,* LV (1938), 471–77.

Strickland, Samuel. *Twenty-Seven Years in Canada West.* London, 1853. Vol. I.

Thomas, W. P. "Millions of Wild Pigeons. A Roost of Immense Extent in the Indian Territory," New York *Sun,* June 14, 1881. Also in *Chicago Field,* XV (1881), 314.

Thompson, W. W. *The Passenger Pigeon.* Coudersport, Penn., *ca.* 1921. Pamphlet.

Thoreau, Henry David. *Journal.* Ed. Bradford Torrey; 14 vols. Vols. 7–20 of *The Writings of Henry David Thoreau.* Boston and N. Y., 1906.

"Tom Tramp." "A Pigeon Roost," *Rod and Gun and Am. Sportsman,* VIII (June 3, 1876), 149.

Whitman, Charles Otis. *Posthumous Works of Charles Otis Whitman.* Washington, D. C., 1919. 3 vols.

Wilson, Alexander. *American Ornithology; or the Natural History of the Birds of the United States.* Phila., 1812. Vol. V.

Wilson, Etta S. "Personal Recollections of the Passenger Pigeon," *Auk,* LI (1934), 157–68.

CHAPTER I

1 Jacques Cartier, *Voyage de Jacques Cartier au Canada en 1534* (ed. M. H. Michelant; Paris, 1865), p. 41.

2 Jacques Cartier, *Brief Recit. & succincte narration, de la nauigation faicte es ysles de Canada* (Boston, 1924), p. 33.

3 John Alphonse of Xanctoigne, "Here Followeth the Course from Belle Isle...up the River of Canada for the Space of 230 Leagues," in Richard Hakluyt, *The Principal Navigations Voyages Traffiques & Discoveries of the English Nation* (Glasgow and N. Y., 1903–5), Extra Ser., VIII, 282.

4 *The Works of Samuel de Champlain* (ed. H. P. Biggar; Toronto, 1922–36), I, 332.

5 Marke Lescarbot, "The Voyage of Monsieur de Monts into New France," in Samuel Purchas, *Hakluytus Posthumus, or Purchas His Pilgrimes* (Glasgow, 1905–7), XVIII, 282.

6 Gabriel Sagard-Theodat, *Le grand Voyage du pays des Hurons* (Paris, 1632), p. 303.

7 Gabriel Sagard-Theodat, *Histoire du Canada* (Paris, 1866), III, 674.

8 *The Jesuit Relations and Allied Documents* (ed. R. G. Thwaites; Cleveland, Ohio, 1896–1901), XLVIII, 177.

9 Pierre Boucher, *Histoire véritable et naturelle des moeurs et productions du pays de la Nouvelle France, vulgairement dite le Canada* (Paris, 1664), pp. 71–72.

10 Louis de Lahontan, *New Voyages to North-America* (London, 1703), I, 61–62.

11 "An Extract of Several Letters from Cotton Mather, D. D. to John Woodward, M. D. and Richard Waller, Esq; S. R. Secr.," *Phil. Trans.*, XXIX (1714), 64; *Abstracts*, VI (1809), 87.

12 Thomas Hariot, "Historical Narrative," in *Sir Walter Ralegh and His Colony in America* (Pub. Prince Soc., Vol. XV; Boston, 1884), p. 218.

13 *Travels and Works of Captain John Smith* (ed. Edward Arber; Edinburgh, 1910), I, 60.

14 William Strachey, *The Historie of Travaile into Virginia Brittania* (Hakluyt Soc., 1st ser., Vol. VI; London, 1849), p. 126.

15 Ralph Hamor, "Notes of Virginian Affaires in the Government of Sir Thomas Dale and Sir Thomas Gates till Anno 1614," in Samuel Purchas, *Hakluytus Posthumus, or Purchas His Pilgrimes* (Glasgow, 1906), XIX, 97.

16 Richard Blome, *The Present State of His Majesties Isles and Territories in America* (London, 1687), p. 94; Thomas Budd, *Good Order Established in Pennsilvania & New Jersey in America* (N. Y., 1865), p. 36; Thomas C. Holm, "A Short Description of the Province of New Sweden Now Called, by the English, Pennsylvania, in America," *Mem. Hist. Soc. Penn.*, III (1834),

Part I, p. 41; Francis D. Pastorius, "A Particular Geographical Description of the Lately Discovered Province of Pennsylvania," *Mem. Hist. Soc. Penn.*, IV (1850), Part II, p. 91; William Penn, in a letter quoted by S. W. Pennypacker, "Collection of Various Pieces concerning Pennsylvania, Printed in 1684," *Penn. Mag. Hist. Biography*, VI (1882), 313.

17 Thomas Paskel, in a letter quoted by S. W. Pennypacker in *Penn. Mag. Hist. Biography*, VI (1882), 326.

18 Thomas Makin quoted in Robert Proud, *The History of Pennsylvania* (Phila., 1797–98), II, 367.

19 John Holme, "True Relation of the Flourishing State of Pennsylvania," *Bull. Hist. Soc. Penn.*, I (1848), 165.

20 "A Brief Relation of the Discovery and Plantation of New England," *Coll. Mass. Hist. Soc.*, 2nd ser., IX (1832), 18.

21 Thomas Dudley, "Letter to the Countess of Lincoln. Boston, March 12, 1631," *ibid.*, 1st ser., VIII (1802), 45.

22 Francis Higginson, "New-Englands Plantation," *ibid.*, I (1792), 121.

23 William Wood, *Wood's New England's Prospect* (Pub. Prince Soc., Vol. III; Boston, 1865), pp. 31–32.

24 John Josselyn, *An Account of Two Voyages to New England, Made during the Years 1638, 1663* (Boston, 1865), p. 79.

25 Thomas Morton, *The New English Canaan* (Pub. Prince Soc., Vol. XIV; Boston, 1883), p. 180.

26 John Winthrop, *The History of New England from 1630 to 1649* (ed. James Savage; Boston, 1843), II, 113 and 404–5.

27 William Hubbard, "A General History of New England," *Coll. Mass. Hist. Soc.*, 2nd ser., V (1848), 25.

28 Cotton Mather, *The Christian Philosopher: A Collection of the Best Discoveries in Nature with Religious Improvements* (London, 1721), pp. 188–89.

29 Nicholas-Jean de Wassenaer, "Description and First Settlement of New Netherland," in E. B. O'Callaghan, *The Documentary History of the State of New-York* (8° ed.; Albany, N. Y., 1849–51), III, 45.

30 David P. De Vries, "Voyages from Holland to America, 1632–1644," *Coll. N. Y. Hist. Soc.*, 2nd ser., III (1857), p. 38.

31 *Ibid.*, pp. 90 and 110.

32 A. Van der Donck, "A Representation of New Netherland" and "Description of the New Netherlands," *ibid.*, II (1849), 265, and I (1841), 173.

33 Hernando de Soto, "A Narrative of the Expedition of Hernando de Soto into Florida," in B. F. French (ed.), *Historical Collections of Louisiana*, Part II (Phila., 1850), p. 220.

34 René Laudonnière, "The Description of the West Indies in Generall, but Chiefly and Particularly of Florida," in Richard Hakluyt, *Principal Navigations*, Extra Ser., VIII, 451.

35   Louis Hennepin, *A New Discovery of a Large Country in America* (London, 1698), pp. 137 and 193.

36   René Menard in *Jesuit Relations,* XLVIII, 119.

37   Jacques Marquette, *ibid.,* LIV, 189.

38   *Ibid.,* LIX, 181.

39   Daniel Coxe, *A Description of the English Province of Carolana by the Spaniards Call'd Florida and by the French, La Louisiane* (4th ed.; London, 1741), p. 96.

40   Le Page Du Pratz, *Histoire de la Louisiane* (Paris, 1758), II, 129–33.

41   N. Bossu, *Nouveaux Voyages aux Indes Occidentales* (Paris, 1768), Part I, p. 128.

42   T. M. (Thomas Mathew), "The Beginning, Progress and Conclusion of Bacon's Rebellion in Virginia, in the Years 1675 and 1676," in Peter Force (col.), *Tracts and Other Papers* (N. Y., 1947), Vol. I, Part VIII, p. 7; also in *Virginia Hist. Reg.,* III (1850), 64.

43   Benjamin S. Barton, *Barton's Fragments of the Natural History of Pennsylvania* (ed. O. Salvin; London, 1883), p. ix. See also John W. Barber, *The History and Antiquities of New England, New York, New Jersey, and Pennsylvania* (Hartford, Conn., 1842), p. 474.

44   John F. Watson, *Annals of Philadelphia and Pennsylvania* (Phila., 1857), II, 411.

CHAPTER 2

1   M. Schaff, *Etna and Kirkersville,* p. 108.

2   W. Craig in *Auk,* XXVIII (1911), 408.

3   *Ibid.,* p. 414.

4   J. J. Audubon, *Ornithol. Biog.,* I (1831), 325.

5   Alexander Wilson, *Am. Ornithology,* V, 111.

6   W. Craig in *Auk,* XXVIII (1911), 417.

7   *Ibid.,* and his "Recollections of the Passenger Pigeon in Captivity," *Bird-Lore,* XV (1913), 93–99.

8   W. Craig in *Auk,* XXVIII (1911), 421.

9   John Mactaggart, *Three Years in Canada: An Account of the Actual State of the Country in 1826–7–8* (London, 1829), I, 233–34.

10   W. B. Mershon, *Passenger Pigeon,* p. 126.

11   J. C. French, *Passenger Pigeon,* p. 205.

12   W. Brewster in *Auk,* VI (1889), 287.

13   J. B. Oviatt quoted in the article of L. E. Scherer, Jr., in *Cardinal,* V (1939), 38.

14   Chief Simon Pokagon in *Chautauquan,* XXII (1895), 203; Edwin Haskell quoted in J. C. French, *Passenger Pigeon,* p. 93.

15   J. J. Audubon, *Ornithol. Biog.,* I (1831), 325.

16 Wallace Craig in *Auk*, XXVIII (1911), 414.

17 *Posthumous Works of C. O. Whitman*, III, 120.

18 Herman Behr, "Recollections of the Passenger Pigeon," *Cassinia*, No. 15 (1911), pp. 25–26.

19 "Backwoods," "In Wild Pigeon Days," *Forest and Stream*, XLIV (1895), 126.

20 L. E. Scherer, Jr., in *Cardinal*, V (1939), 38.

21 H. D. Thoreau, *Journal*, VII, 335; see also V, 415, and VII, 35 and 334.

22 H. T. Blodgett quoted in W. B. Mershon, *Passenger Pigeon*, p. 120. Compare the description in J. C. French, *Passenger Pigeon*, p. 227.

23 A. B. Welford quoted in Percy R. Lowe, "A Reminiscence of the Last Great Flight of the Passenger Pigeon (*Ectopistes migratorius*) in Canada," *Ibis*, 11th ser., IV (1922), 138.

24 James Carnegie, Earl of Southesk, *Saskatchewan and the Rocky Mountains . . . in 1859 and 1860* (Edinburgh, 1875), p. 26; W. Faux, *Memorable Days in America: Being a Journal of a Tour to the United States* (London, 1823), p. 248; Henry Buth in a letter to me; William B. Leffingwell, *Shooting on Upland, Marsh, and Stream* (Chicago, 1890), p. 228; Ben O. Bush quoted in W. B. Mershon, *Passenger Pigeon*, p. 138; Ora W. Knight, *The Birds of Maine* (Bangor, Me., 1908), pp. 210–11; W. B. Mershon, *Passenger Pigeon*, p. 157.

25 H. Howitt in *Can. Field-Naturalist*, XLVI (1932), 27–30.

26 J. B. Oviatt quoted in the article of L. E. Scherer, Jr., in *Cardinal*, V (1939), 38.

27 W. Craig in *Auk*, XXVIII (1911), 419.

28 *Ibid.*, p. 423.

29 W. Brewster in *Bull. Museum Comparative Zool.*, No. 66 (1925), Part II, p. 309.

30 Chief Simon Pokagon in *Chautauquan*, XXII (1895), 202.

31 C. J. S. Bethune in *Ottawa Naturalist*, XVI (1902), 40–44.

32 Ransom A. Moore, "The Hunter of Kewaunee: Passing of the Passenger Pigeon," *Hoard's Dairyman*, LXXIII (1928), 106.

33 C. Dury in *J. Cincinnati Soc. Nat. Hist.*, XXI (1910), 53.

34 John L. Childs, "Personal Recollections of the Passenger Pigeon," *Warbler*, 2nd ser., I (1905), 71–73; Samuel Strickland, *Twenty-Seven Years in Canada West*, I, 297–301.

35 T. G. Gentry, *Life-Histories of Birds*, II, 295.

36 Henry C. Leonard, *Pigeon Cove and Vicinity* (Boston, 1873), pp. 165–67.

37 Pehr Kalm in *Auk*, XXVIII (1911), 64.

38 Isaac Weld, *Travels through the States of North America and the Provinces of Upper and Lower Canada . . .* (London, 1799), pp. 269–70.

39 J. Benwell, *An Englishman's Travels in America* (London, *ca.* 1853), pp. 72–75.

40 Thomas S. Roberts, *The Birds of Minnesota* (Minneapolis, Minn., 1932), I, 576–87.

41 John G. Dillin, "Recollection of Wild Pigeons in Southeastern Pennsylvania, 1864–1881," *Cassinia*, No. 14 (1910), pp. 33–36.

42 William Brewster in *Bull. Museum Comparative Zool.*, No. 66 (1925), Part II, pp. 306–10.

43 *The Writings of Henry David Thoreau*, II, 331.

44 Willis E. Barber, "The Work of the Conservation Commission," in M. M. Quaife, *Wisconsin: Its History and Its People* (Chicago, 1924), II, 383.

45 L. E. Scherer, Jr., in *Cardinal*, V (1939), 37.

46 C. J. Maynard, *Birds of Eastern N. Am.*, p. 336.

47 *Posthumous Works of C. O. Whitman*, III, 119.

48 *Ibid.*, p. 144.

49 J. B. Oviatt quoted in the article of L. E. Scherer, Jr., in *Cardinal*, V (1939), 37.

50 H. D. Thoreau, *Journal*, VI, 402.

51 H. Howitt in *Can. Field-Naturalist*, XLVI (1932), 27–30.

52 Alexander Wilson, *Am. Ornithology*, V, 109.

53 H. Howitt in *Can. Field-Naturalist*, XLVI (1932), 27–30.

54 William Ludlow, *Report of a Reconnaissance of the Black Hills of Dakota in the Summer of 1874* (Wash., 1875), p. 96.

55 Daniel G. Elliot, "The 'Game Birds' of the United States," *Rept. U. S. Dept. Agr.*, 1863–64, pp. 380–81; Elliott Coues, *Key to North American Birds* (5th ed.; Boston, 1903), I, 37.

56 J. J. Audubon, *Ornithol. Biog.*, I, 93 and 326.

57 E. S. Dixon, *The Dovecote and the Aviary* (London, 1851), pp. 215–18.

58 Charles Waterton, "Retrospective Criticism: The Passenger Pigeon," *Mag. Nat. Hist.* (London), VII (1834), 282.

59 Charles Waterton, *Essays on Natural History* (ed. Norman Moore; London, 1871), p. 355.

60 Harry R. Lewis, *Poultry Keeping* (Phila. and London, *ca.* 1915), pp. 286–87; Rudolph Seiden, *Poultry Handbook* (N. Y., 1947), p. 294.

61 C. Howard King, "The Physiology of the 'Stick' in the Dry Picking of Poultry" (B. S. thesis, University of Wisconsin, 1920).

62 J. N. Langley, "On the Sympathetic System of Birds and on the Muscles Which Move the Feathers," *J. Physiol.*, XXX (1904), 241.

63 G. Hapgood Parks, "A Loose-Feathered Nighthawk," *Auk*, LXV (1948), 300–1.

64 Malcolm Davis, "Loose-Feathered Birds," *ibid.*, p. 602.

65 John G. Dillin, "Recollections of Wild Pigeons in Southeastern Pennsylvania, 1864–1881," *Cassinia*, No. 14 (1910), pp. 33–36.

66 *Posthumous Works of C. O. Whitman*, III, 160.

67 Charles Otis Whitman, "Animal Behavior," *Biological Lectures from the Marine Biological Laboratory, Wood's Hole, Mass., 1898* (Boston, 1899), p. 334. See also his *Posthumous Works*, III, 159.

68 R. A. Johnson, "Nesting Behavior of the Atlantic Murre," *Auk*, LVIII (1941), 156.

69 G. K. Noble and D. S. Lehrman, "Egg Recognition in the Laughing Gull," *Auk*, LVII (1940), 36.

70 Quoted in E. S. Dixon, *The Dovecote and the Aviary*, p. 218.

71 H. D. Thoreau, *Journal*, IV, 44.

72 W. Brewster in *Bull. Museum Comparative Zool.*, No. 66 (1925), Part II, p. 309.

73 C. J. Maynard, *Birds of Eastern N. Am.*, p. 336; M. Schaff, *Etna and Kirkersville*, p. 109.

74 John G. Dillin in *Cassinia*, No. 14 (1910), p. 36.

75 E. S. Dixon, *The Dovecote and the Aviary*, p. 218.

76 Charles A. Green, "Wild Pigeons," *Forest and Stream*, LXXXI (1913), 75.

77 W. Craig in *Auk*, XXVIII (1911), 411.

78 *Posthumous Works of C. O. Whitman*, III, 146.

79 C. A. Bryant in *Forest and Stream*, LXXX (1913), 512.

80 Wallace Craig in *Auk*, XXVIII (1911), 411.

81 J. J. Audubon, *Ornithol. Biog.*, I, 326.

82 C. A. Bryant in *Forest and Stream*, LXXX (1913), 494.

83 C. J. Maynard, *Birds of Eastern N. Am.*, p. 337.

84 S. P. Hildreth in *Am. J. Sci.*, XL (1841), 348.

85 W. P. Thomas in *New York Sun*, June 14, 1881, and in *Chicago Field*, XV (1881), 314.

86 C. A. Green in *Forest and Stream*, LXXXI (1913), 75.

87 W. A. Linkletter, "The Passenger Pigeon," *Rod and Gun in Canada*, XXII (Dec., 1920), 755–56.

88 Charles Darwin, *The Variation of Animals and Plants under Domestication* (N. Y., 1896), I, 190; Hoyes Lloyd, "An Aquatic Habit of the Pigeons," *Can. Field-Naturalist*, XXXV (1921), 98–99; Frederick C. Lincoln, "A Note on the Domestic Pigeon," *Proc. Biol. Soc. Wash.*, XXXV (1922), 227; E. H. Forbush, *Birds of Mass.*, II, 53.

89 G. M. Mathews, *The Birds of Australia* (London, 1910–11), I, 153.

90 W. B. Mershon, *Passenger Pigeon*, p. 206.

91 Thomas Nuttall, *A Manual of the Ornithology of the United States and of Canada. . . . The Land Birds* (Cambridge, Mass., 1832), I, 635.

92 *Posthumous Works of C. O. Whitman*, III, 145.

93 L. E. Scherer, Jr., in *Cardinal*, V (1939), 38; W. N. Fenton and M. H. Deardorff in *J. Wash. Acad. Sci.*, XXXIII (1943), 307.

94 E. S. Dixon, *The Dovecote and the Aviary*, p. 218.

95 W. Craig in *Auk,* XXVIII (1911), 412.

96 W. C. Herman in *Auk,* LXV (1948), 79.

97 *Posthumous Works of C. O. Whitman,* III, 141.

98 J. B. Oviatt quoted in the article of L. E. Scherer, Jr., in *Cardinal,* V (1939), 38.

99 *Posthumous Works of C. O. Whitman,* III, 140.

100 T. S. Roberts, *Birds of Minn.,* I, 585; C. J. Maynard, *Birds of Eastern N. Am.,* p. 336.

101 *Posthumous Works of C. O. Whitman,* III, 28.

102 W. B. O. Peabody, "A Report on the Birds of Massachusetts Made to the Legislature in the Session of 1838–9," *J. Boston Soc. Nat. Hist.,* III (1841), 192.

103 W. B. Barrows quoted in W. B. Mershon, *Passenger Pigeon,* p. 158.

104 W. H. Fisher, "Maryland Birds That Interest the Sportsman," *Oologist,* XI (1894), 139.

105 C. S. Webster, "The Wild Pigeon in Iowa," *Forest and Stream,* LII (1899), 305; Emerson Hough, "The Wild Pigeon," *ibid.,* p. 88.

106 T. Martin Trippe, "Some Differences between Western and Eastern Birds," *Am. Naturalist,* V (1871), 634.

107 H. Howitt in *Can. Field-Naturalist,* XLVI (1932), 27; C. S. Osborn quoted in W. B. Mershon, *Passenger Pigeon,* p. 223.

108 Pehr Kalm, *Travels into North America,* I, 164.

109 Pehr Kalm in *Auk,* XXVIII (1911), 65.

110 W. Bullock, *Sketch of a Journey through the Western States of North America* (London, 1827), p. xxi.

111 C. W. Janson, *The Stranger in America* (London, 1807), p. 68.

112 De Witt Clinton in *N. Y. Med. Phys. J.,* II (1823), 210–15.

113 Ruthven Deane in *Auk,* XIII (1896), 236.

114 J. Hunt in *Proc. Zool. Soc. London,* 1833, Part I, p. 10; Emilius Hopkinson, *Records of Birds Bred in Captivity* (London, 1926), p. 104.

115 J. C. French, *Passenger Pigeon,* p. 49.

116 T. M. Owen in *Forest and Stream,* XIII (1879), 533.

117 Ruthven Deane, "Breeding of the Wild Pigeon in Confinement," *Nuttall Bull.,* VI (1881), 60; J. Bebe, "Breeding Wild Pigeons," *Forest and Stream,* XXVII (1887), 485.

118 Frank J. Thompson, "Breeding of the Wild Pigeon in Confinement," *Nuttall Bull.,* VI (1881), 122.

119 C. Dury in *J. Cincinnati Soc. Nat. Hist.,* XXI (1910), 55.

120 S. A. Stephan quoted in Ruthven Deane, "The Passenger Pigeon (*Ectopistes migratorius*) in Confinement," *Auk,* XXV (1908), 183.

121 S. A. Stephan quoted in J. C. French, *Passenger Pigeon,* p. 212, and in Gene

Stratton-Porter, "The Last Passenger Pigeon," *Good Housekeeping*, LXXIX (Aug., 1924), 137.

122 F. J. Thompson in *Nuttall Bull.*, VI (1881), 122; and his "Incubation under Difficulties," *Forest and Stream*, XII (1879), 265.

123 H. M. in *Am. Field*, XLIV (1895), 539.

124 Ruthven Deane in *Auk*, XIII (1896), 235.

125 C. O. Whitman quoted in C. H. Ames, "Breeding of the Wild Pigeon," *Forest and Stream*, LVI (1901), 464. See also W. Wade, "Breeding the Wild Pigeon," *ibid.*, p. 485.

126 W. Craig in *Auk*, XXVIII (1911), 425.

127 C. Bendire, *Life Histories of N. Am. Birds*, Part I, p. 138.

128 Ruthven Deane in *Auk*, XXV (1908), 181–83.

129 J. H. Fleming in *Ottawa Naturalist*, XX (March, 1907), 236–37.

130 Ruthven Deane, "The Passenger Pigeon—Only One Pair Left," *Auk*, XXVI (1909), 429.

131 Ruthven Deane, "The Passenger Pigeon—Only One Bird Left," *Auk*, XXVIII (1911), 262.

132 S. A. Stephan quoted in J. C. French, *Passenger Pigeon*, p. 212; Frank M. Chapman, "The Last Passenger Pigeon," *Bird-Lore*, XVI (1914), 399; Robert W. Shufeldt, "Death of the Last of the Wild Pigeons," *Sci. Am. Supplement*, LXXVIII (1914), 253; Robert W. Shufeldt, "The Last Passenger Pigeon," *Blue-Bird*, VII (1915), 85; Alexander Wetmore, "Game Birds of Prairie, Forest and Tundra," *Nat. Geographic Mag.*, LXX (1936), 495.

133 William Bridges, "The Last of a Species," *Animal Kingdom*, XLIX (1946), 185.

134 Jay Williams, *Fall of the Sparrow* (N. Y., 1951), p. 10.

135 S. A. Stephan quoted in the article of W. C. Herman in *Auk*, LXV (1948), 80.

136 R. W. Shufeldt, "Anatomical and Other Notes on the Passenger Pigeon (Ectopistes migratorius) Lately Living in the Cincinnati Zoological Gardens," *Auk*, XXXII (1915), 29–41.

137 S. A. Stephan quoted in T. Gilbert Pearson, "The Last Pigeon," *Bird-Lore*, XII (1910), 261.

138 S. A. Stephan quoted in Ruthven Deane's articles in *Auk*, XXV (1908), 183, and XXVI (1909), 429.

139 Ruthven Deane in *Auk*, XXVIII (1911), 262.

140 Stephan quoted in R. W. Shufeldt's articles in *Sci. Am. Supplement*, LXXVIII (1914), 253, and in *Blue-Bird*, VII (1915), 85

141 Henry W. Henshaw, "American Game Birds," *Nat. Geographic Mag.*, XXVIII (1915), 136–37; Cincinnati *Enquirer* (Ohio), Jan. 20, 1938; D. H. Eaton, "The Last Surviving Passenger Pigeon," *Forest and Stream*, LXXXII

(1914), 165; Cincinnati *Times Star* (Ohio), July 16, 1947; Witmer Stone in *Auk*, XXXI (1914), 566–67; F. M. Chapman in *Bird-Lore*, XVI (1914), 399; Cincinnati *Enquirer* (Ohio), Sept. 2, 1914.

142 Ruthven Deane in *Auk*, XXV (1908), 182.

CHAPTER 3

1 C. Cottam and P. Knappen, "Food of Some Uncommon North American Birds," *Auk*, LVI (1939), 155–58.

2 "Backwoods," "In Wild Pigeon Days," *Forest and Stream*, XLIV (1895), 126.

3 C. Dury in *J. Cincinnati Soc. Nat. Hist.*, XXI (1910), 53; T. S. Roberts, *Birds of Minn.*, I, 585.

4 J. C. French, *Passenger Pigeon*, p. 95.

5 C. C. Lincoln, "The Passenger Pigeon in Wisconsin" (MS dated Feb. 7, 1910, in the Library of the Wisconsin Historical Society, Madison, Wis).

6 Henry Knapp, "Statements about the Wild Pigeons," *Forest and Stream*, XII (1879), 146.

7 Alexander Wilson, *Am. Ornithology*, V, 107.

8 H. K. (Henry Knapp) in *Am. Sportsman*, IV (Sept. 19, 1874), 387.

9 Lancaster *Herald* (Wis.) quoted in *Milwaukee Democrat*, March 21, 1855.

10 Alexander Wilson, *Am. Ornithology*, V, 108.

11 J. J. Audubon, *Ornithol. Biog.*, I (1831), 322.

12 Bénédict-Henry Révoil, *Chasses dans l'Amérique du Nord* (Tours, 1859), p. 132. A translation from the 1869 edition is printed as *Wild Life Bull.*, No. VIII, Penn. Alpine Club (Altoona, Penn.), and is also printed in part in *Bird-Lore*, XXX (1928), 317–20.

13 Springfield *Republican* (Mass.) quoted in Milwaukee *Wisconsin*, Oct. 4, 1854.

14 H. K. (Henry Knapp), "About Pigeon Catching," *Am. Sportsman*, I (June, 1872), 4.

15 Edward T. Martin in *Outing*, LXIV (1914), 481.

16 Johnson A. Neff, "Habits, Food, and Economic Status of the Band-Tailed Pigeon," *North Am. Fauna*, No. 58 (1947), p. 69.

17 *William Byrd's Histories of the Dividing Line betwixt Virginia and North Carolina* (ed. W. K. Boyd; Raleigh, N. C., 1929), p. 216.

18 Alexander Wilson, *Am. Ornithology*, V, 107.

19 Pehr Kalm in *Auk*, XXVIII (1911), 59.

20 M. Catesby, *Natural History of Carolina*, I, 23. Also see John Lawson, *The History of Carolina . . .* (Raleigh, N. C., 1860), p. 233.

21 [William N. Blane], *An Excursion through the United States and Canada during the Years 1822–23* (London, 1824), pp. 143 and 183.

22 L. E. Scherer, Jr., in *Cardinal*, V (1939), 32.

23 J. M. Wheaton, "Report on the Birds of Ohio," *Report of the Geological Sur-*

vey of Ohio, IV (1882), 442. See also J. J. Audubon, *Ornithol. Biog.*, I, 322; "Backwoods," "In Wild Pigeon Days," *Forest and Stream*, XLIV (1895), 126; John Burroughs, "Recollections of the Passenger Pigeon," *Warbler*, 2nd ser., I (1905), 70–71; John Bradbury, *Travels in the Interior of North America in the Years 1809, 1810, and 1811* (London, 1819), pp. 52–53; Frank W. Langdon, "On the Occurrence in Large Numbers of Seventeen Species of Birds," *J. Cincinnati Soc. Nat. Hist.*, XII (1889), 57–58.

24 Hibbard J. Jewett, "Memories of the Passenger Pigeon," *Bird-Lore*, XX, (1918), 351.

25 James E. Quinlan, *History of Sullivan County* (Liberty, N. Y., 1873), pp. 507–9.

26 John Burroughs in *Warbler*, 2nd ser., I (1905), 70–71.

27 Le Page Du Pratz, *Histoire de la Louisiane* (Paris, 1758), II, 129–33; Alexander Wilson, *Am. Ornithology*, V, 111.

28 J. C. French, *Passenger Pigeon*, p. 51.

29 Jacob Ferris, *The States and Territories of the Great West* (N. Y., 1856), p. 176.

30 C. A. Bryant in *Forest and Stream*, LXXX (1913), 494.

31 E. Haskell quoted in J. C. French, *Passenger Pigeon*, p. 100.

32 T. G. Gentry, *Life-Histories of Birds*, II, 298.

33 J. J. Audubon, *Ornithol. Biog.*, I, 322.

34 Herman Behr, "Recollections of the Passenger Pigeon," *Cassinia*, No. 15 (1911), pp. 24–27.

35 Chief Simon Pokagon quoted in W. B. Mershon, *Passenger Pigeon*, p. 205.

36 "Backwoods," "In Wild Pigeon Days," *Forest and Stream*, XLIV (1895), 126.

37 James B. Purdy quoted in W. B. Mershon, *Passenger Pigeon*, p. 132.

38 *Posthumous Works of C. O. Whitman*, III, 67.

39 Pehr Kalm in *Auk*, XXVIII (1911), 62.

40 James B. Purdy in *Bull. Mich. Ornithol. Club*, IV (1903), 69–71.

41 William T. Cox, "Do Droughts Explain the Prairies?" *Am. Forests*, XLII (1936), 556.

42 Mary Sayle, "Viability of Seeds Passing through the Alimentary Canals of Pigeons," *Auk*, XLI (1924), 474–75.

43 W. W. Bartlett, *History, Tradition and Adventure in the Chippewa Valley* (Chippewa Falls, Wis., 1929), p. 222.

44 New York *Sun*, April 27, 1884.

45 C. Hart Merriam, *Mammals of the Adirondack Region* (N. Y., 1884), p. 225.

46 H. B. Roney in *Chicago Field*, X (1879), 345.

47 Charles W. Gunn, "Notes on the Wild Pigeon," *Western Oologist*, I, No. 4 (1878), 14.

48   William Bartram, *Travels through North & South Carolina, Georgia, East & West Florida* ... (Phila., 1791), p. 469.

49   G. Lincecum in *Am. Sportsman*, IV (June 27, 1874), 194–95; John Lawson, *History of Carolina*, p. 232.

50   Wiley Britton, *Pioneer Life in Southwest Missouri* (Kans. City, Mo., 1929), 51–61.

51   T. G. Gentry, *Life-Histories of Birds*, II, 298; C. Cottam and P. Knappen in *Auk*, LVI (1939), 155–58.

52   E. Sterling, "Food of the Wild Pigeon," *Forest and Stream*, X (1878), 95.

53   Alexander Wilson, *Am. Ornithology*, V, 107; De Witt Clinton in *N. Y. Med. Phys. J.*, II (1823), 210–15; G. Lincecum in *Am. Sportsman*, IV (June 27, 1874), 194–95; J. C. French, *Passenger Pigeon*, p. 15; A. C. Bent, *Life Histories of N. Am. Gallinaceous Birds*, p. 388; Cottam and Knappen in *Auk*, LVI (1939), 155–58.

54   M. H. Mitchell, *Passenger Pigeon*, p. 97.

55   E. H. Forbush, *Game Birds*, p. 471; E. S. Wilson in *Auk*, LI (1934), 158.

56   H. D. Thoreau, *Journal*, XIII, 103.

57   E. Osborn quoted in W. B. Mershon, *Passenger Pigeon*, pp. 111 and 115.

58   J. B. Oviatt quoted in the article of Lloyd E. Scherer, Jr., in *Cardinal*, V (1939), 32 and 35.

59   William B. Mershon, *Passenger Pigeon*, p. 115.

60   James Ingells in Grand Rapids *Press* (Mich.), Oct. 21, 1933; L. E. Scherer, Jr., in *Cardinal*, V (1939), 35; Henry D. Thoreau, *Notes on New England Birds* (ed. F. H. Allen; Boston and N. Y., 1910), pp. 115 and 117.

61   Arthur T. Wayne, *Birds of South Carolina* (Charleston, S. C., 1910), p. 66.

62   T. G. Gentry, *Life-Histories of Birds*, II, 298.

63   T. Hutchins (1782 MS) quoted by Ernest T. Seton, "The Birds of Manitoba," *Proc. U. S. Nat. Museum*, XIII (1891), 522–23.

64   John R. Forster, "An Account of the Birds Sent from Hudson's Bay; with Observations Relative to Their Natural History; and Latin Descriptions of Some of the Most Uncommon," *Phil. Trans.*, LXII (1772), 398.

65   Pehr Kalm, *Travels into North America*, II, 140; and his article in *Auk*, XXVIII (1911), 61.

66   F. E. S., "Netting Wild Pigeons," *Forest and Stream*, XLIII (1894), 28.

67   Henry Knapp in *Am. Sportsman*, IV (Sept. 19, 1874), 387, and *Forest and Stream*, XII (1879), 146; J. C. French, *Passenger Pigeon*, p. 230.

68   Pehr Kalm, *Travels into North America*, II, 140, and his article in *Auk*, XXVIII (1911), 61; De Witt Clinton in *N. Y. Med. Phys. J.*, II (1823), 211.

69   S. C. Bishop, "A Note on the Food of the Passenger Pigeon," *Auk*, XLI (1924), 154.

70   J. C. French, *Passenger Pigeon*, p. 230.

71 T. G. Gentry, *Life-Histories of Birds,* II, 298.

72 C. Cottam and P. Knappen in *Auk,* LVI (1939), 155–58.

73 T. G. Gentry, *Life-Histories of Birds,* II, 298.

74 Alexander Wilson, *Am. Ornithology,* V, 107.

75 De Witt Clinton in *N. Y. Med. Phys. J.,* II (1823), 210–15; Henry C. Leonard, *Pigeon Cove and Vicinity* (Boston, 1873), pp. 165–67; C. J. Maynard, *Birds of Eastern N. Am.,* pp. 335–37; Duncan Cameron, "The Nipigon Country," in L. R. Masson, *Les Bourgeois de la Compagnie du Nord-Ouest* (Quebec, 1890), I, 241; E. S. Wilson in *Auk,* LI (1934), 158.

76 George B. Sudworth, *Check List of the Forest Trees of the United States, Their Names and Ranges* (Bull. U. S. Dept. Agr., Div. Forestry, No. 17; Wash., 1898), p. 76; Willard N. Clute, *American Plant Names* (Indianapolis, Ind., 1940), p. 10.

77 Catherine P. Traill, *Studies of Plant Life in Canada* (Ottawa, 1885), p. 118.

78 Charles Hallock, *The Sportsman's Gazetteer* (N. Y., 1877), p. 235.

79 Samuel Thompson, *Reminiscences of a Canadian Pioneer for the Last Fifty Years* (Toronto, 1884), pp. 75–76.

80 *The Secret Diary of William Byrd of Westover, 1709–1712* (Richmond, Va., 1941), p. 347.

81 C. Douglas quoted in Henry K. Coale, "On the Nesting of Ectopistes migratorius," *Auk,* XXXIX (1922), 254.

82 "Didymus," "The Wild Pigeon," *Forest and Stream,* LII (1899), 444.

83 J. C. French, *Passenger Pigeon,* p. 230; T. G. Gentry, *Life-Histories of Birds,* II, 298; E. S. Wilson in *Auk,* LI (1934), 158.

84 Willard N. Clute, *Am. Plant Names,* p. 218.

85 James G. Cooper, "The Fauna of Montana Territory," *Am. Naturalist,* III (1869), 80.

86 George B. Sudworth, *Check List of Forest Trees,* p. 71.

87 Daniel Agnew, "Wild Pigeon Days," *Forest and Stream,* XLIV (1895), 186–87; J. C. French, *Passenger Pigeon,* p. 230.

88 Alexander Wilson, *Am. Ornithology,* V, 107.

89 W. N. Clute, *Am. Plant Names,* p. 127.

90 C. P. Traill, *Studies of Plant Life in Canada,* p. 147.

91 Pehr Kalm in *Auk,* XXVIII (1911), 63; C. J. Maynard, *Birds of Eastern N. Am.,* pp. 35–57; J. C. French, *Passenger Pigeon,* p. 230.

92 J. M. Wheaton, "The Food of Birds as Related to Agriculture," *29th Ann. Rept. Ohio State Board Agr.,* 1874, p. 571; Daniel Agnew in *Forest and Stream,* XLIV (1895), 186–87; George B. Grinnell, "Recollections of Audubon Park," *Auk,* XXXVII (1920), 375.

93 G. B. Sudworth, *Check List of Forest Trees,* p. 100.

94 W. N. Clute, *Am. Plant Names,* p. 257.

95   John Macoun and James H. Macoun, *Catalogue of Canadian Birds* (Ottawa, 1909), pp. 235–37.

96   Robert Ridgway, "Ornithology," *U. S. Geological Exploration of the Fortieth Parallel,* Vol. IV (1877), Part III, p. 596.

97   Campbell Hardy, *Forest Life in Acadie* (London, 1869), p. 313.

98   Baird, Brewer, and Ridgway, *A History of North American Birds. Land Birds,* III, 372.

99   E. S. Wilson in *Auk,* LI (1934), 158; T. G. Gentry, *Life-Histories of Birds,* II, 298.

100 Pehr Kalm in *Auk,* XXVIII (1911), 62.

101 Maximilian, Prinz von Wied, "Verzeichniss der Vögel, welche auf einer Reise in Nord-America beobachtet wurden," *J. Ornithol.,* VI (1858), 425.

102 U. S. Forest Service, *Woody-Plant Seed Manual* (Wash., 1948), p. 280.

103 Samuel Hearne, *A Journey from Prince of Wales's Fort in Hudson's Bay to the Northern Ocean* . . . (London, 1795), pp. 417–18.

104 William C. Marsden, "What Has Become of the Wild Pigeon?" *Forest and Stream,* LXXXIII (1914), 146–47.

105 T. G. Gentry, *Life-Histories of Birds,* II, 298.

106 C. Cottam and P. Knappen in *Auk,* LVI (1939), 155–58.

107 T. G. Gentry, *Life-Histories of Birds,* II, 298.

108 C. Cottam and P. Knappen in *Auk,* LVI (1939), 155–58.

109 J. B. Purdy in *Bull. Mich. Ornithol. Club,* IV (1903), 69–71.

110 W. J. Beal, "Michigan Weeds," *51st Ann. Rept. State Board Agr. Michigan* (Lansing, Mich., 1912), p. 291.

111 C. Cottam and P. Knappen in *Auk,* LVI (1939), 155–58.

112 G. Lincecum in *Am. Sportsman,* IV (June 27, 1874), 194–95.

113 J. M. Wheaton in *29th Ann. Rept. Ohio State Board Agr.,* 1874, p. 571; T. G. Gentry, *Life-Histories of Birds,* II, 298; Etta S. Wilson in *Auk,* LI (1934), 158.

114 W. N. Clute, *Am. Plant Names,* p. 53.

115 E. S. Wilson in *Auk,* LI (1934), 158.

116 S. P. Hildreth, "Notes on Certain Parts of the State of Ohio," *Am. J. Sci.,* X (1826), 330; W. N. Clute, *Am. Plant Names,* p. 142.

117 George H. Loskiel, *History of the Mission of the United Brethren among the Indians in North America* (London, 1794), pp. 92–93; De Witt Clinton in *N. Y. Med. Phys. J.,* II (1823), 211; J. M. Wheaton in *29th Ann. Rept. Ohio State Board Agr.,* 1874, p. 571.

118 C. Dury in *J. Cincinnati Soc. Nat. Hist.,* XXI (1910), 54.

119 Anne Grant, *Memoirs of an American Lady* (N. Y., 1846), pp. 42–43.

120 Charles W. Townsend, *The Birds of Essex County, Massachusetts* (Cambridge, Mass., 1905), p. 204.

121 Roger Williams, *A Key into the Language of America* (Coll. Rhode Island Hist. Soc., Vol. I; Providence, R. I., 1827), p. 87.

122 "A Brief Relation of the Discovery and Plantation of New England (1607–1622)," *Coll. Mass. Hist. Soc.,* 2nd ser., IX (1832), 18.

123 *The Jesuit Relations and Allied Documents* (ed. R. G. Thwaites; Cleveland, Ohio, 1896–1901), XLVIII, 177.

124 Duncan Cameron, "The Nipigon Country," in L. R. Masson, *Les Bourgeois de la Compagnie du Nord-Ouest,* I, 241; *David Thompson's Narrative of His Explorations in Western America, 1784–1812* (ed. J. B. Tyrrell; Toronto, 1916), p. 61; R. G. A. Levinge, *Echoes from the Backwoods* (London, 1846), I, 127.

125 "Good News from New England," *Coll. Mass. Hist. Soc.,* 4th ser., I (1852), 202.

126 Thomas Morton, *The New English Canaan* (Pub. Prince Soc., Vol. XIV; Boston, 1883), p. 180.

127 W. N. Clute, *Am. Plant Names,* p. 131.

128 C. Cottam and P. Knappen in *Auk,* LVI (1939), 155–58.

129 George Cartwright, *Captain Cartwright and His Labrador Journal* (ed. C. W. Townsend; Boston, 1911), p. 180; W. N. Clute, *Am. Plant Names,* p. 125.

130 W. Brewster in *Bull. Museum Comparative Zool.,* No. 66 (1925), Part II, p. 306; Duncan Cameron in L. R. Masson, *Les Bourgeois de la Compagnie du Nord-Ouest,* I, 241; C. E. I. (C. E. Ingalls), "Wild Pigeon in Massachusetts," *Forest and Stream,* XXXIII (1889), 243; Frederick J. Seaver, *Historical Sketches of Franklin County* (Albany, N. Y., 1918), p. 212; George E. Atkinson, *A Review-History of the Passenger Pigeon of Manitoba* (Trans. Hist. Sci. Soc. Manitoba, No. 68; Winnipeg, 1905), p. 7.

131 J. C. French, *Passenger Pigeon,* p. 230; R. G. A. Levinge, *Echoes from the Backwoods,* I, 127–28; C. J. Maynard, *Birds of Eastern N. Am.,* p. 336; J. M. Wheaton in *29th Ann. Rept. Ohio State Board Agr.,* 1874, p. 571; C. E. I. (C. E. Ingalls) in *Forest and Stream,* XXXIII (1889), 243; Alexander Wilson, *Am. Ornithology,* V, 107; Samuel Strickland, *Twenty-Seven Years in Canada West,* I, 299.

132 J. C. French, *Passenger Pigeon,* p. 226.

133 W. F. Henninger, "A Diary of a New England Ornithologist," *Wilson Bull.,* XXIX (1917), 6; L. E. Scherer, Jr., in *Cardinal,* V (1939), 35.

134 E. S. Wilson in *Auk,* LI (1934), 158.

135 C. A. Bryant in *Forest and Stream,* LXXX (1913), 494.

136 W. F. Henninger in *Wilson Bull.,* XXIX (1917), 6; L. E. Scherer, Jr., in *Cardinal,* V (1939), 35.

137 W. Brewster in *Bull. Museum Comparative Zool.,* No. 66 (1925), Part II, p. 307; Pierre Biard in *Jesuit Relations,* III, 81; Duncan Cameron in L. R. Masson, *Les Bourgeois de la Compagnie du Nord-Ouest,* I, 241; R. G. A. Levinge, *Echoes from the Backwoods,* I, 127–28; C. J. Maynard, *Birds of Eastern N. Am.,* 336; L. E. Scherer, Jr., in *Cardinal,* V (1939), 35; Samuel Strickland, *Twenty-Seven Years in Canada West,* I, 299.

138   Duncan Cameron in L. R. Masson, *Les Bourgeois de la Compagnie du Nord-Ouest,* I, 241.

139   *The Works of Samuel de Champlain* (ed. H. P. Biggar; Toronto, 1922–36), I, 332.

140   Duncan Cameron in L. R. Masson, *Les Bourgeois de la Compagnie du Nord-Ouest,* I, 241.

141   William Brewster, *The Birds of the Cambridge Region of Massachusetts* (Cambridge, Mass., 1906), pp. 177.

142   Duncan Cameron in L. R. Masson, *Les Bourgeois de la Compagnie du Nord-Ouest,* I, 241; R. G. A. Levinge, *Echoes from the Backwoods,* I, 127–28.

143   G. E. Atkinson, *Review-History of Passenger Pigeon of Manitoba,* p. 7.

144   Hector St. John de Crèvecoeur, *Letters from an American Farmer* (London, 1782), p. 37.

145   Alexander Wilson, *Am. Ornithology,* V, 107; P. G. Goodrich, *History of Wayne County* (Honesdale, Pa., 1880), p. 72; *Sketches and Eccentricities of Col. David Crockett, of West Tennessee* (London, 1836), p. 44.

146   J. J. Audubon, *Ornithol. Biog.,* I, 319.

147   Detroit *Free Press* (Mich.), March 13, 1850; Watertown *Chronicle* (Wis.), March 27, 1850.

148   E. Sterling, "Passenger Pigeons and Rice," *Rod and Gun and Am. Sportsman,* VII (Jan. 29, 1876), 277.

149   M. Schaff, *Etna and Kirkersville,* p. 109.

150   *David Thompson's Narrative of His Explorations,* p. 270.

151   Peter Reid, "Pigeons—Food in Crop," *Rod and Gun and Am. Sportsman,* VII (Jan. 8, 1876), 227.

152   John Bachman, "On the Migration of the Birds of North America," *Am. J. Sci.,* XXX (1836), 83.

153   E. Sterling in *Rod and Gun and Am. Sportsman,* VII (Jan. 29, 1876), 277.

154   *Wisconsin Farmer,* III (1851), 151; A. E. Jenks, "The Wild-Rice Gatherers of the Upper Lakes," *19th Ann. Rept. Bur. Am. Ethnology,* 1900, p. 1027.

155   Jedidiah Morse, *A Report to the Secretary of War of the United States on Indian Affairs* . . . (New Haven, Conn., 1822), Appendix, p. 15.

156   "Pistol Grip," "Incidents of Pigeon Shooting on the Saginaw River," *Am. Field,* XXIV (1885), 51–52.

157   Henry Y. Hind, *Narrative of the Canadian Red River Exploring Expedition of 1857 and of the Assinniboine and Saskatchewan Exploring Expedition of 1858* (London, 1860), I, 118.

158   Willard N. Clute, *Am. Plant Names,* pp. 67, 69, 96, 97.

159   Pehr Kalm in *Auk,* XXVIII (1911), 63; Alexander Wilson, *Am. Ornithology,* V, 107; De Witt Clinton in *N. Y. Med. Phys. J.,* II (1823), 211; F. H. King, "Economic Relations of Wisconsin Birds," *Geology of Wisconsin. Survey of 1873–79* (Madison, 1883), I, 589; J. M. Wheaton in *29th Ann. Rept.*

Ohio State Board Agr., 1874, p. 571; J. C. French, *Passenger Pigeon*, p. 230; F. J. Seaver, *Historical Sketches of Franklin County*, p. 212.

160 Pehr Kalm in *Auk*, XXVIII (1911), 62.

161 Alexander Henry, *New Light on the Early History of the Greater Northwest: The Manuscript Journals of Alexander Henry and David Thompson* (ed. E. Coues; N. Y., 1897), II, 605.

162 Pehr Kalm in *Auk*, XXVIII (1911), 62.

163 John Langton, *Early Days in Upper Canada* (Toronto, 1926), pp. 134–35; Etta S. Wilson in *Auk*, LI (1934), 158; W. B. Barrows, *Mich. Bird Life*, p. 242.

164 E. H. Forbush, *Game Birds*, p. 472.

165 Manitowoc *Tribune* (Wis.), June 19, 1860.

166 Alexander Wilson, *Am. Ornithology*, V, 107; J. M. Wheaton in *29th Ann. Rept. Ohio State Board Agr.*, 1874, p. 571; W. B. Barrows, *Mich. Bird Life*, p. 242.

167 Frank Bond, "The Later Flights of the Passenger Pigeon," *Auk*, XXXVIII (1921), 526.

168 Pehr Kalm in *Auk*, XXVIII (1911), 62.

169 W. B. Mershon, *Passenger Pigeon*, p. 115.

170 Alexander Wilson, *Am. Ornithology*, V, 107; J. M. Wheaton in *29th Ann. Rept. Ohio State Board Agr.*, 1874, p. 571.

171 "Journal of Col. James Gordon, of Lancaster County, Va.," *William and Mary College Quarterly Hist. Mag.*, XI (1903), 200.

172 John Langton, *Early Days in Upper Canada*, pp. 134–35.

173 M. H. Mitchell, *Passenger Pigeon*, p. 103.

174 *The Expeditions of Zebulon Montgomery Pike, to Headwaters of the Mississippi River . . . during the Years 1805–6–7* (ed. E. Coues; N. Y., 1895), I, 212.

175 *Posthumous Works of C. O. Whitman*, III, 145.

176 E. S. Wilson in *Auk*, LI (1934), 158.

177 W. B. Barrows, *Mich. Bird Life*, p. 242.

178 Frederick Pursh, "Journal," *Gardener's Monthly*, XI (1869), 15.

179 M. H. Mitchell, *Passenger Pigeon*, p. 97.

180 John Mactaggart, *Three Years in Canada: An Account of the Actual State of the Country in 1826–7–8* (London, 1829), I, 234.

181 B. F. Adamson, "Wild Pigeons Poisoned," New York *Tribune*, April 16, 1878, p. 5.

182 Edward T. Martin in *Chicago Field*, X (1879), 385.

183 C. Bendire, *Life Histories of N. Am. Birds*, Part I, p. 138.

184 E. H. Eaton, *Birds of N. Y.*, I, 383.

185 S. Cook in *Forest and Stream*, LX (1903), 206.

186   W. W. Thompson, *Passenger Pigeon*, p. 12.
187   "Tom Tramp" in *Rod and Gun and Am. Sportsman*, VIII (June 3, 1876), 149.
188   W. B. Barrows, *Mich. Bird Life*, p. 242.
189   E. S. Wilson in *Auk*, LI (1934), 158.
190   W. Craig in *Auk*, XXVIII (1911), 425.
191   E. W. Gifford, "Taxonomy and Habits of Pigeons," *Auk*, LVIII (1941), 245.
192   *Posthumous Works of C. O. Whitman*, III, 144 and 119.
193   *Ibid.*, p. 119.
194   J. M. Wheaton in *29th Ann. Rept. Ohio State Board Agr.*, 1874, p. 571.
195   M. C. Read, "Catalogue of the Birds of Northern Ohio," *Proc. Acad. Nat. Sci. Phila.*, VI (1853), 402.
196   Samuel Aughey, "Notes on the Nature of the Food of the Birds of Nebraska," *First Ann. Rept. U. S. Entomol. Com. for 1877* (Wash., 1878), Appendix II, p. 46.
197   Ned Hollister, "Recent Record of the Passenger Pigeon in Southern Wisconsin," *Auk*, XIII (1896), 341; also in *Wilson Bull.*, IX (1897), 5.
198   F. H. King in *Geology of Wisconsin. Survey of 1873–79*, I, 589.
199   H. H. Hind, *Narrative of Exploring Expedition*, I, 101 and 292.
200   C. Cottam and P. Knappen in *Auk*, LVI (1939), 155–58.
201   T. G. Gentry, *Life-Histories of Birds*, II, 298.
202   W. B. O. Peabody, "A Report on the Birds of Massachusetts Made to the Legislature in the Session of 1838–9," *J. Boston Soc. Nat. Hist.*, III (1841), 194.
203   Grant Powers, *History of Coos County* (Haverhill, N. H., 1841), pp. 110–11.
204   Samuel A. Peters, *A General History of Connecticut* (London, 1781), pp. 154–55.
205   Elsa G. Allen, "The History of American Ornithology before Audubon," *Trans. Am. Phil. Soc.*, XLI (1951), 529.
206   C. W. Nash in Ernest T. Seton, "The Birds of Manitoba," *Proc. U. S. Nat. Museum*, XIII (1891), 522–23.
207   Chief Simon Pokagon in *Chautauquan*, XXII (1895), 204; T. S. Roberts, *Birds of Minn.*, I, 577.
208   H. Elliott McClure, "Ecology and Management of the Mourning Dove, *Zenaidura macroura* (Linn.) in Cass County, Iowa," *Iowa Agr. Expt. Sta. Research Bull.*, No. 310 (1943), p. 404.
209   H. K. (Henry Knapp) in *Am. Sportsman*, IV (Sept. 19, 1874), 387.
210   H. E. McClure in *Iowa Agr. Expt. Sta. Research Bull.*, No. 310 (1943), p. 404.
211   Chief Simon Pokagon quoted in W. B. Mershon, *Passenger Pigeon*, p. 206.
212   Pehr Kalm in *Auk*, XXVIII (1911), 64.
213   Paul Le Jeune in *Jesuit Relations*, XLIII, 153; Raffeix, *ibid.*, LVI, 49; Thomas

Ashe, *Travels in America, Performed in 1806* (London, 1808), pp. 49–50.

214 W. B. Mershon, *Passenger Pigeon*, p. 122; De Witt Clinton in *N. Y. Med. Phys. J.*, II (1823), 211.

215 T. Pennant, *Arctic Zoology*, II, 325; De Witt Clinton in *N. Y. Med. Phys. J.*, II (1823), 211; "Topography and History of Rochester, Mass., 1815," *Coll. Mass. Hist. Soc.*, 2nd ser., IV (1846), 256; Edward E. Bourne, *The History of Wells and Kennebunk* (Portland, Me., 1875), pp. 563–64; Hector St. John de Crèvecoeur, *Sketches of Eighteenth Century America* (New Haven, Conn., 1925), p. 111.

216 [Henry B. Small], *A Canadian Handbook and Tourist's Guide* (Montreal, 1867), p. 97.

217 C. J. Maynard, *Birds of Eastern N. Am.*, p. 337.

218 Charles E. Belknap, *The Yesterdays of Grand Rapids* (Grand Rapids., Mich., 1922), pp. 137–38.

219 J. J. Audubon, *Ornithol. Biog.*, I, 325.

220 Charles L. Mann in *Jahres-Bericht des naturhistorischen Vereins von Wisconsin*, 1880–81, p. 46.

221 Chief Simon Pokagon in *Chautauquan*, XXII (1895), 204; H. B. Roney in *Chicago Field*, X (1879), 345.

222 J. C. French, *Passenger Pigeon*, pp. 209, 227, 243; F. E. S., "Netting Wild Pigeons," *Forest and Stream*, XLIII (1894), 50; L. E. Scherer, Jr., in *Cardinal*, V (1939), 40.

223 W. A. Linkletter, "The Passenger Pigeon," *Rod and Gun in Canada*, XXII (Dec., 1920), 755–56.

224 *Posthumous Works of C. O. Whitman*, III, 145.

225 W. Craig in *Auk*, XXVIII (1911), 425.

226 E. S. Wilson in *Auk*, LI (1934), 158.

227 Nicolas Denys, *The Description and Natural History of the Coasts of North America (Acadia)* (ed. W. F. Ganong; Toronto, 1908), p. 199; S. P. Hildreth in *Am. J. Sci.*, XL (1841), 348; Ralph Ballard, "Passenger Pigeon Recollections," *Jack-Pine Warbler*, XXIV (1946), 135–37; W. P. Thomas in New York *Sun*, June 14, 1881, and in *Chicago Field*, XV (1881), 314.

228 *The Western Journals of Washington Irving* (ed. J. F. McDermott; Norman, Okla., 1944), pp. 155 and 157.

229 "Jack," "Ducks and Pigeons in Arkansas," *Chicago Field*, XII (1879), 250.

230 Jacob H. Studer, *The Birds of North America* (N. Y., 1903), p. 33.

231 John Winthrop, *The History of New England from 1630 to 1649* (ed. James Savage; Boston, 1843), II, 113.

232 Baron Louis de Lahontan, *New Voyages to North-America* (London, 1703), I, 61.

233 Edward A. Samuels, "Mammalogy and Ornithology of New England," *Rept. U. S. Com. Agr. for 1863*, p. 285.

234 E. Michener, "Agricultural Ornithology," *Rept. U. S. Com. Agr. for 1863,* p. 305.

235 R. D. Goss, "Our Boyhood Days," *Iowa Ornithol.,* I (July, 1895), 78.

236 W. J. McGee in *Science,* N. S., XXXII (1910), 959.

237 James Wilson, *An Introduction to the Natural History of Birds* (Edinburgh, 1839), p. 614.

238 Amherst W. Kellogg, "Recollections of Life in Early Wisconsin," *Wis. Mag. Hist.,* VII (1924), 495; R. D. Goss, "Bluebirds and Passenger Pigeons," *Nidologist,* III (1896), 87.

239 Emily C. Blackman, *History of Susquehanna County, Pennsylvania* (Phila., 1873), p. 245.

240 J. M. Judd in *Wis. Farmer,* II (1850), 148.

241 Anon. note *ibid.,* p. 73.

242 St. Paul *Pioneer* (Minn.) quoted in the Horicon *Argus* (Wis.), June 15, 1860.

243 [F. E. Jones], "Oldsters Meet for Birthday," Milwaukee *Journal* (Wis.), Aug. 5, 1945.

244 Samuel Strickland, *Twenty-Seven Years in Canada West,* I, 299.

245 Sebastian Rieber, "Slaughter of Passenger Pigeons Described in Papers of Pioneer," Milwaukee *Journal* (Wis.), June 28, 1942.

246 M. H. Mitchell, *Passenger Pigeon,* p. 105.

247 W. Brewster in *Auk,* VI (1889), 288; L. E. Scherer, Jr., in *Cardinal,* V (1939), 40.

248 Sebastian Rieber in Milwaukee *Journal* (Wis.), June 28, 1942.

249 Milwaukee *Journal* (Wis.), Feb. 25, 1945; P. E. Wadsworth of John Deere Van Brunt Co. in a letter to me.

CHAPTER 4

1 Lena M. Carter, *Twinsburg, Ohio—1817–1917* (Twinsburg, 1917), p. 10.

2 John C. Geikie, *Adventures in Canada; or, Life in the Woods* (Phila., *ca.* 1882), p. 213.

3 G. W. Featherstonhaugh, *Excursion through the Slave States* (London, 1844), II, 11.

4 J. J. Audubon, *Ornithol. Biog.,* I (1831), 319.

5 W. Brewster in *Bull. Museum Comparative Zool.,* No. 66 (1925), Part II, p. 309; Charles W. Townsend in A. C. Bent, *Life Histories of N. Am. Gallinaceous Birds,* p. 395.

6 Pehr Kalm in *Auk,* XXVIII (1911), 64.

7 J. C. French, *Passenger Pigeon,* p. 81.

8 Herbert H. Beck, "Dexterous Alighting Maneuver of Passenger Pigeons," *Auk,* LXVI (1949), 286.

9 J. J. Audubon, *Ornithol. Biog.,* I, 319; H. D. Thoreau, *Journal,* VII, 334.

10 L. E. Scherer, Jr., in *Cardinal,* V (1939), 33.

11 "Wild Pigeon Flights," *Forest and Stream*, LIX (1902), 446–47.

12 J. J. Audubon, *Ornithol. Biog.*, I, 320.

13 John J. Audubon in Maria R. Audubon, *Audubon and His Journals* (ed. E. Coues; N. Y., 1900), I, 141.

14 J. J. Audubon, *Ornithol. Biog.*, I, 320.

15 W. W. Thompson, *Passenger Pigeon*, p. 13.

16 John Bachman, "On the Migration of the Birds of North America," *Am. J. Sci.*, XXX (1836), 83.

17 P. H. Greenleaf, "Observations on the Flight of the American Passenger Pigeon at Madison, Ind., March, 1855," *Proc. Boston Soc. Nat. Hist.*, V (1856), 181–82.

18 George B. Grinnell quoted in William Ludlow, *Report of a Reconnaissance of the Black Hills of Dakota Made in the Summer of 1874* (Wash., 1875), p. 96.

19 C. F. A. Portal, "The Speed of Birds," *Field* (London), CXXXIX (1922), 233–34.

20 William Welsh, "Passenger Pigeon," *Can. Field-Naturalist*, XXXIX (1925), 165–66.

21 J. J. Audubon, *Ornithol. Biog.*, I, 321.

22 *Ibid*.

23 F. S. Stone, *History of Racine County* (Chicago, 1916), I, 488.

24 "Backwoods," "In Wild Pigeon Days," *Forest and Stream*, XLIV (1895), 126.

25 George Heriot, *Travels through the Canadas* ... (London, 1807), pp. 517-18.

26 J. C. French, *Passenger Pigeon*, pp. 33 and 42.

27 T. Blakiston, "On Birds Collected and Observed in the Interior of North America," *Ibis*, 1st ser., V (1863), 121.

28 William Hebert, *A Visit to the Colony of Harmony in Indiana* (London, 1825), p. 10.

29 John Mactaggart, *Three Years in Canada: An Account of the Actual State of the Country in 1826-7-8* (London, 1829), I, 233.

30 John G. Dillin, "Recollection of Wild Pigeons in Southeastern Pennsylvania, 1864–1881," *Cassinia*, No. 14 (1910), p. 36.

31 Herman L. Collins, "Disappearance of the Wild Pigeon," *Forest and Stream*, LXXIX (1912), 235.

32 M. Schaff, *Etna and Kirkersville*, p. 106.

33 J. B. Oviatt quoted in the article of Lloyd E. Scherer, Jr., in *Cardinal*, V (1939), 34.

34 Smith Bennett, "Winter Sports in Northern Louisiana: Shooting Wild Pigeons," *Illustrated Sporting and Dramatic News* (London), III (July 3, 1875), 332; "Shooting Wild Pigeons in Iowa," *Leslie's Illustrated Newspaper*, XXV (Sept. 21, 1867), 8.

35 Alexander Wilson, *Am. Ornithology*, V, 108.
36 James Pender, *History of Benton Harbor* (Chicago, 1915), p. 37.
37 J. J. Audubon, *Ornithol. Biog.*, I, 320.
38 William Brown, *America: A Four Years' Residence in the United States and Canada* (Leeds, 1849), pp. 20–21.
39 Ernest T. Seton in a letter to me and his *Trail of an Artist Naturalist* (N. Y., 1940), p. 115.
40 C. J. S. Bethune in *Ottawa Naturalist*, XVI (1902), 40.
41 C. K. Sober quoted in J. C. French, *Passenger Pigeon*, p. 229.
42 W. J. McGee in *Science*, N. S., XXXII (1910), 959.
43 Frank Bond, "The Later Flights of the Passenger Pigeon," *Auk*, XXXVIII (1921), 523–27.
44 E. D. Nauman, "Vanished Hosts," *Palimpsest*, XVI (June, 1935), 173.
45 William B. Leffingwell, *Shooting on Upland, Marsh, and Stream* (Chicago, 1890), p. 223.
46 William B. Mershon in *Auk*, XXXIX (1922), 300–1.
47 Ashton E. Hemphill, "Passenger Pigeons Not in Company Front," *Auk*, XXXIX (1922), 416.
48 Baynard R. Hall, *The New Purchase: or, Seven and a Half Years in the Far West* (ed. J. A. Woodburn; Princeton, N. J., 1916), p. 466.
49 Charles H. Townsend, "Old Times with the Birds: Autobiographical," *Condor*, XXIX (1927), 224–25.
50 Emerson Hough, "Wild Pigeon Stories," *Forest and Stream*, LX (1903), 51.
51 "Wild Pigeon Flights," *Forest and Stream*, LIX (1902), 446–47.
52 C. Dury in *J. Cincinnati Soc. Nat. Hist.*, XXI (1910), 52.
53 Thomas J. George, "The Passenger Pigeon in Missouri Fifty Years Ago," *Auk*, XXVIII (1911), 259.
54 W. Ross King, *The Sportsman and Naturalist in Canada* (London, 1866), pp. 121–25.
55 H. Howitt in *Can. Field-Naturalist*, XLVI (1932), 28.
56 William Brown, *America: A Four Years' Residence*, pp. 20–21.
57 W. J. McGee in *Science*, N. S., XXXII (1910), 959.
58 H. Howitt in *Can. Field-Naturalist*, XLVI (1932), 28.
59 M. Schaff, *Etna and Kirkersville*, p. 107.
60 J. J. Audubon, *Ornithol. Biog.*, I, 321.
61 W. Ross King, *Sportsman and Naturalist in Canada*, pp. 121–25.
62 B. R. Hall, *The New Purchase*, p. 466.
63 E. T. Seton, *Trail of an Artist Naturalist*, p. 115.
64 William Brown, *America: A Four Years' Residence*, pp. 20–21.
65 "Wild Pigeon Flights," *Forest and Stream*, LIX (1902), 446–47.
66 W. J. McGee in *Science*, N. S., XXXII (1910), 959.

67   C. A. Bryant in *Forest and Stream,* LXXX (1913), 494.

68   Walter L. McClintock, "A Passenger-Pigeon Item," *Cardinal,* III (Jan. 1931), 19.

69   Isaac Weld, *Travels through the States of North America and the Provinces of Upper and Lower Canada . . .* (London, 1799), pp. 269–70.

70   J. J. Audubon, *Ornithol. Biog.,* I, 321.

71   R. P. Robinson, "More about the Passenger Pigeon," *Pennsylvania Sportsman,* May, 1917.

72   W. J. McGee in *Science,* N. S., XXXII (1910), 960.

73   Herman L. Collins, "Disappearance of the Wild Pigeon," *Forest and Stream,* LXXIX (1912), 235.

74   Samuel Smith, *The History of the Colony of Nova-Caesaria, or New Jersey* (Trenton, N. J., 1890), p. 511.

75   John Bachman in *Am. J. Sci.,* XXX (1836), 84.

76   W. J. McGee in *Science,* N. S., XXXII (1910), 959.

77   H. L. Collins in *Forest and Stream,* LXXIX (1912), 235.

78   J. B. Oviatt quoted in Lloyd E. Scherer, Jr., "Passenger Pigeons in Northwestern Pennsylvania," *Cardinal,* V (1939), 34.

79   F. G. McCauley, "An Ohio Pigeon Roost," *Turf, Field and Farm,* XXX (Jan. 9, 1880), 21.

80   Edward Brown, *Wadsworth Memorial* (Wadsworth, Ohio, 1875), p. 52.

81   M. Catesby, *Natural History of Carolina,* I, 23.

82   William Bartram, *Travels through North & South Carolina, Georgia, East & West Florida . . .* (Phila., 1791), p. 469.

83   John Bachman in *Am. J. Sci.,* XXX (1836), 89–90.

84   O. Turner, *History of the Pioneer Settlement of Phelps and Gorman's Purchase* (Rochester, N. Y., 1851), p. 395.

85   W. J. McGee in *Science,* N. S., XXXII (1910), 959.

86   J. G. French, *Passenger Pigeon,* p. 14.

87   Baird, Brewer, and Ridgway, *A History of North American Birds. Land Birds,* III, 370.

88   C. H. Ames, "Breeding of the Wild Pigeon," *Forest and Stream,* LVI (1901), 464.

89   De Witt Clinton in *N. Y. Med. Phys. J.,* II (1823), 211.

90   C. A. Bryant in *Forest and Stream,* LXXX (1913), 494.

91   A. W. Butler in *22nd Ann. Rept. Indiana Dept. Geol. Nat. Resources,* 1897, p. 761.

92   *Albany Daily Advertiser* (N. Y.), March 27, 1830; Joel Munsell, *The Annals of Albany* (Albany, N. Y., 1858), IX, 206.

93   "A Pigeon Storm," *Forest and Stream,* XXVI (1886), 329.

94   O. Edson and G. D. Merrill, *History of Chautauqua County, New York* (Boston, 1894), pp. 268–69.

95 Alexander Henry, *New Light on the Early History of the Greater North-west: The Manuscript Journals of Alexander Henry and of David Thompson* (ed. E. Coues; N. Y., 1897), I, 4.

96 Ruthven Deane in *Auk*, XIII (1896), 237.

97 Charles Lose, "Personal Recollections of the Vanished Wild Pigeons," *Now and Then*, IV (1931), 265.

98 H. L. Collins in *Forest and Stream*, LXXIX (1912), 235.

99 L. E. Scherer, Jr., in *Cardinal*, V (1939), 35.

100 William C. Marsden, "What Has Become of the Wild Pigeon?" *Forest and Stream*, LXXXIII (1914), 146–47.

101 S. Cook in *Forest and Stream*, LX (1903), 205–6.

102 W. B. Mershon, *Passenger Pigeon*, p. 111.

103 W. B. Barrows, *Mich. Bird Life*, p. 246.

104 L. E. Scherer, Jr., in *Cardinal*, V (1939), 36.

105 Paul Radin, "The Winnebago Tribe," *37th Ann. Rept. Bur. Am. Ethnology*, 1923, pp. 112–13.

106 P. H. Greenleaf in *Proc. Boston Soc. Nat. Hist.*, V (1856), 181–82.

107 C. A. Bryant in *Forest and Stream*, LXXX (1913), 494.

108 S. Cook, *ibid.*, LX (1903), 205–6.

109 James Ingells in Grand Rapids *Press* (Mich.), Nov. 4, 1933.

110 W. B. Mershon, *Passenger Pigeon*, p. 137.

111 M. H. Mitchell, *Passenger Pigeon*, p. 80.

112 Charles A. Green, "Memories of the Passenger Pigeon," and "Wild Pigeons," *Forest and Stream*, LXXIV (1910), 614, and LXXXI (1913), 75.

113 E. S. Wilson in *Auk*, LI (1934), 159.

114 Robert Sellar, *The Histories of the Counties of Huntingdon ... to the Year 1838* (Huntingdon, Que., 1888), p. 170.

115 M. H. Mitchell, *Passenger Pigeon*, p. 172.

116 Henry R. Schoolcraft, *Narrative Journal of Travels through the Northwestern Regions of the United States ...* (Albany, 1821), p. 381.

117 J. H. Lanman, *History of Michigan* (N. Y., 1839), p. 278.

118 C. H. Ames, "The Wild Pigeons and Their Fate," *Forest and Stream*, LXV (1905), 211.

119 Amherst W. Kellogg, "Recollections of Life in Early Wisconsin," *Wis. Mag. Hist.*, VII (1924), 495.

120 *Life in the West: Back-Wood Leaves and Prairie Flowers* (London, 1842), p. 286.

121 William L. Dawson, *The Birds of Ohio* (Columbus, Ohio, 1903), p. 426.

122 Sheboygan Falls *News* (Wis.), April 6, 1892, and Oct. 23, 1895.

123 S. S. Stevens quoted in W. Brewster's article in *Auk*, VI (1889), 287.

124 H. B. Roney in *Chicago Field*, X (1879), 349.

125 E. Osborn quoted in W. B. Mershon, *Passenger Pigeon,* p. 116.

126 Harry B. McConnell, "Notes from Eastern Ohio," *Auk,* XXVII (1910), 217; also in *Wilson Bull.,* XX (1908), 214.

127 Thomas Anburey, *Travels through the Interior Parts of America* (London, 1791), I, 243–44.

128 S. S. Stevens quoted in Brewster's article in *Auk,* VI (1889), 289.

129 Susan Fenimore Cooper, *Journal of a Naturalist in the United States* (London, 1856), I, 125.

130 Harriet Martineau, *Society in America* (2nd ed.; London, 1837), II, 9.

131 Ransom A. Moore, "The Hunter of Kewaunee: Passing of the Passenger Pigeon," *Hoard's Dairyman,* LXXIII (1928), 145.

132 George Head, *Forest Scenes and Incidents in the Wilds of North America* (London, 1829), p. 237.

133 Willard Glazier, *Down the Great River* (Phila., 1891), p. 64.

134 E. S. Wilson in *Auk,* LI (1934), 168.

135 Thomas L. McKenney, *Sketches of a Tour of the Lakes* (Baltimore, 1827), p. 353.

136 E. H. Moulton in *Outing,* LXV (1914), 128.

137 Alexander McDougall quoted in W. B. Mershon, *Passenger Pigeon,* p. 134.

138 H. T. Phillips quoted, *ibid.,* p. 107.

139 Witmer Stone in *Abstract Proc. Delaware Valley Ornithol. Club Phila.,* No. 2 (1892–97), p. 17.

140 M. H. Mitchell, *Passenger Pigeon,* pp. 69 and 71.

141 O. Edson and G. D. Merrill, *History of Chautauqua County, New York,* pp. 268–69.

142 Lynds Jones, "The Birds of Cedar Point and Vicinity," *Wilson Bull.,* XXI (1909), 189.

143 John Howison, *Sketches of Upper Canada* (Edinburgh, 1821), p. 160.

144 Charles L. Mann in *Jahres-Bericht des naturhistorischen Vereins von Wisconsin,* 1880–81, p. 46.

145 W. Ross King, *Sportsman and Naturalist in Canada,* pp. 121–25.

146 Isaac Weld, *Travels through the States of North America,* pp. 269–70.

147 C. J. S. Bethune in *Ottawa Naturalist,* XVI (1902), 40.

148 John Townsend quoted in M. H. Mitchell, *Passenger Pigeon,* p. 172.

149 Louis J. P. Vieillot, *Nouveau Dictionnaire d'histoire naturelle* (2nd ed.; Paris, 1818), XXVI, 370.

150 David P. De Vries, "Voyages from Holland to America, 1632–1644," *Coll. N. Y. Hist. Soc.,* 2nd ser., III (1857), 38.

151 Henry C. Leonard, *Pigeon Cove and Vicinity* (Boston, 1873), p. 166.

152 Ludlow Griscom and Edith V. Folger, *The Birds of Nantucket* (Cambridge, Mass., 1948), p. 92.

153 Frederic T. Lewis, "Cotton Mather's Manuscript References to the Passenger Pigeon," *Auk*, LXII (1945), 307.

154 Pehr Kalm in *Auk*, XXVIII (1911), 57.

155 J. P. Giraud, *Birds of Long Island* (N. Y., 1844), pp. 184–85.

CHAPTER 5

1 Alexander Wilson, *Am. Ornithology*, V, 103.

2 J. J. Audubon, *Ornithol. Biog.*, I (1831), 323.

3 Charles Waterton, "Retrospective Criticism: The Passenger Pigeon," *Mag. Nat. Hist.* (London), VII (1834), 282.

4 A. W. Schorger, "Unpublished Manuscripts by Cotton Mather on the Passenger Pigeon," *Auk*, LV (1938), 473.

5 M. Catesby, *Natural History of Carolina*, I, 23.

6 Pehr Kalm in *Auk*, XXVIII (1911), 57.

7 Andrew Burnaby, *Travels through the Middle Settlements in North America, in the Years 1759 and 1760* (London, 1798), pp. 101–2.

8 W. Faux, *Memorable Days in America: Being a Journal of a Tour to the United States* (London, 1823), p. 248.

9 Adelaide L. Fries (ed.), *Records of the Moravians in North Carolina* (Pub. North Carolina Hist. Com.; Raleigh, N. C., 1922–47), VI (1943), 2454.

10 Esau Johnson, "A Pigeon Story of the Early Days," *Wisconsin History Bull.*, Vol. VIII, No. 3 (June, 1921).

11 Frederick S. Barde in *Ann. Rept. Oklahoma State Game and Fish Dept.*, 1912, pp. 110–12.

12 S. P. Hildreth in *Am. J. Sci.*, XXIV (1833), 134–35.

13 S. Cook in *Forest and Stream*, LX (1903), 205–6.

14 "Pigeon-Shooting near Boston," *Cabinet of Natural History and American Rural Sports* (Phila., 1832), II, 136–37; William B. Leffingwell, *Shooting on Upland, Marsh, and Stream* (Chicago, 1890), p. 229.

15 Wallace Craig, "Recollection of the Passenger Pigeon in Captivity," *Bird-Lore*, XV (1913), 96.

16 "The Captain," "Pigeon Shooting in Early Days," *Forest and Stream*, LXVIII (1907), 656–57.

17 "Pigeon-Roosts," *Penny Magazine*, VI (1837), 4.

18 James Hall, *A Brief History of the Mississippi Territory* (Salisbury, N. C., 1801), pp. 56–58.

19 A. W. Schorger, "Unpublished Manuscripts by Cotton Mather on the Passenger Pigeon," *Auk*, LV (1938), 473.

20 Herbert H. Beck, "Historical Sketch of Rural Field Sports in Lancaster County," *Hist. Papers and Addresses Lancaster County Hist. Soc.* (Penn.), XXVII (1923), 152.

21 S. Cook in *Forest and Stream*, LX (1903), 205–6.

22 J. C. French, *Passenger Pigeon*, p. 177.

23 Alexander Wilson, *Am. Ornithology*, V, 103; J. J. Audubon, *Ornithol. Biog.*, I, 323.

24 "The Captain" in *Forest and Stream*, LXVIII (1907), 656–57.

25 S. P. Hildreth in *Am. J. Sci.*, XXIV (1833), 134–35.

26 Thomas Anburey, *Travels through the Interior Parts of America* (London, 1791), I, 243–45; Henry D. Minot, *The Land-Birds and Game-Birds of New England* (Salem, Mass., 1877), 379; "A Pigeon Roost," *Rod and Gun and Am. Sportsman*, VII (Oct. 9, 1875), 27.

27 Herman Behr, "Recollections of the Passenger Pigeon," *Cassinia*, No. 15 (1911), p. 25.

28 Paul Fountain, *The Great North-West* (N. Y., 1904), p. 216.

29 J. B. Oviatt quoted in the article of L. E. Scherer, Jr., in *Cardinal*, V (1939), 34.

30 Frank W. Langdon, "On the Occurrence in Large Numbers of Seventeen Species of Birds," *J. Cincinnati Soc. Nat. Hist.*, XII (1889), 57–58.

31 James Ingells in Grand Rapids *Press* (Mich.), Oct. 21, 1933.

32 S. P. Hildreth in *Am. J. Sci.*, XL (1841), 348.

33 Grand Haven *News* (Mich.), Dec. 20, 1865.

34 "Wild Pigeon Roost in Maryland," *Am. Sportsman*, II (Dec., 1872), 42; *Forest and Stream*, III (1874), 150; Paul Fountain, *The Great North-West*, p. 216.

35 "Pigeon-Roosts," *Penny Magazine*, VI (1837), 4.

36 P. L. W. (P. L. Waller), "Pigeon Shooting in the Alleghanies," *Forest and Stream*, III (1874), 140.

37 Lodi Swamp: S. Cook in *Forest and Stream*, LX (1903), 205–6; F. G. McCauley, "An Ohio Pigeon Roost," *Turf, Field and Farm*, XXX (Jan. 9, 1880), 21. Copley and Mud Brook swamps: Edward Brown, *Wadsworth Memorial* (Wadsworth, Ohio, 1875), p. 52; Samuel A. Lane, *Fifty Years and Over of Akron and Summit County* (Akron, Ohio, 1892), p. 1014. Bloody Run Swamp: M. Schaff, *Etna and Kirkersville*, p. 104; Milton B. Trautman, *The Birds of Buckeye Lake, Ohio* (Ann Arbor, Mich., 1940), p. 270. Bloomfield Swamp: *Forest and Stream*, X (1878), 44; E. M. Green, "The Old Tamarack Swamp," *ibid.*, XXII (1884), 444–45; "Elmer," "Where the Wild Pigeons Are," *ibid.*, X (1878), 85; G. C. Wing, *Early Years on the Western Reserve* (Cleveland, Ohio, 1916), p. 50. Aurora Swamp: Lena M. Carter, *Twinsburg, Ohio—1817–1917* (Twinsburg, 1917), p. 10. Newman's Swamp: Harry C. Oberholser, "A Preliminary List of the Birds of Wayne County, Ohio," *Bull. Ohio Agr. Station*, Tech. Ser., I (1896), 272.

38 M. Schaff, *Etna and Kirkersville*, p. 104.

39 F. G. McCauley in *Turf, Field and Farm*, XXX (Jan. 9, 1880), 21.

40 "The Captain" in *Forest and Stream*, LXVIII (1907), 656–57.

41   J. J. Audubon, *Ornithol. Biog.*, I, 324.

42   Bénédict-Henry Révoil, *The Hunter and Trapper in North America; or Romantic Adventures in Field and Forest* (trans. W. H. Davenport; London, 1874), p. 132.

43   S. P. Hildreth in *Am. J. Sci.*, XXIV (1833), 134–35; Thomas J. George, "The Passenger Pigeon in Missouri Fifty Years Ago," *Auk*, XXVIII (1911), 259; "The Captain" in *Forest and Stream*, LXVIII (1907), 656–57.

44   Editor, "Where the Pigeons Are Now," *Forest and Stream*, XIII (1879), 873.

45   "Wild Pigeon Roost in Maryland," *Am. Sportsman*, II (Dec., 1872), 42.

46   J. J. Audubon, *Ornithol. Biog.*, I, 323.

47   G. Lincecum in *Am. Sportsman*, IV (June 27, 1874), 194.

48   James Hall, *A Brief History of Miss. Territory*, pp. 56–58; Wiley Britton, *Pioneer Life in Southwest Missouri* (Kansas City, Mo., 1929), p. 55 (also in *Missouri Hist. Rev.*, XVI [1922], 57–61); "A Pigeon Roost," *Rod and Gun and Am. Sportsman*, VII (Oct. 9, 1875), 27; James Ingells in Grand Rapids *Press* (Mich.), Oct. 21, 1933; T. H. Harris, *Journal of a Tour into the Territory Northwest of the Alleghany Mountains; Made in the Spring of the Year 1803* (Boston, 1805), p. 179; E. M. Green in *Forest and Stream*, XXII (1884), 444–45.

49   "A Large Pigeon Roost," *Chicago Field*, X (1879), 419.

50   S. P. Hildreth in *Am. J. Sci.*, XXIV (1833), 134–35.

51   S. P. Hildreth, *ibid.*, XL (1841), 348.

52   Rufus Haymond, "Birds of Franklin County, Indiana," *First Ann. Rept. Geol. Survey Indiana*, 1869, p. 226.

53   G. Lincecum in *Am. Sportsman*, IV (June 27, 1874), 194–95.

54   A. L. Fries (ed.), *Records of the Moravians in North Carolina*, I, 235.

55   *Ibid.*, VI, 2623.

56   "Pigeon Roosts Fifty Years Ago," *Indiana Farmer*, XXXI (Feb. 22, 1896), 7.

57   "The Pigeon Roost Massacre," *Forest and Stream*, XIII (1879), 831.

58   B. S. Miner quoted in the article of A. W. Butler in *22nd Ann. Rept. Indiana Dept. Geol. Nat. Resources*, 1897, p. 762.

59   W. C. B. in *Chicago Field*, XIII (1880), 11.

60   Wiley Britton, *Pioneer Life in Southwest Missouri*, pp. 51–55.

61   Daniel Coxe, *A Description of the English Province of Carolana by the Spaniards Call'd Florida and by the French, La Louisiane* (4th ed., London, 1741), p. 96.

62   James Hall, *A Brief History of Miss. Territory*, pp. 56–58.

63   T. H. Harris, *Journal of a Tour into the Territory Northwest of the Alleghany Mountains*, p. 179.

64   Wiley Britton, *Pioneer Life in Southwest Missouri*, p. 55.

65   David Zeisberger, "History of Northern American Indians," *Ohio Arch. Hist. Publ.*, XIX (1910), 66.

66   John Brickell, *The Natural History of North Carolina* (Dublin, 1737), p. 186.

67   Thomas Holme's *Journal of a Tour in the Western Counties of America...* (London, 1828) quoted in William Cobbett, *A Year's Residence in the United States of America* (3rd ed.; London, 1828), p. 291.

68   B. L. C. Wailes, *Report on the Agriculture and Geology of Mississippi* (Miss., 1854), p. 325; T. H. Harris, *Journal of a Tour into the Territory Northwest of the Alleghany Mountains,* p. 179.

69   [Lester Taylor], *Pioneer History of Geauga County* (Geauga County [Ohio] Hist. Soc.; n. p., 1880), p. 604.

70   G. Lincecum in *Am. Sportsman,* IV (June 27, 1874), 194–95.

71   Joseph Simpson, *The Story of Buckeye Lake* (Columbus, Ohio, 1912), p. 73.

72   Andrew Price, "Wild Pigeons in West Virginia," *Forest and Stream,* LIII (1899), 29.

CHAPTER 6

1   A. W. Butler in *22nd Ann. Rept. Indiana Dept. Geol. Nat. Resources,* 1897, pp. 760–64; "The Captain," "Pigeon Shooting in Early Days," *Forest and Stream,* LXVIII (1907), 656–57; J. H. Chatham quoted in J. C. French, *Passenger Pigeon,* p. 241; C. Dury in *J. Cincinnati Soc. Nat. Hist.,* XXI (1910), 52–56; F. L. Grundtvig, "On the Birds of Shiocton in Bovina, Outagamie County, Wisconsin, 1881–83," *Trans. Wis. Acad. Sci.,* X (1895), 106; H. D. Thoreau, *Journal,* VI, 402.

2   A. W. Schorger, "The Great Wisconsin Passenger Pigeon Nesting of 1871," *Proc. Linnæan Soc. N. Y.,* No. 48 (1936), p. 2.

3   J. C. French, *Passenger Pigeon,* p. 56.

4   *Ibid.,* p. 192.

5   *Ibid.,* p. 12.

6   John H. Chatham quoted, *ibid.,* p. 241.

7   G. Lincecum in *Am. Sportsman,* IV (June 27, 1874), 195.

8   John Josselyn, *An Account of Two Voyages to New England, Made in the Years 1638, 1663* (Boston, 1865), p. 79.

9   Jeremy Belknap, *The History of New Hampshire* (Boston, 1792), III, 171–72.

10   George Ord, Vol. IX (Supplement, 1825) of Alexander Wilson's *American Ornithology; or the Natural History of the Birds of the United States* (Phila., 1808–25), pp. cxxx and cxxxviii.

11   Alexander Wilson, *Am. Ornithology,* V, 104.

12   C. W. Dickinson quoted in J. C. French, *Passenger Pigeon,* p. 58.

13   *Ibid.,* p. 57.

14   Edward T. Martin in *Chicago Field,* X (1879), 385–86.

15   Edward T. Martin in *Outing,* LXIV (1914), 479.

16   Charles L. Mann in *Jahres-Bericht des naturhistorischen Vereins von Wisconsin,* 1880–81, p. 44.

17 H. B. Roney in *Chicago Field*, X (1879), 345.

18 Bond and Ellsworth, "Wild Pigeons," *Chicago Field*, XIII (1880), 185.

19 S. S. Stevens quoted in W. Brewster's article in *Auk*, VI (1889), 286–87.

20 C. W. Gunn in *Oologist*, II (1876), 29–30; M. in *Forest and Stream*, XIV (1880), 231–32; *Rod and Gun and Am. Sportsman*, VIII (May 6, 1876), 89.

21 Egbert Bagg, "Birds," *Year Book Oneida Hist. Soc. Utica, N. Y.*, No. 12 (1912), p. 45.

22 "Antler," "With Bow and Arrow among the Wild Pigeons," *Forest and Stream*, XIV (1880), 14.

23 L. E. Scherer, Jr., in *Cardinal*, V (1939), 29.

24 H. K. (Henry Knapp) in *Am. Sportsman*, IV (Sept. 19, 1874), 387.

25 J. B. Oviatt quoted in the article of Lloyd E. Scherer, Jr., in *Cardinal*, V (1939), 29.

26 W. W. Thompson, *Passenger Pigeon*, p. 10.

27 Lafayette H. Bunnell, *Winona and Its Environs on the Mississippi in Ancient and Modern Days* (Winona, Minn., 1897), p. 187.

28 Chief Simon Pokagon quoted in John Muir, *The Story of My Boyhood and Youth* (N. Y., 1913), p. 166.

29 Chief Simon Pokagon quoted in W. B. Mershon, *Passenger Pigeon*, p. 205.

30 H. T. Phillips quoted *ibid.*, p. 107.

31 A. W. Schorger in *Proc. Linnæan Soc. N. Y.*, No. 48 (1936), pp. 1–26.

32 Louis B. Bishop, "Pigeons by the Million," New York *Times*, May 9, 1886, p. 10; also in *Cassinia*, No. 16 (1912), pp. 21–25.

33 G. Lincecum in *Am. Sportsman*, IV (June 27, 1874), 194–95.

34 W. P. Thomas in New York *Sun*, June 14, 1881, and in *Chicago Field*, XV (1881), 314.

35 C. A. Bryant in *Forest and Stream*, LXXX (1913), 515.

36 J. J. Audubon, *Ornithol. Biog.*, I (1831), 320.

37 T. G. Gentry, *Life-Histories of Birds*, II, 296.

38 J. C. French, *Passenger Pigeon*, pp. 12 and 241.

39 C. A. Bryant in *Forest and Stream*, LXXX (1913), 515.

40 J. B. Oviatt quoted in the article of Lloyd E. Scherer, Jr., in *Cardinal*, V (1939), 28.

41 *Posthumous Works of C. O. Whitman*, III, 127; see also pp. 126–29, 149, and 156.

42 James P. Porter, "Further Studies of the English Sparrow and Other Birds," *Am. J. Psychology*, XVII (1906), 258 and 269.

43 Margaret M. Nice and Joost Ter Pelkwyk, "Enemy Recognition by the Song Sparrow," *Auk*, LVIII (1941), 212.

44 Louis B. Bishop in New York *Times*, May 9, 1886, p. 10; also in *Cassinia*, No. 16 (1912), pp. 21–25.

45 William French quoted in J. C. French, *Passenger Pigeon*, p. 31.

46 Otis Lyman quoted, *ibid.*, p. 170.

47 *Ibid.*, pp. 57 and 103.

48 J. B. Oviatt quoted in the article of Lloyd E. Scherer, Jr., in *Cardinal*, V (1939), 28.

49 Zebulon M. Pike, *The Expeditions of Zebulon Montgomery Pike, to Headwaters of the Mississippi River . . . during the Years 1805–6–7* (ed. E. Coues; N. Y., 1895), I, 212.

50 A. C. Bryant in *Forest and Stream*, LXXX (1913), 515; H. B. Roney in *Chicago Field*, X (1879), 346.

51 Paul Fountain, *The Great North-West* (N. Y., 1904), p. 216.

52 Etta S. Wilson, "Personal Recollections of the Passenger Pigeon," *Auk*, LI (1934), 159.

53 Chatfield *Democrat* (Minn.), May 2 and June 6, 1863; April 8 and 23, May 21 and 28, 1864; May 13 and June 3, 1865.

54 J. C. French, *Passenger Pigeon*, pp. 31, 58, 170.

55 *Ibid.*, p. 191.

56 Lloyd E. Scherer, Jr., in *Cardinal*, V (1939), 31.

57 Alexander Wilson, *Am. Ornithology*, V, 104.

58 Edwin Haskell quoted in J. C. French, *Passenger Pigeon*, p. 105.

59 C. K. Sober quoted *ibid.*, p. 225.

60 E. H. Eaton, *Birds of N. Y.*, I, 382.

61 M. W. Mann and M. King, *The History of Ceres* (Olean, N. Y., 1896), p. 99.

62 Charles J. Pennock, "Nesting of the Passenger Pigeon (*Ectopistes migratorius*) in New York," *Auk*, XXIX (1912), 238–39.

63 Samuel H. Hammond, *Hills, Lakes and Forest Streams, or a Tramp in the Chateaugay Woods* (N. Y., 1854), p. 179. Also quoted by Frederick J. Seaver, *Historical Sketches of Franklin County* (Albany, N. Y., 1918), p. 213.

64 H. Howitt in *Can. Field-Naturalist*, XLVI (1932), 29.

65 H. B. Roney in *Chicago Field*, X (1879), 345; "Birds of Passage—the Great Pigeon Nesting in Benzie County," in Detroit *Post and Tribune*, April 29, 1880, in *Forest and Stream*, XIV (1880), 314, and also in *Sci. Am.*, XLII (May 29, 1880), 343–44; Robert Morris Gibbs, "Nesting of the Wild Pigeon," *Forest and Stream*, XLIII (1894), 93.

66 Charles W. Gunn, "Notes on the Passenger Pigeon in Michigan," *Oologist*, XII (1894), 73.

67 E. H. Bowers quoted in C. J. Maynard, *Birds of Eastern N. Am.*, p. 336.

68 "Tom Tramp" in *Rod and Gun and Am. Sportsman*, VIII (June 3, 1876), 149.

69 James Ingells in Grand Rapids *Press* (Mich.), Oct. 28, 1933.

70 C. A. Bryant in *Forest and Stream*, LXXX (1913), 494.

71 Diaries of Franc B. Daniels, while a student at Grand Rapids, Mich., 1863–66 (MS in possession of Professor Farrington Daniels, Madison, Wis.).

72 Henry Knapp (H. K.) in *Am. Sportsman,* IV (Sept. 19, 1874), 387.

73 Henry Nehrling, "Birds of Wisconsin," Milwaukee *Sentinel* (Wis.), April 21, 1898 (Carnival ed.).

74 C. F. Carr, "Passenger Pigeon, (*Ectopistes migratorius*) Nesting in Wisconsin," *Wisconsin Naturalist,* I (1890), 9–10.

75 John Macoun, *Catalogue of Canadian Birds* (Ottawa, 1900–4), Part I, pp. 215–17.

76 Pehr Kalm in *Auk,* XXVIII (1911), 61.

77 "Jacob Lindley's Account of a Journey to Attend the Indian Treaty, Proposed to Be Held at Sandusky, in the Year 1793," *Coll. Mich. Pioneer Hist. Soc.,* XVII (1890), 575.

78 W. H. Rintoul, "The Passenger Pigeon," *Can. Sportsman and Naturalist,* III (1883), 242–43.

79 G. Lincecum in *Am. Sportsman,* IV (June 27, 1874), 194–95.

80 C. W. Dickinson quoted in J. C. French, *Passenger Pigeon,* p. 59.

81 E. Haskell quoted *ibid.,* p. 93.

82 J. B. Oviatt quoted in the article of L. E. Scherer, Jr., in *Cardinal,* V (1939), 28.

83 J. B. Oviatt quoted *ibid.,* p. 31.

84 Samuel H. Hammond, *Hills, Lakes and Forest Streams,* pp. 178–80.

85 Ulysses P. Hedrick, *The Land of the Crooked Tree* (N. Y., 1948), p. 57.

86 H. B. Roney in *Chicago Field,* X (1879), 346.

87 J. J. Audubon, *Ornithol. Biog.,* I, 325.

88 W. Craig in *Auk,* XXVIII (1911), 425.

89 H. F. Witherby *et al., The Handbook of British Birds* (London, 1948), IV, 131.

90 W. Craig in *Auk,* XXVIII (1911), 411.

91 Wallace Craig, "Recollection of the Passenger Pigeon in Captivity," *Bird-Lore,* XV (1913), 98.

92 J. B. Oviatt quoted in the article of L. E. Scherer, Jr., in *Cardinal,* V (1939), 38.

93 Louis B. Bishop in New York *Times,* May 9, 1886, p. 10; also in *Cassinia,* No. 16 (1912), pp. 21–25.

94 J. C. French, *Passenger Pigeon,* p. 96.

95 Chief Simon Pokagon in *Chautauquan,* XXII (1895), 203.

96 *Posthumous Works of C. O. Whitman,* III, 59.

97 *Ibid.,* p. 120.

98 W. Craig in *Auk,* XXVIII (1911), 421.

99 *Posthumous Works of C. O. Whitman,* III, 120.

100 W. Craig in *Auk,* XXVIII (1911), 421.

101 *Posthumous Works of C. O. Whitman,* III, 120; W. Craig in *Auk,* XXVIII (1911), 420.

102 J. Hunt in *Proc. Zool. Soc. London,* 1833, Part I, p. 10; *Posthumous Works of C. O. Whitman,* III, 22.

103 W. Craig in *Auk,* XXVIII (1911), 422.

104 Ruthven Deane in *Auk,* XIII (1896), 235.

105 "Pericles" (R. M. Gibbs) in *Oologist,* XI (1894), 237–40.

106 J. B. Oviatt quoted in the article of L. E. Scherer, Jr., in *Cardinal,* V (1939), 30.

107 T. G. Gentry, *Life-Histories of Birds,* II, 299.

108 "Pericles" (R. M. Gibbs) in *Oologist,* XI (1894), 237–40.

109 Henry D. Thoreau, *The First and Last Journeys of Thoreau* (ed. F. B. Sanborn; Boston, 1905), II, 96.

110 Wendell L. Simpson, "Pigeons and Pigeon-Netting," *Outing,* XXV (Nov., 1894), 164.

111 J. Hunt in *Proc. Zool. Soc. London,* 1833, Part I, p. 10.

112 Chief Simon Pokagon in *Chautauquan,* XXII (1895), 203.

113 "Pericles" (R. M. Gibbs) in *Oologist,* XI (1894), 237–40.

114 W. C. Herman in *Auk,* LXV (1948), 78.

115 Louis B. Bishop in New York *Times,* May 9, 1886, p. 10, and in *Cassinia,* No. 16 (1912), pp. 21–25; John H. Chatham quoted in J. C. French, *Passenger Pigeon,* p. 241; J. C. French, *Passenger Pigeon,* p. 47; J. B. Oviatt quoted in the article of L. E. Scherer, Jr., in *Cardinal,* V (1939), 30.

116 C. W. Gunn in *Oologist,* II (1876), 29–30.

117 Philo L. Hatch, *Notes on the Birds of Minnesota* (Minneapolis, Minn., 1892), p. 171.

118 Chief Simon Pokagon quoted in W. B. Mershon, *Passenger Pigeon,* p. 205.

119 Leaves: Edward A. Samuels, *Ornithology and Oology of New England* (Boston, 1868), p. 373; P. L. Hatch, *Notes on Birds of Minn.,* p. 171. Dry stubble: T. G. Gentry, *Life-Histories of Birds,* II, 299. Feathers: C. W. Gunn in *Oologist,* II (1876), 29–30; "Birds of Passage—the Great Pigeon Nesting in Benzie County," Detroit *Post and Tribune* (Mich.), April 29, 1880, also in *Forest and Stream,* XIV (1880), 314, and in *Sci. Am.,* XLII (May 29, 1880), 343–44; Ruthven Deane in *Auk,* XIII (1896), 235. Moss: H. B. Roney in *Chicago Field,* X (1879), 345; L. B. Bishop in New York *Times,* May 9, 1886, p. 10, and in *Cassinia,* No. 16 (1912), pp. 21–25. Leaves, feathers, and moss are mentioned by H. Howitt in *Can. Field-Naturalist,* XLVI (1932), 28.

120 W. B. Barrows, *Mich. Bird Life,* p. 241.

121 C. H. Merriam quoted in E. H. Eaton, *Birds of N. Y.,* I, 384.

122 "Antler" in *Forest and Stream,* XIV (1880), 14.

123 C. W. Gunn in *Oologist,* II (1876), 29–30.

124   John Burroughs, *Locusts and Wild Honey* (Riverside Ed.; Boston, *ca.* 1904), p. 113.

125   Alexander Wilson, *Am. Ornithology*, V, 104; R. C. Taylor, "On the Geology and Natural History of the North-Eastern Extremity of the Alleghany Mountain Range in Pennsylvania, United States," *Mag. Nat. Hist.* (London), VIII (1835), 535.

126   M. Schaff, *Etna and Kirkersville*, p. 107.

127   "Antler" in *Forest and Stream*, XIV (1880), 14.

128   George H. Harris, "The Life of Horatio Jones," *Pub. Buffalo Hist. Soc.*, VI (1903), 449.

129   G. Lincecum in *Am. Sportsman*, IV (June 27, 1874), 195.

130   *Posthumous Works of C. O. Whitman*, III, 20–21.

131   J. Hunt in *Proc. Zool. Soc. London*, 1833, Part I, p. 10.

132   "Pericles" (R. M. Gibbs) in *Oologist*, XI (1894), 237–40.

133   J. G. French, *Passenger Pigeon*, p. 31; L. E. Scherer, Jr., in *Cardinal*, V (1939), 31; "Ingomar" in *Am. Sportsman*, IV (July 14, 1874), 253; H. Howitt in *Can. Field-Naturalist*, XLVI (1932), 29.

134   Chief Simon Pokagon quoted in W. B. Mershon, *Passenger Pigeon*, p. 206.

135   J. H. Chatham quoted in J. C. French, *Passenger Pigeon*, p. 241; J. B. Oviatt quoted in the article of L. E. Scherer, Jr., in *Cardinal*, V (1939), 31; "Pericles" (R. M. Gibbs) in *Oologist*, XI (1894), 237–40; C. H. Merriam quoted in E. H. Eaton, *Birds of N. Y.*, I, 384; W. B. Barrows, *Mich. Bird Life*, p. 241; C. W. Gunn in *Oologist*, II (1876), 29–30.

136   C. A. Bryant in *Forest and Stream*, LXXX (1913), 515.

137   Hermann Dümling, *Illustrirtes Thierleben. . . . Die Vögel* (Milwaukee, Wis., 1879), p. 182.

138   "Pericles" (R. M. Gibbs) in *Oologist*, XI (1894), 237–40.

139   "Narrative of the Journey of Col. Thomas Proctor, to the Indians of the North-West. 1791," *Penn. Arch.*, 2nd ser., IV (1876), 594; George Henry Loskiel, *History of the Mission of the United Brethren among the Indians in North America* (London, 1794), p. 93.

140   Alexander Wilson, *Am. Ornithology*, V, 105; O. Turner, *History of the Pioneer Settlement of Phelps and Gorman's Purchase* (Rochester, N. Y., 1851), p. 395; R. C. Taylor in *Mag. Nat. Hist.* (London), IX (1836, Suppl.), 73; L. B. Bishop in New York *Times*, May 9, 1886, p. 10, and in *Cassinia*, No. 16 (1912), pp. 21–25; C. W. Gunn in *Oologist*, XII (1895), 73; William Welsh, "Passenger Pigeons," *Can. Field-Naturalist*, XXXIX (1925), 165–66.

141   Chief Simon Pokagon quoted in W. B. Mershon, *Passenger Pigeon*, p. 205.

142   C. W. Dickinson quoted in J. C. French, *Passenger Pigeon*, p. 58.

143   *Posthumous Works of C. O. Whitman*, III, 48.

144   *Ibid.*, p. 45.

145   W. W. Thompson, *Passenger Pigeon*, p. 10.

146 Baird, Brewer, and Ridgway, *History of N. Am. Birds. Land Birds,* III, 370.

147 Bond and Ellsworth in *Am. Field,* XVII (1882), 274.

148 Ruthven Deane in *Auk,* XIII (1896), 236.

149 *Posthumous Works of C. O. Whitman,* III, 4 and 6.

150 "Antler" in *Forest and Stream,* XIV (1880), 14; C. J. Maynard, *Birds of Eastern N. Am.,* p. 336.

151 W. B. Barrows, *Mich. Bird Life,* p. 241.

152 C. Bendire, *Life Histories of N. Am. Birds,* Part I, p. 138; "Pericles" (R. M. Gibbs) in *Oologist,* XI (1894), 237–40.

153 Alexander Wilson, *Am. Ornithology,* V, 107.

154 De Witt Clinton in *N. Y. Med. Phys. J.,* II (1823), 210–15.

155 J. J. Audubon, *Ornithol. Biog.,* I, 326; also in *Edinburgh J. Sci.,* VI (1826–27), 256–65.

156 J. Hunt in *Proc. Zool. Soc. London,* 1833, Part I, p. 10.

157 J. J. Audubon, *Ornithol. Biog.,* V (1839), 552.

158 *Ibid.*

159 J. P. Giraud, *Birds of Long Island* (N. Y., 1844), pp. 184–85.

160 Thomas Nuttall, *A Manual of the Ornithology of the United States and of Canada.... The Land Birds* (Cambridge, Mass., 1832), I, 633.

161 Baird, Brewer, and Ridgway, *History of N. Am. Birds. Land Birds,* III, 373.

162 C. Bendire, *Life Histories of N. Am. Birds,* Part I, p. 142; Harry Harris, *Birds of the Kansas City Region* (Kansas City, Mo., 1919), p. 258; H. Elliott McClure, "Ecology and Management of the Mourning Dove, *Zenaidura macroura* (Linn.) in Cass County, Iowa," *Research Bull. Iowa Agr. Expt. Sta.,* No. 310 (1943), p. 381.

163 "Pericles" (R. M. Gibbs), "Nesting of the Wild Pigeon," *Forest and Stream,* XLIII (1894), 93; W. B. Barrows, *Mich. Bird Life,* p. 241; Clifton E. Hodge, "Passenger Pigeon Investigation," *Forest and Stream,* LXXIV (1910), 812.

164 J. C. French, *Passenger Pigeon,* p. 48.

165 Wallace Craig, "Oviposition Induced by the Male in Pigeons," *J. Morphol.,* XXII (1910), 299–305; *Posthumous Works of C. O. Whitman,* III, 109.

166 C. A. Bryant in *Forest and Stream,* LXXX (1913), 514 and 515.

167 C. W. Gunn in *Oologist,* II (1876), 29; "Pericles" (R. M. Gibbs) in *Forest and Stream,* XLIII (1894), 93.

168 Charles L. Mann in *Jahres-Bericht des naturhistorischen Vereins von Wisconsin,* 1880–81, p. 45; William G. Fargo, "Walter John Hoxie," *Wilson Bull.,* XLVI (1934), 184.

169 Egbert Bagg in *Year Book Oneida Hist. Soc. Utica, N. Y.,* No. 12 (1912), 44; C. Douglas quoted in Henry K. Coale, "On the Nesting of Ectopistes migratorius," *Auk,* XXXIX (1922), 254; Charles R. Keyes and H. S. Williams, "Preliminary Annotated Catalogue of the Birds of Iowa," *Proc. Davenport Acad. Nat. Sci.,* V (1893), 125; George O. Cantwell, "Wild Pigeons,"

Am. Field, XXXIII (1890), 31; William Brewster, *The Birds of the Cambridge Region of Massachusetts* (Cambridge, Mass., 1906), p. 178; F. L. Grundtvig in *Trans. Wis. Acad. Sci.,* X (1895), 106; C. H. Merriam quoted in E. H. Eaton, *Birds of N. Y.,* I, 384; Joel A. Allen, "Catalogue of the Birds Found at Springfield, Mass.," *Proc. Essex Inst.,* 1864, p. 75; C. J. Pennock in *Auk,* XXIX (1912), 239; C. F. Carr, "Passenger Pigeon, (*Ectopistes migratorius*) Nesting in Wisconsin," *Wisconsin Naturalist,* I (1890), 9–10; Henry Nehrling in Milwaukee *Sentinel* (Wis.), April 21, 1898 (Carnival ed.); Thomas S. Roberts, "Spring Notes from Minnesota," *Forest and Stream,* XIV (1880), 428, and Roberts' *Birds of Minn.,* I, 583–84; Elliott Coues, "Field-Notes on Birds Observed in Dakota and Montana Along the Forty-Ninth Parallel during the Seasons of 1873 and 1874," *Bull. U. S. Geol. Geog. Survey Territories,* IV (1878), 628.

170 J. Hunt in *Proc. Zool. Soc. London,* 1833, Part I, p. 10; Philip L. Sclater in *Proc. Zool. Soc. London,* 1865, p. 239; Frank J. Thompson, "Breeding of the Wild Pigeon in Confinement," *Nuttall Bull.,* VI (1881), 122; C. H. Ames, "Breeding of the Wild Pigeon," *Forest and Stream,* LVI (1901), 464; *Posthumous Works of C. O. Whitman,* III, 43; "Pericles" (R. M. Gibbs) in *Forest and Stream,* XLIII (1894), 93; Ruthven Deane in *Auk,* XIII (1896), 235; Clifton F. Hodge in *Forest and Stream,* LXXIV (1910), 812; J. C. French, *Passenger Pigeon,* p. 49.

171 G. Lincecum in *Am. Sportsman,* IV (June 27, 1874), 195; C. W. Gunn in *Oologist,* II (1876), 29–30; "Pericles" (R. M. Gibbs) in *Oologist,* XI (1894), 237–40; Chief Simon Pokagon in *Chautauquan,* XXII (1895), 203; S. Cook in *Forest and Stream,* LX (1903), 206.

172 "Antler" in *Forest and Stream,* XIV (1880), 14; L. B. Bishop in New York *Times,* May 9, 1886, p. 10, and in *Cassinia,* No. 16 (1912), p. 23; H. B. Roney in *Chicago Field,* X (1879), 345; Charles W. Gunn, "Notes on the Wild Pigeon," *Western Oologist,* I, No. 4 (1878), 14, and his article in *Oologist,* XII (1895), 73; "Pericles" (R. M. Gibbs) in *Forest and Stream,* XLIII (1894), 93; Charles F. Goodhue, "The Birds of Webster, New Hampshire, and Adjoining Towns," *Forest and Stream,* VIII (1877), 113; H. Howitt in *Can. Field-Naturalist,* XLVI (1932), 28; R. C. Taylor in *Mag. Nat. Hist.* (London), IX (1836, Suppl.), 73; Henry Knapp in *Am. Sportsman,* IV (Sept. 19, 1874), 387, and his "Statements about the Wild Pigeons," *Forest and Stream,* XII (1879), 146; Philo L. Hatch, *Notes on Birds of Minn.,* p. 171.

173 *Posthumous Works of C. O. Whitman,* III, 6.

174 Willard quoted in Clifton F. Hodge, "Passenger Pigeon Investigation," *Forest and Stream,* LXXIV (1910), 812. See A. W. Schorger, "The Number of Eggs Laid by the Passenger Pigeon, *Ectopistes migratorius,*" *Auk,* LXIX (1952), 201.

175 Charles L. Mann in *Jahres-Bericht des naturhistorischen Vereins von Wisconsin*, 1880–81, p. 44.

176 J. H. Chatham quoted in J. C. French, *Passenger Pigeon*, p. 241.

177 Edward T. Martin in *Outing*, LXIV (1914), 479.

178 Editor, "Wild Pigeons," *Chicago Field*, XIII (1880), 168.

179 "Snap Shot," "Peace and Pigeons in Wisconsin," *Wilkes' Spirit of the Times*, XII (May 27, 1865), 194.

180 H. K. (Henry Knapp) in *Am. Sportsman*, IV (Sept. 19, 1874), 387.

181 *Posthumous Works of C. O. Whitman*, III, 53 and 89.

182 Chief Simon Pokagon in *Chautauquan*, XXII (1895), 203; James Ingells in Grand Rapids *Press* (Mich.), Oct. 28, 1933; S. Cook in *Forest and Stream*, LX (1903), 205–6; L. B. Bishop in New York *Times*, May 9, 1886, p. 10, and in *Cassinia*, No. 16 (1912), p. 23; W. W. Thompson, *Passenger Pigeon*, p. 11; Ruthven Deane in *Auk*, XIII (1896), 236; J. C. French, *Passenger Pigeon*, pp. 47 and 57.

183 C. Bendire, *Life Histories of N. Am. Birds*, Part I, p. 138.

184 *Posthumous Works of C. O. Whitman*, II, 207, and III, 42.

185 *Ibid.*, III, 61.

186 Frank J. Thompson, "Incubation under Difficulties," *Forest and Stream*, XII (1879), 265, and his article in *Nuttall Bull.*, VI (1881), 122.

187 J. B. Oviatt quoted in the article of L. E. Scherer, Jr., in *Cardinal*, V (1939), 36.

188 Ruthven Deane in *Auk*, XIII (1896), 236.

189 *Ibid.*

190 *Posthumous Works of C. O. Whitman*, III, 68 and 89.

191 *Ibid.*, p. 51.

192 W. Brewster in *Auk*, VI (1889), 287.

193 Ben O. Bush quoted in W. B. Mershon, *Passenger Pigeon*, pp. 135 and 137.

194 W. H. Rintoul in *Can. Sportsman and Naturalist*, III (1883), 242–43.

195 S. Cook in *Forest and Stream*, LX (1903), 205–6; L. B. Bishop in New York *Times*, May 9, 1886, p. 10, and in *Cassinia*, No. 16 (1912), p. 23.

196 New York *World*, July 4, 1874.

197 E. S. Starr, "Doves," *Century Illustrated Monthly Mag.*, O. S., XXXVI (1888), 703.

198 James F. Cooper, *The Chainbearer* (N. Y., 1845), Chap. 14.

199 *Posthumous Works of C. O. Whitman*, III, 56.

200 W. Brewster in *Auk*, VI (1889), 287.

201 W. P. Thomas in New York *Sun*, June 14, 1881, and same article in *Chicago Field*, XV (1881), 314.

202 C. W. Dickinson quoted in J. C. French, *Passenger Pigeon*, p. 198.

203 C. W. Dickinson quoted *ibid.*, p. 57.

204 William French quoted *ibid.*, p. 30.

205 J. B. Oviatt quoted in the article of L. E. Scherer, Jr., in *Cardinal*, V (1939), 31.

206 E. Haskell quoted in J. C. French, *Passenger Pigeon*, p. 98; Samuel H. Hammond, *Hills, Lakes and Forest Streams*, p. 180.

207 Paul Fountain, *Great North-West*, p. 216.

208 *Posthumous Works of C. O. Whitman*, III, 55.

209 Ruthven Deane in *Auk*, XIII (1896), 236.

210 *Posthumous Works of C. O. Whitman*, III, 65 and 64.

211 C. W. Dickinson quoted in J. C. French, *Passenger Pigeon*, p. 58.

212 J. J. Audubon, *Ornithol. Biog.*, I, 326.

213 C. W. Dickinson quoted in J. C. French, *Passenger Pigeon*, p. 58; Chief Simon Pokagon in *Chautauquan*, XXII (1895), 203.

214 H. K. (Henry Knapp) in *Am. Sportsman*, IV (Sept. 19, 1874), 387.

215 *Posthumous Works of C. O. Whitman*, III, 64.

216 Chief Simon Pokagon in *Chautauquan*, XXII (1895), 203.

217 Chief Simon Pokagon quoted in W. B. Mershon, *Passenger Pigeon*, p. 206.

218 Charles L. Mann in *Jahres-Bericht des naturhistorischen Vereins von Wisconsin*, 1880–81, p. 45.

219 E. T. Martin in *Chicago Field*, X (1879), 385.

220 W. Craig in *Auk*, XXVIII (1911), 423.

221 *Posthumous Works of C. O. Whitman*, III, 65–66.

222 C. W. Dickinson quoted in J. C. French, *Passenger Pigeon*, p. 60.

223 *Ibid.*, pp. 59 and 67.

224 L. B. Bishop in New York *Times*, May 9, 1886, p. 10, and in *Cassinia*, No. 16 (1912), p. 23; H. K. (Henry Knapp) in *Am. Sportsman*, IV (Sept. 19, 1874), 387; Ruthven Deane in *Auk*, XIII (1896), 236; Whitman quoted in Clifton F. Hodge, "Passenger Pigeon Investigation," *Forest and Stream*, LXXIV (1910), 812; W. W. Thompson, *Passenger Pigeon*, p. 11; C. W. Dickinson quoted in J. C. French, *Passenger Pigeon*, p. 57.

225 *Posthumous Works of C. O. Whitman*, III, 64.

226 H. K. (Henry Knapp) in *Am. Sportsman*, IV (Sept. 19, 1874), 387.

227 James Ingells in Grand Rapids *Press* (Mich.), Oct. 28, 1933.

228 L. E. Scherer, Jr., in *Cardinal*, V (1939), 33.

229 "Tom Tramp" in *Rod and Gun and Am. Sportsman*, VIII (June 3, 1876), 149; New York *World*, July 4, 1874; J. B. Oviatt quoted in the article of L. E. Scherer, Jr., in *Cardinal*, V (1939), 32; W. W. Thompson, *Passenger Pigeon*, p. 11; Chief Simon Pokagon in *Chautauquan*, XXII (1895), 204; S. S. Stevens quoted in W. Brewster's article in *Auk*, VI (1889), 287; H. B. Roney in *Chicago Field*, X (1879), 345; H. K. (Henry Knapp) in *Am. Sportsman*, IV (Sept. 19, 1874), 387.

230 G. Lincecum in *Am. Sportsman*, IV (June 27, 1874), 194–95.

231 Samuel Strickland, *Twenty-Seven Years in Canada West*, I, 301.

232 Chief Simon Pokagon quoted in W. B. Mershon, *Passenger Pigeon*, p. 207.

233 J. J. Audubon, *Ornithol. Biog.*, I, 326.

234 Pehr Kalm in *Auk*, XXVIII (1911), 61.

235 Alexander Wilson, *Am. Ornithology*, V, 107.

236 James Macauley, *The Natural, Statistical and Civil History of the State of New York* (N. Y., 1829), I, 495.

237 H. B. Roney in *Chicago Field*, X (1879), 345.

238 W. B. Mershon, *Passenger Pigeon*, p. xii; J. C. French, *Passenger Pigeon*, pp. 47 and 211; James Heddon, "Will Pigeons Play Out?" *Am. Sportsman*, IV (Sept. 5, 1874), 362.

239 C. W. Dickinson quoted in J. C. French, *Passenger Pigeon*, p. 59.

240 C. Dury in *J. Cincinnati Soc. Nat. Hist.*, XXI (1910), 53–54.

241 "Pericles" (R. M. Gibbs) in *Oologist*, XI (1894), 237–40.

242 George M. Sutton, "The Birds of Pymatuning Swamp and Conneaut Lake, Crawford County, Pennsylvania," *Ann. Carnegie Museum*, XVIII, Part I (1927–28), 117.

243 "Ptarmigan" (T. M. Owen), "Among the Pigeons," *Forest and Stream*, X (1878), 359.

244 S. S. Stevens quoted in W. Brewster's article in *Auk*, VI (1889), 287–88.

245 C. W. Dickinson quoted in J. C. French, *Passenger Pigeon*, pp. 203 and 210.

246 J. B. Oviatt quoted in the article of L. E. Scherer, Jr., in *Cardinal*, V (1939), 26.

247 C. Bendire, *Life Histories of N. Am. Birds*, Part I, p. 138.

248 W. C. Herman in *Auk*, LXV (1948), 78.

249 J. B. Oviatt quoted in the article of L. E. Scherer, Jr. in *Cardinal*, V (1939), 26.

250 W. W. Thompson, *Passenger Pigeon*, p. 11.

251 "Pigeon-Roosts," *Penny Magazine*, VI (1837), 4.

252 J. C. French, *Passenger Pigeon*, p. 48.

253 Leroy Lyman quoted in W. W. Thompson, *Passenger Pigeon*, p. 10.

254 A. W. Schorger in *Proc. Linnæan Soc. N. Y.*, No. 48 (1936), p. 22.

255 G. Lincecum in *Am. Sportsman*, IV (June 27, 1874), 194–95.

256 W. P. Thomas in New York *Sun*, June 14, 1881, and in *Chicago Field*, XV (1881), 314; Editor, "Wild Pigeons," *Forest and Stream*, XVI (1881), 249; W. W. Judy, "Wild Pigeons for the Tournaments," *Chicago Field*, XV (1881), 168.

257 Alexander Wilson, *Am. Ornithology*, V, 106.

258 Z. M. Pike, *Expeditions of Zebulon Montgomery Pike*, I, 212.

259 Vincennes *Gazette* (Ind.), May 1, 1858; also in *Porter's Spirit of the Times*, IV (May 22, 1858), 186.

260 E. T. Martin in *Chicago Field*, X (1879), 385.

261 H. B. Roney, *ibid.*, p. 345.

262 Editor, "Wild Pigeons," *Chicago Field*, XIII (1880), 152.

263 C. A. Bryant in *Forest and Stream*, LXXX (1913), 515.

264 "Wild Pigeons," *Forest and Stream*, X (1878), 99.

265 James Ingells in Grand Rapids *Press* (Mich.), Oct. 28, 1933.

266 E. T. Martin in *Chicago Field*, X (1879), 385–86.

267 *Ibid.*

268 H. T. Phillips quoted in W. B. Mershon, *Passenger Pigeon*, p. 110.

269 E. T. Martin in *Outing*, LXIV (1914), 478.

270 "Birds of Passage—the Great Pigeon Nesting in Benzie County" in Detroit *Post and Tribune* (Mich.), April 29, 1880, in *Forest and Stream*, XIV (1880), 314, and in *Sci. Am.*, XLII (May 29, 1880), 343–44; E. T. Martin in *Outing*, LXIV (1914), 479.

271 H. K. (Henry Knapp) in *Am. Sportsman*, IV (Sept. 19, 1874), 387.

272 E. Osborn quoted in W. B. Mershon, *Passenger Pigeon*, p. 114.

273 J. B. Oviatt quoted in the article of L. E. Scherer, Jr., in *Cardinal*, V (1939), 35.

274 F. E. S., "Netting Wild Pigeons," *Forest and Stream*, XLIII (1894), 50.

275 W. W. Thompson, *Passenger Pigeon*, p. 12.

276 John Burroughs, "Recollections of the Passenger Pigeon," *Warbler*, 2nd ser., I (1905), 71.

277 C. H. Merriam quoted in Sylvester D. Judd, "The Food of Nestling Birds," *Yearbook U. S. Dept. Agr.*, 1900, p. 431.

278 Anon. notes in *Forest and Stream*, X (1878), 10 and 44; "Elmer," "Where the Wild Pigeons Are," *ibid.*, p. 85.

279 Editor, "Interesting to Trap Shooters," *Chicago Field*, IX (1878), 136.

280 E. Osborn quoted in W. B. Mershon, *Passenger Pigeon*, p. 115.

281 Leonard Wing, "Availability Seasons of Some Tennessee Game-Food Plants," *J. Tenn. Acad. Sci.*, XIV (1938), 325–27.

282 E. S. Seymour, *Sketches of Minnesota, the New England of the West* (N. Y., 1850), p. 136.

CHAPTER 7

1 *William Byrd's Histories of the Dividing Line betwixt Virginia and North Carolina* (ed. W. K. Boyd; Raleigh, N. C., 1929), p. 216.

2 Edward T. Martin in *Outing*, LXIV (July, 1914), 481.

3 G. W. Cunningham, "Wild Pigeon Flights Then and Now," *Forest and Stream*, LII (1899), 226; C. Dury in *J. Cincinnati Soc. Nat. Hist.*, XXI (1910), 53.

4 W. M. Cockrum, *Pioneer History of Indiana* (Oakland City, Ind., 1907), pp. 439–40.

5 "Nessmuk" (George W. Sears), *Woodcraft* (12th ed.; N. Y., 1900), p. 106.

6 Alexander Wilson, *Am. Ornithology*, V, 110.

7 Thomas F. De Voe, *The Market Assistant* (N. Y., 1867), p. 175.

8 Pehr Kalm, *Travels into North America,* II, 140, and "A Description of the Wild Pigeons Which Visit the Southern English Colonies in North America, during Certain Years, in Incredible Multitudes," *Auk,* XXVIII (1911), 66.

9 George Henry Loskiel, *History of the Mission of the United Brethren among the Indians in North America* (London, 1794), p. 93; Paul Kane, *Wanderings of an Artist among the Indians of North America* (London, 1859), p. 438.

10 Ransom A. Moore, "The Hunter of Kewaunee: Passing of the Passenger Pigeon," *Hoard's Dairyman,* LXXIII (1928), 145.

11 E. S. Wilson in *Auk,* LI (1934), 164.

12 T. F. De Voe, *Market Assistant,* p. 173; "Backwoods," "In Wild Pigeon Days," *Forest and Stream,* XLIV (1895), 126.

13 Ruthven Deane, "Extracts from the Field Notes of George B. Sennett," *Auk,* XL (1923), 628.

14 P. F. X. de Charlevoix, *Histoire et description generale de la Nouvelle France* (Paris, 1744), I, 273.

15 Pehr Kalm in *Auk,* XXVIII (1911), 61.

16 William Douglass, *A Summary, Historical and Political, of the First Planting, Progressive Improvements, and Present State of the British Settlements in North America* ... (Boston, 1755), II, 218.

17 Philo R. Hoy, "Man's Influence on the Avifauna of Southeastern Wisconsin," *Proc. Nat. Hist. Soc. Wis.,* March, 1885, p. 7.

18 William Douglass, *A Summary of the First Planting,* I, 126.

19 Andrew Burnaby, *Travels through the Middle Settlements in North America, in the Years 1759 and 1760* (London, 1798), pp. 101–2.

20 Nicholas More, "Letter from Green-Spring, Pa. Sept. 13, 1686," *Penn. Mag. Hist. Biography,* IV (1880), 449.

21 Ashton Blackburne quoted in T. Pennant, *Arctic Zoology,* II, 325.

22 James Adair, *The History of the American Indians* (London, 1775), p. 415.

23 Robert Dickson, "Dickson and Grignon Papers—1812–1815," *Coll. State Hist. Soc. Wis.,* XI (1888), 299.

24 David D. Owen, "Preliminary Report, containing Outlines of the Progress of the Geological Survey of Wisconsin and Iowa up to October 11, 1847," in Senate Executive Document No. 2, 30th Congress, 1st Session (Wash., 1847), p. 162.

25 E. Cruikshank, *Ten Years of the Colony of Niagara, 1780–1790* (Pub. Niagara Hist. Soc., No. 17; Welland, Ont., 1908), p. 19.

26 B. A. T. de Montigny, *La Colonisation. Le nord de Montréal ou la région Labelle* (Montreal, 1896), pp. 55–56.

27 W. Faux, *Memorable Days in America: Being a Journal of a Tour to the United States* (London, 1823), p. 22.

28 *The Jesuit Relations and Allied Documents* (ed. R. G. Thwaites; Cleveland, Ohio, 1896–1901), XLVIII, 177.

29 Anne Cary Randolph quoted in *Thomas Jefferson's Garden Book, 1766–1824* ... (Phila., 1944), p. 367.

30 James E. Quinlan, *History of Sullivan County* (Liberty, N. Y., 1873), pp. 507–9.

31 E. S. Wilson in *Auk*, LI (1934), 163.

32 Charles E. Belknap, *The Yesterdays of Grand Rapids* (Grand Rapids, Mich., 1922), pp. 137–38.

33 Mrs. E. S. Earles, "When Wild Pigeons Flew," *Wisconsin History Bull.*, XI, No. 3 (July, 1924).

34 "Last of the Wild Pigeons," New York *Sun*, March 7, 1909, reprinted as "The Wild Pigeons of Old," *Forest and Stream*, LXXII (1909), 755–58; J. C. French, *Passenger Pigeon*, p. 184; "Narrative of the Journey of Col. Thomas Proctor, to the Indians of the North-West. 1791," *Penn. Archives*, 2nd ser., IV (1876), 594.

35 William Byrd, *Natural History of Virginia; or, The Newly Discovered Eden* (ed. and trans. from German version by R. C. Beatty and W. J. Mulloy; Richmond, Va., 1940), p. 63.

36 J. C. French, *Passenger Pigeon*, p. 45.

37 *Ibid.*, p. 206.

38 *Ibid.*, p. 194; *Diary of Christopher Columbus Baldwin* ... *1829–1835* (Trans. Coll. Am. Antiquarian Soc., Vol. VIII; Worcester, Mass., 1901), p. 168; J. E. Quinlan, *History of Sullivan County*, pp. 507–9; Robert Munro (also attributed to Charles Williamson), "Description of the Genesee Country in the State of New York" in E. B. O'Callaghan, *The Documentary History of the State of New-York* (8° ed.; Albany, N. Y., 1849–51), II, 1175.

39 E. S. Wilson in *Auk*, LI (1934), 165.

40 Chauncey E. Kent quoted in Clifton F. Hodge, *The Passenger Pigeon Investigation and Some Photographs of a Long Lost Art* (pamphlet; n. p., *ca.* 1912).

41 Grant Powers, *History of Coos County* (Haverhill, N. H., 1841), p. 110.

42 B. A. T. de Montigny, *La Colonisation*, pp. 55–56.

43 O. Edson and G. D. Merrill, *History of Chautauqua County, New York* (Boston, 1894), pp. 268–69.

44 Sylvester Judd, *History of Hadley* (Northampton, Mass., 1863), pp. 359–60.

45 John Brickell, *The Natural History of North Carolina* (Dublin, 1737), p. 186.

46 A. Larocque, "The Passenger Pigeon in Folklore," *Can. Field-Naturalist*, XLIV (1930), 49.

47 Jedidiah Morse, *A Report to the Secretary of War of the United States on Indian Affairs* ... (New Haven, Conn., 1822), Appendix, p. 61.

48 Susan F. Cooper, *Journal of a Naturalist in the United States* (London, 1856), I, 13.

49 Thomas McIlwraith, *The Birds of Ontario* (2nd ed.; Toronto, 1894), p. 182.

50 A. Montanus, "Description of New Netherland. 1671," in E. B. O'Callaghan, *Documentary History of New-York*, IV, 123; Alexander Wilson, *Am. Ornithology*, V, 104.

51 William Wood, *Wood's New England's Prospect* (Pub. Prince Soc., Vol. III; Boston, 1865), pp. 31–32.

52 John R. Swanton, *The Indians of the Southeastern United States* (Bull. Bur. Am. Ethnology, No. 137; Wash., 1946), p. 298.

53 John Lawson, *The History of Carolina* . . . (Raleigh, N. C., 1860), p. 78.

54 W. J. Wintemberg, *Roebuck Prehistoric Village Site, Grenville County, Ontario* (Bull. Nat. Mus. Canada, No. 83; Ottawa, 1936), p. 14, and *Lawson Prehistoric Village Site, Middlesex County, Ontario* (Bull. Nat. Mus. Canada, No. 94; Ottawa, 1939), p. 9.

55 A. N. Somers, "Prehistoric Cannibalism in America," *Popular Sci. Monthly*, XLII (1892), 204, which is also quoted in S. A. Barrett, *Ancient Aztalan* (Milwaukee, Wis., 1933), p. 386; A. P. Kannenberg, "Ancient Winnebago Use of Birds as Food," *Wis. Archeologist*, XXV (1944), 95.

56 R. P. Jacobo Bruyas, *Radices verborum Iroquaeorum* (N. Y., 1863), pp. 32, 51, and 87.

57 George H. Harris, "The Life of Horatio Jones," *Pub. Buffalo Hist. Soc.*, VI (1903), 450.

58 Benjamin Gilbert, *A Narrative of the Captivity and Suffering of Benjamin Gilbert* . . . (London, 1790), pp. 85–86.

59 Thomas Proctor in *Penn. Archives*, 2nd ser., IV (1876), 591.

60 "Pioneer," "Sketches of Waushara County," *Wautoma Journal* (Wis.), June 29, 1858.

61 Frances Densmore, *Chippewa Customs* (Bull. Bur. Am. Ethnology, No. 86; Wash., 1929), p. 43.

62 Paul Le Jeune in *Jesuit Relations*, X, 143.

63 Mrs. Asher Wright, "An Interview with 'Esq.' Johnson," in Arthur C. Parker, *Seneca Myths and Folk Tales* (Pub. Buffalo Hist. Soc., Vol. XXVII; Buffalo, N. Y., 1923), p. 424.

64 Sarah E. Gunn, "Sarah Whitmore's Captivity in 1772," *Pub. Buffalo Hist. Soc.*, VI (1903), 517.

65 Paul Radin, "The Winnebago Tribe," *37th Ann. Rept. Bur. Am. Ethnology*, 1923, pp. 112–13.

66 Thomas Proctor in *Penn. Archives*, 2nd ser., IV (1876), 594.

67 J. Curtin and J. N. B. Hewitt, "Seneca Fiction, Legends and Myths," *32nd Ann. Rept. Bur. Am. Ethnology*, 1918, pp. 656, 663–66, and 694.

68 J. C. French, *Passenger Pigeon*, p. 37.

69 James Smith, *An Account of the Remarkable Occurrences in the Life and Travels of Col. James Smith . . .* (Cincinnati, Ohio, 1907), p. 10.

70 J. C. French, *Passenger Pigeon,* p. 32; W. N. Fenton and M. H. Deardorff in *J. Wash. Acad. Sci.,* XXXIII (1943), 293.

71 Pehr Kalm in *Auk,* XXVIII (1911), 61.

72 Lafayette H. Bunnell, *Winona and Its Environs on the Mississippi in Ancient and Modern Days* (Winona, Minn., 1897), p. 186.

73 Moritz Fischer, "A Vanished Race," *Bird-Lore,* XV (1913), 81.

74 Chief Simon Pokagon in *Chautauquan,* XXII (1895), 204.

75 G. S. B., "Trapping Wild Pigeons," *Forest and Stream,* XIV (1880), 433.

76 H. B. Roney in *Chicago Field,* X (1879), 346.

77 W. N. Fenton and M. H. Deardorff in *J. Wash. Acad. Sci.,* XXXIII (1943), 289–315.

78 E. S. Dodge, "Notes from Six Nations on the Hunting and Trapping of Wild Turkeys and Passenger Pigeons," *ibid.,* XXXV (1945), 342–43.

79 *Travels and Works of Captain John Smith* (ed. Edward Arber; Edinburgh, 1910), I, 69.

80 Roger Williams, *A Key into the Language of America* (Coll. Rhode Island Hist. Soc., Vol. I; Providence, R. I., 1827), p. 87.

81 Paul Le Jeune in *Jesuit Relations,* X, 221 and 223; Jerome Lalemant, *ibid.,* XXIII, 55.

82 Claude Jean Allouez in *Jesuit Relations,* LIV, 215.

83 Claude Dablon *ibid.,* LVI, 121.

84 Charles C. La Potherie, *Histoire de l'Amerique Septentrionale* (Paris, 1723), II, 61.

85 Pehr Kalm, *Travels into North Am.,* I, 103 and 412.

86 Paul Le Jeune in *Jesuit Relations,* XLIII, 153.

87 Peter E. Radisson, *Radisson's Voyages* (Pub. Prince Soc., Vol. XVI; Boston, 1885), p. 118.

88 Raffeix in *Jesuit Relations,* LVI, 49.

89 Pierre Boucher, *Histoire véritable et naturelle des moeurs et productions du pays de la Nouvelle France, vulgairement dite le Canada* (Paris, 1664), pp. 71–72.

90 Pehr Kalm in *Auk,* XXVIII (1911), 64.

91 C. C. La Potherie, *Histoire de l'Amerique Septentrionale,* II, 80.

92 W. N. Fenton and M. H. Deardorff in *J. Wash. Acad. Sci.,* XXXIII (1943), 290.

93 E. S. Dodge, *ibid.,* XXXV (1945), 342–43.

94 Frances Densmore, *Chippewa Customs,* p. 123.

95 Peter Yarnall quoted in Ruthven Deane, "Abundance of the Passenger Pigeon in Pennsylvania in 1850," *Auk,* XLVIII (1931), 264–65.

96 H. K. (Henry Knapp) in *Am. Sportsman,* IV (Sept. 19, 1874), 387; Chief

Simon Pokagon in *Chautauquan*, XXII (1895), 203; H. B. Roney in *Chicago Field*, X (1879), 345; L. E. Scherer, Jr., in *Cardinal*, V (1939), 33; W. W. Thompson, *Passenger Pigeon*, p. 11; "Tom Tramp" in *Rod and Gun and Am. Sportsman*, VIII (June 3, 1876), 149.

97   S. S. Stevens quoted in W. Brewster's article in *Auk*, VI (1889), 289.

98   F. Curtiss-Wedge, *History of Buffalo and Pepin Counties, Wisconsin* (Winona, Minn., 1919), p. 1031.

99   L. E. Scherer, Jr., in *Cardinal*, V (1939), 41.

100 James Ingells in Grand Rapids *Press* (Mich.), Oct. 28, 1933.

101 H. B. Roney in *Chicago Field*, IX (1878), 10, and X (1879), 346; G. S. B., "Trapping Wild Pigeons," *Forest and Stream*, XIV (1880), 433; J. C. French, *Passenger Pigeon*, p. 98.

102 George H. Harris in *Pub. Buffalo Hist. Soc.*, VI (1903), 450.

103 L. E. Scherer, Jr., in *Cardinal*, V (1939), 41.

104 H. B. Roney in *Chicago Field*, X (1879), 346; "Antler," "With Bow and Arrow among the Wild Pigeons," *Forest and Stream*, XIV (1880), 14; Fond du Lac *Commonwealth* (Wis.), May 20, 1871; S. M. De Golier, "Pigeons Now—and Then," *Forest and Stream*, LXXIII (1909), 212.

105 Chief Simon Pokagon in *Chautauquan*, XXII (1895), 205.

106 E. S. Wilson in *Auk*, LI (1934), 166.

107 E. Haskell quoted in J. C. French, *Passenger Pigeon*, p. 99.

108 Chief Simon Pokagon in *Chautauquan*, XXII (1895), 203.

109 William French quoted in J. C. French, *Passenger Pigeon*, p. 30.

110 H. Howitt in *Can. Field-Naturalist*, XLVI (1932), 29.

111 C. K. Sober quoted in J. C. French, *Passenger Pigeon*, p. 227.

112 H. K. (Henry Knapp) in *Am. Sportsman*, IV (Sept. 19, 1874), 387.

113 J. J. Audubon, *Ornithol. Biog.*, I (1831), 326.

114 C. W. Dickinson quoted in J. C. French, *Passenger Pigeon*, p. 57.

115 *Ibid.*, p. 71.

116 E. Osborn quoted in W. B. Mershon, *Passenger Pigeon*, p. 112.

117 E. T. Martin in *Outing*, LXIV (July, 1914), 478.

118 E. Haskell quoted in J. C. French, *Passenger Pigeon*, pp. 95–96.

119 J. B. Oviatt quoted in the article of L. E. Scherer, Jr., in *Cardinal*, V (1939), 33.

120 Boston *Traveller* quoted in Fredonia *Censor* (N. Y.), June 8, 1842.

121 W. P. Thomas in *Am. Field*, XVII (1882), 259.

122 "Penn," *ibid.*, p. 147.

123 Circleville *Herald* (Ohio), March 22 and April 5, 1861.

124 *Chicago Field*, IX (April 13, 1878), 132, and XI (June 28, 1879), 318.

125 F. E. S., "Netting Wild Pigeons," *Forest and Stream*, XLIII (1894), 28.

126 H. T. Phillips quoted in W. B. Mershon, *Passenger Pigeon*, p. 108; see also p. 117.

127 H. B. Roney in *Chicago Field*, X (1879), 346.

128 James Ingells in Grand Rapids *Press* (Mich.), Nov. 4, 1933.

129 Charles L. Mann in *Jahres-Bericht des naturhistorischen Vereins von Wisconsin*, 1880–81, p. 45.

130 S. Cook in *Forest and Stream*, LX (1903), 205–6.

131 W. B. Mershon, *Passenger Pigeon*, p. 171; William T. Hornaday, *Our Vanishing Wild Life* (N. Y., 1913), pp. 11–14.

132 Edward T. Martin in *Outing*, LXVI (1915), 727.

133 H. T. Phillips quoted in W. B. Mershon, *Passenger Pigeon*, p. 106.

134 Louis M. Hartwick and W. H. Tuller, *Oceana County* (Pentwater, Mich., 1890), p. 81.

135 H. B. Roney, "The Importance of More Effective Legislation for the Protection of Game and Fish," *Chicago Field*, IX (1878), 10.

136 H. B. Roney in *Chicago Field*, X (1879), 346.

137 Edward T. Martin, "Among the Pigeons," *ibid.*, pp. 385–86.

138 "Tom Tramp" in *Rod and Gun and Am. Sportsman*, VIII (June 3, 1876), 149.

139 M. in *Forest and Stream*, XIV (1880), 231–32.

140 *Rod and Gun and Am. Sportsman*, VIII (May 6, 1876), 89.

141 T. M. Owen, "Wild Pigeons," *ibid.*, VIII (June 3, 1876), 148.

142 L. M. Hartwick and W. H. Tuller, *Oceana County*, p. 81.

143 E. S. Bond, "The Game Trade of Chicago," *Chicago Field*, XIV (1881), 347.

144 "Scaup," "Destruction of Pigeons in Wisconsin," *Turf, Field and Farm*, XXXIV (June 9, 1882), 379.

145 "Blue Jay," "Shooting of the Past and Present. The Destruction of the Wild Pigeon," *Am. Field*, XVII (1882), 440.

146 H. B. Roney in *Chicago Field*, X (1879), 345.

147 Edward T. Martin, "Confessions of a Market Shooter," *Outing*, LXIII (1913), 376.

148 H. T. Phillips quoted in W. B. Mershon, *Passenger Pigeon*, pp. 109 and 110.

149 H. K. (Henry Knapp), "About Pigeon Catching," *Am. Sportsman*, I (June, 1872), 4.

150 M. R. B., "Game Protection" and "Treatment of Stool Pigeons," *Am. Field*, XXI (1884), 227 and 395–96.

151 Charles L. Mann in *Jahres-Bericht des naturhistorischen Vereins von Wisconsin*, 1880–81, p. 47.

152 E. T. Martin in *Outing*, LXIV (July, 1914), 481.

153 John Josselyn, *An Account of Two Voyages to New England, Made during the Years 1638, 1663* (Boston, 1865), p. 79.

154 Hector St. John de Crèvecoeur, *Letters from an American Farmer* (London, 1782), p. 38.

155 Sylvester Judd, *History of Hadley*, pp. 359–60.

156 G. K. Clarke, *History of Needham, Massachusetts, 1711–1911* (Cambridge, Mass., *ca.* 1912), p. 49.

157 J. J. Audubon, *Ornithol. Biog.*, I, 325.

158 T. F. De Voe, *Market Assistant*, p. 174.

159 John Lambert, *Travels through Canada, and the United States of North America, in the Years 1806, 1807, & 1808* (2nd ed.; London, 1814), I, 73.

160 J. M. Wheaton, "Report on the Birds of Ohio," *Report of the Geological Survey of Ohio*, IV (1882), 441.

161 C. Dury in *J. Cincinnati Soc. Nat. Hist.*, XXI (1910), 55.

162 E. S. Wilson in *Auk*, LI (1934), 164.

163 Edward T. Martin in *Chicago Field*, XIII (1880), 227.

164 J. B. Oviatt quoted in the article of L. E. Scherer, Jr., in *Cardinal*, V (1939), 42.

165 "Trap-Shooting," *Encyclopaedia Britannica* (14th ed.).

166 Edward Thomas, "Trap-Shooting in the Old Days," *Outing*, LXVI (1915), 368–72.

167 C., "Pigeon Trap-Shooting," *Am. Turf Register and Sporting Mag.*, XIII (July, 1842), 401–2.

168 "Pigeon Shooting," *Cabinet of Natural History and American Rural Sports* (Phila., 1831), I, 165.

169 John Krider, *Sporting Anecdotes* (Phila., 1853), pp. 276–77.

170 William B. Leffingwell, *The Art of Wing Shooting* (Chicago and N. Y., 1895), p. 132.

171 Editor, "Shooting at Pigeons," *Am. Sportsman*, I (Aug., 1872), 4.

172 R. G. A. Levinge, *Echoes from the Backwoods* (London, 1846), I, 127.

173 Etta S. Wilson, "Additional Notes on the Passenger Pigeon," *Auk*, LII (1935), 413.

174 W. B. Leffingwell, *Art of Wing Shooting*, p. 129; C. Dury in *J. Cincinnati Soc. Nat. Hist.*, XXI (1910), 54.

175 C. Dury in *J. Cincinnati Soc. Nat. Hist.*, XXI (1910), 54–55.

176 John Krider, *Sporting Anecdotes*, pp. 276–77.

177 Adam H. Bogardus, *Field, Cover, and Trap Shooting* (N. Y., 1879) p. 338; W. B. Leffingwell, *Art of Wing Shooting*, p. 129.

178 "Marksman," *The Dead Shot; or Sportsman's Complete Guide* (N. Y., 1864), p. 232; see also the description of U. S. Patent No. 149,496 issued to T. Herbert Marsh on April 7, 1874.

179 Nathan B. Tyler, U. S. Patent No. 139,836 issued on June 10, 1873.

180 William H. Hawes, U. S. Patent No. 223,334 issued on January 6, 1880.

181 Henry Knapp, U. S. Patent No. 154,494 issued on August 25, 1874; Wilbur F. Parker, U. S. Patent No. 140,532 issued on July 1, 1873; Horace M. Miller, U. S. Patent No. 227,638 issued on May 18, 1880.

182 See the Parker Brothers' advertisement in *Forest and Stream,* XVI (1881), 380.

183 H. A. Rosenthal, U. S. Patent No. 159,846 issued on February 16, 1875.

184 "Pigeon-starters" were also patented by T. Herbert Marsh, U. S. Patent No. 149,496 issued on April 7, 1874, and Jeremiah J. King, U. S. Patent No. 241,-377 issued on May 10, 1881.

185 John Krider, Sporting Anecdotes, pp. 276–77; Editor, "Principal Rules for Pigeon Shooting of England and U. S.," *Am. Sportsman,* III (1873), 18–20; Baring Blot, *The Laws of Trap Shooting ... Adopted by the Tennessee State Sportsmen's Association* (New Orleans, La., 1875); "The American Shooting Rules," *Forest and Stream,* XXXIV (1890), 14.

186 W. B. Leffingwell, *Art of Wing Shooting,* p. 178.

187 Arthur W. Du Bray quoted, *ibid.,* p. 136.

188 Henry K. Coale, "Notes on Ectopistes migratorius," *Auk,* XXXIX (1922), 255.

189 William Dutcher, "The Passenger or Wild Pigeon," *Bird-Lore,* V (1903), 211.

190 Edward Thomas in *Outing,* LXVI (1915), 372.

191 William B. Mershon, "Pigeon History," *Forest and Stream,* LXX (1908), 92.

192 Editor, "Wild Pigeons," *Chicago Field,* XIII (1880), 152; Tom Stagg's advertisement, *ibid.,* IX (1878), 298.

193 Editor's note in *Forest and Stream,* VI (1876), 273.

194 Editor, "Protecting Wild Pigeons," *ibid.,* VII (1876), 184.

195 Editor's note *ibid.,* VIII (1877), 228.

196 W. P. Thomas in New York *Sun,* June 14, 1881, and in *Chicago Field,* XV (1881), 314; Editor, "The State Shoot," *Forest and Stream,* XVI (1881), 337; Frank M. Chapman, "The Fate of the Passenger Pigeon," *Country Life,* L (Sept., 1926), 49–50.

197 "Mr. Bergh on Pigeons and Snakes," in New York *Herald,* June 12, 1881; and in *Forest and Stream,* XVI (1881), 388.

198 Milwaukee *Sentinel* (Wis.), July 19, 1875; *Forest and Stream,* X (1878), 363.

199 Chicago *Journal* for 1879 quoted in Baldwin *Bulletin* (Wis.), Sept. 6, 1879.

200 Edward Thomas in *Outing,* LXVI (1915), 372.

201 Edward T. Martin, *ibid.,* LXIV (1914), 481.

202 C. Dury in *J. Cincinnati Soc. Nat. Hist.,* XXI (1910), 55.

203 H. W. De L., "An Opinion on Trap-Shooting," *Forest and Stream,* XIV (1880), 233

204 W. B. Leffingwell, *Art of Wing Shooting,* p. 146.

205 A. H. Bogardus, *Field, Cover, and Trap Shooting,* p. 319.

206 Editor's note in *Forest and Stream,* VI (1876), 391.

207 Edward T. Martin in *Outing,* LXIII (1913), 376–78.

208 Knowles, "Another Opinion on Trap-Shooting," *Forest and Stream,* XIV (1880), 253.

209 Henry Hall, *The Tribune Book of Open-Air Sports* (N. Y., 1887), p. 392.

210 Emerson Hough, "Chicago and the West," *Forest and Stream,* XXV (1890), 169.

211 "Wild Pigeons," *Shooting and Fishing,* IX (Mar. 5, 1891), 13.

212 "Mr. Bergh on Pigeons and Snakes" in New York *Herald,* June 12, 1881; and in *Forest and Stream,* XVI (1881), 388.

213 "Mr. Bergh's Anti-Pigeon Shooting Bill," *Forest and Stream,* XVI (1881), 468.

214 These sketches were printed in connection with the article, "The Sportsmen's Tournament at Brighton Beach," *Leslie's Illustrated Newspaper,* LII (July 9, 1881), 319–20, and were reprinted in *Natural History,* LX (Sept., 1951), 328.

215 Charles M. Carter, *Shooting in the Early Days, from 1863 to 1919* (pamphlet; St. Joseph, Mo., 1919), p. 11.

CHAPTER 8

1 T. Jeffreys, *The Natural and Civil History of the French Dominions in North and South America* (London, 1760), Part I, p. 160.

2 Alexander Wilson, *Am. Ornithology,* V, 104; J. J. Audubon, *Ornithol. Biog.,* I (1831), 323.

3 W. J. M. in *Am. Field,* XVI (1881), 362.

4 William G. Hayes quoted in George M. Sutton, "The Birds of Pymatuning Swamp and Conneaut Lake, Crawford County, Pennsylvania," *Ann. Carnegie Museum,* XVIII (1927–28), 118.

5 Le Page Du Pratz, *Histoire de la Louisiane* (Paris, 1758), II, 130.

6 W. Faux, *Memorable Days in America: Being a Journal of a Tour to the United States* (London, 1823), p. 248.

7 Chief Simon Pokagon in *Chautauquan,* XXII (1895), 205.

8 Thomas Tanner quoted in William H. Bishop, *History of Roane County, West Virginia* (Spencer, W. Va., 1927), pp. 34–35.

9 Frederick S. Barde in *Ann. Rept. Oklahoma State Game and Fish Dept.,* 1912, pp. 110–12.

10 Edwin Haskell quoted in J. C. French, *Passenger Pigeon,* p. 99.

11 R. P. Whitfield, "Former Abundance of the Wild Pigeon in Central and Eastern New York," *Auk,* VII (1890), 284–85.

12 F. S. Stone, *History of Racine County* (Chicago, 1916), I, 488.

13 A. Lewis, *The History of Lynn* (Boston, 1829), p. 22.

14 W. Brewster in *Auk,* VI (1889), 289.

15 John May, "Bush Life in the Ottawa Valley Eighty Years Ago," *Papers and Records Ontario Hist. Soc.,* XII (1914), 161.

16 Henry Y. Hind, *Narrative of the Canadian Red River Exploring Expedition*

of 1856 and of the Assinniboine and Saskatchewan Exploring Expedition of 1858 (London, 1860), I, 277.

17   "Canuck" (Michael G. Scherck), *Pen Pictures of Early Life in Upper Canada* (Toronto, 1905), pp. 207–8.

18   J. C. French, *Passenger Pigeon*, p. 254.

19   Peter Yarnall quoted in Ruthven Deane, "Abundance of the Passenger Pigeon in Pennsylvania in 1850," *Auk*, XLVIII (1931), 264.

20   A. W. Schorger, "Unpublished Manuscripts by Cotton Mather on the Passenger Pigeon," *Auk*, LV (1938), 473.

21   John Josselyn, *An Account of Two Voyages to New England, Made in the Years 1638, 1663* (Boston, 1865), p. 79.

22   Sylvester Judd, *History of Hadley* (Northampton, Mass., 1863), pp. 359–60.

23   Frederic T. Lewis, "Cotton Mather's Manuscript References to the Passenger Pigeon," *Auk*, LXII (1945), 306–7; William Douglass, *A Summary, Historical and Political, of the First Planting, Progressive Improvements, and Present State of the British Settlements in North America* ... (Boston, 1755), II, 217.

24   Ashton Blackburne quoted in T. Pennant, *Arctic Zoology*, II, 325.

25   Hector St. John de Crèvecoeur, *Letters from an American Farmer* (London, 1782), pp. 37–38.

26   G. K. Clarke, *History of Needham, Massachusetts, 1711–1911* (Cambridge, Mass., *ca.* 1912), p. 46.

27   Patrick Campbell, *Travels in the Interior Inhabited Parts of North America in the Years 1791 and 1792* (Toronto, 1937), p. 48.

28   H. A. Macpherson, *A History of Fowling* (Edinburgh, 1897), p. 98.

29   P. F. X. de Charlevoix, *Histoire et description genèrale de la Nouvelle France* (Paris, 1744), III, 171.

30   R. A. Cockburn, *Quebec and Its Environments; Being a Picturesque Guide to the Stranger* (Quebec, 1831), pp. 30–31.

31   W. B. Mershon, *Passenger Pigeon*, p. 121.

32   F. S. Stone, *History of Racine County*, I, 488.

33   "The Captain," "Pigeon Shooting in Early Days," *Forest and Stream*, LXVIII (1907), 656–57.

34   W. B. Mershon, *Passenger Pigeon*, p. 127; W. W. Thompson, *Passenger Pigeon*, p. 4.

35   Conyngham, "How Pigeons Are Trapped," *Forest and Stream*, XI (1878), 430; E. R. Inman, "Passenger Pigeons ... Description of Catching These Now Extinct Birds ...," Clinton *Banner* (Wis.), June 14 and 21, 1923; Charles D. Stewart, "The Pigeon Trap," *Wis. Mag. Hist.*, XXIV (1940), 20–24; M. H. Mitchell, *Passenger Pigeon*, p. 124.

36   Henry D. Thoreau, *Notes on New England Birds* (ed. F. H. Allen; Boston and N. Y., 1910), p. 117.

37 E. R. Inman in Clinton *Banner* (Wis.) for June 14 and 21, 1923.

38 H. D. Thoreau, *Journal*, II, 499.

39 J. B. Oviatt quoted in the article of L. E. Scherer, Jr., in *Cardinal*, V (1939), 40.

40 S. S. Stevens quoted in W. Brewster's article in *Auk*, VI (1889), 288.

41 B. C. Allen and R. P. Allen, "Pigeon-Catching," *Am. Sportsman*, V (Oct. 10, 1874), 23; also in *Field and Stream*, II (1874), 321.

42 John Moore, *Columbarium: Or the Pigeon-House* (London, 1735), p. 15.

43 H. A. Macpherson, *History of Fowling*, p. 303.

44 William Douglass, *A Summary of the First Planting*, II, 218.

45 James Ingells in Grand Rapids *Press* (Mich.), Oct. 28, 1933; H. B. Roney in *Chicago Field*, X (1879), 345.

46 M. in *Forest and Stream*, XIV (1880), 231–32.

47 H. T. Phillips quoted in W. B. Mershon, *Passenger Pigeon*, p. 109.

48 H. B. Roney in *Chicago Field*, X (1879), p. 346.

49 F. E. S., "Netting Wild Pigeons," *Forest and Stream*, XLIII (1894), 50.

50 W. P. Thomas in New York *Sun*, June 14, 1881, and in *Chicago Field*, XV (1881), 314.

51 W. H. Baldwin, "1,320 Pigeons Caught in Day," Milwaukee *Journal* (Wis.), Oct. 20, 1929.

52 H. B. Roney in *Chicago Field*, X (1879), 345.

53 J. C. French, *Passenger Pigeon*, p. 195.

54 E. R. Inman in Clinton *Banner* (Wis.), June 14 and 21, 1923; Frank S. Raper in Columbus *Dispatch* (Ohio), April 9, 1939; W. B. Mershon, *Passenger Pigeon*, p. 109; C. C. Lincoln, "The Passenger Pigeon in Wisconsin" (MS dated Feb. 7, 1910, in the Library of the Wisconsin Historical Society, Madison, Wis.).

55 "Mode of Decoying Wild Pigeons in New England" in *Am. J. Sci.*, XVI (1829), 373–74, and in *Mag. Nat. Hist.* (London), V (1832), 452–53; J. C. French, *Passenger Pigeon*, p. 238; B. C. Allen and R. P. Allen in *Am. Sportsman*, V (Oct. 10, 1874), 23, and in *Field and Stream*, II (1874), 321.

56 J. C. French, *Passenger Pigeon*, p. 238.

57 Egbert Bagg, "Birds," *Year Book Oneida Hist. Soc. Utica, N. Y.*, No. 12 (1912), p. 45.

58 M. H. Mitchell, *Passenger Pigeon*, p. 125.

59 Henry B. Tristram, *The Natural History of the Bible* (London, 1889), p. 164.

60 James B. Purdy in *Bull. Mich. Ornithol. Club*, IV (1903), 69–71; "John (X)," "Game Protection—Cruel Treatment of Stool Pigeons," *Am. Field*, XXI (1884), 299.

61 J. H., *ibid.*, p. 396.

62 L. E. Scherer, Jr., in *Cardinal*, V (1939), 39.

63 W. W. Thompson, *Passenger Pigeon*, p. 13.

64   *Ibid.*

65   John H. Chatham quoted in J. C. French, *Passenger Pigeon*, p. 242.

66   H. B. Roney in *Chicago Field*, X (1879), 345.

67   C. C. Lincoln, "The Passenger Pigeon in Wisconsin" (MS dated Feb. 7, 1910, in the Library of the Wisconsin Historical Society, Madison, Wis.).

68   H. S. J. de Crèvecoeur, *Letters from an American Farmer*, pp. 37–38; Thomas F. De Voe, *The Market Assistant* (N. Y., 1867), p. 173; J. B. Purdey in *Bull. Mich. Ornithol. Club*, IV (1903), 69–71; J. C. French, *Passenger Pigeon*, p. 239.

69   J. B. Purdy in *Bull. Mich. Ornithol. Club*, IV (1903), 69–71.

70   M. R. B., "Treatment of Stool Pigeons," *Am. Field*, XXI (1884), 395–96.

71   John L. Sibley, *A History of the Town of Union, in the County of Lincoln, Maine* (Boston, 1851), p. 415.

72   Conyngham in *Forest and Stream*, XI (1878), 430.

73   L. E. Scherer, Jr., in *Cardinal*, V (1939), 40.

74   H. Y. Hind, *Narrative of Canadian Red River Exploring Expedition*, I, 277.

75   H. D. Thoreau, *Journal*, II, 499.

76   J. L. Sibley, *History of Town of Union*, p. 414.

77   J. B. Oviatt quoted in the article of L. E. Scherer, Jr., in *Cardinal*, V (1939), 40.

78   "Birds of Passage—the Great Pigeon Nesting in Benzie County," in Detroit *Post and Tribune* (Mich.), April 29, 1880; in *Forest and Stream*, XIV (1880), 314; and in *Sci. Am.*, XLII (May 29, 1880), 343–44.

79   W. W. Thompson, *Passenger Pigeon*, p. 16.

80   C. C. Lincoln, "The Passenger Pigeon in Wisconsin" (MS dated Feb. 7, 1910, in the Library of the Wisconsin Historical Society, Madison, Wis.).

81   J. B. Purdy in *Bull. Mich. Ornithol. Club*, IV (1903), 69–71.

82   B. C. Allen and R. P. Allen in *Am. Sportsman*, V (Oct. 10, 1874), 23, and in *Field and Stream*, II (1874), 321.

83   C. C. Lincoln, "The Passenger Pigeon in Wisconsin" (MS dated Feb. 7, 1910, in the Library of the Wisconsin Historical Society, Madison, Wis.).

84   S. S. Stevens quoted in W. Brewster's article in *Auk*, VI (1889), 288.

85   J. H. Chatham quoted in J. C. French, *Passenger Pigeon*, p. 240.

86   M. in *Forest and Stream*, XIV (1880), 231–32.

87   F. E. S., *ibid.*, XLIII (1894), 28.

88   L. E. Scherer, Jr., in *Cardinal*, V (1939), 34.

89   W. Brewster in *Auk*, VI (1889), 288.

90   "Tom Tramp" in *Rod and Gun and Am. Sportsman*, VIII (June 3, 1876), 149; Conyngham in *Forest and Stream*, XI (1878), 430; Charles Lose, "Netting Wild Pigeons a Lost Art," *Now and Then*, IV (1931), 224–25.

91   Chief Simon Pokagon in *Chautauquan*, XXII (1895), 204.

92   "Birds of Passage—the Great Pigeon Nesting in Benzie County," in Detroit *Post and Tribune* (Mich.), April 29, 1880; in *Forest and Stream*, XIV (1880), 314; and in *Sci. Am.*, XLII (May 29, 1880), 343–44.

93   Charles R. Weld, *The Pyrenees West and East* (London, 1859), p. 229.

94   H. B. Roney in *Chicago Field*, X (1879), 345; Plattsburg *Republican* (N. Y.), Aug. 2, 1851.

95   H. S. J. de Crèvecoeur, *Letters from an American Farmer*, pp. 37–38.

96   T. F. De Voe, *Market Assistant*, p. 174.

97   Frank S. Raper in Columbus *Dispatch* (Ohio), April 9, 1939.

98   J. C. French, *Passenger Pigeon*, p. 169.

99   "Birds of Passage—the Great Pigeon Nesting in Benzie County," in Detroit *Post and Tribune* (Mich.), April 29, 1880; in *Forest and Stream*, XIV (1880), 314; and in *Sci. Am.*, XLII (May 29, 1880), 343–44.

100 William Brewster in *Auk*, VI (1889), 288.

101 W. B. Barrows, *Mich. Bird Life*, p. 245.

102 H. T. Phillips quoted in W. B. Mershon, *Passenger Pigeon*, p. 109; also see p. 115.

103 James Ingells in Grand Rapids *Press* (Mich.), Oct. 28, 1933; H. B. Roney in *Chicago Field*, X (1879), 345; Edward T. Martin in *Outing*, LXIV (1914), 480; "Birds of Passage—the Great Pigeon Nesting in Benzie County" in Detroit *Post and Tribune* (Mich.), April 29, 1880, in *Forest and Stream*, XIV (1880), 314, and in *Sci. Am.*, XLII (May 29, 1880), 343–44; "Tom Tramp" in *Rod and Gun and Am. Sportsman*, VIII (June 3, 1876), 149.

104 H. B. Roney in *Chicago Field*, X (1879), 345.

105 J. J. Audubon, *Ornithol. Biog.*, I, 325; Milwaukee *Daily Wisconsin*, May 7, 1850.

106 W. P. Thomas in New York *Sun*, June 14, 1881, and in *Chicago Field*, XV (1881), 314; F. E. S. in *Forest and Stream*, XLIII (1894), 29.

107 W. H. Baldwin in Milwaukee *Journal* (Wis.), Oct. 20, 1929.

108 George H. Mackay, "Old Records for Massachusetts and Rhode Island," *Auk*, XXVIII (1911), 119–20.

109 James Ingells in Grand Rapids *Press* (Mich.), Oct. 28, 1933.

110 F. E. S. in *Forest and Stream*, XLIII (1894), 28.

111 W. Brewster in *Auk*, VI (1889), 289.

112 Henry W. Herbert, *Frank Forester's Field Sports of the United States, and British Provinces, of North America* (N. Y., 1852), I, 32.

113 P. F. X. de Charlevoix, *Histoire et description genèrale de la Nouvelle France*, III, 171.

114 M. Catesby, *Natural History of Carolina*, I, 23.

115 Fredericke Charlotte Louise Riedesel, *Letters and Journals Relating to the War of the American Revolution* (trans. W. L. Stone; Albany, N. Y., 1867), pp. 85–86.

116 John G. Dillin, "Recollection of Wild Pigeons in Southeastern Pennsylvania, 1864–1881," *Cassinia*, No. 14 (1910), 33.

117 C. Dury in *J. Cincinnati Soc. Nat. Hist.*, XXI (1910), 53.

118 Samuel Strickland, *Twenty-Seven Years in Canada West*, I, 298.

119 John L. Childs, "Personal Recollections of the Passenger Pigeon," *Warbler*, 2nd ser., I (1905), 71.

120 M. in *Forest and Stream*, XVIII (1882), 507.

121 "Tom Tramp" in *Rod and Gun and Am. Sportsman*, VIII (June 3, 1876), 149.

122 Charles Hallock, *The Sportsman's Gazetteer* (N. Y., 1877), p. 235.

123 George H. Coues, "Pigeon Shooting in Minnesota," *Forest and Stream*, XIX (1882), 188.

124 A. W. Schorger, "Unpublished Manuscripts by Cotton Mather on the Passenger Pigeon," *Auk*, LV (1938), 473.

125 *The Jesuit Relations and Allied Documents* (ed. R. G. Thwaites; Cleveland, Ohio, 1896–1901), XLVIII, 177.

126 Sir William Johnson quoted in T. Pennant, *Arctic Zoology*, II, 325.

127 "Subscriber," "Pigeon-Shooting near Boston," *Cabinet of Natural History and American Rural Sports* (Phila., 1832), II, 137; E. S. Wilson in *Auk*, LI (1934), 161.

128 Thomas Anburey, *Travels through the Interior Parts of America* (London), 1791), I, 244.

129 R. Lamb, *Memoir of His Own Life* (Dublin, 1811), p. 167.

130 T. Pennant, *Arctic Zoology*, II, 325.

131 L., "Old Days in Maine," *Forest and Stream*, XXXIX (1892), 117.

132 T. F. De Voe, *Market Assistant*, p. 173.

133 William B. Leffingwell, *Shooting on Upland, Marsh, and Stream* (Chicago, 1890), p. 229.

134 "Subscriber" in *Cabinet of Natural History and American Rural Sports*, II, 136–37.

135 H. D. Thoreau, *Journal*, V, 71, and VII, 35.

136 F. H. Allen, "Prating for Passenger Pigeons," *Auk*, LXII (1945), 136.

137 R. A. Cockburn, *Quebec and Its Environments*, pp. 30–31.

138 J. H. Sage, L. B. Bishop, and W. P. Bliss, *The Birds of Connecticut* (Bull. Conn. State Geol. and Nat. Hist. Survey, No. 20; Hartford, Conn., 1913), pp. 69–72.

139 John L. Childs in *Warbler*, 2nd ser., I (1905), 73.

140 W. Brewster in *Bull. Museum Comparative Zool.*, No. 66 (1925), Part II, p. 309.

141 Samuel Thompson, *Reminiscences of a Canadian Pioneer for the Last Fifty Years* (Toronto, 1884), pp. 75–76.

142 Godfrey T. Vigne, *Six Months in America* (London, 1832), II, 115.

143 George Heriot, *Travels through the Canadas* ... (London, 1807), pp. 517–18; Samuel Thompson, *Reminiscences of a Canadian Pioneer*, pp. 75–76; Norman Robertson, *A History of the County of Bruce* (Toronto, 1906), p. 79; Ransom A. Moore, "The Hunter of Kewaunee: Passing of the Passenger Pigeon," *Hoard's Dairyman*, LXXIII (1928), 145.

144 J. C. French, *Passenger Pigeon*, p. 56.

145 Christian Schultz, *Travels on an Inland Voyage in the Years 1807 and 1808* (N. Y., 1810), II, 118.

146 "Snipe" in *Forest and Stream*, X (1878), 224.

147 "Hammerless Greener," "Pigeon Shooting," *Can. Sportsman and Naturalist*, I (1881), 20–21.

148 Ralph G. Taber, "Wild Pigeons," *St. Nicholas Mag.*, XLII (March, 1915), 463.

149 E. S. Wilson in *Auk*, LI (1934), 161–62.

150 "Barney," "An Old-Time Pigeon Shot," *Forest and Stream*, XL (1893), 295; A. W. Butler in *22nd Ann. Rept. Indiana Dept. Geol. Nat. Resources*, 1897, p. 761.

151 M. Schaff, *Etna and Kirkersville*, p. 105.

152 *The Secret Diary of William Byrd of Westover, 1709–1712* (Richmond, Va., 1941), p. 347; also see John De Laet, "Extracts from the New World or a Description of the West Indies," *Coll. N. Y. Hist. Soc.*, 2nd ser., I (1841), 300.

153 James Taylor, *Narrative of a Voyage to, and Travels in Upper Canada* (Hull, Eng., 1846), pp. 62–63.

154 James F. Cooper, *The Pioneers, or the Sources of the Susquehanna* (N. Y., 1823), II, 40–50.

155 W. Faux, *Memorable Days in America*, p. 174.

156 W. Brewster in *Bull. Museum Comparative Zool.*, No. 66 (1925), Part II, p. 307.

157 G. Taylor, *A Voyage to North America* ... *in the Years 1768 and 1769* (Nottingham, Eng., 1771), pp. 87–88.

158 E. S. Wilson in *Auk*, LI (1934), 162.

159 Charles A. Post, *Doans Corners* (Cleveland, Ohio, 1930), p. 111.

160 W. B. Leffingwell, *Shooting on Upland, Marsh, and Stream*, p. 220.

161 "Snap Shot," "Peace and Pigeons in Wisconsin," *Wilkes' Spirit of the Times*, XII (May 27, 1865), 194.

162 Aaron Ludwig Kumlien, "Unusual Accidents to Birds," *Field and Forest*, II (Dec., 1876), 106.

163 R. A. Moore in *Hoard's Dairyman*, LXXIII (1928), 145.

164 "Gopher," "Among the Pigeons," *Turf, Field and Farm*, XI (Sept. 16, 1870), 161 and 177.

165   W. R. Manlove, "A Roost of the Wild Pigeon," *Migrant*, IV, No. 2 (June, 1933), 18.

166   Herbert Brandt, *Arizona and Its Bird Life* (Cleveland, Ohio, 1951), p. 529.

167   G. H. Coues in *Forest and Stream*, XIX (1882), 188; Charles A. Green, "Wild Pigeons," *ibid.*, LXXXI (1913), 75.

168   W. B. Leffingwell, *Shooting on Upland, Marsh, and Stream*, p. 222; Rowland E. Robinson, *Uncle Lisha's Outing* (Rutland, Vt., *ca.* 1934), p. 119; W. B. Mershon, *Passenger Pigeon*, p. 8.

169   Anne Grant, *Memoirs of an American Lady* (N. Y., 1846), p. 43.

170   John F. Watson, *Annals of Philadelphia* (Phila., 1830), p. 240.

171   Claude Thomas Dupuy, "Ordonnance de M. Dupuy, Intendant en Canada, portant deffences de tirer des coups de fusils dans la Ville de Quebec," MS in Public Arch. Canada, Ottawa, Moreau St. Merey F3, Vol. XI (1727–31).

172   Antoine D. Raudot, "Ordonnance, Montreal, June 22, 1710," MS in Public Arch. Canada, Ottawa, Ordonnances des Intendances, M 15, p. 432.

173   Gilles Hocquart, "Ordonnance, Montreal, May 12, 1748," MS in Public Arch. Canada, Ottawa, Ordonnances, IV (1725–49).

174   "A Backwoodsman" (William Dunlop), *Statistical Sketches of Upper Canada* (London, 1832), p. 48.

175   "Observer," "Shooting Wild Pigeons," *Forest and Stream*, III (1874), 146.

CHAPTER 9

1   *The Works of Samuel de Champlain* (ed. H. P. Biggar; Toronto, 1922–36), I, 332; Gabriel Sagard-Theodat, *Le grand Voyage du pays des Hurons* (Paris, 1632), p. 303.

2   Louis de Lahontan, *New Voyages to North-America* (London, 1703), I, 61–62.

3   William Strachey, *The Historie of Travaile into Virginia Brittania* (Hakluyt Soc., 1st ser., Vol. VI; London, 1849), p. 126.

4   William Wood, *Wood's New England's Prospect* (Pub. Prince Soc., Vol. III; Boston, 1865), p. 31.

5   A. W. Schorger, "Unpublished Manuscripts by Cotton Mather on the Passenger Pigeon," *Auk*, LV (1938), 473.

6   Samuel Strickland, *Twenty-Seven Years in Canada West*, I, 297.

7   Alexander Wilson, *Am. Ornithology*, V, 106.

8   J. J. Audubon, *Ornithol. Biog.*, I (1831), 322.

9   W. Ross King, *The Sportsman and Naturalist in Canada* (London, 1866), pp. 121–22.

10   Bénédict-Henry Révoil, *The Hunter and Trapper in North America; or Romantic Adventures in Field and Forest* (trans. W. H. Davenport; London, 1874), p. 126.

11 W. B. Mershon, *Passenger Pigeon,* p. 123.

12 Thomas Nuttall, *A Manual of the Ornithology of the United States and of Canada . . . . The Land Birds* (Cambridge, Mass., 1832), I, 630.

13 William B. Mershon, "The Passing of the Passenger Pigeon," *Chambers's Journal,* N. S., LXXXII (1905), 491.

14 W. J. McGee in *Science,* N. S., XXXII (1910), 961.

15 Tom Carter quoted in G. M. Mathews, *The Birds of Australia* (London, 1910–11), I, 153.

16 A. H. Evans, *Birds* (London, 1935), p. 342; Philip L. Sclater in *Proc. Zool. Soc. London,* 1865, p. 239; D. Le Souëf, "Descriptions of Birds'-Eggs from the Port Darwin District, Northern Australia," *Emu,* II (1903), 153–54; G. M. Mathews, *Birds of Australia,* I, 105–27.

17 A. C. Bent, *Life Histories of N. Am. Gallinaceous Birds,* pp. 356 and 367.

18 Johnson A. Neff, "Habits, Food, and Economic Status of the Band-Tailed Pigeon," *North Am. Fauna,* No. 58 (1947), p. 6.

19 S. Grieve, *The Great Auk, or Garefowl* (London, 1885), p. 5.

20 Roger T. Peterson, "How Many Birds Are There?" *Audubon Mag.,* XLIII (1941), 182.

21 Leonard Wing, "Wildlife Populations," mimeographed Washington State Wildlife Management Notes (State College Wash.), III (Dec. 28, 1941), 1.

22 John Josselyn, *An Account of Two Voyages to New England, Made during the Years 1638, 1663* (Boston, 1865), p. 79.

23 Frederic T. Lewis, "Cotton Mather's Manuscript References to the Passenger Pigeon," *Auk,* LXII (1945), 306–7.

24 P. F. X. de Charlevoix, *Histoire et description generale de la Nouvelle France* (Paris, 1744), III, 171.

25 Thomas Dudley, "Letter to the Countess of Lincoln. Boston, March 12, 1631," *Coll. Mass. Hist. Soc.,* 1st ser., VIII (1802), 45.

26 John Clayton, "Letter to the Royal Society, Giving a Further Account of the Soil, and Other Observables of Virginia," *Phil. Trans.,* XVII (1693), 992–93.

27 Pehr Kalm in *Auk,* XXVIII (1911), 58.

28 Samuel Smith, *The History of the Colony of Nova-Caesaria, or New Jersey* (Trenton, N. J., 1890), p. 511.

29 Blackburne quoted in T. Pennant, *Arctic Zoology,* II, 326.

30 Caleb Atwater, *A History of the State of Ohio, Natural and Civil* (Cincinnati, Ohio, 1838), pp. 93–94.

31 S. P. Hildreth in *Am. J. Sci.,* XL (1841), 348.

32 Susan F. Cooper, *Journal of a Naturalist in the United States* (London, 1856), I, 12.

33 John Lambert, *Travels through Canada, and the United States of North America, in the Years 1806, 1807, & 1808* (2nd ed.; London, 1814), I, 78.

34   Richard H. Bonnycastle, *The Canadas in 1841* (London, 1841), I, 168.

35   [Henry B. Small], *A Canadian Handbook and Tourist's Guide* (Montreal, 1867), p. 134.

36   Jeremy Belknap, *The History of New Hampshire* (Boston, 1792), III, 171–72.

37   H. D. Thoreau, *Journal*, IV, 44.

38   Joel A. Allen, "Decrease of Birds in Massachusetts," *Nuttall Bull.*, I (1876), 56.

39   *Diary of Christopher Columbus Baldwin . . . 1829–1835* (Trans. Coll. Am. Antiquarian Soc., Vol. VIII; Worcester, Mass., 1901), p. 168.

40   "Tom Tramp" in *Rod and Gun and Am. Sportsman*, VIII (June 3, 1876), 149.

41   Bénédict-Henry Révoil, *The Hunter and Trapper in North America*, p. 137.

42   J. J. Audubon, *Ornithol. Biog.*, I, 324.

43   J. C. French, *Passenger Pigeon*, p. 32.

44   S. P. Hildreth in *Am. J. Sci.*, XXIV (1833), 134–35.

45   William Welsh, "Passenger Pigeons," *Can. Field-Naturalist*, XXXIX (1925), 165–66.

46   W. J. McKnight, *History of Northwestern Pennsylvania* (Phila., 1905), p. 146.

47   Alexander Wilson, *Am. Ornithology*, V, 110.

48   S. S. Stevens quoted in W. Brewster's article in *Auk*, VI (1889), 289.

49   *Life in the West: Back-Wood Leaves and Prairie Flowers* (London 1842), p. 286.

50   J. C. French, *Passenger Pigeon*, p. 243; N., "Wild Pigeons in Virginia," *Porter's Spirit of the Times*, XX (March 30, 1850), 61.

51   Henry D. Thoreau, *Notes on New England Birds* (ed. F. H. Allen; Boston and N. Y., 1910), p. 117.

52   J. J. Audubon, *Ornithol. Biog.*, I, 187.

53   William Welsh in *Can. Field-Naturalist*, XXXIX (1925), 165–66.

54   J. H. Sage, L. B. Bishop, and W. P. Bliss, *The Birds of Connecticut* (Bull. Conn. State Geol. and Nat. Hist. Survey, No. 20; Hartford, Conn., 1913), p. 72.

55   Milton H. Trautman, *The Birds of Buckeye Lake, Ohio* (Ann Arbor, Mich., 1940), p. 209.

56   S. S. Stevens quoted in W. Brewster's article in *Auk*, VI (1889), 289.

57   J. J. Audubon, *Ornithol. Biog.*, IV (1838), 526.

58   Philo L. Hatch, *Notes on the Birds of Minnesota* (Minneapolis, Minn., 1892), p. 181.

59   Benjamin H. Warren, *Birds of Pennsylvania* (2nd ed.; Harrisburg, Pa., 1890), p. 124; Arthur Cleveland Bent, *Life Histories of North American Birds of Prey* (Bull. U. S. Nat. Museum, No. 167; Wash., 1937), p. 127.

60   P. L. Hatch, *Notes on Birds of Minn.*, p. 184.

61 J. J. Audubon, *Ornithol. Biog.,* II (1834), 242.

62 *Ibid.,* I, 188.

63 Rufus Haymond, "Birds of Franklin County, Indiana," *First Ann. Rept. Geol. Survey Indiana,* 1869, p. 209.

64 J. J. Audubon, *Ornithol. Biog.,* I, 86.

65 George B. Grinnell quoted in William Ludlow, *Report of a Reconnaissance of the Black Hills of Dakota in the Summer of 1874* (Wash., 1875), p. 96.

66 G. F. B., "Extermination of Passenger Pigeons," *Forest and Stream,* LXXXII (1914), 246.

67 L. E. Scherer, Jr., in *Cardinal,* V (1939), 36.

68 Arthur T. Wayne, *Birds of South Carolina* (Charleston, S. C., 1910), p. 66.

69 C. A. Bryant in *Forest and Stream,* LXXX (1913), 515.

70 L. S. Hayes, *History of the Town of Rockingham, Vermont* (Bellows Falls, Vt., 1907), p. 90.

71 Editor, "Pigeon Poll," *Saturday Evening Post,* CCXI (Jan. 14, 1939), 80.

72 Paul Bartsch, "Destruction of Passenger Pigeons in Arkansas," *Auk,* XXXIV (1917), 87.

73 William B. Mershon, "Note on the Passenger Pigeon," *Auk,* XLVIII (1931), 116.

74 J. J. Audubon, *Ornithol. Biog.,* I, 325.

75 S. P. Hildreth in *Am. J. Sci.,* XL (1841), 348.

76 Henry D. Paxson, "The Last of the Wild Pigeons in Bucks County," *Coll. Bucks County Hist. Soc.,* IV (1917), 381.

77 "Wild Pigeons and Trap Shooting," *Turf, Field and Farm,* XXVI (June 21, 1878), 391.

78 Donald C. Peattie, "The Beech and the Pigeon," *Atlantic Monthly,* CLXXXII (Aug., 1948), 58–60.

79 W. W. Thompson, *Passenger Pigeon,* p. 16.

80 W. B. Barrows, *Mich. Bird Life,* p. 248.

81 T. Kenneth Wood, "Strange Story of How Wild Pigeon Passed," Williamsport *Sun* (Pa.), March 8, 1934.

82 Cited by C. William Beebe, *The Bird: Its Form and Function* (N. Y., 1906), p. 446.

83 B. A. Testard de Montigny, *La Colonisation. Le nord de Montreal ou la région Labelle* (Montreal, 1896), pp. 55–56.

84 Quoted in A. Larocque, "The Passenger Pigeon in Folklore," *Can. Field-Naturalist,* XLIV (1930), 49.

85 Paul Paris, "A propos de la Disparition de l'ectopiste migrateur," *Rev. franç. d'ornithol.,* II (1912), 313.

86 H. Howitt in *Can. Field Naturalist,* XLVI (1932), 27–30.

87 C. O. Whitman quoted in C. H. Ames, "Breeding of the Wild Pigeon," *Forest and Stream,* LVI (1901), 464.

88 A. E. Wiedring quoted in Ruthven Deane, "The Passenger Pigeon—Only One Pair Left," *Auk,* XXVI (1909), 429.

89 *Ibid.,* and Deane's article, "The Passenger Pigeon—Only One Bird Left," *Auk,* XXVIII (1911), 262; W. C. Herman in *Auk,* LXV (1948), 78.

90 Edward T. Martin in *Outing,* LXIV (July, 1914), 481.

91 W. W. Thompson, *Passenger Pigeon,* p. 11.

92 R. M. Stabler and C. M. Herman, "Upper Digestive Tract Trichomoniasis in Mourning Doves and Other Birds," *Trans. 16th N. Am. Wildlife Conference,* 1951, p. 159.

93 A. W. Schorger, "Introduction of the Domestic Pigeon," *Auk,* LXIX (1952), 462–63.

94 Thomas McIlwraith, *The Birds of Ontario* (2nd ed.; Toronto, 1894), p. 182.

95 Percy R. Lowe, "A Reminiscence of the Last Great Flight of the Passenger Pigeon (*Ectopistes migratorius*) in Canada," *Ibis,* 11th ser., IV (1922), 140–41.

96 Aretas A. Saunders, *A Distributional List of the Birds of Montana* (Berkeley, Calif., 1921), p. 171.

97 Witmer Stone in *Auk,* XXXI (1914), 567.

98 W. E. C. Todd, *Birds of Western Pennsylvania* (Pittsburgh, Pa., 1940), pp. 266–72.

99 Ludlow Griscom, "The Passing of the Passenger Pigeon," *Am. Scholar,* XV (1946), 215.

100 R. B. Nestler and A. L. Nelson, "Inbreeding among Pen-Reared Quail," *Auk,* LXII (1945), 222.

101 Arthur A. Allen, "Sex Rhythm in the Ruffed Grouse (*Bonasa umbellus* Linn.) and Other Birds," *Auk,* LI (1934), 190.

102 W. J. Breckenridge, "A Century of Minnesota Wild Life," *Minn. History,* XXX (1949), 224.

103 F. F. Darling, *Bird Flocks and the Breeding Cycle* (Cambridge, Eng., 1938) p. 76.

104 Wallace Craig, "The Voices of Pigeons Regarded as Means of Social Control," *Am. J. Sociology,* XIV (1908), 91.

105 B. Waters, "Fate of the Wild Pigeon," *Forest and Stream,* LXVI (1906), 827.

106 W. B. Mershon in *Chambers's Journal,* N. S., LXXXII (1905), 493.

107 Moritz Fischer, "A Vanished Race," *Bird-Lore,* XV (1913), 83.

108 Milwaukee *Sentinel,* June 22, 1882; Green Bay *Data,* June 20, 1882; La Crosse *Chronicle,* May 17, 1882 (all Wis.).

109 Madison *State Journal* (Wis.), May 26, 1882.

110 La Crosse *Republican-Leader* (Wis.), June 19, 1882; C., "The Wild Pigeons," *Forest and Stream,* XXX (1888), 414.

111 "Correspondent," "A Wisconsin Pigeon Roost," *Forest and Stream*, XIX (1882), 8.

112 E. S. Bond quoted by M. R. B. in *Am. Field*, XIX (1883), 513.

113 "A Big Pot-Hunters' Raid," *Forest and Stream*, XXI (1884), 498.

114 W. W. Thompson, *Passenger Pigeon*, p. 6.

115 Shawano *Journal* (Wis.), May 22 and June 5, 1885; Shawano *Advocate*, May 28, 1885.

116 John Lutz in *Outing*, LXV (1915), 640.

117 J. B. Oviatt quoted in the article of L. E. Scherer, Jr., in *Cardinal*, V (1939), 30.

118 Editor in *Am. Field*, XXVI (1886), 415.

119 Louis B. Bishop, "Pigeons by the Million" in New York *Times*, May 9, 1886, p. 10, and in *Cassinia*, No. 16 (1912), pp. 21–25.

120 L. B. Bishop, *ibid.;* also Coudersport *Potter County Journal* (Pa.), May 27, 1886.

121 Editor in *Forest and Stream*, XXVI (1886), 302.

122 W. W. Thompson, *Passenger Pigeon*, p. 6.

123 J. B. Oviatt quoted in the article of L. E. Scherer, Jr., in *Cardinal*, V (1939), 30.

124 J. C. French, *Passenger Pigeon*, pp. 21, 59, 61.

125 W. Brewster in *Auk*, VI (1889), 286.

126 J. L. Smith, "Amount of Game Killed in Missouri," *Am. Field*, XXV (1886), 531.

127 Aaron Ludwig Kumlien, "List of the Birds Known to Nest within the Boundaries of Wisconsin, with a Few Notes Thereon," *Wis. Naturalist*, I (1891), 147.

128 W. Brewster in *Auk*, VI (1889), 286 and 291.

129 F. N. Newton, "The Passenger Pigeon's Nesting," *Forest and Stream*, LXXIV (1910), 934; Herbert H. Beck, "Dexterous Alighting Maneuver of Passenger Pigeons," *Auk*, LXVI (1949), 286.

130 William B. Mershon, "The Wild Pigeons," *Forest and Stream*, XXX (1888), 414.

131 Editor, *ibid.*, p. 429.

132 Stewart E. White, "Birds Observed on Mackinac Island, Michigan, during the Summers of 1889, 1890, and 1891," *Auk*, X (1893), 223.

133 Stewart E. White, "From Michigan," *Oologist*, VII (1890), 11.

134 Stewart E. White quoted in W. B. Mershon, *Passenger Pigeon*, p. 150.

135 George O. Cantwell, "Wild Pigeons," *Am. Field*, XXXIII (1890), 31.

136 "Keokuk," "A Wild Pigeon Flight," *Forest and Stream*, XXXIII (1890), 467.

137 C. F. Carr, "Passenger Pigeon (*Ectopistes migratorius*), Nesting in Wisconsin," *Wis. Naturalist*, I (1890), 9–10.

138 Aaron Ludwig Kumlien's article, *ibid.*, p. 147.

139 Editor, "The Wild Pigeon," *Shooting and Fishing,* IX (Feb. 19, 1891), 5.

140 C. F. Carr, "Passenger Pigeon," *Wis. Naturalist,* I (1891), 143.

141 Emerson Hough, "Wild Pigeons," *Forest and Stream,* XXXIX (1892), 138.

142 Editor's note, *ibid.,* XXXVI (1891), 409.

143 Samuel N. Rhoads, "Notes on Some of the Rarer Birds of Western Pennsylvania," *Auk,* XVI (1899), 310.

144 William Brewster (ed.) in Henry D. Minot, *The Land-Birds and Game-Birds of New England* (2nd ed.; Boston, 1895), p. 395n.

145 J. H. Fleming in *Ottawa Naturalist,* XX (March, 1907), 236–37.

146 Ruthven Deane, "Additional Records of the Passenger Pigeon in Illinois and Indiana," *Auk,* XII (1895), 298.

147 G. D. C. in Whitewater *Register* (Wis.), May 10, 1894, and in *Forest and Stream,* XLII (1894), 422.

148 A. W. Butler in *22nd Ann. Rept. Indiana Dept. Geol. Nat. Resources,* 1897, p. 763.

149 Ruthven Deane, "Additional Records of the Passenger Pigeon (*Ectopistes migratorius*) in Wisconsin and Illinois," *Auk,* XIII (1896), 81.

150 W. B. Mershon, *Passenger Pigeon,* p. 223.

151 A. W. Butler in *22nd Ann. Rept. Indiana Dept. Geol. and Nat. Resources,* 1897, p. 764.

152 Ruthven Deane, "Additional Records of the Passenger Pigeon (*Ectopistes migratorius*)," *Auk,* XIV (1897), 316–17.

153 L. Whitney Watkins *et al.,* "Migration Reports for 1896," *Bull. Mich. Ornithol. Club,* I (1897), 27.

154 Ruthven Deane in *Auk,* XIV (1897), 316–17, and XV (1898), 184–85.

155 Emerson Hough, "Wild Pigeons," *Forest and Stream,* XLVII (1896), 512.

156 Ruthven Deane in *Auk,* XV (1898), 184–85; Emerson Hough, "Wild Pigeons in Wisconsin," *Forest and Stream,* XLIX (1897), 168.

157 W. F. R. (W. F. Rightmire), "Wild Pigeons in Nebraska," *Forest and Stream,* XLIX (1897), 246. See also Ruthven Deane in *Auk,* XV (1898), 184–85.

158 Ned Hollister, "Passenger Pigeon," *Recreation,* XI (Aug., 1899), 134.

159 William Brewster, *The Birds of the Cambridge Region of Massachusetts* (Cambridge, Mass., 1906), p. 178; Robert Hegner, *Parade of the Animal Kingdom* (N. Y., 1940), p. 447.

160 Herbert K. Job, *Propagation of Wild Birds* (N. Y., 1915), p. 100.

161 E. H. Forbush, *Birds of Mass.,* II, 42–44.

162 Clifton F. Hodge, "A Last Effort to Find and Save from Extinction the Passenger Pigeon," *Bird-Lore,* XII (1910), 52.

163 Charles K. Reed, *The Passenger Pigeon* (Worcester, Mass., 1910).

164 Clifton F. Hodge, "To Save the Passenger Pigeon," *Forest and Stream,* LXXIV (1910), 172.

165 Clifton F. Hodge, "The Passenger Pigeon Investigation," *Auk*, XXVIII (1911), 49–53; "Last Call for the Passenger Pigeon," *Forest and Stream*, LXXVII (1911), 557; and "A Last Word on the Passenger Pigeon," *Auk*, XXIX (1912), 169–75.

166 Witmer Stone in *Auk*, XXXI (1914), 567.

167 James F. Cooper, *The Pioneers, or the Sources of the Susquehanna* (N. Y., 1823), II, 41.

168 James F. Clarke, *Memorial and Biographical Sketches* (Boston, 1878), 273.

169 C. W. Gunn in *Oologist*, II (1876), 29–30.

170 "Tom Tramp" in *Rod and Gun and Am. Sportsman*, VIII (June 3, 1876), 149.

171 H. B. Roney, "The Importance of More Effective Legislation for the Protection of Game and Fish," *Chicago Field*, IX (1878), 10.

172 H. B. Roney, *ibid.*, X (1879), 346.

173 Editor, "The Protection of Wild Pigeons," *Forest and Stream*, VII (1876), 104.

174 For an account of the Turner affair and the quotation of his editorial in the Grand Rapids *Eagle* of April 18, 1878, see the article of H. B. Roney in *Chicago Field*, X (1879), 345–47.

175 A. B. Turner, "The Michigan Pigeon Question," *Chicago Field*, X (1879), 401–2; Edward T. Martin, "Among the Pigeons," *ibid.*, p. 385.

176 Ed Lawrence, "The Pigeon Question—A Reply to Messrs. Martin and Turner," *ibid.*, XI (1879), 25.

177 H. B. Roney's article, *ibid.*, X (1879), 346.

178 "Pericles" (Robert Morris Gibbs), "The Effects of Civilization on Our Birds," *Science*, O. S., XX (1892), 183.

179 Louis B. Bishop in New York *Times*, May 9, 1886, p. 10, and in *Cassinia*, No. 16 (1912), pp. 21–25.

180 Editor's note in *Forest and Stream*, XXVI (1886), 302.

181 Editor, "Interesting to Trap Shooters," *Chicago Field*, IX (1878), 136.

182 Editor (N. Rowe), "The Destruction of the Wild Pigeon," *Am. Field*, XVII (1882), 438.

CHAPTER 10

1 Robert Ridgway, *Birds of North and Middle America* (Wash., 1916), Part VII, p. 333.

2 Hubert L. Clark, "Tail-Feathers and Their Major Upper Coverts," *Auk*, XXXV (1918), 118.

3 Robert Ridgway, *Birds of North and Middle America*, Part VII p. 335; Elliott Coues, *Key to North American Birds* (5th ed.; Boston, 1903), II, 712.

4 Elliott Coues, *Key to N. Am. Birds*, II, 712.

5   Elliott Coues, "Field-Notes on Birds Observed in Dakota and Montana along the Forty-Ninth Parallel during the Seasons of 1873 and 1874," *Bull. U. S. Geol. Geog. Survey Territories,* IV (1878), 628.

6   Ruthven Deane, "Extracts from the Field Notes of George B. Sennett," *Auk,* XL (1923), 628.

7   Edgar A. Mearns, "A List of the Birds of the Hudson Highlands, with Annotations," *Bull. Essex Inst.,* XII (1880), 128.

8   Robert Ridgway, *Birds of North and Middle America,* Part VII, p. 335.

9   E. A. Mearns in *Bull. Essex Inst.,* XII (1880), 128.

10 Pehr Kalm in *Auk,* XXVIII (1911), 56.

11 Johann L. Frisch, *Vorstellung der Vögel in Teutschland* (Berlin, 1733–63), Vol. I, Tab. 142.

12 A. C. Bent, *Life Histories of N. Am. Gallinaceous Birds,* p. 387.

13 H. L. Clark, "The Pterylosis of the Wild Pigeon," *Auk,* XXXV (1918), 416.

14 Ruthven Deane in *Auk,* XIII (1896), 237; W. C. Herman in *Auk,* LXV (1948), 79.

15 Henry D. Thoreau, *The First and Last Journeys of Thoreau* (ed. F. B. Sanborn; Boston, 1905), II, 101.

16 *Posthumous Works of C. O. Whitman,* I, 26.

17 Charles A. Keeler, *Evolution of the Colors of North American Land Birds* (San Francisco, 1893), p. 205, and his article of the same title in *Auk,* X (1893), 376.

18 Joel A. Allen, "Keeler on the 'Evolution of the Colors of North American Land Birds,' " *Auk,* X (1893), 194.

19 I. Bickerton Williams, "The Color of Certain Birds, in Relation to Inheritance," *Auk,* XVI (1899), 320.

20 Ruthven Deane, "Albinism and Melanism among North American Birds," *Nuttall Bull.,* I (1876), 22; J. G. Davis in *Forest and Stream,* II (1874), 22.

21 Notice is given in *Jahresbericht des naturhistorischen Vereins von Wisconsin,* 1876, p. 9, and in the Chilton *Times* (Wis.), Sept. 25, 1875.

22 C. W. Dickinson quoted in J. C. French, *Passenger Pigeon,* p. 254.

23 "Teal" (R. L. Newcomb), "Albinoes," *Forest and Stream,* VII (1876), 325.

24 A. C. Bent, *Life Histories of N. Am. Gallinaceous Birds,* p. 388.

25 Ruthven Deane in *Auk,* XIII (1896), 236; W. C. Herman in *Auk,* LXV (1948), 79.

26 E. H. Forbush, *Birds of Mass.,* II, 54.

27 H. D. Thoreau, *Journal,* VII, 36.

28 E. H. Forbush, *Birds of Mass.,* II, 54.

29 A. C. Bent, *Life Histories of N. Am. Gallinaceous Birds,* p. 388.

30 T. G. Gentry, *Life-Histories of Birds,* II, 300.

31 H. L. Clark, "Tail-Feathers and Their Major Upper Coverts," *Auk,* XXXV (1918), 416–20.

32 John R. Forster, "An Account of the Birds Sent from Hudson's Bay; with Observations Relative to Their Natural History; and Latin Descriptions of Some of the Most Uncommon," *Phil. Trans.,* LXII (1772), 398; E. H. Eaton, *Birds of N. Y.,* I, 381.

33 J. C. French, *Passenger Pigeon,* p. 32.

CHAPTER 11

1 Robert W. Shufeldt, "On the Comparative Osteology of the United States *Columbidae,*" *Proc. Zool. Soc. London,* 1891, p. 195; "On the Osteology of the Pigeons (*Columbae*)," *J. Morphol.,* XVII (1901), 487–514; "Osteology of the Passenger Pigeon (*Ectopistes migratorius*)," *Auk,* XXXI (1914), 358–62, plate of skeleton opposite p. 358.

2 Robert W. Shufeldt, "Notes on the Classification of the Pigeons," *Am. Naturalist,* XXV (1891), 158.

3 Frank A. Pitelka and M. D. Bryant, "Available Skeletons of the Passenger Pigeon," *Condor,* XLIV (1942), 74–75.

4 John T. Zimmer, "Skeletons of the Passenger Pigeon," *Auk,* LIX (1942), 459.

5 Edward O. Dodson, "An Additional Available Passenger Pigeon Skeleton," *Condor,* LII (1950), 39–40.

6 F. A. Pitelka and M. D. Bryant in *Condor,* XLIV (1942), 74–75.

7 William Macgillivray quoted in J. J. Audubon, *Ornithol. Biog.,* V (1839), 553.

8 Robert W. Shufeldt, "Anatomical and Other Notes on the Passenger Pigeon (*Ectopistes migratorius*) Lately Living in the Cincinnati Zoölogical Gardens," *Auk,* XXXII (1915), 29–41.

9 T. Jeffrey Parker, *A Course of Instruction in Zoötomy* (London, 1893), pp. 182–261.

10 Elliott Coues, *Key to North American Birds* (4th ed.; Boston, 1894).

11 G. Gulliver, "Observations on the Blood Corpuscles of the Snowy Owl and Passenger Pigeon," *Proc. Zool. Soc. London,* 1839, pp. 43–44.

12 Francesco Romano-Prestia, "Alcune ricerche citologiche sul nevrasse del colombo," *Boll. Soc. Natur. Napoli,* XIX (1906), 248 and 273.

13 J. J. Audubon, *Ornithol. Biog.,* I (1831), 320.

14 E. Sterling, "Passenger Pigeons and Rice," *Rod and Gun and Am. Sportsman,* VII (Jan. 29, 1876), 277.

15 A. W. Schorger, "Unpublished Manuscripts by Cotton Mather on the Passenger Pigeon," *Auk,* LV (1938), 474. See also Frederic T. Lewis, "The Passenger Pigeon as Observed by the Rev. Cotton Mather" and "Cotton Mather's Manuscript References to the Passenger Pigeon," *Auk,* LXI (1944), 587–92, and LXII (1945), 306–7.

16 Cotton Mather, *The Christian Philosopher: A Collection of the Best Discoveries in Nature with Religious Improvements* (London, 1721), p. 192.

17 Georg Litwer, "Die histologischen Veränderungen der Kropfwandung bei

Tauben, zur Zeit der Bebrütung und Ausfütterung ihrer Jungen," *Z. Zellforsch. und mikroskop. Anat.,* III (1926), 695–722.

18 John Hunter, *Observations on Certain Parts of the Animal Economy* (London, 1786), p. 193.

19 Robert Fulton, *The Illustrated Book of Pigeons* (London, Paris, and N. Y., ca. 1876), p. 39.

20 M. D. Patel, "The Physiology of the Formation of 'Pigeon's Milk,'" *Physiol. Zoöl.,* IX (1936), 143.

21 Georg Litwer in *Z. Zellforsch. und mikroskop. Anat.,* III (1926), 695–722; H. W. Beams and R. K. Meyer, "The Formation of 'Pigeon's Milk,'" *Anatomical Record,* XLI (1928), 70, and "The Formation of Pigeon 'Milk,'" *Physiol. Zoöl.,* IV (1931), 486–500; M. D. Patel in *Physiol. Zoöl.,* IX (1936), 129–52.

22 Oscar Riddle and P. F. Braucher, "Control of the Special Secretion of the Crop-Gland in Pigeons by an Anterior Pituitary Hormone," *Am. J. Physiol.* XCVII (1931), 617–25; Oscar Riddle and S. W. Dykshorn, "Secretion of Crop-Milk in the Castrate Male Pigeon," *Proc. Soc. Exp. Biol. Med.,* XXIX (1932), 1213–15.

23 Oscar Riddle, "Prolactin," *Sci. Monthly,* XLVII (1938), 97–113.

24 Oscar Riddle, R. W. Bates, and S. W. Dykshorn, "The Preparation, Identification and Assay of Prolactin—a Hormone of the Anterior Pituitary," *Am. J. Physiol.,* CV (1933), 191–216.

25 M. D. Patel in *Physiol. Zoöl.,* IX (1936), 129–52.

26 Oscar Riddle in *Sci. Monthly,* XLVII (1938), 97–113.

27 D. W. Mitchell, "Notice of a Hybrid Crowned-Pigeon Hatched in the Menagerie," *Proc. Zool. Soc. London,* 1849, pp. 171–72.

28 Christian Ludwig Brehm, *Der völlstandige Vogelfang* (Weimar, 1844), p. 258, and *Verzeichniss des europäischen Vögel nach den Species und Subspecies* (Naumannia, 1855), V, 286; Thommaso Salvadori, *Catalogue of the Columbæ, or Pigeons, in the Collection of the British Museum* (London, 1893), p. 370.

29 T. Salvadori, *Catalogue of Columbæ in British Museum,* p. 414; *Posthumous Works of C. O. Whitman,* II, 189.

30 Alfred Newton and Hans Gadow, *A Dictionary of Birds* (London, 1896), p. 165.

31 James Lee Peters, *Check-List of Birds of the World* (Cambridge, Mass., 1937), III, 92.

32 Charles Darwin, *The Variation of Animals and Plants under Domestication* (N. Y., 1896), I, 203.

33 Michael F. Guyer, *Spermatogenesis of Normal and of Hybrid Pigeons* (Bull. Univ. Cincinnati, No. 22; Cincinnati, Ohio, 1902), p. 43.

34 *Posthumous Works of C. O. Whitman*, II, 5.

35 *Ibid.*, p. 210

36 E. S. Starr, "Doves," *Century Illustrated Monthly Mag.*, O. S., XXXVI (1888), 703.

37 W. Craig in *Auk*, XXVIII (1911), 418.

38 *Posthumous Works of C. O. Whitman*, III, 112.

39 Craig quoted *ibid.*

40 I. Bickerton Williams, "The Color of Certain Birds, in Relation to Inheritance," *Auk*, XVI (1899), 320.

41 Craig quoted in *Posthumous Works of C. O. Whitman*, III, 118–19.

CHAPTER 12

1 James Lee Peters, *Check-List of Birds of the World* (Cambridge, Mass., 1937), III, 11–141.

2 M. Catesby, *Natural History of Carolina*, I, 23.

3 Johann L. Frisch, *Vorstellung der Vögel in Teutschland* (Berlin, 1733–63), Vol. I, Table 142.

4 Jacob T. Klein, *Historiae avium prodromus* . . . (Lübeck, 1750), p. 119; George Edwards, *A Natural History of Uncommon Birds* (London, 1743), Part I, p. 15.

5 William Douglass, *A Summary, Historical and Political, of the First Planting, Progressive Improvements, and Present State of the British Settlements in North America* . . . (Boston, 1755), II, 217.

6 Carolus Linnaeus, *Systema naturae* (10th ed.; Holmiae, 1758), p. 164.

7 George Edwards, *A Natural History of Uncommon Birds*, Part I, p. 15.

8 Pehr Kalm, "Beskrifning på de vilda dufor, som somliga år i så otrolig stor myckenhet komma til de södra Engelska nybyggen i Norra America," *Kong. Svenska Vetenskapsakadimien Handlingar*, XX (1759), 275–95; and his "A Description of the Wild Pigeons Which Visit the Southern English Colonies in North America, during Certain Years, in Incredible Multitudes," *Auk*, XXVIII (1911), 53–66.

9 Pehr Kalm, *En resa til Norra America* (Stockholm, 1761), III, 39; and J. R. Forster's abridged English edition, *Travels into North America* (London, 1772), I, 374.

10 Mathurin J. Brisson, *Ornithologie* (Paris, 1760), I, 100.

11 *Ibid.*, p. 118; see also James Francis Stephens, *Shaw's General Zoology* (London, 1819), XI, 93–96.

12 C. J. Temminck, *Histoire naturelle générale des pigeons et des gallinacés* Amsterdam, 1813), I, 351; Louis J. P. Vieillot, *Nouveau Dictionnaire d'histoire naturelle* (2nd ed.; Paris, 1818), XXVI, 377.

13 Carolus Linnaeus, *Systema naturae* (12th ed.; Holmiae, 1766), I, 284–85.

14   Elliott Coues, "Notes and Queries concerning the Nomenclature of North American Birds," *Nuttall Bull.,* V (1880), 99–100; Harry C. Oberholser, "The Scientific Name of the Passenger Pigeon," *Science,* N. S., XLVIII (1918), 445, and "The Bird Life of Louisiana," *Bull. La. Dept. Conservation,* No. 28, p. 321.

15   Carl E. Hellmayr and Boardman Conover, *Catalogue of Birds of the Americas* (Field Museum Zool. Ser., Vol. XIII; Chicago, 1942), Part I, No. I, pp. 475–76.

16   Georges L. L. Buffon, *Histoire naturella des oiseaux,* III (Paris, 1774), 46.

17   Carolus Linnaeus, *Des Ritters Carl von Linné . . . vollständigen Natursystems . . .* (ed. Philipp L. S. Müller; Nürnberg, 1776), Supplement, p. 134; Carolus Linnaeus, *Systema naturae* (ed. Johann F. Gmelin; Leipzig, 1788–93), Vol. I, Part II, p. 785.

18   John Latham, *A General Synopsis of Birds* (London, *ca.* 1783), Vol. II, Part II, pp. 658 and 661; *Index ornithologicus, sive systema ornithologiae* (London, 1790), II, 612–13.

19   C. J. Temminck, *Histoire naturelle générale des pigeons et des gallinacés,* I, 346–54.

20   William Swainson, "On Several Groups and Forms in Ornithology, Not Hitherto Defined," *Zool. J.,* III (1828), 362.

21   Alexander Sprunt, Jr., and E. B. Chamberlain, *South Carolina Bird Life* (Columbia, S. C., 1949), pp. 289–90.

22   John Richardson and W. Swainson, *Fauna Boreali-Americana; or the Zoology of the Northern Parts of British America* (London, 1829–37), Part II (1831), pp. 363–65.

23   George R. Gray, *The Genera of Birds* (London, 1844), II, 471.

24   J. L. Peters, *Check-List of Birds of the World,* III, 82-83.

25   Elliott Coues, "Field-Notes on Birds Observed in Dakota and Montana along the Forty-Ninth Parallel during the Seasons of 1873 and 1874," *Bull. U. S. Geol. Geog. Survey Territories,* IV (1878), 628; and his article in *Nuttall Bull.,* V (1880), 99–100.

26   Outram Bangs, "The Names of the Passenger Pigeon and the Mourning Dove," *Proc. Biol. Soc. Wash.,* XIX (1906), 43–44.

27   Joel A. Allen, "New Names for North American Birds," *Auk,* XXIII (1906), 474–75; J. L. Peters, *Check-List of Birds of the World,* III, 82–83.

28   F. Hemming, "Proposed Use of the Plenary Powers to Secure that the Name 'Columba migratoria' Linnaeus, 1766, Shall Be the Oldest Available Name for the Passenger Pigeon, the Type Species of the Genus 'Ectopistes' Swainson, 1827," *Bull. Zool. Nomenclature,* IX (1952), 80–84.

29   Christian Ludwig Brehm, *Handbuch der Naturgeschichte aller Vögel Deutschlands* (Ilmenau, 1831), p. 495.

30   Christian Ludwig Brehm, *Der völlstandige Vogelfang* (Weimar, 1855),

p. 258, and *Verzeichniss der europäischen Vögel nach den Species und Subspecies* (Naumannia, 1855), V, 286; Thommaso Salvadori, *Catalogue of the Columbæ, or Pigeons, in the Collection of the British Museum* (London, 1893), p. 370.

31 Hermann Schlegel, *De Dierentuin van het koninklijk zoologisch Genootschap, Natura Artis Magistra* (Amsterdam, 1872), p. 205, and "Rijksmuseum van naturlijke Historie," *Revue méthodique et critique des collections* (Leyden, Muséum d'histoire naturelle des Pays-Bas), IV (1873), 142–43.

32 P. J. E. Mauduyt, "Historie naturelle. Oiseaux," *Encyclopédie méthodique* (Paris and Liège, 1784), II, 369; L. J. P. Vieillot, *Nouveau Dictionnaire d'histoire naturelle* (2nd ed.; Paris, 1818), XXVI, 373.

33 Charles L. Bonaparte, *A Geographical and Comparative List of the Birds of Europe and North America* (London, 1838), p. 41; J. J. Audubon, *Ornithol. Biog.*, IV (1838), 526; Titian R. Peale, *United States Exploring Expedition .... Under the Command of Charles Wilkes* (Phila., 1858), VIII, 278; S. W. Woodhouse, "Description of a New Species of Ectopistes," *Proc. Acad. Nat. Sci. Phila.*, VI (1852), 104–5.

34 E. Billings, "On the Pigeon (*Ectopistes migratoria*)," *Can. Naturalist Geol.*, I (1856), 168–76.

35 Elliott Coues, *Key to North American Birds* (5th ed.; Boston, 1903), II, 711.

36 John Frost, "Game Birds of America," *Graham's Mag.*, XXXII (1848), 185–86.

37 A. W. Schorger, "Unpublished Manuscripts by Cotton Mather on the Passenger Pigeon," *Auk*, LV (1938), 474.

38 Roger Williams, *A Key into the Language of America* (Coll. Rhode Island Hist. Soc., Vol. I; Providence, R. I., 1827), p. 87.

39 A. Lewis, *The History of Lynn* (Boston, 1829), p. 22.

40 Silas T. Rand, *Dictionary of the Language of the Micmac Indians* (Halifax, 1888), p. 196.

CHAPTER 13

1 American Ornithologists' Union, *Check-List of North American Birds* (4th ed.; Lancaster, Penn., 1931), p. 154.

2 John Bartram, "Diary of a Journey through the Carolinas, Georgia, and Florida from July 1, 1765, to April 10, 1766" (ed. Francis Harper), *Trans. Am. Phil. Soc.*, Vol. XXXIII (1942), Part I, p. 45; A. W. Schorger, "John Bartram on the Passenger Pigeon in Florida," *Auk*, LXII (1945), 452.

3 Frank M. Chapman, "A List of Birds Observed at Gainesville, Florida," *Auk*, V (1888), 270; T. Gilbert Pearson in *Abstracts Proc. Linnæan Soc. N. Y.*, No. 5 (1893), p. 5.

4 "John Williams" (C. J. Pennock), "Notes on Birds of Wakulla County, Florida," *Wilson Bull.*, XXXII (1920), 7.

5   M. Lewis and W. Clark, *Original Journals of the Lewis and Clark Expedition 1804–1806* (ed. R. G. Thwaites; N. Y., 1904–5), III, 44.

6   J. C. Merrill, "Notes on the Birds of Fort Sherman, Idaho," *Auk,* XIV (1897), 349; M. Dale Arvey, "A Check-List of the Birds of Idaho," *Pub. Univ. Kansas Museum Nat. Hist.,* I (1947), 202; James G. Cooper, "The Fauna of Montana Territory," *Am. Naturalist,* III (1869), 80.

7   Nathaniel S. Goss, *History of the Birds of Kansas* (Topeka, Kans., 1891), pp. 237–40.

8   James G. Cooper and G. Suckley, *The Natural History of Washington Territory*...(N. Y., 1859), p. 218. This region of Montana is referred to as "Nebraska."

9   M. Lewis and W. Clark, *Original Journals of Lewis and Clark Expedition,* V, 200.

10 Patrick Gass, *Journal of the Voyages and Travels*...*of Captain Lewis and Captain Clarke*...(London, 1808), p. 153.

11 M. Lewis and W. Clark, *Original Journals of Lewis and Clark Expedition,* II, 227.

12 Spencer F. Baird, *Birds,* Vol. IX (U. S. War Dept.; Wash., 1858) of *Reports of Explorations and Surveys to Ascertain the Most Practicable and Economical Route for a Railroad from the Mississippi River to the Pacific Ocean,* p. 600. This is a part of Senate Exec. Doc. No. 78, 33rd Congress, 2nd Session.

13 F. V. Hayden, "On the Geology and Natural History of the Upper Missouri," *Trans. Am. Phil. Soc.,* N. S., XII (1863), 171.

14 M. Lewis and W. Clark, *Original Journals of Lewis and Clark Expedition,* VI, 221.

15 James G. Cooper in *Am. Naturalist,* III (1869), 80.

16 Elliott Coues, "Field-Notes on Birds Observed in Dakota and Montana along the Forty-Ninth Parallel during the Seasons of 1873 and 1874," *Bull. U. S. Geol. Geog. Survey Territories,* IV (1878), 628.

17 Aretas A. Saunders, *A Distributional List of the Birds of Montana* (Berkeley, Calif., 1921), p. 171.

18 Elliott Coues in *Bull. U. S. Geol. Geog. Survey Territories,* IV (1878), 628.

19 Elliott Coues, *Birds of the Northwest* (U. S. Geol. Geog. Survey Territories, Misc. Pub. No. 3; Wash., 1874), p. 388.

20 Robert Ridgway, "The Birds of Colorado," *Bull. Essex Inst.,* V (1873), 178, and his "Ornithology," *U. S. Geological Exploration of the Fortieth Parallel,* Vol. IV (1877), Part III, p. 596; Jean M. Linsdale, *The Birds of Nevada* (Berkeley, Calif., 1936), p. 61.

21 William Ludlow, *Report of a Reconnaissance of the Black Hills of Dakota in the Summer of 1874* (Wash., 1875), p. 98.

22   Elliott Coues in *Bull. U. S. Geol. Geog. Survey Territories,* IV (1878), 628.

23   W. P. Thomas in New York *Sun,* June 14, 1881, and in *Chicago Field,* XV (1881), 314; W. W. Judy, "Wild Pigeons for the Tournaments," *Chicago Field,* XV (1881), 168.

24   John K. Townsend, *Narrative of a Journey across the Rocky Mountains to the Columbia River* (Phila., 1839), p. 335, and "List of the Birds Inhabiting the Region of the Rocky Mountains, the Territory of Oregon, and the North West Coast of America," *J. Acad. Nat. Sci. Phila.,* VIII (1839), 155.

25   James G. Cooper, "Note on Pacific Coast Birds," *Auk,* VII (1890), 216; "The Fauna of Montana Territory" and "Notes on the Fauna of the Upper Missouri," *Am. Naturalist,* III(1869), 80 and 295.

26   Samuel N. Rhoads, "The Wild Pigeon (*Ectopistes migratorius*) on the Pacific Coast," *Auk,* VIII (1891), 310–12.

27   John K. Lord, "List of Birds Collected by J. K. Lord, F. Z. S., and Presented by the British North American Boundary Commission to the Royal Artillery Institution," *Proc. Roy. Artillery Inst.* (Woolwich), IV (1865), 122.

28   W. J. Hoffman, "List of Birds Observed at Grand River Agency, Dakota Ter. from October 7th, 1872, to June 7th, 1873," *Proc. Boston Soc. Nat. Hist.,* XVIII (1877), 174.

29   J. D. Ayers in *Forest and Stream,* LXIX (1907), 772.

30   Wells W. Cooke, *Report on Bird Migration in the Mississippi Valley in the Years 1884 and 1885* (U. S. Dept. Agr., Div. Econ. Ornithol., Bull. No. 2; Wash., 1888), p. 108.

31   William Lloyd, "Birds of Tom Green and Concho Counties, Texas," *Auk,* IV (1887), 187.

32   James G. Cooper and G. Suckley, *Natural History of Washington Territory,* p. 218; and James G. Cooper, "Land Birds," Chapter I of Report No. 3, Part III, in Vol. XII (U. S. War Dept.; Wash., 1860) of *Reports of Explorations and Surveys to Ascertain the Most Practicable and Economical Route for a Railroad from the Mississippi River to the Pacific Ocean,* p. 218 (this being a part of a Senate Exec. Doc. for the 36th Congress, 1st Session).

33   Spencer F. Baird, "Ornithology," Appendix K of *Report of Explorations across the Great Basin of the Territory of Utah . . . in 1859* (Wash., 1876) by J. H. Simpson, p. 380; Wilbur C. Knight, *The Birds of Wyoming* (Univ. Wyoming, Agr. College Dept., Wyo. Experiment Station Bull. No. 55; Laramie, Wyo., 1902), p. 57.

34   Viscount Milton (William Fitzwilliam) and W. B. Cheadle, *The North-West Passage by Land* (4th ed.; London, ca. 1865), p. 208.

35   James Carnegie, Earl of Southesk, *Saskatchewan and the Rocky Mountains . . . in 1859 and 1860* (Edinburgh, 1875), p. 171; Wells W. Cooke, "Passenger Pigeon (*Ectopistes migratorius*) in Alberta," *Auk,* XXIX (1912), 539.

36   John Ross, *Narrative of a Second Voyage in Search of a Northwest Passage*
...(London, 1835), II: *Appendix,* xxix; George Back, *Narrative of the
Arctic Land Expedition to the Mouth of the Great Fish River, and along
the Shores of the Arctic Ocean, in the Years 1833, 1834, and 1835* (London,
1836), p. 508.

37   John Richardson, "Report on North American Zoology," *Rept. 6th Meeting
Brit. Assoc. Advancement Sci.,* V (1836), 180.

38   Viscount Milton (William Fitzwilliam) and W. B. Cheadle, *The North-
West Passage by Land,* p. 208; Theed Pearse, "A Record of the Passenger
Pigeon in British Columbia," *Auk,* LIII (1936), 446.

39   J. A. Munro and I. McT. Cowan, "A Review of the Bird Fauna of British
Columbia," *Special Pub. B. C. Prov. Museum,* No. 2 (1947), p. 239.

40   John K. Lord, *The Naturalist in British Columbia* (London, 1866), II, 298.

41   Allan Brooks and Harry S. Swarth, "A Distributional List of the Birds of
British Columbia," *Pacific Coast Avifauna,* No. 17 (1925), p. 53.

42   H. Whitely, *Catalogue of North American Birds and Eggs...in the Museum of the Royal Artillery Institution, Woolwich* (Woolwich: Roy. Art.
Inst., 1865), p. 15.

43   Thommaso Salvadori, *Catalogue of the Columbæ, or Pigeons, in the Collection of the British Museum* (London, 1893), pp. 369–71.

44   Allen J. Duvall, "An Early Record of the Passenger Pigeon for British
Columbia," *Auk,* LXIII (1946), 598.

45   Robert Ridgway, *Birds of North and Middle America* (Wash., 1916), Part
VII, p. 336.

46   George Cartwright, *Captain Cartwright and His Laborador Journal* (ed.
C. W. Townsend; Boston, 1911), p. 180.

47   Charles W. Townsend and Glover M. Allen, "Birds of Laborador," *Proc.
Boston Soc. Nat. Hist.,* XXXIII (1907), 363–64.

48   *Ibid.*

49   Alexander Mackenzie, *Voyages from Montreal...to the Frozen and Pacific
Oceans; in the Years 1789 and 1793* (London, 1801), p. 81.

50   Thomas Simpson, *Narrative of the Discoveries of the North Coast of America; Effected by the Officers of the Hudson's Bay Company during the Years
1836–39* (London, 1843), p. 93.

51   B. R. Ross, "List of Species of Mammals and Birds—Collected in McKenzie's
River District during 1860–61" and "List of Mammals, Birds, and Eggs,
Observed in the McKenzie's River District, with Notices" *Can. Naturalist
Geol.,* VI (1861), 443, and VII (1862), 148.

52   B. R. Ross, *ibid.,* VI (1861), 443.

53   Alexander Henry, *New Light on the Early History of the Greater Northwest: The Manuscript Journals of Alexander Henry and of David Thompson*
(ed. E. Coues; N. Y., 1897), II, 467 and 469.

54 John Franklin, *Narrative of a Journey to the Shores of the Polar Sea, in the Years 1819, 20, 21, and 22* (London, 1823), p. 186.

55 Samuel Hearne, *A Journey from Prince of Wales's Fort in Hudson's Bay to the Northern Ocean* ... (London, 1795), pp. 417–18.

56 Robert Bell, "Report on Explorations of the Churchill and Nelson Rivers, and around God's and Island Lakes," Part C, Appendix VI, of *Rep. Progress Geol. Survey Canada,* 1878–79, p. 70; W. Eagle Clarke, "On a Collection of Birds from Fort Churchill, Hudson's Bay," *Auk,* VII (1890), 322.

57 T. Huchins (1782 MS) cited in Ernest T. Seton, "The Birds of Manitoba," *Proc. U. S. Nat. Museum,* XIII (1891), 522.

58 Robert Bell in *Rep. Progress Geol. Survey Canada,* 1878–79, Part C, Appendix VI, p. 70.

59 John Richardson and W. Swainson, *Fauna Boreali-Americana; or the Zoology of the Northern Parts of British America* (London, 1829–37), Part II, (1831), pp. 363–65.

60 Henry Reeks, "Notes on the Birds of Newfoundland," *Can. Naturalist Geol.,* N. S., V (1870), 159; Alexander Murray, "Newfoundland—Its Beasts, Birds, and Fishes," *Forest and Stream,* II (1874), 232; Harold S. Peters and Thomas D. Burleigh, *The Birds of Newfoundland* (Boston, 1951), p. 404.

61 Sir George Peckham, "A True Report of the Late Discoveries, and Possession Taken in the Right of the Crowne of England, of the Newfound Lands," in Richard Hakluyt, *The Principal Navigation Voyages Traffiques & Discoveries of the English Nation* (Glasgow and N. Y., 1903–5), Extra Ser., VIII, 115.

62 T. Hutchins cited in the article of Ernest T. Seton in *Proc. U. S. Nat. Museum,* XIII (1891), 522.

63 John R. Forster, "An Account of the Birds Sent from Hudson's Bay; with Observations Relative to Their Natural History; and Latin Descriptions of Some of the Most Uncommon," *Phil. Trans.,* LXII (1772), 398.

64 George Barnston, "Observations on the Progress of the Seasons ... at Martin's Falls, Albany River, Hudson's Bay," *Edinburgh New Phil. J.,* XXX 1841), 255.

65 T. Hutchins cited in E. T. Seton's article in *Proc. U. S. Nat. Museum,* XIII (1891), 522; J. R. Forster in *Phil. Trans.,* LXII (1772), 398.

66 Lucien M. Turner, "List of the Birds of Labrador, including Ungava, East Main, Moose, and Gulf Districts of the Hudson Bay Company, together with the Island of Anticosti," *Proc. U. S. Nat. Museum,* VIII (1885), 245; Alpheus S. Packard, *The Labrador Coast* (N. Y., 1891), pp. 425–26.

67 Jacques Cartier, *Voyage de Jacques Cartier au Canada en 1534* (ed. M. H. Michelant; Paris, 1865), p. 41.

68 A. P. Low, "Report on Explorations in the Labrador Peninsula," Report L,

Appendix II of *Annual Report of the Geological Survey of Canada,* VIII (1895), 325L.

69 J. M. Le Moine, *The Explorations of Jonathan Oldbuck* (Maple Leaves, 5th ser.; Quebec, 1889), p. 211.

70 J. H. Fleming in *Ottawa Naturalist,* XX (1907), 236.

71 C. Hart Merriam, "List of Birds Ascertained to Occur within Ten Miles from Point de Monts, Province of Quebec, Canada; Based Chiefly upon the Notes of Napoleon A. Comeau," *Bull. Nuttall Ornithol. Club,* VII (1882), 238; Napoleon A. Comeau, *Life and Sport on the North Shore of the Lower St. Lawrence and Gulf* (Quebec, 1909), p. 424.

72 A. E. Verrill, "Catalogue of the Birds Observed at Anticosti and Vicinity," *Proc. Boston Soc. Nat. Hist.,* IX (1865), 137.

73 Robert Bell, "Catalogue of Animals and Plants Collected and Observed on the South-East Side of the St. Lawrence from Quebec to Gaspé, and in the Counties of Rimouski, Gaspé and Bonaventure," *Rept. Progress Geol. Survey Canada,* 1858, p. 245; and his "On the Natural History of the St. Lawrence," *Can. Naturalist Geol.,* IV (1859), 203.

74 Nicolas Denys, *The Description and Natural History of the Coasts of North America (Acadia)* (ed. W. F. Ganong; Toronto, 1908), pp. 224–27.

75 Richard King, *Narrative of a Journey to the Shores of the Artic Ocean, in 1833, 1834, and 1835; under the Command of Capt. Back* (London, 1836), II, 220–22.

76 A. R. C. Selwyn, "Notes on a Journey through the Northwest Territory, from Manitoba to Rocky Mountain House," *Can. Naturalist Geol.,* N. S., VII (1875), 200.

77 T. Blakiston, "On Birds Collected and Observed in the Interior of North America," *Ibis.,* 1st ser., V (1863), 121; Eug. Coubeaux, "Contributions to the Natural History of the Northwest," *Ottawa Naturalist,* XIV (1900), 27.

78 Henry Y. Hind, *Narrative of the Canadian Red River Exploring Expedition of 1857 and of the Assinniboine and Saskatchewan Exploring Expedition of 1858* (London, 1860), I, 378; James Carnegie, Earl of Southesk, *Saskatchewan and the Rocky Mountains,* p. 58.

79 George E. Atkinson, *A Review-History of the Passenger Pigeon of Manitoba* (Trans. Hist. Sci. Soc. Manitoba, No. 68; Winnipeg, 1905), p. 7.

80 James Mease, *A Geological Account of the United States* (Phila., 1807), p. 347.

81 J. W. Wedderburn quoted in William Jardine, "Ornithology of the Bermudas," *Contributions to Ornithol.,* II (1849), 87; John R. Willis, "List of Birds of Bermuda, by Lieut. Bland, R. E.," *Ann. Rept. Smithsonian Inst.,* 1858, p. 289.

82 J. L. Hurdis quoted in William Jardine, "Ornithology of the Bermudas,"

Contributions to Ornithol., III (1850), 37; in John M. Jones, *The Naturalist in Bermuda* (London, 1859), p. 55; and in Eduard von Martens, "Die Vögel der Bermuda-Inseln, nach Wedderburn und Hurdis," *J. Ornithol.*, VII (1859), 216.

83 Savile G. Reid, "Birds," Vol. I, Part IV of *Contributions to the Natural History of the Bermudas* (ed. J. M. Jones and G. B. Goode; Bull. U. S. Nat. Museum, No. 25; Wash., 1884), p. 224; T. S. Bradlee, L. L. Mowbray, and W. F. Eaton, "A List of the Birds Recorded from the Bermudas," *Proc. Boston Soc. Nat. Hist.*, XXXIX (1931), 326.

84 Johannes C. Gundlach, "Tabellarische Uebersicht aller bisher auf Cuba beobachteten Vögel," *J. Ornithol.*, IX (1861), 336; Charles B. Cory, "The Birds of the West Indies," *Auk*, IV (1887), 113, and *The Birds of the West Indies* (Boston, 1889), p. 214.

85 Thomas Barbour, *The Birds of Cuba* (Cambridge, Mass., 1923), p. 77; A. C. Bent, *Life Histories of N. Am. Gallinaceous Birds*, p. 401.

86 Johannes C. Gundlach, "Beiträge zur Ornithologie Cuba's," *J. Ornithol.*, IV (1856), 112; "Revista y catalogo de las aves Cubanas," *Repertorio fisico-natural de la isla de Cuba*, I (1866), 302; and "Neue Beiträge zur Ornithologie Cubas," *J. Ornithol.*, XXII (1874), 300.

87 O. Salvin and F. D. Godman, "Biologia Centrali-Americana," *Aves* (London), III (*ca.* 1902), 240–41.

88 Alfonso L. Herrera, "Apuntes de ornithologia, la migration en el Valle de Mexico," *La Naturaleza*, 2nd ser., I (1891), 185.

89 Jesus Sanchez and Manual M. Villada, "Palomas viajeras," *ibid.*, 1st ser., II (1873), 253.

90 Antonio del Castillo, "Noticia sobre estas palomas, por el Sr. Antonio del Castillo," *ibid.*, pp. 254–55.

91 Jesus Sanchez, "Datos para el catálogo de las aves qui viven en México," *Ann. Museo Nacional* (Mexico), I (1877), 104.

92 Come D. Degland, *Ornithologie européenne* (Paris, 1849), II, 12.

93 J. J. Dalgleish, "List of Occurrences of North American Birds in Europe," *Nuttall Bull.*, V (1880), 144.

94 Charles Robert Bree, *A History of the Birds of Europe* . . . (London, 1859–63), I (1859), 182.

95 William Thompson, *The Natural History of Ireland* (London, 1850–51), II (1850), 18; Howard Saunders, *An Illustrated Manual of British Birds* (2nd ed.; London, 1899), p. 487.

96 E. S. Dixon, *The Dovecote and the Aviary* (London, 1851), p. 217.

97 J. J. Audubon, *Ornithol. Biog.*, I (1831), 326, and V (1839), 552–53.

98 Philip L. Sclater, "The Passenger Pigeon," *Ibis*, 9th ser., VI (1912), 217–18.

99 William Yarrell, *A History of British Birds* (3rd ed.; London, 1856), II, 316.

100 James E. Harting, "Passenger Pigeon in Yorkshire," *Zoologist*, 3rd ser., I (1877), 180.

101 J. J. Dalgleish in *Nuttall Bull.*, V. (1880), 144; Percy E. Freke, "North-American Birds Crossing the Atlantic," *Sci. Proc. Roy. Dublin Soc.*, III (1881), 6; William Yarrell, *A History of British Birds* (4th ed.; rev. A. Newton and H. Saunders; London, 1882–84), III, 26–30; Howard Saunders, *An Illustrated Manual of British Birds*, p. 487; H. F. Witherby et al., *The Handbook of British Birds* (London, 1948), IV, 146.

102 H. Blanc's brochure, *Le Musée zoologique de Lausanne*, cited by A. Menegaux in *Rev. franç. d'ornithol.*, II (1912), 426.

103 Pehr Kalm in *Auk*, XXVIII (1911), 66.

104 Henry Seebohm, *A History of British Birds* (London, 1896), II, 414–15.

105 Henri Gadeau de Kerville, *Fauna de la Normandie* (Paris, 1887–97), III, 217; Louis-Marcellin Bureau, "Sur la Capture en France d'un pigeon migrateur d'Amerique *Ectopistes migratorius* (Lin.)," *Bull. soc. nat. d'acclimatation de France*, LVIII (1911), 353–56.

106 H. W. Shoemaker quoted in J. C. French, *Passenger Pigeon*, p. 176.

107 William Thompson, *Natural History of Ireland*, III, 443.

108 Edmond de Selys-Longchamps, "Sur les Oiseaux americains, admis dans la fauna européenne," *Mem. Soc. Roy. Sci. Liege*, IV (1846), 7; Come D. Degland, *Ornithologie européenne* (Paris, 1849), II, 12; Come D. Degland and Z. Gerbe, *Ornithologie européenne* (2nd ed.; Paris, 1867), II, 12; Jean C. L. T. d'Hamonville, *Catalogue des oiseaux d'Europe*... (Paris, 1876), p. 42.

109 John Fleming, *A History of British Animals* (Edinburgh, 1828), p. 145; George Montagu, *Ornithological Dictionary of British Birds* (London, 1831), p. 357; Leonard Jenyns, *A Manual of British Vertebrate Animals* (London, 1835), pp. 163–64; T. C. Eyton, *A History of the Rarer British Birds* (London, 1836), pp. 30–32.

110 William Macgillivray, *A History of British Birds* (London, 1837), I, 294; Alfred Newton and Hans Gadow, *A Dictionary of Birds* (London, 1896), pp. 696–97.

111 Alexander F. von Keyserling and J. H. Blasius, *Die Wirbelthiere Europa's* (Braunschweig, 1840), p. lxii.

112 William P. Turnbull, *The Birds of East Lothian, and a Portion of the Adjoining Counties* (Glasgow, 1867), p. 41.

113 S. W. Wilson quoted in H. B. Bailey, "Memoranda of a Collection of Eggs from Georgia," *Nuttall Bull.*, VIII (1883), 41.

114 Nathaniel S. Goss, *History of the Birds of Kansas*, pp. 237–40.

115 Alexander Wilson, *Am. Ornithology*, V, 111.

116 G. Lincecum in *Am. Sportsman*, IV (June 27, 1874), 194–95.

117 James G. Cooper in *Am. Naturalist*, III (1870), 295.

118 Charles C. Abbott, "Birds," in George H. Cook, *Geology of New Jersey* (Newark, N. J., 1868), p. 783.

119 Samuel Smith, *The History of the Colony of Nova-Caesaria, or New Jersey* (Trenton, N. J., 1890), p. 511.

120 Arthur T. Wayne, "A Contribution to the Ornithology of South Carolina, Chiefly the Coastal Region," *Auk*, XXIII (1906), 61.

121 Elliott Coues, *Birds of the Northwest*, p. 388; and in *Bull. U. S. Geol. Geog. Survey Territories*, IV (1878), 628.

122 James G. Cooper in *Am. Naturalist*, III (1869), 80.

123 Editor, "Wild Pigeons," *Forest and Stream*, XVI (1881), 249.

124 W. P. Thomas in New York *Sun*, June 14, 1881, and same article in *Chicago Field*, XV (1881), 314.

125 W. W. Judy, "Wild Pigeons for the Tournaments" and "The Atoka Nesting" in *Chicago Field*, XV (1881), 168 and 233.

126 G. S. Agersborg, "The Birds of Southeastern Dakota," *Auk*, II (1885), 285.

127 James G. Cooper in *Am. Naturalist*, III (1869), 80.

128 Samuel N. Rhoads, "Contributions of the Zoology of Tennessee," *Proc. Acad. Nat. Sci. Phila.*, 1895, pp. 475–76.

129 Maurice Brooks, *A Check-List of West Virginia Birds* (Univ. W. Va., College Agr., Forestry, Home Econ., Agr. Exp. Sta., Bull. No. 316; Morgantown, W. Va., 1944), p. 25.

130 John Macoun and James H. Macoun, *Catalogue of Canadian Birds* (Ottawa, 1909), p. 236.

131 Ernest E. Thompson, "The Birds of Manitoba," *Proc. U. S. Nat. Museum*, XIII (1891), 522–23.

132 Harold Herrick, "A Partial Catalogue of the Birds of Grand Menan, New Brunswick," *Bull. Essex Inst.*, V (1873), 36.

133 Charles F. Batchelder, "Notes on the Summer Birds of the Upper St. John," *Nuttall Bull.*, VII (1882), 151.

134 Andrew Downs, "A Catalogue of the Birds of Nova Scotia," *Proc. Trans. Nova Scotian Inst. Nat. Sci.*, VII (1890), 157.

135 W. J. McLean quoted in George E. Atkinson, *A Review-History of the Passenger Pigeon of Manitoba*, p. 7.

136 M. H. Mitchell, *Passenger Pigeon*, p. 38.

137 "Dogwhip," "Three Days at a Pigeon Rookery," *Am. Sportsman*, IV (July 25, 1874), 263.

138 Hutchins quoted in the article of E. E. Thompson in *Proc. U. S. Nat. Museum*, XIII (1891), 522–23.

139 John Macoun, *Catalogue of Canadian Birds* (Ottawa, 1900–4), Part I, pp. 215–17.

140 M. H. Mitchell, *Passenger Pigeon*, p. 28.

141 Pehr Kalm in *Auk*, XXVIII (1911), 60.

142   Hugh Gray, *Letters from Canada Written during a Residence There in the Years 1806, 1807, and 1808* (London, 1809), pp. 245–46.

CHAPTER 14

1   Anne Grant, *Memoirs of an American Lady* (N. Y., 1846), pp. 42–43.

2   James Macauley, *The Natural, Statistical and Civil History of the State of New York* (N. Y., 1829), I, 495.

3   C. A. Bryant in *Forest and Stream*, LXXX (1913), 494.

4   "Pericles" (R. M. Gibbs) in *Oologist*, XI (1894), 237–40.

5   Wells W. Cooke, *Report on Bird Migration in the Mississippi Valley in the Years 1884 and 1885* (ed. and rev. C. Hart Merriam; U. S. Dept. Agr., Div. Econ. Ornithol., Bull. No. 2; Wash., 1888), p. 108.

6   *William Byrd's Histories of the Dividing Line betwixt Virginia and North Carolina* (ed. W. K. Boyd; Raleigh, N. C., 1929), p. 216; M. Catesby, *Natural History of Carolina*, I, 23.

7   Wells W. Cooke, *Rept. on Bird Migration in Miss. Valley*, p. 108.

8   American Ornithologists' Union, *Check-List of North American Birds* (4th ed.; Lancaster, Penn., 1931).

9   A. W. Schorger, "The Migration of the Passenger Pigeon in Wisconsin," *Passenger Pigeon*, XIII (1951), 101–4 and 144–46.

10   "Edisto" in *Am. Field*, XX (1883), 509.

11   *The Western Journals of Washington Irving* (ed. J. F. McDermott; Norman, Okla., 1944), pp. 155 and 157.

12   L. W. B. in *Am. Field*, XVI (1881), 266.

13   Arthur H. Howell, *Birds of Arkansas* (U. S. Dept. Agr., Biol. Survey, Bull. No. 38; Wash., 1911), p. 35.

14   "Dardanelle," "Arkansas Notes," *Forest and Stream*, XIV (1880), 232.

15   Note in *Spirit of the Times*, XI (Nov. 20, 1841), 450, previously appearing in the Little Rock *Gazette* (Ark.) of that year.

16   J. H. Sage quoted in C. Hart Merriam, "A Review of the Birds of Connecticut, with Remarks on Their Habits," *Trans. Conn. Acad. Arts Sci.*, IV (1877–82), 93.

17   J. H. Sage, L. B. Bishop, and W. P. Bliss, *The Birds of Connecticut* (Bull. Conn. State Geol. and Nat. Hist. Survey, No. 20; Hartford, Conn., 1913), pp. 69–72.

18   Note cancelled.

19   F. in *Forest and Stream*, XV (1880), 189.

20   Departed by then.—Johann D. Schoepf, *Travels in the Confederation* (trans. and ed. A. J. Morrison; Phila., 1911), I, 378.

21   Elliott Coues and D. Webster Prentiss, *Avifauna Columbiana* (Bull. U. S. Nat. Mus., No. 26; 2nd ed.; Wash., 1883), pp. 90–91.

22 Eugene E. Murphey, *Observations on the Bird Life of the Middle Savannah Valley, 1890–1937* (Contrib. Charleston Museum, Vol. IX; Charleston, S. C., 1937), pp. 22–24.

23 William Bartram, *Travels through North & South Carolina, Georgia, East & West Florida* ... (Phila., 1791), p. 469. Date suggested by Francis Harper.

24 Sometimes arrived in Feb.—E. W. Nelson, "Birds of North-Eastern Illinois," *Bull Essex Inst.*, VIII (1876), 120.

25 Robert Ridgway, "Catalogue of the Birds Ascertained to Occur in Illinois," *Ann. Lyceum Nat. Hist. N. Y.*, X (1874), 382.

26 *Intimate Letters of Carl Schurz* (trans. and ed. Joseph Schafer; Coll. State Hist. Soc. Wis., Vol. XXX; Madison, Wis., 1928), p. 137.

27 Frank M. Woodruff, *The Birds of the Chicago Area* (Chicago, 1907), pp. 86–90; Henry K. Coale in *Auk*, XLII (1925), 137–38.

28 J. B. D. in *Am. Field*, XVII (1882), 162, and XI (1878), 193.

29 A late spring.—Jacques Marquette in *The Jesuit Relations and Allied Documents* (ed. R. G. Thwaites; Cleveland, Ohio, 1896–1901), LIX, 181.

30 E. Duis, *The Good Old Times in McClean County, Illinois* (Bloomington, Ill., 1874), p. 234; Chicago *Daily Journal*, Sept. 3, 1844.

31 Chicago *Daily Journal*, Mar. 12, 1850, and Sept. 7, 1853.

32 *Ibid.*, Mar. 14, 1855. J. O. Dunn, "The Passenger Pigeon in the Upper Mississippi Valley," *Auk*, XII (1895), 389.

33 Chicago *Daily Journal*, Mar. 26, 1856.

34 Chicago *Tribune*, Mar. 5, 1860.

35 Chicago *Daily Journal*, Mar. 7, 1865.

36 "Ten-Bore" in *Forest and Stream*, XVIII (1882), 129.

37 D. A. in *Am. Field*, XVII (1882), 132.

38 "Sangamon," *ibid.*, XXXI (1889), 267.

39 C. W. W., *ibid.*, XVII (1882), 132.

40 J. O. A., *ibid.*, p. 66.

41 Freeport *Journal* (Ill.), April 10 and May 1, 1867; Freeport *Bulletin* (Ill.), Sept. 13, 1866.

42 Freeport *Bulletin*, Mar. 19, 1868.

43 Galena *Gazette and Advertiser* (Ill.), Mar. 17, 1846.

44 B. T. Gault, "The Passenger Pigeon in Aitkin County, Minn., with a Recent Record for Northeastern Illinois," *Auk*, XII (1895), 80.

45 Pierce Brodkorb, "Notes on Some Uncommon Birds in the Chicago Region," *Auk*, XLIV (1927), 260.

46 A. B. W. in *Forest and Stream*, XVIII (1882), 72.

47 Wells W. Cooke, *Rept. on Bird Migration in Miss. Valley*, p. 108.

48 Harry Hunter in *Forest and Stream*, XVIII (1882), 71.

49 L. S. Hansell, "Wild Pigeons in Illinois," *ibid.*, XLVII (1896), 244.

50 Ruthven Deane, "Additional Records of the Passenger Pigeon (*Ectopistes migratorius*) in Wisconsin and Illinois," *Auk*, XIII (1896), 81.

51 W. L. Jones, "March Memoranda," *Forest and Stream*, VI (1876), 338.

52 "Ptarmigan," "Bird Notes from Illinois," *ibid.*, X (1878), 359.

53 Moving south and in Feb. abundant along Kaskaskia River for a few weeks. —W. L. J., "Wild Pigeons," *ibid.*, p. 65.

54 Freeport *Bulletin* (Ill.), Mar. 2, 1882.

55 H. W. Merrill in *Forest and Stream*, VII (1876), 134.

56 B. in *Am. Field*, XX (1883), 319.

57 Jacques Gravier in *Jesuit Relations*, LXV, 109.

58 Christian Schultz, *Travels on an Inland Voyage in the Years 1807 and 1808* (N. Y., 1810), II, 17.

59 Have departed.—T. J. F. in *Forest and Stream*, III (1874), 170.

60 Notice in Platteville *American* (Wis.), Mar. 27, 1846, previously appearing in Quincy *Whig* (Ill.) of that year.

61 "Jack Snipe" in *Am. Field*, XIX (1883), 191.

62 Mabry, "Pigeons in Illinois," *Field*, III (April 3, 1875), 100.

63 C. W. W. in *Am. Field*, XVII (1882), 132.

64 R. H. P., *ibid.*, p. 66.

65 Robert Ridgway, "The Times of Migrating and Nesting of the Birds of the Lower Wabash Valley," *Proc. Boston Soc. Nat. Hist.*, XVI (1874), 318–19.

66 Frank M. Woodruff, *Birds of Chicago Area*, pp. 86–90; E. R. Ford, C. C. Sanborn, and C. B. Coursen, "Birds of the Chicago Region," *Program of Activities Chicago Acad. Sci.*, V (1934), 45.

67 James H. Fleming, "The Disappearance of the Passenger Pigeon," *Ottawa Field Naturalist*, XX (1907), 236.

68 Usually returned in force in Feb. and Mar. and some found dead in severe winters.—A. W. Butler in *22nd Ann. Rept. Indiana Dept. Geol. Nat. Resources*, 1897, pp. 760–64.

69 Rufus Haymond, "Birds of Franklin County, Indiana," *First Ann. Rept. Geol. Survey Indiana*, 1869, p. 226.

70 Waldo L. McAtee, "Ecological Notes on the Birds Occurring within a Radius of Five Miles of the Indiana University Campus," *Proc. Ind. Acad. Sci.*, 1904, p. 174.

71 *Ibid.*

72 Passed over daily from roost at Scottsburg.—Notice signed C. B. W. in *Chicago Field*, XIII (1880), 11.

73 Large roost.—[William N. Blane], *An Excursion through the United States and Canada during the Years 1822–23* (London, 1824), p. 143.

74 C. U. Agen, "Wild Pigeons in Indiana," *Am. Field*, XIX (1883), 299.

75 J. O. Dunn in *Auk*, XII (1895), 389.

76 *Ibid.*

77 P. H. Greenleaf, "Observations on the Flight of the American Passenger Pigeon at Madison, Ind., March, 1855," *Proc. Boston Soc. Nat. Hist.,* V (1856), 181–82.

78 Barton W. Evermann, "Birds of Carroll County, Indiana," *Auk,* V (1888), 349.

79 "Henry Hay's Journal from Detroit to the Miami River," *Proc. Wis. Hist. Soc.,* 1914, p. 258.

80 Quite large flocks in Jan.—Maximilian, Prinz von Wied, *Travels in the Interior of North America* (London, 1843), p. 92, and "Verzeichniss der Vögel, welche auf einer Reise in Nord-America beobachtet wurden," *J. Ornithol.,* VI (1858), 425.

81 Flying over for several months from roost in Scott Co.—W. G. M., "Wild Pigeons," *Forest and Stream,* XIV (1880), 132.

82 Note in Horicon *Argus* (Wis.), March 23, 1855, previously appearing in the Terre Haute *American* (Ind.) of that year.

83 Large roost.—A. W. Butler in *22nd Ann. Rept. Indiana Dept. Geol. Nat. Resources,* 1897, pp. 760–64.

84 Present for a month.—"Wapsiepinicon" in *Am. Field,* XVII (1882), 211.

85 "Journal of Stephan Watts Kearney," *Coll. Mo. Hist. Soc.,* III (1908), 119.

86 Departed by this date.—W. H. S. in *Am. Field,* XVII (1882), 211.

87 Violet S. Williams in *Forest and Stream,* XVIII (1882), 166.

88 Immense numbers for past two weeks.—Manchester *Union,* May 2, 1867.

89 Dubuque *Herald* (Iowa), Feb. 18, 1882.

90 Bond and Ellsworth, "Wild Pigeons Moving North," *Chicago Field,* XV (1881), 217.

91 Keokuk *Dispatch* (Iowa), Mar. 15, 1855; Otto Widmann, *A Preliminary Catalog of the Birds of Missouri* (St. Louis, Mo., 1907), pp. 84–85.

92 Scott in *Am. Field,* XVII (1882), 132; Otto Widmann, *Preliminary Catalog of Birds of Missouri,* pp. 84–85.

93 Otto Widman, *Preliminary Catalog of Birds of Missouri,* pp. 84–85.

94 Nathaniel S. Goss, *History of the Birds of Kansas* (Topeka, Kans., 1891), p. 237.

95 John Bradbury, *Travels in the Interior of North America in the Years 1809, 1810, and 1811* (London, 1819), pp. 52–53.

96 Abundant.—Grand Haven *News* (Mich.), December 20, 1865.

97 Richard Butler, "Journal of General Butler," *The Olden Time,* II (1848), 495.

98 James F. Clarke, *Memorial and Biographical Sketches* (Boston, 1878), pp. 273–76.

99 Louisville *Courier* (Ky.), Jan. 11, 1854.

100 Millions flying northward.—*Ibid.,* Jan. 23, 1858.

101 A great flight southward.—Elizabeth Coombs, "Brief History of the Shaker Colony at South Union, Kentucky," *Filson Club Hist. Quarterly,* XIV (1940), 162.

102 W. Brewster in *Bull. Museum Comparative Zool.,* No. 66 (1925), Part II, p. 308.

103 James C. Mead, "The Last of the Passenger Pigeons Breeding at North Bridgton, Maine," *J. Maine Ornithol. Soc.,* XII (1910), 1–3.

104 A. E. Verrill, "Catalogue of the Birds Found at Norway, Oxford Co., Maine," *Proc. Essex Inst.,* III (1862), 151.

105 Ralph S. Palmer, "Maine Birds," *Bull. Museum Comp. Zool.,* No. 102 (1949), p. 292.

106 Cyrus Eaton, *Annals of the Town of Warren* . . . (Hallowell, Me., 1851), p. 304.

107 Hiner in *Forest and Stream,* IX (1878), 454.

108 "Alleghany," *ibid.,* IV (1875), 106 and 122; P. L. Waller, "Pigeon Shooting in the Alleghanies," *ibid.,* III (1874), 140.

109 "Natax," *ibid.,* XIX (1882), 310.

110 "Chief," "Wild Pigeons," *ibid.,* XI (1878), 224.

111 Cumberland *Daily News* (Md.), Oct. 2, 1872.

112 Editor, "The Wild Pigeon," *Forest and Stream,* XXXIII (1889), 261.

113 Absent only in severest part of winter.—Edward A. Samuels, *Ornithology and Oology of New England* (Boston, 1868), pp. 373–75.

114 Joel A. Allen, "Calendar," *Forest and Stream,* VI (1876), 116; C. J. Maynard, *Birds of Eastern N. Am.* p. 337.

115 E. H. Forbush, *Birds of Mass.,* II, 55. Cotton Mather wrote, "One worthy person of my Acquaintance had a Descent of them in his Neighborhood in the month of December, a very unusual Time of the Year; while there was yett no Snow, but many Acorns, which 'tis thought, might then draw them thither."—A. W. Schorger, "Unpublished Manuscripts by Cotton Mather on the Passenger Pigeon," *Auk,* LV (1938), 474.

116 Glover M. Allen, "An Essex County Ornithologist," *Auk,* XXX (1913), 24.

117 *Ibid.*

118 H. C. Newell, "Wild Pigeons in Massachusetts," *Forest and Stream,* XLVI (1896), 292.

119 Boston *Evening Transcript,* Sept. 9, 1834.

120 Bradford A. Scudder, "Ectopistes migratorius . . . in Bristol Co., Mass.," *Auk,* XV (1898), 333.

121 William Brewster, *The Birds of the Cambridge Region of Massachusetts* (Cambridge, Mass., 1906), p. 178.

122 H. D. Thoreau, *Journal,* VII, 334.

123 C. E. I. (C. E. Ingalls), "Wild Pigeon in Massachusetts," *Forest and Stream,* XXXIII (1889), 243.

124 March 23, new style.—Thomas Dudley, "Letter to the Countess of Lincoln. Boston, March 12, 1631," *Coll. Mass. Hist. Soc.,* VIII (1802), 45.

125 F. C. Browne in *Forest and Stream,* XII (1879), 385.

126 R. L. N[ewcomb], *ibid.,* p. 216.

127 George H. Mackay, "Old Records for Massachusetts and Rhode Island," *Auk,* XXVIII (1911), 119.

128 *The Diary of William Bentley, p.p. Pastor of the East Church. Salem, Massachusetts* (Salem, Mass., 1905–14), II, 39.

129 George H. Mackay, "Old Notes on the Passenger Pigeon (*Ectopistes migratorius*)," *Auk,* XXVIII (1911), 261–62.

130 *Ibid.*

131 W. E. S. in *Forest and Stream,* XI (1878), 213.

132 "Pericles" (R. M. Gibbs) in *Oologist,* XI (1894), 237–40; Adolph B. Covert, "Birds of Lower Michigan," *Forest and Stream,* VI (1876), 402; Robert Morris Gibbs, "Annotated List of the Birds of Michigan," *Bull. U. S. Geol. Geog. Survey Territories,* V (1879), 491.

133 A. B. Covert in *Forest and Stream,* VI (1876), 402.

134 Two feet of snow in woods.—"Peep Sight" in *Chicago Field,* XV (1881), 218.

135 Ruthven Deane in *Auk,* XIII (1896), 81.

136 James H. Fleming, "Recent Records of the Wild Pigeon," *Auk,* XX (1903), 66.

137 Grand Haven *News* (Mich.), March 22, 1865.

138 Chandler R. Gilman, *Life on the Lakes: A Trip to the Pictured Rocks of Lake Superior* (N. Y., 1836), II, 39 and 68.

139 Reverse migration on March 20.—Diaries of Franc B. Daniels, while a student at Grand Rapids, Mich., 1863–66 (MS in possession of Professor Farrington Daniels, Madison, Wis.).

140 *The John Askin Papers* (ed. Milo M. Quaife; Detroit, Mich., 1928), I, 54–55.

141 Stewart E. White, "Birds Observed on Mackinac Island, Michigan, during the Summers of 1889, 1890, and 1891," *Auk,* X (1893), 223.

142 Ralph Ballard, "Passenger Pigeon Recollections," *Jack-Pine Warbler,* XXIV (1946), 135–37.

143 Main flight arrived.—C. A. Bryant in *Forest and Stream,* LXXX (1913), 515.

144 S., *ibid.,* V (1875), 106.

145 S. Kneeland, "On the Birds of Keweenaw Point, Lake Superior," *Proc. Boston Soc. Nat. Hist.,* VI (1859), 237.

146 Alexander Henry, *Travels and Adventures in the Years 1760–1776* (Chicago, 1921), p. 62.

147 Exceptionally mild winter.—Rezarf in *Am. Field*, XVII (1882), 178.

148 J. Claire Wood, "Michigan Randoms," *Auk*, XXII (1905), 217.

149 Average arrival April 7, with March 9, 11, 22, and 24, and April 6, 21, and 24 also given.—T. S. Roberts, *Birds of Minn.*, I, 576. Most have departed by Nov. 1, but a few remain until snow covers the mast.—Philo L. Hatch, *Notes on the Birds of Minnesota* (Minneapolis, Minn., 1892), p. 172.

150 Average was April 5, but arrived as early as March 27.—P. L. Hatch, *Notes on Birds of Minnesota*, pp. 171–72; T. S. Roberts, *Birds of Minn.*, I, 576–87.

151 Chatfield *Democrat* (Minn.), April 8, 1864.

152 Duluth *Minnesotian*, Sept. 3, 1870, and Milwaukee *Evening Wisconsin*, Sept. 6, 1870.

153 T. S. Roberts, *Birds of Minn.*, I, 576.

154 Wells W. Cooke, *Rept. on Bird Migration in Miss. Valley*, p. 108.

155 Ruthven Deane, "Extracts from the Field Notes of George B. Sennett," *Auk*, XL (1923), 629.

156 "Will" in *Chicago Field*, XI (1879), 66.

157 D. C. Estes, *ibid.*, VI (1876), 266.

158 T. S. Roberts, *Birds of Minn.* I, 576.

159 *Ibid.*

160 T. S. Roberts, "Spring Notes from Minneapolis, Minn.," *Forest and Stream*, XIV (1880), 224.

161 Rochester *Free Press* (Minn.), March 24, 1859.

162 Rochester *Post* (Minn.), April 24, 1869.

163 St. Paul *Pioneer* (Minn.), Sept. 6, 1859.

164 Winona *Herald* (Minn.), April 12, 1872.

165 Henry R. Schoolcraft, *Journal of a Tour into the Interior of Missouri and Arkansaw* ... (London, 1821), p. 23.

166 W. W. Judy in *Am. Field*, XVII (1882), 243.

167 Ruthven Deane in *Auk*, XV (1898), 184–85.

168 "A Big Pot-Hunters' Raid," *Forest and Stream*, XXI (1884), 498.

169 St. Louis *Republican* (Mo.), Mar. 21, 1879.

170 H. C. M. in *Forest and Stream*, VII (1876), 134.

171 William E. D. Scott, "Notes on Birds Observed during the Spring Migration in Western Missouri," *Nuttall Bull.*, IV (1879), 147.

172 Flying for two weeks.—*Forest and Stream*, X (1878), 100.

173 St. Louis *Republican* (Mo.), Mar. 21, 1879

174 John K. Townsend, *Narrative of a Journey across the Rocky Mountains to the Columbia River* (Phila., 1839), p. 13.

175 Otto Widmann, *Preliminary Catalog of Birds of Missouri*, pp. 84–85; St. Louis *Republican* (Mo.), Sept. 30 and Dec. 24, 1851.

176 Otto Widmann, *Preliminary Catalog of Birds of Missouri*, pp. 84–85.

177 St. Louis *Republican* (Mo.), Mar. 21, 1879.

178 Large roost.—*Ibid.,* Oct. 18, 1877; notice also in *Forest and Stream,* IX (1877), 289.

179 "Sassafras" in *Am. Field,* XVII (1882), 132.

180 Ruthven Deane in *Auk,* XV (1898), 184–85.

181 Lawrence Bruner, *Some Notes on Nebraska Birds* (Lincoln, Nebr., 1896), p. 84.

182 *Ibid.*

183 Glover M. Allen, *A List of the Birds of New Hampshire* (Manchester, N. H., 1903), pp. 94–95.

184 *Ibid.*

185 W. H. Fox, "Three Migrations Compared," *Forest and Stream,* VI (1876), 354.

186 *Ibid.*

187 *Ibid.*

188 Webb in *Forest and Stream,* XV (1880), 169.

189 Charles C. Abbott, "Birds," in George H. Cook, *Geology of New Jersey* (Newark, N. J., 1868), p. 783; W. Holberton in *Forest and Stream,* XXII (1884), 83.

190 "A Brick," *ibid.,* III (1874), 118.

191 Annie M. Alexander, "A Further Chronicle of the Passenger Pigeon and Methods Employed in Hunting It," *Condor,* XXIX (1927), 273.

192 Witmer Stone, *The Birds of New Jersey* (Trenton, N. J., 1909), p. 154.

193 M. in *Forest and Stream,* V (1875), 26.

194 E. Carleton Thurber, "A List of Birds of Morris County, New Jersey," Morristown *Democratic Banner* (N. J.), Nov. 10, 1887.

195 Witmer Stone, *Birds of New Jersey,* p. 154.

196 Pehr Kalm, *Travels into North America,* I, 374.

197 "A Brick" in *Forest and Stream,* III (1874), 86.

198 Large numbers present when Hudson River was frozen and there was a foot of snow.—James E. De Kay, *Zoology of New York* (Albany, N. Y., 1844), Part II, pp. 196–97.

199 H. G. Fowler, "Birds of Central New York," *Forest and Stream,* VII (1876), 36.

200 J. E. De Kay, *Zoology of New York,* Part II, pp. 196–97.

201 Albany *Daily Advertiser* (N. Y.), March 27, 1830, and New York *Evening Post,* March 29, 1830.

202 "Uncas" in *Forest and Stream,* X (1878), 99.

203 E. H. Eaton, *Birds of N. Y.,* I, 385.

204 Franklin B. Hough, *Results of a Series of Meteorological Observations Made ...in the State of New York, 1850–1863* (Albany, N. Y., 1872), pp. 340–52.

205 Susan F. Cooper, *Journal of a Naturalist in the United States* (London, 1856), I, 12, and II, 9.

206 *Ibid.,* II, 29.

207 Robert Rodgers, letter quoted in E. B. O'Callaghan, *The Documentary History of the State of New-York* (8° ed.; Albany, N. Y., 1849–51), IV, 259.

208 G. Taylor, *A Voyage to North America . . . in the Years 1768 and 1769* (Nottingham, Eng., 1771), pp. 87–88.

209 F. Sturdevant in *Forest and Stream,* VII (1876), 134.

210 J. M. B., *ibid.,* XII (1879), 216.

211 Franklin B. Hough, *Results of Meteorological Observations Made in New York,* pp. 340–52.

212 E. B. Gleason, "Notes on Familiar Birds," *Forest and Stream,* X (1878), 503.

213 Immense numbers.—Fredonia *Censor* (N. Y.), Dec. 22, 1846.

214 C. E. Sanford, *Early History of the Town of Hopkinton* (Boston, 1903), p. 331.

215 *Ibid.,* p. 378.

216 John in *Forest and Stream,* VII (1876), 134, and X (1878), 100.

217 J. Otis Fellows, "Spring Notes Hornellsville, N. Y.," *ibid.,* XVI (1881), 187.

218 Edgar A. Mearns, "A List of the Birds of the Hudson Highlands, with Annotations," *Bull. Essex Inst.,* XII (1880), 128.

219 When found weather was usually mild.—Edgar A. Mearns, "Notes on Some of the Less Hardy Winter Residents in the Hudson River Valley," *Nuttall Bull.,* IV (1879), 37.

220 Jamestown *Democrat* (N. Y.), April 13, 1872.

221 C. Hart Merriam, "Winter Notes. The Winter of 1881–82 in Lewis County, Northern New York," *Forest and Stream,* XVIII (1882), 207.

222 Franklin B. Hough, *Results of Meteorological Observations Made in New York,* pp. 340–52.

223 Mayville *Sentinel* (N. Y.), March 5, 1840.

224 A. R. Fuller, "Spring at Meachan Lake," *Forest and Stream,* VI (1876), 301.

225 "Explosive Target," *ibid.,* XIV (1880), 112.

226 Mild winter.—New York *Mirror,* Feb. 1, 1858.

227 F. B. Hough, *Results of Meteorological Observations Made in New York,* pp. 340–52.

228 *Ibid.* Huge flocks.—Notice in *Magazine Nat. Hist.* (London), II (1829), 369, previously appearing in the Rochester *Register* (N. Y.) of Dec., 1828.

229 F. B. Hough, *Results of Meteorological Observations Made in New York,* pp. 340–52.

230 *Ibid.*

231 *Forest and Stream,* VI (1876), 171.

232 Migrating recently.— E. W. B., *ibid.,* XVIII (1882), 107.

233 William Brewster, "An Ornithological Reconnaissance in Western North Carolina," *Auk,* III (1886), 179.

234 Adelaide L. Fries (ed.), *Records of the Moravians in North Carolina* (Pub. North Carolina Hist. Com.; Raleigh, N. C., 1922–47), I, 235. Huge flocks in "January or February, 1701–2."—John Lawson, *The History of Carolina* ... (Raleigh, 1860), p. 234.

235 Hard winter.—John Lawson, *History of Carolina*, pp. 231–32.

236 Abundant.—Raleigh *Register* (N. C.), Feb. 19, 1838.

237 A large roost on South Fork from Nov. 20, 1760, to the first week in Jan., 1761.—A. L. Fries (ed.), *Records of Moravians in North Carolina*, I, 233, VI, 2454.

238 *Ibid.*, VI, 2623.

239 *Ibid.*, p. 2855.

240 W. J. Holland, "The Passenger Pigeon (Ectopistes migratorius) in North Carolina," *Auk*, XL (1923), 530–32.

241 W. W. Cooke, *Rept. on Bird Migration in Miss. Valley*, p. 108.

242 Maria R. Audubon, *Audubon and His Journals* (ed. E. Coues; N. Y., 1900), II, 156.

243 "Taxi," "Wild Pigeons," *Forest and Stream*, XXXVIII (1892), 418.

244 Alexander Henry, *New Light on the Early History of the Greater Northwest: The Manuscript Journals of Alexander Henry and of David Thompson* (ed. E. Coues; N. Y., 1897), I, 195.

245 *Ibid.*, p. 243.

246 J. M. Wheaton, "The Food of Birds as Related to Agriculture," *29th Ann. Rept. Ohio State Board Agr.*, 1874, p. 571.

247 "Elmer," "Where the Wild Pigeons Are," *Forest and Stream*, X (1878), 85.

248 Warren *Trumbull County Democrat* (Ohio), Dec. 22, 1855.

249 *Forest and Stream*, X (1878), 10 and 44.

250 Canton *Repository* (Ohio), Oct. 29, 1843, and Racine *Advocate* (Wis.), Nov. 23, 1843.

251 W. E. G. in *Porter's Spirit of the Times*, II (March 14, 1857), 23.

252 Circleville *Watchman* (Ohio), Mar. 29, 1861.

253 Cleveland *Plain Dealer* (Ohio), Jan. 24, 1851, and Watertown *Chronicle* (Wis.), Feb. 12, 1851.

254 "K Nine" in *Chicago Field*, XII (1880), 379.

255 Present for two months.—F. in *Forest and Stream*, VI (1876), 204.

256 M. C. R., "Wild Pigeons in Ohio," *ibid.*, XIV (1880), 166.

257 "Wild Pigeons," *ibid.*, p. 112; anon. note, *ibid.*, X (1878), 10.

258 Anon. note, *ibid.*, X (1878), 44.

259 W. P. Cutler and J. P. Cutler, *Life, Journals and Correspondence of Rev. Manasseh Cutler* (Cincinnati, Ohio, 1888), I, 418; John Heckewelder, "Journey to the Wabash in 1792," *Penn. Mag. Hist. Biog.*, XII (1888), 182.

260 S. P. Hildreth in *Am. J. Sci.*, XXIV (1833), 134–35.

261 Flying for several days.—S. M. H. in *Am. Field*, XVII (1882), 162.

262 Last week.—*Ibid.,* XIX (1883), 230.

263 "Rob Roy" in *Forest and Stream,* XIII (1879), 733.

264 "Ire-Land," "Wild Pigeons," *ibid.,* XIV (1880), 12.

265 Ravenna *Star* (Ohio), Oct. 9, 1850.

266 W. F. Henninger, "A Preliminary List of the Birds of Middle Southern Ohio," *Wilson Bull.,* XIV (1902), 82.

267 "The Kid" in *Am. Field,* XVII (1882), 227.

268 W. S. A. in *Forest and Stream,* XVIII (1882), 89.

269 Anon. note, *ibid.,* VI (1876), 90.

270 Harry C. Oberholser, "A Preliminary List of the Birds of Wayne County, Ohio," *Bull. Ohio Agr. Station,* Tech. Ser., I (1896), 272.

271 *Ibid.*

272 T. M. in *Forest and Stream,* XIV (1880), 72.

273 "Buckeye Boy," *ibid.,* XIII (1879), 773.

274 W. Faux, *Memorable Days in America: Being a Journal of a Tour to the United States* (London, 1823), p. 174.

275 Immense numbers in some winters.—Pehr Kalm, *Travels into North America,* I, 164.

276 J. W. F. in *Forest and Stream,* VI (1876), 91.

277 "Plenty last week."—S. T., *ibid.,* XIII (1879), 853.

278 "A Summer Jaunt in 1773," *Penn. Mag. Hist. and Biog.,* X (1886), 208.

279 Abundant in "winter of 1875 or 1876," the weather being mild, at the boundary between Cambria and Somerset counties. Probably 1876/77.—J. C. French, *Passenger Pigeon,* p. 14.

280 W. M. Baird and Spencer F. Baird, "List of Birds Found in the Vicinity of Carlisle, Cumberland County, Pa., *Am. J. Sci.,* XLVI (1844), 270; Phillips B. Street, "The Edward Harris Collection of Birds," *Wilson Bull.,* LX (1948), 182.

281 W. M. Baird and S. F. Baird in *Am. J. Sci.,* XLVI (1844), 270.

282 *Ibid.*

283 Franklin L. Burns, *The Ornithology of Chester County, Pennsylvania* (Boston, 1919), p. 49.

284 Witmer Stone in *Abstract Proc. Delaware Valley Ornithol. Club Phila.,* No. 2 (1892–97), p. 17.

285 Coudersport *Potter County Journal* (Pa.), Mar. 25, 1886.

286 W. W. D. in *Forest and Stream,* X (1878), 85.

287 A few flocks.—"Penn" in *Am. Field,* XVII (1882), 147.

288 "Keokuk," "A Wild Pigeon Flight," *Forest and Stream,* XXXII (1890), 467.

289 Herbert H. Beck, "Historical Sketch of Rural Field Sports in Lancaster County," *Hist. Papers and Addresses Lancaster County Hist. Soc.* (Penn.), XXVII (1923), 152.

290 W. H. Spera, "The Coming of the Birds," *Forest and Stream,* VI (1876), 52.

291 *Ibid.*

292 J. C. French, *Passenger Pigeon,* p. 222.

293 A few wintered.—G. S. B., "Trapping Wild Pigeons," *Forest and Stream,* XIV (1880), 433.

294 Witmer Stone in *Cassinia,* No. 11 (1907), p. 84.

295 Edward Norris, "A Pennsylvania Wild Pigeon," *Forest and Stream,* XLV (1895), 489.

296 J. A. Schoepf, *Travels in the Confederation,* I, 161.

297 Flying southward (Mar. 22–Apr. 2, new style).—Pehr Kalm in *Auk,* XXVIII (1911), 53–66. Large flocks seldom wintered but there were immense numbers near Phila. during the mild winter of 1792/93 and individuals were believed to winter commonly.—Benjamin S. Barton, *Barton's Fragments of the Natural History of Pennsylvania* (ed. O. Salvin; London, 1883), p. ix.

298 Witmer Stone, "Bird Migration Records of William Bartram," *Auk,* XXX (1913), 338.

299 James Mease, *A Geological Account of the United States* (Phila., 1807), pp. 347–49.

300 William Bartram in Witmer Stone's article in *Auk,* XXX (1913), 338.

301 *Ibid.*

302 During past week—"Homo" and R. F. in *Forest and Stream,* XVIII (1882), 150, and XI (1878), 193.

303 Lake Geneva *Herald* (Wis.), May 13, 1876.

304 *Turf, Field and Farm,* XXII (1876), 246.

305 "X Tempore," *ibid.,* XXVI (1886), 182.

306 Anon. note, *ibid.,* IX (1877), 175.

307 "Passenger Pigeon Reminiscences," *Cardinal,* I, No. 3 (Jan., 1924), 7–11.

308 In winter, occasionally a few, but in open winters hundreds would sometimes remain until the storms drove them south.—L. E. Scherer, Jr., in *Cardinal,* V (1939), 25–42.

309 *Ibid.*

310 Abundant the "winter of 1875 or 1876," the weather being mild, at the boundary between Cambria and Somerset counties.—John C. French, *Passenger Pigeon,* p. 14.

311 Immense numbers.—The diary of S. J. Miller of Springs, Somerset County, quoted by W. E. C. Todd, *Birds of Western Pennsylvania* (Pittsburgh, Pa., 1940), p. 267.

312 Stroudsburg *Jeffersonian* (Pa.), April 16, 1868.

313 Numerous all winter.—McK. in *Forest and Stream,* X (1878), 99.

314 "A Pigeon Storm," *Forest and Stream,* XXVI (1886), 329.

315 G. H. W., *ibid.,* X (1878), 99.

316 "Penn" in *Am. Field,* XVII (1882), 147.

317   Mild winter.—C. C. P. *ibid.,* p. 132.

318   Herbert H. Beck, "Dexterous Alighting Maneuver of Passenger Pigeons," *Auk,* LXVI (1949), 286.

319   Harry S. Hathaway, "Notes on the Occurrence and Nesting of Certain Birds in Rhode Island," *Auk,* XXX (1913), 552.

320   *Nailer Tom's Diary; Otherwise, the Journal of Thomas B. Hazard of Kingston, Rhode Island, 1778 to 1840* . . . (Boston, 1930), pp. 68–88.

321   *Ibid.*

322   Andrew Burnaby, *Travels through the Middle Settlements in North America, in the Years 1759 and 1760* (London, 1798), pp. 101–2.

323   H. S. Hathaway in *Auk,* XXX (1913), 552.

324   Maria R. Audubon, *Audubon and His Journals,* II, 160 and 163.

325   Jane M. Parker, "Louis Philippe in the United States," *Century Illustrated Monthly Mag.,* N. S., XL (1901), 751.

326   Arrived last week.—W. W. L. in *Forest and Stream,* IX (1877), 216.

327   W. J. M. in *Am. Field,* XVI (1881), 362.

328   Guyon, Jr., *ibid.,* XX (1883), 509.

329   Nashville *Gazette* (Tenn.), Oct. 25, 1844; Chicago *Daily Journal,* Nov. 16, 1844.

330   "Will" in *Forest and Stream,* XI (1878), 270.

331   *Ibid.,* XIX (1882), 269.

332   *Porter's Spirit of the Times,* III (Nov. 21, 1857), 181.

333   "In winter beyond number or imagination."—Ralph Hamor, "Notes of Virginian Affaires in the Government of Sir Thomas Dale and Sir Thomas Gates till Anno 1614," in Samuel Purchas, *Hakluytus Posthumeus, or Purchas His Pilgrimes* (Glasgow, 1906), XIX, 97.

334   *William Byrd's Histories of the Dividing Line betwixt Virginia and North Carolina,* p. 216.

335   N., "Wild Pigeons in Virginia," *Porter's Spirit of the Times,* XX (Mar. 30, 1850), 61.

336   E. (M. G. Elzey) in *Forest and Stream,* VII (1876), 122.

337   Every year in Sept. and Oct.—"Chief," "Wild Pigeons," *ibid.,* XI (1878), 224.

338   *Forest and Stream,* III (1874), 170.

339   *Thomas Jefferson's Garden Book, 1766–1824* (Phila., 1944), p. 367.

340   "Chief" in *Forest and Stream,* XI (1878), 224.

341   Stanstead, "Spring Notes," *ibid.,* XL (1893), 403.

342   "Vast quantities of wild pigeons about."—"Journal of Col. James Gordon of Lancaster County, Va.," *William and Mary College Quarterly Hist. Mag.,* XII (1903–4), 1.

343   Thomas Williamson in *Forest and Stream,* VI (1876), 163; T. W., *ibid.,* XI (1878), 213.

344   E. (M. G. Elzey), *ibid.,* XI (1878), 224.

345   Daniel Boone in L. Draper's "Life of Boone" (Draper MS 3B319, Library, Wisconsin Hist. Soc., Madison), p. 219.

346   Wild pigeons in city market.—G. H., "Wild Pigeons," *Forest and Stream,* XXXVIII (1892), 79.

347   "Flag" in *Porter's Spirit of the Times,* III (Nov. 14, 1857), 167.

348   D., "Wild Pigeons in Virginia," *Forest and Stream,* XXXV (1890), 190.

349   June 1, new style.—*The Secret Diary of William Byrd of Westover* (Richmond, Va., 1941), p. 347.

350   J. S. Buckingham, *The Slave States of America* (London, 1842), II, 330.

351   *Forest and Stream,* III (1874), 150.

352   Record questionable. C. L. S., "Passenger Pigeons Seen," *Forest and Stream,* LIII (1899), 405.

353   Alexander S. Withers, *Chronicles of Border Warfare* (Clarksburg, Va., 1831), p. 226.

354   W. P. Cutler and J. P. Cutler, *Life, Journals and Correspondence of Rev. Manasseh Cutler,* I, 422.

355   "Last week" (about Feb. 21).

356   One shot between these dates.

357   Zebulon M. Pike, *The Expeditions of Zebulon Montgomery Pike, to Headwaters of the Mississippi River ... during the Years 1805–6–7* (ed. E. Coues; N. Y., 1895), I, 32.

358   "A few days since."

359   Henry R. Schoolcraft, *Narrative Journal of Travels through the Northwestern Regions of the United States ...* (Albany, N.Y., 1821), p. 381.

360   "The last few days."

361   On April 2, 1856, "the past few days."

362   Very late spring.

363   "For a day or two."

364   About Mar. 14, 1855.

365   "For several days" around March 12, 1846; Dec. date from Madison *Democrat* (Wis.) of Dec. 14, 1875.

366   "Flying for several days" around Mar. 28, 1864.

367   "For a few days."

368   Report on Thursday, April 3, 1883, states "flying the past week."

369   B I. D., "Flight of Wild Pigeons," Am. Field, XVII (1882), 52.

370   "Last week."

371   "About a week ago."

372   Jan. date from Watertown *Democrat* (Wis.), Jan. 6, 1876.

373   John Richardson and W. Swainson, *Fauna Boreali-Americana: or the Zoology of the Northern Parts of British America* (London, 1829–37), Part II (1831), p. 363; Ernest T. Seton, "The Birds of Western Manitoba," *Auk,* III (1886), 153.

374   Robert M. Christy, "Notes on the Birds of Manitoba," *Zoologist,* 3rd ser., IX (1885), 130.

375   George Mercer Dawson, *Report on the Geology and Resources of the Region in the Vicinity of the Forty-Ninth Parallel* ... (Brit. N. Am. Boundary Com.; Montreal, 1875), p. 281.

376   A bird collected.—George E. Atkinson, *Rare Bird Records of Manitoba* (Trans. Hist. Sci. Soc. Manitoba, No. 65; Winnipeg, 1904), p. 1.

377   This may refer to the specimen collected on April 10.—James H. Fleming in *Auk,* XX (1903), 66.

378   This may refer to the specimen collected on April 10.—Ernest T. Seton, "Recent Bird Records for Manitoba," *Auk,* XXV (1908), 452.

379   Wells W. Cooke, *Rept. on Bird Migration in Miss. Valley,* p. 108.

380   *Ibid.*

381   Alexander Henry, *New Light on Early History of Greater Northwest,* I, 176.

382   *Ibid.,* II, 469.

383   A few earlier.—Wells W. Cooke, *Rept. on Bird Migration in Miss. Valley,* p. 108.

384   J. H. Fleming in *Ottawa Naturalist,* XX (1907), 236.

385   Daniel W. Harmon, *A Journal of Voyages and Travels in the Interior of North America* (N. Y., 1922), p. 63.

386   Alexander Henry, *New Light on Early History of Greater Northwest,* II, 622.

387   *Ibid.,* I, 4.

388   M. H. Mitchell, *Passenger Pigeon,* pp. 65–69. Large flocks were observed in Canada in the coldest winters; however, the ground was free from snow.— John Bachman, "On the Migration of the Birds of North America," *Am. J. Sci.,* XXX (1836), 89.

389   M. H. Mitchell, *Passenger Pigeon,* p. 69.

390   "Au Sable" (J. W. Dutton) in *Forest and Stream,* XVII (1881), 148.

391   G. A. MacCallum, "Wild Pigeons," *Forest and Stream,* XLIII (1894), 443.

392   Wild pigeons in a starving condition were reported wandering about in western Ontario, particularly in the vicinity of Galt.—*Chicago Daily Journal,* Jan. 27, 1851; Cleveland *Plain Dealer* (Ohio), Jan. 24, 1851; Watertown *Chronicle* (Wis.), Feb. 12, 1851.

393   Thomas Rolph, *A Brief Account, together with Observations, Made during a Visit in the West Indies, and a Tour through the United States of America, in Parts of the Years 1832-3* (Dundas, 1836), p. 121.

394   George Head, *Forest Scenes and Incidents in the Wilds of North America* (London, 1829), p. 237.

395   Earliest previous arrival April 21.—"Correspondent," "Unusual Migration of Wild Pigeons," *Can. Naturalist Geol.,* III (1858), 150–51.

396   M. H. Mitchell, *Passenger Pigeon,* p. 79.

397   C. J. S. Bethune in *Ottawa Naturalist,* XVI (1902), 43.

398   George Barnston, "Observations on the Progress of the Seasons . . . at Martin's Falls, Albany River, Hudson's Bay," *Edinburgh New Phil. J.,* XXX (1841), 255.

399   Lucien M. Turner, "List of the Birds of Labrador, including Ungava, East Main, Moose, and Gulf Districts of the Hudson Bay Company, together with the Island of Anticosti," *Proc. U. S. Nat. Museum,* VIII (1885), 245.

400   E. Cruikshank, "The Journal of Captain Walter Butler, on a Voyage along the North Shore of Lake Ontario, from the 8th to the 16th of March, 1779," *Trans. Can. Inst.,* IV (1892–93), 279.

401   M. H. Mitchell, *Passenger Pigeon,* p. 70.

402   *Ibid.*

403   C. E. L., "Wild Pigeons," *Forest and Stream,* XX (1883), 170.

404   "Hammerless Greener," "Pigeon Shooting," *Can. Sportsman and Naturalist,* I (1881), 20–21; Hoyes Lloyd, "The Birds of Ottawa," *Can. Field-Naturalist,* XXXVII (1923), 151.

405   George R. White and J. M. Macoun, "Report of the Ornithological Branch for the Year 1886–87" and "Report of the Ornithological Branch for 1887," *Ottawa Naturalist,* I (1887), 99, and II (1888), 52.

406   Thomas Need, *Six Years in the Bush . . . 1832–1838* (London, 1838), p. 48.

407   None in April, 1837.—*Ibid.,* pp. 83 and 123.

408   Charles Fothergill quoted in M. H. Mitchell, *Passenger Pigeon,* p. 162.

409   J. H. Fleming in *Auk,* XXIV (1907), 72.

410   William Henry Smith, *Canada: Past, Present and Future* (Toronto, *ca.* 1851), II, 426; John Edmonds, "Ornithological Report, Nov. 11, 1890," *Trans. Can. Inst.,* III (1891–92), 89.

411   M. H. Mitchell, *Passenger Pigeon,* p. 89; J. H. Fleming in *Ottawa Naturalist,* XX (1907), 236.

412   C. J. S. Bethune in *Ottawa Naturalist,* XVI (1902), 40–44.

413   M. H. Mitchell, *Passenger Pigeon,* pp. 89–90.

414   *Ibid.*

415   *Ibid.*

416   *Ibid.*

417   *Ibid.*

418   *Ibid.*

419   *Ibid.*

420   *Ibid.*

421   *Ibid.*

422   E. Deacon, "Ornithological Report, April 14, 1891," *Trans. Can. Inst.,* III (1891–92), 102.

423 Robert Bell, "Catalogue of Animals and Plants Collected and Observed on the South-East Side of the St. Lawrence from Quebec to Gaspé and Bonaventure," *Rept. Progress Geol. Survey Canada,* 1858, p. 245.

424 Isaac Weld, *Travels through the States of North America and the Provinces of Upper and Lower Canada . . .* (London, 1799), p. 269.

425 J. H. Fleming in *Ottawa Naturalist,* XX (1907), 236.

426 Ernest D. Wintle, *The Birds of Montreal* (Montreal, 1896), pp. 51–52.

427 Abundant.—S. K. Stevens *et al.* (eds.), *Travels in New France by J. C. B.* (Harrisburg, Pa., 1941), p. 15.

428 W. S. M. D'Urban, "Observations on the Natural History of the Valley of the River Rouge, and Surrounding Townships in the Counties of Argenteuil and Ottawa," *Can. Naturalist Geol.,* IV (1859), 265–66.

429 T. Blakiston, "On Birds Collected and Observed in the Interior of North America," *Ibis,* 1st ser., V (1863), 121.

CHAPTER 15

1 W. Brewster in *Bull. Museum Comparative Zool.,* No. 66 (1925), Part II, p. 309.

2 Henry D. Paxson, "The Last of the Wild Pigeon in Bucks County," *Coll. Bucks County Hist. Soc.,* IV (1917), 372.

3 W. B. Barrows quoted in W. B. Mershon, *Passenger Pigeon,* p. 158.

4 George E. Atkinson quoted *ibid.,* p. 160.

5 W. C. Avery, "Birds Observed in Alabama," *Am. Field,* XXXIV (1890), 584.

6 Paul R. Litzke, "Wild Pigeons," *Forest and Stream,* LIV (1900), 24.

7 Otto Widmann quoted in Edward H. Forbush, "The Last Passenger Pigeon," *Bird-Lore,* XV (1913), 100.

8 J. H. Sage, L. B. Bishop, and W. P. Bliss, *The Birds of Connecticut* (Bull. Conn. State Geol. and Nat. Hist. Survey, No. 20; Hartford, Conn., 1913), p. 69.

9 L. E. Wyman, "A Very Late Record of the Passenger Pigeon (*Ectopistes migratorius*)," *Auk,* XXXVIII (1921), 274.

10 James H. Fleming quoted in A. C. Bent, *Life Histories of N. Am. Gallinaceous Birds,* p. 380.

11 Outram Bangs quoted in J. H. Sage, L. B. Bishop, and W. P. Bliss, *Birds of Connecticut,* p. 69.

12 Eugene E. Murphey, *Observations on the Bird Life of the Middle Savannah Valley, 1890–1937* (Contrib. Charleston Museum, Vol. IX; Charleston, S. C., 1937), p. 23.

13 Ruthven Deane, "Additional Records of the Passenger Pigeon (*Ectopistes migratorius*) in Wisconsin and Illinois," *Auk,* XIII (1896), 81.

14 E. R. Ford, C. C. Sanborn, and C. B. Coursen, "Birds of the Chicago Region," *Program of Activities Chicago Acad. Sci.,* V, Nos. 2–3 (1934), 45.

15   Henry K. Coale in *Auk,* XLII (1925), 137.

16   J. O. Dunn, "The Passenger Pigeon in the Upper Mississippi Valley," *Auk,* XII (1895), 389.

17   A. W. Butler in *22nd Ann. Rept. Indiana Dept. Geol. and Nat. Resources,* 1897, p. 764.

18   Waldo L. McAtee, "Ecological Notes on the Birds Occurring within a Radius of Five Miles of the Indiana University Campus," *Proc. Ind. Acad. Sci.,* 1904, p. 174.

19   A. W. Butler in *22nd Ann. Rept. Indiana Dept. Geol. and Nat. Resources,* 1897, p. 764.

20   Joseph F. Honecker quoted in Amos W. Butler, "Some Notes on Indiana Birds," *Auk,* XXIII (1906), 273.

21   Otto Widmann, *A Preliminary Catalog of the. Birds of Missouri* (St. Louis, Mo., 1907), p. 85; Sept. 7 is given by R. M. Anderson, *The Birds of Iowa,* p. 239.

22   C. S. Webster, "The Wild Pigeon in Iowa," *Forest and Stream,* LII (1899), 305.

23   H. E. James, *ibid.,* LVIII (1902), 447.

24   Nathaniel S. Goss, *History of the Birds of Kansas* (Topeka, Kans., 1891), pp. 237–38.

25   David E. Lantz, "A Review of Kansas Ornithology," *Trans. Kansas Acad. Sci.,* XVI (1897–98), 254.

26   Alexander Wetmore, "Game Birds of Prairie, Forest, and Tundra," *Nat. Geographic Mag.,* LXX (1936), 495.

27   Lucien Beckner, "The Last Wild Pigeon in Kentucky," *Trans. Ky. Acad. Sci.,* II (1924–26), 55–56.

28   J. G. Taylor in Osprey, III (1898), 12; J. H. Fleming in *Ottawa Naturalist,* XX (1907), 237.

29   George E. Beyer quoted in E. H. Forbush, *Game Birds,* p. 461.

30   George E. Beyer, A. Allison, and H. H. Kopman, "List of the Birds of Louisiana," *Auk,* XXV (1908), 440.

31   Harry C. Oberholser, "The Bird Life of Louisiana," *Bull. La. Dept. Conservation,* No. 28 (1938), p. 320; E. A. McIlhenny, "Major Changes in the Bird Life of Southern Louisiana during Sixty Years," *Auk,* LX (1943), 546.

32   Ora W. Knight in *Maine Sportsman,* IV (Nov., 1896), 8; his *The Birds of Maine* (Bangor, Me., 1908), pp. 210–11.

33   Ora W. Knight, "Latest Authentic Record of the Passenger Pigeon in Maine," *J. Maine Ornithol. Soc.,* X (1908), 54.

34   Ralph S. Palmer, "Maine Birds," *Bull. Museum Comp. Zool.,* No. 102 (1949), 299.

35   W. H. Fisher, "Maryland Birds that Interest the Sportsman," *Oologist,* XI (1894), 139.

36　Gustave Eifrig, "Birds of Alleghany and Garrett Counties, Western Maryland," *Auk,* XXI (1904), 250.

37　Unsigned note by George Fowle in *Shooting and Fishing,* VIII (Oct. 2, 1890), 13; editor's note, *ibid.,* VIII (Oct. 9, 1890), 13; "Gulch" (Herbert W. Bartlett), "Notes from Plymouth, Mass.," *ibid.,* VIII (June 19, 1890), 146; T. H. B. in *Forest and Stream,* XXXVII (1891), 183.

38　E. H. Forbush, *Game Birds,* p. 461.

39　Ludlow Griscom, *The Birds of Concord* (Cambridge, Mass., 1949), p. 17.

40　Ruthven Deane in *Auk,* XIII (1896), 81.

41　Emerson Hough, "The Wild Pigeon," *Forest and Stream,* LII (1899), 88.

42　"Frank Clements" (Philip E. Moody), "A Recent Record of the Wild Pigeon," *Bull. Michigan Ornithol. Club,* IV (1903), 81; J. H. Fleming in *Auk,* XX (1903), 66; J. Claire Wood, "The Last Passenger Pigeons in Wayne County, Michigan," *Auk,* XXVII (1910), 208; Norman A. Wood, *The Birds of Michigan* (Misc. Publ. Museum Zool., Univ. Mich., No. 75; Ann Arbor, Mich., 1951), p. 225.

43　J. C. French, *Passenger Pigeon,* p. 175.

44　Oliver V. Jones, "The Passenger Pigeon," *Oologist,* XIV (1897), 14; T. S. Roberts, *Birds of Minn.,* I, 584

45　Guyon in *Forest and Stream,* III (1874), 201.

46　W. W. T. in *Am. Field,* XIX (1883), 170.

47　Ruthven Deane in *Auk,* XIV (1897), 316–17, and XV (1898), 185.

48　Otto Widmann, *Preliminary Catalog of the Birds of Missouri,* pp. 84–85.

49　Lawrence Bruner, *Some Notes on Nebraska Birds* (Rept. Nebr. State Agr. Soc.; Lincoln, Nebr., 1896), p. 84.

50　W. F. R. (W. F. Rightmire), "Wild Pigeons in Nebraska," *Forest and Stream,* XLIX (1897), 246; Ruthven Deane in *Auk,* XV (1898), 184–85.

51　Glover M. Allen, *A List of the Birds of New Hampshire* (Manchester, N. H., 1903), pp. 94–95.

52　"Swain" in *Shooting and Fishing,* X (Oct. 1, 1891), 10.

53　E. Carleton Thurber, "A List of Birds of Morris County, New Jersey," Morristown *Democratic Banner* (N. J.), Nov. 10, 1887.

54　Witmer Stone in *Cassinia,* No. 11 (1907), p. 84, and his *The Birds of New Jersey* (Trenton, N. J., 1909), p. 154.

55　Frank M. Chapman, "The Wild Pigeon at Englewood, N. J.," *Auk,* XIII 1896), 341.

56　W. S. Johnson, "The Passenger Pigeon (*Ectopistes migratorius*) in Lewis County, N. Y.," *Auk,* XIV (1897), 88.

57　E. H. Eaton, *Birds of N. Y.,* I, 385.

58　Editor, "Wild Pigeon in New York," *Forest and Stream,* XLIII (1899), 164.

59　S. C. Bishop and A. H. Wright, "Note on the Passenger Pigeon," *Auk,* XXXIV (1917), 208–9.

60 A. C. Bent, *Life Histories of N. Am. Gallinaceous Birds,* p. 380.

61 C. S. Brimley, "Thirty-Two Years of Bird Migration at Raleigh, North Carolina," *Auk,* XXXIV (1917), 305.

62 E. H. Forbush, *Game Birds,* p. 461; T. Gilbert Pearson, C. S. Brimley, and H. H. Brimley, *Birds of North Carolina* (Raleigh, N. C., 1919), pp. 156–57.

63 H. V. Williams, "Birds of the Red River Valley of Northeastern North Dakota," *Wilson Bull.,* XXXVIII (1926), 30.

64 "Taxi," "Wild Pigeons," *Forest and Stream,* XXXVIII (1892), 418.

65 Harry C. Oberholser, "A Preliminary List of the Birds of Wayne County, Ohio," *Bull. Ohio Agr. Station, Tech.* Ser., I, No. 4 (1896), 272.

66 W. F. Henninger, "A Preliminary List of the Birds of Middle Southern Ohio," *Wilson Bull.,* XIV (1902), 82; William L. Dawson, *The Birds of Ohio* (Columbus, Ohio, 1903), p. 427; Frank S. Raper in Columbus *Dispatch* (Ohio), April 9, 1939; Donald J. Borror, "A Check List of the Birds of Ohio, with the Migration Dates for the Birds of Central Ohio," *Ohio J. Sci.,* L (1950), 12.

67 E. H. Forbush, *Birds of Mass.,* II, 76; Henry T. Bannon, *Stories Old and Often Told. Being Chronicles of Scioto County, Ohio* (Baltimore, Md., 1927), p. 86.

68 Ernest T. Seton, "Recent Bird Records for Manitoba," *Auk,* XXV (1908), 451–52.

69 William Brewster (ed.) in Henry D. Minot, *The Land-Birds and Game-Birds of New England* (2nd ed.; Boston, 1895), p. 395n.; J. H. Fleming in *Ottawa Naturalist,* XX (1907), 236.

70 W. O. Blaisdell, "Wild Pigeons in Oklahoma," *Forest and Stream,* LIV (1900), 265.

71 Edward Norris, "A Pennsylvania Wild Pigeon," *ibid.,* XLV (1895), 489.

72 Witmer Stone in *Cassinia,* No. 11 (1907), p. 84.

73 Henry D. Paxson in *Coll. Bucks County Hist. Soc.,* IV (1917), 372.

74 J. H. Fleming in *Ottawa Naturalist,* XX (1907), 237.

75 W. E. C. Todd, *Birds of Western Pennsylvania* (Pittsburgh, Pa., 1940), p. 271.

76 Harvey A. Surface, "Report of the Ornithologist," *Tenth Ann. Rept. Penn. Dept. Agr.,* 1904, p. 422.

77 Harry S. Hathaway, "Notes on the Occurrence and Nesting of Certain Birds in Rhode Island," *Auk,* XXX (1913), 552.

78 *Ibid.*

79 Reginald H. Howe and Edward Sturtevant, *The Birds of Rhode Island* (Middletown, R. I., 1899), p. 88.

80 Arthur T. Wayne, "A Contribution to the Ornithology of South Carolina, Chiefly the Coastal Region," *Auk,* XXIII (1906), 61.

81 W. J. Hoxie, "Passenger Pigeon, *Ectopistes migratorius,*" *Wilson Bull.,* XIII (May, 1901), 44.

82   Henry E. Davis, *The American Wild Turkey* (Georgetown, S. C., 1949), p. 34.

83   W. J. Hoffman, "List of Birds Observed at Grand River Agency, Dakota Ter. from October 7th, 1872, to June 7th, 1873," *Proc. Boston Soc. Nat. Hist.*, XVIII (1877), 174.

84   G. S. Agersborg, "The Birds of Southeastern Dakota," *Auk*, II (1885), 285.

85   Samuel N. Rhoads, "Contributions to the Zoology of Tennessee," *Proc. Acad. Nat. Sci. Phila.*, 1895, pp. 475–76.

86   A. S. Eldredge quoted in E. H. Forbush, *Game Birds*, p. 461; J. D. Ayers in *Forest and Stream*, LXIX (1907), 772.

87   G. F. Simmons, *Birds of the Austin Region* (Austin, Tex., 1925), p. 86.

88   George H. Perkins and Clifton D. Howe, "A Preliminary List of the Birds Found in Vermont," *21st Ann. Rept. Vt. State Board Agr.*, 1901, p. 101; also appeared separately in Dec., 1901, with reference on p. 17 of this publication.

89   "Kenewah," "Green Mountain Notes," *Forest and Stream*, LII (1899), 248.

90   D., "Wild Pigeons in Virginia," *ibid.*, XXXV (1890), 190.

91   G. H., "Wild Pigeons," *ibid.*, XXXVIII (1892), 79.

92   Stanstead, "Spring Notes," *ibid.*, XL (1893), 403.

93   Maurice Brooks, *A Check-List of West Virginia Birds* (Univ. W. Va., College Agr., Forestry, Home Econ., Agr. Exp. Sta., Bull. No. 316; Morgantown, W. Va., 1944), p. 25.

94   William H. Bishop, *History of Roane County, West Virginia* (Spencer, W. Va., 1927), pp. 34–35.

95   "Backwoods," "In Wild Pigeon Days," *Forest and Stream*, XLIV (1895), 126.

96   C. L. S., "Passenger Pigeon Seen," *ibid.*, LIII (1899), 405.

97   Delavan *Republican* (Wis.), Sept. 10, 1896; Ned Hollister, "Recent Record of the Passenger Pigeon in Southern Wisconsin," in *Auk*, XIII (1896), 341, and in *Wilson Bull.*, IX (Jan. 30, 1897), 5.

98   Emerson Hough, "Wild Pigeons in Wisconsin," *Forest and Stream*, XLIX (1897), 168; Ruthven Deane in *Auk*, XV (1898), 184–85.

99   Emerson Hough, "A Genuine Wild Pigeon," *Forest and Stream*, LIII (1899), 248; A. W. Schorger, "The Last Passenger Pigeon Killed in Wisconsin," *Auk*, LV (1938), 531.

100 Emerson Hough, "The Past Participle in Pigeons," *Saturday Evening Post*, CLXXXIII (Oct. 15, 1910), 30.

101 Henry K. Coale, "Passenger Pigeon in Wisconsin," *Auk*, XXXVIII (1921), 456.

102 J. H. Fleming in *Ottawa Naturalist*, XX (1907), 236.

103 George E. Atkinson, *Rare Bird Records of Manitoba* (Trans. Hist. Sci. Soc. Manitoba, No. 65; Winnipeg, 1904), p. 8.

104 *Ibid.*

105 J. H. Fleming in *Auk*, XX (1903), 66.

106 E. T. Seton in *Auk*, XXV (1908), 451–52.

107 Charles F. Batchelder, "Notes on the Summer Birds of the Upper St. John," *Nuttall Bull.*, VII (1882), 151.

108 Montague Chamberlain, "A Catalogue of the Birds of New Brunswick," *Bull. Nat. Hist. Soc. New Brunswick*, No. 1 (1882), p. 50.

109 J. Matthew Jones, "List of the Birds of Nova Scotia. Land Birds," *Forest and Stream*, XII (1879), 245; Andrew Downs, "A Catalogue of the Birds of Nova Scotia," *Proc. Trans. Nova Scotian Inst. Nat. Sci.*, VII (1890), 157.

110 John Edmonds, "Ornithological Report, Nov. 11, 1890," *Trans. Can. Inst.*, III (1891–92), 89.

111 J. H. Fleming in *Ottawa Naturalist*, XX (1907), 236.

112 E. Deacon, "Ornithological Report, April 14, 1891," *Trans. Can. Inst.*, III (1891–92), 102.

113 J. H. Fleming in *Auk*, XX (1903), 66.

114 J. H. Fleming in *Ottawa Naturalist*, XX (1907), 236.

115 Napoleon A. Comeau, *Life and Sport on the North Shore of the Lower St. Lawrence and Gulf* (Quebec, 1909), p. 424.

116 E. H. Forbush, *Game Birds*, p. 462.

CHAPTER 16

1 Robert W. Shufeldt, "Published Figures and Plates of the Extinct Passenger Pigeon," *Sci. Monthly*, XII (1921), 458–81; Nettie W. Park, "Pigeons of Passage," *Nature Mag.*, XLII (Oct., 1949), 372–75.

2 M. Catesby, *Natural History of Carolina*, I, 23.

3 Johann L. Frisch, *Vorstellung der Vögel in Teutschland* (Berlin, 1733–63), Vol. II, Plate 142.

4 George L. L. Buffon, *Histoire naturelle des oiseaux*, Vol. III (Paris, 1774), Plate 175.

5 Walter Faxon, "John Abbot's Drawings of the Birds of Georgia," *Auk*, XIII (1896), 215; Samuel N. Rhoads, "Georgia's Rarities Further Discovered in a Second American Portfolio of John Abbot's Bird Plates," *Auk*, XXXV (1918), 282.

6 Pauline Knip, *Les Pigeons* (Paris, 1838–43), Vol. I, Plates 48 and 49.

7 Alexander Wilson, *Am. Ornithology*, V, 103.

8 Thomas Brown, *Illustrations of the American Ornithology of Alexander Wilson and Charles Lucien Bonaparte, Prince of Musignano* (Edinburgh, 1835), Plate 65, No. 1.

9 W. B. Mershon, *Passenger Pigeon*, p. 24.

10 Francis H. Herrick, *Audubon the Naturalist* (N. Y., 1917), I, 292.

11 P. J. Selby, *Pigeons*, Vol. V (Edinburgh, 1835) of *The Naturalists's Library* (ed. Wm. Jardine), Plate 19.

12   M. H. Mitchell, *Passenger Pigeon;* Walter E. Scott (ed.), *Silent Wings—A Memorial to the Passenger Pigeon* (Madison, Wis., 1947).

13   H. L. Mëyer, *Illustrations of British Birds* (London, 1839), Vol. II.

14   James E. DeKay, *Zoology of New York* (Albany, N. Y., 1844), Part II, Plate 74, Fig. 167.

15   Heinrich G. L. Reichenbach, *Die vollständigste Naturgeschichte der Tauben und taubenartigen Vögel* (Dresden and Leipzig, 1861–62).

16   Baird, Brewer, and Ridgway, *History of N. Am. Birds. Land Birds,* Vol. III, Plate 57, Fig. 4.

17   Hermann Dümling, *Illustrirtes Thierleben.... Die Vögel* (Milwaukee, Wis., 1879), Plate 10.

18   Benjamin H. Warren, *Birds of Pennsylvania* (2nd ed.; Harrisburg, Pa., 1890), Plate 71, Fig. 3.

19   Theodore Jasper, *Ornithology; or, the Science of Birds* (Columbus, 1878), Plate 24, Fig. 3.

20   Jacob H. Studer, *The Birds of North America* (N. Y., 1903), Plate 29.

21   William L. Dawson, *The Birds of Ohio* (Columbus, Ohio, 1903).

22   Mr. and Mrs. I. N. Mitchell, "Passenger Pigeon," *Wisconsin Arbor and Bird Day Annual,* 1911, pp. 106–8.

23   Charles K. Reed, *The Passenger Pigeon* (Worcester, Mass., 1910).

24   W. B. Mershon, *Passenger Pigeon.*

25   E. H. Eaton, *Birds of N. Y.,* Vol. I, Plate 42.

26   E. H. Forbush, *Birds of Mass.,* Vol. II, Plate 36.

27   *Posthumous Works of C. O. Whitman,* Vol. II, Plates 28–30.

28   W. B. Barrows, *Mich. Bird Life,* Plate 16.

29   Edward H. Forbush, *The Passenger Pigeon* (Nat. Assoc. Audubon Soc. Leaflet, No. 6; N. Y., 1920).

30   Harry C. Oberholser, "The Bird Life of Louisiana," Bull. *La. Dept. Conservation,* No. 28 (1938), Plate 33.

31   William T. Hornaday, *The American Natural History* (N. Y., 1914), p. 86.

32   Hennessey plate in Percy A. Taverner, *Birds of Eastern Canada* (Ottawa, 1919), Plate 11; Brooks plate in Percy A. Taverner, *Birds of Western Canada* Ottawa, 1926), Plate 24.

33   Alexander Wetmore, "Game Birds of Prairie, Forest, and Tundra," *Nat. Geographic Mag.,* LXX (1936), 497, Plate 15.

34   Thomas S. Roberts, *The Birds of Minnesota* (Minneapolis, Minn., 1932), Vol. I, Plate 41.

35   Nettie W. Park in *Nature Mag.,* XLII (Oct. 1949), 372–75.

36   W. E. Scott (ed.), *Silent Wings—A Memorial to the Passenger Pigeon,* p. 5.

37   J. C. French, *Passenger Pigeon,* pp. 82 and 246.

38   Frank Bond, "The Later Flights of the Passenger Pigeon," *Auk,* XXXVIII (1921), 524.

39   Bénédict-Henry Révoil, *The Hunter and Trapper in North America; or Ro-*

mantic Adventures in Field and Forest (trans. W. H. Davenport; London, 1874).

40 Marc de Villiers, *Les Raretés des Indes. "Codex Canadensis"* (Paris, 1930), Plate 45, Fig. 1.

41 Pehr Kalm, *Travels into North America*, I, 374.

42 T. Pennant, *Arctic Zoology*, Vol. II, Plate 14.

43 T. C. Eyton, *A History of the Rarer British Birds* (London, 1836), p. 30; William Yarrell, *A History of British Birds* (1st ed. London, 1843) II, 272.

44 Thomas Nuttall, *A Manual of the Ornithology of the United States and of Canada.... The Land Birds* (Cambridge, Mass., 1832), I, 629.

45 John Frost, "Game Birds of America," *Graham's Mag.*, XXXII (1848), 185–86.

46 Elliott Coues, *Key to North American Birds* (1st ed.; N. Y. and Boston, 1872), p. 225.

47 James G. Cooper, *Ornithology. Land Birds* (Cambridge, Mass., 1870), p. 510; Baird, Brewer, and Ridgway, *History of N. Am. Birds. Land Birds*, III, 369.

48 J. G. Cooper, *Ornithology. Land Birds*, p. 509; Robert Ridgway, *A Manual of North American Birds* (Phila., 1887), Plate 63, Fig. 1; and Ridgway's *Birds of North and Middle America* (Wash., 1916), Part VII, Plate 21.

49 Parker Gillmore, *Prairie and Forest* (N. Y., 1874), pp. 125–26; A. E. Brehm, *Thierleben, allgemeine Kunde des Thierreichs. Die Vögel* Leipzig, 1876–79), II (1879), 639.

50 Gene Stratton-Porter, "The Last Passenger Pigeon," *Good Housekeeping*, LXXIX (Aug., 1924), 54; E. J. Sawyer, "Some Extinct American Birds," *St. Nicholas Mag.*, XLII (Nov., 1914), 73.

51 C. W. Nash, "Passing of the Pigeons," *Canadian Mag.*, XX (1903), 315–17.

52 William Dutcher, "The Passenger or Wild Pigeon," *Bird-Lore*, V (1903), 209.

53 W. E. C. Todd, *Birds of Western Pennsylvania* (Pittsburgh, Penn., 1940), p. 267.

54 Albert H. Wright, "The Passenger Pigeon," *Youth's Companion*, LXXXV (Feb. 9, 1911), 75; Alexander Sprunt, Jr., "Echoes of a Vanished Host," *Nature Mag.*, XII (1928), 302.

55 T. S. Roberts, *Birds of Minnesota*, I, 580.

56 Samuel G. Goodrich, *Recollections of a Lifetime* (N. Y., 1857), I, p. 100.

57 "Netting Wild Pigeons in New England," *Leslie's Illustrated Newspaper*, XXV (Sept. 21, 1867), 8.

58 R. A. Cockburn, *Quebec and Its Environments; Being a Picturesque Guide to the Stranger* (Quebec, 1831), p. 30.

59 Smith Bennett, "Winter Sports in Northern Louisiana: Shooting Wild Pigeons," *Illustrated Sporting and Dramatic News* (London), III (July 3, 1875), 332.

60 "Shooting Wild Pigeons in Iowa," *Leslie's Illustrated Newspaper*, XXV (Sept. 21, 1867), 8.

61 "The Sportsmen's Tournament at Coney Island. Methods of Trapping and Transporting the Pigeons for Use in the Contests," *ibid.*, LII (July 2, 1881), 300.

62 "The Sportsmen's Tournament at Brighton Beach," *ibid.* LII (July 9, 1881), 319–20; also in *Natural History*, LX (Sept., 1951), 328.

63 Frank M. Chapman, *Handbook of Birds of Eastern North America* (2nd rev. ed.; N. Y., 1937), p. 327.

64 Charles H. Townsend, "Old Times with the Birds: Autobiographical," *Condor*, XXIX (1927), 224–25.

65 E. H. Forbush, *Game Birds*, Plate 19.

66 W. B. Barrows, *Mich. Bird Life*, Plate 17.

67 Robert W. Shufeldt in *Sci. Monthly*, XII (1921), 458–81, Fig. 6.

68 H. O. Bishop, "The Wild Pigeon," *Am. Forests*, XXXVIII (Nov., 1932), 597.

69 T. S. Roberts, *Birds of Minnesota*, I, 578; A. C. Bent, *Life Histories of N. Am. Gallinaceous Birds*, Plate 83.

70 E. H. Forbush, *Game Birds*, Plate 18.

71 Robert W. Shufeldt, "Death of the Last of the Wild Pigeons," *Sci. American Supplement*, LXXVIII (1914), 253.

72 Robert W. Shufeldt, "Anatomical and Other Notes on the Passenger Pigeon (*Ectopistes migratorius*) Lately Living in the Cincinnati Zoological Gardens," *Auk*, XXXII (1915), 29–41, Plates 4–6.

73 Robert W. Shufeldt, "Osteology of the Passenger Pigeon (*Ectopistes migratorius*)," *Auk*, XXXI (1914), 358–62, Plate 34.

74 Moritz Fischer. "A Vanished Race," *Bird-Lore*, XV (1913), 79.

75 Albert H. Wright, "The Passenger Pigeon: Early Historical Records, 1534–1860," *ibid.*, p. 89.

76 Moritz Fischer, *ibid.*, p. 82.

77 A. H. Wright, *ibid.*, p. 86.

78 Wallace Craig, "Recollection of the Passenger Pigeon in Captivity," *ibid.*, p. 94.

79 Alexander Wetmore in *Nat. Geographic Mag.*, LXX (1936), 465.

80 A. H. Wright in *Bird-Lore*, XV (1913), 91.

81 A. H. Cole, "What Became of 2,230,270,000 Passenger-Pigeons," *World To-Day*, XVIII (1910), 531–32; Robert Hegner, *Parade of the Animal Kingdom* (N. Y., 1940), p. 447; W. B. Barrows *Mich. Bird Life*, Plate 15; W. B. Mershon, *Passenger Pigeon*, p. 198.

82 W. T. Hornaday, *Our Vanishing Wild Life;* Frank M. Chapman, "The Last Passenger Pigeon," *Bird-Lore*, XVI (1914), 399.

83 A. C. Bent, *Life Histories of N. Am. Gallinaceous Birds*, Plate 83.

84 Wallace Craig in *Bird-Lore*, XV (1913), 96.

France: occurrence of passenger pigeon
in, 263–64
Franklin, John, 261
Freezing: as cause of death, 66, 67
French, John C.: on food, 34; on shape
of flocks, 59; on nesting, 87, 96, 110,
116, 121, 208; on Indians, 136, 208
French, William, 95, 143
Fright: from presence of blood, 131;
from presence of feathers, 181
Frightening: from fields, 52, 53
Frisch, J. L., 248, 294
Frost, John, 251, 299
Fuertes, Louis Agassiz, 297, 300
Fulton, Robert, 242–43

Galissoniere, Marquis de la, 263
Gass, Patrick, 258
Gaultheria procumbens, 42
Gaylussacia, 42
Gehr, Nelson, 121
Geikie, John C., 54
Gentry, Thomas G., 18, 48, 236
Geometra, 49
Georgia: as breeding area, 264; migra-
tion records for, 270; late record for,
287
Gibbs, Robert Morris: on nesting, 103–
6 *passim,* 111, 121; on migration in
Michigan, 268
Gifford, E. W., 47
Gilbert, Benjamin, 135
Gillmore, Parker, 299
Giraud, J. P., 77, 110
Glazier, Willard, 74
Gordon, James, 45
Goss, N. S., 288
Goss, R. D., 51
Grading pigeons for market, 147
Grain: as food, 35, 52–53
Grant, Anne, 267
Granville, Charles B. de, 299
Grass: as food, 46
Grasshoppers, 48
Gray, George R., 250
Gray, Hugh, 266

Green, Charles A., 23, 24
Greenleaf, P. H., 57, 69
Grinnell, George B., 58, 210
Griscom, L., 214–15
Grit, 50–51
Gromme, Owen J., 298
Ground beetle, 48
Grow, Elisha A., 52
Guatemala: as limit of range, 262
Gum berries, 40
Gunfire: effect on pigeons, 194
Gunn, Charles W.: on nesting in Michi-
gan, 36, 97, 227; on nest, 104, 111; on
protective laws, 227
Guyer, M. F., 245

Hackberries, 39
Hall, Baynard R., 63, 64
Hall, James, 81, 85
Hallock, Charles, 40, 189
Hammond, Samuel H., 99, 117
Hamor, Ralph, 5
"H" and "T" releasers, 158
Hariot, Thomas, 5
Harpalus: compar, 48; *pennsylvanicus,*
48
Harvestman, 48
Haskell, Edwin: on voice, 15; on feed-
ing, 34, 144; on nesting, 96, 99, 117,
144; on capture with poles, 169
Hastings, N. S., 30
Hatch, Philo L., 209
Hawes, W. H., 158–60
Hawk: effect on pigeons, 58, 208–9, 211;
duck, 58, 210; Cooper's, 209; sharp-
shinned, 209; goshawk, 209–10; pi-
geon, 210; red-tailed, 210–11
Hayashi, K., 297
Hayden, F. V., 258
Hayes, William G., 167
Head, George, 74
Hearne, Samuel, 41
Hebert, William, 60
Heddon, James, 121
Hedrick, U. P., 90, 99
Hegner, Robert, 222, 302